2013/14
FACTS & FIGURES

TABLES FOR THE CALCULATION OF DAMAGES

2013/14
FACTS & FIGURES

TABLES FOR THE CALCULATION OF DAMAGES

Compiled and Edited by:

Members of the
Professional Negligence Bar Association

General Editor: Robin de Wilde QC

Editors:

Michael Jarvis, FCA
Peter Jennings
Simon Levene
Tejina Mangat
Harry Trusted

SWEET & MAXWELL

THOMSON REUTERS

Published in 2013 by Thomson Reuters (Legal) Limited
(Registered in England & Wales, Company No 167046.
Registered office and address for service:
100 Avenue Road, London, NW3 3PF)
Trading as Sweet & Maxwell Limited

Designed and typeset by Interactive Sciences Ltd, Gloucester
Printed in Great Britain by TJ International Ltd, Padstow, Cornwall

No natural forests were destroyed to make this product:
only farmed timber was used and re-planted.

ISBN 9780414028418

A CIP catalogue record for this book is available from the British Library.

ACKNOWLEDGMENTS

HMSO gave us kind permission to use Table A3 (Life tables), Table A8 (The Ogden Tables), Table C2 (Real and nominal interest rates and price inflation), Table F5 (Average weekly earnings index), Table F6 (Average weekly earnings), Table F7 (Average earnings statistics), and the material from the NHS leaflet HC12, NHS charges. The Inland Revenue and HMSO gave us permission to use the material in Table L2 (Taxation of car and fuel benefits).

We are grateful to Adrian Gallop, Government Actuary's Department, for his assistance in preparing A3 (Life tables and projected life tables).

Crown Copyright is reproduced with the permission of HMSO.

We are extremely grateful to Dr Victoria Wass of Cardiff Business School for updating her step-by-step guide to finding the annual estimates for hourly pay in ASHE SOC2000 6115 at B6 and the guide to the ASHE earnings tables at F7 and her input into F4, F5 and F6.

Permission to use the tables from Kemp & Kemp: The Quantum of Damages at C3 (Special investment account rates), C8 (Judgment debt interest rates), E1 (Retail prices index) and E2 (Inflation table) was given by Sweet & Maxwell Ltd.

We are grateful to Rodney Nelson Jones of Field Fisher Waterhouse and Lexis Nexis for allowing us to use and to develop his table for the calculation of special damages interest in C4.

Permission to use Table C9 (Judicial Rates of Interest) was given by W. Green.

Tim Higginson of Dixon Wilson has for many years been involved in the meticulous preparation and updating of various annually changing tables in sections C, F, G, H and L. We thank him once again.

The FTSE group gave us permission to use the FTSE 100 Index at Table D1.

We are grateful to Barclays Capital for the use of their table at D2 (Barclays Equity Index).

We are grateful to Maurice Faull for helping us with Table D3 (Index-linked stock).

Halifax plc provided the up-to-date material for Tables E3 and E4 showing House price indices.

We are grateful to Keith Carter, Isabelle Symons and Lynn Bourne of Keith Carter & Associates for the research undertaken for the preparation of the tables in F4 to F7.

We wish to thank Lynne Bradey of Wrigleys for preparing Table I4.

Permission to produce the Code of Best Practice on Rehabilitation at K6 and K7 was given to us by the Bodily Injury Claims Management Association.

Permission to use Table L1 (AA motoring costs) was given by the Automobile Association.

Our thanks go to Nicholas Leviseur for preparing the notes on the Motability Scheme at L3.

We are grateful to the Family Law Bar Association and Melissa Chapman for their permission to use table F8 (Public sector comparable earnings), I1 and I2 (Social security benefits) and I6 (Foster care allowances) taken from At A Glance.

We are grateful to Bauer Media, publishers of Parker's Car Price Guide on whose figures the calculations in Table L4 are based.

Table M3 (Perpetual calendar) is reproduced with permission from the International Management Diary published by Collins Debden Australia.

We are grateful to Mike Perrett and Debra Smith of BWCI Consulting Ltd for their assistance with E2 (Inflation table).

We are grateful to Margaret McDonald, specialist costs counsel of Kenworthy's Chambers, for permission to reproduce her table of Senior Court Costs Office Guideline Rates for Summary Assessment at M1.

We are grateful to Alison Somek, of Somek & Associates, and to James Rowley, of Byrom Street Chambers, for their work on Carer Rates in at K1.

We are grateful to Hugh Jones of Pannone LLP for J1 (Editor's Note on the Court of Protection). Finally, our thanks go to Tom Cook and Adrian Mundell, Kester Cunningham John, for J2 (The Incidence of Deputyship Costs over a Claimant's Life) and J3 (Deputyship Costs).

FOREWORD TO THE FIRST EDITION

by the Hon. Mr Justice Bell

The assessment of damages for personal injuries and consequential losses has become a matter of increasingly intricate calculation. Detailed schedules of damages and counter-schedules are vital to the proper portrayal of claim and defence to claim but they are arduous and time consuming to compile. Much the same building blocks of information and aids to calculation are required over and over again. This volume has gathered many of the most frequently used building blocks and aids together in a readily accessible form and those who prepare, argue and settle such cases should be grateful for it. Robin de Wilde and his committee have put a lot of work into what is in fact a manual of very practical assistance and they are to be congratulated on a new venture which should mature year by year with the help of your own suggestions.

May 1996

INTRODUCTION TO THE EIGHTEENTH EDITION

"He was blessed with several other qualities not always conjoined with a first-class mind: humility, common sense, an instinct for fairness, consideration for others and sparkling wit . . . . He was quite simply the best appellate judge of his generation and an admirable human being."

Sir Christopher Rose, Lives Remembered,
Lord Bingham of Cornhill,
The Times, September 22, 2010

Who we are?

For 17 years, Michael Jarvis, FCA, of Dixon Wilson, has been at the heart of this enterprise, to make it as easy as it can be for the ordinary practitioner, to find the answer to the practical problems of drafting a credible Schedule of Damages or the appropriate Counter Schedule.

He has left us, because he is taking up a post of distinction in a Livery Company, whose members have appreciated his qualities, both as an accountant and as an outstanding individual who cares about the people he represented and who always ended up being respected by his clients, though some were involved in some fairly egregious conduct.

It was he, to his own surprise who, as an articled clerk, discovered the nature and extent of the late John Stonehouse's financial misconduct, which led John Stonehouse, who pretended to have died on a beach in Florida, to be found in Australia, brought back to England and face a trial at the Old Bailey, leading to imprisonment.

Michael Jarvis has left us with a whole series of Tables of the greatest clarity, which enable anyone to work out and appreciate how much the real take home pay is, when the ramifications of the tax and national insurance are taken into account.

For those of us who have worked with him, he has been a delightful companion in a task (when none of us receives any benefit apart from an annual dinner from the publishers); the fruits of this operation going into the funds of the Professional Negligence Bar Association, and which supports the training of younger barristers whether on discrete particular courses or on the celebrated Clinical Negligence Residential Course and other weekends run by an open minded Committee of officers and members of the Association.

He possesses a delicious sense of humour in which neither he, nor anyone else, is spared from his dry observations of the passing scene. Though I trust he continues as a friend of mine, I will miss the regularity of our meetings.

The rest of us are as before: Peter Jennings, Simon Levene, Harry Trusted and Tejina Mangat.

We continue to be supported by others in the background, who we try to fully appreciate in the preceding pages, entitled "Acknowledgements". New people come forward every year, as we try and encompass other specialist areas outside our own expertise and/or correct our errors.

The financial background

We continue to struggle through the worst financial crash of our economic history as a nation, the like of which the present Governor of the Bank of England acknowledges we have never experienced before. He said on May 15, 2013 at his final Press Conference as Governor that: "This hasn't been a typical recession and it won't be a typical recovery. Nevertheless, a recovery is in sight." We all hope that he is right in that prediction.

The present discussion is now about whether or not the final figures reveal whether we experienced a "double dip recession". It is unlikely that our children will ever live through this sort of financial and economic crisis. However, that does not mean or guarantee that those who manage our affairs will have learned all the lessons that they should. The Bank lending rates are as low as they have ever been, but the CPI rate is still running at 2.8 per cent, although the target is 2.0 per cent. We appear to be entering our sixth year of the crisis. The only redeeming feature is that the power house which is the United States appears to be coming out of it.

The Discount Rate

This is a scandal, but no one, not even Lord Pannick, seems to care. When it was set by Lord Chancellor Irvine in July 2001, he set it at 2.5 per cent. At the time when he set it, we argued that it was too high by about 0.5 per cent. The best advice that I have received (that is from someone who knows what he is talking about) the rate today for Index Linked Gilt Stock is either −0.5 per cent or 0 per cent. That means that in a substantial case, where the claimant is going to get in excess of £100,000 by way of compensation, if they do not qualify for a Periodical Payment Order (and not everyone does for a series of reasons with which I will not trouble you) then if they are compensated in the best way, by Gilts, then they are going to be under compensated either five or six times the proper sum.

For, as every good reader of this volume knows the discount rate informs the calculation of the multiplier to give you the most accurate figure for calculating the future loss. As no one deliberately injures themselves to make a financial claim for personal injuries, one would think, even in the brave new world of Mr Cameron and Mr Grayling that the injured would be classed as being the most vulnerable members of society and they should be properly protected. Why does this not happen? No, don't bother to write to me about it.

Compensation culture and the hanging flower baskets of Bury St Edmunds

It is always a pleasure to have one's strong views (others might call them prejudices) confirmed. I have written about this on a number of occasions, notably when I discussed "The hanging flower baskets of Bury St Edmunds". The more discerning of my readers will recall that this is a topic to which I have returned, again and again. In the "Introduction to the Fifteenth Edition" in a paragraph entitled: "Misconceptions and the hanging flower baskets of Bury St Edmunds"[1] I told the story of those hanging flower baskets. The Sun newspaper had reported on February 10, 2004 that the local authority had voted to have the Victorian metal flower baskets removed as they were no longer safe and they should be removed lest they should fall on innocent members of the public. This story appeared a further 31 times in the following 30 months. All but two reports, save for The Guardian and The Independent newspapers, treated the story as the unquestioned, gospel truth.

This cycle was repeated by Mr Blair, the then Prime Minister, who cited the removal of the Bury St Edmunds's hanging baskets as a true story which justified the need for s.1 of the Compensation Act

[1] Facts & Figures, 2010/11, p.x.

2006. As far as I know, those hanging baskets continue to hang in their usual manner in Bury St Edmunds. I have not been to that delightful place for many years.

Lord Dyson, MR, in his Handsworth Club Lecture entitled "Compensation Culture: Fact or Fantasy?" delivered on March 15, 2013[2] has, once more, exposed the idleness of the newspapers and media generally by following the same route and he follows through the whole sorry saga of misreporting of "compensation culture" and then proceeds to destroy the whole myth.

He also deals with the question of costs and ADR, following the reform of the conditional fee agreements by the Access to Justice Act 1999. He speaks about the intention of those reforms to make CFAs more attractive to claimants in order to increase access to justice to those who previously would not have qualified for legal aid, as well as to provide funding for those for whom legal aid was no longer available. He goes onto say that "an unintended consequence of this reform was to inflate legal costs, specifically costs that defendants are liable to pay." He speaks of the rise of unmeritorious claims and the increase in claims management firms, as well as the increase in advertising and other practices aimed at drumming up work.

However, what he does not say, and what I have repeatedly said, is that the merits of the legal aid system for civil work has been destroyed by political chicanery and lies. The power and influence on successive Governments of the ABI is amazing.

We know that 92 per cent of civil legal aid certificates in personal injury work were satisfied and that the sums recovered more than covered the 8 per cent of cases which were lost, including benefits paid out by the state, whether in CRU payments or other benefits or payments to the NHS, and that together with income tax and VAT paid by the lawyers on the litigation and their earnings satisfied the balance of the 8 per cent lost claims.

In real terms the legal aid system made a profit for the state. There were solicitors in every high street, available to the public and as early as the 1950s it had been discovered that 83 per cent of the population could obtain legal aid, subject to a contribution, assessed by the local benefits office. It was a system run by lawyers and supervised by other lawyers, the local legal aid area committee, who gave up their time for free and the Law Society effectively ran the whole scheme.

There were the occasional abuses, but because sadly those abuses were not followed up and punished. It also relied on the good faith of counsel and their honest advices and opinions. For the most part, counsel gave honest advice and opinions.

Apart from fraud, which is deliberate, no one enters into a marriage with the intention of it breaking down or deliberately injures themselves unless they are a sadomasochist. Bad things happen to people; things go wrong and civil servants and public bodies often treat the ordinary citizen abysmally. That is why an open system of justice is vital in a healthy society.

We had what Lord Mackay of Clashfern, in a recent letter to *The Times*, described as: "the best legal aid system in the world." Both the criminal and civil legal aid systems are being destroyed and ordinary people (the 83 per cent) are being denied justice in the courts, provided by an independent legal profession.

After the defence of the realm, provision of an effective system of justice must be the second duty of the state towards its citizens. It should not be as the Victorian judge remarked about the law that it was, "like the doors of the Ritz Hotel, open to all the world".

---

[2] *http://www.judiciary.gov.uk/Resources/JCO/Documents/Speeches/mr-speech-compensation-culture.pdf.*

However, Lord Dyson simply could not say that, because he is a judge and not a politician.

This is a murky area, where politicians end up hurling abuse at the judiciary for supposed interference, when it is usually nothing of the kind. It is merely the incompetence and short-term aspirations of the politicians, together with lack of understanding that they make the law, they have to suffer for those reckless and foolish ambitions when they pass a statute which is either misconceived incomprehensible or stupid. The judges merely interpret or make the law, when the opportunity presents itself.

I trust that this excellent Speech from Lord Dyson may be the end of the spread of the myth of compensation culture, but I doubt it.

New ideas and improvements

If any reader or user (and there may be discrete differences between the two classes) has a new idea or thought for improving the Tables, layout, or the need for some useful addition, please let us know. Sometimes, the best ideas for change in the come from outside the "magic circle" of those who run the organisation, or in this case the Editorial Committee.

Let me illustrate that with an example: if every time a credit card was used (not a debit card) a tax was imposed on its use of 10p, to be collected on behalf of the Government, by the credit card company, then the Government would benefit by millions of pounds every day, perhaps even allowing them to fund Legal Aid properly. Also, those idiots who pay for the coffee or other commodity in a coffee shop or elsewhere with a credit card, such a taxation process would be helping Starbucks, Amazon and Google or whoever, to make a positive contribution to the general taxation fund of the United Kingdom. When I first heard of it as an idea, I thought it was a good idea and not falling into the "mad as a box of frogs" category.

We are not interested in those ideas that I would describe as being in the "mad as a box of frogs" class, though those who tender such ideas will never know what I think, because they will still receive a courteous reply. That is described as "editorial discretion"!

So, we are still interested in new ideas.

Bernie Ecclestone and why he receives a mention

If you turn forward a page or two, you will find the "Introduction to the First Edition" written in May 1996. In those days, when we first thought of dealing with comparative and comparable earnings, I was looking for someone whose earnings were so enormous that they would never enter any such Table. Such is the smallness of my world, that I had never previously come across Mr Ecclestone whose earnings I discovered to have been in 1993, as a director of his company, Formula One Promotions and International Sports World, to have been £30,750,109.00.

Since that time, I have followed his activities with enthusiasm, as I discovered more about his origins, skill and rapidly increasing acquisition of wealth.

He still does not appear in the Table of Comparable Earnings, Table F8.

Envoi

We continue to accept criticisms, corrections and amendments, for which I am grateful. The sheer mass of the material is a problem. Do check anything that causes you any doubt. We try to provide sources for all public figures we quote. The Care Rates for Domestic Care continue to provide problems, as has been previously explained.

Large cases continue to be reported. There have been two in the last year in the region of £24/25 million for very serious injuries, where, doubtless, there were a mass of specialist reports. They will be useful for anyone who stumbles into such a case, not only for a sense of the measure of the awards in the largest cases, but also the amount of work that has to be done to prepare such cases properly.

This volume is also intended to be used in hearings before the District Judge as well, when each penny can be as hotly contested as in the largest cases.

Please keep sending in the correspondence, when appropriate. I will acknowledge it as quickly as I can.

Some of you will be pleased to know that a Scots advocate who produces a similar volume to this in Edinburgh, but not quite as extensive, has recently written to tell me that I was "mad". I do my best to bring sunshine into the world for the benefit of others!

Robin de Wilde, QC

218 Strand Chambers
218 Strand
London
WC2R 1AT

rdewilde@218strand.com
020 7427 0841 (direct)

July 1, 2013

INTRODUCTION TO THE FIRST EDITION

Schedules of Damages have become more complex. These tables are intended as an assistance to those who have to check the details which support a Schedule. The Tables themselves come from a variety of primary sources. In one volume they should be easier to use.

The task of compiling this volume has proved more onerous than any of the members of the Committee assigned to the task would have imagined. The discussions as to what should be included or excluded became intense. When dealing with comparative and comparable earnings, should not Mr Bernie Ecclestone of Formula One Promotions and International Sports World receive a mention? He was paid in 1993 the sum of £30,750,109 and became easily the highest paid director by £8,000,000 or so. He is not included in the Table of Comparable Earnings.

We are also conscious that the application of each Table may or may not be easy depending on the contents. We do not intend to triple the size of the volume by setting out worked examples, but would refer the reader to the appropriate text books. It is intended as a source book, easily to hand, so that the practitioner may find what is needed quickly and easily in a single volume.

As this is our first foray into the world of tables, we appreciate that some matters will have been omitted that should be included and some of that which is included should not be present. We rely on our readers to tell us what is wanted and needed, so that the next annual update can be improved. The intention is that each edition is published in late January or early February of each year, incorporating the declarations announced in the Budget in November the previous year.

We have plundered shamelessly from a variety of sources. The final stimulus has been the Family Law Bar Association's "At A Glance" annual publication, but it is designed for practitioners in a different world, facing other demands and needs.

We are also grateful to Mr Justice Bell, who attended the final Advisory Committee Meeting and agreed to write a Foreword to this venture.

We conclude with the thought expressed by the historian Edward Gibbon in *The Decline and Fall of the Roman Empire*, when he states in a footnote about one Emperor that:

"Twenty-two acknowledged concubines and a library of sixty-two thousand volumes, attested the variety of his inclinations; and from the productions which he left behind him, it appears that the former as well as the latter were designed for use rather than ostentation."

These Tables, too, are designed for use rather than ostentation.

199 Strand
London WC2R 1DR
May 1996   Robin de Wilde, QC

CONTENTS

Group A—Odgen Tables and Related Materials

A1 2.5% discount tables "at a glance" 3
A2 Nil discount tables "at a glance" 8
A3 Life tables and projected life tables 12
A4 Loss of earnings multipliers adjusted for education, disability and employment status 17
A5 Multipliers for fixed periods and at intervals 31
A6 Combination tables 39
A7 Table of adjustments to multiplier for Fatal Accidents Acts dependency 43
A8 The Ogden Tables 44
A9 The Lord Chancellor's statement, July 27, 2001 121

Group B—Damages

B1 General damages table following Heil v Rankin and Jackson 129
B2 Bereavement damages 133
B3 Auty analysis (pension claims) 134
B4 Roberts v Johnstone analysis (accommodation claims) 135
B5 "Model Order" for periodical payments 136
B6 Step-by-step guide to finding the annual estimates for hourly pay in ASHE SOC2000 6115 ... 137

Group C—Interest Rates

C1 Interest base rates 141
C2 Real and nominal interest rates and price inflation 143
C3 Special investment account rates 145
C4 Special and general damages interest 146
C5 Base rate + 10% 148
C6 Number of days between two dates 149
C7 Decimal years 150
C8 Judgment debt interest rates (England and Wales) 151
C9 Judicial rates of interest (Scotland) 151

Group D—Investment

D1 Share price index (FTSE 100) 155
D2 Barclays Equity Index 156
D3 Index-linked stock 157

Group E—Prices

E1 Retail prices index 163
E2 Inflation table 165
E3 House price indices 166
E4 Average semi-detached house prices by region 168
E5 How prices have changed over 12 years 168

Group F—Earnings

F1 Earnings losses in personal injury and fatal accident cases 171
F2 Payroll documents 175

Contents

F3   National minimum wage 177
F4   Regional unemployment statistics 179
F5   Average weekly earnings index 185
F6   Average weekly earnings 187
F7   Average earnings statistics 188
F8   Public sector comparable earnings 209
F9   Public sector earnings websites 210

Group G—Tax and National Insurance
G1   Net equivalents to a range of gross annual income figures 213
G2   Illustrative net earnings calculations 221
G3   Income tax reliefs and rates 222
G4   National Insurance contributions 226
G5   VAT registration thresholds and rates 229

Group H—Pension
H1   Net equivalents to a range of gross annual pension figures 233
H2   Illustrative net pension calculations 235
H3   Note on pension losses 239

Group I—Benefits, Allowances, Charges
I1   Social security benefits (non-means-tested) 245
I2   Social security benefits and tax credits (means-tested) 248
I3   Personal injury trusts 252
I4   Claims for loss of earnings and maintenance at public expense 261
I5   Foster care allowances 261

Group J—Court of Protection
J1   Note on the Court of Protection 265
J2   The incidence of Deputyship costs over a claimant's life 274
J3   Deputyship costs 277

Group K—Carer Rates and Rehabilitation
K1   Care and attendance 281
K2   Nannies, cleaners and school fees 296
K3   DIY, gardening and housekeeping 297
K4   Hospital self-pay (uninsured) charges 299
K5   NHS charges 301
K6   The 2007 Rehabilitation Code 302
K7   Rehabilitation: a practitioner's guide 306

Group L—Motoring and Allied Material
L1   AA motoring costs 323
L2   Taxation of car and fuel benefits 327
L3   The Motability Scheme 329
L4   Calculations involving motor cars 330
L5   Time, speed and distance 338

Group M—Other Information
M1 Senior Court Costs Office Guideline Rates for Summary Assessment 343

M2 Conversion formulae 346
M3 Perpetual calendar... 349
M4 Religious festivals 352
M5 Medical reference intervals and scales.. 353
M6 Websites.. 358
M7 Addresses of useful organisations 359

Group A
Ogden Tables and Related Materials

A

A1:   **2.5% discount tables "at a glance"**

A2:   **Nil discount tables "at a glance"**

A3:   **Life tables and projected life tables**

A4:   **Loss of earnings multipliers adjusted for education, disability and employment status**

A5:   **Multipliers for fixed periods and at intervals**

A6:   **Combination tables**

A7:   **Table of adjustments to multiplier for Fatal Accidents Acts dependency**

A8:   **The Ogden Tables**

A9:   **The Lord Chancellor's statement, July 27, 2001**

A1: 2.5% discount tables "at a glance"

The following two tables comprise the 2.5% columns from Ogden Tables 1–26.

If 2.5% is the appropriate discount factor, these tables contain all the appropriate multipliers.

Readers are reminded that the figures for loss of earnings must be adjusted in accordance with Section B of the Explanatory Notes to the Ogden Tables (Contingencies Other than Mortality) reproduced in Part A8. Multipliers already adjusted for these contingencies are set out in Table A4.

2.5% discount tables "at a glance"—MALE

	Table 1 Pecuniary loss for life	Table 3 Loss of earnings to age 50	Table 5 Loss of earnings to age 55	Table 7 Loss of earnings to age 60	Table 9 Loss of earnings to age 65	Table 11 Loss of earnings to age 70	Table 13 Loss of earnings to age 75	Table 15 Loss of pension from age 50	Table 17 Loss of pension from age 55	Table 19 Loss of pension from age 60	Table 21 Loss of pension from age 65	Table 23 Loss of pension from age 70	Table 25 Loss of pension from age 75
0	35.41							7.00	5.69	4.54	3.54	2.69	1.97
1	35.46							7.20	5.85	4.66	3.64	2.76	2.02
2	35.33							7.37	5.98	4.77	3.72	2.82	2.06
3	35.19							7.54	6.12	4.88	3.80	2.88	2.10
4	35.05							7.72	6.26	4.98	3.88	2.94	2.14
5	34.90							7.89	6.40	5.10	3.97	3.00	2.19
6	34.75							8.08	6.54	5.21	4.05	3.06	2.23
7	34.59							8.26	6.69	5.32	4.14	3.13	2.27
8	34.42							8.45	6.84	5.44	4.23	3.19	2.32
9	34.25							8.65	7.00	5.56	4.32	3.26	2.36
10	34.08							8.84	7.15	5.68	4.41	3.33	2.41
11	33.90							9.05	7.32	5.81	4.51	3.39	2.46
12	33.72							9.26	7.48	5.94	4.60	3.46	2.50
13	33.53							9.47	7.65	6.07	4.70	3.54	2.55
14	33.34							9.69	7.82	6.20	4.80	3.61	2.60
15	33.14							9.91	8.00	6.34	4.91	3.68	2.65
16	32.94	22.80	24.76	26.46	27.92	29.18	30.23	10.14	8.18	6.48	5.01	3.76	2.71
17	32.73	22.36	24.37	26.11	27.61	28.89	29.97	10.37	8.37	6.62	5.12	3.84	2.76
18	32.52	21.91	23.97	25.75	27.29	28.61	29.71	10.61	8.56	6.77	5.23	3.92	2.81
19	32.31	21.45	23.56	25.39	26.97	28.31	29.44	10.86	8.75	6.92	5.34	4.00	2.87
20	32.10	20.99	23.14	25.02	26.64	28.01	29.17	11.11	8.95	7.08	5.46	4.08	2.92
21	31.87	20.50	22.72	24.64	26.30	27.71	28.89	11.37	9.16	7.23	5.58	4.17	2.98
22	31.64	20.01	22.28	24.25	25.95	27.39	28.61	11.63	9.37	7.40	5.70	4.25	3.04
23	31.41	19.51	21.83	23.85	25.59	27.07	28.31	11.90	9.58	7.56	5.82	4.34	3.10
24	31.17	18.99	21.37	23.44	25.22	26.74	28.01	12.18	9.80	7.73	5.95	4.43	3.16
25	30.92	18.46	20.90	23.02	24.85	26.40	27.70	12.46	10.02	7.90	6.08	4.52	3.22
26	30.67	17.92	20.42	22.59	24.47	26.06	27.39	12.76	10.25	8.08	6.21	4.62	3.29
27	30.42	17.36	19.93	22.16	24.07	25.70	27.07	13.06	10.49	8.26	6.34	4.71	3.35
28	30.15	16.79	19.42	21.71	23.67	25.34	26.74	13.36	10.73	8.45	6.48	4.81	3.42
29	29.88	16.21	18.91	21.25	23.26	24.97	26.40	13.67	10.97	8.63	6.62	4.91	3.48
30	29.60	15.61	18.38	20.78	22.84	24.59	26.05	13.99	11.23	8.83	6.76	5.01	3.55
31	29.32	15.00	17.83	20.29	22.41	24.20	25.70	14.33	11.49	9.03	6.91	5.12	3.62
32	29.04	14.37	17.28	19.80	21.97	23.81	25.35	14.67	11.76	9.23	7.07	5.23	3.69
33	28.75	13.73	16.72	19.30	21.53	23.41	24.98	15.02	12.03	9.45	7.22	5.34	3.77
34	28.46	13.08	16.14	18.79	21.07	23.00	24.61	15.38	12.32	9.66	7.38	5.45	3.84
35	28.15	12.41	15.55	18.27	20.60	22.58	24.23	15.75	12.61	9.89	7.55	5.57	3.92
36	27.84	11.72	14.94	17.73	20.13	22.15	23.84	16.13	12.90	10.11	7.72	5.69	4.00
37	27.53	11.01	14.32	17.18	19.64	21.72	23.45	16.51	13.21	10.35	7.89	5.81	4.08
38	27.20	10.29	13.68	16.61	19.13	21.27	23.04	16.91	13.52	10.58	8.07	5.93	4.16
39	26.86	9.54	13.02	16.04	18.62	20.80	22.62	17.32	13.84	10.83	8.24	6.06	4.24
40	26.52	8.78	12.35	15.44	18.09	20.33	22.19	17.74	14.17	11.08	8.43	6.19	4.33
41	26.17	8.00	11.67	14.84	17.55	19.85	21.75	18.17	14.50	11.33	8.62	6.32	4.42
42	25.81	7.20	10.96	14.21	17.00	19.36	21.31	18.61	14.85	11.60	8.81	6.46	4.51
43	25.45	6.38	10.24	13.58	16.44	18.85	20.85	19.07	15.21	11.87	9.01	6.60	4.60
44	25.08	5.54	9.50	12.93	15.86	18.34	20.39	19.54	15.57	12.15	9.21	6.74	4.69
45	24.70	4.68	8.74	12.26	15.27	17.81	19.91	20.02	15.95	12.44	9.43	6.89	4.79
46	24.31	3.79	7.97	11.58	14.67	17.27	19.42	20.52	16.34	12.73	9.64	7.04	4.88
47	23.91	2.88	7.17	10.88	14.05	16.72	18.93	21.03	16.74	13.03	9.86	7.19	4.99
48	23.51	1.95	6.35	10.16	13.42	16.16	18.42	21.56	17.15	13.35	10.09	7.35	5.09
49	23.10	0.99	5.52	9.43	12.77	15.58	17.90	22.11	17.58	13.67	10.33	7.52	5.20
50	22.69		4.66	8.68	12.11	15.00	17.38	22.69	18.03	14.01	10.58	7.69	5.31
51	22.27		3.78	7.91	11.44	14.40	16.85		18.49	14.36	10.83	7.87	5.42
52	21.85		2.87	7.12	10.75	13.80	16.31		18.98	14.72	11.10	8.05	5.54
53	21.42		1.94	6.32	10.05	13.18	15.76		19.48	15.11	11.37	8.24	5.67
54	20.99		0.99	5.49	9.33	12.55	15.20		20.01	15.50	11.66	8.44	5.80

2.5% discount tables "at a glance"—MALE *continued*

	Table 1 Pecuniary loss for life	Table 3 Loss of earnings to age 50	Table 5 Loss of earnings to age 55	Table 7 Loss of earnings to age 60	Table 9 Loss of earnings to age 65	Table 11 Loss of earnings to age 70	Table 13 Loss of earnings to age 75	Table 15 Loss of pension from age 50	Table 17 Loss of pension from age 55	Table 19 Loss of pension from age 60	Table 21 Loss of pension from age 65	Table 23 Loss of pension from age 70	Table 25 Loss of pension from age 75
55	20.56			4.64	8.59	11.90	14.63		20.56	15.92	11.97	8.65	5.93
56	20.12			3.76	7.84	11.25	14.05			16.36	12.29	8.88	6.08
57	19.68			2.86	7.06	10.57	13.46			16.82	12.62	9.11	6.23
58	19.23			1.94	6.26	9.88	12.85			17.29	12.97	9.35	6.38
59	18.77			0.98	5.45	9.18	12.23			17.79	13.32	9.59	6.54
60	18.30				4.60	8.45	11.60			18.30	13.69	9.85	6.70
61	17.81				3.74	7.71	10.95				14.08	10.11	6.87
62	17.33				2.85	6.94	10.28				14.48	10.38	7.04
63	16.84				1.93	6.16	9.61				14.91	10.67	7.23
64	16.35				0.98	5.36	8.93				15.37	10.98	7.42
65	15.86					4.54	8.23				15.86	11.32	7.63
66	15.38					3.70	7.52					11.68	7.86
67	14.90					2.82	6.79					12.07	8.11
68	14.42					1.92	6.04					12.50	8.38
69	13.93					0.98	5.27					12.96	8.67
70	13.44						4.47					13.44	8.97
71	12.94						3.65						9.30
72	12.43						2.79						9.64
73	11.90						1.90						10.00
74	11.36						0.97						10.39
75	10.81												10.81
76	10.25												
77	9.69												
78	9.15												
79	8.61												
80	8.09												
81	7.60												
82	7.13												
83	6.69												
84	6.28												
85	5.88												
86	5.50												
87	5.14												
88	4.78												
89	4.43												
90	4.10												
91	3.79												
92	3.49												
93	3.21												
94	2.96												
95	2.74												
96	2.54												
97	2.37												
98	2.22												
99	2.08												
100	1.95												

2.5% discount tables "at a glance"—FEMALE

	Table 2 Pecuniary loss for life	Table 4 Loss of earnings to age 50	Table 6 Loss of earnings to age 55	Table 8 Loss of earnings to age 60	Table 10 Loss of earnings to age 65	Table 12 Loss of earnings to age 70	Table 14 Loss of earnings to age 75	Table 16 Loss of pension from age 50	Table 18 Loss of pension from age 55	Table 20 Loss of pension from age 60	Table 22 Loss of pension from age 65	Table 24 Loss of pension from age 70	Table 26 Loss of pension from age 75
0	35.94							7.43	6.09	4.92	3.90	3.01	2.25
1	35.97							7.64	6.26	5.06	4.00	3.09	2.31
2	35.86							7.82	6.41	5.17	4.09	3.16	2.36
3	35.73							8.00	6.56	5.29	4.19	3.23	2.41
4	35.60							8.19	6.71	5.41	4.28	3.30	2.46
5	35.47							8.39	6.87	5.54	4.38	3.37	2.51
6	35.34							8.58	7.03	5.66	4.47	3.44	2.56
7	35.19							8.78	7.19	5.79	4.57	3.52	2.61
8	35.05							8.99	7.36	5.92	4.68	3.59	2.67
9	34.90							9.20	7.53	6.06	4.78	3.67	2.72
10	34.75							9.42	7.70	6.20	4.89	3.75	2.78
11	34.59							9.64	7.88	6.34	4.99	3.83	2.84
12	34.42							9.86	8.06	6.48	5.11	3.92	2.90
13	34.26							10.09	8.25	6.63	5.22	4.00	2.96
14	34.09							10.33	8.44	6.78	5.33	4.09	3.02
15	33.91							10.57	8.63	6.93	5.45	4.17	3.08
16	33.73	22.91	24.90	26.64	28.16	29.47	30.59	10.82	8.83	7.09	5.57	4.26	3.14
17	33.55	22.47	24.51	26.29	27.85	29.19	30.34	11.07	9.03	7.25	5.70	4.36	3.21
18	33.36	22.02	24.11	25.94	27.53	28.91	30.08	11.33	9.24	7.42	5.82	4.45	3.27
19	33.16	21.56	23.71	25.58	27.21	28.62	29.82	11.60	9.46	7.58	5.95	4.55	3.34
20	32.97	21.09	23.29	25.21	26.88	28.32	29.56	11.87	9.68	7.76	6.09	4.64	3.41
21	32.76	20.61	22.86	24.83	26.54	28.02	29.28	12.15	9.90	7.93	6.22	4.74	3.48
22	32.56	20.12	22.42	24.44	26.20	27.71	29.00	12.44	10.13	8.12	6.36	4.85	3.55
23	32.34	19.61	21.97	24.04	25.84	27.39	28.71	12.73	10.37	8.30	6.50	4.95	3.63
24	32.12	19.09	21.51	23.63	25.47	27.06	28.42	13.03	10.61	8.49	6.65	5.06	3.70
25	31.89	18.56	21.04	23.21	25.10	26.73	28.12	13.33	10.85	8.68	6.79	5.16	3.78
26	31.66	18.01	20.56	22.78	24.72	26.39	27.81	13.65	11.10	8.88	6.94	5.28	3.85
27	31.42	17.45	20.06	22.34	24.33	26.03	27.49	13.97	11.36	9.08	7.10	5.39	3.93
28	31.18	16.88	19.56	21.89	23.93	25.68	27.17	14.30	11.62	9.29	7.26	5.50	4.01
29	30.93	16.30	19.04	21.43	23.51	25.31	26.84	14.64	11.89	9.50	7.42	5.62	4.10
30	30.68	15.70	18.51	20.96	23.09	24.93	26.50	14.98	12.17	9.71	7.58	5.74	4.18
31	30.41	15.08	17.96	20.48	22.66	24.55	26.15	15.33	12.45	9.94	7.75	5.87	4.27
32	30.15	14.45	17.40	19.98	22.22	24.15	25.79	15.70	12.74	10.16	7.92	6.00	4.35
33	29.87	13.80	16.83	19.48	21.77	23.75	25.43	16.07	13.04	10.40	8.10	6.13	4.44
34	29.59	13.14	16.25	18.96	21.31	23.34	25.06	16.45	13.35	10.64	8.28	6.26	4.54
35	29.31	12.46	15.65	18.43	20.84	22.91	24.68	16.84	13.66	10.88	8.47	6.39	4.63
36	29.01	11.77	15.03	17.88	20.35	22.48	24.29	17.24	13.98	11.13	8.66	6.53	4.73
37	28.71	11.06	14.40	17.32	19.86	22.04	23.89	17.65	14.30	11.38	8.85	6.67	4.82
38	28.40	10.33	13.76	16.75	19.35	21.58	23.48	18.07	14.64	11.65	9.05	6.82	4.92
39	28.09	9.58	13.10	16.17	18.83	21.12	23.06	18.50	14.98	11.92	9.25	6.97	5.02
40	27.76	8.82	12.42	15.57	18.30	20.65	22.63	18.95	15.34	12.19	9.46	7.12	5.13
41	27.43	8.03	11.73	14.96	17.76	20.16	22.20	19.40	15.70	12.47	9.67	7.27	5.23
42	27.09	7.22	11.02	14.33	17.20	19.66	21.75	19.87	16.07	12.76	9.89	7.43	5.34
43	26.75	6.40	10.29	13.69	16.63	19.15	21.29	20.35	16.45	13.06	10.12	7.59	5.45
44	26.39	5.55	9.55	13.03	16.05	18.63	20.82	20.84	16.84	13.36	10.35	7.76	5.57
45	26.03	4.69	8.79	12.36	15.45	18.10	20.35	21.35	17.25	13.68	10.58	7.93	5.69
46	25.67	3.80	8.00	11.67	14.84	17.56	19.86	21.87	17.66	14.00	10.83	8.11	5.81
47	25.29	2.88	7.20	10.96	14.22	17.01	19.36	22.41	18.09	14.33	11.08	8.29	5.93
48	24.91	1.95	6.38	10.24	13.58	16.44	18.86	22.97	18.53	14.67	11.33	8.47	6.06
49	24.53	0.99	5.54	9.50	12.93	15.86	18.34	23.54	18.99	15.03	11.60	8.67	6.19
50	24.14		4.68	8.74	12.26	15.27	17.82	24.14	19.46	15.39	11.88	8.86	6.32
51	23.74		3.79	7.97	11.58	14.67	17.28		19.95	15.77	12.16	9.07	6.46
52	23.33		2.88	7.17	10.88	14.05	16.73		20.45	16.16	12.45	9.28	6.60
53	22.92		1.95	6.36	10.17	13.42	16.17		20.97	16.56	12.75	9.49	6.75
54	22.50		0.99	5.52	9.43	12.78	15.60		21.51	16.98	13.06	9.72	6.90

2.5% discount tables "at a glance"—FEMALE *continued*

	Table 2 Pecuniary loss for life	Table 4 Loss of earnings to age 50	Table 6 Loss of earnings to age 55	Table 8 Loss of earnings to age 60	Table 10 Loss of earnings to age 65	Table 12 Loss of earnings to age 70	Table 14 Loss of earnings to age 75	Table 16 Loss of pension from age 50	Table 18 Loss of pension from age 55	Table 20 Loss of pension from age 60	Table 22 Loss of pension from age 65	Table 24 Loss of pension from age 70	Table 26 Loss of pension from age 75
55	22.07			4.66	8.68	12.12	15.02		22.07	17.41	13.39	9.95	7.06
56	21.64			3.78	7.92	11.45	14.42			17.86	13.73	10.19	7.22
57	21.21			2.87	7.13	10.76	13.81			18.33	14.08	10.44	7.39
58	20.76			1.94	6.32	10.05	13.19			18.81	14.44	10.70	7.56
59	20.30			0.99	5.49	9.33	12.56			19.31	14.81	10.97	7.74
60	19.83				4.64	8.59	11.91			19.83	15.19	11.24	7.92
61	19.35				3.76	7.83	11.24				15.59	11.52	8.11
62	18.86				2.86	7.05	10.56				16.00	11.81	8.30
63	18.37				1.94	6.25	9.86				16.43	12.11	8.50
64	17.87				0.98	5.44	9.16				16.89	12.43	8.71
65	17.38					4.60	8.43				17.38	12.78	8.94
66	16.88					3.74	7.70					13.15	9.19
67	16.39					2.85	6.94					13.54	9.45
68	15.89					1.93	6.17					13.96	9.72
69	15.39					0.98	5.37					14.40	10.02
70	14.87						4.55					14.87	10.33
71	14.35						3.70						10.65
72	13.80						2.82						10.98
73	13.24						1.92						11.32
74	12.66						0.98						11.68
75	12.06												12.06
76	11.45												
77	10.84												
78	10.24												
79	9.64												
80	9.07												
81	8.51												
82	7.99												
83	7.49												
84	7.01												
85	6.55												
86	6.11												
87	5.68												
88	5.26												
89	4.86												
90	4.47												
91	4.11												
92	3.77												
93	3.46												
94	3.18												
95	2.94												
96	2.74												
97	2.56												
98	2.39												
99	2.23												
100	2.08												

A2: Nil discount tables "at a glance"

MALE

	Table 1 Pecuniary loss for life	Table 3 Loss of earnings to age 50	Table 5 Loss of earnings to age 55	Table 7 Loss of earnings to age 60	Table 9 Loss of earnings to age 65	Table 11 Loss of earnings to age 70	Table 13 Loss of earnings to age 75	Table 15 Loss of pension from age 50	Table 17 Loss of pension from age 55	Table 19 Loss of pension from age 60	Table 21 Loss of pension from age 65	Table 23 Loss of pension from age 70	Table 25 Loss of pension from age 75
0	88.96							39.61	34.80	30.06	25.41	20.90	16.58
1	88.31							39.70	34.87	30.10	25.44	20.91	16.56
2	87.22							39.59	34.76	30.00	25.33	20.81	16.47
3	86.12							39.49	34.65	29.89	25.23	20.70	16.37
4	85.01							39.37	34.54	29.78	25.12	20.60	16.28
5	83.89							39.26	34.43	29.67	25.01	20.50	16.18
6	82.78							39.14	34.32	29.56	24.90	20.39	16.08
7	81.66							39.03	34.20	29.45	24.80	20.29	15.98
8	80.55							38.91	34.09	29.34	24.69	20.19	15.88
9	79.43							38.80	33.97	29.22	24.58	20.08	15.79
10	78.31							38.68	33.86	29.11	24.47	19.97	15.69
11	77.19							38.56	33.74	29.00	24.36	19.87	15.59
12	76.07							38.44	33.63	28.88	24.25	19.76	15.49
13	74.96							38.33	33.51	28.77	24.14	19.66	15.39
14	73.84							38.21	33.40	28.66	24.03	19.56	15.29
15	72.73							38.10	33.29	28.55	23.92	19.45	15.20
16	71.61	33.63	38.44	43.18	47.80	52.26	56.51	37.99	33.17	28.44	23.82	19.35	15.10
17	70.51	32.63	37.44	42.18	46.80	51.26	55.50	37.88	33.06	28.33	23.71	19.25	15.01
18	69.41	31.64	36.45	41.18	45.80	50.25	54.49	37.77	32.96	28.23	23.61	19.15	14.92
19	68.31	30.65	35.46	40.19	44.80	49.26	53.49	37.67	32.85	28.12	23.51	19.06	14.82
20	67.22	29.66	34.47	39.20	43.81	48.26	52.48	37.57	32.75	28.02	23.41	18.96	14.74
21	66.13	28.66	33.48	38.21	42.82	47.26	51.48	37.46	32.65	27.92	23.31	18.87	14.65
22	65.04	27.67	32.49	37.21	41.82	46.27	50.48	37.36	32.55	27.82	23.21	18.77	14.55
23	63.94	26.68	31.49	36.22	40.83	45.27	49.48	37.26	32.45	27.72	23.11	18.67	14.46
24	62.85	25.69	30.50	35.23	39.84	44.27	48.48	37.16	32.34	27.62	23.01	18.58	14.37
25	61.76	24.70	29.52	34.24	38.85	43.28	47.48	37.06	32.24	27.52	22.91	18.48	14.28
26	60.68	23.71	28.53	33.25	37.86	42.29	46.48	36.96	32.15	27.42	22.82	18.39	14.20
27	59.59	22.72	27.54	32.27	36.87	41.29	45.48	36.87	32.06	27.33	22.73	18.30	14.11
28	58.51	21.73	26.55	31.28	35.88	40.30	44.48	36.77	31.96	27.23	22.63	18.21	14.02
29	57.42	20.74	25.56	30.29	34.89	39.31	43.49	36.68	31.86	27.13	22.53	18.11	13.93
30	56.34	19.76	24.57	29.30	33.90	38.32	42.49	36.58	31.76	27.04	22.44	18.02	13.85
31	55.27	18.77	23.59	28.32	32.92	37.33	41.50	36.50	31.68	26.95	22.35	17.93	13.76
32	54.20	17.78	22.61	27.34	31.94	36.35	40.52	36.42	31.60	26.86	22.26	17.85	13.69
33	53.15	16.80	21.63	26.36	30.96	35.37	39.54	36.35	31.52	26.79	22.18	17.77	13.61
34	52.09	15.82	20.65	25.38	29.99	34.40	38.56	36.27	31.44	26.71	22.10	17.69	13.53
35	51.03	14.83	19.67	24.40	29.01	33.42	37.58	36.20	31.36	26.63	22.02	17.61	13.45
36	49.98	13.85	18.69	23.43	28.03	32.45	36.60	36.13	31.29	26.55	21.94	17.53	13.38
37	48.93	12.86	17.71	22.45	27.06	31.47	35.62	36.06	31.22	26.47	21.87	17.45	13.30
38	47.87	11.88	16.73	21.48	26.08	30.50	34.64	35.99	31.14	26.40	21.79	17.37	13.23
39	46.82	10.89	15.75	20.50	25.11	29.52	33.67	35.92	31.07	26.32	21.71	17.30	13.15
40	45.76	9.91	14.76	19.52	24.13	28.55	32.69	35.85	31.00	26.24	21.63	17.22	13.07
41	44.71	8.92	13.78	18.54	23.16	27.57	31.71	35.79	30.93	26.17	21.55	17.14	13.00
42	43.67	7.93	12.80	17.57	22.19	26.60	30.74	35.73	30.86	26.10	21.48	17.07	12.93
43	42.62	6.95	11.82	16.59	21.22	25.63	29.77	35.68	30.80	26.03	21.41	16.99	12.86
44	41.59	5.96	10.84	15.62	20.25	24.66	28.80	35.63	30.74	25.97	21.34	16.92	12.79
45	40.55	4.97	9.86	14.64	19.28	23.70	27.83	35.58	30.69	25.91	21.27	16.85	12.72
46	39.52	3.98	8.88	13.67	18.31	22.73	26.87	35.54	30.64	25.85	21.21	16.79	12.65
47	38.49	2.99	7.90	12.70	17.34	21.77	25.90	35.50	30.59	25.79	21.15	16.72	12.59
48	37.47	1.99	6.92	11.73	16.38	20.81	24.95	35.47	30.55	25.74	21.09	16.66	12.52
49	36.45	1.00	5.93	10.75	15.41	19.85	23.99	35.46	30.52	25.70	21.04	16.60	12.46
50	35.45		4.95	9.78	14.46	18.90	23.04	35.45	30.50	25.66	20.99	16.55	12.41
51	34.45		3.97	8.81	13.50	17.95	22.10		30.49	25.64	20.96	16.51	12.36
52	33.47		2.98	7.84	12.54	17.00	21.16		30.49	25.62	20.93	16.47	12.31
53	32.49		1.99	6.87	11.59	16.06	20.23		30.50	25.62	20.91	16.43	12.27
54	31.53		1.00	5.90	10.63	15.12	19.30		30.53	25.63	20.90	16.41	12.23

Nil discount tables "at a glance"—MALE *continued*

	Table 1 Pecuniary loss for life	Table 3 Loss of earnings to age 50	Table 5 Loss of earnings to age 55	Table 7 Loss of earnings to age 60	Table 9 Loss of earnings to age 65	Table 11 Loss of earnings to age 70	Table 13 Loss of earnings to age 75	Table 15 Loss of pension from age 50	Table 17 Loss of pension from age 55	Table 19 Loss of pension from age 60	Table 21 Loss of pension from age 65	Table 23 Loss of pension from age 70	Table 25 Loss of pension from age 75
55	30.58			4.93	9.68	14.19	18.37		30.58	25.65	20.90	16.39	12.20
56	29.64			3.95	8.73	13.25	17.46			25.69	20.91	16.39	12.18
57	28.71			2.97	7.77	12.32	16.54			25.74	20.94	16.39	12.17
58	27.78			1.99	6.82	11.39	15.63			25.80	20.97	16.40	12.16
59	26.85			1.00	5.85	10.45	14.71			25.86	21.00	16.40	12.15
60	25.92				4.89	9.51	13.79			25.92	21.03	16.41	12.13
61	25.00				3.92	8.58	12.87				21.07	16.42	12.12
62	24.08				2.95	7.64	11.96				21.12	16.44	12.12
63	23.17				1.98	6.70	11.05				21.20	16.47	12.12
64	22.28				0.99	5.77	10.15				21.29	16.52	12.13
65	21.42					4.83	9.25				21.42	16.59	12.16
66	20.57					3.88	8.36					16.69	12.21
67	19.74					2.93	7.46					16.81	12.28
68	18.93					1.97	6.56					16.96	12.37
69	18.12					0.99	5.66					17.13	12.47
70	17.32						4.75					17.32	12.58
71	16.53						3.83						12.70
72	15.72						2.89						12.83
73	14.92						1.95						12.97
74	14.10						0.99						13.12
75	13.29												13.29
76	12.48												
77	11.70												
78	10.93												
79	10.19												
80	9.49												
81	8.83												
82	8.22												
83	7.65												
84	7.13												
85	6.63												
86	6.16												
87	5.71												
88	5.27												
89	4.86												
90	4.47												
91	4.10												
92	3.76												
93	3.44												
94	3.16												
95	2.91												
96	2.69												
97	2.50												
98	2.34												
99	2.18												
100	2.04												

Nil discount tables "at a glance"—FEMALE

	Table 2 Pecuniary loss for life	Table 4 Loss of earnings to age 50	Table 6 Loss of earnings to age 55	Table 8 Loss of earnings to age 60	Table 10 Loss of earnings to age 65	Table 12 Loss of earnings to age 70	Table 14 Loss of earnings to age 75	Table 16 Loss of pension from age 50	Table 18 Loss of pension from age 55	Table 20 Loss of pension from age 60	Table 22 Loss of pension from age 65	Table 24 Loss of pension from age 70	Table 26 Loss of pension from age 75
0	92.57							42.98	38.10	33.26	28.47	23.78	19.22
1	91.86							43.07	38.16	33.30	28.50	23.79	19.21
2	90.77							42.97	38.06	33.20	28.40	23.69	19.12
3	89.68							42.87	37.96	33.10	28.30	23.60	19.02
4	88.58							42.77	37.86	33.00	28.21	23.50	18.93
5	87.49							42.67	37.76	32.90	28.11	23.41	18.84
6	86.38							42.56	37.66	32.80	28.01	23.31	18.75
7	85.28							42.46	37.56	32.70	27.91	23.21	18.65
8	84.18							42.36	37.45	32.60	27.81	23.11	18.56
9	83.07							42.25	37.35	32.49	27.70	23.01	18.46
10	81.97							42.15	37.24	32.39	27.60	22.92	18.37
11	80.86							42.04	37.14	32.29	27.50	22.82	18.28
12	79.76							41.94	37.04	32.18	27.40	22.72	18.18
13	78.65							41.83	36.93	32.08	27.30	22.62	18.09
14	77.55							41.73	36.83	31.98	27.20	22.53	18.00
15	76.44							41.62	36.72	31.88	27.10	22.43	17.91
16	75.34	33.82	38.72	43.57	48.34	53.01	57.53	41.52	36.62	31.78	27.00	22.33	17.81
17	74.24	32.82	37.72	42.57	47.34	52.01	56.52	41.42	36.52	31.67	26.90	22.24	17.72
18	73.14	31.83	36.72	41.57	46.34	51.00	55.51	41.32	36.42	31.58	26.80	22.14	17.63
19	72.05	30.83	35.73	40.57	45.34	50.00	54.51	41.22	36.32	31.48	26.71	22.05	17.54
20	70.96	29.83	34.73	39.57	44.34	49.00	53.50	41.12	36.23	31.38	26.61	21.96	17.45
21	69.86	28.84	33.73	38.58	43.34	48.00	52.50	41.03	36.13	31.29	26.52	21.86	17.36
22	68.77	27.84	32.74	37.58	42.34	47.00	51.49	40.93	36.03	31.19	26.42	21.77	17.27
23	67.67	26.85	31.74	36.58	41.35	46.00	50.49	40.82	35.93	31.09	26.32	21.67	17.18
24	66.57	25.85	30.74	35.58	40.35	44.99	49.48	40.72	35.83	30.99	26.23	21.58	17.09
25	65.48	24.85	29.75	34.59	39.35	43.99	48.48	40.62	35.73	30.89	26.13	21.48	17.00
26	64.38	23.86	28.75	33.59	38.35	42.99	47.47	40.53	35.63	30.79	26.03	21.39	16.91
27	63.29	22.86	27.76	32.59	37.35	41.99	46.47	40.43	35.54	30.70	25.94	21.30	16.82
28	62.20	21.87	26.76	31.60	36.36	40.99	45.46	40.33	35.44	30.60	25.84	21.21	16.74
29	61.11	20.87	25.77	30.60	35.36	39.99	44.46	40.24	35.34	30.51	25.75	21.11	16.65
30	60.02	19.88	24.77	29.61	34.36	39.00	43.46	40.15	35.25	30.41	25.66	21.03	16.56
31	58.94	18.88	23.78	28.62	33.37	38.00	42.46	40.06	35.16	30.32	25.57	20.94	16.48
32	57.86	17.89	22.79	27.62	32.38	37.01	41.46	39.97	35.07	30.23	25.48	20.85	16.39
33	56.77	16.89	21.79	26.63	31.38	36.01	40.46	39.88	34.98	30.14	25.39	20.76	16.31
34	55.69	15.90	20.80	25.64	30.39	35.02	39.47	39.79	34.89	30.05	25.30	20.68	16.23
35	54.61	14.91	19.81	24.65	29.40	34.02	38.47	39.70	34.80	29.96	25.21	20.59	16.14
36	53.53	13.92	18.82	23.66	28.41	33.03	37.47	39.62	34.72	29.88	25.13	20.50	16.06
37	52.46	12.92	17.83	22.67	27.42	32.04	36.48	39.54	34.63	29.79	25.04	20.42	15.98
38	51.38	11.93	16.84	21.68	26.43	31.05	35.49	39.45	34.55	29.71	24.95	20.33	15.90
39	50.31	10.94	15.85	20.69	25.44	30.06	34.49	39.37	34.46	29.62	24.87	20.25	15.82
40	49.24	9.95	14.86	19.70	24.45	29.07	33.50	39.29	34.38	29.54	24.79	20.17	15.73
41	48.17	8.95	13.87	18.71	23.47	28.08	32.51	39.22	34.30	29.46	24.70	20.08	15.66
42	47.10	7.96	12.88	17.73	22.48	27.10	31.53	39.14	34.23	29.38	24.62	20.00	15.58
43	46.04	6.97	11.89	16.74	21.50	26.11	30.54	39.07	34.15	29.30	24.54	19.93	15.50
44	44.98	5.97	10.90	15.75	20.51	25.13	29.55	39.01	34.08	29.23	24.47	19.85	15.43
45	43.93	4.98	9.91	14.77	19.53	24.15	28.57	38.94	34.02	29.16	24.40	19.78	15.35
46	42.87	3.99	8.92	13.79	18.55	23.17	27.59	38.89	33.95	29.09	24.32	19.70	15.28
47	41.83	2.99	7.93	12.80	17.57	22.19	26.62	38.83	33.89	29.02	24.26	19.63	15.21
48	40.79	2.00	6.95	11.82	16.59	21.22	25.64	38.79	33.84	28.97	24.19	19.57	15.14
49	39.76	1.00	5.96	10.84	15.62	20.25	24.67	38.76	33.80	28.92	24.14	19.51	15.08
50	38.73		4.97	9.86	14.65	19.28	23.71	38.73	33.76	28.87	24.08	19.45	15.02
51	37.71		3.98	8.88	13.67	18.31	22.75		33.73	28.83	24.03	19.39	14.96
52	36.69		2.99	7.90	12.70	17.35	21.78		33.70	28.79	23.99	19.34	14.90
53	35.68		1.99	6.92	11.73	16.39	20.83		33.68	28.76	23.95	19.29	14.85
54	34.68		1.00	5.94	10.76	15.43	19.87		33.68	28.74	23.91	19.25	14.80

Nil discount tables "at a glance"—FEMALE *continued*

	Table 2 Pecuniary loss for life	Table 4 Loss of earnings to age 50	Table 6 Loss of earnings to age 55	Table 8 Loss of earnings to age 60	Table 10 Loss of earnings to age 65	Table 12 Loss of earnings to age 70	Table 14 Loss of earnings to age 75	Table 16 Loss of pension from age 50	Table 18 Loss of pension from age 55	Table 20 Loss of pension from age 60	Table 22 Loss of pension from age 65	Table 24 Loss of pension from age 70	Table 26 Loss of pension from age 75
55	33.68			4.95	9.79	14.47	18.92	33.68		28.73	23.89	19.21	14.76
56	32.69			3.97	8.82	13.51	17.97			28.73	23.87	19.19	14.72
57	31.71			2.98	7.85	12.55	17.02			28.73	23.86	19.16	14.69
58	30.74			1.99	6.88	11.59	16.08			28.74	23.86	19.14	14.66
59	29.76			1.00	5.91	10.64	15.13			28.76	23.85	19.12	14.62
60	28.78				4.93	9.68	14.19		28.78		23.85	19.10	14.59
61	27.80				3.95	8.72	13.24				23.85	19.08	14.55
62	26.83				2.97	7.76	12.30				23.86	19.06	14.52
63	25.86				1.99	6.80	11.36				23.88	19.06	14.50
64	24.91				1.00	5.85	10.43				23.92	19.07	14.48
65	23.98					4.89	9.50			23.98		19.10	14.49
66	23.07					3.92	8.57					19.15	14.51
67	22.18					2.95	7.64					19.22	14.54
68	21.29					1.98	6.70					19.32	14.59
69	20.42					0.99	5.77					19.43	14.65
70	19.55						4.83				19.55		14.72
71	18.67						3.88						14.79
72	17.79						2.93						14.86
73	16.89						1.97						14.93
74	15.99						0.99						15.00
75	15.08												15.08
76	14.17												
77	13.28												
78	12.40												
79	11.56												
80	10.77												
81	10.02												
82	9.31												
83	8.65												
84	8.03												
85	7.45												
86	6.89												
87	6.36												
88	5.85												
89	5.36												
90	4.90												
91	4.47												
92	4.08												
93	3.72												
94	3.41												
95	3.14												
96	2.91												
97	2.70												
98	2.52												
99	2.35												
100	2.18												

A3: Life tables and projected life tables

Period expectation of life, United Kingdom
Based on data for the years 2008–2010

Age	Males					Females				
x	m_x	q_x	l_x	d_x	e_x	m_x	q_x	l_x	d_x	e_x
0	0.005006	0.004993	100000.0	499.3	78.05	0.004152	0.004143	100000.0	414.3	82.12
1	0.000335	0.000335	99500.7	33.4	77.44	0.000292	0.000292	99585.7	29.1	81.46
2	0.000189	0.000189	99467.3	18.8	76.46	0.000179	0.000179	99556.6	17.8	80.49
3	0.000144	0.000144	99448.5	14.3	75.48	0.000155	0.000155	99538.7	15.4	79.50
4	0.000107	0.000107	99434.2	10.6	74.49	0.000120	0.000120	99523.3	11.9	78.51
5	0.000119	0.000119	99423.6	11.9	73.50	0.000096	0.000096	99511.4	9.6	77.52
6	0.000112	0.000112	99411.7	11.1	72.51	0.000084	0.000084	99501.8	8.3	76.53
7	0.000087	0.000087	99400.6	8.7	71.51	0.000084	0.000084	99493.5	8.4	75.54
8	0.000115	0.000115	99391.9	11.4	70.52	0.000088	0.000088	99485.1	8.8	74.54
9	0.000102	0.000102	99380.5	10.2	69.53	0.000100	0.000100	99476.3	9.9	73.55
10	0.000098	0.000098	99370.3	9.7	68.54	0.000079	0.000079	99466.4	7.9	72.56
11	0.000100	0.000100	99360.6	9.9	67.54	0.000088	0.000088	99458.6	8.7	71.56
12	0.000107	0.000107	99350.7	10.6	66.55	0.000094	0.000094	99449.8	9.3	70.57
13	0.000121	0.000121	99340.1	12.0	65.56	0.000102	0.000102	99440.5	10.1	69.58
14	0.000143	0.000143	99328.1	14.2	64.56	0.000126	0.000126	99430.4	12.5	68.58
15	0.000220	0.000220	99313.9	21.8	63.57	0.000158	0.000158	99417.8	15.7	67.59
16	0.000298	0.000298	99292.1	29.6	62.59	0.000179	0.000179	99402.2	17.8	66.60
17	0.000472	0.000472	99262.5	46.9	61.61	0.000225	0.000225	99384.4	22.4	65.61
18	0.000563	0.000563	99215.6	55.9	60.63	0.000250	0.000250	99362.0	24.8	64.63
19	0.000573	0.000573	99159.8	56.8	59.67	0.000260	0.000260	99337.2	25.8	63.64
20	0.000630	0.000630	99103.0	62.5	58.70	0.000247	0.000247	99311.4	24.5	62.66
21	0.000629	0.000629	99040.5	62.3	57.74	0.000243	0.000243	99286.9	24.1	61.68
22	0.000608	0.000608	98978.2	60.1	56.78	0.000229	0.000229	99262.8	22.7	60.69
23	0.000658	0.000658	98918.1	65.1	55.81	0.000257	0.000257	99240.1	25.5	59.70
24	0.000645	0.000645	98853.0	63.7	54.85	0.000254	0.000254	99214.6	25.2	58.72
25	0.000659	0.000659	98789.3	65.1	53.88	0.000280	0.000280	99189.5	27.7	57.73
26	0.000736	0.000736	98724.2	72.6	52.92	0.000307	0.000307	99161.7	30.4	56.75
27	0.000738	0.000738	98651.6	72.8	51.95	0.000344	0.000344	99131.3	34.1	55.77
28	0.000810	0.000809	98578.7	79.8	50.99	0.000365	0.000365	99097.3	36.2	54.79
29	0.000843	0.000843	98499.0	83.0	50.03	0.000371	0.000371	99061.1	36.8	53.81
30	0.000922	0.000922	98416.0	90.7	49.08	0.000427	0.000427	99024.3	42.2	52.83
31	0.000917	0.000916	98325.2	90.1	48.12	0.000429	0.000429	98982.1	42.5	51.85
32	0.000970	0.000970	98235.2	95.3	47.16	0.000504	0.000504	98939.6	49.8	50.87
33	0.001027	0.001027	98139.9	100.7	46.21	0.000521	0.000521	98889.8	51.5	49.90
34	0.001161	0.001161	98039.1	113.8	45.26	0.000588	0.000588	98838.2	58.1	48.92
35	0.001261	0.001261	97925.3	123.5	44.31	0.000627	0.000627	98780.1	61.9	47.95
36	0.001251	0.001250	97801.9	122.3	43.36	0.000652	0.000652	98718.1	64.4	46.98
37	0.001317	0.001316	97679.6	128.6	42.42	0.000741	0.000741	98653.8	73.1	46.01
38	0.001487	0.001485	97551.0	144.9	41.47	0.000807	0.000807	98580.7	79.5	45.04
39	0.001549	0.001548	97406.1	150.8	40.53	0.000836	0.000835	98501.2	82.3	44.08
40	0.001681	0.001680	97255.3	163.4	39.60	0.000974	0.000973	98418.9	95.8	43.12
41	0.001789	0.001787	97092.0	173.5	38.66	0.001069	0.001069	98323.1	105.1	42.16
42	0.001847	0.001845	96918.5	178.8	37.73	0.001103	0.001102	98218.0	108.3	41.20
43	0.001989	0.001987	96739.6	192.2	36.80	0.001218	0.001217	98109.8	119.4	40.25
44	0.002215	0.002213	96547.4	213.6	35.87	0.001370	0.001369	97990.4	134.2	39.30
45	0.002414	0.002411	96333.8	232.3	34.95	0.001464	0.001463	97856.2	143.1	38.35
46	0.002548	0.002545	96101.5	244.6	34.03	0.001601	0.001600	97713.1	156.3	37.40
47	0.002723	0.002719	95856.9	260.7	33.12	0.001710	0.001708	97556.8	166.6	36.46
48	0.002942	0.002937	95596.2	280.8	32.21	0.001892	0.001890	97390.1	184.1	35.52
49	0.003170	0.003165	95315.4	301.7	31.30	0.002075	0.002073	97206.0	201.5	34.59
50	0.003530	0.003524	95013.7	334.8	30.40	0.002396	0.002393	97004.5	232.1	33.66

Period expectation of life, United Kingdom
Based on data for the years 2008–2010

Age	Males					Females				
x	m_x	q_x	l_x	d_x	e_x	m_x	q_x	l_x	d_x	e_x
51	0.003878	0.003870	94678.9	366.5	29.50	0.002505	0.002502	96772.4	242.1	32.74
52	0.004242	0.004233	94312.5	399.3	28.62	0.002836	0.002832	96530.3	273.4	31.82
53	0.004637	0.004626	93913.2	434.4	27.74	0.003045	0.003041	96256.9	292.7	30.91
54	0.005020	0.005008	93478.8	468.1	26.86	0.003507	0.003501	95964.2	335.9	30.00
55	0.005718	0.005702	93010.6	530.3	26.00	0.003611	0.003605	95628.3	344.7	29.11
56	0.006253	0.006233	92480.3	576.5	25.14	0.003977	0.003969	95283.6	378.1	28.21
57	0.006751	0.006728	91903.9	618.3	24.30	0.004325	0.004315	94905.4	409.5	27.32
58	0.007307	0.007280	91285.5	664.6	23.46	0.004692	0.004681	94495.9	442.3	26.44
59	0.007964	0.007933	90621.0	718.9	22.63	0.005208	0.005195	94053.6	488.6	25.56
60	0.008759	0.008720	89902.1	784.0	21.80	0.005642	0.005626	93565.0	526.4	24.69
61	0.009329	0.009286	89118.1	827.6	20.99	0.006160	0.006141	93038.6	571.4	23.83
62	0.010190	0.010138	88290.6	895.1	20.18	0.006529	0.006508	92467.3	601.8	22.97
63	0.011501	0.011435	87395.4	999.3	19.38	0.007255	0.007229	91865.5	664.1	22.12
64	0.012718	0.012638	86396.1	1091.9	18.60	0.008064	0.008032	91201.4	732.5	21.28
65	0.013800	0.013706	85304.2	1169.1	17.83	0.008732	0.008694	90468.9	786.6	20.44
66	0.015430	0.015312	84135.1	1288.3	17.07	0.009647	0.009601	89682.3	861.0	19.62
67	0.016766	0.016627	82846.8	1377.5	16.33	0.010473	0.010418	88821.3	925.3	18.80
68	0.018938	0.018760	81469.3	1528.4	15.60	0.011741	0.011673	87896.0	1026.0	18.00
69	0.020779	0.020566	79940.9	1644.0	14.89	0.012944	0.012861	86870.0	1117.2	17.20
70	0.022354	0.022107	78296.9	1730.9	14.19	0.014566	0.014461	85752.7	1240.1	16.42
71	0.024741	0.024439	76566.0	1871.2	13.50	0.015806	0.015682	84512.7	1325.4	15.66
72	0.027459	0.027087	74694.8	2023.3	12.83	0.017528	0.017376	83187.3	1445.5	14.90
73	0.030389	0.029934	72671.5	2175.4	12.17	0.019717	0.019525	81741.8	1596.0	14.15
74	0.033228	0.032685	70496.2	2304.1	11.53	0.021965	0.021727	80145.9	1741.3	13.42
75	0.037273	0.036591	68192.0	2495.2	10.90	0.024360	0.024067	78404.6	1887.0	12.71
76	0.041569	0.040723	65696.8	2675.3	10.30	0.027670	0.027292	76517.6	2088.4	12.01
77	0.046058	0.045021	63021.5	2837.3	9.71	0.030802	0.030335	74429.3	2257.8	11.33
78	0.051369	0.050083	60184.1	3014.2	9.15	0.035082	0.034477	72171.5	2488.3	10.67
79	0.057359	0.055760	57170.0	3187.8	8.60	0.039853	0.039074	69683.2	2722.8	10.04
80	0.065073	0.063023	53982.1	3402.1	8.08	0.045161	0.044163	66960.4	2957.2	9.42
81	0.072653	0.070106	50580.0	3546.0	7.59	0.050967	0.049701	64003.2	3181.0	8.84
82	0.080487	0.077374	47034.1	3639.2	7.13	0.057234	0.055642	60822.2	3384.3	8.27
83	0.088707	0.084940	43394.9	3686.0	6.68	0.064903	0.062863	57437.9	3610.7	7.73
84	0.100893	0.096048	39708.9	3814.0	6.26	0.073008	0.070437	53827.2	3791.4	7.22
85	0.112822	0.106798	35895.0	3833.5	5.87	0.082500	0.079232	50035.8	3964.4	6.73
86	0.125527	0.118114	32061.5	3786.9	5.51	0.093064	0.088926	46071.4	4096.9	6.26
87	0.137888	0.128995	28274.5	3647.3	5.18	0.104812	0.099593	41974.5	4180.4	5.82
88	0.151168	0.140545	24627.3	3461.2	4.87	0.118831	0.112166	37794.1	4239.2	5.41
89	0.157285	0.145818	21166.0	3086.4	4.59	0.127718	0.120051	33554.9	4028.3	5.03
90	0.169348	0.156128	18079.7	2822.7	4.29	0.146019	0.136084	29526.6	4018.1	4.65
91	0.182353	0.167116	15256.9	2549.7	3.99	0.159555	0.147766	25508.5	3769.3	4.30
92	0.207208	0.187756	12707.2	2385.9	3.68	0.186047	0.170213	21739.2	3700.3	3.96
93	0.233790	0.209322	10321.4	2160.5	3.42	0.208554	0.188860	18038.9	3406.8	3.67
94	0.257552	0.228169	8160.9	1862.1	3.19	0.232079	0.207948	14632.1	3042.7	3.41
95	0.284003	0.248689	6298.8	1566.4	2.99	0.254768	0.225981	11589.3	2619.0	3.18
96	0.306861	0.266042	4732.4	1259.0	2.81	0.280161	0.245738	8970.4	2204.4	2.96
97	0.334772	0.286771	3473.4	996.1	2.65	0.303297	0.263359	6766.0	1781.9	2.76
98	0.357008	0.302933	2477.3	750.5	2.52	0.336476	0.288020	4984.1	1435.5	2.57
99	0.372453	0.313981	1726.8	542.2	2.40	0.357586	0.303349	3548.6	1076.5	2.41
100	0.417865	0.345648	1184.7	409.5	2.27	0.391877	0.327673	2472.1	810.1	2.24

Source: Office for National Statistics licensed under the Open Government license V.I.O.

Expectations of life table

Expectations of life for age attained in 2013 allowing for projected changes in mortality assumed in the 2010-based population projections produced by the Office for National Statistics.

	United Kingdom					
Age	Males	Females	Age	Males	Females
0	90.7	94.1	51	34.7	38.0
1	89.9	93.3	52	33.7	36.9
2	88.8	92.2	53	32.7	35.9
3	87.7	91.1	54	31.7	34.8
4	86.5	90.0	55	30.7	33.8
5	85.4	88.9	56	29.7	32.8
6	84.2	87.7	57	28.7	31.8
7	83.1	86.6	58	27.7	30.8
8	81.9	85.5	59	26.8	29.8
9	80.8	84.3	60	25.9	28.8
10	79.7	83.2	61	25.0	27.9
11	78.5	82.1	62	24.1	26.9
12	77.3	80.9	63	23.2	26.0
13	76.2	79.8	64	22.3	25.0
14	75.1	78.7	65	21.4	24.1
15	73.9	77.5	66	20.6	23.1
16	72.8	76.4	67	19.7	22.2
17	71.6	75.3	68	18.8	21.3
18	70.5	74.2	69	18.0	20.4
19	69.4	73.1	70	17.2	19.5
20	68.3	71.9	71	16.4	18.6
21	67.1	70.8	72	15.6	17.7
22	66.0	69.7	73	14.8	16.9
23	64.9	68.6	74	14.1	16.0
24	63.8	67.5	75	13.3	15.2
25	62.7	66.3	76	12.6	14.4
26	61.6	65.2	77	11.9	13.6
27	60.4	64.1	78	11.2	12.8
28	59.3	63.0	79	10.5	12.0
29	58.2	61.9	80	9.8	11.2
30	57.1	60.8	81	9.2	10.4
31	56.0	59.7	82	8.5	9.7
32	54.9	58.6	83	7.9	9.0
33	53.9	57.5	84	7.4	8.3
34	52.8	56.4	85	6.9	7.7
35	51.7	55.3	86	6.4	7.1
36	50.6	54.2	87	6.0	6.6
37	49.6	53.1	88	5.6	6.1
38	48.5	52.0	89	5.2	5.6
39	47.4	50.9	90	4.8	5.2
40	46.3	49.8	91	4.5	4.8
41	45.3	48.7	92	4.2	4.4
42	44.2	47.6	93	3.9	4.1
43	43.1	46.5	94	3.7	3.8
44	42.1	45.4	95	3.4	3.5
45	41.0	44.3	96		
46	40.0	43.3	97		
47	38.9	42.2	98		
48	37.9	41.1	99		
49	36.8	40.1	100		
50	35.8	39.0			

Source: Office for National Statistics

Notes:

1. National life tables of various kinds and population projections have been produced for a considerable period, formerly by the Government Actuary's Department and, since February 2006, by the Office for National Statistics. The Decennial Life Tables for England and Wales combined and for Scotland are based on data for the three-year period around a Census. Between Censuses, life tables known as Interim Life Tables are produced which are based on data for the numbers in the population and the deaths by age and sex for the latest three-year period available. These Interim Life Tables are produced for the United Kingdom as a whole, Great Britain, England and Wales and also for each individual country of the United Kingdom. It is intended to update the life tables in Facts and Figures every year, using the latest data then available.

The historical life tables

2. The latest published Decennial Life Tables are the English Life Tables No.16 and the Scottish Life Tables 2000–2002. These are based on data on the numbers in the population and the numbers of deaths by age and sex for 2000–2002 (the three years around the 2001 Census).

3. Data from the preceding Decennial Life Table, ELT No.15, formed the mortality assumptions underlying the calculations of the multipliers in Tables 1–18 of the 4th edn of the Ogden Tables. Tables of multipliers using mortality from the Decennial Life Tables are no longer reproduced in the Ogden Tables.

4. The tables we produce are the latest available Interim Life Tables for the United Kingdom (based on data for 2008–2010).

5. The Ogden Tables take account of the possibilities that a claimant will live for different periods, e.g. die soon or live to be very old. The mortality assumptions for the 7th edn relate to the general population of the United Kingdom. Unless there is clear evidence in an individual case to support the view that the individual concerned is atypical and will experience a rather shorter or longer than average life, no further increase or reduction is required for mortality alone. Examples of atypical individuals would be a lifelong heavy smoker, someone suffering from a head injury or epilepsy or an immobile patient.

Projected mortality

6. The life tables referred to above are based on historical data (and expectations of life which are calculated using these data), and effectively assume that the mortality rate for a given age and sex will remain constant in future years. However, there have been large improvements in mortality rates over the last 100 years or so. If improvements in mortality rates carry on into the future, awards of damages calculated on the basis of historical mortality rates are likely to under-compensate claimants, on average.

7. At Appendix A to the Introduction to the 4th edn of the Ogden Tables there is an extract from ELT No.15, which shows graphs indicating rates of mortality expressed in percentages of the 1911 rates of mortality on a logarithmic scale. They demonstrate in stark fashion the improvement in longevity which has taken place since 1911.

8. The sole exception in some recent years has been small increases in the mortality of young males in their 30s due to increases in deaths caused by HIV infection and AIDS; suicide rates and

alcohol-related mortality have also increased for men at young ages in some years. However, even if this slight worsening of mortality were to continue, the effects on the tables of multipliers (in the Ogden Tables) would not be significant.

9. The Office for National Statistics carries out official population projections for the United Kingdom and constituent countries, usually every two years. In particular, these projections include assumptions of improving mortality rates at most ages in the years following the base year of the projections.

10. Tables 1–26 of the 7th edn of the Ogden Tables give multipliers based on the projected mortality rates underlying the 2008-based population projections for the United Kingdom by the Government Actuary. These take as their base the estimated numbers in the population by sex and age in the constituent countries of the United Kingdom in mid-2008. The projections and the underlying assumptions are available on the website of the Office for National Statistics at: *http://www.ons .gov.uk/ons/rel/npp/national-population-projections/index.html*.

11. Multipliers in earlier editions of the Ogden Tables were based on historical or projected mortality rates for the population of England and Wales combined. However, the Ogden Tables are used extensively in Scotland and Northern Ireland. Although it would be possible to produce separate Tables based on projected mortality rates for Scotland and for Northern Ireland, it was agreed for the 6th edn that rather than have three separate sets of tables there should be one set calculated using mortality rates from the population projections of the United Kingdom as a whole and this has been continued in the 7th edn.

12. Past official projections have tended to assume that the high rates of mortality improvement seen over the 20th century as a result of technical, medical and environmental changes were unlikely to be sustained indefinitely. However, expectations of life at birth have continued to increase at relatively constant rates over the last 20 years for both males and females, suggesting that, based on current trends, previous long-term assumptions were too pessimistic. As a result, recent successive projections have generally increased the projected expectations of life for the population at most ages.

13. The 2010-based national population projections were published in October 2011. Table A3, "Expectation of Life Table", shows expectations of life in the year 2013 by age and sex allowing for future improvements based on the mortality assumptions underlying the 2010-based population projections for the United Kingdom combined, setting out the expectation of life to specific ages attained in the year 2013.

14. As mentioned earlier, the mortality rates used are for the population as a whole. In difficult cases, where the sums involved are large and the matter is in doubt, an actuary should be consulted. Expert medical evidence should be obtained in atypical cases.

A4: Loss of earnings multipliers adjusted for education, disability and employment status

The Ogden Tables dealing with loss of earnings (Ogden tables 3–14) are subject to adjustment for contingencies other than mortality (Ogden paras 26–44). The tables which follow incorporate those factors without the need for further calculation.

The contingencies are whether the claimant was in employment or not, whether he was disabled or not, and his educational or skill level. Earlier editions (1st–5th) of the Ogden Tables and of Facts & Figures, based on earlier research, made adjustments for the general state of the economy; the nature of the claimant's employment, whether clerical or manual; and for different geographical areas of the country. These are not used in the latest edition as more recent research has shown that when adjustments are made for education, disability and educational attainment the difference made by these other factors is small.

Employment

Employed
Those who at the time of the accident are employed, self-employed or on a government training scheme.

Not employed
All others (including those temporarily out of work, full-time students and unpaid family workers).

Disability

Disabled
A person is classified as being disabled if all three of the following conditions in relation to the ill-health or disability are met:

(i) he or she has either a progressive illness or an illness which has or is expected to last for over a year,

   and

(ii) he or she satisfies the Equality Act definition that the impact of the disability substantially limits the person's ability to carry out normal day-to-day activities,

   and

(iii) his or her condition affects either the kind **or** the amount of paid work they can do.

Not disabled.
All others.

Paragraph 35 of the Ogden notes (section A8 in this book) gives examples of the ways in which a disability may limit one's day-to-day activities.

Educational attainment means the highest level of education attained by the claimant. It is a shorthand for the level of skill and includes equivalent non-academic qualifications.

Degree or equivalent.
This includes professional qualifications, for example as a nurse.

GCSE grades A–C, O levels, or CSE grade 1, up to A-levels or equivalent.
In the tables which follow this is called "Good GCSE level education or equivalent".

Qualifications below GCSE grade C or CSE grade 1 or equivalent, or no qualifications. In the tables which follow this is called "Education below good GCSE level".

There are 12 tables each for men and women arranged in the following order.

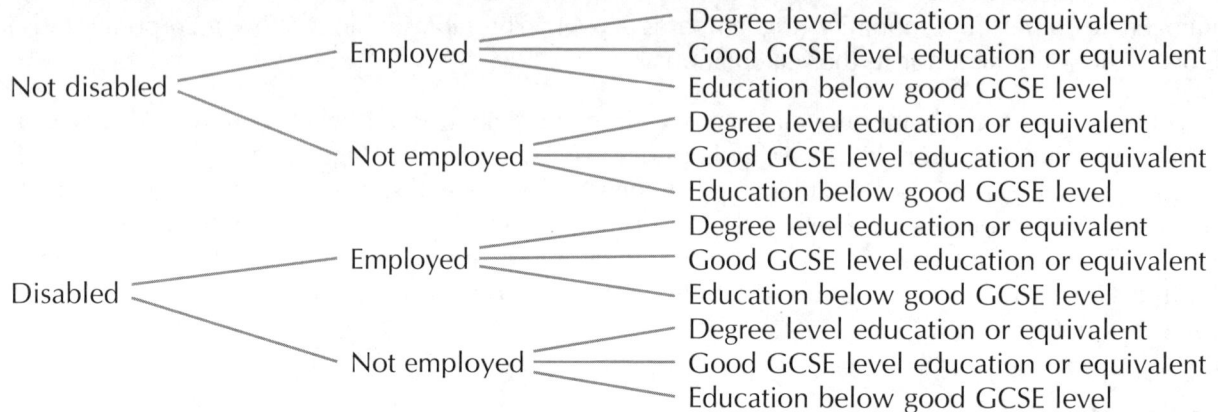

```
                                        ┌── Degree level education or equivalent
                        ┌── Employed ───┼── Good GCSE level education or equivalent
                        │               └── Education below good GCSE level
Not disabled ───────────┤               ┌── Degree level education or equivalent
                        └── Not employed┼── Good GCSE level education or equivalent
                                        └── Education below good GCSE level
                                        ┌── Degree level education or equivalent
                        ┌── Employed ───┼── Good GCSE level education or equivalent
                        │               └── Education below good GCSE level
Disabled ───────────────┤               ┌── Degree level education or equivalent
                        └── Not employed┼── Good GCSE level education or equivalent
                                        └── Education below good GCSE level
```

Thus if the claimant is a 32-year-old male solicitor, employed before the accident at a salary of £40,000, not disabled and proposing to retire at 60, the first table on the next page gives the multiplier for loss of earnings to age 60 as 18.22.

By using the tables for disabled claimants it is possible to obtain an estimate of the claimant's residual earning capacity, with an "inbuilt" allowance for employment risks which would otherwise require a separate *Smith v Manchester* award. Thus if the accident has seriously affected the solicitor's ability to work as a solicitor, and he is now employed at a salary of £25,000, the seventh table gives a multiplier of 11.68 for his new earning capacity to age 60. This approach will not always be suitable and there will be cases where a *Smith v Manchester* or *Blamire* award is still needed.

The 6th edn of the Ogden Tables had an adjustment factor for persons aged 16–19 with a degree level education. This caused difficulties. The 7th edn (para.41) recommends that in the case of someone who has not yet reached the age at which it is likely that he would start work, there should be an assessment of the level of education he would have attained, the age he would have started work, and whether he would have been employed or not. The multiplier appropriate to that age and those conditions should then be discounted for early receipt (for the period between the date of trial and the putative date of starting work).

The notes to the Ogden Tables do not provide specific adjustment factors for ages above 54 on the basis that, above that age, the likely course of someone's employment will depend on individual circumstances and the use of statistical averages may be inappropriate.

The adjustment factors as stated in the Ogden Tables are usually constant over a five year age range. This sometimes gives the appearance of anomalies or discontinuities in the figures—for example, in some tables a claimant of 18 or 19 has a smaller multiplier than one in his or her early 20s. The editors have been advised that this is the correct approach.

The tables assume a 2.5 per cent discount rate.

ND E Deg

Loss of earnings: not disabled; employed; degree level education or equivalent

Age	Male to retiring age						Age	Female to retiring age					
	50	55	60	65	70	75		50	55	60	65	70	75
16							16						
17			See introductory notes				17			See introductory notes			
18							18						
19							19						
20	19.31	21.29	23.02	24.51	25.77	26.84	20	18.77	20.73	22.44	23.92	25.20	26.31
21	18.86	20.90	22.67	24.20	25.49	26.58	21	18.34	20.35	22.10	23.62	24.94	26.06
22	18.41	20.50	22.31	23.87	25.20	26.32	22	17.91	19.95	21.75	23.32	24.66	25.81
23	17.95	20.08	21.94	23.54	24.90	26.05	23	17.45	20.44	21.40	23.00	24.38	25.55
24	17.47	19.66	21.56	23.20	24.60	25.77	24	16.99	19.14	21.03	22.67	24.08	25.29
25	17.17	19.44	21.41	23.11	24.55	25.76	25	16.52	18.73	20.66	22.34	23.79	25.03
26	16.67	18.99	21.01	22.76	24.24	25.47	26	16.03	18.30	20.27	22.00	23.49	24.75
27	16.14	18.53	20.61	22.39	23.90	25.18	27	15.53	17.85	19.88	21.65	23.17	24.47
28	15.61	18.06	20.19	22.01	23.57	24.87	28	15.02	17.41	19.48	21.30	22.86	24.18
29	15.08	17.59	19.76	21.63	23.22	24.55	29	14.51	16.95	19.07	20.92	22.53	23.89
30	14.36	16.91	19.12	21.01	22.62	23.97	30	13.97	16.47	18.65	20.55	22.19	23.59
31	13.80	16.40	18.67	20.62	22.26	23.64	31	13.42	15.98	18.23	20.17	21.85	23.27
32	13.22	15.90	18.22	20.21	21.91	23.32	32	12.86	15.49	17.78	19.78	21.49	22.95
33	12.63	15.38	17.76	19.81	21.54	22.98	33	12.28	14.98	17.34	19.38	21.14	22.63
34	12.03	14.85	17.29	19.38	21.16	22.64	34	11.69	14.46	16.87	18.97	20.77	22.30
35	11.17	14.00	16.44	18.54	20.32	21.81	35	11.09	13.93	16.40	18.55	20.39	21.97
36	10.55	13.45	15.96	18.12	19.94	21.46	36	10.48	13.38	15.91	18.11	20.01	21.62
37	9.91	12.89	15.46	17.68	19.55	21.11	37	9.84	12.82	15.41	17.68	19.62	21.26
38	9.26	12.31	14.95	17.22	19.14	20.74	38	9.19	12.25	14.91	17.22	19.21	20.90
39	8.59	11.72	14.44	16.76	18.72	20.36	39	8.52	11.66	14.39	16.76	18.80	20.52
40	7.72	10.87	13.59	15.92	17.89	19.53	40	7.85	11.05	13.86	16.29	18.38	20.14
41	7.04	10.27	13.06	15.44	17.47	19.14	41	7.15	10.44	13.31	15.81	17.94	19.76
42	6.33	9.64	12.50	14.96	17.04	18.75	42	6.43	9.81	12.75	15.31	17.50	19.36
43	5.61	9.01	11.95	14.47	16.59	18.35	43	5.70	9.16	12.18	14.80	17.04	18.95
44	4.88	8.36	11.38	13.96	16.14	17.94	44	4.94	8.50	11.60	14.28	16.58	18.53
45	4.02	7.52	10.54	13.13	15.32	17.12	45	4.08	7.65	10.75	13.44	15.75	17.70
46	3.26	6.85	9.96	12.62	14.85	16.70	46	3.31	6.96	10.15	12.91	15.28	17.28
47	2.47	6.17	9.36	12.08	14.38	16.28	47	2.51	6.26	9.54	12.37	14.80	16.84
48	1.68	5.46	8.74	11.54	13.90	15.84	48	1.69	5.55	8.91	11.81	14.30	16.41
49	0.85	4.75	8.11	10.98	13.40	15.39	49	0.86	4.82	8.27	11.25	13.80	15.96
50		3.87	7.20	10.05	12.45	14.43	50		4.02	7.52	10.54	13.13	15.33
51		3.10	6.49	9.38	11.81	13.82	51		3.22	6.77	9.84	12.47	14.69
52		2.33	5.77	8.71	11.18	13.21	52		2.42	6.02	9.14	11.80	14.05
53		1.55	5.06	8.04	10.54	12.61	53		1.61	5.28	8.44	11.14	13.42
54		0.78	4.34	7.37	9.91	12.01	54		0.82	4.58	7.83	10.61	12.95

See introductory notes as regards claimants
over 54 at date of trial

See introductory notes as regards claimants
over 54 at date of trial

A4: Loss of earnings multipliers adjusted for education, etc.

Loss of earnings: not disabled; employed; good GCSE level education or equivalent

Age	Male to retiring age						Age	Female to retiring age					
	50	55	60	65	70	75		50	55	60	65	70	75
16	20.52	22.28	23.81	25.13	26.26	27.21	16	18.56	20.17	21.58	22.81	23.87	24.78
17	20.12	21.93	23.50	24.85	26.00	26.97	17	18.20	19.85	21.29	22.56	23.64	24.58
18	19.72	21.57	23.18	24.56	25.75	26.74	18	17.84	19.53	21.01	22.30	23.42	24.36
19	19.31	21.20	22.85	24.27	25.48	26.50	19	17.46	19.21	20.72	22.04	23.18	24.15
20	19.31	21.29	23.02	24.51	25.77	26.84	20	17.29	19.10	20.67	22.04	23.22	24.24
21	18.86	20.90	22.67	24.20	25.49	26.58	21	16.90	18.75	20.36	21.76	22.98	24.01
22	18.41	20.50	22.31	23.87	25.20	26.32	22	16.50	18.38	20.04	21.48	22.72	23.78
23	17.95	20.08	21.94	23.54	24.90	26.05	23	16.08	18.84	19.71	21.19	22.46	23.54
24	17.47	19.66	21.56	23.20	24.60	25.77	24	15.65	17.64	19.38	20.89	22.19	23.30
25	16.98	19.23	21.18	22.86	24.29	25.48	25	15.59	17.67	19.50	21.08	22.45	23.62
26	16.49	18.79	20.78	22.51	23.98	25.20	26	15.13	17.27	19.14	20.76	22.17	23.36
27	15.97	18.34	20.39	22.14	23.64	24.90	27	14.66	16.85	18.77	20.44	21.87	23.09
28	15.45	17.87	19.97	21.78	23.31	24.60	28	14.18	16.43	18.39	20.10	21.57	22.82
29	14.91	17.40	19.55	21.40	22.97	24.29	29	13.69	15.99	18.00	19.75	21.26	22.55
30	14.20	16.73	18.91	20.78	22.38	23.71	30	13.35	15.73	17.82	19.63	21.19	22.53
31	13.65	16.23	18.46	20.39	22.02	23.39	31	12.82	15.27	17.41	19.26	20.87	22.23
32	13.08	15.72	18.02	19.99	21.67	23.07	32	12.28	14.79	16.98	18.89	20.53	21.92
33	12.50	15.22	17.56	19.59	21.30	22.73	33	11.73	14.31	16.56	18.50	20.19	21.62
34	11.90	14.69	17.10	19.17	20.93	22.40	34	11.17	13.81	16.12	18.11	19.84	21.30
35	11.17	14.00	16.44	18.54	20.32	21.81	35	10.71	13.46	15.85	17.92	19.70	21.22
36	10.55	13.45	15.96	18.12	19.94	21.46	36	10.12	12.93	15.38	17.50	19.33	20.89
37	9.91	12.89	15.46	17.68	19.55	21.11	37	9.51	12.38	14.90	17.08	18.95	20.55
38	9.26	12.31	14.95	17.22	19.14	20.74	38	8.88	11.83	14.41	16.64	18.56	20.19
39	8.59	11.72	14.44	16.76	18.72	20.36	39	8.23	11.27	13.91	16.19	18.16	19.83
40	7.72	10.87	13.59	15.92	17.89	19.53	40	7.59	10.68	13.39	15.74	17.76	19.46
41	7.04	10.27	13.06	15.44	17.47	19.14	41	6.91	10.09	12.87	15.27	17.34	19.09
42	6.33	9.64	12.50	14.96	17.04	18.75	42	6.21	9.48	12.32	14.79	16.91	18.71
43	5.61	9.01	11.95	14.47	16.59	18.35	43	5.50	8.85	11.77	14.30	16.47	18.31
44	4.88	8.36	11.38	13.96	16.14	17.94	44	4.77	8.21	11.21	13.80	16.02	17.91
45	4.02	7.52	10.54	13.13	15.32	17.12	45	3.99	7.47	10.51	13.13	15.39	17.30
46	3.26	6.85	9.96	12.62	14.85	16.70	46	3.23	6.80	9.92	12.61	14.93	16.88
47	2.47	6.17	9.36	12.08	14.38	16.28	47	2.45	6.12	9.32	12.09	14.46	16.46
48	1.68	5.46	8.74	11.54	13.90	15.84	48	1.66	5.42	8.70	11.54	13.97	16.03
49	0.85	4.75	8.11	10.98	13.40	15.39	49	0.84	4.71	8.08	10.99	13.48	15.59
50		3.87	7.20	10.05	12.45	14.43	50		3.93	7.34	10.30	12.83	14.97
51		3.10	6.49	9.38	11.81	13.82	51		3.18	6.69	9.73	12.32	14.52
52		2.33	5.77	8.71	11.18	13.21	52		2.42	6.02	9.14	11.80	14.05
53		1.55	5.06	8.04	10.54	12.61	53		1.61	5.28	8.44	11.14	13.42
54		0.78	4.34	7.37	9.91	12.01	54		0.82	4.58	7.83	10.61	12.95

See introductory notes as regards claimants
over 54 at date of trial

See introductory notes as regards claimants
over 54 at date of trial

Loss of earnings: not disabled; employed; education below good GCSE level

Age	Male to retiring age						Age	Female to retiring age					
	50	55	60	65	70	75		50	55	60	65	70	75
16	19.38	21.05	22.49	23.73	24.80	25.70	16	14.66	15.94	17.05	18.02	18.86	19.58
17	19.01	20.71	22.19	23.47	24.56	25.47	17	14.38	15.69	16.83	17.82	18.68	19.42
18	18.62	20.37	21.89	23.20	24.32	25.25	18	14.09	15.43	16.60	17.62	18.50	19.25
19	18.23	20.03	21.58	22.92	24.06	25.02	19	13.80	15.17	16.37	17.41	18.32	19.08
20	18.26	20.13	21.77	23.18	24.37	25.38	20	14.34	15.84	17.14	18.28	19.26	20.10
21	17.84	19.77	21.44	22.88	24.11	25.13	21	14.01	15.54	16.88	18.05	19.05	19.91
22	17.41	19.38	21.10	22.58	23.83	24.89	22	13.68	15.25	16.62	17.82	18.84	19.72
23	16.97	18.99	20.75	22.26	23.55	24.63	23	13.33	15.62	16.35	17.57	18.63	19.52
24	16.52	18.59	20.39	21.94	23.26	24.37	24	12.98	14.63	16.07	17.32	18.40	19.33
25	16.43	18.60	20.49	22.12	23.50	24.65	25	13.36	15.15	16.71	18.07	19.25	20.25
26	15.95	18.17	20.11	21.78	23.19	24.38	26	12.97	14.80	16.40	17.80	19.00	20.02
27	15.45	17.74	19.72	21.42	22.87	24.09	27	12.56	14.44	16.08	17.52	18.74	19.79
28	14.94	17.28	19.32	21.07	22.55	23.80	28	12.15	14.08	15.76	17.23	18.49	19.56
29	14.43	16.83	18.91	20.70	22.22	23.50	29	11.74	13.71	15.43	16.93	18.22	19.32
30	13.89	16.36	18.49	20.33	21.89	23.18	30	11.78	13.88	15.72	17.32	18.70	19.88
31	13.35	15.87	18.06	19.94	21.54	22.87	31	11.31	13.47	15.36	17.00	18.41	19.61
32	12.79	15.38	17.62	19.55	21.19	22.56	32	10.84	13.05	14.99	16.67	18.11	19.34
33	12.22	14.88	17.18	19.16	20.83	22.23	33	10.35	12.62	14.61	16.33	17.81	19.07
34	11.64	14.36	16.72	18.75	20.47	21.90	34	9.85	12.19	14.22	15.98	17.51	18.80
35	11.04	13.84	16.26	18.33	20.10	21.56	35	9.72	12.21	14.38	16.26	17.87	19.25
36	10.43	13.30	15.78	17.92	19.71	21.22	36	9.18	11.72	13.95	15.87	17.53	18.95
37	9.80	12.74	15.29	17.48	19.33	20.87	37	8.63	11.23	13.51	15.49	17.19	18.63
38	9.16	12.18	14.78	17.03	18.93	20.51	38	8.06	10.73	13.07	15.09	16.83	18.31
39	8.49	11.59	14.28	16.57	18.51	20.13	39	7.47	10.22	12.61	14.69	16.47	17.99
40	7.72	10.87	13.59	15.92	17.89	19.53	40	7.06	9.94	12.46	14.64	16.52	18.10
41	7.04	10.27	13.06	15.44	17.47	19.14	41	6.42	9.38	11.97	14.21	16.13	17.76
42	6.33	9.64	12.50	14.96	17.04	18.75	42	5.78	8.82	11.46	13.76	15.73	17.40
43	5.61	9.01	11.95	14.47	16.59	18.35	43	5.12	8.23	10.95	13.30	15.32	17.03
44	4.88	8.36	11.38	13.96	16.14	17.94	44	4.44	7.64	10.42	12.84	14.90	16.66
45	4.02	7.52	10.54	13.13	15.32	17.12	45	3.80	7.12	10.01	12.51	14.66	16.48
46	3.26	6.85	9.96	12.62	14.85	16.70	46	3.08	6.48	9.45	12.02	14.22	16.09
47	2.47	6.17	9.36	12.08	14.38	16.28	47	2.34	5.83	8.88	11.52	13.78	15.68
48	1.68	5.46	8.74	11.54	13.90	15.84	48	1.58	5.17	8.29	11.00	13.32	15.28
49	0.85	4.75	8.11	10.98	13.40	15.39	49	0.80	4.49	7.70	10.47	12.85	14.86
50		3.87	7.20	10.05	12.45	14.43	50		3.79	7.08	9.93	12.37	14.43
51		3.10	6.49	9.38	11.81	13.82	51		3.07	6.46	9.38	11.88	14.00
52		2.33	5.77	8.71	11.18	13.21	52		2.33	5.81	8.81	11.38	13.55
53		1.55	5.06	8.04	10.54	12.61	53		1.58	5.15	8.24	10.87	13.10
54		0.78	4.34	7.37	9.91	12.01	54		0.81	4.53	7.73	10.48	12.79

See introductory notes as regards claimants
over 54 at date of trial

See introductory notes as regards claimants
over 54 at date of trial

A4: Loss of earnings multipliers adjusted for education, etc.

Loss of earnings: not disabled; not employed; degree level education or equivalent

Age	Male to retiring age						Age	Female to retiring age					
	50	55	60	65	70	75		50	55	60	65	70	75
16							16						
17			See introductory notes				17			See introductory notes			
18							18						
19							19						
20	18.68	20.59	22.27	23.71	24.93	25.96	20	17.72	19.56	21.18	22.58	23.79	24.83
21	18.25	20.22	21.93	23.41	24.66	25.71	21	17.31	19.20	20.86	22.29	23.54	24.60
22	17.81	19.83	21.58	23.10	24.38	25.46	22	16.90	18.83	20.53	22.01	23.28	24.36
23	17.36	19.43	21.23	22.78	24.09	25.20	23	16.47	19.29	20.19	21.71	23.01	24.12
24	16.90	19.02	20.86	22.45	23.80	24.93	24	16.04	18.07	19.85	21.39	22.73	23.87
25	16.43	18.60	20.49	22.12	23.50	24.65	25	15.40	17.46	19.26	20.83	22.19	23.34
26	15.95	18.17	20.11	21.78	23.19	24.38	26	14.95	17.06	18.91	20.52	21.90	23.08
27	15.45	17.74	19.72	21.42	22.87	24.09	27	14.48	16.65	18.54	20.19	21.60	22.82
28	14.94	17.28	19.32	21.07	22.55	23.80	28	14.01	16.23	18.17	19.86	21.31	22.55
29	14.43	16.83	18.91	20.70	22.22	23.50	29	13.53	15.80	17.79	19.51	21.01	22.28
30	13.58	15.99	18.08	19.87	21.39	22.66	30	12.72	14.99	16.98	18.70	20.19	21.47
31	13.05	15.51	17.65	19.50	21.05	22.36	31	12.21	14.55	16.59	18.35	19.89	21.18
32	12.50	15.03	17.23	19.11	20.71	22.05	32	11.70	14.09	16.18	18.00	19.56	20.89
33	11.95	14.55	16.79	18.73	20.37	21.73	33	11.18	13.63	15.78	17.63	19.24	20.60
34	11.38	14.04	16.35	18.33	20.01	21.41	34	10.64	13.16	15.36	17.26	18.91	20.30
35	10.55	13.22	15.53	17.51	19.19	20.60	35	9.97	12.52	14.74	16.67	18.33	19.74
36	9.96	12.70	15.07	17.11	18.83	20.26	36	9.42	12.02	14.30	16.28	17.98	19.43
37	9.36	12.17	14.60	16.69	18.46	19.93	37	8.85	11.52	13.86	15.89	17.63	19.11
38	8.75	11.63	14.12	16.26	18.08	19.58	38	8.26	11.01	13.40	15.48	17.26	18.78
39	8.11	11.07	13.63	15.83	17.68	19.23	39	7.66	10.48	12.94	15.06	16.90	18.45
40	7.20	10.13	12.66	14.83	16.67	18.20	40	6.88	9.69	12.14	14.27	16.11	17.65
41	6.56	9.57	12.17	14.39	16.28	17.84	41	6.26	9.15	11.67	13.85	15.72	17.32
42	5.90	8.99	11.65	13.94	15.88	17.47	42	5.63	8.60	11.18	13.42	15.33	16.97
43	5.23	8.40	11.14	13.48	15.46	17.10	43	4.99	8.03	10.68	12.97	14.94	16.61
44	4.54	7.79	10.60	13.01	15.04	16.72	44	4.33	7.45	10.16	12.52	14.53	16.24
45	3.60	6.73	9.44	11.76	13.71	15.33	45	3.38	6.33	8.90	11.12	13.03	14.65
46	2.92	6.14	8.92	11.30	13.30	14.95	46	2.74	5.76	8.40	10.68	12.64	14.30
47	2.22	5.52	8.38	10.82	12.87	14.58	47	2.08	5.18	7.89	10.24	12.25	13.94
48	1.50	4.89	7.82	10.33	12.44	14.18	48	1.40	4.59	7.37	9.78	11.84	13.58
49	0.76	4.25	7.26	9.83	12.00	13.78	49	0.71	3.99	6.84	9.31	11.42	13.20
50		3.36	6.25	8.72	10.80	12.51	50		3.00	5.59	7.85	9.77	11.40
51		2.64	5.54	8.01	10.08	11.80	51		2.27	4.78	6.95	8.80	10.37
52		1.92	4.77	7.20	9.25	10.93	52		1.61	4.02	6.09	7.87	9.37
53		1.22	3.98	6.33	8.30	9.93	53		0.97	3.18	5.09	6.71	8.09
54		0.58	3.24	5.50	7.40	8.97	54		0.43	2.43	4.15	5.62	6.86

See introductory notes as regards claimants
over 54 at date of trial

See introductory notes as regards claimants
over 54 at date of trial

Loss of earnings: not disabled; not employed; good GCSE level education or equivalent

Age	Male to retiring age						Age	Female to retiring age					
	50	55	60	65	70	75		50	55	60	65	70	75
16	19.38	21.05	22.49	23.73	24.80	25.70	16	17.64	19.17	20.51	21.68	22.69	23.55
17	19.01	20.71	22.19	23.47	24.56	25.47	17	17.30	18.87	20.24	21.44	22.48	23.36
18	18.62	20.37	21.89	23.20	24.32	25.25	18	16.96	18.56	19.97	21.20	22.26	23.16
19	18.23	20.03	21.58	22.92	24.06	25.02	19	16.60	18.26	19.70	20.95	22.04	22.96
20	18.47	20.36	22.02	23.44	24.65	25.67	20	16.03	17.70	19.16	20.43	21.52	22.47
21	18.04	19.99	21.68	23.14	24.38	25.42	21	15.66	17.37	18.87	20.17	21.30	22.25
22	17.61	19.61	21.34	22.84	24.10	25.18	22	15.29	17.04	18.57	19.91	21.06	22.04
23	17.17	19.21	20.99	22.52	23.82	24.91	23	14.90	17.46	18.27	19.64	20.82	21.82
24	16.71	18.81	20.63	22.19	23.53	24.65	24	14.51	16.35	17.96	19.36	20.57	21.60
25	16.24	18.39	20.26	21.87	23.23	24.38	25	13.92	15.78	17.41	18.83	20.05	21.09
26	15.77	17.97	19.88	21.53	22.93	24.10	26	13.51	15.42	17.09	18.54	19.79	20.86
27	15.28	17.54	19.50	21.18	22.62	23.82	27	13.09	15.05	16.76	18.25	19.52	20.62
28	14.78	17.09	19.10	20.83	22.30	23.53	28	12.66	14.67	16.42	17.95	19.26	20.38
29	14.26	16.64	18.70	20.47	21.97	23.23	29	12.23	14.28	16.07	17.63	18.98	20.13
30	13.42	15.81	17.87	19.64	21.15	22.40	30	11.78	13.88	15.72	17.32	18.70	19.88
31	12.90	15.33	17.45	19.27	20.81	22.10	31	11.31	13.47	15.36	17.00	18.41	19.61
32	12.36	14.86	17.03	18.89	20.48	21.80	32	10.84	13.05	14.99	16.67	18.11	19.34
33	11.81	14.38	16.60	18.52	20.13	21.48	33	10.35	12.62	14.61	16.33	17.81	19.07
34	11.24	13.88	16.16	18.12	19.78	21.16	34	9.85	12.19	14.22	15.98	17.51	18.80
35	10.42	13.06	15.35	17.30	18.97	20.35	35	9.22	11.58	13.64	15.42	16.95	18.26
36	9.84	12.55	14.89	16.91	18.61	20.03	36	8.71	11.12	13.23	15.06	16.64	17.97
37	9.25	12.03	14.43	16.50	18.24	19.70	37	8.18	10.66	12.82	14.70	16.31	17.68
38	8.64	11.49	13.95	16.07	17.87	19.35	38	7.64	10.18	12.40	14.32	15.97	17.38
39	8.01	10.94	13.47	15.64	17.47	19.00	39	7.09	9.69	11.97	13.93	15.63	17.06
40	7.11	10.00	12.51	14.65	16.47	17.97	40	6.35	8.94	11.21	13.18	14.87	16.29
41	6.48	9.45	12.02	14.22	16.08	17.62	41	5.78	8.45	10.77	12.79	14.52	15.98
42	5.83	8.88	11.51	13.77	15.68	17.26	42	5.20	7.93	10.32	12.38	14.16	15.66
43	5.16	8.29	11.00	13.32	15.27	16.89	43	4.61	7.41	9.86	11.97	13.79	15.33
44	4.49	7.70	10.47	12.85	14.86	16.52	44	4.00	6.88	9.38	11.56	13.41	14.99
45	3.60	6.73	9.44	11.76	13.71	15.33	45	3.00	5.63	7.91	9.89	11.58	13.02
46	2.92	6.14	8.92	11.30	13.30	14.95	46	2.43	5.12	7.47	9.50	11.24	12.71
47	2.22	5.52	8.38	10.82	12.87	14.58	47	1.84	4.61	7.01	9.10	10.89	12.39
48	1.50	4.89	7.82	10.33	12.44	14.18	48	1.25	4.08	6.55	8.69	10.52	12.07
49	0.76	4.25	7.26	9.83	12.00	13.78	49	0.63	3.55	6.08	8.28	10.15	11.74
50		3.36	6.25	8.72	10.80	12.51	50		2.57	4.81	6.74	8.40	9.80
51		2.64	5.54	8.01	10.08	11.80	51		1.93	4.06	5.91	7.48	8.81
52		1.92	4.77	7.20	9.25	10.93	52		1.32	3.30	5.00	6.46	7.70
53		1.22	3.98	6.33	8.30	9.93	53		0.80	2.61	4.17	5.50	6.63
54		0.58	3.24	5.50	7.40	8.97	54		0.35	1.93	3.30	4.47	5.46

See introductory notes as regards claimants
over 54 at date of trial

See introductory notes as regards claimants
over 54 at date of trial

A4: Loss of earnings multipliers adjusted for education, etc.

Loss of earnings: not disabled; not employed; education below good GCSE level

Age	Male to retiring age						Age	Female to retiring age					
	50	55	60	65	70	75		50	55	60	65	70	75
16	18.70	20.30	21.70	22.89	23.93	24.79	16	13.52	14.69	15.72	16.61	17.39	18.05
17	18.34	19.98	21.41	22.64	23.69	24.58	17	13.26	14.46	15.51	16.43	17.22	17.90
18	17.97	19.66	21.12	22.38	23.46	24.36	18	12.99	14.22	15.30	16.24	17.06	17.75
19	17.59	19.32	20.82	22.12	23.21	24.14	19	12.72	13.99	15.09	16.05	16.89	17.59
20	17.42	19.21	20.77	22.11	23.25	24.21	20	12.65	13.97	15.13	16.13	16.99	17.74
21	17.02	18.86	20.45	21.83	23.00	23.98	21	12.37	13.72	14.90	15.92	16.81	17.57
22	16.61	18.49	20.13	21.54	22.73	23.75	22	12.07	13.45	14.66	15.72	16.63	17.40
23	16.19	18.12	19.80	21.24	22.47	23.50	23	11.77	13.78	14.42	15.50	16.43	17.23
24	15.76	17.74	19.46	20.93	22.19	23.25	24	11.45	12.91	14.18	15.28	16.24	17.05
25	15.14	17.14	18.88	20.38	21.65	22.71	25	11.32	12.83	14.16	15.31	16.31	17.15
26	14.69	16.74	18.52	20.07	21.37	22.46	26	10.99	12.54	13.90	15.08	16.10	16.96
27	14.24	16.34	18.17	19.74	21.07	22.20	27	10.64	12.24	13.63	14.84	15.88	16.77
28	13.77	15.92	17.80	19.41	20.78	21.93	28	10.29	11.93	13.35	14.60	15.66	16.57
29	13.29	15.51	17.43	19.07	20.48	21.65	29	9.94	11.61	13.07	14.34	15.44	16.37
30	12.64	14.89	16.83	18.50	19.92	21.10	30	9.89	11.66	13.20	14.55	15.71	16.70
31	12.15	14.44	16.43	18.15	19.60	20.82	31	9.50	11.31	12.90	14.28	15.47	16.47
32	11.64	14.00	16.04	17.80	19.29	20.53	32	9.10	10.96	12.59	14.00	15.21	16.25
33	11.12	13.54	15.63	17.44	18.96	20.23	33	8.69	10.60	12.27	13.72	14.96	16.02
34	10.59	13.07	15.22	17.07	18.63	19.93	34	8.28	10.24	11.94	13.43	14.70	15.79
35	9.93	12.44	14.62	16.48	18.06	19.38	35	7.85	9.86	11.61	13.13	14.43	15.55
36	9.38	11.95	14.18	16.10	17.72	19.07	36	7.42	9.47	11.26	12.82	14.16	15.30
37	8.81	11.46	13.74	15.71	17.38	18.76	37	6.97	9.07	10.91	12.51	13.89	15.05
38	8.23	10.94	13.29	15.30	17.02	18.43	38	6.51	8.67	10.55	12.19	13.60	14.79
39	7.63	10.42	12.83	14.90	16.64	18.10	39	6.03	8.25	10.19	11.86	13.31	14.53
40	6.85	9.63	12.04	14.11	15.86	17.31	40	5.29	7.45	9.34	10.98	12.39	13.58
41	6.24	9.10	11.58	13.69	15.48	16.97	41	4.82	7.04	8.98	10.66	12.10	13.32
42	5.61	8.55	11.08	13.26	15.10	16.62	42	4.33	6.61	8.60	10.32	11.80	13.05
43	4.97	7.99	10.59	12.82	14.70	16.26	43	3.84	6.17	8.21	9.98	11.49	12.77
44	4.32	7.41	10.09	12.37	14.31	15.90	44	3.33	5.73	7.82	9.63	11.18	12.49
45	3.46	6.47	9.07	11.30	13.18	14.73	45	2.44	4.57	6.43	8.03	9.41	10.58
46	2.80	5.90	8.57	10.86	12.78	14.37	46	1.98	4.16	6.07	7.72	9.13	10.33
47	2.13	5.31	8.05	10.40	12.37	14.01	47	1.50	3.74	5.70	7.39	8.85	10.07
48	1.44	4.70	7.52	9.93	11.96	13.63	48	1.01	3.32	5.32	7.06	8.55	9.81
49	0.73	4.08	6.98	9.45	11.53	13.25	49	0.51	2.88	4.94	6.72	8.25	9.54
50		3.26	6.08	8.48	10.50	12.17	50		2.01	3.76	5.27	6.57	7.66
51		2.57	5.38	7.78	9.79	11.46	51		1.51	3.19	4.63	5.87	6.91
52		1.90	4.70	7.10	9.11	10.76	52		1.04	2.58	3.92	5.06	6.02
53		1.22	3.98	6.33	8.30	9.93	53		0.62	2.04	3.25	4.29	5.17
54		0.58	3.24	5.50	7.40	8.97	54		0.27	1.49	2.55	3.45	4.21

See introductory notes as regards claimants
over 54 at date of trial

See introductory notes as regards claimants
over 54 at date of trial

D E Deg

Loss of earnings: disabled; employed; degree level education or equivalent

Age	Male to retiring age						Age	Female to retiring age					
	50	55	60	65	70	75		50	55	60	65	70	75
16							16						
17			See introductory notes				17			See introductory notes			
18							18						
19							19						
20	12.80	14.12	15.26	16.25	17.09	17.79	20	13.50	14.91	16.13	17.20	18.12	18.92
21	12.51	13.86	15.03	16.04	16.90	17.62	21	13.19	14.63	15.89	16.99	17.93	18.74
22	12.21	13.59	14.79	15.83	16.71	17.45	22	12.88	14.35	15.64	16.77	17.73	18.56
23	11.90	13.32	14.55	15.61	16.51	17.27	23	12.55	14.70	15.39	16.54	17.53	18.37
24	11.58	13.04	14.30	15.38	16.31	17.09	24	12.22	13.77	15.12	16.30	17.32	18.19
25	11.08	12.54	13.81	14.91	15.84	16.62	25	11.69	13.26	14.62	15.81	16.84	17.72
26	10.75	12.25	13.55	14.68	15.64	16.43	26	11.35	12.95	14.35	15.57	16.63	17.52
27	10.42	11.96	13.30	14.44	15.42	16.24	27	10.99	12.64	14.07	15.33	16.40	17.32
28	10.07	11.65	13.03	14.20	15.20	16.04	28	10.63	12.32	13.79	15.08	16.18	17.12
29	9.73	11.35	12.75	13.96	14.98	15.84	29	10.27	12.00	13.50	14.81	15.95	16.91
30	9.21	10.84	12.26	13.48	14.51	15.37	30	9.73	11.48	13.00	14.32	15.46	16.43
31	8.85	10.52	11.97	13.22	14.28	15.16	31	9.35	11.14	12.70	14.05	15.22	16.21
32	8.48	10.20	11.68	12.96	14.05	14.96	32	8.96	10.79	12.39	13.78	14.97	15.99
33	8.10	9.86	11.39	12.70	13.81	14.74	33	8.55	10.43	12.08	13.50	14.73	15.77
34	7.71	9.52	11.09	12.43	13.57	14.52	34	8.14	10.08	11.76	13.21	14.47	15.54
35	7.20	9.02	10.60	11.95	13.10	14.05	35	7.60	9.55	11.24	12.71	13.98	15.05
36	6.80	8.67	10.28	11.68	12.85	13.83	36	7.18	9.17	10.91	12.41	13.71	14.82
37	6.38	8.31	9.96	11.39	12.60	13.60	37	6.75	8.78	10.57	12.11	13.44	14.57
38	5.97	7.93	9.63	11.10	12.34	13.36	38	6.30	8.39	10.22	11.80	13.16	14.32
39	5.53	7.55	9.30	10.80	12.06	13.12	39	5.84	7.99	9.86	11.49	12.88	14.07
40	5.00	7.04	8.80	10.31	11.59	12.65	40	5.29	7.45	9.34	10.98	12.39	13.58
41	4.56	6.65	8.46	10.00	11.31	12.40	41	4.82	7.04	8.98	10.66	12.10	13.32
42	4.10	6.25	8.10	9.69	11.04	12.15	42	4.33	6.61	8.60	10.32	11.80	13.05
43	3.63	5.84	7.74	9.37	10.74	11.88	43	3.84	6.17	8.21	9.98	11.49	12.77
44	3.16	5.42	7.37	9.04	10.45	11.62	44	3.33	5.73	7.82	9.63	11.18	12.49
45	2.57	4.81	6.74	8.40	9.80	10.95	45	2.81	5.27	7.42	9.27	10.86	12.21
46	2.08	4.38	6.37	8.07	9.50	10.68	46	2.28	4.80	7.00	8.90	10.54	11.92
47	1.58	3.94	5.98	7.73	9.20	10.41	47	1.73	4.32	6.58	8.53	10.21	11.62
48	1.07	3.49	5.59	7.38	8.89	10.13	48	1.17	3.83	6.14	8.15	9.86	11.32
49	0.54	3.04	5.19	7.02	8.57	9.85	49	0.59	3.32	5.70	7.76	9.52	11.00
50		2.47	4.60	6.42	7.95	9.21	50		2.81	5.24	7.36	9.16	10.69
51		2.00	4.19	6.06	7.63	8.93	51		2.31	4.86	7.06	8.95	10.54
52		1.55	3.84	5.81	7.45	8.81	52		1.76	4.37	6.64	8.57	10.21
53		1.05	3.41	5.43	7.12	8.51	53		1.21	3.94	6.31	8.32	10.03
54		0.53	2.96	5.04	6.78	8.21	54		0.62	3.48	5.94	8.05	9.83

See introductory notes as regards claimants
over 54 at date of trial

See introductory notes as regards claimants
over 54 at date of trial

A4: Loss of earnings multipliers adjusted for education, etc.

Loss of earnings: disabled; employed; good GCSE level education or equivalent

Age	Male to retiring age						Age	Female to retiring age					
	50	55	60	65	70	75		50	55	60	65	70	75
16	12.54	13.62	14.55	15.36	16.05	16.63	16	9.85	10.71	11.46	12.11	12.67	13.15
17	12.30	13.40	14.36	15.19	15.89	16.48	17	9.66	10.54	11.30	11.98	12.55	13.05
18	12.05	13.18	14.16	15.01	15.74	16.34	18	9.47	10.37	11.15	11.84	12.43	12.93
19	11.80	12.96	13.96	14.83	15.57	16.19	19	9.27	10.20	11.00	11.70	12.31	12.82
20	11.54	12.73	13.76	14.65	15.41	16.04	20	9.28	10.25	11.09	11.83	12.46	13.01
21	11.28	12.50	13.55	14.47	15.24	15.89	21	9.07	10.06	10.93	11.68	12.33	12.88
22	11.01	12.25	13.34	14.27	15.06	15.74	22	8.85	9.86	10.75	11.53	12.19	12.76
23	10.73	12.01	13.12	14.07	14.89	15.57	23	8.63	10.11	10.58	11.37	12.05	12.63
24	10.44	11.75	12.89	13.87	14.71	15.41	24	8.40	9.46	10.40	11.21	11.91	12.50
25	9.97	11.29	12.43	13.42	14.26	14.96	25	8.35	9.47	10.44	11.30	12.03	12.65
26	9.68	11.03	12.20	13.21	14.07	14.79	26	8.10	9.25	10.25	11.12	11.88	12.51
27	9.37	10.76	11.97	13.00	13.88	14.62	27	7.85	9.03	10.05	10.95	11.71	12.37
28	9.07	10.49	11.72	12.78	13.68	14.44	28	7.59	8.80	9.85	10.77	11.56	12.23
29	8.75	10.21	11.48	12.56	13.48	14.26	29	7.34	8.57	9.64	10.58	11.39	12.08
30	8.12	9.56	10.81	11.88	12.79	13.55	30	7.22	8.51	9.64	10.62	11.47	12.19
31	7.80	9.27	10.55	11.65	12.58	13.36	31	6.94	8.26	9.42	10.42	11.29	12.03
32	7.47	8.99	10.30	11.42	12.38	13.18	32	6.65	8.00	9.19	10.22	11.11	11.86
33	7.14	8.69	10.04	11.20	12.17	12.99	33	6.35	7.74	8.96	10.01	10.93	11.70
34	6.80	8.39	9.77	10.96	11.96	12.80	34	6.04	7.48	8.72	9.80	10.74	11.53
35	5.96	7.46	8.77	9.89	10.84	11.63	35	5.98	7.51	8.85	10.00	11.00	11.85
36	5.63	7.17	8.51	9.66	10.63	11.44	36	5.65	7.21	8.58	9.77	10.79	11.66
37	5.28	6.87	8.25	9.43	10.43	11.26	37	5.31	6.91	8.31	9.53	10.58	11.47
38	4.94	6.57	7.97	9.18	10.21	11.06	38	4.96	6.60	8.04	9.29	10.36	11.27
39	4.58	6.25	7.70	8.94	9.98	10.86	39	4.60	6.29	7.76	9.04	10.14	11.07
40	4.21	5.93	7.41	8.68	9.76	10.65	40	4.50	6.33	7.94	9.33	10.53	11.54
41	3.84	5.60	7.12	8.42	9.53	10.44	41	4.10	5.98	7.63	9.06	10.28	11.32
42	3.45	5.26	6.82	8.16	9.29	10.23	42	3.68	5.62	7.31	8.77	10.03	11.09
43	3.06	4.92	6.52	7.89	9.05	10.01	43	3.26	5.25	6.98	8.48	9.77	10.86
44	2.66	4.56	6.21	7.61	8.80	9.79	44	2.83	4.87	6.65	8.19	9.50	10.62
45	2.25	4.20	5.88	7.33	8.55	9.56	45	2.53	4.75	6.67	8.34	9.77	10.99
46	1.82	3.83	5.56	7.04	8.29	9.32	46	2.05	4.32	6.30	8.01	9.48	10.72
47	1.38	3.44	5.22	6.74	8.03	9.09	47	1.56	3.89	5.92	7.68	9.19	10.45
48	0.94	3.05	4.88	6.44	7.76	8.84	48	1.05	3.45	5.53	7.33	8.88	10.18
49	0.47	2.65	4.53	6.13	7.48	8.59	49	0.53	2.99	5.13	6.98	8.56	9.90
50		2.28	4.25	5.93	7.35	8.52	50		2.62	4.89	6.87	8.55	9.98
51		1.85	3.88	5.61	7.06	8.26	51		2.20	4.62	6.72	8.51	10.02
52		1.41	3.49	5.27	6.76	7.99	52		1.73	4.30	6.53	8.43	10.04
53		0.95	3.10	4.92	6.46	7.72	53		1.21	3.94	6.31	8.32	10.03
54		0.49	2.75	4.67	6.28	7.60	54		0.65	3.64	6.22	8.43	10.30

See introductory notes as regards claimants
over 54 at date of trial

See introductory notes as regards claimants
over 54 at date of trial

D E <GCSE

Loss of earnings: disabled; employed; education below good GCSE level

Age	Male to retiring age						Age	Female to retiring age					
	50	55	60	65	70	75		50	55	60	65	70	75
16	7.30	7.92	8.47	8.93	9.34	9.67	16	5.73	6.23	6.66	7.04	7.37	7.65
17	7.16	7.80	8.36	8.84	9.24	9.59	17	5.62	6.13	6.57	6.96	7.30	7.59
18	7.01	7.67	8.24	8.73	9.16	9.51	18	5.51	6.03	6.49	6.88	7.23	7.52
19	6.86	7.54	8.12	8.63	9.06	9.42	19	5.39	5.93	6.40	6.80	7.16	7.46
20	7.98	8.79	9.51	10.12	10.64	11.08	20	5.27	5.82	6.30	6.72	7.08	7.39
21	7.79	8.63	9.36	9.99	10.53	10.98	21	5.15	5.72	6.21	6.64	7.01	7.32
22	7.60	8.47	9.22	9.86	10.41	10.87	22	5.03	5.61	6.11	6.55	6.93	7.25
23	7.41	8.30	9.06	9.72	10.29	10.76	23	4.90	5.74	6.01	6.46	6.85	7.18
24	7.22	8.12	8.91	9.58	10.16	10.64	24	4.77	5.38	5.91	6.37	6.77	7.11
25	7.75	8.78	9.67	10.44	11.09	11.63	25	4.64	5.26	5.80	6.28	6.68	7.03
26	7.53	8.58	9.49	10.28	10.95	11.50	26	4.50	5.14	5.70	6.18	6.60	6.95
27	7.29	8.37	9.31	10.11	10.79	11.37	27	4.36	5.02	5.59	6.08	6.51	6.87
28	7.05	8.16	9.12	9.94	10.64	11.23	28	4.22	4.89	5.47	5.98	6.42	6.79
29	6.81	7.94	8.93	9.77	10.49	11.09	29	4.08	4.76	5.36	5.88	6.33	6.71
30	6.24	7.35	8.31	9.14	9.84	10.42	30	4.71	5.55	6.29	6.93	7.48	7.95
31	6.00	7.13	8.12	8.96	9.68	10.28	31	4.52	5.39	6.14	6.80	7.37	7.85
32	5.75	6.91	7.92	8.79	9.52	10.14	32	4.34	5.22	5.99	6.67	7.25	7.74
33	5.49	6.69	7.72	8.61	9.36	9.99	33	4.14	5.05	5.84	6.53	7.13	7.63
34	5.23	6.46	7.52	8.43	9.20	9.84	34	3.94	4.88	5.69	6.39	7.00	7.52
35	4.84	6.06	7.13	8.03	8.81	9.45	35	4.24	5.32	6.27	7.09	7.79	8.39
36	4.57	5.83	6.91	7.85	8.64	9.30	36	4.00	5.11	6.08	6.92	7.64	8.26
37	4.29	5.58	6.70	7.66	8.47	9.15	37	3.76	4.90	5.89	6.75	7.49	8.12
38	4.01	5.34	6.48	7.46	8.30	8.99	38	3.51	4.68	5.70	6.58	7.34	7.98
39	3.72	5.08	6.26	7.26	8.11	8.82	39	3.26	4.45	5.50	6.40	7.18	7.84
40	3.42	4.82	6.02	7.06	7.93	8.65	40	3.35	4.72	5.92	6.95	7.85	8.60
41	3.12	4.55	5.79	6.84	7.74	8.48	41	3.05	4.46	5.68	6.75	7.66	8.44
42	2.81	4.27	5.54	6.63	7.55	8.31	42	2.74	4.19	5.45	6.54	7.47	8.27
43	2.49	3.99	5.30	6.41	7.35	8.13	43	2.43	3.91	5.20	6.32	7.28	8.09
44	2.16	3.71	5.04	6.19	7.15	7.95	44	2.11	3.63	4.95	6.10	7.08	7.91
45	1.83	3.41	4.78	5.96	6.95	7.76	45	1.97	3.69	5.19	6.49	7.60	8.55
46	1.48	3.11	4.52	5.72	6.74	7.57	46	1.60	3.36	4.90	6.23	7.38	8.34
47	1.12	2.80	4.24	5.48	6.52	7.38	47	1.21	3.02	4.60	5.97	7.14	8.13
48	0.76	2.48	3.96	5.23	6.30	7.18	48	0.82	2.68	4.30	5.70	6.90	7.92
49	0.38	2.15	3.68	4.98	6.08	6.98	49	0.41	2.33	3.99	5.43	6.66	7.70
50		1.86	3.47	4.84	6.00	6.95	50		2.20	4.11	5.76	7.18	8.38
51		1.55	3.24	4.69	5.90	6.91	51		1.86	3.91	5.67	7.19	8.47
52		1.18	2.92	4.41	5.66	6.69	52		1.47	3.66	5.55	7.17	8.53
53		0.82	2.65	4.22	5.54	6.62	53		1.05	3.43	5.49	7.25	8.73
54		0.42	2.36	4.01	5.40	6.54	54		0.56	3.15	5.38	7.28	8.89

See introductory notes as regards claimants
over 54 at date of trial

See introductory notes as regards claimants
over 54 at date of trial

A4: Loss of earnings multipliers adjusted for education, etc.

Loss of earnings: disabled; not employed; degree level education or equivalent

Age	Male to retiring age						Age	Female to retiring age					
	50	55	60	65	70	75		50	55	60	65	70	75
16							16						
17			See introductory notes				17			See introductory notes			
18							18						
19							19						
20	11.12	12.26	13.26	14.12	14.85	15.46	20	12.23	13.51	14.62	15.59	16.43	17.14
21	10.87	12.04	13.06	13.94	14.69	15.31	21	11.95	13.26	14.40	15.39	16.25	16.98
22	10.61	11.81	12.85	13.75	14.52	15.16	22	11.67	13.00	14.18	15.20	16.07	16.82
23	10.34	11.57	12.64	13.56	14.35	15.00	23	11.37	13.32	13.94	14.99	15.89	16.65
24	10.06	11.33	12.42	13.37	14.17	14.85	24	11.07	12.48	13.71	14.77	15.69	16.48
25	8.86	10.03	11.05	11.93	12.67	13.30	25	9.28	10.52	11.61	12.55	13.37	14.06
26	8.60	9.80	10.84	11.75	12.51	13.15	26	9.01	10.28	11.39	12.36	13.20	13.91
27	8.33	9.57	10.64	11.55	12.34	12.99	27	8.72	10.03	11.17	12.17	13.02	13.75
28	8.06	9.32	10.42	11.36	12.16	12.84	28	8.44	9.78	10.95	11.97	12.84	13.59
29	7.78	9.08	10.20	11.16	11.99	12.67	29	8.15	9.52	10.72	11.76	12.66	13.42
30	6.71	7.90	8.94	9.82	10.57	11.20	30	6.91	8.14	9.22	10.16	10.97	11.66
31	6.45	7.67	8.72	9.64	10.41	11.05	31	6.64	7.90	9.01	9.97	10.80	11.51
32	6.18	7.43	8.51	9.45	10.24	10.90	32	6.36	7.66	8.79	9.78	10.63	11.35
33	5.90	7.19	8.30	9.26	10.07	10.74	33	6.07	7.41	8.57	9.58	10.45	11.19
34	5.62	6.94	8.08	9.06	9.89	10.58	34	5.78	7.15	8.34	9.38	10.27	11.03
35	4.72	5.91	6.94	7.83	8.58	9.21	35	5.23	6.57	7.74	8.75	9.62	10.37
36	4.45	5.68	6.74	7.65	8.42	9.06	36	4.94	6.31	7.51	8.55	9.44	10.20
37	4.18	5.44	6.53	7.46	8.25	8.91	37	4.65	6.05	7.27	8.34	9.26	10.03
38	3.91	5.20	6.31	7.27	8.08	8.76	38	4.34	5.78	7.04	8.13	9.06	9.86
39	3.62	4.95	6.10	7.08	7.90	8.60	39	4.02	5.50	6.79	7.91	8.87	9.69
40	2.90	4.08	5.10	5.97	6.71	7.32	40	3.35	4.72	5.92	6.95	7.85	8.60
41	2.64	3.85	4.90	5.79	6.55	7.18	41	3.05	4.46	5.68	6.75	7.66	8.44
42	2.37	3.62	4.69	5.61	6.39	7.03	42	2.74	4.19	5.45	6.54	7.47	8.27
43	2.10	3.38	4.48	5.43	6.22	6.88	43	2.43	3.91	5.20	6.32	7.28	8.09
44	1.83	3.14	4.27	5.23	6.05	6.73	44	2.11	3.63	4.95	6.10	7.08	7.91
45	1.22	2.27	3.19	3.97	4.63	5.18	45	1.31	2.46	3.46	4.33	5.07	5.70
46	0.98	2.07	3.01	3.81	4.49	5.05	46	1.06	2.24	3.27	4.16	4.92	5.56
47	0.75	1.86	2.83	3.65	4.35	4.92	47	0.81	2.02	3.07	3.98	4.76	5.42
48	0.51	1.65	2.64	3.49	4.20	4.79	48	0.55	1.79	2.87	3.80	4.60	5.28
49	0.26	1.44	2.45	3.32	4.05	4.65	49	0.28	1.55	2.66	3.62	4.44	5.14
50		1.12	2.08	2.91	3.60	4.17	50		1.08	2.01	2.82	3.51	4.10
51		0.87	1.82	2.63	3.31	3.88	51		0.80	1.67	2.43	3.08	3.63
52		0.63	1.57	2.37	3.04	3.59	52		0.58	1.43	2.18	2.81	3.35
53		0.41	1.33	2.11	2.77	3.31	53		0.35	1.14	1.83	2.42	2.91
54		0.20	1.10	1.87	2.51	3.04	54		0.16	0.88	1.51	2.04	2.50

See introductory notes as regards claimants
over 54 at date of trial

See introductory notes as regards claimants
over 54 at date of trial

D NE GCSE

Loss of earnings: disabled; not employed; good GCSE level education or equivalent

Age	Male to retiring age						Age	Female to retiring age					
	50	55	60	65	70	75		50	55	60	65	70	75
16	11.17	12.13	12.97	13.68	14.30	14.81	16	8.02	8.72	9.32	9.86	10.31	10.71
17	10.96	11.94	12.79	13.53	14.16	14.69	17	7.86	8.58	9.20	9.75	10.22	10.62
18	10.74	11.75	12.62	13.37	14.02	14.56	18	7.71	8.44	9.08	9.64	10.12	10.53
19	10.51	11.54	12.44	13.22	13.87	14.43	19	7.55	8.30	8.95	9.52	10.02	10.44
20	9.66	10.64	11.51	12.25	12.88	13.42	20	6.96	7.69	8.32	8.87	9.35	9.75
21	9.43	10.45	11.33	12.10	12.75	13.29	21	6.80	7.54	8.19	8.76	9.25	9.66
22	9.20	10.25	11.16	11.94	12.60	13.16	22	6.64	7.40	8.07	8.65	9.14	9.57
23	8.97	10.04	10.97	11.77	12.45	13.02	23	6.47	7.58	7.93	8.53	9.04	9.47
24	8.74	9.83	10.78	11.60	12.30	12.88	24	6.30	7.10	7.80	8.41	8.93	9.38
25	7.57	8.57	9.44	10.19	10.82	11.36	25	5.94	6.73	7.43	8.03	8.55	9.00
26	7.35	8.37	9.26	10.03	10.68	11.23	26	5.76	6.58	7.29	7.91	8.44	8.90
27	7.12	8.17	9.09	9.87	10.54	11.10	27	5.58	6.42	7.15	7.79	8.33	8.80
28	6.88	7.96	8.90	9.70	10.39	10.96	28	5.40	6.26	7.00	7.66	8.22	8.69
29	6.65	7.75	8.71	9.54	10.24	10.82	29	5.22	6.09	6.86	7.52	8.10	8.59
30	5.31	6.25	7.07	7.77	8.36	8.86	30	4.87	5.74	6.50	7.16	7.73	8.22
31	5.10	6.06	6.90	7.62	8.23	8.74	31	4.67	5.57	6.35	7.02	7.61	8.11
32	4.89	5.88	6.73	7.47	8.10	8.62	32	4.48	5.39	6.19	6.89	7.49	7.99
33	4.67	5.68	6.56	7.32	7.96	8.49	33	4.28	5.22	6.04	6.75	7.36	7.88
34	4.45	5.49	6.39	7.16	7.82	8.37	34	4.07	5.04	5.88	6.61	7.24	7.77
35	3.47	4.35	5.12	5.77	6.32	6.78	35	3.49	4.38	5.16	5.84	6.41	6.91
36	3.28	4.18	4.96	5.64	6.20	6.68	36	3.30	4.21	5.01	5.70	6.29	6.80
37	3.08	4.01	4.81	5.50	6.08	6.57	37	3.10	4.03	4.85	5.56	6.17	6.69
38	2.88	3.83	4.65	5.36	5.96	6.45	38	2.89	3.85	4.69	5.42	6.04	6.57
39	2.67	3.65	4.49	5.21	5.82	6.33	39	2.68	3.67	4.53	5.27	5.91	6.46
40	2.02	2.84	3.55	4.16	4.68	5.10	40	2.03	2.86	3.58	4.21	4.75	5.20
41	1.84	2.68	3.41	4.04	4.57	5.00	41	1.85	2.70	3.44	4.08	4.64	5.11
42	1.66	2.52	3.27	3.91	4.45	4.90	42	1.66	2.53	3.30	3.96	4.52	5.00
43	1.47	2.36	3.12	3.78	4.34	4.80	43	1.47	2.37	3.15	3.82	4.40	4.90
44	1.27	2.19	2.97	3.65	4.22	4.69	44	1.28	2.20	3.00	3.69	4.28	4.79
45	0.94	1.75	2.45	3.05	3.56	3.98	45	0.84	1.58	2.22	2.78	3.26	3.66
46	0.76	1.59	2.32	2.93	3.45	3.88	46	0.68	1.44	2.10	2.67	3.16	3.57
47	0.58	1.43	2.18	2.81	3.34	3.79	47	0.52	1.30	1.97	2.56	3.06	3.48
48	0.39	1.27	2.03	2.68	3.23	3.68	48	0.35	1.15	1.84	2.44	2.96	3.39
49	0.20	1.10	1.89	2.55	3.12	3.58	49	0.18	1.00	1.71	2.33	2.85	3.30
50		0.84	1.56	2.18	2.70	3.13	50		0.70	1.31	1.84	2.29	2.67
51		0.64	1.34	1.94	2.45	2.86	51		0.53	1.12	1.62	2.05	2.42
52		0.46	1.14	1.72	2.21	2.61	52		0.37	0.93	1.41	1.83	2.17
53		0.29	0.95	1.51	1.98	2.36	53		0.21	0.70	1.12	1.48	1.78
54		0.14	0.77	1.31	1.76	2.13	54		0.09	0.50	0.85	1.15	1.40

See introductory notes as regards claimants over 54 at date of trial

See introductory notes as regards claimants over 54 at date of trial

A4: Loss of earnings multipliers adjusted for education, etc.

Loss of earnings: disabled; not employed; education below good GCSE level

Age	Male to retiring age						Age	Female to retiring age					
	50	55	60	65	70	75		50	55	60	65	70	75
16	5.70	6.19	6.62	6.98	7.30	7.56	16	4.35	4.73	5.06	5.35	5.60	5.81
17	5.59	6.09	6.53	6.90	7.22	7.49	17	4.27	4.66	5.00	5.29	5.55	5.76
18	5.48	5.99	6.44	6.82	7.15	7.43	18	4.18	4.58	4.93	5.23	5.49	5.72
19	5.36	5.89	6.35	6.74	7.08	7.36	19	4.10	4.50	4.86	5.17	5.44	5.67
20	5.04	5.55	6.00	6.39	6.72	7.00	20	3.59	3.96	4.29	4.57	4.81	5.03
21	4.92	5.45	5.91	6.31	6.65	6.93	21	3.50	3.89	4.22	4.51	4.76	4.98
22	4.80	5.35	5.82	6.23	6.57	6.87	22	3.42	3.81	4.15	4.45	4.71	4.93
23	4.68	5.24	5.72	6.14	6.50	6.79	23	3.33	3.90	4.09	4.39	4.66	4.88
24	4.56	5.13	5.63	6.05	6.42	6.72	24	3.25	3.66	4.02	4.33	4.60	4.83
25	4.43	5.02	5.52	5.96	6.34	6.65	25	2.97	3.37	3.71	4.02	4.28	4.50
26	4.30	4.90	5.42	5.87	6.25	6.57	26	2.88	3.29	3.64	3.96	4.22	4.45
27	4.17	4.78	5.32	5.78	6.17	6.50	27	2.79	3.21	3.57	3.89	4.16	4.40
28	4.03	4.66	5.21	5.68	6.08	6.42	28	2.70	3.13	3.50	3.83	4.11	4.35
29	3.89	4.54	5.10	5.58	5.99	6.34	29	2.61	3.05	3.43	3.76	4.05	4.29
30	3.59	4.23	4.78	5.25	5.66	5.99	30	2.36	2.78	3.14	3.46	3.74	3.98
31	3.45	4.10	4.67	5.15	5.57	5.91	31	2.26	2.69	3.07	3.40	3.68	3.92
32	3.31	3.97	4.55	5.05	5.48	5.83	32	2.17	2.61	3.00	3.33	3.62	3.87
33	3.16	3.85	4.44	4.95	5.38	5.75	33	2.07	2.52	2.92	3.27	3.56	3.81
34	3.01	3.71	4.32	4.85	5.29	5.66	34	1.97	2.44	2.84	3.20	3.50	3.76
35	2.48	3.11	3.65	4.12	4.52	4.85	35	1.74	2.19	2.58	2.92	3.21	3.46
36	2.34	2.99	3.55	4.03	4.43	4.77	36	1.65	2.10	2.50	2.85	3.15	3.40
37	2.20	2.86	3.44	3.93	4.34	4.69	37	1.55	2.02	2.42	2.78	3.09	3.34
38	2.06	2.74	3.32	3.83	4.25	4.61	38	1.45	1.93	2.35	2.71	3.02	3.29
39	1.91	2.69	3.21	3.72	4.16	4.52	39	1.34	1.83	2.26	2.64	2.96	3.23
40	1.32	1.85	2.32	2.71	3.05	3.33	40	1.15	1.61	2.02	2.38	2.68	2.94
41	1.20	1.75	2.23	2.63	2.98	3.26	41	1.04	1.52	1.94	2.31	2.62	2.89
42	1.08	1.64	2.13	2.55	2.90	3.20	42	0.94	1.43	1.86	2.24	2.56	2.83
43	0.96	1.54	2.04	2.47	2.83	3.13	43	0.83	1.34	1.78	2.16	2.49	2.77
44	0.83	1.43	1.94	2.38	2.75	3.06	44	0.72	1.24	1.69	2.09	2.42	2.71
45	0.51	0.96	1.35	1.68	1.96	2.19	45	0.52	0.97	1.36	1.70	1.99	2.24
46	0.42	0.88	1.27	1.61	1.90	2.14	46	0.42	0.88	1.28	1.63	1.93	2.18
47	0.32	0.79	1.20	1.55	1.84	2.08	47	0.32	0.79	1.21	1.56	1.87	2.13
48	0.21	0.70	1.12	1.48	1.78	2.03	48	0.21	0.70	1.13	1.49	1.81	2.07
49	0.11	0.61	1.04	1.40	1.71	1.97	49	0.11	0.61	1.05	1.42	1.74	2.02
50		0.47	0.87	1.21	1.50	1.74	50		0.47	0.87	1.23	1.53	1.78
51		0.34	0.71	1.03	1.30	1.52	51		0.34	0.72	1.04	1.32	1.56
52		0.23	0.57	0.86	1.10	1.30	52		0.23	0.57	0.87	1.12	1.34
53		0.14	0.44	0.70	0.92	1.10	53		0.14	0.45	0.71	0.94	1.13
54		0.06	0.33	0.56	0.75	0.91	54		0.06	0.33	0.57	0.77	0.94

See introductory notes as regards claimants
over 54 at date of trial

See introductory notes as regards claimants
over 54 at date of trial

A5: Multipliers for fixed periods and at intervals

Introductory notes

1.   The purpose of the tables is to provide a means of calculating an appropriate multiplier which will produce the present day equivalent of a cost recurring, either continuously or at fixed intervals, over a given number of years. It does not allow for mortality or contingencies.

2.   The three tables are based on discount rates of −1.5%, 1% and 2.5% per annum. The Lord Chancellor fixed the discount rate under the Damages Act 1996 (June 27, 2001) at 2.5%, leaving open the possibility of a different rate in exceptional cases such as the effect of tax on large sums. The range of discount rates has been extended as a result of the decision in *Helmot v Simon*.[1]

3.   It is assumed that yearly loss is incurred at the *end* of each year in which the loss arises. (Continuous loss obviously accrues from day to day throughout the period. Weekly and monthly losses can in practice be treated as continuous.) For example:

> For expenditure assumed to recur every seven years the expenditure is shown as arising at the end of years seven, 14, and so on.

4.   The table contains a number of columns: the number of years; the multiplier for a single payment in *n* years' time; that for a continuous loss over that period of *n* years; that for annual payments in the sense of a series of payments at intervals of one year; and those for payments at intervals of two, three, four and so on years.

5.   The multiplier for a single payment in *n* years' time (second column) is the same as the discount factor for deferment for the next *n* years.

6.   The table shows a multiplier appropriate to each year in which expenditure is to be incurred, and also cumulative multipliers for expenditure up to the end of that year. For example, at 2.5% discount:

> The multiplier for expenditure at the end of year 10 is 0.781. Thus the current lump sum required to provide £100 in 10 years' time is £78.10.

And similarly:

- £100 a year continuously over the next 10 years has a present value of £886;

- £100 at the end of each of the next 10 years a present value of £875;

- £100 at the end of two, four, six, eight and 10 years a present value of £432 (row 10, two-yearly column); and

- £100 at the end of three, six and nine years a present value of £259 (row 9, three-yearly column).

The cumulative multipliers do not include an immediate payment: where one is needed in addition to the recurring payments add 1.00 to the multiplier.

7.   The calculations have been rounded to two places of decimals.

---

[1] [2010] GCA 31.

Multipliers where there is evidence of life expectancy

8. In some cases there is medical evidence of the particular claimant's life expectancy. As more distant losses have lower present value, the possibility of dying earlier than expected has more effect on the multiplier than that of dying later than expected. The multiplier for life of someone whose life expectancy is *n* years will therefore be lower than the multiplier for a fixed period of *n* years. The difference varies with sex and age. It is not large but at a discount rate of 2.5% it is not negligible.

Reduction of fixed multipliers for mortality

9. For the reasons discussed above in relation to cases where there is evidence of life expectancy, in all cases where the period of loss is dependent on someone's life the multiplier for a fixed period will be slightly higher than the true multiplier. In appropriate cases the fixed term multipliers can be reduced by the method discussed in paras 20–23 of the Ogden notes (section A8 of this book).

10. For example:

    The claimant is aged 53 and seven months. His life expectancy is 30 years. For the first 12 years he will need care at £10,000 a year and incur expenditure on equipment of £5,000 every four years. For the remaining 18 years he will need care at £20,000 a year and expenditure on equipment of £6,000 every three years.

    For a fixed term of 30 years the multipliers at 2.5%—from Table A5 at 2.5%—are:

First 12 years: care	equipment	Remaining 18 years: care	equipment	30 years
10.39	2.47	10.80	3.47	21.19

    The claimant's multiplier for life at 2.5% (Table A1) is 20.33. It is not 21.19, because the possibility of dying earlier than expected affects the multiplier more than the possibility of dying later. The fixed term multipliers for care and equipment are therefore high and need to be reduced by a factor of 20.33/21.19 = 0.96.

    Multipliers adjusted for mortality (that is multiplied by 0.96):

First 12 years: care	equipment	Remaining 18 years: care	equipment	Life
9.97	2.37	10.36	3.33	20.33

Modifications

11. Multipliers for continuous loss for periods other than entire years can be obtained by interpolation:

    For continuous payments for 10 and 11 years the multipliers are 8.86 and 9.63.

    So for weekly payments for $10\frac{1}{2}$ years the multiplier is approximately $\frac{1}{2}(8.86 + 9.63) = 9.25$.

12. Multipliers for payments beginning after a deferred period can be derived by subtraction or by multiplying by a factor from the single payment column:

    Multipliers for five-yearly payments for 15 and for 50 years are 2.36 and 5.40;

    So the multiplier for five-yearly payments from years 20 to 50 inclusive is 5.40 − 2.36 = 3.14;

    Multiplier for one payment after 18 years is 0.641;

    So that for five-yearly payments from years 23–68 inclusive is 5.40 × 0.641 = 3.46.

13. Multipliers for irregular payments can be found by adding individual figures from the single payment column.

Multipliers at −1.5% discount

n	Single payment	Continuous loss	1	2	3	4	5	6	7	8	10	12	15	20
							Frequency of payments in years							
1	1.015	1.01	1.02											
2	1.031	2.03	2.05	1.03										
3	1.046	3.07	3.09		1.05									
4	1.062	4.12	4.15	2.09		1.06								
5	1.078	5.19	5.23				1.08							
6	1.095	6.28	6.33	3.19	2.14			1.09						
7	1.112	7.38	7.44						1.11					
8	1.129	8.50	8.57	4.32		2.19				1.13				
9	1.146	9.64	9.71		3.29									
10	1.163	10.80	10.88	5.48			2.24				1.16			
11	1.181	11.97	12.06											
12	1.199	13.16	13.26	6.68	4.49	3.39		2.29				1.20		
13	1.217	14.37	14.47											
14	1.236	15.59	15.71	7.91					2.35					
15	1.254	16.84	16.96		5.74		3.50						1.25	
16	1.274	18.10	18.24	9.19		4.66				2.40				
17	1.293	19.38	19.53											
18	1.313	20.69	20.84	10.50	7.05			3.61						
19	1.333	22.01	22.18											
20	1.353	23.35	23.53	11.85		6.02	4.85				2.52			1.35
21	1.374	24.72	24.90		8.43				3.72					
22	1.394	26.10	26.30	13.25										
23	1.416	27.50	27.71											
24	1.437	28.93	29.15	14.68	9.86	7.45		5.04		3.84		2.64		
25	1.459	30.38	30.61				6.31							
26	1.481	31.85	32.09	16.17										
27	1.504	33.34	33.59		11.37									
28	1.527	34.86	35.12	17.69		8.98			5.25					
29	1.550	36.40	36.67											
30	1.574	37.96	38.24	19.27	12.94		7.88	6.62			4.09		2.83	
31	1.598	39.54	39.84											
32	1.622	41.15	41.46	20.89		10.60				5.46				
33	1.647	42.79	43.11		14.59									
34	1.672	44.45	44.78	22.56										
35	1.697	46.13	46.48				9.58		6.94					
36	1.723	47.84	48.20	24.28	16.31	12.33		8.34				4.36		
37	1.749	49.58	49.95											
38	1.776	51.34	51.73	26.06										
39	1.803	53.13	53.53		18.11									
40	1.830	54.95	55.36	27.89		14.16	11.41			7.29	5.92			3.18
41	1.858	56.79	57.22											
42	1.887	58.66	59.11	29.78	20.00			10.23	8.83					
43	1.915	60.56	61.02											
44	1.944	62.49	62.97	31.72		16.10								
45	1.974	64.45	64.94		21.97		13.38						4.80	
46	2.004	66.44	66.94	33.73										
47	2.035	68.46	68.98											
48	2.066	70.51	71.04	35.79	24.04	18.17		12.29		9.36		6.42		
49	2.097	72.59	73.14						10.93					
50	2.129	74.71	75.27	37.92			15.51				8.05			
51	2.161	76.85	77.43		26.20									
52	2.194	79.03	79.63	40.11		20.36								
53	2.228	81.24	81.85											
54	2.262	83.49	84.12	42.38	28.46			14.55						
55	2.296	85.76	86.41				17.81							
56	2.331	88.08	88.74	44.71		22.69			13.26	11.69				
57	2.367	90.43	91.11		30.83									
58	2.403	92.81	93.51	47.11										
59	2.439	95.23	95.95											
60	2.476	97.69	98.43	49.59	33.31	25.17	20.29	17.03			10.53	8.90	7.28	5.66

Multipliers at −1.5% discount

n	Single payment	Continuous loss	1	2	3	4	5	6	7	8	10	12	15	20
61	2.514	100.19	100.94												
62	2.552	102.72	103.50		52.14										
63	2.591	105.29	106.09			35.90				15.85					
64	2.631	107.90	108.72		54.77		27.80				14.32				
65	2.671	110.55	111.39					22.96							
66	2.711	113.24	114.10		57.48	38.61			19.74						
67	2.753	115.98	116.85												
68	2.795	118.75	119.65		60.28		30.59								
69	2.837	121.57	122.48			41.45									
70	2.880	124.42	125.36		63.16			25.84		18.73		13.41			
71	2.924	127.33	128.29												
72	2.969	130.27	131.26		66.12	44.42	33.56		22.71		17.29		11.87		
73	3.014	133.27	134.27												
74	3.060	136.30	137.33		69.18										
75	3.107	139.39	140.44			47.52		28.94						10.39	
76	3.154	142.52	143.59		72.34		36.72								
77	3.202	145.69	146.79							21.93					
78	3.251	148.92	150.05		75.59	50.77			25.96						
79	3.300	152.20	153.35												
80	3.350	155.52	156.70		78.94		40.07	32.29			20.64	16.76			9.01
81	3.401	158.90	160.10			54.17									
82	3.453	162.32	163.55		82.39										
83	3.506	165.80	167.06												
84	3.559	169.34	170.62		85.95	57.73	43.63		29.52	25.49			15.43		
85	3.613	172.92	174.23					35.91							
86	3.668	176.56	177.90		89.62										
87	3.724	180.26	181.62			61.46									
88	3.781	184.01	185.40		93.40		47.41				24.42				
89	3.839	187.82	189.24												
90	3.897	191.69	193.14		97.30	65.35		39.80	33.42			20.65		14.28	
91	3.956	195.62	197.10							29.45					
92	4.017	199.60	201.11		101.32		51.42								
93	4.078	203.65	205.19			69.43									
94	4.140	207.76	209.33		105.46										
95	4.203	211.93	213.53					44.01							
96	4.267	216.17	217.80		109.72	73.70	55.69		37.69		28.69		19.70		
97	4.332	220.47	222.13												
98	4.398	224.83	226.53		114.12					33.85					
99	4.465	229.26	230.99			78.16									
100	4.533	233.76	235.53		118.65		60.22	48.54				25.19			13.54

1. The single payment column is the appropriate multiplier for one payment in *n* years' time.

2. The continuous loss column is for loss accruing from day to day: in practice it is appropriate for weekly and monthly losses as well.

3. The column headed "1" is for a series of payments at yearly intervals at the *end of each year* for *n* years. If you want an immediate payment as well, add 1.

4. The remaining columns similarly show the multiplier for a series of payments at intervals of two, three, four and so on years.

5. Thus at −1.5% discount £100 paid after 10 years has a present value of £116.30;

    – £100 a year continuously over the next 10 years has a present value of £1,080;

    – £100 at the end of each of the next 10 years has a present value of £1,088;

    – £100 at the end of two, four, six, eight and 10 years has a present value of £548 (row 10, two-yearly column);

    – £100 at the end of three, six and nine years has a present value of £329 (row 9, three-yearly column); and

    – £100 now and after two, four, six and eight years (but not the 10th year) has a present value of £532 (row 8, two-yearly column, plus one).

Multipliers at 1.0% discount

n	Single payment	Continuous loss	1	2	3	4	5	6	7	8	10	12	15	20
			Frequency of payments in years											
1	0.990	1.00	0.99											
2	0.980	1.98	1.97	0.98										
3	0.971	2.96	2.94		0.97									
4	0.961	3.92	3.90	1.94		0.96								
5	0.951	4.88	4.85				0.95							
6	0.942	5.82	5.80	2.88	1.91			0.94						
7	0.933	6.76	6.73						0.93					
8	0.923	7.69	7.65	3.81		1.88				0.92				
9	0.914	8.61	8.57		2.83									
10	0.905	9.52	9.47	4.71			1.86				0.91			
11	0.896	10.42	10.37											
12	0.887	11.31	11.26	5.60	3.71	2.77		1.83				0.89		
13	0.879	12.19	12.13											
14	0.870	13.07	13.00	6.47					1.80					
15	0.861	13.93	13.87		4.58		2.72						0.86	
16	0.853	14.79	14.72	7.32		3.62				1.78				
17	0.844	15.64	15.56											
18	0.836	16.48	16.40	8.16	5.41			2.67						
19	0.828	17.31	17.23											
20	0.820	18.14	18.05	8.98		4.44	3.54				1.72			0.82
21	0.811	18.95	18.86		6.22			2.61						
22	0.803	19.76	19.66	9.78										
23	0.795	20.56	20.46											
24	0.788	21.35	21.24	10.57	7.01	5.23		3.45		2.56		1.68		
25	0.780	22.13	22.02				4.32							
26	0.772	22.91	22.80	11.34										
27	0.764	23.68	23.56		7.78									
28	0.757	24.44	24.32	12.10		5.99			3.37					
29	0.749	25.19	25.07											
30	0.742	25.94	25.81	12.84	8.52		5.06	4.20			2.47		1.60	
31	0.735	26.67	26.54											
32	0.727	27.41	27.27	13.57		6.72				3.29				
33	0.720	28.13	27.99		9.24									
34	0.713	28.85	28.70	14.28										
35	0.706	29.56	29.41				5.77		4.08					
36	0.699	30.26	30.11	14.98	9.94	7.41		4.89				2.37		
37	0.692	30.95	30.80											
38	0.685	31.64	31.48	15.66										
39	0.678	32.32	32.16		10.61									
40	0.672	33.00	32.83	16.34		8.09	6.44			3.96	3.14			1.49
41	0.665	33.67	33.50											
42	0.658	34.33	34.16	16.99	11.27			5.55	4.74					
43	0.652	34.98	34.81											
44	0.645	35.63	35.46	17.64		8.73								
45	0.639	36.27	36.09		11.91		7.08						2.24	
46	0.633	36.91	36.73	18.27										
47	0.626	37.54	37.35											
48	0.620	38.16	37.97	18.89	12.53	9.35		6.17		4.58		2.99		
49	0.614	38.78	38.59						5.35					
50	0.608	39.39	39.20	19.50			7.68				3.75			
51	0.602	40.00	39.80		13.13									
52	0.596	40.60	40.39	20.10		9.95								
53	0.590	41.19	40.98											
54	0.584	41.78	41.57	20.68	13.72			6.76						
55	0.579	42.36	42.15				8.26							
56	0.573	42.93	42.72	21.25		10.52			5.92	5.16				
57	0.567	43.50	43.29		14.29									
58	0.562	44.07	43.85	21.82										
59	0.556	44.63	44.40											
60	0.550	45.18	44.96	22.37	14.84	11.07	8.81	7.31			4.30	3.54	2.79	2.04

Multipliers at 1.0% discount

n	Single payment	Continuous loss	1	2	3	4	5	6	7	8	10	12	15	20
			*			Frequency of payments in years								
61	0.545	45.73	45.50											
62	0.540	46.27	46.04	22.91										
63	0.534	46.81	46.57			15.37				6.46				
64	0.529	47.34	47.10	23.43			11.60				5.68			
65	0.524	47.86	47.63					9.34						
66	0.519	48.39	48.15	23.95		15.89			7.83					
67	0.513	48.90	48.66											
68	0.508	49.41	49.17	24.46			12.11							
69	0.503	49.92	49.67			16.39								
70	0.498	50.42	50.17	24.96				9.84		6.95		4.80		
71	0.493	50.92	50.66											
72	0.488	51.41	51.15	25.45		16.88	12.60		8.31		6.17		4.03	
73	0.484	51.89	51.63											
74	0.479	52.37	52.11	25.93										
75	0.474	52.85	52.59			17.35		10.31					3.27	
76	0.469	53.32	53.06	26.40			13.07							
77	0.465	53.79	53.52							7.42				
78	0.460	54.25	53.98	26.86		17.82			8.77					
79	0.456	54.71	54.44											
80	0.451	55.16	54.89	27.31			13.52	10.76			6.62	5.25		2.49
81	0.447	55.61	55.33			18.26								
82	0.442	56.06	55.78	27.75										
83	0.438	56.50	56.21											
84	0.434	56.93	56.65	28.18		18.70	13.95		9.21	7.85			4.47	
85	0.429	57.36	57.08					11.19						
86	0.425	57.79	57.50	28.61										
87	0.421	58.21	57.92			19.12								
88	0.417	58.63	58.34	29.02			14.37				7.04			
89	0.412	59.05	58.75											
90	0.408	59.46	59.16	29.43		19.52		11.60	9.62			5.65	3.68	
91	0.404	59.86	59.57							8.26				
92	0.400	60.27	59.97	29.83			14.77							
93	0.396	60.66	60.36			19.92								
94	0.392	61.06	60.75	30.23										
95	0.389	61.45	61.14					11.99						
96	0.385	61.84	61.53	30.61		20.31	15.15		10.00		7.43		4.85	
97	0.381	62.22	61.91											
98	0.377	62.60	62.29	30.99						8.63				
99	0.373	62.97	62.66			20.68								
100	0.370	63.34	63.03	31.36			15.52	12.36				6.02		2.86

1. The single payment column is the appropriate multiplier for one payment in *n* years' time.

2. The continuous loss column is for loss accruing from day to day: in practice it is appropriate for weekly and monthly losses as well.

3. The column headed "1" is for a series of payments at yearly intervals *at the end of each year* for *n* years. If you want an immediate payment as well, add 1.

4. The remaining columns similarly show the muliplier for a series of payments at intervals of two, three, four and so on years.

5. Thus at 1.0% discount £100 paid after 10 years has a present value of £90.50;

   – £100 a year continuously over the next 10 years has a present value of £952;
   – £100 at the end of each of the next 10 years has a present value of £947;
   – £100 at the end of two, four, six, eight and 10 years has a present value of £471 (row 10, two-yearly column);
   – £100 at the end of three, six and nine years has a present value of £283 (row 9, three-yearly column); and
   – £100 now and after two, four, six and eight years (but not the 10th year) has a present value of £481 (row 8, two-yearly column, plus one).

Multipliers at 2.5% discount

n	Single payment	Continuous loss	1	2	3	4	5	6	7	8	10	12	15	20
			\
			Frequency of payments in years											

n	Single payment	Continuous loss	1	2	3	4	5	6	7	8	10	12	15	20
1	0.976	0.99	0.98											
2	0.952	1.95	1.93	0.95										
3	0.929	2.89	2.86		0.93									
4	0.906	3.81	3.76	1.86		0.91								
5	0.884	4.70	4.65				0.88							
6	0.862	5.58	5.51	2.72	1.79			0.86						
7	0.841	6.43	6.35						0.84					
8	0.821	7.26	7.17	3.54		1.73				0.82				
9	0.801	8.07	7.97		2.59									
10	0.781	8.86	8.75	4.32			1.67				0.78			
11	0.762	9.63	9.51											
12	0.744	10.39	10.26	5.07	3.34	2.47		1.61				0.74		
13	0.725	11.12	10.98											
14	0.708	11.84	11.69	5.77					1.55					
15	0.690	12.54	12.38		4.03		2.36						0.69	
16	0.674	13.22	13.06	6.45		3.14				1.49				
17	0.657	13.88	13.71											
18	0.641	14.53	14.35	7.09	4.67			2.25						
19	0.626	15.17	14.98											
20	0.610	15.78	15.59	7.70		3.75	2.97				1.39			0.61
21	0.595	16.39	16.18		5.26				2.14					
22	0.581	16.97	16.77	8.28										
23	0.567	17.55	17.33											
24	0.553	18.11	17.88	8.83	5.82	4.31		2.80		2.05		1.30		
25	0.539	18.65	18.42				3.51							
26	0.526	19.19	18.95	9.36										
27	0.513	19.71	19.46		6.33									
28	0.501	20.21	19.96	9.86		4.81			2.65					
29	0.489	20.71	20.45											
30	0.477	21.19	20.93	10.34	6.81		3.98	3.28			1.87		1.17	
31	0.465	21.66	21.40											
32	0.454	22.12	21.85	10.79		5.26				2.50				
33	0.443	22.57	22.29		7.25									
34	0.432	23.01	22.72	11.22										
35	0.421	23.43	23.15				4.40		3.07					
36	0.411	23.85	23.56	11.63	7.66	5.67		3.69				1.71		
37	0.401	24.26	23.96											
38	0.391	24.65	24.35	12.02										
39	0.382	25.04	24.73		8.04									
40	0.372	25.42	25.10	12.40		6.05	4.78			2.87	2.24			0.98
41	0.363	25.78	25.47											
42	0.354	26.14	25.82	12.75	8.40			4.04	3.42					
43	0.346	26.49	26.17											
44	0.337	26.84	26.50	13.09		6.38								
45	0.329	27.17	26.83		8.72		5.10						1.50	
46	0.321	27.49	27.15	13.41										
47	0.313	27.81	27.47											
48	0.306	28.12	27.77	13.72	9.03	6.69		4.35		3.18		2.01		
49	0.298	28.42	28.07						3.72					
50	0.291	28.72	28.36	14.01			5.40				2.53			
51	0.284	29.00	28.65		9.31									
52	0.277	29.28	28.92	14.28		6.97								
53	0.270	29.56	29.19											
54	0.264	29.83	29.46	14.55	9.58			4.61						
55	0.257	30.09	29.71				5.65							
56	0.251	30.34	29.96	14.80		7.22			3.97	3.43				
57	0.245	30.59	30.21		9.82									
58	0.239	30.83	30.45	15.04										
59	0.233	31.06	30.68											
60	0.227	31.30	30.91	15.26	10.05	7.44	5.88	4.84			2.76	2.24	1.72	1.21

Multipliers at 2.5% discount

n	Single payment	Continuous loss	1	2	3	4	5	6	7	8	10	12	15	20
						Frequency of payments in years								
61	0.222	31.52	31.13											
62	0.216	31.74	31.35	15.48										
63	0.211	31.95	31.56		10.26				4.18					
64	0.206	32.16	31.76	15.69		7.65				3.64				
65	0.201	32.36	31.96				6.08							
66	0.196	32.56	32.16	15.88	10.46			5.04						
67	0.191	32.76	32.35											
68	0.187	32.95	32.54	16.07		7.84								
69	0.182	33.13	32.72		10.64									
70	0.178	33.31	32.90	16.25			6.26		4.36		2.94			
71	0.173	33.48	33.07											
72	0.169	33.66	33.24	16.41	10.81	8.00		5.20		3.80		2.41		
73	0.165	33.82	33.40											
74	0.161	33.99	33.57	16.58										
75	0.157	34.14	33.72		10.96		6.42						1.88	
76	0.153	34.30	33.88	16.73		8.16								
77	0.149	34.45	34.03						4.51					
78	0.146	34.60	34.17	16.87	11.11			5.35						
79	0.142	34.74	34.31											
80	0.139	34.88	34.45	17.01		8.30	6.55			3.94	3.08			1.35
81	0.135	35.02	34.59		11.25									
82	0.132	35.15	34.72	17.15										
83	0.129	35.28	34.85											
84	0.126	35.41	34.97	17.27	11.37	8.42		5.48	4.63			2.54		
85	0.123	35.53	35.10				6.68							
86	0.120	35.66	35.22	17.39										
87	0.117	35.77	35.33		11.49									
88	0.114	35.89	35.45	17.50		8.54				4.06				
89	0.111	36.00	35.56											
90	0.108	36.11	35.67	17.61	11.60		6.79	5.58			3.18		1.99	
91	0.106	36.22	35.77						4.74					
92	0.103	36.32	35.87	17.72		8.64								
93	0.101	36.42	35.98		11.70									
94	0.098	36.52	36.07	17.81										
95	0.096	36.62	36.17				6.88							
96	0.093	36.72	36.26	17.91	11.79	8.73		5.68		4.15		2.63		
97	0.091	36.81	36.35											
98	0.089	36.90	36.44	18.00					4.83					
99	0.087	36.99	36.53		11.88									
100	0.085	37.07	36.61	18.08		8.82	6.97				3.27			1.43

1. The single payment column is the appropriate multiplier for one payment in n years' time.

2. The continuous loss column is for loss accruing from day to day: in practice it is appropriate for weekly and monthly losses as well.

3. The column headed "1" is for a series of payments at yearly intervals *at the end of each year* for n years. If you want an immediate payment as well, add 1.

4. The remaining columns similarly show the muliplier for a series of payments at intervals of two, three, four and so on years.

5. Thus at 2.5% discount £100 paid after 10 years has a present value of £78.10;
   - £100 a year continuously over the next 10 years has a present value of £886;
   - £100 at the end of each of the next 10 years has a present value of £875;
   - £100 at the end of two, four, six, eight and 10 years has a present value of £432 (row 10, two-yearly column);
   - £100 at the end of three, six and nine years has a present value of £259 (row 9, three-yearly column); and
   - £100 now and after two, four, six and eight years (but not the 10th year) has a present value of £454 (row 8, two-yearly column, plus one).

A6: Combination tables

Introductory notes

1. The following tables are intended for use when a claimant will suffer a loss over a known number of years, but that loss will not start to run immediately. They have been derived from first principles, but tables at discount rates between 0% and 5% could be obtained by combining Ogden Tables 27 and 28.

2. For example:

   a. The claimant is now 30 years old. He has a reduced life expectation, to the age of 60. For the last 10 years of his life, he will need nursing care at a cost of £7,500 a year. His nursing needs will therefore start in 20 years.

   b. At 2.5% discount, the multiplier for a period of 10 years is 8.86 [Ogden Table 28].

   c. At 2.5% discount, a loss that will not occur for a further 20 years must be discounted by multiplying it by 0.6103 [Ogden Table 27].

   d. The appropriate multiplier is therefore [8.86×0.6103] = 5.41 (to two decimal places).

   But see paras 20–33 of the Ogden notes.

3. The following points should also be remembered:

   a. When applying the multipliers to claims for loss of earnings, Ogden Tables 3–14 only take the ordinary risks of mortality into account. They do *not* take into account any other factors such as educational attainment or disability. A further discount must be made for these risks: see Section B of the Introduction to the Ogden Tables (Contingencies other than Mortality).

   b. Ogden Table 27 (Discounting Factors for Term Certain) gives the discount factor for a period of *complete* years. So in the example above, where the date of trial is August 23, 2012, the need for nursing care will start on August 23, 2032.

   c. Ogden Table 28 (Multipliers for Pecuniary Loss for Term Certain) assumes that the loss will occur regularly throughout the year, e.g. a monthly nursing bill.

Combination grid (Discount rate −1.5%)

Years of loss	Years before loss starts to run																	Years of loss
	1	2	3	4	5	6	7	8	9	10	12.5	15	20	25	30	35	40	
1	1.02	1.04	1.05	1.07	1.09	1.10	1.12	1.14	1.15	1.17	1.22	1.26	1.36	1.47	1.59	1.71	1.84	1
2	2.06	2.09	2.12	2.16	2.19	2.22	2.26	2.29	2.33	2.36	2.45	2.55	2.75	2.96	3.20	3.45	3.72	2
3	3.12	3.16	3.21	3.26	3.31	3.36	3.41	3.46	3.52	3.57	3.71	3.85	4.15	4.48	4.83	5.21	5.62	3
4	4.19	4.25	4.31	4.38	4.45	4.51	4.58	4.65	4.72	4.80	4.98	5.17	5.58	6.02	6.49	7.00	7.55	4
5	5.27	5.35	5.43	5.52	5.60	5.69	5.77	5.86	5.95	6.04	6.27	6.52	7.03	7.58	8.17	8.82	9.51	5
6	6.38	6.47	6.57	6.67	6.77	6.88	6.98	7.09	7.20	7.31	7.59	7.88	8.50	9.16	9.88	10.66	11.50	6
7	7.50	7.61	7.73	7.84	7.96	8.08	8.21	8.33	8.46	8.59	8.92	9.26	9.99	10.77	11.62	12.53	13.52	7
8	8.63	8.76	8.90	9.03	9.17	9.31	9.45	9.60	9.74	9.89	10.27	10.67	11.51	12.41	13.38	14.43	15.57	8
9	9.79	9.94	10.09	10.24	10.40	10.56	10.72	10.88	11.05	11.21	11.65	12.09	13.04	14.07	15.17	16.36	17.65	9
10	10.96	11.13	11.30	11.47	11.64	11.82	12.00	12.18	12.37	12.56	13.04	13.54	14.61	15.75	16.99	18.32	19.76	10
11	12.15	12.33	12.52	12.71	12.91	13.10	13.30	13.51	13.71	13.92	14.46	15.01	16.19	17.46	18.83	20.31	21.91	11
12	13.36	13.56	13.77	13.98	14.19	14.41	14.63	14.85	15.07	15.30	15.89	16.51	17.80	19.20	20.71	22.33	24.08	12
13	14.58	14.81	15.03	15.26	15.49	15.73	15.97	16.21	16.46	16.71	17.35	18.02	19.44	20.96	22.61	24.38	26.29	13
14	15.83	16.07	16.31	16.56	16.82	17.07	17.33	17.60	17.86	18.14	18.83	19.56	21.09	22.75	24.54	26.46	28.54	14
15	17.09	17.35	17.62	17.89	18.16	18.43	18.72	19.00	19.29	19.58	20.34	21.12	22.78	24.57	26.50	28.58	30.82	15
16	18.38	18.66	18.94	19.23	19.52	19.82	20.12	20.43	20.74	21.05	21.86	22.71	24.49	26.41	28.48	30.72	33.13	16
17	19.68	19.98	20.28	20.59	20.91	21.22	21.55	21.88	22.21	22.55	23.41	24.32	26.23	28.28	30.50	32.90	35.48	17
18	21.00	21.32	21.65	21.98	22.31	22.65	23.00	23.35	23.70	24.06	24.99	25.95	27.99	30.18	32.55	35.11	37.87	18
19	22.34	22.68	23.03	23.38	23.74	24.10	24.47	24.84	25.22	25.60	26.59	27.61	29.78	32.11	34.64	37.35	40.29	19
20	23.71	24.07	24.44	24.81	25.19	25.57	25.96	26.35	26.75	27.16	28.21	29.29	31.59	34.07	36.75	39.63	42.74	20
21	25.09	25.47	25.86	26.26	26.66	27.06	27.47	27.89	28.32	28.75	29.85	31.00	33.44	36.06	38.89	41.95	45.24	21
22	26.50	26.90	27.31	27.73	28.15	28.58	29.01	29.45	29.90	30.36	31.53	32.74	35.31	38.08	41.07	44.30	47.77	22
23	27.92	28.35	28.78	29.22	29.66	30.12	30.57	31.04	31.51	31.99	33.22	34.50	37.21	40.13	43.28	46.68	50.34	23
24	29.37	29.82	30.27	30.73	31.20	31.68	32.16	32.65	33.15	33.65	34.95	36.29	39.14	42.21	45.53	49.10	52.96	24
25	30.84	31.31	31.79	32.27	32.76	33.26	33.77	34.28	34.81	35.34	36.70	38.11	41.10	44.33	47.81	51.56	55.61	25
26	32.33	32.83	33.33	33.83	34.35	34.87	35.40	35.94	36.49	37.05	38.47	39.95	43.09	46.47	50.12	54.05	58.30	26
27	33.85	34.37	34.89	35.42	35.96	36.51	37.06	37.63	38.20	38.78	40.28	41.83	45.11	48.65	52.47	56.59	61.03	27
28	35.39	35.93	36.47	37.03	37.59	38.17	38.75	39.34	39.94	40.54	42.11	43.73	47.16	50.86	54.85	59.16	63.80	28
29	36.95	37.51	38.08	38.66	39.25	39.85	40.46	41.07	41.70	42.33	43.96	45.66	49.24	53.11	57.27	61.77	66.62	29
30	38.54	39.12	39.72	40.32	40.94	41.56	42.19	42.84	43.49	44.15	45.85	47.62	51.35	55.39	59.73	64.42	69.48	30
31	40.15	40.76	41.38	42.01	42.65	43.30	43.96	44.63	45.31	46.00	47.77	49.61	53.50	57.70	62.23	67.11	72.38	31
32	41.78	42.42	43.06	43.72	44.38	45.06	45.75	46.44	47.15	47.87	49.71	51.62	55.68	60.05	64.76	69.84	75.33	32
33	43.44	44.10	44.77	45.45	46.15	46.85	47.56	48.29	49.02	49.77	51.68	53.68	57.89	62.43	67.33	72.62	78.32	33
34	45.12	45.81	46.51	47.22	47.94	48.67	49.41	50.16	50.92	51.70	53.69	55.76	60.13	64.85	69.94	75.43	81.36	34
35	46.83	47.55	48.27	49.01	49.75	50.51	51.28	52.06	52.85	53.66	55.72	57.87	62.41	67.31	72.60	78.29	84.44	35
36	48.57	49.31	50.06	50.82	51.60	52.38	53.18	53.99	54.81	55.65	57.79	60.01	64.73	69.81	75.29	81.20	87.57	36
37	50.33	51.10	51.88	52.67	53.47	54.28	55.11	55.95	56.80	57.67	59.89	62.19	67.07	72.34	78.02	84.14	90.75	37
38	52.12	52.92	53.72	54.54	55.37	56.21	57.07	57.94	58.82	59.72	62.02	64.40	69.46	74.91	80.79	87.13	93.97	38
39	53.94	54.76	55.59	56.44	57.30	58.17	59.06	59.96	60.87	61.80	64.18	66.65	71.88	77.52	83.61	90.17	97.25	39
40	55.78	56.63	57.49	58.37	59.26	60.16	61.08	62.01	62.95	63.91	66.37	68.93	74.34	80.17	86.47	93.25	100.57	40
41	57.66	58.53	59.42	60.33	61.25	62.18	63.13	64.09	65.07	66.06	68.60	71.24	76.83	82.86	89.37	96.38	103.95	41
42	59.56	60.46	61.38	62.32	63.27	64.23	65.21	66.20	67.21	68.23	70.86	73.59	79.37	85.60	92.32	99.56	107.38	42
43	61.49	62.42	63.37	64.34	65.32	66.31	67.32	68.35	69.39	70.45	73.16	75.97	81.94	88.37	95.31	102.79	110.86	43
44	63.45	64.41	65.39	66.39	67.40	68.43	69.47	70.53	71.60	72.69	75.49	78.40	84.55	91.19	98.34	106.06	114.39	44
45	65.43	66.43	67.44	68.47	69.51	70.57	71.65	72.74	73.84	74.97	77.86	80.85	87.20	94.05	101.43	109.39	117.98	45
Years of loss	1	2	3	4	5	6	7	8	9	10	12.5	15	20	25	30	35	40	Years of loss

Combination grid (Discount rate 1%)

Years of loss	Years before loss starts to run																	Years of loss
	1	2	3	4	5	6	7	8	9	10	12.5	15	20	25	30	35	40	
1	0.99	0.98	0.97	0.96	0.95	0.94	0.93	0.92	0.91	0.90	0.88	0.86	0.82	0.78	0.74	0.70	0.67	1
2	1.96	1.94	1.92	1.90	1.88	1.87	1.85	1.83	1.81	1.79	1.75	1.71	1.62	1.54	1.47	1.40	1.33	2
3	2.93	2.90	2.87	2.84	2.81	2.78	2.76	2.73	2.70	2.68	2.61	2.55	2.42	2.30	2.19	2.09	1.99	3
4	3.88	3.84	3.81	3.77	3.73	3.69	3.66	3.62	3.59	3.55	3.46	3.38	3.21	3.06	2.91	2.77	2.63	4
5	4.83	4.78	4.73	4.69	4.64	4.60	4.55	4.50	4.46	4.42	4.31	4.20	4.00	3.80	3.62	3.44	3.28	5
6	5.77	5.71	5.65	5.60	5.54	5.49	5.43	5.38	5.33	5.27	5.14	5.02	4.77	4.54	4.32	4.11	3.91	6
7	6.69	6.63	6.56	6.50	6.43	6.37	6.31	6.24	6.18	6.12	5.97	5.82	5.54	5.27	5.02	4.77	4.54	7
8	7.61	7.54	7.46	7.39	7.32	7.24	7.17	7.10	7.03	6.96	6.79	6.62	6.30	6.00	5.71	5.43	5.16	8
9	8.52	8.44	8.36	8.27	8.19	8.11	8.03	7.95	7.87	7.79	7.60	7.42	7.06	6.71	6.39	6.08	5.78	9
10	9.42	9.33	9.24	9.15	9.06	8.97	8.88	8.79	8.70	8.62	8.41	8.20	7.80	7.42	7.06	6.72	6.39	10
11	10.32	10.21	10.11	10.01	9.91	9.82	9.72	9.62	9.53	9.43	9.20	8.97	8.54	8.12	7.73	7.36	7.00	11
12	11.20	11.09	10.98	10.87	10.76	10.66	10.55	10.45	10.34	10.24	9.99	9.74	9.27	8.82	8.39	7.98	7.60	12
13	12.07	11.95	11.84	11.72	11.60	11.49	11.37	11.26	11.15	11.04	10.77	10.50	9.99	9.51	9.05	8.61	8.19	13
14	12.94	12.81	12.68	12.56	12.43	12.31	12.19	12.07	11.95	11.83	11.54	11.26	10.71	10.19	9.70	9.23	8.78	14
15	13.80	13.66	13.52	13.39	13.26	13.13	13.00	12.87	12.74	12.61	12.30	12.00	11.42	10.87	10.34	9.84	9.36	15
16	14.65	14.50	14.36	14.21	14.07	13.93	13.80	13.66	13.52	13.39	13.06	12.74	12.12	11.53	10.97	10.44	9.93	16
17	15.49	15.33	15.18	15.03	14.88	14.73	14.59	14.44	14.30	14.16	13.81	13.47	12.82	12.20	11.60	11.04	10.50	17
18	16.32	16.16	16.00	15.84	15.68	15.53	15.37	15.22	15.07	14.92	14.55	14.20	13.51	12.85	12.23	11.63	11.07	18
19	17.14	16.97	16.80	16.64	16.47	16.31	16.15	15.99	15.83	15.67	15.29	14.91	14.19	13.50	12.84	12.22	11.63	19
20	17.96	17.78	17.60	17.43	17.26	17.08	16.92	16.75	16.58	16.42	16.01	15.62	14.86	14.14	13.46	12.80	12.18	20
21	18.76	18.58	18.39	18.21	18.03	17.85	17.68	17.50	17.33	17.16	16.73	16.32	15.53	14.78	14.06	13.38	12.73	21
22	19.56	19.37	19.18	18.99	18.80	18.61	18.43	18.25	18.07	17.89	17.45	17.02	16.19	15.41	14.66	13.95	13.27	22
23	20.35	20.15	19.95	19.76	19.56	19.37	19.17	18.99	18.80	18.61	18.15	17.71	16.85	16.03	15.25	14.51	13.81	23
24	21.14	20.93	20.72	20.52	20.31	20.11	19.91	19.72	19.52	19.33	18.85	18.39	17.50	16.65	15.84	15.07	14.34	24
25	21.91	21.70	21.48	21.27	21.06	20.85	20.64	20.44	20.24	20.04	19.54	19.06	18.14	17.26	16.42	15.62	14.87	25
26	22.68	22.46	22.24	22.02	21.80	21.58	21.37	21.16	20.95	20.74	20.23	19.73	18.78	17.86	17.00	16.17	15.39	26
27	23.44	23.21	22.98	22.75	22.53	22.31	22.08	21.87	21.65	21.43	20.91	20.39	19.40	18.46	17.57	16.71	15.90	27
28	24.20	23.96	23.72	23.48	23.25	23.02	22.79	22.57	22.34	22.12	21.58	21.05	20.03	19.06	18.13	17.25	16.41	28
29	24.94	24.69	24.45	24.21	23.97	23.73	23.50	23.26	23.03	22.81	22.24	21.70	20.65	19.64	18.69	17.78	16.92	29
30	25.68	25.43	25.17	24.92	24.68	24.43	24.19	23.95	23.72	23.48	22.90	22.34	21.26	20.22	19.24	18.31	17.42	30
31	26.41	26.15	25.89	25.63	25.38	25.13	24.88	24.63	24.39	24.15	23.56	22.98	21.86	20.80	19.79	18.83	17.92	31
32	27.13	26.87	26.60	26.34	26.08	25.82	25.56	25.31	25.06	24.81	24.20	23.61	22.46	21.37	20.33	19.35	18.41	32
33	27.85	27.58	27.30	27.03	26.76	26.50	26.24	25.98	25.72	25.47	24.84	24.23	23.05	21.93	20.87	19.86	18.89	33
34	28.56	28.28	28.00	27.72	27.45	27.17	26.91	26.64	26.38	26.11	25.47	24.85	23.64	22.49	21.40	20.36	19.37	34
35	29.26	28.97	28.69	28.40	28.12	27.84	27.57	27.29	27.02	26.76	26.10	25.46	24.22	23.05	21.93	20.86	19.85	35
36	29.96	29.66	29.37	29.08	28.79	28.50	28.22	27.94	27.67	27.39	26.72	26.06	24.80	23.59	22.45	21.36	20.32	36
37	30.65	30.34	30.04	29.75	29.45	29.16	28.87	28.59	28.30	28.02	27.33	26.66	25.37	24.14	22.97	21.85	20.79	37
38	31.33	31.02	30.71	30.41	30.11	29.81	29.51	29.22	28.93	28.65	27.94	27.25	25.93	24.67	23.48	22.34	21.25	38
39	32.00	31.69	31.37	31.06	30.76	30.45	30.15	29.85	29.55	29.26	28.54	27.84	26.49	25.21	23.98	22.82	21.71	39
40	32.67	32.35	32.03	31.71	31.40	31.09	30.78	30.47	30.17	29.87	29.14	28.42	27.04	25.73	24.48	23.29	22.16	40
41	33.33	33.00	32.68	32.35	32.03	31.72	31.40	31.09	30.78	30.48	29.73	29.00	27.59	26.25	24.98	23.77	22.61	41
42	33.99	33.65	33.32	32.99	32.66	32.34	32.02	31.70	31.39	31.08	30.31	29.57	28.13	26.77	25.47	24.23	23.06	42
43	34.64	34.29	33.96	33.62	33.29	32.96	32.63	32.31	31.99	31.67	30.89	30.13	28.67	27.28	25.96	24.70	23.50	43
44	35.28	34.93	34.58	34.24	33.90	33.57	33.24	32.91	32.58	32.26	31.47	30.69	29.20	27.79	26.44	25.15	23.93	44
45	35.92	35.56	35.21	34.86	34.51	34.17	33.83	33.50	33.17	32.84	32.03	31.25	29.73	28.29	26.91	25.61	24.36	45
Years of loss	1	2	3	4	5	6	7	8	9	10	12.5	15	20	25	30	35	40	Years of loss

Combination grid (Discount rate 2.5%)

Years of loss	\multicolumn{10}{c}{Years before loss starts to run}										12.5	15	20	25	30	35	40	Years of loss
	1	2	3	4	5	6	7	8	9	10	12.5	15	20	25	30	35	40	
1	0.96	0.94	0.92	0.89	0.87	0.85	0.83	0.81	0.79	0.77	0.73	0.68	0.60	0.53	0.47	0.42	0.37	1
2	1.90	1.86	1.81	1.77	1.72	1.68	1.64	1.60	1.56	1.52	1.43	1.35	1.19	1.05	0.93	0.82	0.73	2
3	2.82	2.75	2.69	2.62	2.56	2.49	2.43	2.37	2.32	2.26	2.12	2.00	1.76	1.56	1.38	1.22	1.08	3
4	3.72	3.63	3.54	3.45	3.37	3.28	3.20	3.13	3.05	2.98	2.80	2.63	2.32	2.05	1.82	1.61	1.42	4
5	4.59	4.48	4.37	4.26	4.16	4.06	3.96	3.86	3.77	3.67	3.45	3.25	2.87	2.54	2.24	1.98	1.75	5
6	5.44	5.31	5.18	5.05	4.93	4.81	4.69	4.58	4.47	4.36	4.10	3.85	3.40	3.01	2.66	2.35	2.08	6
7	6.27	6.12	5.97	5.82	5.68	5.54	5.41	5.28	5.15	5.02	4.72	4.44	3.92	3.47	3.06	2.71	2.39	7
8	7.08	6.91	6.74	6.58	6.42	6.26	6.11	5.96	5.81	5.67	5.33	5.01	4.43	3.92	3.46	3.06	2.70	8
9	7.87	7.68	7.49	7.31	7.13	6.96	6.79	6.62	6.46	6.30	5.93	5.57	4.93	4.35	3.85	3.40	3.01	9
10	8.65	8.43	8.23	8.03	7.83	7.64	7.45	7.27	7.10	6.92	6.51	6.12	5.41	4.78	4.22	3.73	3.30	10
11	9.40	9.17	8.95	8.73	8.51	8.31	8.10	7.91	7.71	7.53	7.07	6.65	5.88	5.20	4.59	4.06	3.59	11
12	10.13	9.89	9.64	9.41	9.18	8.96	8.74	8.52	8.32	8.11	7.63	7.17	6.34	5.60	4.95	4.38	3.87	12
13	10.85	10.58	10.33	10.07	9.83	9.59	9.36	9.13	8.90	8.69	8.17	7.68	6.79	6.00	5.30	4.69	4.14	13
14	11.55	11.27	10.99	10.72	10.46	10.21	9.96	9.72	9.48	9.25	8.69	8.17	7.22	6.38	5.64	4.99	4.41	14
15	12.23	11.93	11.64	11.36	11.08	10.81	10.55	10.29	10.04	9.79	9.21	8.66	7.65	6.76	5.98	5.28	4.67	15
16	12.90	12.58	12.27	11.98	11.68	11.40	11.12	10.85	10.58	10.33	9.71	9.13	8.07	7.13	6.30	5.57	4.92	16
17	13.54	13.21	12.89	12.58	12.27	11.97	11.68	11.39	11.12	10.85	10.20	9.59	8.47	7.49	6.62	5.85	5.17	17
18	14.18	13.83	13.50	13.17	12.84	12.53	12.23	11.93	11.64	11.35	10.67	10.03	8.87	7.84	6.93	6.12	5.41	18
19	14.80	14.44	14.08	13.74	13.40	13.08	12.76	12.45	12.14	11.85	11.14	10.47	9.26	8.18	7.23	6.39	5.65	19
20	15.40	15.02	14.66	14.30	13.95	13.61	13.28	12.95	12.64	12.33	11.59	10.90	9.63	8.51	7.52	6.65	5.88	20
21	15.99	15.60	15.22	14.85	14.48	14.13	13.79	13.45	13.12	12.80	12.04	11.31	10.00	8.84	7.81	6.90	6.10	21
22	16.56	16.16	15.76	15.38	15.00	14.64	14.28	13.93	13.59	13.26	12.47	11.72	10.36	9.16	8.09	7.15	6.32	22
23	17.12	16.70	16.30	15.90	15.51	15.13	14.76	14.40	14.05	13.71	12.89	12.12	10.71	9.47	8.37	7.39	6.54	23
24	17.67	17.24	16.82	16.41	16.01	15.61	15.23	14.86	14.50	14.15	13.30	12.50	11.05	9.77	8.63	7.63	6.74	24
25	18.20	17.76	17.32	16.90	16.49	16.09	15.69	15.31	14.94	14.57	13.70	12.88	11.38	10.06	8.89	7.86	6.95	25
26	18.72	18.26	17.82	17.38	16.96	16.55	16.14	15.75	15.36	14.99	14.09	13.25	11.71	10.35	9.15	8.09	7.15	26
27	19.23	18.76	18.30	17.85	17.42	16.99	16.58	16.17	15.78	15.40	14.47	13.61	12.03	10.63	9.40	8.30	7.34	27
28	19.72	19.24	18.77	18.31	17.87	17.43	17.01	16.59	16.19	15.79	14.85	13.96	12.34	10.90	9.64	8.52	7.53	28
29	20.20	19.71	19.23	18.76	18.30	17.86	17.42	17.00	16.58	16.18	15.21	14.30	12.64	11.17	9.87	8.73	7.71	29
30	20.68	20.17	19.68	19.20	18.73	18.27	17.83	17.39	16.97	16.56	15.56	14.63	12.93	11.43	10.10	8.93	7.89	30
31	21.13	20.62	20.12	19.63	19.15	18.68	18.22	17.78	17.35	16.92	15.91	14.96	13.22	11.68	10.33	9.13	8.07	31
32	21.58	21.06	20.54	20.04	19.55	19.08	18.61	18.16	17.71	17.28	16.25	15.27	13.50	11.93	10.55	9.32	8.24	32
33	22.02	21.48	20.96	20.45	19.95	19.46	18.99	18.52	18.07	17.63	16.58	15.58	13.77	12.17	10.76	9.51	8.41	33
34	22.45	21.90	21.37	20.84	20.34	19.84	19.36	18.88	18.42	17.97	16.90	15.89	14.04	12.41	10.97	9.69	8.57	34
35	22.86	22.31	21.76	21.23	20.71	20.21	19.71	19.23	18.76	18.31	17.21	16.18	14.30	12.64	11.17	9.87	8.73	35
36	23.27	22.70	22.15	21.61	21.08	20.57	20.06	19.58	19.10	18.63	17.52	16.47	14.56	12.86	11.37	10.05	8.88	36
37	23.67	23.09	22.52	21.98	21.44	20.92	20.41	19.91	19.42	18.95	17.81	16.75	14.80	13.08	11.56	10.22	9.03	37
38	24.05	23.47	22.89	22.33	21.79	21.26	20.74	20.23	19.74	19.26	18.11	17.02	15.04	13.30	11.75	10.39	9.18	38
39	24.43	23.83	23.25	22.68	22.13	21.59	21.06	20.55	20.05	19.56	18.39	17.29	15.28	13.51	11.94	10.55	9.33	39
40	24.80	24.19	23.60	23.03	22.46	21.92	21.38	20.86	20.35	19.86	18.67	17.55	15.51	13.71	12.12	10.71	9.47	40
41	25.16	24.54	23.94	23.36	22.79	22.23	21.69	21.16	20.65	20.14	18.94	17.80	15.74	13.91	12.29	10.86	9.60	41
42	25.51	24.88	24.28	23.68	23.11	22.54	21.99	21.46	20.93	20.42	19.20	18.05	15.95	14.10	12.46	11.02	9.74	42
43	25.85	25.22	24.60	24.00	23.42	22.85	22.29	21.74	21.21	20.70	19.46	18.29	16.17	14.29	12.63	11.16	9.87	43
44	26.18	25.54	24.92	24.31	23.72	23.14	22.58	22.02	21.49	20.96	19.71	18.53	16.38	14.47	12.79	11.31	9.99	44
45	26.51	25.86	25.23	24.61	24.01	23.43	22.86	22.30	21.75	21.22	19.95	18.76	16.58	14.65	12.95	11.45	10.12	45
Years of loss	1	2	3	4	5	6	7	8	9	10	12.5	15	20	25	30	35	40	Years of loss

A7: Table of adjustments to multiplier for Fatal Accidents Acts dependency

These tables deal with factors to be applied in fatal accident cases to allow for the possibility that the deceased would not have survived until trial. These tables are derived from the Explanatory Notes of the Ogden Tables, para.64 onwards. They are set out here on one page for convenience. (The user will need to consider the current state of authority on the acceptability of this approach.)

PRE-TRIAL damages (factor to be applied to damages from date of accident to trial)

Age of deceased at date of accident	Period from accident to trial (or cessation of dependency if earlier)							
	Male	3	6	9	Female	3	6	9
10		1.00	1.00	1.00		1.00	1.00	1.00
20		1.00	1.00	1.00		1.00	1.00	1.00
30		1.00	1.00	0.99		1.00	1.00	1.00
40		1.00	0.99	0.99		1.00	1.00	0.99
50		0.99	0.99	0.98		1.00	0.99	0.99
60		0.99	0.97	0.94		0.99	0.98	0.97
65		0.98	0.95	0.91		0.99	0.97	0.95
70		0.97	0.92	0.86		0.98	0.95	0.91
75		0.94	0.87	0.78		0.96	0.91	0.84
80		0.90	0.79	0.67		0.93	0.84	0.75

POST-TRIAL damages (factor to be applied to damages from date of trial to retirement age)

Age of deceased at date of accident	Period from accident to trial							
	Male	3	6	9	Female	3	6	9
10		1.00	1.00	1.00		1.00	1.00	1.00
20		1.00	1.00	0.99		1.00	1.00	1.00
30		1.00	0.99	0.99		1.00	1.00	0.99
40		0.99	0.99	0.98		1.00	0.99	0.99
50		0.99	0.97	0.95		0.99	0.98	0.97
60		0.97	0.93	0.88		0.98	0.96	0.92
65		0.96	0.90	0.82		0.97	0.93	0.88
70		0.93	0.84	0.71		0.96	0.89	0.80
75		0.88	0.73	0.55		0.92	0.81	0.66
80		0.83	0.59	0.37		0.86	0.68	0.48

POST-RETIREMENT damages (for the period of dependency after retirement age)

1. First obtain the multiplier for the whole of life dependency by the following steps:

    (a) determine, from 0% tables, the expectation of life which the deceased would have had at the date of trial (or the shorter period for which the deceased would have provided the dependency);

    (b) determine the expected period for which the dependant would have been able to receive the dependency (for a widow, normally her life expectancy from 0% tables; for a child, normally the period until it reaches adulthood);

    (c) take the lesser of the two periods; and

    (d) treat the resulting period as a term certain and look up the multiplier for that period (Table A5, continuous loss column).

2. Obtain the multiplier for dependency from date of trial to retirement age. Do not adjust it for contingencies other than mortality. Do not apply the factors in the Post-Trial table above.

3. Subtract the multiplier for dependency to retirement age (2) from the whole life multiplier (1). Multiply by the factor in the Post-Trial table above.

    Post-retirement multiplier = [Stage 1 figure *minus* Stage 2 figure] × Post-Trial factor.

A8: The Ogden Tables

Actuarial tables with explanatory notes for use in personal injury and fatal accident cases.

Prepared by an Inter-Professional Working Party of Actuaries, Lawyers, Accountants and other interested parties.

7th edn prepared by the Government Actuary's Department.

Table of Contents	*Page*
Introduction to 7th edn	46
Explanatory Notes	50
Section A: General	50
Section B: Contingencies other than mortality	57
Section C: Summary of personal injury applications	64
Section D: Application of tables to fatal accident cases	69
Section E: Concluding remarks	80

Tables 1–26

Table 1: Multipliers for pecuniary loss for life (males)	81
Table 2: Multipliers for pecuniary loss for life (females)	83
Table 3: Multipliers for loss of earnings to pension age 50 (males)	85
Table 4: Multipliers for loss of earnings to pension age 50 (females)	86
Table 5: Multipliers for loss of earnings to pension age 55 (males)	87
Table 6: Multipliers for loss of earnings to pension age 55 (females)	88
Table 7: Multipliers for loss of earnings to pension age 60 (males)	89
Table 8: Multipliers for loss of earnings to pension age 60 (females)	90
Table 9: Multipliers for loss of earnings to pension age 65 (males)	91
Table 10: Multipliers for loss of earnings to pension age 65 (females)	92
Table 11: Multipliers for loss of earnings to pension age 70 (males)	93
Table 12: Multipliers for loss of earnings to pension age 70 (females)	94
Table 13: Multipliers for loss of earnings to pension age 75 (males)	95
Table 14: Multipliers for loss of earnings to pension age 75 (females)	96
Table 15: Multipliers for loss of pension commencing age 50 (males)	97
Table 16: Multipliers for loss of pension commencing age 50 (females)	98
Table 17: Multipliers for loss of pension commencing age 55 (males)	99
Table 18: Multipliers for loss of pension commencing age 55 (females)	100
Table 19: Multipliers for loss of pension commencing age 60 (males)	101

Table 20: Multipliers for loss of pension commencing age 60 (females)   103

Table 21: Multipliers for loss of pension commencing age 65 (males)   105

Table 22: Multipliers for loss of pension commencing age 65 (females)   107

Table 23: Multipliers for loss of pension commencing age 70 (males)   109

Table 24: Multipliers for loss of pension commencing age 70 (females)   111

Table 25: Multipliers for loss of pension commencing age 75 (males)   113

Table 26: Multipliers for loss of pension commencing age 75 (females)   115

Tables 27 and 28 (Tables for term certain)

Table 27: Discounting factors for term certain   117

Table 28: Multipliers for pecuniary loss for term certain   119

Actuarial formulae and basis   120

Introduction to the 7th edn

"When it comes to the explanatory notes we must make sure that they are readily comprehensible. We must assume the most stupid circuit judge in the country and before him are the two most stupid advocates. All three of them must be able to understand what we are saying"

Sir Michael Ogden QC, on his explanatory notes to the 1st edn of the Ogden Tables.[1]

1. The Working Party has been eager to see a new set of these tables published, as there have been changes in the official projections of future mortality rates for the UK since the previous, 6th edn was published which produce significant changes in the values of some of the multipliers. The Working Party is grateful that the Ministry of Justice has agreed to fund the production of this edition of the Ogden Tables.

Purpose of the tables

2. These tables are designed to assist those concerned with calculating lump sum damages for future losses in personal injury and fatal accident cases in the UK.

3. The methodology is long-established whereby multipliers are applied to the present day value of a future annual loss (net of tax in the case of a loss of earnings and pension) with the aim of producing a lump sum equivalent to the capitalised value of the future losses. In essence, the multiplier is the figure by which an annual loss is multiplied in order to calculate a capitalised sum, taking into account accelerated receipt, mortality risks and, in relation to claims for loss of earnings and pension, discounts for contingencies other than mortality.

4. This methodology was endorsed by the House of Lords in the famous case of **Wells v Wells**.[2] In that case the court determined that the discount rate should be based on the yields on Index Linked Government Stock. The discount rate is now fixed by the Lord Chancellor of the day pursuant to his powers under the Damages Act 1996. The above method was further endorsed by Lord Chancellor Irvine in his decision of July 2001, when he fixed the Discount Rate as being 2.5 per cent. He also gave his reasons for his decision, which reasons appear now to be less than happy in the light of the financial turmoil which has since occurred. I will deal with this below. In my view, this present rate is long out of date and does not reflect the substantial reduction in yields on Index Linked Government Stocks since 2001. The present Lord Chancellor Clarke has agreed to review it although his decision may not be available for several months.

First decision of the Working Party

5. It was decided that, with funding now obtained, a new set of tables, based on the most recent mortality rates produced by the Office for National Statistics (ONS), with as few other revisions as possible, should be issued as quickly as was realistically achievable.

Second decision of the Working Party

6. It was decided that, due to the passage of time and the changed circumstances since the tables were first produced, the text of the Explanatory Notes will require a substantial re-write in order to bolster

---

[1] Memoirs of Sir Michael Ogden QC, *Variety is the Spice of Legal Life*, p.182 (Lewes: The Book Guild, 2002).
[2] [1999] 1 A.C. 345.

its usefulness to practitioners. Not only is there a need to change the language, but the effect of other decided cases has made this a task of importance. The intention of the Working party is to accomplish this re-writing in the next (eighth) edition, which will rely on the further updated mortality projections due to be produced by the ONS later in 2011. It is hoped that the 8th edition will be available in autumn 2012.

Third decision of the Working Party

7. Developments in Guernsey and the review of the discount rate currently being carried out by the Lord Chancellor (see further, below, in respect of both matters) caused the Working Party to decide to include in this edition tables with discount rate columns which range between minus 2 per cent and plus 3 per cent.

8. It is not, we believe, the purpose of these tables or the role of the Working Party to advocate a discount rate, but merely to provide the tools so that, whatever the rate should be, personal injury and fatal accident claims may be quantified.

9. The revised spread of discount rates will assist comparison between lump sums and periodical payments, a process required by the Damages Act 1996, to be more accurately appreciated. The present value of periodical payments is substantially higher than lump sums calculated using the current discount rate of 2.5 per cent. Brooke L.J. remarked in para.34 of the *Flora v Wakom*[3] judgment: "The fact that these two quite different mechanisms now sit side by side in the same Act of Parliament does not in my judgment mean that the problems that infected the operation of the one should be allowed to infect the operation of the other." This imbalance is a factor which any Lord Chancellor ought to take into account.

Fourth decision of the Working Party

10. The Working Party decided not to increase further the number of tables to reflect different possible retirement ages. The multipliers for retirement ages which do not conform strictly with the five-yearly intervals between 50 and 75 can be calculated with reasonable accuracy by interpolation. We would be interested to learn of other views on this decision which might cause us to think again.

Helmot v Simon

11. The judgment in *Helmot v Simon*[4] in the Court of Appeal of the Island of Guernsey (September 14, 2010), presided over by Sumption J.A., could be truly described as a decision which has had after-effects. The results have rippled the waters within the English legal establishment, even though the decision creates no precedent in England.

12. The first point to make about the case is that the Damages Act 1996 (as amended) does not apply in Guernsey. Consequentally, neither the 2.5 per cent discount rate prescribed under the power provided by s.1 applies nor is there any power to make an award by way of a periodical payment.

13. The original lump sum award made at first instance on January 14, 2010 was for damages in the sum of £9.3 million plus interest. The court used a single discount rate of 1 per cent for all future losses. The claimant had argued for differential rates of 0.5 per cent for non-earnings-related losses and of

---

[3] [2006] EWCA Civ 1103; [2007] 1 W.L.R. 282.
[4] [2009–10] G.L.R. 465.

minus 1.5 per cent for earnings-related losses. Some eight months later these arguments succeeded on appeal and the final amount of the award was increased to more than £14 million. Permission has been granted to appeal the decision to the Privy Council.

14. The consequences in England and Wales have been profound. The Lord Chancellor has indicated his intention to reconsider the discount rate and at the time of writing is in the process of doing so. It has also emphasised the disparity between lump sum awards and the provision of periodical payments, to the detriment of lump sum awards, when the discount rate is inappropriate, it not having been revised for a period of 10 years.

Mortality data

15. Projections of future mortality rates are usually produced on a two-yearly basis by the ONS as part of the production of national population projections for the United Kingdom and its constituent countries. Multipliers published in the 6th edition of the Ogden Tables were calculated using mortality rates from the 2004-based projections; this new edition provides multipliers based on mortality rates from the most recent, 2008-based, projections. The 2006-based projections showed rather higher projected life expectancies at many ages than those in the 2004-based projections. The 2008-based projections suggest slightly higher projected life expectancies than those in the 2006-based projections, but which are of relatively little significance in terms of the values of the multipliers at most ages.

16. There is much debate among demographers about whether the factors that have led to the significant improvements in mortality in recent years can continue unabated, thus adding some uncertainty to any projections of future mortality. While the Working Party has continued to use the official projections made by the ONS of future mortality rates in the UK, we propose to monitor developments as new evidence becomes available.

Contingencies other than mortality

17. We have persuaded Dr Victoria Wass to join the Working Party. She has suggested changes to the definition of "disabled" and also clarified some of the language in the Explanatory Notes. We anticipate some further suggestions for amendment in the 8th edn.

18. The Working Party notes that there have been a number of cases in which judges have made significant adjustments to the suggested discount factors. In particular the approach of the trial judges to the calculation of future loss of earnings in **Conner v Bradman**[5] and **Clarke v Maltby**[6] has generated some debate. These issues will be discussed in detail when drafting the 8th edn and consideration will be given to whether or not the Explanatory Notes need amendment, especially as regards the circumstances in which it might be appropriate to depart from the suggested non-mortality reduction factors and the size of any adjustments that are made. In the meantime, practitioners performing such calculations are referred to the helpful article by Dr Wass, *"Discretion in the Application of the New Ogden Six Multipliers: The Case of Conner v Bradman and Company"*,[7] which highlights some of the relevant issues.

---

[5] [2007] EWHC 2789 (QB).
[6] [2010] EWHC 1201 (QB).
[7] [2008] J.P.I.L. 2, 154–163.

Fatal Accidents Act calculations and the "Actuarially Recommended Approach"

19. This is dealt with in detail in Section D of the Explanatory Notes. To those comments I would add one qualification which is that the Court of Appeal in *Fletcher v A Train & Sons Ltd*[8] was sufficiently concerned with the consequence of following the reasoning of the House of Lords in *Cookson v Knowles*[9] that it unanimously gave the unsuccessful appellant permission to appeal to the House of Lords on the point; the appeal was subsequently compromised.

20. The Scottish Parliament has since enacted the Damages (Scotland) Act 2011 dealing with the same point and in so doing has demonstrated that it agrees with the point that our predecessors had made on this topic.

21. Section 7(1)(d) of the Damages (Scotland) Act 2011 provides for the multiplier to be calculated at the date of the proof (trial) and the losses over the period between the fatal accident and the proof to be calculated separately, subject to a factor for possible early death, with interest added. Multipliers are determined from the tables based on the age of the deceased had he/she survived to the date of proof. This is the same as our actuarially recommended approach.

Concluding remarks

22. The changes to the Explanatory Notes in this edition are minor; it is the figures that have been updated.

23. As I have previously stated, the figures for the tables themselves are produced by the Government Actuary's Department according to long-established principles.

24. The other matters discussed are the subject of careful and detailed analysis by the members of the Working Party. Its discussions are never less than uninhibited and I am grateful to those members of the Working Party (listed inside the front cover) who give their time and energy to attend the meetings and ensure that all is done which ought to be done.

25. I begin to believe that the journey made by Jason and the Argonauts in search of the Golden Fleece is as nothing in comparison with the desire of those involved in these tables to make the assessment of future losses as simple and accurate as they possibly can be, whilst remaining as clear as we can be in explaining the actual process of calculating the figures. I am conscious that we may not always succeed in that ambition.

Robin de Wilde QC   August 1, 2012

---

[8] [2008] EWCA Civ 413; [2008] 4 All E.R. 699.
[9] [1979] A.C. 566.

Explanatory Notes

Section A: General

Purpose of tables

1. The tables have been prepared by the Government Actuary's Department. They provide an aid for those assessing the lump sum appropriate as compensation for a continuing future pecuniary loss or consequential expense or cost of care in personal injury and fatal accident cases.

Application of tables

2. The tables set out multipliers. These multipliers enable the user to assess the present capital value of future annual loss (net of tax) or annual expense calculated on the basis of various assumptions which are explained below. Accordingly, to find the present capital value of a given annual loss or expense, it is necessary to select the appropriate table, find the appropriate multiplier and then multiply the amount of the annual loss or expense by that figure.

3. Tables 1–26 deal with annual loss or annual expense extending over three different periods of time. In each case there are separate tables for men and women.

— In Tables 1 and 2 the loss or expense is assumed to begin immediately and to continue for the whole of the rest of the claimant's life.

— In Tables 3–14 the loss or expense is assumed to begin immediately but to continue only until the claimant's retirement or earlier death.

— In Tables 15–26 it is assumed that the annual loss or annual expense will not begin until the claimant reaches retirement but will then continue for the whole of the rest of his or her life. These tables all make due allowance for the chance that the claimant may not live to reach the age of retirement.

Mortality assumptions

4. The tables are based on a reasonable estimate of the future mortality likely to be experienced by average members of the population alive today and are based on projected mortality rates for the United Kingdom as a whole. The Office for National Statistics publishes population projections on a regular basis which include estimates of the extent of future improvements in mortality. Tables 1–26 in this edition show the multipliers which result from the application of these projected mortality rates which were derived from the principal 2008-based population projections for the United Kingdom, which were published in October 2009. (Further details of these projections can be found on the ONS website at: *http://www.ons.gov.uk/ons/rel/npp/national-population-projections/2008-based-projections/index/html.*)

5. The tables do not assume that the claimant dies after a period equating to the expectation of life, but take account of the possibilities that the claimant will live for different periods, e.g. die soon or live to be very old. The mortality assumptions relate to the general population of the United Kingdom. However, unless there is clear evidence in an individual case to support the view that the individual is atypical and will enjoy longer or shorter expectation of life, no further increase or reduction is required for mortality alone.

Use of tables

6. To find the appropriate figure for the present value of a particular loss or expense, the user must first choose that table which relates to the period of loss or expense for which the individual claimant is to be compensated and to the gender of the claimant, or, where appropriate, the claimant's dependants.

7. If, for some reason, the facts in a particular case do not correspond with the assumptions on which one of the tables is based (e.g. it is known that the claimant will have a different retiring age from that assumed in the tables), then the tables can only be used if an appropriate allowance is made for this difference; for this purpose the assistance of an actuary should be sought, except for situations where specific guidance is given in these explanatory notes.

Rate of return

8. The basis of the multipliers set out in the tables is that the lump sum will be invested and yield income (but that over the period in question the claimant will gradually reduce the capital sum, so that at the end of the period it is exhausted). Accordingly, an essential factor in arriving at the right figure is the choice of the appropriate rate of return.

9. The annual rate of return currently to be applied is 2.5 per cent (net of tax), as fixed by the Lord Chancellor on June 25, 2001, and reassessed on July 27, 2001, under the provisions of the Damages Act 1996 s.1. An annual rate of return of 2.5 per cent was also set for Scotland by the Scottish Ministers on February 8, 2002. The Lord Chancellor may make a fresh determination of this rate, after receiving advice from the Government Actuary and the Treasury (and, in Scotland, the Scottish Ministers after consultation with the Government Actuary). In order to allow the tables to continue to be used should a new discount rate be specified, the tables are accordingly shown for a range of possible annual rates of return ranging from –2 per cent to 3 per cent, in steps of 0.5 per cent, rather than the range 0.0 per cent to 5.0 per cent as in the 6th edn. This change has been made because multipliers at negative rates are useful for the financial evaluation of periodical payments in the exercise which is required by the Damages Act in all cases for comparison with lump sums. In addition, it is recognised that multipliers based on discount rates of more than 3 per cent are currently not generally required, and a recent case heard in the Channel Islands (**Helmot v Simon**[10]) has made an award based on negative discount rates.

10. The figures in the 0% column show the multiplier without any discount for interest and provide the expectations of life (Tables 1 and 2) or the expected period over which a person would have provided a dependency (up to retirement age Tables 3–14 or from pension age Tables 15–26). These are supplied to assist in the calculation of multipliers in Fatal Accidents Act cases (see Section D).

11. Section 1(2) of the Damages Act 1996 makes provision for the courts to make variations to the discount rate if any party to the proceedings shows that it is more appropriate in the case in question. Variations to the discount rate under this provision have, however, been rejected by the Court of Appeal in the cases of **Warriner v Warriner**[11] and **Cooke & Others v United Bristol Health Care & Others**.[12]

12. Previous editions of these tables explained how the current yields on index-linked government bonds could be used as an indicator of the appropriate real rate of return for valuing future income streams. Such considerations were endorsed by the House of Lords in **Wells v Wells** and the same

---

[10] [2009–10] G.L.R. 465.
[11] [2002] EWCA Civ 81; [2002] 1 W.L.R. 1703.
[12] [2003] EWCA Civ 1370; [2004] 1 W.L.R. 251.

argumentation was adopted by the Lord Chancellor when he set the rate on commencement of s.1 of the Damages Act 1996. In cases outwith the scope of these tables, the advice of an actuary should be sought.

Different retirement ages

13. In para.7 above, reference was made to the problem that will arise when the claimant's retiring age is different from that assumed in the tables. Such a problem may arise in valuing a loss or expense beginning immediately but ending at retirement; or in valuing a loss or expense which will not begin until the claimant reaches retirement but will then continue until death. Tables are provided for retirement ages of 50, 55, 60, 65, 70 and 75. Where the claimant's actual retiring age would have been between two of the retirement ages for which tables are provided, the correct multiplier can be obtained by consideration of the tables for retirement age immediately above and below the actual retirement age, keeping the period to retirement age the same. Thus a woman of 42 who would have retired at 58 can be considered as being in between the cases of a woman of 39 with a retirement age of 55 and a woman of 44 with a retirement age of 60. The steps to take are as follows:

(1) Determine between which retirement ages, for which tables are provided, the claimant's actual retirement age R lies. Let the lower of these ages be A and the higher be B.

(2) Determine how many years must be subtracted from the claimant's actual retirement age to get to A and subtract that period from the claimant's age. If the claimant's age is x, the result of this calculation is $(x + A - R)$.

(3) Look up this new reduced age in the table corresponding to retirement age A at the appropriate rate of return. Let the resulting multiplier be M.

(4) Determine how many years must be added to the claimant's actual retirement age to get to B and add that period to the claimant's age. The result of this calculation is $(x + B - R)$.

(5) Look up this new increased age in the table corresponding to retirement age B at the appropriate rate of return. Let the resulting multiplier be N.

(6) Interpolate between M and N. In other words, calculate:

$(B - R) \times M + (R - A) \times N$

and divide the result by $[(B - R) + (R - A)]$, (or equivalently $[B - A]$).

14. In the example given in para.13, the steps would be as follows:

(1) R is 58, A is 55 and B is 60.

(2) Subtracting three years from the claimant's age gives 39.

(3) Looking up age 39 in Table 6 (for retirement age 55) gives 13.10 at a rate of return of 2.5 per cent.

(4) Adding two years to the claimant's age gives 44.

(5) Looking up age 44 in Table 8 (for retirement age 60) gives 13.03 at a rate of return of 2.5 per cent.

(6) Calculating $2 \times 13.10 + 3 \times 13.03$ and dividing by $(60 - 58) + (58 - 55)$ [equals 5] gives 13.06 as the multiplier.

15. When the loss or expense to be valued is that from the date of retirement to death, and the claimant's date of retirement differs from that assumed in the tables, a different approach is necessary, involving the following three steps.

(1)   Assume that there is a present loss which will continue for the rest of the claimant's life and from Table 1 or 2 establish the value of that loss or expense over the whole period from the date of assessment until the claimant's death.

(2)   Establish the value of such loss or expense over the period from the date of assessment until the claimant's expected date of retirement following the procedure explained in paras 13 and 14, above.

(3)   Subtract the second figure from the first. The balance remaining represents the present value of the claimant's loss or expense between retirement and death.

16. If the claimant's actual retirement age would have been earlier than 50, or later than 75, the advice of an actuary should be sought.

Younger ages

17. Tables 1 and 2, which concern pecuniary loss for life, and Tables 15–26, which concern loss of pension from retirement age, have been extended down to age 0. In some circumstances the multiplier at age 0 is slightly lower than that at age 1; this arises because of the relatively high incidence of deaths immediately after birth.

18. Tables for multipliers for loss of earnings (Tables 3–14) have not been extended below age 16. In order to determine the multiplier for loss of earnings for someone who has not yet started work, it is first necessary to determine an assumed age at which the claimant would have commenced work and to find the appropriate multiplier for that age from Tables 3–14, according to the assumed retirement age. This multiplier should then be multiplied by the deferment factor from Table 27 which corresponds to the appropriate rate of return and the period from the date of the trial to the date on which it is assumed that the claimant would have started work. A similar approach can be used for determining a multiplier for pecuniary loss for life where the loss is assumed to commence a fixed period of years from the date of the trial. For simplicity the factors in Table 27 relate purely to the impact of compound interest and ignore mortality. At ages below 30 this is a reasonable approximation but at higher ages it would normally be appropriate to allow explicitly for mortality and the advice of an actuary should be sought.

Contingencies

19. Tables 1–26 make reasonable provision for the levels of mortality which members of the population of the United Kingdom alive today may expect to experience in future. The tables do not take account of the other risks and vicissitudes of life, such as the possibility that the claimant would for periods have ceased to earn due to ill-health or loss of employment. Nor do they take account of the fact that many people cease work for substantial periods to care for children or other dependants. Section B suggests ways in which allowance may be made to the multipliers for loss of earnings, to allow for certain risks other than mortality.

Impaired lives

20. In some cases, medical evidence may be available which asserts that a claimant's health impairments are equivalent to adding a certain number of years to their current age, or to treating the

individual as having a specific age different from their actual age. In such cases, Tables 1 and 2 can be used with respect to the deemed higher age. For the other tables the adjustment is not so straightforward, as adjusting the age will also affect the assumed retirement age, but the procedures described in paras 13–15 may be followed, or the advice of an actuary should be sought. In other cases, the medical evidence may state that the claimant is likely to live for a stated number of years. This is often then treated as requiring payment to be made for a fixed period equal to the stated life expectancy and using Table 28 to ascertain the value of the multiplier. In general, this is likely to give a multiplier which is too high since this approach does not allow for the distribution of deaths around the expected length of life. For a group of similarly impaired lives of the same age, some will die before the average life expectancy and some after; allowing for this spread of deaths results in a lower multiplier than assuming payment for a term certain equal to the life expectancy. In such cases, it is preferable to look up the age in the 0 per cent column in Tables 1 or 2 for which the value of the multiplier at 0 per cent is equal to the stated life expectancy. The relevant multipliers are then obtained from the relevant tables using this age. Take, for example, an impaired male life which is stated to have a life expectancy of 20 years. By interpolation, the age for which the multiplier in the 0 per cent column in Table 1 is 20 is:

$$(20 - 19.74)/(20.57 - 19.74) \times 66 + (20.57 - 20)/(20.57 - 19.74) \times 67$$

which equals 66.7 years.

The value of the whole of life multiplier is then obtained from the 2.5 per cent column of Table 1 for age 66.7 years:

$$(67 - 66.7) \times 15.38 + (66.7 - 66) \times 14.90$$

which equals 15.04 (compared to 15.78 for the value for a term certain of 20 years using the 2.5 per cent column of Table 28).

Fixed period

21. In cases where pecuniary loss is to be valued for a fixed period, the multipliers in Table 28 may be used. These make no allowance for mortality or any other contingency but assume that regular frequent payments (e.g. weekly or monthly) will continue throughout the period. These figures should in principle be adjusted if the periodicity of payment is less frequent, especially if the payments in question are annually in advance or in arrears.

Variable future losses or expenses

22. The tables do not provide an immediate answer when the annual future loss or expense is likely to change at given points in time in the future. The most common examples will be where:

(a) the claimant's lost earnings would have increased on a sliding scale or changed due to promotion; or

(b) the claimant's care needs are likely to change in the future, perhaps because it is anticipated that a family carer will not be able to continue to provide help.

In such situations it is usually necessary to split the overall multiplier, whether for working life or whole of life, into segments, and then to apply those smaller segmented multipliers to the multiplicand appropriate for each period.

There are a variety of methods which could be used for splitting a multiplier, especially where the age at which a payment is increased or decreased, or stops or begins, is one which is tabulated in Tables 1–26. The following examples serve to illustrate how multipliers might be split using the "apportionment method". This method can be extended for use in cases where none of the ages at which payments change are tabulated.

Example 1—Variable future earnings

23. The claimant is female, a graduate with a degree, aged 25 at date of settlement/trial. Her probable career progression, in the absence of injury, would have provided her with salary increases at ages 30, 35 and 40; thereafter she would have continued at the same level to age 60, when she would have stepped down from full-time work to work part-time until 70. Post-accident she is now incapable of working.

The multiplicands for lost future earnings are:

Age 25–30:   £16,000 a year

Age 30–35:   £25,000 a year

Age 35–40:   £35,000 a year

Age 40–60:   £40,000 a year

Age 60–70:   £20,000 a year

The multipliers for each stage of her career are calculated as follows:

(1)   The working-life will be 45 years and the Multiplier from Table 12 for that period taking into account mortality risks but without any discounts for any other contingencies will be 26.73.

(2)   The multiplier for a term certain of 45 years (ignoring mortality risks) from Table 28 is 27.17.

(3)   The multiplier from Table 28 should be split so that each individual segment of the whole working life period (45 years) is represented by a figure. So, the first five years is represented by a multiplier for a term certain of five years, namely 4.70; the next five years is represented by a multiplier of 4.16 (being the difference between the figure for a term certain of 10 years, namely 8.86 and the figure for a term certain of five years, namely 4.70); the next five years by 3.68 (i.e. the 15-year figure of 12.54 less the 10 year figure of 8.86); the next 20 years by 10.89 (i.e. the difference between the 35-year figure which is 23.43 and the 15-year figure of 12.54); then, the final 10 years by the balance of 3.74 (the residual figure being 27.17 less 23.43).

(4)   Each of those smaller segmented multipliers can be shown as a percentage or fraction of the whole: so, for the first five years the segmented multiplier of 4.70 is 17.30 per cent of the whole figure of 27.17, and so on for each segment of the 45-year period.

(5)   The working life multiplier from Table 12 can now be split up in identical proportions to the way in which the Table 28 multiplier has been treated above: thus the first five-year period is now represented by a multiplier of 4.62, which is calculated by taking 17.30 per cent of 26.73. Each segmented multiplier is calculated in the same way.

(6)   Having now obtained multipliers for each segment of working life, taking into account mortality risks, it is then necessary to discount those figures for "contingencies other than mortality". The discount factor from Table C (using the column for a female, not disabled, with degree level

education) is 0.89. So, the figure of 4.62 for the first five-year period now becomes 4.11 (i.e. 4.62 × 0.89). Again, treat each segmented multiplier in the same way.

(7) The multiplicand for each segment of working life is now multiplied by the appropriate segmented multiplier to calculate the loss for that period. The sum total of those losses represents the full sum for loss of future earnings (ignoring any mitigation).

(8) The figures are set out in tabular form below and give a total lump sum award of £716,260:

Ages	Period (years)	Table 28	% Split	Table 12	Discounted Multipliers (Table C) (× 0.89)	Net Annual Earnings £	£ Loss
25–30	5	4.70	17.30	4.62	4.11	16,000	65,760
30–35	5	4.16	15.31	4.09	3.64	25,000	91,000
35–40	5	3.68	13.54	3.62	3.22	35,000	112,700
40–60	20	10.89	40.08	10.71	9.53	40,000	381,200
60–70	10	3.74	13.77	3.68	3.28	20,000	65,600
Totals:	45 years	27.17	100.00	26.73	23.79		**716, 260**

N.B. the figures in the above table have been rounded at each step of the calculation so the totals shown are not necessarily the sum of the individual multipliers in the columns

Example 2—Variable future care costs

24. A male aged 20 years at the date of settlement/trial requires personal care support for life. He has a normal life expectation for his age. Significant changes in his care regime are anticipated at age 30 and again at age 50.

The multiplicands for care costs are:

Age 20–30:   £30,000 a year

Age 30–50:   £60,000 a year

Age 50 for rest of life: £80,000 a year

The multipliers for each stage of the care regime are calculated as follows:

(1) The life expectation will be 67.22 years (from the 0 per cent column of Table 1) and the multiplier for that period taking into account mortality risks (from Table 1) will be 32.10.

(2) The multiplier for a term certain of 67.22 years (ignoring mortality risks) from Table 28 lies between 32.75 (for 67 years) and 32.94 (for 68 years) and is calculated thus:

$$(68 - 67.22) \times 32.75 + (67.22 - 67) \times 32.94 = 32.79.$$

(3) The multiplier from Table 28 should be split so that each individual segment of the whole period of life expectation is represented by a figure. So, the first 10 years (20–30) are represented by a multiplier of 8.86; the next 20 years (30–50) are represented by a multiplier of 12.33 (being the difference between the 30-year figure of 21.19 and the 10-year figure of 8.86); then, the final years (50 to death) are represented by the balance of 11.60 (being the difference between the term certain multiplier of 32.79 and the 30-year figure of 21.19).

(4) Each of those smaller segmented multipliers can be shown as a percentage or fraction of the whole: so, for the first 10 years the segmented multiplier of 8.86 is 27.02 per cent of the whole figure of 32.79, and so on for each segment of the life period.

(5) The life multiplier from Table 1 can now be split up in the way in which the Table 28 multiplier was treated above and in identical proportions: thus the first 10-year period is now represented by a multiplier of 8.67 which is calculated by taking 27.02 per cent of 32.10.

(6) The figures are set out in tabular form below and give a total lump sum award of £1,893,100:

Age (years)	Table 28 (67.22 years) Split multipliers	% Split (of Table 28) figure	Table 1 (multiplier allowing for mortality)	Care costs £ a year	Total £
20–30	8.86	27.02%	8.67	30,000	260,100
30–50	12.33	37.60%	12.07	60,000	724,200
50 till death	11.60	35.38%	11.36	80,000	908,800
Totals	32.79 (no mortality discount)	100.00%	32.10 life multiplier		**1,893,100**

N.B. the figures in the above table have been rounded at each step of the calculation.

Spouse's pensions

25. If doubt exists whether the tables are appropriate to a particular case which appears to present significant difficulties of substance, it would be prudent to take actuarial advice. This might be appropriate in relation to the level of spouse's benefits, if these are to be assessed, since these are not readily valued using Tables 1–26. As a rough rule of thumb, if spouse's benefits are to be included when valuing pension loss from normal pension age, the multipliers in Tables 15–26 should be increased by 5 per cent for a female claimant (i.e. benefits to the male spouse) and by 14 per cent for a male claimant if the spouse's pension would be half of the pension that the member was receiving at death. If the spouse's pension would be payable at a rate of two-thirds the member's pension at death the multipliers should be increased by 7 per cent for a female claimant and by 18 per cent for a male claimant.

Section B: Contingencies other than mortality

26. As stated in para.19, the tables for loss of earnings (Tables 3–14) take no account of risks other than mortality. This section shows how the multipliers in these tables may be reduced to take account of these risks.

27. Tables of factors to be applied to the existing multipliers were first introduced in the 2nd edn of the Ogden Tables. These factors were based on work commissioned by the Institute of Actuaries and carried out by Professor S. Haberman and Mrs D. S. F. Bloomfield.[13] Although there was some debate within the actuarial profession about the details of the work, and in particular about the scope for developing it further, the findings were broadly accepted and were adopted by the Government Actuary and the other actuaries who were members of the Working Party when the 2nd edn of the Tables was published and remained unchanged until the 6th edn.

---

[13] "Work time lost to sickness, unemployment and stoppages: measurement and application" (1990) 117 *Journal of the Institute of Actuaries*, 533–595.

28. Some related work was published in 2002 by Lewis, McNabb and Wass.[14] For the publication of the 6th edn of the Ogden Tables, the Ogden Working Party was involved in further research into the impact of contingencies other than mortality carried out by Professor Richard Verrall, Professor Steven Haberman and Mr Zoltan Butt of City University, London and, in a separate exercise, by Dr Victoria Wass of Cardiff University. Their findings were combined to produce the tables of factors given in section B of the 6th edn and repeated here.

29. The Haberman and Bloomfield paper relied on data from the Labour Force Surveys for 1973, 1977, 1981 and 1985 and English Life Tables No. 14 (1980–82). The Labour Force Survey (LFS) was originally designed to produce a periodic cross-sectional snapshot of the working age population and collects information on an extensive range of socio-economic and labour force characteristics. Since the winter of 1992/3, the LFS has been carried out on a quarterly basis, with respondents being included in the survey over five successive quarters. The research of Professor Verrall *et al.* and Dr Wass used data from the Labour Force Surveys conducted from 1998–2003 to estimate the probabilities of movement of males and females between different states of economic activity, dependent on age, sex, employment activity and level of disability. These probabilities permit the calculation of the expected periods in employment until retirement age, dependent on the initial starting state of economic activity, disability and educational attainment. These can then be discounted at the same discount rate that is used for obtaining the relevant multiplier from Tables 3–14, in order to give a multiplier which takes into account only those periods the claimant would be expected, on average, to be in work. These discounted working life expectancy multipliers can be compared to those obtained assuming the person remained in work throughout, to obtain reduction factors which give the expected proportion of time to retirement age which will be spent in employment.

30. The factors described in subsequent paragraphs are for use in calculating loss of earnings up to retirement age. The research work did not investigate the impact of contingencies other than mortality on the value of future pension rights. Some reduction to the multiplier for loss of pension would often be appropriate when a reduction is being applied for loss of earnings. This may be a smaller reduction than in the case of loss of earnings because the ill-health contingency (as opposed to the unemployment contingency) may give rise to significant ill-health retirement pension rights. A bigger reduction may be necessary in cases where there is significant doubt whether pension rights would have continued to accrue (to the extent not already allowed for in the post-retirement multiplier) or in cases where there may be doubt over the ability of the pension fund to pay promised benefits. In the case of a defined contribution pension scheme, loss of pension rights may be allowed for, simply by increasing the future earnings loss (adjusted for contingencies other than mortality) by the percentage of earnings which the employer contributes to the scheme represent.

31. The methodology proposed in paras 33–42 describes one method for dealing with contingencies other than mortality. If this methodology is followed, in many cases it will be appropriate to increase or reduce the discount in the tables to take account of the nature of a particular claimant's disabilities. It should be noted that the methodology does not take into account the pre-accident employment history. The methodology also provides for the possibility of valuing more appropriately the possible mitigation of loss of earnings in cases where the claimant is employed after the accident or is considered capable of being employed. This will in many cases enable a more accurate assessment to be made of the mitigation of loss. However, there may be some cases when the *Smith v Manchester Corporation* or *Blamire* approach remains applicable or otherwise where a precise mathematical approach is inapplicable.

32. The suggestions which follow are intended as a "ready reckoner" which provides an initial adjustment to the multipliers according to the employment status, disability status and educational

---

[14] "Methods of calculating damages for loss of future earnings" (2002) 2 *Journal of Personal Injury Law*, 151–165.

attainment of the claimant when calculating awards for loss of earnings and for any mitigation of this loss in respect of potential future post-injury earnings. Such a ready reckoner cannot take into account all circumstances and it may be appropriate to argue for higher or lower adjustments in particular cases. In particular, it can be difficult to place a value on the possible mitigating income when considering the potential range of disabilities and their effect on post-work capability, even within the interpretation of disability set out in para.35. However, the methodology does offer a framework for consideration of a range of possible figures with the maximum being effectively provided by the post-injury multiplier assuming the claimant was not disabled and the minimum being the case where there is no realistic prospect of post-injury employment.

The deduction for contingencies other than mortality

33. Under this method, multipliers for loss of earnings obtained from Tables 3–14 are multiplied by factors to allow for the risk of periods of non-employment and absence from the workforce because of sickness.

34. The research by Professor Verrall et al. and Dr Wass referred to in paras 28 and 29 demonstrated that the key issues affecting a person's future working life are employment status, disability status and educational attainment.

35. The definitions of employed/not employed, disabled/not disabled and educational attainment used in this analysis and which should be used for determining which factors to apply to the multipliers to allow for contingencies other than mortality are as follows:

Employed   Those who at the time of the accident are employed, self-employed or on a government training scheme.

Not employed   All others (including those temporarily out of work, full-time students and unpaid family workers).

Disabled   A person is classified as being disabled if all three of the following conditions in relation to the ill-health or disability are met:

(i)   the person has an illness or a disability which has lasted or is expected to last for over a year or is a progressive illness,

(ii)   the person satisfies the Equality Act 2010 definition that the impact of the disability substantially limits the person's ability to carry out normal day to day activities, and

(iii)   their condition affects either the kind **or** the amount of paid work they can do.

Not disabled   All others.

Normal day to day activities are those which are carried out by most people on a daily basis, and we are interested in disabilities/health problems which have a substantial adverse effect on respondent's ability to carry out these activities.

There are several ways in which a disability or health problem may affect the respondent's day to day activities:

Mobility—for example, unable to travel short journeys as a passenger in a car, unable to walk other than at a slow pace or with jerky movements, difficulty in negotiating stairs, unable to use one or more forms of public transport, unable to go out of doors unaccompanied.

Manual dexterity—for example, loss of functioning in one or both hands, inability to use a knife and fork at the same time, or difficulty in pressing buttons on a keyboard.

Physical co-ordination—for example, the inability to feed or dress oneself; or to pour liquid from one vessel to another except with unusual slowness or concentration.

Problems with bowel/bladder control—for example, frequent or regular loss of control of the bladder or bowel. Occasional bedwetting is not considered a disability.

Ability to lift, carry or otherwise move everyday objects (for example, books, kettles, light furniture)—for example, inability to pick up a weight with one hand but not the other, or to carry a tray steadily.

Speech—for example, unable to communicate (clearly) orally with others, taking significantly longer to say things. A minor stutter, difficulty in speaking in front of an audience, or inability to speak a foreign language would not be considered impairments.

Hearing—for example, not being able to hear without the use of a hearing aid, the inability to understand speech under normal conditions or over the telephone.

Eyesight—for example, while wearing spectacles or contact lenses—being unable to pass the standard driving eyesight test, total inability to distinguish colours (excluding ordinary red/green colour blindness), or inability to read newsprint.

Memory or ability to concentrate, learn or understand—for example, intermittent loss of consciousness or confused behaviour, inability to remember names of family or friends, unable to write a cheque without assistance, or an inability to follow a recipe.

Perception of risk of physical danger—for example, reckless behaviour putting oneself or others at risk, mobility to cross the road safely. This excludes (significant) fear of heights or under-estimating risk of dangerous hobbies.

Three levels of educational attainment are defined for the purposes of the tables as follows:

D   Degree or equivalent or higher.

GE–A   GCSE grades A–C up to A levels or equivalents.

O   Below GCSE C or CSE 1 or equivalent or no qualifications.

The following table gives a more detailed breakdown of the allocation of various types of educational qualification to each of the three categories above and is based on the allocations used in the research by Professor Verrall, et al. and Dr Wass.

Categories of highest educational attainment

D Degree or equivalent or higher	GE–A GCSE grades A–C up to A levels or equivalent	O Below GCSE grade C or CSE grade 1 or equivalent or no qualifications
Any degree (first or higher) Other higher education qualification below degree level Diploma in higher education	A or AS level or equivalent O level, GCSE grade A–C or equivalent	CSE below grade 1 GCSE below grade C
NVQ level 4 or 5	NVQ level 2 or 3	NVQ level 1 or equivalent
HNC/HND, BTEC higher, etc	BTEC/SCOTVEC first or general diploma OND/ONC, BTEC/SCOTVEC national	BTEC first or general certificate SCOTVEC modules or equivalent
RSA higher diploma	RSA diploma, advanced diploma or certificate	RSA other
Teaching, Nursing, etc	GNVQ intermediate or advanced	GNVQ/GVSQ foundation level
	City and Guilds craft or advanced craft	City and Guilds other
	SCE higher or equivalent Trade apprenticeship Scottish 6th year certificate (CSYS)	YT/ YTP certificate Other qualifications No qualification Don't know

Note: "educational attainment" is used here as a proxy for skill level, so that those in professional occupations such as law, accountancy, nursing, etc. who do not have a degree ought to be treated as if they do have one.

36. The research also considered the extent to which a person's future working life expectancy is affected by individual circumstances such as occupation and industrial sector, geographical region and education. The researchers concluded that the most significant consideration was the highest level of education achieved by the claimant and that, if this was allowed for, the effect of the other factors was relatively small. As a result, the Working Party decided to propose adjustment factors which allow for employment status, disability status and educational attainment only. This is a change from earlier editions of the Ogden Tables where adjustments were made for types of occupation and for geographical region.

37. A separate assessment is made for: (a) the value of earnings the claimant would have received if the injury had not been suffered, and (b) the value of the claimant's earnings (if any) taking account of the injuries sustained. The risk of non-employment is significantly higher post-injury due to the impairment. The loss is arrived at by deducting (b) from (a).

38. In order to calculate the value of the earnings the claimant would have received, if the injury had not been suffered, the claimant's employment status and the disability status need to be determined as at the date of the accident (or the onset of the medical condition) giving rise to the claim, so that the correct table can be applied. For the calculation of future loss of earnings (based on actual pre-accident earnings and also future employment prospects), Tables A and C should be used for claimants who were not disabled at the time of the accident, and Tables B and D should be used for those with a pre-existing disability. In all of these tables the three left hand columns are for those who were employed at the time of the accident and the three right hand columns are for those who were not.

39. In order to calculate the value of the actual earnings that a claimant is likely to receive in the future (i.e. after settlement or trial), the employment status and the disability status need to be determined as at the date of settlement or trial. For claimants with a work-affecting disability at that point in time, Tables B and D should be used. The three left hand columns will apply in respect of claimants actually in employment at date of settlement or trial and the three right hand columns will apply in respect of those who remain non-employed at that point in time.

40. The factors in Tables A–D allow for the interruption of employment for bringing up children and caring for other dependants.

41. In the case of those who at the date of the accident have not yet reached the age at which it is likely they would have started work, the relevant factor will be chosen based on a number of assessments of the claimant's likely employment had the injury not occurred. The relevant factor from the tables would be chosen on the basis of the level of education the claimant would have been expected to have attained, the age at which it is likely the claimant would have started work, together with an assessment as to whether the claimant would have become employed or not. The work multiplier will also have to be discounted for early receipt using the appropriate factor from Table 27 for the number of years between the claimant's age at the date of trial and the age at which it is likely that he/she would have started work.

42. Tables A–D include factors up to age 54 only. For older ages the reduction factors increase towards 1 at retirement age for those who are employed and fall towards 0 for those who are not employed. However, where the claimant is older than 54, it is anticipated that the likely future course of employment status will be particularly dependent on individual circumstances, so that the use of factors based on averages would not be appropriate. Hence reduction factors are not provided for these older ages.

Table A
Loss of earnings to pension age 65 (males—not disabled)

Age at date of trial	Employed			Not employed		
	D	GE–A	O	D	GE–A	O
16–19		0.90	0.85		0.85	0.82
20–24	0.92	0.92	0.87	0.89	0.88	0.83
25–29	0.93	0.92	0.89	0.89	0.88	0.82
30–34	0.92	0.91	0.89	0.87	0.86	0.81
35–39	0.90	0.90	0.89	0.85	0.84	0.80
40–44	0.88	0.88	0.88	0.82	0.81	0.78
45–49	0.86	0.86	0.86	0.77	0.77	0.74
50	0.83	0.83	0.83	0.72	0.72	0.70
51	0.82	0.82	0.82	0.70	0.70	0.68
52	0.81	0.81	0.81	0.67	0.67	0.66
53	0.80	0.80	0.80	0.63	0.63	0.63
54	0.79	0.79	0.79	0.59	0.59	0.59

Table B
Loss of earnings to pension age 65 (males—disabled)

Age at date of trial	Employed			Not employed		
	D	GE–A	O	D	GE–A	O
16–19		0.55	0.32		0.49	0.25
20–24	0.61	0.55	0.38	0.53	0.46	0.24
25–29	0.60	0.54	0.42	0.48	0.41	0.24
30–34	0.59	0.52	0.40	0.43	0.34	0.23
35–39	0.58	0.48	0.39	0.38	0.28	0.20
40–44	0.57	0.48	0.39	0.33	0.23	0.15
45–49	0.55	0.48	0.39	0.26	0.20	0.11
50	0.53	0.49	0.40	0.24	0.18	0.10
51	0.53	0.49	0.41	0.23	0.17	0.09
52	0.54	0.49	0.41	0.22	0.16	0.08
53	0.54	0.49	0.42	0.21	0.15	0.07
54	0.54	0.50	0.43	0.20	0.14	0.06

Table C
Loss of earnings to pension age 60 (females—not disabled)

Age at date of trial	Employed			Not employed		
	D	GE–A	O	D	GE–A	O
16–19		0.81	0.64		0.77	0.59
20–24	0.89	0.82	0.68	0.84	0.76	0.60
25–29	0.89	0.84	0.72	0.83	0.75	0.61
30–34	0.89	0.85	0.75	0.81	0.75	0.63
35–39	0.89	0.86	0.78	0.80	0.74	0.63
40–44	0.89	0.86	0.80	0.78	0.72	0.60
45–49	0.87	0.85	0.81	0.72	0.64	0.52
50	0.86	0.84	0.81	0.64	0.55	0.43
51	0.85	0.84	0.81	0.60	0.51	0.40
52	0.84	0.84	0.81	0.56	0.46	0.36
53	0.83	0.83	0.81	0.50	0.41	0.32
54	0.83	0.83	0.82	0.44	0.35	0.27

Table D
Loss of earnings to pension age 60 (females—disabled)

Age at date of trial	Employed D	Employed GE–A	Employed O	Not employed D	Not employed GE–A	Not employed O
16–19		0.43	0.25		0.35	0.19
20–24	0.64	0.44	0.25	0.58	0.33	0.17
25–29	0.63	0.45	0.25	0.50	0.32	0.16
30–34	0.62	0.46	0.30	0.44	0.31	0.15
35–39	0.61	0.48	0.34	0.42	0.28	0.14
40–44	0.60	0.51	0.38	0.38	0.23	0.13
45–49	0.60	0.54	0.42	0.28	0.18	0.11
50	0.60	0.56	0.47	0.23	0.15	0.10
51	0.61	0.58	0.49	0.21	0.14	0.09
52	0.61	0.60	0.51	0.20	0.13	0.08
53	0.62	0.62	0.54	0.18	0.11	0.07
54	0.63	0.66	0.57	0.16	0.09	0.06

The factors in Tables A–D will need to be reviewed if the discount rate changes.

Different pension ages

43. The factors in the preceding tables assume retirement at age 65 for males and age 60 for females. It is not possible to calculate expected working life times assuming alternative retirement ages from the LFS data, since the employment data in the LFS are collected only for the working population, assumed to be aged between 16 and 64 for males and between 16 and 59 for females. Where the retirement age is different from age 65 for males or age 60 for females, it is suggested that this should be ignored and the reduction factor and the adjustments thereto be taken from the above tables for the age of the claimant as at the date of trial with no adjustment, i.e. assume that the retirement age is age 65 for males and age 60 for females. However, if the retirement age is close to the age at the date of trial, then it may be more appropriate to take into account the circumstances of the individual case.

44. It should be noted that the reduction factors in Tables A, B, C and D are based on data for the period 1998–2003. Whilst the reduction factors and adjustments allow for the age-specific probabilities of moving into, or out of, employment over future working life time, based on data for the period 1998–2003, the methodology assumes that these probabilities remain constant over time; there is no allowance for changes in these age-specific probabilities beyond this period. It is also assumed that there will be no change in disability status or educational achievement after the date of the accident. Future changes in the probabilities of moving into, and out of, employment are especially difficult to predict with any certainty. It is the intention that the factors should be reassessed from time to time as new data becomes available.

Section C: Summary of personal injury applications

45. To use the tables the guidance below should be followed:

(1) Choose the table relating to the appropriate sex of the claimant and period of loss or expense (e.g. loss for life, or loss of earnings to a set retirement age). Where loss of earnings is concerned, and none of the tables is relevant because the claimant's expected age of retirement differs from that assumed in the tables, the procedure in paras 13–16 of the explanatory notes should be followed.

(2) Choose the appropriate discount column (currently 2.5 per cent).

(3)   In that column find the appropriate figure for the claimant's age at trial ("the basic multiplier").

Loss of earnings

(4)   When calculating **loss of earnings**, the tables should be used when a multiplier/multiplicand approach is appropriate. If it is, the basic multiplier should be adjusted to take account of contingencies other than mortality. These contingencies include the claimant's employment and disability status and educational qualifications. The basic multiplier should be multiplied by the appropriate figure taken from Tables A–D. It may be necessary at this stage to modify the resulting figure further to allow for circumstances specific to the claimant.

This process gives "the adjusted table multiplier".

(5)   Multiply the net annual loss (the multiplicand) by the adjusted table multiplier to arrive at a figure which represents the capitalised value of the future loss of earnings.

(6)   If the claimant has a residual earning capacity, allowance should be made for any post-accident vulnerability on the labour market: the following paragraphs show one way of doing this, although there may still be cases where a conventional ***Smith v City of Manchester*** award is appropriate.

Where it is appropriate to do so, repeat steps 1–5 above, replacing the pre-accident employment and disability status with the post-accident employment and disability status in step 4 and replacing the net annual loss by the assumed new level of net earnings at step 5. It will only be necessary to reconsider the claimant's educational attainments if these have changed between the accident and the date of trial or settlement.

The result will represent the capitalised value of the claimant's likely post-accident earnings. It is important to note that, when carrying out this exercise, the *degree* of residual disability may have a different effect on residual earnings depending on its relevance to the claimant's likely field of work. For example, the loss of a leg may have less effect on a sedentary worker's earnings than on a manual worker's.

(7)   Deduct the sum yielded by step 6 from that yielded by step 5 to obtain the net amount of loss of earnings allowing for residual earning capacity. Where the above methodology is used there will usually be no need for a separate ***Smith v City of Manchester*** award.

Lifetime losses

(8)   Where a **loss** will continue **for life**, follow steps 1–3, above, to find the appropriate multiplier in the table.

Where the normal life expectancy given by the table is inapplicable the approach set out in para.20, using the lifetime tables rather than Table 28, is the correct approach.

(9)   This figure may need adjustment to allow for the particular circumstances of the claimant.

(10) Multiply the annual loss or expense by the multiplier as adjusted.

Variable annual losses

(11) In cases where there will be different losses at different periods it may be necessary to split the multiplier. The approach set out at paras 22–24 should be followed.

Fixed period and deferred losses

(12) Where a loss will continue over a fixed period, the appropriate multiplier can be found in Table 28.

(13) Where a loss will not commence until some future date, multiply the appropriate multiplier by a discount figure taken from Table 27 (the use of which is explained in para.18). This paragraph does not apply to loss of pensions, which have their own tables.

Examples

46. The following are examples of the use of the tables in illustrative personal injury cases with simplified assumptions.

Example 3

47. The claimant is female, aged 35 at the date of the trial. She has three A levels, but not a degree, and was in employment at the date of the accident at a salary of £25,000 a year net of tax. She was not disabled before the accident. As a result of her injuries, she is now disabled and has lost her job but has found part-time employment at a salary of £5,000 a year net of tax. Her loss of earnings to retirement age of 60 is assessed as follows:

(1) Look up Table 8 for loss of earnings to pension age 60 for females.

(2) The appropriate rate of return is determined to be 2.5 per cent (the rate currently set under s.1 of the Damages Act 1996).

(3) Table 8 shows that, on the basis of a 2.5 per cent rate of return, the multiplier for a female aged 35 is 18.43.

(4) Now take account of risks other than mortality. Allowing for the claimant being employed, not disabled and having achieved A levels at the date of trial, Table C would require 18.43 to be multiplied by 0.86, resulting in a revised multiplier of 15.85.

(5) The damages for loss of earnings are assessed as £396,250 (15.85 × £25,000).

(6) Allow for mitigation of loss of earnings in respect of post-injury earnings. As before, Table 8 shows that, on the basis of a 2.5 per cent rate of return, the multiplier for a female aged 35 is 18.43.

(7) Now take account of risks other than mortality. Allowing for the claimant being employed, disabled and having achieved A levels at the date of trial, Table D would require 18.43 to be multiplied by 0.48, resulting in a revised multiplier of 8.85.

(8) The amount of mitigation for post-injury earnings is assessed as £44,150 (8.85 × £5,000).

(9) Hence award for loss of earnings after allowing for mitigation is £396,250 – £44,250 = £352,00.

Example 4

48. The claimant is male, aged 48 at the date of the trial. He has no educational qualifications. His retirement age was 65, he was employed at the time of the accident and his pre-retirement multiplicand has been determined as £20,000 a year net of tax. He was not disabled before the accident.

As a result of his injuries, he is now disabled and has lost his job. The multiplicand for costs of care is deemed to be £50,000 a year. He is unemployed at the date of trial but has been assessed as capable of finding work with possible future earnings of £5,000 a year net of tax. His loss of earnings to retirement age of 65 is assessed as follows:

(1)   Look up Table 9 for loss of earnings to pension age 65 for males.

(2)   The appropriate rate of return is determined to be 2.5 per cent (the rate currently set under s.1 of the Damages Act 1996).

(3)   Table 9 shows that, on the basis of a 2.5 per cent rate of return, the multiplier for a male aged 48 is 13.42.

(4)   Now take account of risks other than mortality. Allowing for the claimant being employed, not disabled and having no educational qualifications at the date of trial, Table A would require 13.42 to be multiplied by 0.86, resulting in a revised multiplier of 11.54.

(5)   The damages for loss of earnings are assessed as £230,800 (11.54 × £20,000).

(6)   Allow for mitigation of loss of earnings in respect of post-injury earnings. As before, Table 9 shows that, on the basis of a 2.5 per cent rate of return, the multiplier for a male aged 48 is 13.42.

(7)   Now take account of risks other than mortality. Allowing for the claimant being unemployed and disabled with no educational qualifications at the date of trial, Table B would require 13.42 to be multiplied by 0.11, resulting in a revised multiplier of 1.48.

(8)   The amount of mitigation for post-injury earnings is assessed as £7,400 (1.48 × £5,000).

(9)   Hence award for loss of earnings after allowing for mitigation is £230,800 − £7,400 = £223,400.

49. The damages for cost of care are assessed as follows:

(1)   Look up Table 1 for the multiplier at age 48.

(2)   The appropriate rate of return is 2.5 per cent.

(3)   Table 1 shows that, on the basis of a 2.5 per cent rate of return, the multiplier at age 48 is 23.51.

(4)   No adjustment is made for risks other than mortality.

(5)   The damages for cost of care are assessed at £1,175,500 (23.51 × £50,000).

Example 5

50. The claimant is female, aged 14 at the date of the trial. She is expected to achieve a degree and to be in employment thereafter on a salary, in current terms, of £30,000 a year net of tax. She was not disabled before the accident. As a result of her injuries, she is now disabled—she is still expected to achieve a degree and to be in employment, but with an average salary in current terms of £20,000 net of tax. She will be aged 21 when she completes her degree. Her loss of earnings to retirement age of 60 is assessed as follows:

(1)　Look up Table 8 for loss of earnings to pension age 60 for females.

(2)　The appropriate rate of return is determined to be 2.5 per cent (the rate currently set under s.1 of the Damages Act 1996).

(3)　Table 8 shows that, on the basis of a 2.5 per cent rate of return, the multiplier for a female graduate aged 21 is 24.83. This needs to be discounted back to age 14. The factor at 2.5 per cent for a period for deferment for seven years is 0.8413 from Table 27, giving a total multiplier of 24.83 × 0.8413 = 20.89.

(4)　Now take account of risks other than mortality. Allowing for the claimant at age 21 assessed as achieving a degree, being employed and not disabled, Table C would require 20.89 to be multiplied by 0.89, resulting in a revised multiplier of 18.59.

(5)　The damages for loss of earnings are assessed as £557,700 (18.59 × £30,000).

(6)　Allow for mitigation of loss of earnings in respect of post-injury earnings. As before, Table 8 shows that, on the basis of a 2.5 per cent rate of return, the multiplier for a female graduate aged 21 is 24.83. As before, after discounting for seven years to age 14 the multiplier is reduced to 24.83 × 0.8413 = 20.89.

(7)　Now take account of risks other than mortality. Allowing for the claimant at age 21 assessed as achieving a degree, being employed and disabled, Table D would require 20.89 to be multiplied by 0.64, resulting in a revised multiplier of 13.37.

(8)　The amount of mitigation for post-injury earnings is assessed as £267,400 (13.37 × £20,000).

(9)　Hence award for loss of earnings after allowing for mitigation is £557,700 − £267,400 = £290,300.

Example 6

51. The claimant is male, aged 40 at the date of the trial. He has achieved O levels. He was unemployed at the time of the accident. His potential pre-retirement multiplicand has been determined as £15,000 a year net of tax. He was disabled before the accident. As a result of his injuries, he has been assessed as having no future prospect of employment. His loss of earnings to retirement age of 65 is assessed as follows:

(1)　Look up Table 9 for loss of earnings to pension age 65 for males.

(2)　The appropriate rate of return is determined to be 2.5 per cent (the rate currently set under s.1 of the Damages Act 1996).

(3)　Table 9 shows that, on the basis of a 2.5 per cent rate of return, the multiplier for a male aged 40 is 18.09.

(4)　Now take account of risks other than mortality. Allowing for the claimant being unemployed, disabled and having achieved O levels at the date of trial, Table A would require 18.09 to be multiplied by 0.23, resulting in a revised multiplier of 4.16.

(5)　The damages for loss of earnings are assessed as £62,400 (4.16 × £15,000).

(6)   As the claimant has been assessed as having no future prospect of employment following the accident, there is no mitigation of loss of earnings in respect of post-injury earnings.

(7)   Hence award for loss of earnings after allowing for mitigation is £62,400.

Section D: Application of tables to fatal accident cases

52. The current approach of the courts, except in Scotland, is to assess the multiplier as at the date of death (*Cookson v Knowles*[15]).

53. That approach was criticised by the Law Commission in their Report 263 (*Claims for Wrongful Death*). The Law Commission recommended that multipliers should be assessed as at the date of trial and that the multipliers derived from the Ogden Tables should only take effect from the date of trial. The Law Commission stressed that the current approach incorporates an actuarial flaw in that it incorporates a discount for early receipt in the period prior to trial or assessment.

54. The Working Party, then under the Chairmanship of the late Sir Michael Ogden QC, considered that the Law Commission's criticism was valid. In the Fourth Edition of the Tables published in August 2000, the Working Party set out guidance in Section D of the Explanatory Notes on how damages should be calculated in such cases. We refer to that guidance below as the actuarially recommended approach. We note that the actuarially recommended approach has been adopted in the Damages (Scotland) Act 2011. For further details see paras 20–21 in the Introduction.

55. However, the courts have considered themselves bound by *Cookson v Knowles* and hence have not followed the actuarially recommended approach (*White v Esab*,[16] *H v S*[17] and *Fletcher v A Train & Sons Ltd*[18]).

The basic law in England and Wales

56. Under the Fatal Accidents Act the loss is that of the dependants, i.e. those who relied upon the deceased for support. They may claim that part of the deceased's income (whether earnings, pension, unearned income or state benefits) that the deceased would have spent on them. They may also claim the loss of the services such as DIY, domestic/household or childcare which the deceased would have undertaken and from which they would have benefited. The position of each dependant must be considered separately.

57. Each head of dependency must be considered separately. For each head of claim for each dependant the court calculates a multiplicand. This is calculated on the basis of what is known at the date of trial. For pre-trial losses, the actual loss to date of trial is calculated. Interest is added. For post-trial losses the multiplicand is calculated as at the date of trial.

58. A multiplier for the period of dependency is applied to the multiplicand to arrive at an overall lump sum for each head of dependency.

59. The remainder of section D deals with how to approach the calculations in fatal accident claims. Three approaches are put forward. Paragraphs 60–63 set out the current approach. The actuarially

[15] [1979] A.C. 556.
[16] [2002] P.I.Q.R. Q6.
[17] [2002] EWCA Civ. 792, [2003] Q.B. 965.
[18] [2008] EWCA Civ. 413, [2008] 4 All E.R. 699.

recommended approach is then set out at paras 64–81. Example 7 illustrates the application of both these approaches whilst Examples 8 and 9 show the actuarially recommended approach applied to more complex situations—these examples make up paras 82–87. The final paragraphs of section D, 88–90, offer an alternative approach using multipliers selected from the date of death.

The current approach

60. Under the approach currently followed by the courts, the multiplier is calculated as at the date of death. However, when making that calculation the court is entitled to take into account matters that have arisen between death and trial. For example, **Williamson v Thorneycroft**[19] in which the deceased's widow died after her husband but before trial, her dependency terminated at her death. See also, **Corbett v Barking, Havering & Brentwood HA**.[20]

61. There are two periods to be determined:

(i) the expected period from date of death in which the deceased would have been capable of providing the dependency; and

(ii) the expected period from the date of the death in which the dependant would have been able to receive the dependency.

The shorter of those two periods provides the basis for the multiplier.

62. In respect of each of those periods consideration must be given as to what discount should be made for contingencies other than mortality. The most obvious contingencies other than mortality fall into the following three categories:

(i) Factors relating to the deceased. For example, the deceased's health may have been such as to seriously affect his ability to provide services or work until retirement age. In relation to earnings the starting point for the adjustment factor should be the figures contained in Tables A–D.

(ii) Factors relating to the dependant. For example, at trial it may be proved that a dependant has a significantly reduced life expectancy.

(iii) Factors relating to the relationship of the deceased and the dependant. For example, an unmarried couple who were on the point of separation before the deceased died. See also s.3 (4) of the Act and **Drew v Abassi**.[21]

63. The assessment of the multiplier involves the following steps:

(1) Determine the expected period from the date of death for which the deceased would have been capable of providing the dependency.

(2) Discount that period for early receipt using the appropriate table as at the date of death and a discount rate of 2.5 per cent.

(3) Apply any adjustment to the above figure to reflect contingencies other than mortality.

[19] [1940] 2 K.B. 658.
[20] [1991] 2 Q.B. 408.
[21] Court of Appeal, May 24, 1995.

(4) Determine the expected period from date of death for which the dependant would have been able to receive the dependency.

(5) Discount that period for early receipt using the appropriate table as at the date of death at a discount rate of 2.5 per cent.

(6) Apply any adjustment to the figure in (5) to reflect contingencies other than mortality.

(7) Take the lower of the figures in (3) and (6) above. That is the overall multiplier from date of death.

(8) Subtract the period elapsed from date of death to date of trial. Losses in this period will be treated as in effect special damages and will attract an award of interest.

(9) The balance of the multiplier will be the multiplier for the post-trial multiplicand.

The actuarially recommended approach

64. Whereas in personal injury cases the problem to be solved is that of setting a value on an income stream during the potential life of one person (the claimant), the situation is generally more complicated in fatal accident cases. Here the compensation is intended to reflect the value of an income stream during the lifetime of one or more dependants of the deceased (or the expected period for which the dependants would have expected to receive the dependency, if shorter) but limited according to the expectation of how long the deceased would have been able to provide the financial support, had he or she not been involved in the fatal accident.

65. In principle, therefore, the compensation for post-trial dependency should be based on the present value at the date of the trial of the dependency during the expected future joint lifetime of the deceased and the dependant or claimant (had the deceased survived naturally to the date of the trial), subject to any limitations on the period of dependency and any expected future changes in the level of dependency, for example, on attaining retirement age. In addition there should be compensation for the period between the date of accident and the date of trial.

66. A set of actuarial tables to make such calculations accurately would require tables similar to Tables 1–26 but for each combination of ages as at the date of the trial of the deceased and the dependant to whom compensation is to be paid. The Working Party concluded that this would not meet the criterion of simplicity of application which was a central objective of these tables and recommends that, in complex cases, or cases where the accuracy of the multiplier is thought by the parties to be of critical importance and material to the resulting amount of compensation (for example, in cases potentially involving very large claims where the level of the multiplicand is unambiguously established), the advice of a professionally qualified actuary should be sought. However, for the majority of cases, a certain amount of approximation will be appropriate, bearing in mind the need for a simple and streamlined process, and taking into consideration the other uncertainties in the determination of an appropriate level of compensation. The following paragraphs describe a methodology using Tables 1–26 which can be expected to yield satisfactory answers.

(i) Damages for the period from the fatal accident to the date of trial

67. The period of pre-trial dependency will normally be equal to the period between the date of the fatal accident and the date of the trial, substituting where appropriate the lower figure of the expected period for which the deceased would have provided the dependency, had he or she not been killed in

the accident, or if the period of dependency would have been limited in some way, for example, if the dependant is a child.

68. A deduction may be made for the risk that the deceased might have died anyway, in the period between the date of the fatal accident and the date at which the trial takes place. In many cases this deduction will be small and could usually be regarded as de minimis. The need for a deduction becomes more necessary the longer the period from the date of accident to the date of trial and the older the deceased at the date of death. As an illustration of the order of magnitude of the deduction, Table E shows some examples of factors by which the multiplier should be multiplied for different ages of the deceased and for different periods from the date of accident to the date of the trial.

Table E
Factor by which pre-trial damages should be multiplied to allow for the likelihood that the deceased would not in any case have survived to provide the dependency for the full period to the date of trial

Age of deceased at date of accident	Period from date of accident to date of trial or date of cessation of dependency, if earlier (years)					
	Male deceased			Female deceased		
	3	6	9	3	6	9
10	1.00	1.00	1.00	1.00	1.00	1.00
20	1.00	1.00	1.00	1.00	1.00	1.00
30	1.00	1.00	0.99	1.00	1.00	1.00
40	1.00	0.99	0.99	1.00	1.00	0.99
50	0.99	0.99	0.98	1.00	0.99	0.99
60	0.99	0.97	0.94	0.99	0.98	0.97
65	0.98	0.95	0.91	0.99	0.97	0.95
70	0.97	0.92	0.86	0.98	0.95	0.91
75	0.94	0.87	0.78	0.96	0.91	0.84
80	0.90	0.79	0.67	0.93	0.84	0.75

N.B. The factor for a period of zero years is clearly 1.00. Factors for other ages and periods not shown in the table may be obtained approximately by interpolation.

69. The resultant multiplier, after application of any discount for the possibility of early death of the deceased before the date of trial, even had the accident not taken place, is to be applied to the multiplicand, which is determined in the usual way. Interest will then be added up to the date of trial on the basis of special damages.

(ii) Damages from the date of trial to retirement age

70. The assessment of the multiplier involves the following steps:

(1)   Determine the expected period from the date of the trial for which the deceased would have been able to provide the dependency (see para.71).

(2)   Determine the expected period for which the dependant would have been able to receive the dependency (see paras 71 and 72).

(3)   Take the lesser of the two periods.

(4)   Treat the resulting period as a term certain for which the multiplier is to be determined and look up the figure in Table 28 for this period at the appropriate rate of interest.

(5)   Apply any adjustment for contingencies other than mortality in accordance with section B.

(6)   If necessary, make an allowance for the risk that the deceased might have died anyway before the date of the trial (see para.73).

71. The expected periods at (1) and (2) of para.70 may be obtained from the 0% column of the appropriate table at the back of this booklet. For (1), Tables 3–14 will be relevant, according to the sex of the deceased and the expected age of retirement. The age at which the table should be entered is the age which the deceased would have been at the date of the trial. For (2), Tables 1 and 2 can be used, according to the sex of the dependant and looking up the table at the age of the dependant at the date of the trial.

72. If the period for which the dependency would have continued is a short fixed period, as in the case of a child, the figure at (2) would be the outstanding period at the date of the trial.

73. A deduction may be made for the risk that the deceased might have died anyway before the date of trial. The need for such a deduction becomes more necessary the longer the period from the date of accident to the date of trial and the older the deceased at the date of death. As an illustration of the order of magnitude of the deduction, Table F shows some examples of the factor by which the multiplier, determined as above, should be multiplied for different ages of the deceased and for different periods from the date of accident to the date of the trial.

Table F
Factor by which post-trial damages should be multiplied to allow for the likelihood that the deceased would not in any case have survived to the date of trial in order to provide any post-trial dependency

Age of deceased at date of accident	Period from date of accident to date of trial (years)					
	Male deceased			Female deceased		
	3	6	9	3	6	9
10	1.00	1.00	1.00	1.00	1.00	1.00
20	1.00	1.00	0.99	1.00	1.00	1.00
30	1.00	0.99	0.99	1.00	1.00	0.99
40	0.99	0.99	0.98	1.00	0.99	0.99
50	0.99	0.97	0.95	0.99	0.98	0.97
60	0.97	0.93	0.88	0.98	0.96	0.92
65	0.96	0.90	0.82	0.97	0.93	0.88
70	0.93	0.84	0.71	0.96	0.89	0.80
75	0.88	0.73	0.55	0.92	0.81	0.66
80	0.83	0.59	0.37	0.86	0.68	0.48

N.B. The factor for a period of zero years is clearly 1.00. Factors for other ages and periods not shown in the table may be obtained approximately by interpolation.

74. The resulting multiplier, after application of any discount for the possibility of early death of the deceased before the date of trial, even had the accident not taken place, is to be applied to the appropriate multiplicand, determined in relation to dependency as assessed for the period up to retirement age.

75. If there are several dependants, to whom damages are to be paid in respect of their own particular lifetime (or for a fixed period of dependency), separate multipliers should be determined for each and multiplied by the appropriate multiplicand using the procedure in paras 70–74. The total amount of damages is then obtained by adding the separate components. If a single multiplicand is determined, but the damages are to be shared among two or more dependants so long as they are each alive, or during a period of common dependency, then the multiplier will be calculated using the procedure in paras 70–74. However, at step (2) of para.70 the expected period will be the longest of the expected periods for which the dependency might last.

(iii) Damages for the period of dependency after retirement age

76. The method described in paras 70–75 for pre-retirement age dependency cannot satisfactorily be applied directly to post-retirement age dependency with a sufficient degree of accuracy. We therefore propose a method which involves determining the multiplier by looking at dependency for the rest of life from the date of trial and then subtracting the multiplier for dependency up to retirement age.

77. The assessment of the multiplier for whole of life dependency involves the following steps:

(1)   Determine the expectation of life which the deceased would have had as at the date of trial, or such lesser period for which the deceased would have been able to provide the dependency (see para.78).

(2)   Determine the expected period for which the dependant would have been able to receive the dependency (see para.78).

(3)   Take the lesser of the two periods.

(4)   Treat the resulting period as a term certain for which the multiplier is to be determined and look up the figure in Table 28 for this period at the appropriate rate of interest.

78. The expected periods at (1) and (2) of para.77 may be obtained from the 0% column of the appropriate table at the back of this booklet. For (1), Tables 1 or 2 will be relevant, according to the sex of the deceased. The age at which the table should be entered is the age which the deceased would have attained at the date of the trial. For (2), Tables 1 and 2 can be used, according to the sex of the dependant and looking up the table at the age of the dependant at the date of the trial.

79. Deduct the corresponding multiplier for post-trial pre-retirement dependency, as determined in paras 70–75, but without any adjustment for contingencies other than mortality, or that the deceased may have died anyway before the date of trial. The result is the multiplier for post-retirement dependency, which must then be applied to the appropriate multiplicand, assessed in relation to dependency after retirement age. The adjustment for contingencies other than mortality in respect of the damages for the period of dependency after retirement age will often be less than that required for pre-retirement age damages (see para.30).

80. A deduction may finally be made for the risk that the deceased might have died anyway before the date of trial. The need for such a deduction becomes more necessary the longer the period from the date of accident to the date of trial and the older the deceased at the date of death. As an illustration of the order of magnitude of the deduction, Table F shows some examples of the factor by which the multiplier, determined as above, should be multiplied for different ages of the deceased and for different periods from the date of accident to the date of the trial. The factors for this purpose are exactly the same deductions as used in the calculation at paras 70–75.

81. The layout of paras 70–80 is based on the assumption that the dependency provided by the deceased would have changed at retirement age. This may not be appropriate in some cases, particularly in the important case of the deceased wife and mother whose contribution has been solely in the home or in the case of an adult child caring for an elderly parent or parents. In cases like this, where the deceased might have provided the dependency throughout their lifetime, paras 76–80 should be ignored and paras 70–75 used, with the difference that the expected period required at step (1) of para.70 should be a whole of life expectancy, taken from Tables 1 and 2. This is also the approach to use when the deceased was already a pensioner.

Examples

82. Paragraphs 83 and 84 give calculations of damages awards for Example 7, calculated using first the current approach and then the actuarially recommended approach.

Example 7

83. The dependant is female, aged 38 at the date of the trial, which is taking place three years after the date of the fatal accident which killed her husband, at that time aged 37, on whom she was financially dependent. The deceased had A levels, was in employment and in good health with no disability at the time of the fatal accident. The dependant was, at the date of death, and is at the date of trial, in good health. Their relationship was stable. The court has determined a multiplicand of £30,000 up to the deceased's normal retirement age of 65 with no financial dependency post-age 65, nor any services dependency. The damages are to be calculated as follows:

The current approach

(1) The deceased would have been capable of providing the financial dependency to the dependant for the period of 28 years from the date of his death aged 37 to his 65th birthday.

(2) The appropriate Table is 9. Using the 2.5 per cent column the multiplier = 19.64.

(3) Adjustment factor for contingencies other than mortality (in accordance with section B) for an employed male aged 37 with A levels and who is not disabled = 0.9 to give a multiplier of 19.64 × 0.9 = 17.68.

(4) The expected period for which the dependant would have been able to receive the dependency was between the ages of 35 and 63.

(5) The appropriate Tables are 8 and 10, and using the 2.5 per cent column the multiplier = 19.91.

(6) The parties were married so section 3(4) does not apply. The relationship was stable. The dependant was and is in good health. The court is unlikely to make much of an adjustment to the figure in (5) above to reflect contingencies other than mortality.

(7) The lower of the two figures is that in (3) above, namely 17.68.

(8) The period that has elapsed between date of death and date of trial is three years. The pre-trial loss is therefore £30,000 × 3 = £90,000.

(9) Interest at half rate from date of death to date of trial: three years at 3 per cent a year = 9 per cent.
£90,000 × 9% = £8,100.

(10) The post-trial multiplier is 14.68 (17.68 − 3).

(11) The post trial loss is therefore 14.68 × £30,000 = £440,400.

(12) Total financial dependency is therefore £90,000 + £8,100 + £440,400 = £538,500.

The actuarially recommended approach

84. Applying this approach to Example 7 set out above:

Pre-trial damages:

(1) Period between fatal accident and trial: three years.

(2)   Factor for possible early death (Table E for male aged 37 and three years) = 1.00.

(3)   Pre-trial damages = 3 × 1.00 × £30,000 = £90,000 (plus interest as special damages).

(4)   Interest at half rate from date of death to date of trial: three years at 3 per cent a year = 9 per cent.
£90,000 × 9% = £8,100.

Post-trial damages:

(1)   Expected period for which the deceased would have provided the dependency (Table 9 at 0 per cent for male aged 40, the age as at the date of trial): 24.13.

(2)   Expected period for which the dependant would have been able to receive the dependency (Table 2 at 0 per cent for female aged 38): 51.38.

(3)   Lesser of two periods at (1) and (2) = 24.13.

(4)   Multiplier for term certain of 24.13 years at 2.5 per cent rate of return = 18.18.

(5)   Adjustment factor for contingencies other than mortality (in accordance with section B) for an employed male aged 40 with A levels and who was not disabled = 0.88 to give a multiplier of 18.18 × 0.88 = 16.00.

(6)   Adjustment factor for the risk that the deceased might have died anyway before the date of trial (Table F for male aged 37 and three years): 0.99 to give a multiplier of 16.00 × 0.99 = 15.84.

(7)   Post-trial damages = 15.84 × £30,000 = £475,200.

(8)   Total financial dependency is therefore £90,000 + £8,100 + £475,200 = £573,300.

85. Examples 8 and 9 in the following paragraphs set out two further examples to show the application of the actuarially recommended approach to more complex examples.

Example 8

86. The dependant is female, aged 50 at the date of the trial, which is taking place four years after the date of the fatal accident which killed the man, at that time aged 47, on whom she was financially dependent. The deceased was in employment at the time of the fatal accident, was not disabled and had achieved A levels. The court has determined a multiplicand, up to the deceased's normal retirement age of 60, of £50,000 and has decided that post-retirement damages should be payable based on a multiplicand of £30,000. The damages are to be calculated as follows:

Pre-trial damages:

(1)   Period between fatal accident and trial: four years.

(2)   Factor for possible early death (Table E for male aged 47 and four years): 0.99.

(3)   Pre-trial damages = 4 × 0.99 × £50,000 = £198,000 (plus interest as special damages).

Post-trial pre-retirement damages:

(1)   Expected period for which the deceased would have provided the dependency (Table 7 at 0% for male aged 51, the age as at the date of trial): 8.81.

(2) Expected period for which the dependant would have been able to receive the dependency (Table 2 at 0 per cent for female aged 50): 38.73.

(3) Lesser of two periods at (1) and (2) = 8.81.

(4) Multiplier for term certain of 8.81 years at 2.5 per cent rate of return (interpolating between the values for 8 and 9 in Table 28) = (9 − 8.81) × 7.26 + (8.81 − 8) × 8.07 = 7.92.

(5) Adjustment factor for contingencies other than mortality (in accordance with section B) for an employed male aged 51 with A levels and who was not disabled = 0.82 to give a multiplier of 7.92 × 0.82 = 6.49.

(6) Adjustment factor for the risk that the deceased might have died anyway before the date of trial (Table F for male aged 47 and four years): 0.99 to give a multiplier of 6.49 × 0.99 = 6.43.

(7) Post-trial pre-retirement damages = 6.43 × £50,000 = £321,500.

Post-retirement damages:

(1) Expectation of life of deceased at date of trial (Table 1 at 0 per cent for male aged 51): 34.45.

(2) Expected period for which the dependant would have been able to receive the dependency (Table 2 at 0 per cent for female aged 50): 38.73.

(3) Lesser of two periods at (1) and (2) = 34.45.

(4) Multiplier for term certain of 34.45 years at 2.5 per cent rate of return (interpolating between the values for 34 and 35 in Table 28) = (35 − 34.45) × 23.01 + (34.45 − 34) × 23.43 = 23.20.

(5) Deduct multiplier for post-trial pre-retirement damages before application of adjustment factors for contingencies other than mortality and for the risk that the deceased might have died anyway before the date of trial: 23.20 − 7.92 = 15.28.

(6) Adjustment factor for the risk that the deceased might have died anyway before the date of trial (Table F for male aged 47 and four years): 0.99 to give a multiplier of 15.28 × 0.99 = 15.13.

(7) Post-retirement damages = 15.13 × £30,000 = £453,900.

Example 9

87. There are two dependants, respectively a child aged 10 and a male aged 41 at the date of the trial, which is taking place three years after the date of the fatal accident which killed the woman, at that time aged 35, on whom both were financially dependent. She had a degree and worked in London for a computer company. The court has determined a multiplicand, up to the deceased's normal retirement age of 62, of £50,000 for the male dependant and £10,000 for the child, up to the age of 21, and has decided that post-retirement damages should be payable based on a multiplicand of £20,000. The damages are to be calculated as follows:

Pre-trial damages:

(1) Period between fatal accident and trial: three years.

(2) Factor for possible early death (Table E for female aged 35 and three years): 1.00.

(3)   Pre-trial damages = 3 × 1.00 × (£50,000 + £10,000) = £180,000 (plus interest as special damages).

Post-trial pre-retirement damages:

(1)   Expected period for which the deceased would have provided the dependency should be based on female aged 38 at the date of trial with retirement age of 62. First calculate as though deceased were aged 36 and had retirement age of 60 (Table 8 at 0% for female aged 36): 23.66.

Then calculate as though deceased were aged 41 and had retirement age of 65 (Table 10 at 0 per cent for female aged 41): 23.47.

Interpolate for age 38 with retirement age of 62 = (3 × 23.66 + 2 × 23.47)/5 = 23.58.

(2)   Expected period for which the male dependant would have been able to receive the dependency (Table 1 at 0 per cent for male aged 41): 44.71.

Expected period for which child would have been able to receive the dependency = 11.00.

(3)   Lesser of two periods at (1) and (2) = 11.00 (in case of child)

= 23.58 (in case of man).

(4)   Multiplier for term certain of 11 years at 2.5 per cent (Table 28): 9.63.

Multiplier for term certain of 23.58 years at 2.5 per cent rate of return (interpolating between the values for 23 and 24 in Table 28)

= (24 − 23.58) × 17.55 + (23.58 − 23) × 18.11= 17.87.

(5)   Adjustment factor for contingencies other than mortality (in accordance with section B) for an employed female aged 38 with a degree and who was not disabled = 0.89 (does not apply to child) to give a multiplier of 17.87 × 0.89 = 15.90.

(6)   Adjustment factor for the risk that the deceased might have died anyway before the date of trial (Table F for female aged 35 and three years): 1.00, so multipliers are 9.63 and 15.90 respectively.

(7)   Pre-retirement damages = 9.63 × £10,000 + 15.90 × £50,000

= £96,300 + £795,000 = £891,300.

Post-retirement damages:

(1)   Expectation of life of deceased at date of trial (Table 2 at 0 per cent for female aged 38): 51.38.

(2)   Expected period for which the dependant would have been able to receive the dependency (Table 1 at 0 per cent for male aged 41): 44.71 (no post retirement dependency for child).

(3)   Lesser of two periods at (1) and (2) = 44.71.

(4)   Multiplier for term certain of 44.71 years at 2.5 per cent rate of return (interpolating between the values for 42 and 43 in Table 28)

= (45 − 44.71) × 26.83 + (44.71 − 44) × 27.17 = 27.07.

(5)   Deduct multiplier for post-trial pre-retirement damages before application of adjustment factors for contingencies other than mortality and for the risk that the deceased might have died anyway before the date of trial: 27.07 − 17.87 = 9.20.

(6)   Adjustment factor for the risk that the deceased might have died anyway before the date of trial (Table F for female aged 35 and three years) = 1.00, so multiplier is 9.20 × 1.00 = 9.20.

(7)   Post-retirement damages = 9.20 × £20,000 = £184,000.

An Alternative approach

88. If the court wishes to select multipliers from the date of death, it is essential to ensure that the period before the trial does not include a discount for early receipt. This could be achieved by selecting multipliers from the 0% columns of the appropriate tables and then applying the discount for early receipt to the period after the trial (using the discount rate set under s.1 of the Damages Act 1996). The calculation of the multiplier involves the following steps:

(1)   Determine the expected period for which the deceased would have provided the dependency at the date of death.

(2)   Deduct the period between accidental death and date of trial to give post-trial period.

(3)   Determine the expected post-trial period for which the dependant would have been able to receive the dependency.

(4)   Take the lesser of two periods at (2) and (3).

(5)   Take the multiplier for term certain for the period calculated at (4) at 2.5 per cent rate of return (from Table 28).

(6)   Apply any adjustment factor to the figure in (5) to reflect contingencies other than mortality (in accordance with section B). This will give the multiplier for the post-trial multiplicand.

89. Applying this approach to Example 7 set out above:

(1)   Expected period for which the deceased would have provided the dependency (Table 9 at 0 per cent for male aged 37, the age as at the date of death): 27.06.

(2)   Deduct period between accidental death and date of trial of three years to give post-trial period: 24.06.

(3)   Expected post-trial period for which the dependant would have been able to receive the dependency (Table 2 at 0 per cent for female aged 38): 51.38.

(4)   Lesser of two periods at (2) and (3) = 24.06.

(5)   Multiplier for term certain of 24.06 years at 2.5 per cent rate of return (Table 28) = 18.14.

(6)   Adjustment factor for contingencies other than mortality (in accordance with section B) for an employed male aged 37 with A levels and who was not disabled = 0.90 to give a multiplier of 18.14 × 0.90 = 16.33.

(7) Pre-trial damages = 3 × £30,000 = £90,000 (plus interest as special damages of £8,100).

(8) Post-trial damages = 16.33 × £30,000 = £489,900.

(9) Total financial dependency therefore £90,000 + £8,100 + £489,900 = £588,000.

90. As can be seen, the three methodologies (the current approach, the actuarially recommended approach and this alternative approach) give three different amounts of damages in relation to Example 7, namely £538,500 for the current approach used by the courts, £573,300 using the actuarially recommended approach, and £588,000 using this alternative approach. The size of the disparities between the three methods depends on the length of the period between the date of death and the date of trial; if the example had assumed a period of six years then the differences would have been greater.

Section E: Concluding remarks

91. These tables are designed to assist the courts to arrive at suitable multipliers in a range of possible situations. However, they do not cover all possibilities and in more complex situations, such as where there are significant pension rights, advice should be sought from a Fellow of the Institute and Faculty of Actuaries.

GEORGE RUSSELL FIA
Deputy Government Actuary
London
August 2012

Table 1: Multipliers for pecuniary loss for life (males)

Age at date of trial	Multiplier calculated with allowance for projected mortality from the 2008–based population projections and rate of return of											Age at date of trial
	–2.0%	–1.5%	–1.0%	–0.5%	0.0%	0.5%	1.0%	1.5%	2.0%	2.5%	3.0%	
0	264.76	195.32	147.14	113.22	88.96	71.35	58.34	48.60	41.17	35.41	30.89	0
1	259.11	191.95	145.15	112.06	88.31	71.00	58.18	48.54	41.18	35.46	30.96	1
2	252.28	187.68	142.46	110.35	87.22	70.30	57.73	48.24	40.98	35.33	30.87	2
3	245.58	183.46	139.78	108.64	86.12	69.58	57.26	47.94	40.78	35.19	30.78	3
4	239.02	179.29	137.12	106.93	85.01	68.86	56.78	47.62	40.56	35.05	30.68	4
5	232.59	175.19	134.48	105.22	83.89	68.12	56.30	47.29	40.34	34.90	30.58	5
6	226.29	171.15	131.87	103.52	82.78	67.39	55.80	46.96	40.12	34.75	30.47	6
7	220.14	167.18	129.29	101.83	81.66	66.65	55.31	46.63	39.89	34.59	30.36	7
8	214.13	163.28	126.74	100.15	80.55	65.90	54.80	46.28	39.65	34.42	30.24	8
9	208.23	159.43	124.21	98.48	79.43	65.15	54.29	45.93	39.41	34.25	30.13	9
10	202.47	155.64	121.71	96.81	78.31	64.39	53.78	45.58	39.16	34.08	30.00	10
11	196.83	151.92	119.23	95.15	77.19	63.63	53.25	45.22	38.91	33.90	29.87	11
12	191.33	148.26	116.79	93.50	76.07	62.86	52.72	44.85	38.65	33.72	29.74	12
13	185.95	144.67	114.37	91.87	74.96	62.09	52.19	44.47	38.39	33.53	29.61	13
14	180.69	141.14	111.98	90.24	73.84	61.32	51.65	44.10	38.12	33.34	29.47	14
15	175.56	137.67	109.62	88.63	72.73	60.55	51.11	43.71	37.84	33.14	29.32	15
16	170.55	134.27	107.30	87.02	71.61	59.77	50.56	43.32	37.57	32.94	29.17	16
17	165.66	130.93	105.00	85.44	70.51	58.99	50.01	42.93	37.28	32.73	29.02	17
18	160.89	127.66	102.74	83.86	69.41	58.22	49.46	42.53	37.00	32.52	28.87	18
19	156.25	124.45	100.52	82.31	68.31	57.44	48.91	42.14	36.71	32.31	28.71	19
20	151.72	121.31	98.32	80.76	67.22	56.66	48.35	41.73	36.41	32.10	28.55	20
21	147.28	118.22	96.15	79.23	66.13	55.88	47.78	41.32	36.11	31.87	28.39	21
22	142.94	115.17	94.00	77.70	65.04	55.09	47.21	40.90	35.81	31.64	28.22	22
23	138.69	112.17	91.87	76.18	63.94	54.30	46.63	40.48	35.49	31.41	28.04	23
24	134.54	109.22	89.77	74.67	62.85	53.51	46.05	40.05	35.17	31.17	27.86	24
25	130.49	106.33	87.69	73.17	61.76	52.71	45.46	39.61	34.85	30.92	27.67	25
26	126.54	103.50	85.65	71.69	60.68	51.91	44.87	39.17	34.51	30.67	27.48	26
27	122.69	100.72	83.63	70.22	59.59	51.11	44.28	38.73	34.18	30.42	27.28	27
28	118.90	97.98	81.63	68.74	58.51	50.30	43.67	38.27	33.83	30.15	27.08	28
29	115.20	95.28	79.64	67.28	57.42	49.49	43.06	37.81	33.48	29.88	26.87	29
30	111.59	92.63	77.69	65.83	56.34	48.68	42.45	37.34	33.12	29.60	26.65	30
31	108.09	90.04	75.78	64.40	55.27	47.87	41.83	36.87	32.76	29.32	26.44	31
32	104.68	87.52	73.89	62.99	54.20	47.06	41.22	36.40	32.39	29.04	26.21	32
33	101.36	85.04	72.04	61.60	53.15	46.26	40.60	35.92	32.02	28.75	25.99	33
34	98.10	82.61	70.21	60.21	52.09	45.45	39.98	35.44	31.65	28.46	25.75	34
35	94.92	80.21	68.39	58.83	51.03	44.63	39.35	34.95	31.26	28.15	25.51	35
36	91.82	77.86	66.60	57.46	49.98	43.82	38.71	34.45	30.87	27.84	25.27	36
37	88.78	75.55	64.83	56.10	48.93	43.00	38.07	33.95	30.47	27.53	25.01	37
38	85.81	73.27	63.08	54.74	47.87	42.18	37.42	33.44	30.06	27.20	24.75	38
39	82.89	71.03	61.35	53.39	46.82	41.35	36.77	32.91	29.65	26.86	24.48	39
40	80.05	68.83	59.63	52.05	45.76	40.51	36.11	32.39	29.22	26.52	24.20	40
41	77.27	66.67	57.94	50.72	44.71	39.68	35.44	31.85	28.79	26.17	23.91	41
42	74.56	64.55	56.28	49.41	43.67	38.84	34.77	31.31	28.35	25.81	23.62	42
43	71.92	62.47	54.63	48.10	42.62	38.01	34.10	30.76	27.91	25.45	23.32	43
44	69.34	60.43	53.01	46.81	41.59	37.17	33.42	30.21	27.45	25.08	23.01	44
45	66.82	58.43	51.41	45.52	40.55	36.33	32.73	29.65	26.99	24.70	22.69	45
46	64.36	56.46	49.83	44.25	39.52	35.49	32.05	29.08	26.53	24.31	22.37	46
47	61.96	54.53	48.28	42.99	38.49	34.65	31.35	28.51	26.05	23.91	22.04	47
48	59.63	52.64	46.74	41.74	37.47	33.81	30.66	27.94	25.57	23.51	21.70	48
49	57.35	50.79	45.24	40.50	36.45	32.97	29.97	27.36	25.09	23.10	21.36	49
50	55.14	48.99	43.76	39.29	35.45	32.14	29.27	26.78	24.60	22.69	21.01	50
51	52.99	47.23	42.31	38.09	34.45	31.31	28.58	26.19	24.11	22.27	20.65	51
52	50.90	45.51	40.89	36.91	33.47	30.48	27.88	25.61	23.61	21.85	20.29	52
53	48.87	43.83	39.49	35.74	32.49	29.67	27.19	25.02	23.11	21.42	19.92	53
54	46.90	42.19	38.12	34.60	31.53	28.85	26.50	24.43	22.61	20.99	19.55	54

Table 1: Multipliers for pecuniary loss for life (males) *continued*

Age at date of trial	Multiplier calculated with allowance for projected mortality from the 2008–based population projections and rate of return of											Age at date of trial
	-2.0%	*-1.5%*	*-1.0%*	*-0.5%*	*0.0%*	*0.5%*	*1.0%*	*1.5%*	*2.0%*	*2.5%*	*3.0%*	
55	44.99	40.60	36.79	33.47	30.58	28.04	25.81	23.85	22.11	20.56	19.18	55
56	43.15	39.04	35.48	32.37	29.64	27.25	25.13	23.26	21.60	20.12	18.80	56
57	41.35	37.53	34.19	31.28	28.71	26.45	24.45	22.67	21.09	19.68	18.42	57
58	39.59	36.04	32.93	30.19	27.78	25.65	23.76	22.08	20.58	19.23	18.02	58
59	37.87	34.57	31.67	29.11	26.85	24.85	23.07	21.47	20.05	18.77	17.62	59
60	36.17	33.12	30.42	28.04	25.92	24.04	22.36	20.86	19.51	18.30	17.20	60
61	34.52	31.69	29.19	26.97	25.00	23.23	21.65	20.24	18.96	17.81	16.77	61
62	32.91	30.30	27.98	25.92	24.08	22.43	20.95	19.62	18.41	17.33	16.34	62
63	31.36	28.95	26.80	24.89	23.17	21.63	20.25	19.00	17.86	16.84	15.90	63
64	29.85	27.63	25.65	23.88	22.28	20.85	19.55	18.38	17.31	16.35	15.47	64
65	28.40	26.37	24.54	22.90	21.42	20.08	18.87	17.77	16.77	15.86	15.03	65
66	27.02	25.14	23.46	21.94	20.57	19.33	18.20	17.17	16.24	15.38	14.60	66
67	25.68	23.96	22.41	21.01	19.74	18.59	17.54	16.58	15.70	14.90	14.16	67
68	24.38	22.81	21.39	20.10	18.93	17.86	16.88	15.99	15.17	14.42	13.73	68
69	23.13	21.69	20.39	19.21	18.12	17.14	16.23	15.40	14.64	13.93	13.29	69
70	21.91	20.60	19.41	18.32	17.32	16.41	15.58	14.81	14.10	13.44	12.84	70
71	20.70	19.52	18.43	17.44	16.53	15.69	14.92	14.21	13.55	12.94	12.38	71
72	19.52	18.44	17.46	16.56	15.72	14.96	14.25	13.60	12.99	12.43	11.91	72
73	18.34	17.38	16.49	15.67	14.92	14.22	13.57	12.97	12.42	11.90	11.42	73
74	17.18	16.32	15.52	14.79	14.10	13.47	12.89	12.34	11.83	11.36	10.92	74
75	16.04	15.27	14.56	13.90	13.29	12.72	12.19	11.70	11.24	10.81	10.40	75
76	14.93	14.25	13.62	13.03	12.48	11.97	11.50	11.05	10.64	10.25	9.88	76
77	13.86	13.26	12.70	12.18	11.70	11.24	10.82	10.42	10.05	9.69	9.36	77
78	12.83	12.31	11.82	11.36	10.93	10.53	10.15	9.79	9.46	9.15	8.85	78
79	11.86	11.40	10.97	10.57	10.19	9.84	9.50	9.19	8.89	8.61	8.34	79
80	10.94	10.55	10.17	9.82	9.49	9.18	8.88	8.60	8.34	8.09	7.85	80
81	10.10	9.75	9.43	9.12	8.83	8.56	8.30	8.05	7.82	7.60	7.38	81
82	9.33	9.03	8.74	8.47	8.22	7.98	7.75	7.53	7.33	7.13	6.94	82
83	8.62	8.36	8.11	7.88	7.65	7.44	7.24	7.05	6.87	6.69	6.53	83
84	7.97	7.74	7.53	7.32	7.13	6.94	6.76	6.59	6.43	6.28	6.13	84
85	7.36	7.16	6.98	6.80	6.63	6.47	6.31	6.16	6.02	5.88	5.75	85
86	6.79	6.62	6.46	6.31	6.16	6.02	5.88	5.75	5.62	5.50	5.39	86
87	6.25	6.11	5.97	5.83	5.71	5.58	5.46	5.35	5.24	5.14	5.04	87
88	5.74	5.62	5.50	5.38	5.27	5.16	5.06	4.96	4.87	4.78	4.69	88
89	5.26	5.15	5.05	4.95	4.86	4.76	4.68	4.59	4.51	4.43	4.35	89
90	4.81	4.72	4.64	4.55	4.47	4.39	4.31	4.24	4.17	4.10	4.03	90
91	4.40	4.32	4.25	4.17	4.10	4.04	3.97	3.91	3.85	3.79	3.73	91
92	4.01	3.94	3.88	3.82	3.76	3.70	3.65	3.59	3.54	3.49	3.44	92
93	3.65	3.59	3.54	3.49	3.44	3.39	3.34	3.30	3.25	3.21	3.17	93
94	3.33	3.29	3.24	3.20	3.16	3.11	3.07	3.03	2.99	2.96	2.92	94
95	3.06	3.02	2.98	2.94	2.91	2.87	2.84	2.80	2.77	2.74	2.71	95
96	2.83	2.79	2.76	2.72	2.69	2.66	2.63	2.60	2.57	2.54	2.52	96
97	2.62	2.59	2.56	2.53	2.50	2.48	2.45	2.42	2.40	2.37	2.35	97
98	2.44	2.41	2.38	2.36	2.34	2.31	2.29	2.27	2.24	2.22	2.20	98
99	2.27	2.25	2.22	2.20	2.18	2.16	2.14	2.12	2.10	2.08	2.06	99
100	2.11	2.09	2.07	2.06	2.04	2.02	2.00	1.98	1.97	1.95	1.93	100

Table 2: Multipliers for pecuniary loss for life (females)

Age at date of trial	Multiplier calculated with allowance for projected mortality from the 2008–based population projections and rate of return of											Age at date of trial
	–2.0%	**–1.5%**	**–1.0%**	**–0.5%**	**0.0%**	**0.5%**	**1.0%**	**1.5%**	**2.0%**	**2.5%**	**3.0%**	
0	285.20	208.39	155.57	118.70	92.57	73.74	59.95	49.69	41.92	35.94	31.26	0
1	279.01	204.72	153.41	117.45	91.86	73.36	59.76	49.62	41.91	35.97	31.32	1
2	271.81	200.28	150.65	115.73	90.77	72.67	59.33	49.34	41.73	35.86	31.24	2
3	264.75	195.89	147.91	114.00	89.68	71.97	58.88	49.05	41.55	35.73	31.16	3
4	257.83	191.56	145.19	112.28	88.58	71.27	58.43	48.75	41.35	35.60	31.08	4
5	251.06	187.30	142.49	110.56	87.49	70.56	57.97	48.45	41.15	35.47	30.99	5
6	244.43	183.11	139.83	108.85	86.38	69.85	57.50	48.14	40.95	35.34	30.89	6
7	237.94	178.98	137.18	107.15	85.28	69.13	57.03	47.83	40.74	35.19	30.80	7
8	231.59	174.92	134.57	105.46	84.18	68.40	56.55	47.51	40.52	35.05	30.70	8
9	225.38	170.93	131.98	103.77	83.07	67.67	56.06	47.18	40.30	34.90	30.60	9
10	219.31	167.00	129.43	102.10	81.97	66.94	55.57	46.85	40.08	34.75	30.49	10
11	213.37	163.14	126.90	100.43	80.86	66.20	55.07	46.52	39.85	34.59	30.38	11
12	207.57	159.34	124.40	98.78	79.76	65.46	54.57	46.18	39.62	34.42	30.27	12
13	201.89	155.60	121.92	97.13	78.65	64.71	54.07	45.83	39.38	34.26	30.15	13
14	196.33	151.93	119.48	95.49	77.55	63.96	53.55	45.47	39.13	34.09	30.03	14
15	190.91	148.32	117.06	93.86	76.44	63.21	53.03	45.12	38.88	33.91	29.90	15
16	185.61	144.77	114.67	92.25	75.34	62.45	52.51	44.75	38.62	33.73	29.77	16
17	180.42	141.28	112.31	90.64	74.24	61.70	51.99	44.38	38.37	33.55	29.64	17
18	175.36	137.86	109.98	89.05	73.14	60.94	51.46	44.01	38.10	33.36	29.51	18
19	170.42	134.50	107.68	87.46	72.05	60.17	50.92	43.63	37.83	33.16	29.37	19
20	165.60	131.20	105.42	85.89	70.96	59.41	50.38	43.25	37.56	32.97	29.22	20
21	160.88	127.95	103.17	84.33	69.86	58.64	49.84	42.86	37.28	32.76	29.08	21
22	156.26	124.76	100.95	82.78	68.77	57.86	49.28	42.47	36.99	32.56	28.92	22
23	151.72	121.60	98.74	81.22	67.67	57.08	48.72	42.06	36.70	32.34	28.76	23
24	147.29	118.50	96.56	79.68	66.57	56.29	48.16	41.65	36.40	32.12	28.60	24
25	142.97	115.46	94.41	78.15	65.48	55.50	47.58	41.23	36.09	31.89	28.43	25
26	138.74	112.47	92.28	76.63	64.38	54.71	47.01	40.81	35.78	31.66	28.26	26
27	134.61	109.53	90.18	75.12	63.29	53.92	46.43	40.38	35.46	31.42	28.08	27
28	130.57	106.65	88.11	73.62	62.20	53.12	45.84	39.95	35.14	31.18	27.90	28
29	126.63	103.81	86.05	72.13	61.11	52.32	45.25	39.51	34.81	30.93	27.71	29
30	122.78	101.02	84.03	70.65	60.02	51.52	44.65	39.06	34.47	30.68	27.51	30
31	119.02	98.29	82.03	69.18	58.94	50.71	44.05	38.61	34.13	30.41	27.31	31
32	115.34	95.60	80.06	67.72	57.86	49.90	43.44	38.15	33.78	30.15	27.11	32
33	111.75	92.97	78.11	66.27	56.77	49.09	42.83	37.68	33.42	29.87	26.89	33
34	108.24	90.37	76.18	64.83	55.69	48.27	42.21	37.21	33.06	29.59	26.67	34
35	104.80	87.81	74.27	63.40	54.61	47.45	41.58	36.73	32.69	29.31	26.45	35
36	101.45	85.31	72.39	61.98	53.53	46.63	40.95	36.24	32.31	29.01	26.22	36
37	98.17	82.84	70.53	60.57	52.46	45.81	40.31	35.75	31.93	28.71	25.98	37
38	94.97	80.42	68.69	59.17	51.38	44.98	39.67	35.25	31.54	28.40	25.74	38
39	91.83	78.04	66.88	57.78	50.31	44.15	39.03	34.74	31.14	28.09	25.48	39
40	88.77	75.71	65.08	56.39	49.24	43.31	38.37	34.23	30.73	27.76	25.23	40
41	85.78	73.41	63.31	55.02	48.17	42.48	37.71	33.71	30.32	27.43	24.96	41
42	82.86	71.16	61.56	53.66	47.10	41.64	37.05	33.18	29.90	27.09	24.69	42
43	80.01	68.94	59.84	52.31	46.04	40.80	36.38	32.65	29.47	26.75	24.41	43
44	77.23	66.77	58.14	50.97	44.98	39.95	35.71	32.11	29.03	26.39	24.12	44
45	74.52	64.65	56.46	49.64	43.93	39.11	35.03	31.56	28.59	26.03	23.82	45
46	71.87	62.56	54.81	48.32	42.87	38.27	34.35	31.01	28.14	25.67	23.52	46
47	69.28	60.51	53.17	47.02	41.83	37.42	33.67	30.45	27.69	25.29	23.21	47
48	66.77	58.50	51.57	45.73	40.79	36.58	32.98	29.89	27.23	24.91	22.90	48
49	64.32	56.54	50.00	44.46	39.76	35.74	32.30	29.33	26.76	24.53	22.58	49
50	61.93	54.62	48.44	43.20	38.73	34.90	31.61	28.76	26.29	24.14	22.25	50
51	59.60	52.73	46.91	41.95	37.71	34.06	30.91	28.19	25.81	23.74	21.92	51
52	57.33	50.88	45.40	40.71	36.69	33.22	30.22	27.61	25.33	23.33	21.57	52
53	55.11	49.07	43.92	39.49	35.68	32.38	29.52	27.02	24.84	22.92	21.22	53
54	52.96	47.30	42.46	38.28	34.68	31.55	28.82	26.44	24.34	22.50	20.87	54

Table 2: Multipliers for pecuniary loss for life (females) *continued*

Age at date of trial	Multiplier calculated with allowance for projected mortality from the 2008–based population projections and rate of return of											Age at date of trial
	–2.0%	*–1.5%*	*–1.0%*	*–0.5%*	*0.0%*	*0.5%*	*1.0%*	*1.5%*	*2.0%*	*2.5%*	*3.0%*	
55	50.86	45.57	41.02	37.09	33.68	30.71	28.12	25.84	23.84	22.07	20.51	55
56	48.83	43.88	39.61	35.91	32.69	29.88	27.42	25.25	23.34	21.64	20.14	56
57	46.84	42.22	38.23	34.75	31.71	29.05	26.72	24.65	22.83	21.21	19.76	57
58	44.89	40.60	36.86	33.59	30.74	28.22	26.01	24.05	22.31	20.76	19.37	58
59	42.99	38.99	35.50	32.44	29.76	27.39	25.29	23.43	21.78	20.30	18.98	59
60	41.12	37.41	34.16	31.30	28.78	26.55	24.57	22.81	21.24	19.83	18.57	60
61	39.30	35.86	32.83	30.16	27.80	25.70	23.84	22.18	20.69	19.35	18.15	61
62	37.52	34.33	31.52	29.03	26.83	24.86	23.11	21.54	20.13	18.86	17.72	62
63	35.79	32.84	30.24	27.92	25.86	24.02	22.38	20.90	19.57	18.37	17.28	63
64	34.11	31.39	28.98	26.83	24.91	23.19	21.65	20.26	19.01	17.87	16.84	64
65	32.50	29.99	27.76	25.77	23.98	22.38	20.93	19.63	18.45	17.38	16.40	65
66	30.94	28.64	26.58	24.73	23.07	21.58	20.23	19.00	17.89	16.88	15.96	66
67	29.44	27.32	25.43	23.72	22.18	20.78	19.52	18.38	17.34	16.39	15.52	67
68	27.99	26.05	24.30	22.72	21.29	20.00	18.83	17.76	16.78	15.89	15.07	68
69	26.57	24.80	23.19	21.74	20.42	19.22	18.13	17.13	16.22	15.39	14.62	69
70	25.19	23.57	22.10	20.76	19.55	18.44	17.43	16.50	15.65	14.87	14.15	70
71	23.83	22.35	21.01	19.79	18.67	17.65	16.72	15.86	15.07	14.35	13.68	71
72	22.47	21.14	19.92	18.81	17.79	16.85	16.00	15.20	14.48	13.80	13.18	72
73	21.13	19.93	18.83	17.82	16.89	16.04	15.25	14.53	13.86	13.24	12.66	73
74	19.80	18.72	17.73	16.82	15.99	15.21	14.50	13.84	13.23	12.66	12.13	74
75	18.48	17.53	16.64	15.83	15.08	14.38	13.74	13.14	12.58	12.06	11.58	75
76	17.20	16.35	15.57	14.84	14.17	13.55	12.97	12.43	11.92	11.45	11.01	76
77	15.95	15.21	14.51	13.87	13.28	12.72	12.20	11.72	11.27	10.84	10.45	77
78	14.75	14.10	13.50	12.93	12.40	11.91	11.45	11.02	10.62	10.24	9.88	78
79	13.62	13.05	12.52	12.03	11.56	11.13	10.72	10.34	9.98	9.64	9.32	79
80	12.56	12.07	11.61	11.17	10.77	10.38	10.02	9.69	9.37	9.07	8.78	80
81	11.58	11.15	10.75	10.37	10.02	9.68	9.36	9.06	8.78	8.51	8.26	81
82	10.67	10.30	9.95	9.62	9.31	9.02	8.74	8.48	8.23	7.99	7.76	82
83	9.83	9.51	9.21	8.92	8.65	8.39	8.15	7.92	7.70	7.49	7.29	83
84	9.06	8.78	8.52	8.27	8.03	7.81	7.59	7.39	7.19	7.01	6.83	84
85	8.34	8.10	7.87	7.65	7.45	7.25	7.06	6.88	6.71	6.55	6.40	85
86	7.66	7.45	7.25	7.07	6.89	6.72	6.56	6.40	6.25	6.11	5.97	86
87	7.01	6.84	6.67	6.51	6.36	6.21	6.07	5.93	5.80	5.68	5.56	87
88	6.41	6.26	6.11	5.98	5.85	5.72	5.60	5.48	5.37	5.26	5.16	88
89	5.84	5.71	5.59	5.47	5.36	5.25	5.15	5.05	4.95	4.86	4.77	89
90	5.31	5.20	5.10	5.00	4.90	4.81	4.72	4.64	4.55	4.47	4.40	90
91	4.82	4.73	4.64	4.55	4.47	4.40	4.32	4.25	4.18	4.11	4.04	91
92	4.37	4.29	4.22	4.15	4.08	4.01	3.95	3.89	3.83	3.77	3.71	92
93	3.97	3.90	3.84	3.78	3.72	3.67	3.61	3.56	3.51	3.46	3.41	93
94	3.62	3.56	3.51	3.46	3.41	3.36	3.31	3.27	3.22	3.18	3.14	94
95	3.32	3.27	3.23	3.18	3.14	3.10	3.06	3.02	2.98	2.94	2.91	95
96	3.06	3.02	2.98	2.94	2.91	2.87	2.84	2.80	2.77	2.74	2.71	96
97	2.84	2.80	2.77	2.74	2.70	2.67	2.64	2.61	2.58	2.56	2.53	97
98	2.64	2.61	2.58	2.55	2.52	2.49	2.47	2.44	2.42	2.39	2.37	98
99	2.45	2.42	2.40	2.37	2.35	2.32	2.30	2.28	2.26	2.23	2.21	99
100	2.27	2.25	2.22	2.20	2.18	2.16	2.14	2.12	2.10	2.08	2.06	100

Table 3: Multipliers for loss of earnings to pension age 50 (males)

Age at date of trial	Multiplier calculated with allowance for projected mortality from the 2008–based population projections and rate of return of											Age at date of trial
	–2.0%	*–1.5%*	*–1.0%*	*–0.5%*	*0.0%*	*0.5%*	*1.0%*	*1.5%*	*2.0%*	*2.5%*	*3.0%*	
16	48.26	43.90	40.05	36.65	33.63	30.94	28.55	26.42	24.51	22.80	21.26	16
17	46.31	42.26	38.66	35.47	32.63	30.10	27.84	25.81	24.00	22.36	20.89	17
18	44.40	40.64	37.29	34.30	31.64	29.25	27.12	25.20	23.47	21.91	20.51	18
19	42.54	39.04	35.93	33.14	30.65	28.41	26.39	24.57	22.94	21.45	20.11	19
20	40.71	37.48	34.58	31.99	29.66	27.55	25.66	23.94	22.39	20.99	19.71	20
21	38.91	35.93	33.25	30.84	28.66	26.70	24.92	23.30	21.84	20.50	19.29	21
22	37.16	34.41	31.94	29.70	27.67	25.84	24.17	22.65	21.27	20.01	18.86	22
23	35.44	32.92	30.63	28.56	26.68	24.97	23.41	21.99	20.69	19.51	18.42	23
24	33.75	31.44	29.34	27.43	25.69	24.10	22.65	21.32	20.11	18.99	17.96	24
25	32.10	29.99	28.06	26.31	24.70	23.23	21.88	20.65	19.51	18.46	17.49	25
26	30.48	28.56	26.80	25.19	23.71	22.36	21.11	19.96	18.90	17.92	17.01	26
27	28.89	27.15	25.55	24.08	22.72	21.47	20.32	19.26	18.27	17.36	16.52	27
28	27.34	25.76	24.31	22.97	21.73	20.59	19.53	18.55	17.64	16.79	16.00	28
29	25.81	24.40	23.08	21.87	20.74	19.70	18.73	17.83	16.99	16.21	15.48	29
30	24.32	23.05	21.87	20.78	19.76	18.81	17.92	17.10	16.33	15.61	14.94	30
31	22.86	21.73	20.67	19.69	18.77	17.91	17.11	16.36	15.66	15.00	14.38	31
32	21.43	20.43	19.49	18.61	17.78	17.01	16.29	15.61	14.97	14.37	13.81	32
33	20.03	19.15	18.31	17.53	16.80	16.11	15.46	14.85	14.28	13.73	13.22	33
34	18.66	17.88	17.15	16.47	15.82	15.20	14.63	14.08	13.57	13.08	12.62	34
35	17.31	16.64	16.00	15.40	14.83	14.29	13.78	13.30	12.84	12.41	11.99	35
36	16.00	15.42	14.87	14.34	13.85	13.38	12.93	12.51	12.10	11.72	11.35	36
37	14.70	14.21	13.74	13.29	12.86	12.46	12.07	11.70	11.35	11.01	10.69	37
38	13.44	13.02	12.62	12.24	11.88	11.53	11.20	10.88	10.58	10.29	10.01	38
39	12.19	11.85	11.52	11.20	10.89	10.60	10.32	10.05	9.79	9.54	9.31	39
40	10.98	10.69	10.42	10.16	9.91	9.67	9.43	9.21	8.99	8.78	8.58	40
41	9.78	9.55	9.34	9.13	8.92	8.72	8.53	8.35	8.17	8.00	7.84	41
42	8.61	8.43	8.26	8.10	7.93	7.78	7.63	7.48	7.34	7.20	7.07	42
43	7.46	7.33	7.20	7.07	6.95	6.83	6.71	6.60	6.49	6.38	6.28	43
44	6.33	6.24	6.14	6.05	5.96	5.87	5.78	5.70	5.62	5.54	5.46	44
45	5.23	5.16	5.10	5.03	4.97	4.91	4.85	4.79	4.73	4.68	4.62	45
46	4.14	4.10	4.06	4.02	3.98	3.94	3.90	3.86	3.83	3.79	3.75	46
47	3.08	3.06	3.03	3.01	2.99	2.97	2.94	2.92	2.90	2.88	2.86	47
48	2.03	2.02	2.01	2.00	1.99	1.98	1.97	1.96	1.96	1.95	1.94	48
49	1.01	1.01	1.00	1.00	1.00	1.00	0.99	0.99	0.99	0.99	0.98	49

Table 4: Multipliers for loss of earnings to pension age 50 (females)

Age at date of trial	Multiplier calculated with allowance for projected mortality from the 2008–based population projections and rate of return of											Age at date of trial
	-2.0%	*-1.5%*	*-1.0%*	*-0.5%*	*0.0%*	*0.5%*	*1.0%*	*1.5%*	*2.0%*	*2.5%*	*3.0%*	
16	48.58	44.19	40.30	36.87	33.82	31.12	28.71	26.56	24.63	22.91	21.36	16
17	46.62	42.53	38.91	35.69	32.82	30.27	27.99	25.95	24.12	22.47	20.99	17
18	44.71	40.91	37.53	34.52	31.83	29.42	27.27	25.33	23.59	22.02	20.60	18
19	42.83	39.30	36.16	33.35	30.83	28.57	26.54	24.71	23.06	21.56	20.21	19
20	40.98	37.73	34.81	32.19	29.83	27.72	25.80	24.08	22.51	21.09	19.80	20
21	39.18	36.17	33.47	31.03	28.84	26.85	25.06	23.43	21.96	20.61	19.39	21
22	37.41	34.64	32.14	29.89	27.84	25.99	24.31	22.78	21.39	20.12	18.96	22
23	35.68	33.13	30.83	28.74	26.85	25.12	23.55	22.12	20.81	19.61	18.51	23
24	33.98	31.65	29.53	27.60	25.85	24.25	22.78	21.44	20.22	19.09	18.06	24
25	32.31	30.18	28.24	26.47	24.85	23.37	22.01	20.76	19.61	18.56	17.59	25
26	30.68	28.74	26.97	25.35	23.86	22.49	21.23	20.07	19.00	18.01	17.10	26
27	29.08	27.33	25.71	24.23	22.86	21.60	20.44	19.37	18.37	17.45	16.60	27
28	27.52	25.93	24.46	23.11	21.87	20.71	19.64	18.65	17.74	16.88	16.09	28
29	25.98	24.55	23.23	22.01	20.87	19.82	18.84	17.93	17.08	16.30	15.56	29
30	24.48	23.20	22.01	20.90	19.88	18.92	18.03	17.20	16.42	15.70	15.02	30
31	23.01	21.86	20.80	19.81	18.88	18.02	17.21	16.45	15.74	15.08	14.46	31
32	21.56	20.55	19.60	18.72	17.89	17.11	16.38	15.70	15.05	14.45	13.88	32
33	20.15	19.26	18.42	17.63	16.89	16.20	15.55	14.93	14.35	13.80	13.29	33
34	18.76	17.98	17.25	16.55	15.90	15.28	14.70	14.15	13.63	13.14	12.68	34
35	17.41	16.73	16.09	15.48	14.91	14.37	13.85	13.36	12.90	12.46	12.05	35
36	16.08	15.49	14.94	14.41	13.92	13.44	12.99	12.56	12.16	11.77	11.40	36
37	14.77	14.28	13.80	13.35	12.92	12.51	12.12	11.75	11.40	11.06	10.73	37
38	13.50	13.08	12.68	12.30	11.93	11.58	11.25	10.93	10.62	10.33	10.05	38
39	12.25	11.90	11.56	11.24	10.94	10.64	10.36	10.09	9.83	9.58	9.34	39
40	11.02	10.73	10.46	10.20	9.95	9.70	9.47	9.24	9.02	8.82	8.61	40
41	9.82	9.59	9.37	9.16	8.95	8.76	8.56	8.38	8.20	8.03	7.86	41
42	8.64	8.46	8.29	8.12	7.96	7.80	7.65	7.51	7.36	7.22	7.09	42
43	7.48	7.35	7.22	7.09	6.97	6.85	6.73	6.62	6.51	6.40	6.29	43
44	6.35	6.25	6.16	6.06	5.97	5.89	5.80	5.72	5.63	5.55	5.48	44
45	5.24	5.17	5.11	5.04	4.98	4.92	4.86	4.80	4.74	4.69	4.63	45
46	4.15	4.11	4.07	4.03	3.99	3.95	3.91	3.87	3.83	3.80	3.76	46
47	3.08	3.06	3.04	3.01	2.99	2.97	2.95	2.93	2.90	2.88	2.86	47
48	2.04	2.03	2.02	2.01	2.00	1.99	1.98	1.97	1.96	1.95	1.94	48
49	1.01	1.01	1.00	1.00	1.00	1.00	0.99	0.99	0.99	0.99	0.98	49

Table 5: Multipliers for loss of earnings to pension age 55 (males)

Age at date of trial	Multiplier calculated with allowance for projected mortality from the 2008–based population projections and rate of return of											Age at date of trial
	–2.0%	*–1.5%*	*–1.0%*	*–0.5%*	*0.0%*	*0.5%*	*1.0%*	*1.5%*	*2.0%*	*2.5%*	*3.0%*	
16	58.33	52.26	47.00	42.43	38.44	34.96	31.90	29.22	26.85	24.76	22.90	16
17	56.17	50.49	45.54	41.22	37.44	34.13	31.22	28.65	26.38	24.37	22.58	17
18	54.07	48.74	44.09	40.02	36.45	33.30	30.53	28.08	25.90	23.97	22.24	18
19	52.00	47.03	42.67	38.83	35.46	32.48	29.84	27.50	25.42	23.56	21.90	19
20	49.99	45.34	41.26	37.65	34.47	31.65	29.14	26.91	24.92	23.14	21.55	20
21	48.01	43.68	39.86	36.48	33.48	30.81	28.44	26.31	24.42	22.72	21.19	21
22	46.07	42.04	38.47	35.31	32.49	29.97	27.72	25.71	23.90	22.28	20.82	22
23	44.17	40.43	37.11	34.14	31.49	29.13	27.00	25.10	23.38	21.83	20.43	23
24	42.31	38.84	35.75	32.98	30.50	28.28	26.28	24.47	22.85	21.37	20.04	24
25	40.49	37.28	34.41	31.83	29.52	27.43	25.54	23.84	22.30	20.90	19.63	25
26	38.70	35.74	33.08	30.69	28.53	26.57	24.81	23.20	21.75	20.42	19.21	26
27	36.95	34.23	31.77	29.55	27.54	25.71	24.06	22.55	21.18	19.93	18.78	27
28	35.24	32.74	30.47	28.42	26.55	24.85	23.30	21.89	20.60	19.42	18.34	28
29	33.56	31.27	29.18	27.29	25.56	23.98	22.54	21.22	20.01	18.91	17.89	29
30	31.91	29.82	27.91	26.17	24.57	23.11	21.78	20.55	19.42	18.38	17.42	30
31	30.30	28.40	26.66	25.06	23.59	22.24	21.00	19.86	18.81	17.83	16.94	31
32	28.73	27.00	25.41	23.95	22.61	21.37	20.22	19.17	18.19	17.28	16.44	32
33	27.19	25.63	24.19	22.86	21.63	20.49	19.44	18.46	17.56	16.72	15.94	33
34	25.68	24.27	22.97	21.76	20.65	19.61	18.65	17.75	16.92	16.14	15.41	34
35	24.20	22.94	21.77	20.68	19.67	18.72	17.85	17.03	16.26	15.55	14.88	35
36	22.75	21.63	20.58	19.60	18.69	17.83	17.04	16.29	15.59	14.94	14.32	36
37	21.33	20.33	19.40	18.52	17.71	16.94	16.22	15.55	14.91	14.32	13.76	37
38	19.94	19.06	18.23	17.46	16.73	16.04	15.40	14.79	14.22	13.68	13.17	38
39	18.57	17.80	17.07	16.39	15.75	15.14	14.56	14.02	13.51	13.02	12.56	39
40	17.23	16.56	15.93	15.33	14.76	14.23	13.72	13.24	12.79	12.35	11.94	40
41	15.92	15.34	14.79	14.28	13.78	13.32	12.87	12.45	12.05	11.67	11.30	41
42	14.63	14.14	13.67	13.23	12.80	12.40	12.01	11.65	11.30	10.96	10.64	42
43	13.37	12.96	12.56	12.18	11.82	11.48	11.15	10.83	10.53	10.24	9.96	43
44	12.13	11.79	11.46	11.14	10.84	10.55	10.27	10.01	9.75	9.50	9.26	44
45	10.92	10.64	10.37	10.11	9.86	9.62	9.39	9.17	8.95	8.74	8.54	45
46	9.73	9.51	9.29	9.08	8.88	8.68	8.50	8.31	8.14	7.97	7.80	46
47	8.57	8.39	8.22	8.06	7.90	7.74	7.59	7.45	7.31	7.17	7.04	47
48	7.43	7.29	7.17	7.04	6.92	6.80	6.68	6.57	6.46	6.35	6.25	48
49	6.31	6.21	6.12	6.02	5.93	5.85	5.76	5.68	5.60	5.52	5.44	49
50	5.21	5.14	5.08	5.01	4.95	4.89	4.83	4.77	4.72	4.66	4.60	50
51	4.13	4.09	4.05	4.01	3.97	3.93	3.89	3.85	3.81	3.78	3.74	51
52	3.07	3.05	3.03	3.00	2.98	2.96	2.94	2.91	2.89	2.87	2.85	52
53	2.03	2.02	2.01	2.00	1.99	1.98	1.97	1.96	1.95	1.94	1.93	53
54	1.01	1.01	1.00	1.00	1.00	1.00	0.99	0.99	0.99	0.99	0.98	54

Table 6: Multipliers for loss of earnings to pension age 55 (females)

Age at date of trial	Multiplier calculated with allowance for projected mortality from the 2008–based population projections and rate of return of											Age at date of trial
	–2.0%	*–1.5%*	*–1.0%*	*–0.5%*	*0.0%*	*0.5%*	*1.0%*	*1.5%*	*2.0%*	*2.5%*	*3.0%*	
16	58.83	52.69	47.37	42.75	38.72	35.20	32.11	29.40	27.01	24.90	23.03	16
17	56.66	50.91	45.90	41.54	37.72	34.37	31.43	28.84	26.54	24.51	22.70	17
18	54.54	49.15	44.45	40.34	36.72	33.55	30.74	28.26	26.07	24.11	22.37	18
19	52.46	47.43	43.02	39.14	35.73	32.71	30.05	27.68	25.58	23.71	22.03	19
20	50.43	45.73	41.60	37.95	34.73	31.88	29.35	27.09	25.09	23.29	21.68	20
21	48.43	44.05	40.19	36.77	33.73	31.04	28.64	26.50	24.58	22.86	21.32	21
22	46.48	42.41	38.80	35.59	32.74	30.20	27.92	25.89	24.06	22.42	20.95	22
23	44.56	40.78	37.42	34.42	31.74	29.35	27.20	25.27	23.54	21.97	20.56	23
24	42.69	39.18	36.05	33.25	30.74	28.49	26.47	24.65	23.00	21.51	20.17	24
25	40.85	37.60	34.70	32.09	29.75	27.64	25.73	24.01	22.46	21.04	19.76	25
26	39.04	36.05	33.36	30.94	28.75	26.78	24.99	23.37	21.90	20.56	19.34	26
27	37.28	34.52	32.04	29.79	27.76	25.91	24.24	22.72	21.33	20.06	18.91	27
28	35.55	33.02	30.73	28.65	26.76	25.04	23.48	22.05	20.75	19.56	18.46	28
29	33.86	31.54	29.43	27.51	25.77	24.17	22.72	21.38	20.16	19.04	18.01	29
30	32.20	30.08	28.15	26.38	24.77	23.30	21.94	20.70	19.56	18.51	17.54	30
31	30.57	28.64	26.88	25.26	23.78	22.42	21.16	20.01	18.94	17.96	17.05	31
32	28.98	27.23	25.62	24.15	22.79	21.53	20.38	19.31	18.32	17.40	16.56	32
33	27.42	25.84	24.38	23.03	21.79	20.64	19.58	18.60	17.68	16.83	16.04	33
34	25.89	24.46	23.15	21.93	20.80	19.75	18.78	17.87	17.03	16.25	15.52	34
35	24.39	23.11	21.93	20.83	19.81	18.86	17.97	17.14	16.37	15.65	14.97	35
36	22.92	21.78	20.73	19.74	18.82	17.96	17.15	16.40	15.69	15.03	14.41	36
37	21.48	20.48	19.53	18.65	17.83	17.05	16.33	15.65	15.01	14.40	13.84	37
38	20.07	19.19	18.35	17.57	16.84	16.14	15.49	14.88	14.30	13.76	13.25	38
39	18.69	17.92	17.19	16.50	15.85	15.23	14.65	14.11	13.59	13.10	12.64	39
40	17.34	16.67	16.03	15.43	14.86	14.32	13.80	13.32	12.86	12.42	12.01	40
41	16.02	15.44	14.89	14.36	13.87	13.40	12.95	12.52	12.12	11.73	11.36	41
42	14.72	14.22	13.75	13.30	12.88	12.47	12.08	11.71	11.36	11.02	10.70	42
43	13.45	13.03	12.63	12.25	11.89	11.54	11.21	10.89	10.59	10.29	10.01	43
44	12.20	11.85	11.52	11.20	10.90	10.61	10.33	10.06	9.80	9.55	9.31	44
45	10.98	10.70	10.42	10.16	9.91	9.67	9.43	9.21	8.99	8.79	8.58	45
46	9.78	9.56	9.34	9.13	8.92	8.73	8.54	8.35	8.17	8.00	7.84	46
47	8.61	8.43	8.26	8.09	7.93	7.78	7.63	7.48	7.34	7.20	7.07	47
48	7.46	7.33	7.20	7.07	6.95	6.83	6.71	6.60	6.49	6.38	6.28	48
49	6.33	6.24	6.14	6.05	5.96	5.87	5.78	5.70	5.62	5.54	5.46	49
50	5.23	5.16	5.10	5.03	4.97	4.91	4.85	4.79	4.73	4.68	4.62	50
51	4.14	4.10	4.06	4.02	3.98	3.94	3.90	3.86	3.83	3.79	3.75	51
52	3.08	3.06	3.03	3.01	2.99	2.97	2.94	2.92	2.90	2.88	2.86	52
53	2.03	2.02	2.01	2.00	1.99	1.98	1.97	1.96	1.96	1.95	1.94	53
54	1.01	1.01	1.00	1.00	1.00	1.00	0.99	0.99	0.99	0.99	0.98	54

Table 7: Multipliers for loss of earnings to pension age 60 (males)

Age at date of trial	Multiplier calculated with allowance for projected mortality from the 2008–based population projections and rate of return of											Age at date of trial
	–2.0%	–1.5%	–1.0%	–0.5%	0.0%	0.5%	1.0%	1.5%	2.0%	2.5%	3.0%	
16	69.28	61.13	54.18	48.26	43.18	38.81	35.03	31.77	28.93	26.46	24.29	16
17	66.90	59.22	52.65	47.02	42.18	38.00	34.38	31.24	28.50	26.11	24.01	17
18	64.58	57.34	51.13	45.79	41.18	37.19	33.73	30.71	28.07	25.75	23.72	18
19	62.30	55.49	49.63	44.57	40.19	36.38	33.06	30.17	27.62	25.39	23.42	19
20	60.08	53.68	48.15	43.36	39.20	35.57	32.40	29.62	27.17	25.02	23.11	20
21	57.90	51.89	46.68	42.15	38.21	34.75	31.72	29.06	26.71	24.64	22.80	21
22	55.76	50.13	45.23	40.95	37.21	33.93	31.04	28.50	26.25	24.25	22.47	22
23	53.66	48.40	43.79	39.76	36.22	33.11	30.36	27.93	25.77	23.85	22.14	23
24	51.61	46.69	42.37	38.57	35.23	32.28	29.66	27.35	25.28	23.44	21.80	24
25	49.60	45.01	40.96	37.40	34.24	31.45	28.97	26.76	24.79	23.02	21.44	25
26	47.64	43.35	39.57	36.22	33.25	30.61	28.26	26.16	24.28	22.59	21.08	26
27	45.71	41.72	38.19	35.06	32.27	29.77	27.55	25.56	23.77	22.16	20.71	27
28	43.82	40.12	36.83	33.90	31.28	28.93	26.83	24.94	23.24	21.71	20.32	28
29	41.97	38.54	35.48	32.74	30.29	28.09	26.10	24.32	22.70	21.25	19.92	29
30	40.15	36.99	34.14	31.59	29.30	27.24	25.37	23.69	22.16	20.78	19.52	30
31	38.38	35.46	32.83	30.46	28.32	26.39	24.64	23.05	21.61	20.29	19.10	31
32	36.65	33.96	31.53	29.33	27.34	25.53	23.89	22.40	21.04	19.80	18.67	32
33	34.96	32.48	30.24	28.21	26.36	24.68	23.15	21.75	20.47	19.30	18.23	33
34	33.30	31.03	28.97	27.09	25.38	23.82	22.39	21.09	19.89	18.79	17.78	34
35	31.67	29.60	27.71	25.98	24.40	22.96	21.63	20.42	19.30	18.27	17.32	35
36	30.07	28.19	26.46	24.88	23.43	22.09	20.87	19.74	18.69	17.73	16.84	36
37	28.51	26.80	25.23	23.78	22.45	21.22	20.09	19.04	18.08	17.18	16.35	37
38	26.98	25.43	24.01	22.69	21.48	20.35	19.31	18.34	17.45	16.61	15.84	38
39	25.48	24.08	22.80	21.60	20.50	19.47	18.52	17.63	16.81	16.04	15.32	39
40	24.00	22.76	21.60	20.52	19.52	18.59	17.72	16.91	16.15	15.44	14.78	40
41	22.56	21.45	20.41	19.45	18.54	17.70	16.91	16.17	15.48	14.84	14.23	41
42	21.15	20.16	19.24	18.38	17.57	16.81	16.10	15.43	14.80	14.21	13.66	42
43	19.76	18.90	18.08	17.31	16.59	15.92	15.28	14.68	14.11	13.58	13.07	43
44	18.41	17.65	16.93	16.26	15.62	15.02	14.45	13.91	13.41	12.93	12.47	44
45	17.08	16.42	15.79	15.20	14.64	14.12	13.61	13.14	12.69	12.26	11.85	45
46	15.78	15.21	14.67	14.16	13.67	13.21	12.77	12.35	11.95	11.58	11.22	46
47	14.50	14.02	13.56	13.12	12.70	12.30	11.92	11.55	11.21	10.88	10.56	47
48	13.26	12.85	12.46	12.08	11.73	11.38	11.06	10.75	10.45	10.16	9.89	48
49	12.03	11.69	11.37	11.05	10.75	10.47	10.19	9.93	9.67	9.43	9.19	49
50	10.83	10.56	10.29	10.03	9.78	9.55	9.32	9.10	8.88	8.68	8.48	50
51	9.66	9.44	9.22	9.01	8.81	8.62	8.43	8.25	8.08	7.91	7.75	51
52	8.51	8.34	8.17	8.00	7.84	7.69	7.54	7.40	7.26	7.12	6.99	52
53	7.38	7.25	7.12	7.00	6.87	6.76	6.64	6.53	6.42	6.32	6.21	53
54	6.27	6.18	6.08	5.99	5.90	5.82	5.73	5.65	5.57	5.49	5.41	54
55	5.18	5.12	5.05	4.99	4.93	4.87	4.81	4.75	4.69	4.64	4.58	55
56	4.12	4.07	4.03	3.99	3.95	3.91	3.87	3.84	3.80	3.76	3.73	56
57	3.06	3.04	3.02	2.99	2.97	2.95	2.93	2.91	2.89	2.86	2.84	57
58	2.03	2.02	2.01	2.00	1.99	1.98	1.97	1.96	1.95	1.94	1.93	58
59	1.01	1.00	1.00	1.00	1.00	0.99	0.99	0.99	0.99	0.98	0.98	59

Table 8: Multipliers for loss of earnings to pension age 60 (females)

Age at date of trial	Multiplier calculated with allowance for projected mortality from the 2008–based population projections and rate of return of											Age at date of trial
	−2.0%	−1.5%	−1.0%	−0.5%	0.0%	0.5%	1.0%	1.5%	2.0%	2.5%	3.0%	
16	70.04	61.77	54.73	48.72	43.57	39.14	35.32	32.02	29.14	26.64	24.45	16
17	67.65	59.85	53.18	47.48	42.57	38.33	34.67	31.49	28.72	26.29	24.17	17
18	65.30	57.96	51.66	46.24	41.57	37.52	34.01	30.96	28.28	25.94	23.88	18
19	63.01	56.10	50.15	45.02	40.57	36.71	33.35	30.41	27.84	25.58	23.59	19
20	60.76	54.27	48.66	43.80	39.57	35.90	32.68	29.87	27.39	25.21	23.28	20
21	58.56	52.46	47.18	42.58	38.58	35.08	32.01	29.31	26.93	24.83	22.97	21
22	56.40	50.69	45.71	41.37	37.58	34.25	31.32	28.74	26.46	24.44	22.64	22
23	54.29	48.94	44.26	40.17	36.58	33.42	30.64	28.17	25.98	24.04	22.31	23
24	52.21	47.21	42.83	38.98	35.58	32.59	29.94	27.59	25.50	23.63	21.97	24
25	50.18	45.51	41.41	37.79	34.59	31.75	29.24	27.00	25.00	23.21	21.61	25
26	48.19	43.84	40.00	36.60	33.59	30.91	28.53	26.40	24.49	22.78	21.25	26
27	46.24	42.20	38.61	35.43	32.59	30.07	27.81	25.79	23.98	22.34	20.87	27
28	44.33	40.58	37.24	34.26	31.60	29.22	27.09	25.17	23.45	21.89	20.49	28
29	42.46	38.98	35.87	33.09	30.60	28.37	26.36	24.55	22.91	21.43	20.09	29
30	40.63	37.41	34.53	31.94	29.61	27.51	25.62	23.91	22.37	20.96	19.69	30
31	38.83	35.86	33.19	30.79	28.62	26.65	24.88	23.27	21.81	20.48	19.27	31
32	37.08	34.34	31.87	29.64	27.62	25.79	24.13	22.62	21.24	19.98	18.83	32
33	35.35	32.84	30.57	28.50	26.63	24.93	23.37	21.96	20.66	19.48	18.39	33
34	33.67	31.37	29.28	27.37	25.64	24.06	22.61	21.29	20.07	18.96	17.93	34
35	32.01	29.91	28.00	26.25	24.65	23.18	21.84	20.60	19.47	18.43	17.46	35
36	30.40	28.48	26.73	25.13	23.66	22.30	21.06	19.91	18.86	17.88	16.98	36
37	28.81	27.08	25.48	24.02	22.67	21.42	20.28	19.21	18.23	17.32	16.48	37
38	27.26	25.69	24.24	22.91	21.68	20.54	19.48	18.50	17.60	16.75	15.97	38
39	25.73	24.32	23.02	21.81	20.69	19.65	18.68	17.78	16.95	16.17	15.44	39
40	24.24	22.98	21.81	20.72	19.70	18.76	17.88	17.05	16.29	15.57	14.90	40
41	22.78	21.66	20.61	19.63	18.71	17.86	17.06	16.31	15.61	14.96	14.34	41
42	21.35	20.35	19.42	18.55	17.73	16.96	16.24	15.56	14.93	14.33	13.77	42
43	19.95	19.07	18.24	17.47	16.74	16.05	15.41	14.80	14.23	13.69	13.18	43
44	18.58	17.81	17.08	16.40	15.75	15.15	14.57	14.03	13.52	13.03	12.57	44
45	17.24	16.57	15.93	15.33	14.77	14.23	13.73	13.25	12.79	12.36	11.95	45
46	15.92	15.34	14.80	14.28	13.79	13.32	12.87	12.45	12.05	11.67	11.30	46
47	14.63	14.14	13.67	13.23	12.80	12.40	12.01	11.65	11.30	10.96	10.64	47
48	13.37	12.95	12.56	12.18	11.82	11.48	11.15	10.83	10.53	10.24	9.96	48
49	12.13	11.79	11.46	11.14	10.84	10.55	10.27	10.00	9.75	9.50	9.26	49
50	10.92	10.64	10.37	10.11	9.86	9.62	9.39	9.17	8.95	8.74	8.54	50
51	9.73	9.51	9.29	9.08	8.88	8.69	8.50	8.31	8.14	7.97	7.80	51
52	8.57	8.39	8.22	8.06	7.90	7.75	7.60	7.45	7.31	7.17	7.04	52
53	7.43	7.30	7.17	7.04	6.92	6.80	6.68	6.57	6.46	6.36	6.25	53
54	6.31	6.21	6.12	6.03	5.94	5.85	5.76	5.68	5.60	5.52	5.44	54
55	5.21	5.14	5.08	5.02	4.95	4.89	4.83	4.77	4.72	4.66	4.61	55
56	4.13	4.09	4.05	4.01	3.97	3.93	3.89	3.85	3.82	3.78	3.74	56
57	3.07	3.05	3.03	3.00	2.98	2.96	2.94	2.92	2.89	2.87	2.85	57
58	2.03	2.02	2.01	2.00	1.99	1.98	1.97	1.96	1.95	1.94	1.93	58
59	1.01	1.01	1.00	1.00	1.00	1.00	0.99	0.99	0.99	0.99	0.98	59

Table 9: Multipliers for loss of earnings to pension age 65 (males)

Age at date of trial	Multiplier calculated with allowance for projected mortality from the 2008–based population projections and rate of return of											Age at date of trial
	−2.0%	−1.5%	−1.0%	−0.5%	0.0%	0.5%	1.0%	1.5%	2.0%	2.5%	3.0%	
16	81.11	70.46	61.56	54.09	47.80	42.47	37.95	34.08	30.77	27.92	25.46	16
17	78.49	68.41	59.95	52.82	46.80	41.68	37.32	33.59	30.38	27.61	25.21	17
18	75.93	66.39	58.35	51.56	45.80	40.89	36.69	33.09	29.98	27.29	24.96	18
19	73.42	64.40	56.78	50.31	44.80	40.10	36.06	32.58	29.58	26.97	24.70	19
20	70.97	62.45	55.22	49.07	43.81	39.30	35.42	32.07	29.16	26.64	24.43	20
21	68.57	60.53	53.68	47.83	42.82	38.50	34.78	31.55	28.74	26.30	24.15	21
22	66.21	58.63	52.16	46.60	41.82	37.70	34.13	31.02	28.31	25.95	23.87	22
23	63.90	56.77	50.65	45.38	40.83	36.89	33.47	30.49	27.88	25.59	23.57	23
24	61.64	54.93	49.15	44.16	39.84	36.08	32.81	29.94	27.43	25.22	23.27	24
25	59.43	53.12	47.68	42.95	38.85	35.27	32.14	29.39	26.98	24.85	22.96	25
26	57.26	51.35	46.22	41.75	37.86	34.45	31.46	28.84	26.52	24.47	22.65	26
27	55.14	49.60	44.77	40.56	36.87	33.63	30.78	28.27	26.05	24.07	22.32	27
28	53.06	47.87	43.34	39.37	35.88	32.81	30.10	27.70	25.57	23.67	21.98	28
29	51.02	46.17	41.92	38.18	34.89	31.98	29.40	27.11	25.08	23.26	21.63	29
30	49.03	44.50	40.52	37.01	33.90	31.15	28.70	26.52	24.58	22.84	21.28	30
31	47.08	42.86	39.14	35.84	32.92	30.32	28.00	25.93	24.07	22.41	20.91	31
32	45.17	41.25	37.78	34.69	31.94	29.49	27.29	25.33	23.56	21.97	20.54	32
33	43.31	39.67	36.43	33.54	30.96	28.65	26.58	24.72	23.04	21.53	20.16	33
34	41.48	38.11	35.10	32.40	29.99	27.81	25.86	24.10	22.51	21.07	19.77	34
35	39.69	36.57	33.78	31.27	29.01	26.97	25.14	23.48	21.97	20.60	19.36	35
36	37.94	35.06	32.47	30.14	28.03	26.13	24.41	22.84	21.42	20.13	18.95	36
37	36.22	33.57	31.18	29.02	27.06	25.28	23.67	22.20	20.86	19.64	18.52	37
38	34.54	32.11	29.90	27.90	26.08	24.43	22.92	21.55	20.29	19.13	18.08	38
39	32.89	30.66	28.64	26.79	25.11	23.57	22.17	20.88	19.70	18.62	17.62	39
40	31.27	29.24	27.38	25.69	24.13	22.71	21.41	20.21	19.11	18.09	17.16	40
41	29.69	27.84	26.14	24.59	23.16	21.85	20.64	19.53	18.50	17.55	16.68	41
42	28.14	26.46	24.92	23.50	22.19	20.98	19.87	18.84	17.88	17.00	16.18	42
43	26.62	25.10	23.70	22.41	21.22	20.11	19.09	18.14	17.26	16.44	15.68	43
44	25.13	23.77	22.50	21.33	20.25	19.24	18.30	17.43	16.62	15.86	15.16	44
45	23.68	22.45	21.32	20.26	19.28	18.36	17.51	16.71	15.97	15.27	14.62	45
46	22.25	21.16	20.14	19.19	18.31	17.48	16.71	15.98	15.30	14.67	14.07	46
47	20.86	19.89	18.98	18.14	17.34	16.60	15.90	15.24	14.63	14.05	13.50	47
48	19.49	18.64	17.84	17.08	16.38	15.71	15.09	14.50	13.94	13.42	12.92	48
49	18.15	17.41	16.70	16.04	15.41	14.82	14.27	13.74	13.24	12.77	12.33	49
50	16.85	16.20	15.58	15.00	14.46	13.94	13.44	12.98	12.53	12.11	11.71	50
51	15.57	15.01	14.48	13.98	13.50	13.04	12.61	12.20	11.81	11.44	11.09	51
52	14.32	13.84	13.39	12.95	12.54	12.15	11.77	11.42	11.08	10.75	10.44	52
53	13.09	12.69	12.30	11.94	11.59	11.25	10.93	10.62	10.33	10.05	9.78	53
54	11.89	11.56	11.24	10.93	10.63	10.35	10.08	9.82	9.57	9.33	9.10	54
55	10.71	10.44	10.18	9.92	9.68	9.45	9.22	9.00	8.79	8.59	8.40	55
56	9.56	9.34	9.13	8.93	8.73	8.54	8.35	8.17	8.00	7.84	7.67	56
57	8.43	8.26	8.09	7.93	7.77	7.62	7.47	7.33	7.19	7.06	6.93	57
58	7.32	7.19	7.06	6.94	6.82	6.70	6.59	6.48	6.37	6.26	6.16	58
59	6.22	6.13	6.03	5.94	5.85	5.77	5.68	5.60	5.52	5.45	5.37	59
60	5.14	5.08	5.01	4.95	4.89	4.83	4.77	4.71	4.66	4.60	4.55	60
61	4.09	4.04	4.00	3.96	3.92	3.89	3.85	3.81	3.77	3.74	3.70	61
62	3.04	3.02	3.00	2.98	2.95	2.93	2.91	2.89	2.87	2.85	2.83	62
63	2.02	2.01	2.00	1.99	1.98	1.97	1.96	1.95	1.94	1.93	1.92	63
64	1.00	1.00	1.00	1.00	0.99	0.99	0.99	0.99	0.98	0.98	0.98	64

Table 10: Multipliers for loss of earnings to pension age 65 (females)

Age at date of trial	Multiplier calculated with allowance for projected mortality from the 2008–based population projections and rate of return of											Age at date of trial
	-2.0%	*-1.5%*	*-1.0%*	*-0.5%*	*0.0%*	*0.5%*	*1.0%*	*1.5%*	*2.0%*	*2.5%*	*3.0%*	
16	82.26	71.41	62.34	54.74	48.34	42.93	38.33	34.41	31.05	28.16	25.66	16
17	79.62	69.34	60.72	53.47	47.34	42.14	37.71	33.91	30.66	27.85	25.41	17
18	77.03	67.31	59.12	52.20	46.34	41.35	37.08	33.42	30.26	27.53	25.16	18
19	74.50	65.30	57.53	50.95	45.34	40.55	36.45	32.91	29.86	27.21	24.91	19
20	72.02	63.33	55.96	49.70	44.34	39.75	35.81	32.40	29.45	26.88	24.64	20
21	69.59	61.39	54.41	48.45	43.34	38.95	35.16	31.88	29.03	26.54	24.37	21
22	67.20	59.48	52.87	47.21	42.34	38.15	34.51	31.35	28.60	26.20	24.08	22
23	64.87	57.59	51.35	45.98	41.35	37.33	33.85	30.82	28.16	25.84	23.79	23
24	62.58	55.73	49.84	44.75	40.35	36.52	33.19	30.27	27.72	25.47	23.49	24
25	60.34	53.91	48.35	43.53	39.35	35.70	32.51	29.72	27.27	25.10	23.19	25
26	58.14	52.11	46.87	42.32	38.35	34.88	31.84	29.16	26.80	24.72	22.87	26
27	55.99	50.33	45.41	41.11	37.35	34.05	31.15	28.60	26.33	24.33	22.54	27
28	53.88	48.59	43.96	39.91	36.36	33.23	30.46	28.02	25.85	23.93	22.21	28
29	51.82	46.87	42.53	38.72	35.36	32.39	29.77	27.44	25.36	23.51	21.86	29
30	49.80	45.18	41.12	37.53	34.36	31.56	29.06	26.84	24.87	23.09	21.51	30
31	47.82	43.52	39.72	36.35	33.37	30.72	28.35	26.25	24.36	22.66	21.14	31
32	45.88	41.88	38.33	35.18	32.38	29.87	27.64	25.64	23.84	22.22	20.77	32
33	43.98	40.27	36.96	34.01	31.38	29.03	26.92	25.02	23.31	21.77	20.38	33
34	42.12	38.68	35.60	32.85	30.39	28.18	26.19	24.39	22.78	21.31	19.98	34
35	40.30	37.11	34.26	31.70	29.40	27.32	25.45	23.76	22.23	20.84	19.57	35
36	38.51	35.58	32.93	30.56	28.41	26.47	24.71	23.12	21.67	20.35	19.15	36
37	36.76	34.06	31.62	29.42	27.42	25.61	23.96	22.47	21.10	19.86	18.72	37
38	35.05	32.57	30.32	28.28	26.43	24.74	23.21	21.81	20.52	19.35	18.28	38
39	33.38	31.10	29.04	27.16	25.44	23.88	22.44	21.14	19.93	18.83	17.82	39
40	31.73	29.66	27.76	26.04	24.45	23.00	21.68	20.46	19.33	18.30	17.35	40
41	30.12	28.24	26.51	24.92	23.47	22.13	20.90	19.77	18.72	17.76	16.86	41
42	28.55	26.84	25.26	23.81	22.48	21.25	20.12	19.07	18.10	17.20	16.37	42
43	27.01	25.46	24.03	22.71	21.50	20.37	19.33	18.36	17.46	16.63	15.85	43
44	25.49	24.10	22.81	21.62	20.51	19.48	18.53	17.64	16.82	16.05	15.33	44
45	24.02	22.77	21.61	20.53	19.53	18.60	17.73	16.92	16.16	15.45	14.79	45
46	22.57	21.46	20.42	19.45	18.55	17.71	16.92	16.18	15.49	14.84	14.23	46
47	21.15	20.17	19.24	18.38	17.57	16.81	16.10	15.43	14.81	14.22	13.66	47
48	19.77	18.90	18.08	17.31	16.59	15.92	15.28	14.68	14.11	13.58	13.08	48
49	18.41	17.65	16.93	16.26	15.62	15.02	14.45	13.91	13.41	12.93	12.47	49
50	17.08	16.42	15.80	15.21	14.65	14.12	13.62	13.14	12.69	12.26	11.85	50
51	15.78	15.21	14.67	14.16	13.67	13.21	12.77	12.35	11.96	11.58	11.22	51
52	14.51	14.02	13.56	13.12	12.70	12.30	11.92	11.56	11.21	10.88	10.56	52
53	13.26	12.85	12.46	12.09	11.73	11.39	11.06	10.75	10.45	10.17	9.89	53
54	12.04	11.70	11.37	11.06	10.76	10.47	10.20	9.93	9.68	9.43	9.20	54
55	10.84	10.56	10.30	10.04	9.79	9.55	9.32	9.10	8.89	8.68	8.49	55
56	9.67	9.44	9.23	9.02	8.82	8.63	8.44	8.26	8.09	7.92	7.75	56
57	8.52	8.34	8.17	8.01	7.85	7.70	7.55	7.40	7.26	7.13	7.00	57
58	7.39	7.25	7.13	7.00	6.88	6.76	6.65	6.53	6.43	6.32	6.22	58
59	6.28	6.18	6.09	5.99	5.91	5.82	5.73	5.65	5.57	5.49	5.41	59
60	5.19	5.12	5.05	4.99	4.93	4.87	4.81	4.75	4.69	4.64	4.58	60
61	4.11	4.07	4.03	3.99	3.95	3.91	3.87	3.84	3.80	3.76	3.73	61
62	3.06	3.04	3.02	2.99	2.97	2.95	2.93	2.91	2.88	2.86	2.84	62
63	2.03	2.02	2.01	2.00	1.99	1.98	1.97	1.96	1.95	1.94	1.93	63
64	1.01	1.00	1.00	1.00	1.00	0.99	0.99	0.99	0.99	0.98	0.98	64

Table 11: Multipliers for loss of earnings to pension age 70 (males)

Age at date of trial	Multiplier calculated with allowance for projected mortality from the 2008–based population projections and rate of return of											Age at date of trial
	−2.0%	−1.5%	−1.0%	−0.5%	0.0%	0.5%	1.0%	1.5%	2.0%	2.5%	3.0%	
16	93.75	80.18	69.05	59.87	52.26	45.93	40.62	36.16	32.38	29.18	26.44	16
17	90.86	77.97	67.35	58.57	51.26	45.15	40.02	35.69	32.02	28.89	26.22	17
18	88.04	75.80	65.68	57.27	50.25	44.37	39.41	35.22	31.65	28.61	25.99	18
19	85.28	73.67	64.03	55.99	49.26	43.59	38.81	34.74	31.28	28.31	25.76	19
20	82.58	71.57	62.39	54.71	48.26	42.81	38.19	34.26	30.90	28.01	25.52	20
21	79.94	69.50	60.78	53.44	47.26	42.03	37.58	33.78	30.52	27.71	25.28	21
22	77.35	67.47	59.17	52.18	46.27	41.24	36.95	33.28	30.12	27.39	25.03	22
23	74.81	65.46	57.59	50.93	45.27	40.45	36.32	32.78	29.72	27.07	24.77	23
24	72.32	63.49	56.02	49.68	44.27	39.65	35.68	32.26	29.31	26.74	24.50	24
25	69.89	61.55	54.47	48.44	43.28	38.85	35.04	31.75	28.89	26.40	24.23	25
26	67.50	59.64	52.93	47.20	42.29	38.05	34.39	31.22	28.47	26.06	23.95	26
27	65.17	57.76	51.42	45.98	41.29	37.25	33.74	30.69	28.03	25.70	23.66	27
28	62.88	55.91	49.92	44.76	40.30	36.44	33.08	30.15	27.59	25.34	23.36	28
29	60.64	54.08	48.43	43.54	39.31	35.63	32.41	29.61	27.14	24.97	23.05	29
30	58.45	52.29	46.96	42.34	38.32	34.81	31.74	29.05	26.68	24.59	22.74	30
31	56.31	50.53	45.51	41.14	37.33	34.00	31.07	28.49	26.22	24.20	22.42	31
32	54.21	48.80	44.08	39.96	36.35	33.18	30.39	27.93	25.75	23.81	22.09	32
33	52.17	47.10	42.67	38.79	35.37	32.37	29.71	27.36	25.27	23.41	21.75	33
34	50.16	45.43	41.28	37.62	34.40	31.55	29.02	26.78	24.79	23.00	21.41	34
35	48.20	43.78	39.89	36.46	33.42	30.73	28.33	26.20	24.29	22.58	21.05	35
36	46.28	42.16	38.53	35.31	32.45	29.90	27.63	25.60	23.79	22.15	20.69	36
37	44.39	40.57	37.18	34.16	31.47	29.07	26.93	25.00	23.27	21.72	20.31	37
38	42.55	39.00	35.84	33.02	30.50	28.24	26.21	24.39	22.75	21.27	19.93	38
39	40.74	37.45	34.51	31.88	29.52	27.40	25.49	23.77	22.21	20.80	19.53	39
40	38.96	35.92	33.20	30.75	28.55	26.56	24.76	23.14	21.67	20.33	19.12	40
41	37.23	34.42	31.90	29.63	27.57	25.71	24.03	22.50	21.11	19.85	18.70	41
42	35.53	32.95	30.62	28.51	26.60	24.87	23.29	21.86	20.55	19.36	18.26	42
43	33.86	31.50	29.35	27.40	25.63	24.02	22.55	21.20	19.98	18.85	17.82	43
44	32.23	30.07	28.10	26.30	24.66	23.17	21.80	20.54	19.39	18.34	17.36	44
45	30.64	28.66	26.86	25.21	23.70	22.31	21.04	19.87	18.80	17.81	16.90	45
46	29.08	27.28	25.63	24.12	22.73	21.45	20.28	19.19	18.19	17.27	16.41	46
47	27.55	25.92	24.42	23.04	21.77	20.59	19.51	18.51	17.58	16.72	15.92	47
48	26.06	24.58	23.22	21.97	20.81	19.73	18.74	17.81	16.95	16.16	15.41	48
49	24.60	23.27	22.04	20.91	19.85	18.87	17.96	17.11	16.32	15.58	14.90	49
50	23.17	21.98	20.88	19.85	18.90	18.01	17.18	16.40	15.68	15.00	14.37	50
51	21.78	20.72	19.73	18.81	17.95	17.14	16.39	15.69	15.02	14.40	13.82	51
52	20.42	19.48	18.60	17.78	17.00	16.28	15.60	14.96	14.36	13.80	13.27	52
53	19.09	18.26	17.48	16.75	16.06	15.41	14.81	14.23	13.69	13.18	12.70	53
54	17.79	17.06	16.38	15.73	15.12	14.55	14.01	13.49	13.01	12.55	12.11	54
55	16.51	15.88	15.29	14.72	14.19	13.68	13.20	12.75	12.31	11.90	11.52	55
56	15.27	14.73	14.21	13.72	13.25	12.81	12.39	11.99	11.61	11.25	10.90	56
57	14.05	13.59	13.14	12.72	12.32	11.94	11.57	11.22	10.89	10.57	10.27	57
58	12.85	12.46	12.09	11.73	11.39	11.06	10.75	10.45	10.16	9.88	9.62	58
59	11.68	11.35	11.04	10.74	10.45	10.17	9.91	9.66	9.41	9.18	8.95	59
60	10.52	10.26	10.00	9.75	9.51	9.28	9.06	8.85	8.65	8.45	8.26	60
61	9.39	9.18	8.97	8.77	8.58	8.39	8.21	8.04	7.87	7.71	7.55	61
62	8.28	8.11	7.95	7.79	7.64	7.49	7.35	7.21	7.07	6.94	6.82	62
63	7.19	7.06	6.94	6.82	6.70	6.59	6.48	6.37	6.27	6.16	6.06	63
64	6.12	6.03	5.94	5.85	5.77	5.68	5.60	5.52	5.44	5.36	5.29	64
65	5.07	5.01	4.95	4.89	4.83	4.77	4.71	4.65	4.60	4.54	4.49	65
66	4.04	4.00	3.96	3.92	3.88	3.84	3.81	3.77	3.73	3.70	3.66	66
67	3.02	3.00	2.97	2.95	2.93	2.91	2.89	2.86	2.84	2.82	2.80	67
68	2.01	2.00	1.99	1.98	1.97	1.96	1.95	1.94	1.93	1.92	1.91	68
69	1.00	1.00	1.00	0.99	0.99	0.99	0.99	0.98	0.98	0.98	0.98	69

Table 12: Multipliers for loss of earnings to pension age 70 (females)

Age at date of trial	Multiplier calculated with allowance for projected mortality from the 2008–based population projections and rate of return of											Age at date of trial
	-2.0%	*-1.5%*	*-1.0%*	*-0.5%*	*0.0%*	*0.5%*	*1.0%*	*1.5%*	*2.0%*	*2.5%*	*3.0%*	
16	95.47	81.58	70.18	60.79	53.01	46.54	41.12	36.57	32.73	29.47	26.68	16
17	92.56	79.35	68.47	59.48	52.01	45.76	40.53	36.11	32.37	29.19	26.46	17
18	89.71	77.16	66.79	58.18	51.00	44.99	39.93	35.65	32.01	28.91	26.24	18
19	86.92	75.00	65.12	56.89	50.00	44.21	39.32	35.18	31.64	28.62	26.02	19
20	84.18	72.88	63.47	55.61	49.00	43.43	38.71	34.70	31.27	28.32	25.79	20
21	81.50	70.79	61.84	54.33	48.00	42.64	38.09	34.21	30.88	28.02	25.55	21
22	78.87	68.73	60.22	53.06	47.00	41.85	37.47	33.72	30.49	27.71	25.30	22
23	76.30	66.70	58.62	51.79	46.00	41.06	36.84	33.22	30.09	27.39	25.04	23
24	73.77	64.70	57.04	50.53	44.99	40.26	36.20	32.71	29.68	27.06	24.78	24
25	71.30	62.73	55.47	49.28	43.99	39.46	35.56	32.19	29.27	26.73	24.51	25
26	68.88	60.80	53.91	48.03	42.99	38.65	34.91	31.67	28.85	26.39	24.23	26
27	66.51	58.89	52.38	46.80	41.99	37.85	34.26	31.13	28.41	26.03	23.95	27
28	64.19	57.01	50.86	45.56	40.99	37.03	33.59	30.60	27.98	25.68	23.65	28
29	61.91	55.17	49.36	44.34	39.99	36.22	32.93	30.05	27.53	25.31	23.35	29
30	59.68	53.35	47.87	43.12	39.00	35.40	32.25	29.50	27.07	24.93	23.04	30
31	57.50	51.56	46.40	41.91	38.00	34.58	31.58	28.94	26.61	24.55	22.72	31
32	55.37	49.79	44.94	40.71	37.01	33.75	30.89	28.37	26.13	24.15	22.39	32
33	53.27	48.06	43.51	39.52	36.01	32.92	30.20	27.79	25.65	23.75	22.05	33
34	51.22	46.35	42.08	38.33	35.02	32.09	29.50	27.21	25.16	23.34	21.70	34
35	49.22	44.67	40.67	37.14	34.02	31.26	28.80	26.61	24.66	22.91	21.35	35
36	47.25	43.02	39.28	35.97	33.03	30.42	28.09	26.01	24.15	22.48	20.98	36
37	45.32	41.39	37.90	34.80	32.04	29.58	27.37	25.40	23.63	22.04	20.60	37
38	43.44	39.79	36.54	33.64	31.05	28.73	26.65	24.78	23.10	21.58	20.21	38
39	41.59	38.21	35.19	32.48	30.06	27.88	25.92	24.16	22.56	21.12	19.81	39
40	39.78	36.66	33.85	31.34	29.07	27.03	25.19	23.52	22.01	20.65	19.40	40
41	38.01	35.13	32.53	30.20	28.08	26.18	24.45	22.88	21.46	20.16	18.98	41
42	36.28	33.62	31.23	29.06	27.10	25.32	23.70	22.23	20.89	19.66	18.54	42
43	34.58	32.14	29.94	27.93	26.11	24.46	22.95	21.57	20.31	19.15	18.10	43
44	32.92	30.69	28.66	26.81	25.13	23.59	22.19	20.90	19.72	18.63	17.64	44
45	31.29	29.26	27.40	25.70	24.15	22.73	21.42	20.22	19.12	18.10	17.17	45
46	29.70	27.85	26.15	24.60	23.17	21.86	20.65	19.54	18.51	17.56	16.68	46
47	28.15	26.47	24.92	23.50	22.19	20.99	19.87	18.84	17.89	17.01	16.19	47
48	26.63	25.11	23.71	22.41	21.22	20.11	19.09	18.14	17.26	16.44	15.68	48
49	25.14	23.77	22.51	21.34	20.25	19.24	18.30	17.43	16.62	15.86	15.16	49
50	23.68	22.46	21.32	20.27	19.28	18.36	17.51	16.71	15.97	15.27	14.62	50
51	22.26	21.17	20.15	19.20	18.31	17.49	16.71	15.99	15.31	14.67	14.07	51
52	20.87	19.90	18.99	18.14	17.35	16.60	15.91	15.25	14.63	14.05	13.51	52
53	19.50	18.65	17.85	17.09	16.39	15.72	15.09	14.50	13.95	13.42	12.93	53
54	18.17	17.42	16.72	16.05	15.43	14.83	14.28	13.75	13.25	12.78	12.33	54
55	16.86	16.21	15.60	15.02	14.47	13.95	13.45	12.99	12.54	12.12	11.72	55
56	15.58	15.02	14.49	13.99	13.51	13.05	12.62	12.21	11.82	11.45	11.09	56
57	14.33	13.85	13.40	12.96	12.55	12.16	11.78	11.43	11.09	10.76	10.45	57
58	13.10	12.70	12.31	11.95	11.59	11.26	10.94	10.63	10.34	10.05	9.78	58
59	11.89	11.56	11.24	10.93	10.64	10.35	10.08	9.82	9.57	9.33	9.10	59
60	10.71	10.44	10.18	9.92	9.68	9.44	9.22	9.00	8.79	8.59	8.39	60
61	9.55	9.33	9.12	8.92	8.72	8.53	8.35	8.17	8.00	7.83	7.67	61
62	8.42	8.25	8.08	7.92	7.76	7.61	7.46	7.32	7.18	7.05	6.92	62
63	7.30	7.17	7.05	6.92	6.80	6.69	6.57	6.47	6.36	6.25	6.15	63
64	6.21	6.12	6.02	5.93	5.85	5.76	5.68	5.59	5.51	5.44	5.36	64
65	5.14	5.07	5.01	4.95	4.89	4.83	4.77	4.71	4.65	4.60	4.54	65
66	4.08	4.04	4.00	3.96	3.92	3.88	3.85	3.81	3.77	3.74	3.70	66
67	3.04	3.02	3.00	2.98	2.95	2.93	2.91	2.89	2.87	2.85	2.83	67
68	2.02	2.01	2.00	1.99	1.98	1.97	1.96	1.95	1.94	1.93	1.92	68
69	1.00	1.00	1.00	1.00	0.99	0.99	0.99	0.99	0.98	0.98	0.98	69

Table 13: Multipliers for loss of earnings to pension age 75 (males)

Age at date of trial	Multiplier calculated with allowance for projected mortality from the 2008–based population projections and rate of return of											Age at date of trial
	–2.0%	**–1.5%**	**–1.0%**	**–0.5%**	**0.0%**	**0.5%**	**1.0%**	**1.5%**	**2.0%**	**2.5%**	**3.0%**	
16	107.05	90.16	76.55	65.51	56.51	49.13	43.04	37.99	33.77	30.23	27.24	16
17	103.88	87.79	74.76	64.17	55.50	48.37	42.46	37.55	33.44	29.97	27.04	17
18	100.78	85.45	73.01	62.84	54.49	47.60	41.88	37.10	33.10	29.71	26.84	18
19	97.75	83.16	71.27	61.52	53.49	46.83	41.29	36.65	32.75	29.44	26.63	19
20	94.79	80.91	69.55	60.21	52.48	46.06	40.70	36.20	32.40	29.17	26.42	20
21	91.89	78.69	67.86	58.91	51.48	45.29	40.11	35.74	32.04	28.89	26.20	21
22	89.04	76.51	66.17	57.61	50.48	44.52	39.50	35.27	31.67	28.61	25.98	22
23	86.25	74.36	64.51	56.32	49.48	43.74	38.89	34.79	31.30	28.31	25.74	23
24	83.52	72.24	62.86	55.04	48.48	42.95	38.28	34.31	30.92	28.01	25.51	24
25	80.85	70.15	61.23	53.76	47.48	42.17	37.66	33.82	30.53	27.70	25.26	25
26	78.23	68.10	59.63	52.50	46.48	41.38	37.04	33.32	30.14	27.39	25.01	26
27	75.67	66.09	58.03	51.24	45.48	40.59	36.41	32.82	29.74	27.07	24.75	27
28	73.16	64.10	56.46	49.99	44.48	39.79	35.77	32.31	29.32	26.74	24.48	28
29	70.70	62.14	54.90	48.74	43.49	38.99	35.13	31.79	28.91	26.40	24.21	29
30	68.29	60.22	53.35	47.50	42.49	38.19	34.48	31.27	28.48	26.05	23.93	30
31	65.95	58.33	51.84	46.28	41.50	37.39	33.83	30.74	28.05	25.70	23.64	31
32	63.65	56.48	50.34	45.06	40.52	36.59	33.18	30.21	27.62	25.35	23.35	32
33	61.41	54.66	48.86	43.86	39.54	35.79	32.52	29.67	27.18	24.98	23.05	33
34	59.22	52.87	47.40	42.66	38.56	34.98	31.86	29.13	26.73	24.61	22.74	34
35	57.06	51.11	45.95	41.47	37.58	34.17	31.19	28.58	26.27	24.23	22.43	35
36	54.96	49.37	44.52	40.29	36.60	33.36	30.52	28.02	25.80	23.84	22.10	36
37	52.90	47.67	43.11	39.12	35.62	32.55	29.84	27.45	25.33	23.45	21.77	37
38	50.87	45.98	41.70	37.95	34.64	31.73	29.16	26.87	24.85	23.04	21.42	38
39	48.89	44.33	40.31	36.78	33.67	30.91	28.46	26.29	24.35	22.62	21.07	39
40	46.95	42.69	38.94	35.62	32.69	30.08	27.76	25.70	23.85	22.19	20.70	40
41	45.05	41.09	37.58	34.47	31.71	29.25	27.06	25.10	23.34	21.75	20.33	41
42	43.19	39.51	36.24	33.33	30.74	28.42	26.35	24.49	22.81	21.31	19.95	42
43	41.37	37.96	34.91	32.20	29.77	27.59	25.63	23.87	22.29	20.85	19.55	43
44	39.59	36.43	33.60	31.07	28.80	26.76	24.91	23.25	21.75	20.39	19.15	44
45	37.85	34.93	32.31	29.95	27.83	25.92	24.19	22.62	21.20	19.91	18.73	45
46	36.14	33.45	31.03	28.84	26.87	25.08	23.46	21.98	20.64	19.42	18.31	46
47	34.47	32.00	29.76	27.74	25.90	24.24	22.72	21.34	20.08	18.93	17.87	47
48	32.84	30.58	28.52	26.65	24.95	23.39	21.98	20.69	19.50	18.42	17.42	48
49	31.25	29.18	27.29	25.56	23.99	22.55	21.24	20.03	18.92	17.90	16.97	49
50	29.70	27.81	26.07	24.49	23.04	21.71	20.49	19.37	18.33	17.38	16.50	50
51	28.18	26.46	24.88	23.43	22.10	20.87	19.74	18.70	17.74	16.85	16.03	51
52	26.70	25.14	23.70	22.38	21.16	20.03	18.99	18.03	17.13	16.31	15.54	52
53	25.26	23.85	22.54	21.34	20.23	19.19	18.24	17.35	16.52	15.76	15.04	53
54	23.85	22.58	21.40	20.31	19.30	18.35	17.48	16.66	15.90	15.20	14.53	54
55	22.48	21.34	20.28	19.29	18.37	17.52	16.72	15.98	15.28	14.63	14.02	55
56	21.13	20.12	19.17	18.28	17.46	16.68	15.96	15.28	14.64	14.05	13.49	56
57	19.82	18.92	18.07	17.28	16.54	15.85	15.19	14.58	14.00	13.46	12.95	57
58	18.53	17.74	16.99	16.29	15.63	15.00	14.42	13.86	13.34	12.85	12.39	58
59	17.27	16.57	15.91	15.29	14.71	14.16	13.63	13.14	12.67	12.23	11.81	59
60	16.03	15.42	14.85	14.30	13.79	13.30	12.84	12.40	11.99	11.60	11.22	60
61	14.81	14.29	13.79	13.32	12.87	12.45	12.04	11.66	11.29	10.95	10.61	61
62	13.62	13.18	12.75	12.35	11.96	11.59	11.24	10.91	10.59	10.28	9.99	62
63	12.46	12.09	11.73	11.38	11.05	10.74	10.44	10.15	9.88	9.61	9.36	63
64	11.33	11.02	10.72	10.43	10.15	9.89	9.63	9.39	9.15	8.93	8.71	64
65	10.22	9.97	9.72	9.48	9.25	9.03	8.82	8.61	8.42	8.23	8.04	65
66	9.14	8.93	8.73	8.54	8.36	8.18	8.00	7.83	7.67	7.52	7.36	66
67	8.08	7.92	7.76	7.61	7.46	7.32	7.18	7.04	6.91	6.79	6.66	67
68	7.04	6.91	6.79	6.67	6.56	6.45	6.34	6.24	6.14	6.04	5.94	68
69	6.01	5.92	5.83	5.74	5.66	5.58	5.50	5.42	5.34	5.27	5.19	69
70	4.99	4.93	4.87	4.81	4.75	4.69	4.63	4.58	4.52	4.47	4.42	70
71	3.98	3.94	3.90	3.86	3.83	3.79	3.75	3.72	3.68	3.65	3.61	71
72	2.98	2.96	2.94	2.92	2.89	2.87	2.85	2.83	2.81	2.79	2.77	72
73	1.99	1.98	1.97	1.96	1.95	1.94	1.93	1.92	1.91	1.90	1.89	73
74	1.00	0.99	0.99	0.99	0.99	0.98	0.98	0.98	0.98	0.97	0.97	74

Table 14: Multipliers for loss of earnings to pension age 75 (females)

Age at date of trial	Multiplier calculated with allowance for projected mortality from the 2008–based population projections and rate of return of											Age at date of trial
	-2.0%	**-1.5%**	**-1.0%**	**-0.5%**	**0.0%**	**0.5%**	**1.0%**	**1.5%**	**2.0%**	**2.5%**	**3.0%**	
16	109.63	92.19	78.15	66.79	57.53	49.95	43.70	38.52	34.21	30.59	27.53	16
17	106.42	89.80	76.36	65.44	56.52	49.19	43.13	38.09	33.88	30.34	27.34	17
18	103.28	87.44	74.59	64.11	55.51	48.43	42.55	37.65	33.55	30.08	27.15	18
19	100.20	85.12	72.84	62.78	54.51	47.66	41.97	37.21	33.21	29.82	26.95	19
20	97.19	82.84	71.11	61.47	53.50	46.90	41.38	36.76	32.86	29.56	26.74	20
21	94.24	80.59	69.39	60.15	52.50	46.13	40.79	36.30	32.51	29.28	26.53	21
22	91.35	78.38	67.69	58.85	51.49	45.35	40.19	35.84	32.15	29.00	26.31	22
23	88.51	76.19	66.01	57.55	50.49	44.57	39.58	35.37	31.78	28.71	26.08	23
24	85.73	74.04	64.34	56.25	49.48	43.79	38.97	34.89	31.40	28.42	25.85	24
25	83.01	71.93	62.69	54.97	48.48	43.00	38.35	34.40	31.02	28.12	25.61	25
26	80.34	69.84	61.06	53.69	47.47	42.21	37.73	33.91	30.63	27.81	25.37	26
27	77.73	67.79	59.45	52.42	46.47	41.41	37.10	33.41	30.23	27.49	25.11	27
28	75.17	65.77	57.85	51.15	45.46	40.62	36.47	32.90	29.83	27.17	24.85	28
29	72.67	63.79	56.27	49.90	44.46	39.82	35.83	32.39	29.42	26.84	24.59	29
30	70.22	61.83	54.71	48.65	43.46	39.01	35.18	31.87	29.00	26.50	24.31	30
31	67.82	59.91	53.17	47.40	42.46	38.20	34.53	31.34	28.57	26.15	24.03	31
32	65.47	58.01	51.64	46.17	41.46	37.40	33.87	30.81	28.13	25.79	23.74	32
33	63.16	56.15	50.13	44.94	40.46	36.58	33.21	30.26	27.69	25.43	23.44	33
34	60.91	54.31	48.63	43.72	39.47	35.77	32.54	29.72	27.24	25.06	23.13	34
35	58.70	52.51	47.15	42.51	38.47	34.95	31.86	29.16	26.78	24.68	22.82	35
36	56.54	50.73	45.69	41.30	37.47	34.12	31.18	28.59	26.31	24.29	22.49	36
37	54.42	48.98	44.24	40.10	36.48	33.30	30.49	28.02	25.83	23.89	22.16	37
38	52.35	47.26	42.81	38.91	35.49	32.47	29.80	27.44	25.34	23.48	21.81	38
39	50.32	45.57	41.40	37.73	34.49	31.64	29.10	26.85	24.85	23.06	21.46	39
40	48.33	43.90	40.00	36.55	33.50	30.80	28.40	26.26	24.35	22.63	21.10	40
41	46.38	42.26	38.61	35.38	32.51	29.96	27.69	25.65	23.83	22.20	20.73	41
42	44.48	40.64	37.24	34.22	31.53	29.12	26.97	25.04	23.31	21.75	20.34	42
43	42.61	39.06	35.89	33.06	30.54	28.28	26.25	24.42	22.78	21.29	19.95	43
44	40.79	37.49	34.55	31.92	29.55	27.43	25.52	23.79	22.24	20.82	19.55	44
45	39.00	35.96	33.23	30.78	28.57	26.58	24.79	23.16	21.69	20.35	19.13	45
46	37.26	34.45	31.93	29.65	27.59	25.73	24.05	22.52	21.13	19.86	18.71	46
47	35.55	32.97	30.64	28.53	26.62	24.88	23.30	21.87	20.56	19.36	18.27	47
48	33.88	31.51	29.37	27.42	25.64	24.03	22.56	21.21	19.98	18.86	17.83	48
49	32.25	30.08	28.11	26.31	24.67	23.18	21.81	20.55	19.40	18.34	17.37	49
50	30.66	28.68	26.87	25.22	23.71	22.32	21.05	19.88	18.81	17.82	16.90	50
51	29.10	27.30	25.65	24.14	22.75	21.47	20.29	19.20	18.20	17.28	16.42	51
52	27.58	25.94	24.44	23.06	21.78	20.61	19.52	18.52	17.59	16.73	15.93	52
53	26.08	24.61	23.25	21.99	20.83	19.75	18.75	17.83	16.97	16.17	15.43	53
54	24.63	23.30	22.07	20.93	19.87	18.89	17.98	17.13	16.34	15.60	14.91	54
55	23.20	22.01	20.91	19.88	18.92	18.03	17.20	16.42	15.69	15.02	14.38	55
56	21.81	20.75	19.76	18.83	17.97	17.16	16.41	15.70	15.04	14.42	13.84	56
57	20.45	19.50	18.62	17.80	17.02	16.30	15.62	14.98	14.38	13.81	13.28	57
58	19.11	18.28	17.50	16.77	16.08	15.43	14.82	14.25	13.70	13.19	12.71	58
59	17.80	17.07	16.39	15.74	15.13	14.56	14.02	13.50	13.02	12.56	12.12	59
60	16.52	15.88	15.29	14.72	14.19	13.68	13.20	12.75	12.32	11.91	11.52	60
61	15.26	14.71	14.20	13.71	13.24	12.80	12.38	11.98	11.60	11.24	10.89	61
62	14.03	13.56	13.12	12.70	12.30	11.92	11.56	11.21	10.88	10.56	10.26	62
63	12.83	12.43	12.06	11.70	11.36	11.04	10.72	10.42	10.14	9.86	9.60	63
64	11.65	11.33	11.01	10.71	10.43	10.15	9.89	9.63	9.39	9.16	8.93	64
65	10.50	10.24	9.98	9.73	9.50	9.27	9.05	8.84	8.63	8.43	8.24	65
66	9.38	9.16	8.96	8.76	8.57	8.38	8.20	8.03	7.86	7.70	7.54	66
67	8.28	8.11	7.95	7.79	7.64	7.49	7.35	7.21	7.07	6.94	6.81	67
68	7.19	7.07	6.94	6.82	6.70	6.59	6.48	6.37	6.27	6.17	6.07	68
69	6.13	6.04	5.95	5.86	5.77	5.69	5.60	5.52	5.44	5.37	5.29	69
70	5.08	5.01	4.95	4.89	4.83	4.77	4.71	4.66	4.60	4.55	4.49	70
71	4.04	4.00	3.96	3.92	3.88	3.85	3.81	3.77	3.73	3.70	3.66	71
72	3.02	3.00	2.97	2.95	2.93	2.91	2.89	2.86	2.84	2.82	2.80	72
73	2.01	2.00	1.99	1.98	1.97	1.96	1.95	1.94	1.93	1.92	1.91	73
74	1.00	1.00	1.00	0.99	0.99	0.99	0.99	0.98	0.98	0.98	0.98	74

Table 15: Multipliers for loss of pension commencing age 50 (males)

Age at date of trial	Multiplier calculated with allowance for projected mortality from the 2008–based population projections and rate of return of											Age at date of trial
	−2.0%	−1.5%	−1.0%	−0.5%	0.0%	0.5%	1.0%	1.5%	2.0%	2.5%	3.0%	
0	179.64	121.70	83.09	57.16	39.61	27.64	19.42	13.74	9.78	7.00	5.04	0
1	176.24	120.05	82.40	56.99	39.70	27.85	19.67	13.99	10.01	7.20	5.21	1
2	172.05	117.83	81.32	56.54	39.59	27.92	19.83	14.17	10.19	7.37	5.36	2
3	167.93	115.64	80.24	56.09	39.49	27.99	19.98	14.35	10.37	7.54	5.51	3
4	163.90	113.48	79.16	55.63	39.37	28.06	20.13	14.53	10.56	7.72	5.67	4
5	159.97	111.36	78.10	55.18	39.26	28.12	20.28	14.72	10.75	7.89	5.83	5
6	156.12	109.27	77.05	54.73	39.14	28.19	20.43	14.91	10.94	8.08	5.99	6
7	152.36	107.22	76.01	54.28	39.03	28.25	20.59	15.10	11.14	8.26	6.16	7
8	148.69	105.21	74.99	53.83	38.91	28.32	20.74	15.29	11.33	8.45	6.34	8
9	145.10	103.23	73.98	53.39	38.80	28.38	20.90	15.48	11.54	8.65	6.52	9
10	141.59	101.28	72.97	52.95	38.68	28.44	21.05	15.68	11.74	8.84	6.70	10
11	138.17	99.37	71.98	52.51	38.56	28.51	21.21	15.87	11.95	9.05	6.89	11
12	134.83	97.50	71.01	52.07	38.44	28.57	21.36	16.07	12.16	9.26	7.08	12
13	131.57	95.66	70.04	51.64	38.33	28.63	21.52	16.28	12.38	9.47	7.28	13
14	128.40	93.86	69.10	51.21	38.21	28.70	21.68	16.48	12.60	9.69	7.48	14
15	125.31	92.10	68.16	50.79	38.10	28.76	21.85	16.69	12.82	9.91	7.69	15
16	122.29	90.37	67.24	50.38	37.99	28.83	22.01	16.90	13.05	10.14	7.91	16
17	119.35	88.68	66.34	49.96	37.88	28.89	22.17	17.12	13.29	10.37	8.13	17
18	116.49	87.02	65.46	49.56	37.77	28.96	22.34	17.34	13.53	10.61	8.36	18
19	113.71	85.41	64.59	49.16	37.67	29.03	22.52	17.56	13.77	10.86	8.60	19
20	111.01	83.83	63.74	48.78	37.57	29.11	22.69	17.79	14.02	11.11	8.85	20
21	108.37	82.28	62.90	48.39	37.46	29.18	22.87	18.02	14.28	11.37	9.10	21
22	105.78	80.76	62.06	48.00	37.36	29.26	23.04	18.25	14.53	11.63	9.36	22
23	103.25	79.25	61.24	47.62	37.26	29.33	23.22	18.49	14.80	11.90	9.62	23
24	100.79	77.78	60.42	47.24	37.16	29.40	23.40	18.73	15.06	12.18	9.90	24
25	98.39	76.35	59.63	46.86	37.06	29.48	23.58	18.97	15.34	12.46	10.18	25
26	96.06	74.95	58.85	46.50	36.96	29.56	23.77	19.22	15.62	12.76	10.47	26
27	93.80	73.57	58.08	46.14	36.87	29.64	23.96	19.47	15.90	13.06	10.77	27
28	91.57	72.22	57.32	45.77	36.77	29.71	24.14	19.72	16.19	13.36	11.08	28
29	89.39	70.88	56.56	45.41	36.68	29.79	24.33	19.98	16.49	13.67	11.39	29
30	87.27	69.58	55.82	45.06	36.58	29.87	24.52	20.24	16.79	13.99	11.72	30
31	85.23	68.32	55.10	44.71	36.50	29.96	24.72	20.51	17.10	14.33	12.05	31
32	83.24	67.09	54.41	44.38	36.42	30.05	24.93	20.79	17.42	14.67	12.40	32
33	81.32	65.90	53.73	44.06	36.35	30.15	25.14	21.07	17.75	15.02	12.77	33
34	79.44	64.72	53.05	43.74	36.27	30.24	25.35	21.36	18.08	15.38	13.14	34
35	77.60	63.57	52.39	43.42	36.20	30.34	25.56	21.65	18.42	15.75	13.52	35
36	75.82	62.44	51.74	43.11	36.13	30.44	25.78	21.95	18.77	16.13	13.92	36
37	74.08	61.34	51.09	42.81	36.06	30.54	26.00	22.25	19.12	16.51	14.32	37
38	72.37	60.25	50.46	42.50	35.99	30.64	26.22	22.55	19.49	16.91	14.74	38
39	70.70	59.18	49.83	42.19	35.92	30.74	26.45	22.86	19.85	17.32	15.17	39
40	69.07	58.13	49.21	41.89	35.85	30.85	26.67	23.18	20.23	17.74	15.62	40
41	67.49	57.11	48.61	41.60	35.79	30.96	26.91	23.50	20.62	18.17	16.08	41
42	65.95	56.11	48.01	41.31	35.73	31.07	27.14	23.83	21.01	18.61	16.55	42
43	64.46	55.14	47.44	41.03	35.68	31.18	27.39	24.16	21.42	19.07	17.04	43
44	63.01	54.19	46.87	40.76	35.63	31.30	27.63	24.51	21.84	19.54	17.55	44
45	61.60	53.26	46.32	40.49	35.58	31.42	27.89	24.86	22.26	20.02	18.07	45
46	60.22	52.36	45.77	40.23	35.54	31.55	28.14	25.22	22.70	20.52	18.62	46
47	58.88	51.47	45.24	39.98	35.50	31.68	28.41	25.59	23.15	21.03	19.18	47
48	57.59	50.62	44.73	39.73	35.47	31.83	28.69	25.97	23.62	21.56	19.76	48
49	56.34	49.79	44.23	39.50	35.46	31.98	28.97	26.37	24.10	22.11	20.37	49
50	55.14	48.99	43.76	39.29	35.45	32.14	29.27	26.78	24.60	22.69	21.01	50

Table 16: Multipliers for loss of pension commencing age 50 (females)

Age at date of trial	Multiplier calculated with allowance for projected mortality from the 2008–based population projections and rate of return of											Age at date of trial
	–2.0%	–1.5%	–1.0%	–0.5%	0.0%	0.5%	1.0%	1.5%	2.0%	2.5%	3.0%	
0	199.59	134.37	91.19	62.37	42.98	29.85	20.87	14.70	10.42	7.43	5.33	0
1	195.74	132.49	90.40	62.16	43.07	30.06	21.13	14.95	10.65	7.64	5.51	1
2	191.18	130.11	89.25	61.69	42.97	30.15	21.30	15.16	10.85	7.82	5.67	2
3	186.71	127.75	88.10	61.23	42.87	30.24	21.48	15.36	11.05	8.00	5.83	3
4	182.34	125.44	86.97	60.76	42.77	30.32	21.65	15.56	11.26	8.19	6.00	4
5	178.06	123.16	85.85	60.30	42.67	30.41	21.82	15.77	11.46	8.39	6.17	5
6	173.88	120.92	84.74	59.84	42.56	30.49	22.00	15.97	11.67	8.58	6.35	6
7	169.79	118.72	83.65	59.38	42.46	30.58	22.17	16.18	11.89	8.78	6.53	7
8	165.80	116.55	82.56	58.92	42.36	30.66	22.35	16.40	12.10	8.99	6.72	8
9	161.89	114.43	81.49	58.47	42.25	30.75	22.53	16.61	12.33	9.20	6.91	9
10	158.08	112.34	80.43	58.02	42.15	30.83	22.70	16.83	12.55	9.42	7.11	10
11	154.36	110.29	79.39	57.57	42.04	30.92	22.89	17.05	12.78	9.64	7.31	11
12	150.73	108.28	78.36	57.12	41.94	31.00	23.07	17.27	13.01	9.86	7.52	12
13	147.17	106.30	77.34	56.68	41.83	31.08	23.25	17.50	13.25	10.09	7.73	13
14	143.71	104.36	76.34	56.24	41.73	31.17	23.43	17.73	13.49	10.33	7.95	14
15	140.33	102.45	75.35	55.81	41.62	31.25	23.62	17.96	13.74	10.57	8.18	15
16	137.02	100.58	74.37	55.38	41.52	31.34	23.81	18.20	13.99	10.82	8.41	16
17	133.80	98.75	73.41	54.95	41.42	31.42	24.00	18.44	14.25	11.07	8.65	17
18	130.66	96.95	72.46	54.53	41.32	31.51	24.19	18.68	14.51	11.33	8.90	18
19	127.60	95.19	71.52	54.11	41.22	31.60	24.38	18.92	14.78	11.60	9.16	19
20	124.61	93.47	70.61	53.70	41.12	31.69	24.58	19.18	15.05	11.87	9.42	20
21	121.70	91.78	69.70	53.30	41.03	31.78	24.78	19.43	15.32	12.15	9.69	21
22	118.85	90.11	68.80	52.89	40.93	31.87	24.97	19.69	15.61	12.44	9.97	22
23	116.05	88.47	67.91	52.48	40.82	31.96	25.17	19.94	15.89	12.73	10.25	23
24	113.32	86.85	67.03	52.08	40.72	32.05	25.37	20.21	16.18	13.03	10.54	24
25	110.66	85.27	66.16	51.68	40.62	32.14	25.57	20.47	16.48	13.33	10.85	25
26	108.06	83.73	65.31	51.28	40.53	32.23	25.78	20.74	16.78	13.65	11.16	26
27	105.53	82.21	64.47	50.89	40.43	32.32	25.99	21.02	17.09	13.97	11.48	27
28	103.06	80.72	63.64	50.50	40.33	32.41	26.19	21.29	17.40	14.30	11.81	28
29	100.65	79.26	62.82	50.12	40.24	32.50	26.41	21.58	17.72	14.64	12.14	29
30	98.30	77.82	62.02	49.74	40.15	32.60	26.62	21.86	18.05	14.98	12.49	30
31	96.01	76.42	61.23	49.37	40.06	32.69	26.84	22.15	18.38	15.33	12.85	31
32	93.78	75.05	60.46	49.00	39.97	32.79	27.06	22.45	18.73	15.70	13.22	32
33	91.61	73.71	59.69	48.64	39.88	32.89	27.28	22.75	19.07	16.07	13.61	33
34	89.48	72.38	58.93	48.28	39.79	32.99	27.50	23.05	19.43	16.45	14.00	34
35	87.39	71.08	58.18	47.92	39.70	33.09	27.73	23.36	19.79	16.84	14.40	35
36	85.37	69.81	57.45	47.57	39.62	33.19	27.96	23.68	20.16	17.24	14.82	36
37	83.40	68.57	56.73	47.22	39.54	33.29	28.19	24.00	20.53	17.65	15.25	37
38	81.47	67.35	56.02	46.87	39.45	33.40	28.43	24.32	20.92	18.07	15.69	38
39	79.59	66.15	55.31	46.53	39.37	33.50	28.66	24.65	21.31	18.50	16.14	39
40	77.75	64.97	54.62	46.19	39.29	33.61	28.90	24.99	21.71	18.95	16.61	40
41	75.96	63.82	53.94	45.86	39.22	33.72	29.15	25.33	22.11	19.40	17.10	41
42	74.22	62.69	53.27	45.54	39.14	33.83	29.40	25.67	22.53	19.87	17.60	42
43	72.53	61.59	52.62	45.22	39.07	33.95	29.65	26.03	22.96	20.35	18.11	43
44	70.88	60.52	51.98	44.90	39.01	34.07	29.91	26.39	23.40	20.84	18.64	44
45	69.28	59.47	51.35	44.60	38.94	34.19	30.17	26.76	23.85	21.35	19.19	45
46	67.72	58.45	50.74	44.30	38.89	34.32	30.44	27.14	24.31	21.87	19.76	46
47	66.20	57.45	50.14	44.01	38.83	34.45	30.72	27.53	24.78	22.41	20.35	47
48	64.73	56.48	49.56	43.73	38.79	34.59	31.01	27.93	25.27	22.97	20.96	48
49	63.31	55.54	48.99	43.46	38.76	34.74	31.30	28.34	25.77	23.54	21.59	49
50	61.93	54.62	48.44	43.20	38.73	34.90	31.61	28.76	26.29	24.14	22.25	50

Table 17: Multipliers for loss of pension commencing age 55 (males)

Age at date of trial	Multiplier calculated with allowance for projected mortality from the 2008–based population projections and rate of return of											Age at date of trial
	–2.0%	–1.5%	–1.0%	–0.5%	0.0%	0.5%	1.0%	1.5%	2.0%	2.5%	3.0%	
0	165.74	111.07	74.94	50.90	34.80	23.94	16.57	11.54	8.08	5.69	4.02	0
1	162.56	109.52	74.30	50.73	34.87	24.11	16.78	11.74	8.26	5.85	4.16	1
2	158.64	107.46	73.29	50.31	34.76	24.17	16.90	11.89	8.41	5.98	4.27	2
3	154.79	105.43	72.29	49.89	34.65	24.22	17.02	12.04	8.56	6.12	4.39	3
4	151.03	103.43	71.30	49.47	34.54	24.27	17.15	12.19	8.71	6.26	4.52	4
5	147.35	101.46	70.32	49.05	34.43	24.31	17.27	12.34	8.86	6.40	4.64	5
6	143.76	99.52	69.35	48.63	34.32	24.36	17.39	12.49	9.02	6.54	4.77	6
7	140.25	97.62	68.39	48.22	34.20	24.41	17.52	12.64	9.17	6.69	4.90	7
8	136.83	95.76	67.44	47.80	34.09	24.45	17.64	12.80	9.33	6.84	5.04	8
9	133.48	93.92	66.51	47.39	33.97	24.50	17.77	12.96	9.50	7.00	5.18	9
10	130.21	92.11	65.58	46.98	33.86	24.54	17.89	13.11	9.66	7.15	5.32	10
11	127.02	90.34	64.67	46.57	33.74	24.59	18.02	13.27	9.83	7.32	5.47	11
12	123.91	88.61	63.77	46.17	33.63	24.63	18.14	13.44	10.00	7.48	5.62	12
13	120.87	86.91	62.88	45.77	33.51	24.68	18.27	13.60	10.18	7.65	5.78	13
14	117.91	85.24	62.00	45.37	33.40	24.72	18.40	13.77	10.35	7.82	5.94	14
15	115.03	83.61	61.14	44.98	33.29	24.77	18.53	13.94	10.53	8.00	6.10	15
16	112.22	82.01	60.30	44.60	33.17	24.81	18.66	14.11	10.72	8.18	6.27	16
17	109.49	80.45	59.47	44.22	33.06	24.86	18.79	14.28	10.90	8.37	6.45	17
18	106.83	78.92	58.65	43.84	32.96	24.91	18.93	14.46	11.10	8.56	6.63	18
19	104.24	77.42	57.85	43.47	32.85	24.96	19.07	14.64	11.29	8.75	6.81	19
20	101.73	75.97	57.07	43.11	32.75	25.02	19.21	14.82	11.49	8.95	7.00	20
21	99.28	74.54	56.29	42.76	32.65	25.07	19.35	15.01	11.70	9.16	7.20	21
22	96.87	73.13	55.52	42.40	32.55	25.12	19.49	15.19	11.90	9.37	7.40	22
23	94.52	71.74	54.76	42.04	32.45	25.17	19.63	15.38	12.11	9.58	7.61	23
24	92.23	70.38	54.02	41.69	32.34	25.23	19.77	15.58	12.33	9.80	7.82	24
25	90.00	69.05	53.28	41.34	32.24	25.28	19.92	15.77	12.54	10.02	8.04	25
26	87.84	67.76	52.56	41.00	32.15	25.34	20.07	15.97	12.77	10.25	8.27	26
27	85.73	66.49	51.86	40.67	32.06	25.40	20.22	16.17	13.00	10.49	8.50	27
28	83.67	65.24	51.16	40.33	31.96	25.45	20.37	16.38	13.23	10.73	8.74	28
29	81.64	64.01	50.46	39.99	31.86	25.51	20.52	16.58	13.46	10.97	8.98	29
30	79.68	62.81	49.78	39.66	31.76	25.56	20.67	16.79	13.70	11.23	9.24	30
31	77.78	61.65	49.12	39.35	31.68	25.63	20.83	17.01	13.95	11.49	9.50	31
32	75.95	60.52	48.48	39.04	31.60	25.69	20.99	17.23	14.20	11.76	9.77	32
33	74.17	59.42	47.86	38.74	31.52	25.77	21.16	17.46	14.46	12.03	10.05	33
34	72.42	58.34	47.24	38.44	31.44	25.84	21.33	17.69	14.73	12.32	10.34	34
35	70.72	57.27	46.62	38.15	31.36	25.91	21.50	17.92	15.00	12.61	10.64	35
36	69.07	56.24	46.03	37.86	31.29	25.98	21.68	18.16	15.28	12.90	10.94	36
37	67.45	55.22	45.44	37.57	31.22	26.06	21.85	18.40	15.56	13.21	11.26	37
38	65.87	54.22	44.85	37.29	31.14	26.13	22.03	18.65	15.85	13.52	11.58	38
39	64.33	53.23	44.27	37.00	31.07	26.21	22.21	18.89	16.14	13.84	11.91	39
40	62.82	52.27	43.70	36.72	31.00	26.28	22.38	19.14	16.44	14.17	12.26	40
41	61.36	51.33	43.15	36.45	30.93	26.36	22.57	19.40	16.74	14.50	12.61	41
42	59.93	50.41	42.60	36.18	30.86	26.45	22.76	19.66	17.06	14.85	12.98	42
43	58.55	49.51	42.07	35.92	30.80	26.53	22.95	19.93	17.38	15.21	13.36	43
44	57.21	48.64	41.55	35.66	30.74	26.62	23.15	20.21	17.71	15.57	13.75	44
45	55.90	47.78	41.04	35.41	30.69	26.71	23.35	20.49	18.04	15.95	14.15	45
46	54.63	46.95	40.54	35.16	30.64	26.81	23.55	20.77	18.39	16.34	14.57	46
47	53.39	46.14	40.05	34.93	30.59	26.91	23.76	21.06	18.74	16.74	15.00	47
48	52.20	45.35	39.58	34.70	30.55	27.01	23.98	21.37	19.11	17.15	15.45	48
49	51.04	44.58	39.12	34.48	30.52	27.12	24.20	21.68	19.49	17.58	15.92	49
50	49.93	43.85	38.68	34.27	30.50	27.25	24.44	22.00	19.88	18.03	16.40	50
51	48.86	43.14	38.26	34.08	30.49	27.38	24.69	22.34	20.29	18.49	16.91	51
52	47.83	42.46	37.86	33.91	30.49	27.53	24.95	22.69	20.72	18.98	17.44	52
53	46.84	41.81	37.48	33.74	30.50	27.68	25.22	23.06	21.16	19.48	17.99	53
54	45.90	41.19	37.12	33.60	30.53	27.86	25.51	23.44	21.62	20.01	18.57	54
55	44.99	40.60	36.79	33.47	30.58	28.04	25.81	23.85	22.11	20.56	19.18	55

Table 18: Multipliers for loss of pension commencing age 55 (females)

Age at date of trial	Multiplier calculated with allowance for projected mortality from the 2008–based population projections and rate of return of											Age at date of trial
	−2.0%	**−1.5%**	**−1.0%**	**−0.5%**	**0.0%**	**0.5%**	**1.0%**	**1.5%**	**2.0%**	**2.5%**	**3.0%**	
0	185.47	123.56	82.90	56.01	38.10	26.08	17.97	12.46	8.69	6.09	4.30	0
1	181.85	121.80	82.16	55.81	38.16	26.26	18.19	12.68	8.88	6.26	4.44	1
2	177.57	119.58	81.09	55.37	38.06	26.33	18.33	12.84	9.05	6.41	4.57	2
3	173.37	117.38	80.03	54.94	37.96	26.40	18.48	13.01	9.21	6.56	4.69	3
4	169.26	115.23	78.98	54.51	37.86	26.47	18.62	13.18	9.38	6.71	4.83	4
5	165.25	113.10	77.94	54.08	37.76	26.54	18.76	13.35	9.55	6.87	4.97	5
6	161.33	111.01	76.92	53.65	37.66	26.60	18.91	13.52	9.72	7.03	5.11	6
7	157.49	108.96	75.90	53.22	37.56	26.67	19.05	13.69	9.89	7.19	5.25	7
8	153.74	106.95	74.89	52.79	37.45	26.73	19.20	13.87	10.07	7.36	5.40	8
9	150.08	104.96	73.90	52.37	37.35	26.80	19.35	14.04	10.25	7.53	5.55	9
10	146.51	103.02	72.92	51.95	37.24	26.86	19.49	14.22	10.44	7.70	5.71	10
11	143.02	101.11	71.95	51.53	37.14	26.93	19.64	14.41	10.63	7.88	5.87	11
12	139.61	99.24	71.00	51.12	37.04	26.99	19.79	14.59	10.82	8.06	6.04	12
13	136.29	97.39	70.05	50.71	36.93	27.06	19.94	14.78	11.01	8.25	6.21	13
14	133.04	95.59	69.12	50.30	36.83	27.12	20.09	14.97	11.21	8.44	6.38	14
15	129.87	93.82	68.21	49.90	36.72	27.19	20.25	15.16	11.41	8.63	6.56	15
16	126.78	92.08	67.30	49.50	36.62	27.26	20.40	15.35	11.61	8.83	6.75	16
17	123.76	90.37	66.41	49.10	36.52	27.32	20.55	15.55	11.82	9.03	6.94	17
18	120.82	88.70	65.53	48.71	36.42	27.39	20.71	15.75	12.03	9.24	7.13	18
19	117.96	87.07	64.67	48.32	36.32	27.46	20.87	15.95	12.25	9.46	7.34	19
20	115.17	85.47	63.82	47.94	36.23	27.53	21.03	16.16	12.47	9.68	7.54	20
21	112.45	83.90	62.98	47.56	36.13	27.60	21.20	16.37	12.70	9.90	7.76	21
22	109.78	82.35	62.15	47.19	36.03	27.67	21.36	16.58	12.93	10.13	7.98	22
23	107.16	80.82	61.33	46.81	35.93	27.73	21.52	16.79	13.16	10.37	8.20	23
24	104.61	79.32	60.51	46.43	35.83	27.80	21.68	17.00	13.40	10.61	8.43	24
25	102.12	77.86	59.71	46.06	35.73	27.87	21.85	17.22	13.64	10.85	8.67	25
26	99.70	76.42	58.92	45.69	35.63	27.94	22.02	17.44	13.88	11.10	8.92	26
27	97.34	75.01	58.15	45.33	35.54	28.01	22.19	17.67	14.13	11.36	9.17	27
28	95.02	73.63	57.38	44.97	35.44	28.08	22.36	17.89	14.39	11.62	9.43	28
29	92.77	72.27	56.62	44.61	35.34	28.15	22.53	18.12	14.65	11.89	9.70	29
30	90.58	70.94	55.88	44.26	35.25	28.22	22.71	18.36	14.91	12.17	9.97	30
31	88.45	69.65	55.15	43.92	35.16	28.29	22.88	18.60	15.18	12.45	10.26	31
32	86.37	68.38	54.44	43.58	35.07	28.37	23.06	18.84	15.46	12.74	10.55	32
33	84.34	67.13	53.73	43.24	34.98	28.45	23.24	19.09	15.74	13.04	10.85	33
34	82.35	65.90	53.03	42.90	34.89	28.52	23.43	19.33	16.03	13.35	11.16	34
35	80.41	64.70	52.34	42.57	34.80	28.60	23.61	19.59	16.32	13.66	11.48	35
36	78.53	63.52	51.66	42.24	34.72	28.67	23.80	19.84	16.62	13.98	11.80	36
37	76.69	62.37	51.00	41.92	34.63	28.75	23.99	20.10	16.92	14.30	12.14	37
38	74.89	61.24	50.34	41.60	34.55	28.83	24.18	20.37	17.23	14.64	12.49	38
39	73.14	60.13	49.69	41.28	34.46	28.91	24.37	20.64	17.55	14.98	12.85	39
40	71.43	59.04	49.05	40.97	34.38	29.00	24.57	20.91	17.87	15.34	13.22	40
41	69.76	57.97	48.43	40.66	34.30	29.08	24.77	21.19	18.20	15.70	13.60	41
42	68.14	56.93	47.81	40.35	34.23	29.17	24.97	21.47	18.54	16.07	13.99	42
43	66.56	55.91	47.21	40.05	34.15	29.25	25.17	21.76	18.88	16.45	14.39	43
44	65.03	54.92	46.62	39.76	34.08	29.35	25.38	22.05	19.23	16.84	14.81	44
45	63.54	53.95	46.04	39.48	34.02	29.44	25.60	22.35	19.60	17.25	15.24	45
46	62.09	53.00	45.47	39.20	33.95	29.54	25.82	22.66	19.97	17.66	15.68	46
47	60.68	52.07	44.91	38.93	33.89	29.64	26.04	22.97	20.35	18.09	16.14	47
48	59.31	51.18	44.38	38.66	33.84	29.75	26.27	23.30	20.74	18.53	16.62	48
49	57.99	50.31	43.85	38.41	33.80	29.87	26.51	23.63	21.14	18.99	17.12	49
50	56.70	49.46	43.35	38.17	33.76	29.99	26.76	23.97	21.56	19.46	17.63	50
51	55.46	48.63	42.85	37.93	33.73	30.12	27.01	24.32	21.99	19.95	18.16	51
52	54.25	47.83	42.37	37.70	33.70	30.25	27.27	24.68	22.43	20.45	18.71	52
53	53.08	47.05	41.90	37.49	33.68	30.40	27.54	25.06	22.88	20.97	19.29	53
54	51.95	46.30	41.45	37.28	33.68	30.55	27.83	25.44	23.35	21.51	19.88	54
55	50.86	45.57	41.02	37.09	33.68	30.71	28.12	25.84	23.84	22.07	20.51	55

Table 19: Multipliers for loss of pension commencing age 60 (males)

Age at date of trial	Multiplier calculated with allowance for projected mortality from the 2008–based population projections and rate of return of											Age at date of trial
	–2.0%	**–1.5%**	**–1.0%**	**–0.5%**	**0.0%**	**0.5%**	**1.0%**	**1.5%**	**2.0%**	**2.5%**	**3.0%**	
0	150.59	99.76	66.49	44.58	30.06	20.38	13.89	9.52	6.56	4.54	3.16	0
1	147.63	98.33	65.89	44.41	30.10	20.52	14.06	9.69	6.70	4.66	3.26	1
2	144.02	96.44	64.97	44.02	30.00	20.55	14.16	9.80	6.82	4.77	3.35	2
3	140.47	94.58	64.06	43.63	29.89	20.59	14.26	9.92	6.94	4.88	3.44	3
4	137.00	92.74	63.15	43.25	29.78	20.62	14.35	10.04	7.06	4.98	3.54	4
5	133.61	90.93	62.25	42.86	29.67	20.65	14.45	10.16	7.18	5.10	3.63	5
6	130.29	89.16	61.36	42.47	29.56	20.68	14.54	10.28	7.30	5.21	3.73	6
7	127.06	87.42	60.49	42.09	29.45	20.71	14.64	10.40	7.42	5.32	3.83	7
8	123.91	85.71	59.63	41.71	29.34	20.74	14.74	10.52	7.55	5.44	3.94	8
9	120.82	84.03	58.77	41.33	29.22	20.77	14.84	10.65	7.68	5.56	4.05	9
10	117.81	82.38	57.93	40.95	29.11	20.80	14.93	10.77	7.81	5.68	4.16	10
11	114.87	80.76	57.09	40.58	29.00	20.82	15.03	10.90	7.94	5.81	4.27	11
12	112.01	79.17	56.27	40.21	28.88	20.85	15.13	11.03	8.07	5.94	4.39	12
13	109.22	77.62	55.46	39.84	28.77	20.88	15.23	11.16	8.21	6.07	4.50	13
14	106.50	76.10	54.67	39.48	28.66	20.91	15.33	11.29	8.35	6.20	4.63	14
15	103.85	74.61	53.88	39.12	28.55	20.94	15.43	11.42	8.49	6.34	4.75	15
16	101.27	73.15	53.11	38.77	28.44	20.96	15.53	11.55	8.63	6.48	4.88	16
17	98.76	71.72	52.36	38.42	28.33	20.99	15.63	11.69	8.78	6.62	5.02	17
18	96.32	70.32	51.61	38.07	28.23	21.03	15.74	11.83	8.93	6.77	5.15	18
19	93.94	68.96	50.88	37.74	28.12	21.06	15.84	11.97	9.08	6.92	5.30	19
20	91.64	67.63	50.17	37.41	28.02	21.09	15.95	12.11	9.24	7.08	5.44	20
21	89.39	66.33	49.47	37.08	27.92	21.13	16.06	12.26	9.40	7.23	5.59	21
22	87.18	65.04	48.77	36.75	27.82	21.16	16.17	12.41	9.56	7.40	5.74	22
23	85.02	63.77	48.08	36.42	27.72	21.19	16.28	12.55	9.72	7.56	5.90	23
24	82.92	62.54	47.40	36.09	27.62	21.23	16.39	12.70	9.89	7.73	6.06	24
25	80.88	61.33	46.73	35.78	27.52	21.26	16.50	12.86	10.06	7.90	6.23	25
26	78.91	60.15	46.08	35.46	27.42	21.30	16.61	13.01	10.23	8.08	6.40	26
27	76.98	59.00	45.44	35.16	27.33	21.34	16.73	13.17	10.41	8.26	6.58	27
28	75.09	57.86	44.80	34.85	27.23	21.37	16.84	13.33	10.59	8.45	6.76	28
29	73.23	56.74	44.17	34.54	27.13	21.41	16.96	13.49	10.77	8.63	6.95	29
30	71.44	55.65	43.55	34.24	27.04	21.44	17.08	13.65	10.96	8.83	7.14	30
31	69.70	54.59	42.95	33.95	26.95	21.48	17.20	13.82	11.15	9.03	7.34	31
32	68.02	53.56	42.37	33.66	26.86	21.53	17.32	13.99	11.35	9.23	7.54	32
33	66.40	52.56	41.80	33.39	26.79	21.58	17.45	14.17	11.55	9.45	7.75	33
34	64.81	51.58	41.24	33.12	26.71	21.63	17.58	14.35	11.76	9.66	7.97	34
35	63.25	50.61	40.68	32.84	26.63	21.67	17.71	14.53	11.96	9.89	8.20	35
36	61.74	49.67	40.14	32.58	26.55	21.72	17.85	14.72	12.18	10.11	8.43	36
37	60.27	48.75	39.60	32.31	26.47	21.78	17.98	14.90	12.40	10.35	8.66	37
38	58.83	47.84	39.07	32.05	26.40	21.83	18.12	15.09	12.62	10.58	8.91	38
39	57.42	46.95	38.55	31.79	26.32	21.88	18.25	15.28	12.84	10.83	9.16	39
40	56.04	46.07	38.03	31.53	26.24	21.93	18.39	15.48	13.07	11.08	9.42	40
41	54.71	45.22	37.53	31.28	26.17	21.98	18.53	15.68	13.31	11.33	9.68	41
42	53.42	44.38	37.04	31.03	26.10	22.03	18.67	15.88	13.55	11.60	9.96	42
43	52.16	43.57	36.55	30.79	26.03	22.09	18.82	16.09	13.80	11.87	10.24	43
44	50.93	42.78	36.08	30.55	25.97	22.15	18.97	16.30	14.05	12.15	10.54	44
45	49.74	42.01	35.62	30.32	25.91	22.22	19.12	16.51	14.31	12.44	10.84	45
46	48.58	41.25	35.16	30.09	25.85	22.28	19.28	16.73	14.57	12.73	11.15	46
47	47.46	40.51	34.72	29.87	25.79	22.35	19.44	16.96	14.84	13.03	11.48	47
48	46.37	39.80	34.29	29.65	25.74	22.42	19.60	17.19	15.12	13.35	11.81	48
49	45.32	39.10	33.87	29.45	25.70	22.50	19.77	17.43	15.41	13.67	12.16	49
50	44.30	38.43	33.47	29.26	25.66	22.59	19.95	17.68	15.71	14.01	12.52	50
51	43.33	37.79	33.09	29.07	25.64	22.69	20.14	17.94	16.03	14.36	12.90	51
52	42.39	37.17	32.72	28.91	25.62	22.79	20.34	18.21	16.35	14.72	13.30	52
53	41.49	36.58	32.37	28.75	25.62	22.91	20.55	18.49	16.69	15.11	13.71	53
54	40.63	36.01	32.04	28.61	25.63	23.04	20.77	18.79	17.04	15.50	14.14	54

Table 19: Multipliers for loss of pension commencing age 60 (males) *continued*

Age at date of trial	Multiplier calculated with allowance for projected mortality from the 2008–based population projections and rate of return of											Age at date of trial
	−2.0%	−1.5%	−1.0%	−0.5%	0.0%	0.5%	1.0%	1.5%	2.0%	2.5%	3.0%	
55	39.81	35.48	31.73	28.48	25.65	23.18	21.01	19.10	17.41	15.92	14.60	55
56	39.03	34.97	31.45	28.37	25.69	23.33	21.26	19.43	17.80	16.36	15.07	56
57	38.29	34.49	31.18	28.28	25.74	23.50	21.52	19.77	18.21	16.82	15.57	57
58	37.56	34.02	30.92	28.20	25.80	23.68	21.79	20.12	18.63	17.29	16.09	58
59	36.86	33.56	30.67	28.12	25.86	23.86	22.07	20.49	19.06	17.79	16.64	59
60	36.17	33.12	30.42	28.04	25.92	24.04	22.36	20.86	19.51	18.30	17.20	60

Table 20: Multipliers for loss of pension commencing age 60 (females)

Age at date of trial	Multiplier calculated with allowance for projected mortality from the 2008–based population projections and rate of return of											Age at date of trial
	–2.0%	*–1.5%*	*–1.0%*	*–0.5%*	*0.0%*	*0.5%*	*1.0%*	*1.5%*	*2.0%*	*2.5%*	*3.0%*	
0	169.99	112.01	74.27	49.55	33.26	22.45	15.24	10.40	7.14	4.92	3.41	0
1	166.62	110.38	73.58	49.35	33.30	22.59	15.42	10.58	7.30	5.06	3.52	1
2	162.64	108.33	72.60	48.95	33.20	22.65	15.53	10.71	7.43	5.17	3.62	2
3	158.74	106.30	71.62	48.55	33.10	22.70	15.65	10.85	7.56	5.29	3.72	3
4	154.93	104.31	70.66	48.15	33.00	22.75	15.77	10.98	7.69	5.41	3.83	4
5	151.21	102.36	69.71	47.75	32.90	22.80	15.88	11.12	7.83	5.54	3.93	5
6	147.57	100.43	68.76	47.36	32.80	22.85	16.00	11.26	7.97	5.66	4.04	6
7	144.01	98.54	67.83	46.96	32.70	22.89	16.11	11.40	8.11	5.79	4.16	7
8	140.54	96.68	66.91	46.57	32.60	22.94	16.23	11.54	8.25	5.92	4.27	8
9	137.14	94.85	65.99	46.18	32.49	22.99	16.35	11.69	8.39	6.06	4.39	9
10	133.83	93.06	65.09	45.79	32.39	23.03	16.47	11.83	8.54	6.20	4.51	10
11	130.60	91.31	64.21	45.41	32.29	23.08	16.59	11.98	8.69	6.34	4.64	11
12	127.45	89.58	63.33	45.02	32.18	23.13	16.71	12.13	8.84	6.48	4.77	12
13	124.36	87.89	62.47	44.65	32.08	23.17	16.83	12.28	9.00	6.63	4.90	13
14	121.36	86.23	61.62	44.27	31.98	23.22	16.95	12.43	9.16	6.78	5.04	14
15	118.43	84.60	60.77	43.90	31.88	23.27	17.07	12.58	9.32	6.93	5.18	15
16	115.57	83.00	59.95	43.53	31.78	23.31	17.19	12.74	9.48	7.09	5.32	16
17	112.78	81.44	59.13	43.16	31.67	23.36	17.32	12.90	9.65	7.25	5.47	17
18	110.06	79.90	58.33	42.80	31.58	23.41	17.44	13.06	9.82	7.42	5.62	18
19	107.41	78.40	57.53	42.45	31.48	23.46	17.57	13.22	9.99	7.58	5.78	19
20	104.83	76.93	56.76	42.10	31.38	23.51	17.70	13.38	10.17	7.76	5.94	20
21	102.32	75.49	55.99	41.75	31.29	23.56	17.83	13.55	10.35	7.93	6.11	21
22	99.85	74.07	55.23	41.40	31.19	23.61	17.96	13.72	10.53	8.12	6.28	22
23	97.44	72.67	54.48	41.05	31.09	23.66	18.09	13.89	10.71	8.30	6.45	23
24	95.08	71.29	53.73	40.70	30.99	23.70	18.22	14.06	10.90	8.49	6.63	24
25	92.79	69.95	53.00	40.36	30.89	23.75	18.35	14.24	11.09	8.68	6.82	25
26	90.55	68.63	52.28	40.03	30.79	23.80	18.48	14.41	11.29	8.88	7.01	26
27	88.37	67.34	51.57	39.69	30.70	23.85	18.62	14.59	11.49	9.08	7.20	27
28	86.24	66.07	50.87	39.36	30.60	23.90	18.75	14.77	11.69	9.29	7.41	28
29	84.17	64.83	50.18	39.03	30.51	23.95	18.89	14.96	11.90	9.50	7.61	29
30	82.15	63.61	49.50	38.71	30.41	24.00	19.03	15.15	12.11	9.71	7.83	30
31	80.18	62.43	48.84	38.39	30.32	24.05	19.17	15.34	12.32	9.94	8.04	31
32	78.27	61.26	48.19	38.08	30.23	24.11	19.31	15.53	12.54	10.16	8.27	32
33	76.40	60.12	47.54	37.77	30.14	24.16	19.45	15.72	12.76	10.40	8.50	33
34	74.57	59.00	46.90	37.46	30.05	24.22	19.60	15.92	12.99	10.64	8.74	34
35	72.79	57.90	46.27	37.15	29.96	24.27	19.74	16.12	13.22	10.88	8.99	35
36	71.05	56.82	45.66	36.85	29.88	24.33	19.89	16.33	13.45	11.13	9.24	36
37	69.36	55.77	45.05	36.55	29.79	24.38	20.04	16.53	13.69	11.38	9.50	37
38	67.71	54.73	44.45	36.26	29.71	24.44	20.19	16.74	13.94	11.65	9.77	38
39	66.10	53.72	43.86	35.97	29.62	24.50	20.34	16.96	14.19	11.92	10.04	39
40	64.53	52.73	43.28	35.68	29.54	24.56	20.50	17.17	14.44	12.19	10.32	40
41	63.00	51.75	42.70	35.39	29.46	24.62	20.65	17.39	14.70	12.47	10.62	41
42	61.51	50.80	42.14	35.11	29.38	24.68	20.81	17.62	14.97	12.76	10.92	42
43	60.06	49.87	41.59	34.84	29.30	24.74	20.97	17.85	15.24	13.06	11.23	43
44	58.65	48.97	41.06	34.57	29.23	24.81	21.14	18.08	15.52	13.36	11.55	44
45	57.28	48.08	40.53	34.31	29.16	24.88	21.31	18.32	15.80	13.68	11.88	45
46	55.95	47.21	40.01	34.05	29.09	24.95	21.48	18.56	16.09	14.00	12.22	46
47	54.65	46.37	39.50	33.79	29.02	25.02	21.65	18.81	16.39	14.33	12.57	47
48	53.40	45.55	39.01	33.55	28.97	25.10	21.84	19.06	16.70	14.67	12.94	48
49	52.19	44.75	38.54	33.32	28.92	25.19	22.03	19.33	17.01	15.03	13.32	49
50	51.01	43.98	38.07	33.09	28.87	25.28	22.22	19.60	17.34	15.39	13.71	50
51	49.86	43.22	37.62	32.87	28.83	25.38	22.42	19.87	17.67	15.77	14.11	51
52	48.76	42.49	37.17	32.65	28.79	25.47	22.62	20.16	18.02	16.16	14.53	52
53	47.68	41.78	36.75	32.45	28.76	25.58	22.83	20.45	18.38	16.56	14.97	53
54	46.65	41.09	36.34	32.26	28.74	25.70	23.06	20.76	18.74	16.98	15.43	54

Table 20: Multipliers for loss of pension commencing age 60 (females) *continued*

Age at date of trial	Multiplier calculated with allowance for projected mortality from the 2008–based population projections and rate of return of											Age at date of trial
	–2.0%	*–1.5%*	*–1.0%*	*–0.5%*	*0.0%*	*0.5%*	*1.0%*	*1.5%*	*2.0%*	*2.5%*	*3.0%*	
55	45.65	40.43	35.94	32.08	28.73	25.82	23.29	21.07	19.13	17.41	15.90	55
56	44.69	39.79	35.57	31.91	28.73	25.95	23.53	21.40	19.52	17.86	16.39	56
57	43.76	39.18	35.20	31.75	28.73	26.09	23.78	21.74	19.93	18.33	16.91	57
58	42.86	38.57	34.85	31.59	28.74	26.24	24.04	22.09	20.35	18.81	17.44	58
59	41.98	37.99	34.50	31.44	28.76	26.39	24.30	22.44	20.79	19.31	17.99	59
60	41.12	37.41	34.16	31.30	28.78	26.55	24.57	22.81	21.24	19.83	18.57	60

Table 21: Multipliers for loss of pension commencing age 65 (males)

Age at date of trial	Multiplier calculated with allowance for projected mortality from the 2008–based population projections and rate of return of											Age at date of trial
	–2.0%	–1.5%	–1.0%	–0.5%	0.0%	0.5%	1.0%	1.5%	2.0%	2.5%	3.0%	
0	134.16	87.81	57.78	38.22	25.41	16.98	11.40	7.69	5.21	3.54	2.42	0
1	131.46	86.50	57.23	38.06	25.44	17.08	11.53	7.82	5.32	3.64	2.50	1
2	128.17	84.80	56.40	37.70	25.33	17.10	11.60	7.91	5.41	3.72	2.57	2
3	124.95	83.11	55.57	37.35	25.23	17.12	11.67	8.00	5.50	3.80	2.64	3
4	121.80	81.45	54.76	37.00	25.12	17.14	11.75	8.09	5.59	3.88	2.71	4
5	118.72	79.82	53.95	36.64	25.01	17.15	11.82	8.18	5.68	3.97	2.78	5
6	115.71	78.22	53.15	36.29	24.90	17.17	11.89	8.27	5.78	4.05	2.85	6
7	112.78	76.65	52.36	35.95	24.80	17.18	11.96	8.36	5.87	4.14	2.93	7
8	109.92	75.11	51.59	35.60	24.69	17.20	12.03	8.46	5.97	4.23	3.01	8
9	107.13	73.60	50.82	35.26	24.58	17.21	12.11	8.55	6.07	4.32	3.09	9
10	104.40	72.11	50.06	34.91	24.47	17.22	12.18	8.65	6.17	4.41	3.17	10
11	101.74	70.65	49.31	34.57	24.36	17.23	12.25	8.74	6.27	4.51	3.26	11
12	99.15	69.23	48.57	34.24	24.25	17.25	12.32	8.84	6.37	4.60	3.34	12
13	96.62	67.83	47.84	33.91	24.14	17.26	12.39	8.94	6.47	4.70	3.43	13
14	94.16	66.46	47.13	33.58	24.03	17.27	12.47	9.04	6.58	4.80	3.52	14
15	91.77	65.12	46.43	33.25	23.92	17.28	12.54	9.14	6.68	4.91	3.62	15
16	89.44	63.81	45.74	32.93	23.82	17.30	12.62	9.24	6.79	5.01	3.71	16
17	87.17	62.53	45.06	32.61	23.71	17.31	12.69	9.34	6.90	5.12	3.81	17
18	84.97	61.27	44.39	32.30	23.61	17.33	12.77	9.45	7.02	5.23	3.91	18
19	82.83	60.05	43.74	32.00	23.51	17.34	12.85	9.55	7.13	5.34	4.02	19
20	80.75	58.86	43.10	31.70	23.41	17.36	12.93	9.66	7.25	5.46	4.13	20
21	78.72	57.69	42.47	31.40	23.31	17.38	13.01	9.77	7.37	5.58	4.24	21
22	76.73	56.54	41.84	31.10	23.21	17.39	13.09	9.88	7.49	5.70	4.35	22
23	74.79	55.40	41.22	30.80	23.11	17.41	13.17	9.99	7.61	5.82	4.47	23
24	72.90	54.29	40.61	30.51	23.01	17.42	13.25	10.11	7.74	5.95	4.59	24
25	71.06	53.21	40.01	30.22	22.91	17.44	13.33	10.22	7.87	6.08	4.71	25
26	69.28	52.16	39.43	29.94	22.82	17.46	13.41	10.34	8.00	6.21	4.83	26
27	67.55	51.13	38.86	29.66	22.73	17.48	13.50	10.46	8.13	6.34	4.97	27
28	65.85	50.11	38.29	29.38	22.63	17.50	13.58	10.58	8.26	6.48	5.10	28
29	64.18	49.10	37.72	29.10	22.53	17.51	13.66	10.69	8.40	6.62	5.23	29
30	62.57	48.13	37.17	28.82	22.44	17.53	13.75	10.82	8.54	6.76	5.38	30
31	61.01	47.18	36.64	28.56	22.35	17.55	13.83	10.94	8.68	6.91	5.52	31
32	59.50	46.27	36.12	28.30	22.26	17.58	13.93	11.07	8.83	7.07	5.67	32
33	58.05	45.38	35.61	28.06	22.18	17.61	14.02	11.20	8.98	7.22	5.83	33
34	56.62	44.50	35.11	27.81	22.10	17.63	14.12	11.34	9.14	7.38	5.99	34
35	55.23	43.64	34.61	27.56	22.02	17.66	14.21	11.47	9.29	7.55	6.15	35
36	53.87	42.80	34.13	27.32	21.94	17.69	14.31	11.61	9.45	7.72	6.32	36
37	52.56	41.97	33.65	27.08	21.87	17.72	14.41	11.75	9.61	7.89	6.49	37
38	51.26	41.16	33.18	26.84	21.79	17.75	14.50	11.89	9.78	8.07	6.67	38
39	50.00	40.37	32.71	26.60	21.71	17.77	14.60	12.03	9.95	8.24	6.85	39
40	48.77	39.59	32.25	26.36	21.63	17.80	14.70	12.18	10.12	8.43	7.04	40
41	47.58	38.83	31.80	26.13	21.55	17.83	14.80	12.32	10.29	8.62	7.24	41
42	46.42	38.09	31.36	25.91	21.48	17.86	14.90	12.47	10.47	8.81	7.44	42
43	45.30	37.36	30.93	25.69	21.41	17.90	15.01	12.63	10.65	9.01	7.64	43
44	44.21	36.66	30.51	25.47	21.34	17.93	15.12	12.78	10.84	9.21	7.86	44
45	43.15	35.97	30.09	25.26	21.27	17.97	15.23	12.94	11.03	9.43	8.08	45
46	42.11	35.30	29.69	25.05	21.21	18.01	15.34	13.10	11.22	9.64	8.30	46
47	41.11	34.64	29.29	24.85	21.15	18.05	15.46	13.27	11.42	9.86	8.54	47
48	40.14	34.01	28.91	24.65	21.09	18.10	15.57	13.44	11.63	10.09	8.78	48
49	39.20	33.39	28.53	24.46	21.04	18.15	15.70	13.62	11.84	10.33	9.03	49
50	38.29	32.79	28.18	24.28	20.99	18.20	15.83	13.80	12.07	10.58	9.29	50
51	37.42	32.22	27.83	24.11	20.96	18.27	15.97	13.99	12.29	10.83	9.56	51
52	36.58	31.67	27.50	23.96	20.93	18.34	16.11	14.19	12.53	11.10	9.85	52
53	35.78	31.14	27.19	23.81	20.91	18.41	16.26	14.40	12.78	11.37	10.15	53
54	35.01	30.64	26.89	23.67	20.90	18.50	16.42	14.62	13.04	11.66	10.46	54

Table 21: Multipliers for loss of pension commencing age 65 (males) *continued*

Age at date of trial	Multiplier calculated with allowance for projected mortality from the 2008–based population projections and rate of return of											Age at date of trial
	–2.0%	–1.5%	–1.0%	–0.5%	0.0%	0.5%	1.0%	1.5%	2.0%	2.5%	3.0%	
55	34.28	30.15	26.61	23.55	20.90	18.60	16.59	14.85	13.31	11.97	10.78	55
56	33.59	29.70	26.35	23.44	20.91	18.71	16.78	15.09	13.60	12.29	11.13	56
57	32.92	29.27	26.10	23.35	20.94	18.83	16.97	15.34	13.90	12.62	11.49	57
58	32.28	28.85	25.87	23.26	20.97	18.95	17.18	15.60	14.21	12.97	11.86	58
59	31.65	28.44	25.64	23.17	21.00	19.08	17.38	15.87	14.53	13.32	12.25	59
60	31.03	28.04	25.41	23.09	21.03	19.21	17.59	16.14	14.85	13.69	12.65	60
61	30.43	27.65	25.19	23.01	21.07	19.35	17.81	16.43	15.19	14.08	13.07	61
62	29.87	27.28	24.99	22.94	21.12	19.50	18.04	16.73	15.55	14.48	13.51	62
63	29.34	26.94	24.81	22.90	21.20	19.67	18.29	17.05	15.93	14.91	13.98	63
64	28.85	26.63	24.65	22.88	21.29	19.86	18.56	17.39	16.33	15.37	14.49	64
65	28.40	26.37	24.54	22.90	21.42	20.08	18.87	17.77	16.77	15.86	15.03	65

Table 22: Multipliers for loss of pension commencing age 65 (females)

Age at date of trial	Multiplier calculated with allowance for projected mortality from the 2008–based population projections and rate of return of											Age at date of trial
	–2.0%	*–1.5%*	*–1.0%*	*–0.5%*	*0.0%*	*0.5%*	*1.0%*	*1.5%*	*2.0%*	*2.5%*	*3.0%*	
0	153.09	99.71	65.31	43.01	28.47	18.95	12.67	8.52	5.75	3.90	2.66	0
1	149.98	98.22	64.68	42.82	28.50	19.06	12.81	8.66	5.87	4.00	2.74	1
2	146.34	96.35	63.78	42.45	28.40	19.10	12.90	8.76	5.98	4.09	2.82	2
3	142.77	94.51	62.90	42.08	28.30	19.13	12.99	8.87	6.08	4.19	2.90	3
4	139.29	92.70	62.02	41.72	28.21	19.16	13.08	8.98	6.18	4.28	2.98	4
5	135.88	90.92	61.16	41.36	28.11	19.20	13.17	9.08	6.29	4.38	3.06	5
6	132.55	89.17	60.30	40.99	28.01	19.23	13.26	9.19	6.40	4.47	3.14	6
7	129.30	87.45	59.46	40.63	27.91	19.26	13.35	9.30	6.51	4.57	3.23	7
8	126.13	85.76	58.62	40.27	27.81	19.29	13.45	9.41	6.62	4.68	3.32	8
9	123.03	84.10	57.80	39.92	27.70	19.32	13.54	9.53	6.73	4.78	3.41	9
10	120.00	82.48	56.98	39.56	27.60	19.35	13.63	9.64	6.85	4.89	3.50	10
11	117.06	80.89	56.18	39.21	27.50	19.38	13.72	9.75	6.97	4.99	3.60	11
12	114.18	79.32	55.39	38.87	27.40	19.41	13.81	9.87	7.08	5.11	3.69	12
13	111.37	77.79	54.61	38.52	27.30	19.44	13.90	9.99	7.20	5.22	3.79	13
14	108.63	76.28	53.84	38.18	27.20	19.47	14.00	10.11	7.33	5.33	3.90	14
15	105.96	74.81	53.08	37.84	27.10	19.50	14.09	10.23	7.45	5.45	4.00	15
16	103.35	73.36	52.33	37.50	27.00	19.53	14.19	10.35	7.58	5.57	4.11	16
17	100.81	71.94	51.59	37.17	26.90	19.56	14.28	10.47	7.71	5.70	4.23	17
18	98.33	70.55	50.86	36.84	26.80	19.59	14.38	10.60	7.84	5.82	4.34	18
19	95.92	69.19	50.15	36.52	26.71	19.62	14.47	10.72	7.97	5.95	4.46	19
20	93.58	67.87	49.45	36.20	26.61	19.65	14.57	10.85	8.11	6.09	4.58	20
21	91.29	66.56	48.76	35.88	26.52	19.69	14.67	10.98	8.25	6.22	4.71	21
22	89.05	65.28	48.07	35.56	26.42	19.72	14.77	11.11	8.39	6.36	4.84	22
23	86.86	64.01	47.39	35.24	26.32	19.74	14.87	11.24	8.53	6.50	4.97	23
24	84.71	62.77	46.72	34.93	26.23	19.77	14.97	11.38	8.68	6.65	5.11	24
25	82.63	61.55	46.06	34.62	26.13	19.80	15.07	11.51	8.83	6.79	5.25	25
26	80.60	60.37	45.41	34.31	26.03	19.83	15.17	11.65	8.98	6.94	5.39	26
27	78.62	59.20	44.77	34.01	25.94	19.86	15.27	11.79	9.13	7.10	5.54	27
28	76.69	58.06	44.14	33.71	25.84	19.89	15.38	11.93	9.29	7.26	5.69	28
29	74.81	56.94	43.52	33.41	25.75	19.93	15.48	12.07	9.44	7.42	5.84	29
30	72.98	55.84	42.91	33.12	25.66	19.96	15.58	12.21	9.61	7.58	6.00	30
31	71.20	54.77	42.32	32.83	25.57	19.99	15.69	12.36	9.77	7.75	6.17	31
32	69.46	53.73	41.73	32.54	25.48	20.03	15.80	12.51	9.94	7.92	6.34	32
33	67.77	52.70	41.15	32.26	25.39	20.06	15.91	12.66	10.11	8.10	6.51	33
34	66.12	51.69	40.58	31.98	25.30	20.09	16.02	12.81	10.28	8.28	6.69	34
35	64.50	50.70	40.01	31.70	25.21	20.13	16.13	12.97	10.46	8.47	6.88	35
36	62.93	49.73	39.45	31.43	25.13	20.16	16.24	13.12	10.64	8.66	7.06	36
37	61.41	48.78	38.91	31.15	25.04	20.20	16.35	13.28	10.83	8.85	7.26	37
38	59.91	47.85	38.37	30.89	24.95	20.23	16.47	13.44	11.01	9.05	7.46	38
39	58.46	46.94	37.84	30.62	24.87	20.27	16.58	13.61	11.20	9.25	7.67	39
40	57.04	46.05	37.32	30.36	24.79	20.31	16.70	13.77	11.40	9.46	7.88	40
41	55.66	45.17	36.80	30.10	24.70	20.35	16.81	13.94	11.60	9.67	8.10	41
42	54.31	44.32	36.30	29.84	24.62	20.38	16.93	14.11	11.80	9.89	8.32	42
43	53.01	43.48	35.81	29.59	24.54	20.43	17.05	14.29	12.00	10.12	8.55	43
44	51.74	42.67	35.33	29.35	24.47	20.47	17.18	14.46	12.22	10.35	8.79	44
45	50.50	41.88	34.85	29.11	24.40	20.51	17.31	14.65	12.43	10.58	9.04	45
46	49.30	41.10	34.39	28.87	24.32	20.56	17.44	14.83	12.65	10.83	9.29	46
47	48.13	40.34	33.93	28.64	24.26	20.61	17.57	15.02	12.88	11.08	9.55	47
48	47.00	39.61	33.49	28.42	24.19	20.66	17.70	15.22	13.11	11.33	9.82	48
49	45.91	38.89	33.06	28.20	24.14	20.72	17.85	15.42	13.35	11.60	10.10	49
50	44.85	38.20	32.64	27.99	24.08	20.78	17.99	15.62	13.60	11.88	10.40	50
51	43.82	37.52	32.23	27.79	24.03	20.85	18.14	15.83	13.85	12.16	10.70	51
52	42.82	36.86	31.84	27.59	23.99	20.92	18.29	16.05	14.12	12.45	11.01	52
53	41.85	36.22	31.45	27.40	23.95	20.99	18.45	16.27	14.38	12.75	11.33	53
54	40.92	35.60	31.08	27.22	23.91	21.07	18.62	16.50	14.66	13.06	11.67	54

Table 22: Multipliers for loss of pension commencing age 65 (females) *continued*

Age at date of trial	Multiplier calculated with allowance for projected mortality from the 2008–based population projections and rate of return of											Age at date of trial
	–2.0%	*–1.5%*	*–1.0%*	*–0.5%*	*0.0%*	*0.5%*	*1.0%*	*1.5%*	*2.0%*	*2.5%*	*3.0%*	
55	40.02	35.01	30.73	27.05	23.89	21.16	18.80	16.74	14.95	13.39	12.02	55
56	39.16	34.44	30.38	26.89	23.87	21.26	18.98	16.99	15.25	13.73	12.38	56
57	38.32	33.88	30.05	26.74	23.86	21.36	19.17	17.25	15.56	14.08	12.76	57
58	37.51	33.34	29.73	26.59	23.86	21.46	19.36	17.51	15.88	14.44	13.16	58
59	36.72	32.81	29.42	26.45	23.85	21.57	19.56	17.78	16.21	14.81	13.56	59
60	35.94	32.29	29.10	26.31	23.85	21.68	19.76	18.06	16.54	15.19	13.98	60
61	35.18	31.78	28.80	26.17	23.85	21.79	19.97	18.34	16.89	15.59	14.42	61
62	34.46	31.29	28.51	26.04	23.86	21.91	20.18	18.63	17.25	16.00	14.87	62
63	33.76	30.83	28.23	25.93	23.88	22.05	20.41	18.94	17.62	16.43	15.35	63
64	33.10	30.39	27.98	25.83	23.92	22.20	20.66	19.27	18.02	16.89	15.86	64
65	32.50	29.99	27.76	25.77	23.98	22.38	20.93	19.63	18.45	17.38	16.40	65

Table 23: Multipliers for loss of pension commencing age 70 (males)

Age at date of trial	Multiplier calculated with allowance for projected mortality from the 2008–based population projections and rate of return of											Age at date of trial
	–2.0%	–1.5%	–1.0%	–0.5%	0.0%	0.5%	1.0%	1.5%	2.0%	2.5%	3.0%	
0	116.52	75.30	48.89	31.89	20.90	13.76	9.09	6.04	4.02	2.69	1.81	0
1	114.10	74.13	48.39	31.74	20.91	13.83	9.19	6.13	4.11	2.76	1.87	1
2	111.17	72.62	47.66	31.42	20.81	13.84	9.24	6.20	4.17	2.82	1.91	2
3	108.30	71.12	46.93	31.10	20.70	13.84	9.29	6.27	4.24	2.88	1.96	3
4	105.50	69.65	46.20	30.78	20.60	13.85	9.34	6.33	4.31	2.94	2.02	4
5	102.76	68.21	45.49	30.47	20.50	13.85	9.39	6.40	4.37	3.00	2.07	5
6	100.08	66.80	44.78	30.16	20.39	13.85	9.44	6.46	4.44	3.06	2.12	6
7	97.48	65.41	44.09	29.84	20.29	13.85	9.49	6.53	4.51	3.13	2.18	7
8	94.95	64.05	43.40	29.54	20.19	13.85	9.54	6.60	4.58	3.19	2.23	8
9	92.47	62.71	42.72	29.23	20.08	13.85	9.59	6.67	4.65	3.26	2.29	9
10	90.04	61.40	42.05	28.92	19.97	13.85	9.64	6.74	4.73	3.33	2.35	10
11	87.69	60.11	41.39	28.62	19.87	13.85	9.69	6.81	4.80	3.39	2.41	11
12	85.39	58.86	40.74	28.32	19.76	13.85	9.74	6.88	4.87	3.46	2.47	12
13	83.16	57.63	40.10	28.02	19.66	13.85	9.79	6.95	4.95	3.54	2.54	13
14	80.98	56.42	39.47	27.73	19.56	13.85	9.84	7.02	5.02	3.61	2.60	14
15	78.87	55.24	38.85	27.44	19.45	13.85	9.89	7.09	5.10	3.68	2.67	15
16	76.81	54.09	38.25	27.15	19.35	13.85	9.94	7.16	5.18	3.76	2.74	16
17	74.80	52.96	37.65	26.87	19.25	13.85	9.99	7.24	5.26	3.84	2.81	17
18	72.86	51.86	37.06	26.59	19.15	13.85	10.05	7.31	5.34	3.92	2.88	18
19	70.97	50.79	36.49	26.32	19.06	13.85	10.10	7.39	5.43	4.00	2.95	19
20	69.13	49.74	35.93	26.05	18.96	13.85	10.15	7.47	5.51	4.08	3.03	20
21	67.34	48.71	35.38	25.79	18.87	13.85	10.21	7.55	5.60	4.17	3.11	21
22	65.59	47.70	34.82	25.52	18.77	13.85	10.26	7.63	5.69	4.25	3.19	22
23	63.88	46.71	34.28	25.25	18.67	13.85	10.31	7.70	5.77	4.34	3.27	23
24	62.22	45.74	33.75	24.99	18.58	13.85	10.37	7.78	5.86	4.43	3.36	24
25	60.60	44.79	33.22	24.74	18.48	13.86	10.42	7.87	5.96	4.52	3.44	25
26	59.04	43.87	32.71	24.48	18.39	13.86	10.48	7.95	6.05	4.62	3.53	26
27	57.52	42.97	32.21	24.24	18.30	13.86	10.54	8.03	6.14	4.71	3.63	27
28	56.02	42.07	31.71	23.99	18.21	13.86	10.59	8.12	6.24	4.81	3.72	28
29	54.56	41.20	31.22	23.74	18.11	13.86	10.65	8.20	6.34	4.91	3.82	29
30	53.15	40.34	30.73	23.49	18.02	13.87	10.70	8.29	6.44	5.01	3.92	30
31	51.78	39.52	30.27	23.26	17.93	13.87	10.76	8.38	6.54	5.12	4.02	31
32	50.46	38.72	29.81	23.03	17.85	13.88	10.82	8.47	6.64	5.23	4.12	32
33	49.19	37.94	29.37	22.81	17.77	13.89	10.89	8.56	6.75	5.34	4.23	33
34	47.94	37.18	28.93	22.59	17.69	13.90	10.95	8.66	6.86	5.45	4.35	34
35	46.72	36.43	28.50	22.37	17.61	13.91	11.02	8.75	6.97	5.57	4.46	35
36	45.54	35.70	28.08	22.15	17.53	13.92	11.08	8.85	7.08	5.69	4.58	36
37	44.39	34.98	27.66	21.94	17.45	13.93	11.15	8.95	7.20	5.81	4.70	37
38	43.26	34.27	27.24	21.72	17.37	13.94	11.21	9.04	7.32	5.93	4.82	38
39	42.16	33.58	26.84	21.51	17.30	13.95	11.28	9.14	7.43	6.06	4.95	39
40	41.09	32.90	26.43	21.30	17.22	13.95	11.34	9.24	7.55	6.19	5.08	40
41	40.05	32.24	26.04	21.10	17.14	13.97	11.41	9.35	7.68	6.32	5.22	41
42	39.04	31.60	25.66	20.90	17.07	13.98	11.48	9.45	7.80	6.46	5.36	42
43	38.06	30.97	25.28	20.70	16.99	13.99	11.55	9.56	7.93	6.60	5.50	43
44	37.11	30.36	24.92	20.51	16.92	14.01	11.62	9.67	8.06	6.74	5.65	44
45	36.18	29.76	24.56	20.32	16.85	14.02	11.69	9.78	8.20	6.89	5.80	45
46	35.28	29.18	24.20	20.13	16.79	14.04	11.77	9.89	8.33	7.04	5.96	46
47	34.41	28.61	23.86	19.95	16.72	14.06	11.85	10.01	8.47	7.19	6.12	47
48	33.57	28.06	23.52	19.77	16.66	14.08	11.92	10.13	8.62	7.35	6.29	48
49	32.75	27.52	23.19	19.60	16.60	14.10	12.01	10.25	8.77	7.52	6.46	49
50	31.96	27.01	22.88	19.43	16.55	14.13	12.09	10.38	8.92	7.69	6.64	50
51	31.21	26.51	22.58	19.28	16.51	14.17	12.19	10.51	9.08	7.87	6.83	51
52	30.48	26.03	22.29	19.13	16.47	14.21	12.28	10.65	9.25	8.05	7.02	52
53	29.79	25.57	22.01	19.00	16.43	14.25	12.39	10.79	9.42	8.24	7.23	53
54	29.12	25.13	21.75	18.87	16.41	14.30	12.50	10.94	9.60	8.44	7.44	54

Table 23: Multipliers for loss of pension commencing age 70 (males) *continued*

Age at date of trial	Multiplier calculated with allowance for projected mortality from the 2008–based population projections and rate of return of											Age at date of trial
	-2.0%	-1.5%	-1.0%	-0.5%	0.0%	0.5%	1.0%	1.5%	2.0%	2.5%	3.0%	
55	28.48	24.71	21.50	18.75	16.39	14.36	12.61	11.10	9.79	8.65	7.66	55
56	27.88	24.32	21.27	18.65	16.39	14.43	12.74	11.27	9.99	8.88	7.90	56
57	27.30	23.94	21.05	18.55	16.39	14.51	12.88	11.45	10.20	9.11	8.15	57
58	26.74	23.58	20.84	18.46	16.40	14.59	13.02	11.63	10.42	9.35	8.40	58
59	26.19	23.22	20.63	18.38	16.40	14.68	13.16	11.82	10.64	9.59	8.67	59
60	25.65	22.86	20.42	18.29	16.41	14.76	13.30	12.01	10.86	9.85	8.94	60
61	25.13	22.52	20.22	18.20	16.42	14.84	13.44	12.20	11.10	10.11	9.23	61
62	24.63	22.19	20.03	18.13	16.44	14.94	13.60	12.41	11.34	10.38	9.52	62
63	24.16	21.88	19.86	18.07	16.47	15.04	13.77	12.63	11.60	10.67	9.84	63
64	23.72	21.60	19.71	18.03	16.52	15.17	13.95	12.86	11.87	10.98	10.18	64
65	23.33	21.35	19.59	18.01	16.59	15.31	14.16	13.12	12.17	11.32	10.54	65
66	22.97	21.14	19.50	18.02	16.69	15.48	14.39	13.40	12.50	11.68	10.93	66
67	22.66	20.96	19.44	18.06	16.81	15.68	14.65	13.71	12.86	12.07	11.36	67
68	22.38	20.82	19.40	18.12	16.96	15.90	14.93	14.05	13.24	12.50	11.82	68
69	22.13	20.70	19.40	18.21	17.13	16.15	15.24	14.42	13.66	12.96	12.31	69
70	21.91	20.60	19.41	18.32	17.32	16.41	15.58	14.81	14.10	13.44	12.84	70

Table 24: Multipliers for loss of pension commencing age 70 (females)

Age at date of trial	Multiplier calculated with allowance for projected mortality from the 2008–based population projections and rate of return of											Age at date of trial
	–2.0%	–1.5%	–1.0%	–0.5%	0.0%	0.5%	1.0%	1.5%	2.0%	2.5%	3.0%	
0	134.74	86.70	56.06	36.43	23.78	15.60	10.28	6.80	4.52	3.01	2.02	0
1	131.93	85.35	55.49	36.25	23.79	15.68	10.38	6.91	4.61	3.09	2.08	1
2	128.66	83.68	54.69	35.92	23.69	15.70	10.45	6.99	4.69	3.16	2.14	2
3	125.45	82.03	53.90	35.58	23.60	15.72	10.52	7.07	4.77	3.23	2.20	3
4	122.32	80.42	53.12	35.25	23.50	15.74	10.58	7.15	4.85	3.30	2.25	4
5	119.26	78.83	52.35	34.93	23.41	15.76	10.65	7.23	4.93	3.37	2.32	5
6	116.28	77.27	51.59	34.60	23.31	15.77	10.72	7.31	5.01	3.44	2.38	6
7	113.36	75.74	50.83	34.27	23.21	15.79	10.78	7.39	5.09	3.52	2.44	7
8	110.51	74.23	50.09	33.95	23.11	15.80	10.85	7.48	5.18	3.59	2.51	8
9	107.73	72.75	49.35	33.63	23.01	15.82	10.92	7.56	5.26	3.67	2.57	9
10	105.03	71.30	48.63	33.31	22.92	15.83	10.98	7.65	5.35	3.75	2.64	10
11	102.39	69.89	47.92	33.00	22.82	15.85	11.05	7.73	5.43	3.83	2.71	11
12	99.81	68.49	47.21	32.68	22.72	15.86	11.12	7.82	5.52	3.92	2.79	12
13	97.30	67.13	46.52	32.37	22.62	15.87	11.18	7.91	5.61	4.00	2.86	13
14	94.85	65.79	45.83	32.07	22.53	15.89	11.25	8.00	5.71	4.09	2.94	14
15	92.46	64.48	45.16	31.76	22.43	15.90	11.32	8.09	5.80	4.17	3.01	15
16	90.13	63.19	44.49	31.46	22.33	15.92	11.39	8.18	5.89	4.26	3.09	16
17	87.86	61.93	43.84	31.16	22.24	15.93	11.46	8.27	5.99	4.36	3.18	17
18	85.65	60.70	43.19	30.86	22.14	15.95	11.53	8.36	6.09	4.45	3.26	18
19	83.51	59.49	42.56	30.57	22.05	15.96	11.60	8.46	6.19	4.55	3.35	19
20	81.42	58.32	41.94	30.29	21.96	15.98	11.67	8.55	6.29	4.64	3.44	20
21	79.38	57.16	41.33	30.00	21.86	15.99	11.74	8.65	6.40	4.74	3.53	21
22	77.38	56.02	40.72	29.72	21.77	16.01	11.81	8.75	6.50	4.85	3.62	22
23	75.43	54.90	40.12	29.43	21.67	16.02	11.88	8.85	6.61	4.95	3.72	23
24	73.52	53.80	39.52	29.15	21.58	16.03	11.95	8.94	6.71	5.06	3.82	24
25	71.67	52.72	38.94	28.87	21.48	16.05	12.03	9.04	6.82	5.16	3.92	25
26	69.86	51.67	38.37	28.60	21.39	16.06	12.10	9.14	6.93	5.28	4.03	26
27	68.11	50.64	37.80	28.32	21.30	16.07	12.17	9.25	7.05	5.39	4.13	27
28	66.39	49.63	37.25	28.05	21.21	16.09	12.24	9.35	7.16	5.50	4.24	28
29	64.72	48.64	36.70	27.79	21.11	16.10	12.32	9.46	7.28	5.62	4.36	29
30	63.09	47.68	36.16	27.52	21.03	16.12	12.39	9.56	7.40	5.74	4.47	30
31	61.51	46.73	35.63	27.27	20.94	16.13	12.47	9.67	7.52	5.87	4.59	31
32	59.98	45.81	35.11	27.01	20.85	16.15	12.55	9.78	7.65	6.00	4.72	32
33	58.48	44.91	34.60	26.76	20.76	16.16	12.62	9.89	7.77	6.13	4.84	33
34	57.02	44.02	34.10	26.51	20.68	16.18	12.70	10.00	7.90	6.26	4.97	34
35	55.59	43.14	33.60	26.26	20.59	16.20	12.78	10.12	8.03	6.39	5.10	35
36	54.20	42.29	33.11	26.01	20.50	16.21	12.86	10.23	8.16	6.53	5.24	36
37	52.85	41.45	32.63	25.77	20.42	16.23	12.94	10.35	8.30	6.67	5.38	37
38	51.53	40.64	32.16	25.53	20.33	16.25	13.02	10.46	8.44	6.82	5.53	38
39	50.24	39.83	31.69	25.29	20.25	16.26	13.10	10.58	8.57	6.97	5.67	39
40	48.99	39.05	31.23	25.06	20.17	16.28	13.18	10.70	8.72	7.12	5.83	40
41	47.77	38.28	30.78	24.82	20.08	16.30	13.27	10.83	8.86	7.27	5.98	41
42	46.58	37.53	30.34	24.60	20.00	16.32	13.35	10.95	9.01	7.43	6.14	42
43	45.43	36.80	29.90	24.37	19.93	16.34	13.44	11.08	9.16	7.59	6.31	43
44	44.31	36.08	29.48	24.15	19.85	16.36	13.52	11.21	9.31	7.76	6.48	44
45	43.23	35.39	29.06	23.94	19.78	16.39	13.61	11.34	9.47	7.93	6.66	45
46	42.17	34.70	28.65	23.73	19.70	16.41	13.70	11.47	9.63	8.11	6.84	46
47	41.14	34.04	28.25	23.52	19.63	16.44	13.80	11.61	9.80	8.29	7.03	47
48	40.14	33.39	27.86	23.32	19.57	16.47	13.89	11.75	9.97	8.47	7.22	48
49	39.18	32.77	27.49	23.12	19.51	16.50	13.99	11.90	10.14	8.67	7.42	49
50	38.25	32.16	27.12	22.93	19.45	16.54	14.10	12.05	10.32	8.86	7.63	50
51	37.34	31.56	26.76	22.75	19.39	16.57	14.20	12.20	10.51	9.07	7.84	51
52	36.46	30.99	26.41	22.57	19.34	16.62	14.31	12.36	10.69	9.28	8.06	52
53	35.61	30.43	26.07	22.40	19.29	16.66	14.42	12.52	10.89	9.49	8.30	53
54	34.79	29.89	25.74	22.23	19.25	16.71	14.54	12.69	11.09	9.72	8.53	54

Table 24: Multipliers for loss of pension commencing age 70 (females) *continued*

Age at date of trial	Multiplier calculated with allowance for projected mortality from the 2008–based population projections and rate of return of											Age at date of trial
	–2.0%	**–1.5%**	**–1.0%**	**–0.5%**	**0.0%**	**0.5%**	**1.0%**	**1.5%**	**2.0%**	**2.5%**	**3.0%**	
55	34.00	29.36	25.43	22.08	19.21	16.77	14.67	12.86	11.30	9.95	8.78	55
56	33.24	28.86	25.12	21.93	19.19	16.83	14.80	13.04	11.52	10.19	9.04	56
57	32.51	28.37	24.83	21.79	19.16	16.89	14.93	13.23	11.74	10.44	9.31	57
58	31.79	27.90	24.54	21.65	19.14	16.96	15.07	13.42	11.97	10.70	9.59	58
59	31.10	27.43	24.26	21.51	19.12	17.03	15.21	13.61	12.21	10.97	9.88	59
60	30.41	26.97	23.98	21.37	19.10	17.10	15.35	13.81	12.44	11.24	10.17	60
61	29.74	26.52	23.71	21.24	19.08	17.17	15.49	14.01	12.69	11.52	10.48	61
62	29.10	26.09	23.44	21.11	19.06	17.25	15.64	14.22	12.94	11.81	10.80	62
63	28.48	25.67	23.19	21.00	19.06	17.33	15.80	14.43	13.21	12.11	11.13	63
64	27.90	25.28	22.96	20.90	19.07	17.43	15.97	14.67	13.49	12.43	11.48	64
65	27.36	24.92	22.75	20.82	19.10	17.55	16.17	14.92	13.79	12.78	11.86	65
66	26.86	24.60	22.58	20.77	19.15	17.69	16.38	15.19	14.12	13.15	12.26	66
67	26.40	24.30	22.43	20.74	19.22	17.85	16.61	15.49	14.47	13.54	12.69	67
68	25.97	24.04	22.30	20.73	19.32	18.03	16.87	15.81	14.84	13.96	13.15	68
69	25.57	23.79	22.19	20.74	19.43	18.23	17.14	16.15	15.24	14.40	13.64	69
70	25.19	23.57	22.10	20.76	19.55	18.44	17.43	16.50	15.65	14.87	14.15	70

Table 25: Multipliers for loss of pension commencing age 75 (males)

Age at date of trial	Multiplier calculated with allowance for projected mortality from the 2008–based population projections and rate of return of											Age at date of trial
	-2.0%	**-1.5%**	**-1.0%**	**-0.5%**	**0.0%**	**0.5%**	**1.0%**	**1.5%**	**2.0%**	**2.5%**	**3.0%**	
0	97.81	62.36	39.93	25.68	16.58	10.74	6.99	4.57	2.99	1.97	1.30	0
1	95.69	61.34	39.49	25.52	16.56	10.79	7.06	4.63	3.05	2.02	1.34	1
2	93.15	60.03	38.85	25.24	16.47	10.79	7.09	4.68	3.10	2.06	1.37	2
3	90.66	58.74	38.22	24.97	16.37	10.78	7.12	4.73	3.15	2.10	1.41	3
4	88.23	57.47	37.59	24.69	16.28	10.77	7.16	4.77	3.19	2.14	1.44	4
5	85.86	56.23	36.98	24.41	16.18	10.76	7.19	4.82	3.24	2.19	1.48	5
6	83.55	55.01	36.37	24.14	16.08	10.75	7.22	4.86	3.29	2.23	1.52	6
7	81.31	53.82	35.77	23.86	15.98	10.74	7.25	4.91	3.33	2.27	1.55	7
8	79.12	52.65	35.18	23.59	15.88	10.73	7.28	4.95	3.38	2.32	1.59	8
9	76.97	51.50	34.59	23.32	15.79	10.72	7.31	5.00	3.43	2.36	1.63	9
10	74.89	50.37	34.02	23.06	15.69	10.71	7.34	5.05	3.48	2.41	1.67	10
11	72.85	49.27	33.45	22.79	15.59	10.70	7.37	5.09	3.53	2.46	1.71	11
12	70.88	48.19	32.89	22.53	15.49	10.69	7.40	5.14	3.58	2.50	1.76	12
13	68.96	47.14	32.34	22.27	15.39	10.67	7.43	5.19	3.63	2.55	1.80	13
14	67.09	46.10	31.80	22.02	15.29	10.66	7.46	5.23	3.68	2.60	1.84	14
15	65.27	45.10	31.27	21.76	15.20	10.65	7.49	5.28	3.74	2.65	1.89	15
16	63.50	44.11	30.75	21.51	15.10	10.64	7.52	5.33	3.79	2.71	1.94	16
17	61.78	43.15	30.24	21.27	15.01	10.63	7.55	5.38	3.85	2.76	1.98	17
18	60.12	42.21	29.74	21.03	14.92	10.62	7.58	5.43	3.90	2.81	2.03	18
19	58.50	41.29	29.25	20.79	14.82	10.61	7.61	5.48	3.96	2.87	2.08	19
20	56.93	40.40	28.77	20.55	14.74	10.60	7.65	5.53	4.02	2.92	2.13	20
21	55.40	39.52	28.29	20.32	14.65	10.59	7.68	5.59	4.08	2.98	2.19	21
22	53.90	38.66	27.82	20.09	14.55	10.58	7.71	5.64	4.13	3.04	2.24	22
23	52.44	37.81	27.36	19.86	14.46	10.57	7.74	5.69	4.19	3.10	2.30	23
24	51.02	36.99	26.90	19.63	14.37	10.55	7.77	5.74	4.25	3.16	2.35	24
25	49.64	36.18	26.46	19.41	14.28	10.54	7.81	5.80	4.31	3.22	2.41	25
26	48.31	35.40	26.02	19.19	14.20	10.53	7.84	5.85	4.38	3.29	2.47	26
27	47.02	34.64	25.60	18.98	14.11	10.52	7.87	5.91	4.44	3.35	2.53	27
28	45.74	33.88	25.17	18.76	14.02	10.51	7.90	5.96	4.51	3.42	2.60	28
29	44.50	33.14	24.75	18.54	13.93	10.50	7.94	6.01	4.57	3.48	2.66	29
30	43.30	32.41	24.34	18.33	13.85	10.49	7.97	6.07	4.64	3.55	2.73	30
31	42.14	31.71	23.94	18.13	13.76	10.48	8.00	6.13	4.70	3.62	2.79	31
32	41.02	31.04	23.56	17.93	13.69	10.48	8.04	6.19	4.77	3.69	2.86	32
33	39.94	30.38	23.18	17.74	13.61	10.47	8.08	6.25	4.85	3.77	2.94	33
34	38.89	29.74	22.81	17.54	13.53	10.47	8.12	6.31	4.92	3.84	3.01	34
35	37.86	29.10	22.44	17.35	13.45	10.46	8.15	6.37	4.99	3.92	3.09	35
36	36.86	28.49	22.08	17.16	13.38	10.46	8.19	6.43	5.07	4.00	3.16	36
37	35.88	27.88	21.73	16.98	13.30	10.45	8.23	6.50	5.14	4.08	3.24	37
38	34.93	27.29	21.38	16.79	13.23	10.44	8.27	6.56	5.22	4.16	3.33	38
39	34.00	26.71	21.03	16.61	13.15	10.44	8.31	6.62	5.30	4.24	3.41	39
40	33.10	26.14	20.69	16.43	13.07	10.43	8.34	6.69	5.38	4.33	3.49	40
41	32.22	25.58	20.36	16.25	13.00	10.43	8.38	6.75	5.46	4.42	3.58	41
42	31.38	25.04	20.04	16.07	12.93	10.42	8.42	6.82	5.54	4.51	3.67	42
43	30.55	24.51	19.72	15.90	12.86	10.42	8.46	6.89	5.62	4.60	3.77	43
44	29.75	24.00	19.41	15.73	12.79	10.42	8.50	6.96	5.71	4.69	3.86	44
45	28.98	23.50	19.10	15.57	12.72	10.41	8.55	7.03	5.79	4.79	3.96	45
46	28.22	23.01	18.80	15.41	12.65	10.41	8.59	7.10	5.88	4.88	4.06	46
47	27.49	22.53	18.51	15.25	12.59	10.41	8.63	7.17	5.97	4.99	4.17	47
48	26.78	22.07	18.23	15.09	12.52	10.41	8.68	7.25	6.07	5.09	4.28	48
49	26.10	21.62	17.95	14.94	12.46	10.42	8.73	7.33	6.16	5.20	4.39	49
50	25.44	21.18	17.68	14.80	12.41	10.43	8.78	7.41	6.26	5.31	4.50	50
51	24.80	20.77	17.43	14.66	12.36	10.44	8.83	7.49	6.37	5.42	4.62	51
52	24.20	20.37	17.18	14.53	12.31	10.45	8.89	7.58	6.48	5.54	4.75	52
53	23.61	19.98	16.95	14.41	12.27	10.47	8.96	7.67	6.59	5.67	4.88	53
54	23.05	19.61	16.72	14.29	12.23	10.50	9.02	7.77	6.70	5.80	5.02	54

Table 25: Multipliers for loss of pension commencing age 75 (males) *continued*

Age at date of trial	Multiplier calculated with allowance for projected mortality from the 2008–based population projections and rate of return of											Age at date of trial
	–2.0%	*–1.5%*	*–1.0%*	*–0.5%*	*0.0%*	*0.5%*	*1.0%*	*1.5%*	*2.0%*	*2.5%*	*3.0%*	
55	22.52	19.26	16.51	14.18	12.20	10.53	9.09	7.87	6.83	5.93	5.16	55
56	22.01	18.93	16.31	14.08	12.18	10.56	9.17	7.98	6.96	6.08	5.31	56
57	21.53	18.61	16.12	13.99	12.17	10.60	9.26	8.10	7.09	6.23	5.47	57
58	21.06	18.30	15.94	13.91	12.16	10.65	9.34	8.21	7.23	6.38	5.64	58
59	20.60	18.00	15.76	13.82	12.15	10.69	9.43	8.33	7.38	6.54	5.81	59
60	20.15	17.70	15.58	13.73	12.13	10.74	9.52	8.45	7.52	6.70	5.98	60
61	19.71	17.41	15.40	13.65	12.12	10.78	9.61	8.58	7.67	6.87	6.16	61
62	19.29	17.13	15.23	13.57	12.12	10.84	9.71	8.71	7.83	7.04	6.35	62
63	18.89	16.86	15.08	13.51	12.12	10.89	9.81	8.85	7.99	7.23	6.55	63
64	18.52	16.62	14.94	13.45	12.13	10.96	9.92	8.99	8.16	7.42	6.76	64
65	18.18	16.40	14.82	13.41	12.16	11.05	10.05	9.16	8.35	7.63	6.99	65
66	17.87	16.21	14.73	13.40	12.21	11.15	10.20	9.34	8.56	7.86	7.23	66
67	17.60	16.04	14.65	13.40	12.28	11.27	10.36	9.53	8.79	8.11	7.50	67
68	17.35	15.90	14.60	13.42	12.37	11.41	10.54	9.75	9.03	8.38	7.78	68
69	17.12	15.78	14.56	13.46	12.47	11.56	10.73	9.98	9.30	8.67	8.09	69
70	16.92	15.67	14.54	13.51	12.58	11.72	10.94	10.23	9.58	8.97	8.42	70
71	16.72	15.57	14.53	13.57	12.70	11.90	11.17	10.49	9.87	9.30	8.77	71
72	16.53	15.48	14.52	13.64	12.83	12.08	11.40	10.77	10.18	9.64	9.14	72
73	16.36	15.40	14.52	13.71	12.97	12.28	11.64	11.05	10.51	10.00	9.53	73
74	16.19	15.33	14.53	13.80	13.12	12.49	11.90	11.36	10.86	10.39	9.95	74
75	16.04	15.27	14.56	13.90	13.29	12.72	12.19	11.70	11.24	10.81	10.40	75

Table 26: Multipliers for loss of pension commencing age 75 (females)

Age at date of trial	Multiplier calculated with allowance for projected mortality from the 2008–based population projections and rate of return of											Age at date of trial
	–2.0%	*–1.5%*	*–1.0%*	*–0.5%*	*0.0%*	*0.5%*	*1.0%*	*1.5%*	*2.0%*	*2.5%*	*3.0%*	
0	114.99	73.05	46.61	29.87	19.22	12.42	8.06	5.25	3.43	2.25	1.48	0
1	112.51	71.86	46.09	29.69	19.21	12.48	8.13	5.33	3.50	2.31	1.53	1
2	109.64	70.40	45.40	29.40	19.12	12.48	8.18	5.38	3.56	2.36	1.57	2
3	106.83	68.96	44.71	29.10	19.02	12.49	8.23	5.44	3.61	2.41	1.61	3
4	104.08	67.55	44.02	28.81	18.93	12.49	8.27	5.50	3.67	2.46	1.65	4
5	101.41	66.16	43.35	28.52	18.84	12.49	8.32	5.56	3.73	2.51	1.69	5
6	98.79	64.80	42.69	28.23	18.75	12.50	8.36	5.62	3.79	2.56	1.74	6
7	96.24	63.47	42.03	27.94	18.65	12.50	8.41	5.67	3.84	2.61	1.78	7
8	93.75	62.16	41.38	27.66	18.56	12.50	8.45	5.73	3.90	2.67	1.83	8
9	91.32	60.87	40.74	27.37	18.46	12.50	8.50	5.79	3.97	2.72	1.88	9
10	88.95	59.61	40.11	27.09	18.37	12.50	8.54	5.85	4.03	2.78	1.92	10
11	86.65	58.38	39.49	26.82	18.28	12.50	8.59	5.92	4.09	2.84	1.97	11
12	84.41	57.17	38.88	26.54	18.18	12.51	8.63	5.98	4.15	2.90	2.03	12
13	82.21	55.99	38.27	26.26	18.09	12.51	8.68	6.04	4.22	2.96	2.08	13
14	80.08	54.83	37.68	25.99	18.00	12.51	8.72	6.10	4.28	3.02	2.13	14
15	78.00	53.69	37.09	25.73	17.91	12.51	8.77	6.16	4.35	3.08	2.19	15
16	75.98	52.58	36.52	25.46	17.81	12.51	8.81	6.23	4.42	3.14	2.24	16
17	74.00	51.48	35.95	25.20	17.72	12.51	8.86	6.29	4.49	3.21	2.30	17
18	72.08	50.42	35.39	24.94	17.63	12.51	8.90	6.36	4.55	3.27	2.36	18
19	70.22	49.37	34.84	24.68	17.54	12.51	8.95	6.42	4.63	3.34	2.42	19
20	68.41	48.36	34.31	24.43	17.45	12.51	9.00	6.49	4.70	3.41	2.48	20
21	66.64	47.36	33.78	24.18	17.36	12.51	9.05	6.56	4.77	3.48	2.55	21
22	64.91	46.38	33.26	23.93	17.27	12.51	9.09	6.63	4.85	3.55	2.61	22
23	63.22	45.41	32.73	23.68	17.18	12.51	9.14	6.69	4.92	3.63	2.68	23
24	61.56	44.46	32.22	23.43	17.09	12.51	9.18	6.76	4.99	3.70	2.75	24
25	59.96	43.53	31.71	23.18	17.00	12.51	9.23	6.83	5.07	3.78	2.82	25
26	58.40	42.63	31.22	22.94	16.91	12.51	9.28	6.90	5.15	3.85	2.89	26
27	56.88	41.74	30.73	22.70	16.82	12.51	9.32	6.97	5.23	3.93	2.97	27
28	55.40	40.87	30.25	22.47	16.74	12.50	9.37	7.04	5.31	4.01	3.04	28
29	53.96	40.02	29.78	22.23	16.65	12.50	9.42	7.12	5.39	4.10	3.12	29
30	52.56	39.19	29.32	22.00	16.56	12.50	9.47	7.19	5.47	4.18	3.20	30
31	51.20	38.38	28.86	21.78	16.48	12.50	9.52	7.26	5.56	4.27	3.28	31
32	49.88	37.59	28.42	21.55	16.39	12.51	9.57	7.34	5.65	4.35	3.37	32
33	48.59	36.82	27.98	21.33	16.31	12.51	9.62	7.42	5.73	4.44	3.45	33
34	47.33	36.05	27.55	21.11	16.23	12.51	9.67	7.49	5.82	4.54	3.54	34
35	46.10	35.30	27.12	20.89	16.14	12.51	9.72	7.57	5.91	4.63	3.63	35
36	44.91	34.57	26.70	20.68	16.06	12.51	9.77	7.65	6.00	4.73	3.73	36
37	43.75	33.86	26.29	20.47	15.98	12.51	9.82	7.73	6.10	4.82	3.82	37
38	42.62	33.16	25.88	20.26	15.90	12.51	9.87	7.81	6.19	4.92	3.92	38
39	41.52	32.48	25.48	20.05	15.82	12.51	9.92	7.89	6.29	5.02	4.02	39
40	40.44	31.81	25.09	19.84	15.73	12.51	9.97	7.97	6.39	5.13	4.13	40
41	39.40	31.15	24.70	19.64	15.66	12.51	10.03	8.05	6.49	5.23	4.23	41
42	38.38	30.51	24.32	19.44	15.58	12.52	10.08	8.14	6.59	5.34	4.34	42
43	37.40	29.89	23.95	19.24	15.50	12.52	10.13	8.22	6.69	5.45	4.46	43
44	36.44	29.28	23.59	19.05	15.43	12.52	10.19	8.31	6.80	5.57	4.57	44
45	35.52	28.69	23.23	18.86	15.35	12.53	10.25	8.40	6.90	5.69	4.69	45
46	34.61	28.10	22.88	18.68	15.28	12.53	10.31	8.49	7.01	5.81	4.82	46
47	33.73	27.54	22.54	18.49	15.21	12.54	10.36	8.58	7.13	5.93	4.94	47
48	32.89	26.99	22.21	18.32	15.14	12.55	10.43	8.68	7.24	6.06	5.07	48
49	32.07	26.46	21.88	18.15	15.08	12.56	10.49	8.78	7.36	6.19	5.21	49
50	31.27	25.94	21.57	17.98	15.02	12.58	10.56	8.88	7.48	6.32	5.35	50
51	30.50	25.43	21.26	17.81	14.96	12.59	10.62	8.98	7.61	6.46	5.49	51
52	29.75	24.94	20.96	17.65	14.90	12.61	10.69	9.09	7.74	6.60	5.64	52
53	29.03	24.47	20.67	17.50	14.85	12.63	10.77	9.20	7.87	6.75	5.80	53
54	28.33	24.01	20.39	17.35	14.80	12.66	10.84	9.31	8.01	6.90	5.96	54

Table 26: Multipliers for loss of pension commencing age 75 (females) *continued*

Age at date of trial	Multiplier calculated with allowance for projected mortality from the 2008–based population projections and rate of return of											Age at date of trial
	–2.0%	*–1.5%*	*–1.0%*	*–0.5%*	*0.0%*	*0.5%*	*1.0%*	*1.5%*	*2.0%*	*2.5%*	*3.0%*	
55	27.66	23.56	20.12	17.21	14.76	12.69	10.92	9.43	8.15	7.06	6.12	55
56	27.02	23.14	19.86	17.08	14.72	12.72	11.01	9.55	8.30	7.22	6.30	56
57	26.39	22.72	19.60	16.95	14.69	12.75	11.10	9.67	8.45	7.39	6.48	57
58	25.78	22.32	19.36	16.83	14.66	12.79	11.19	9.80	8.60	7.56	6.66	58
59	25.19	21.92	19.11	16.70	14.62	12.83	11.28	9.93	8.76	7.74	6.85	59
60	24.61	21.53	18.87	16.57	14.59	12.86	11.37	10.06	8.92	7.92	7.05	60
61	24.04	21.14	18.63	16.45	14.55	12.90	11.46	10.19	9.08	8.11	7.25	61
62	23.49	20.77	18.40	16.33	14.52	12.94	11.55	10.33	9.25	8.30	7.46	62
63	22.96	20.41	18.17	16.22	14.50	12.99	11.65	10.47	9.43	8.50	7.68	63
64	22.46	20.07	17.97	16.12	14.48	13.04	11.76	10.63	9.62	8.71	7.91	64
65	22.00	19.76	17.78	16.04	14.49	13.11	11.89	10.79	9.82	8.94	8.16	65
66	21.56	19.48	17.62	15.97	14.51	13.20	12.03	10.98	10.03	9.19	8.42	66
67	21.16	19.22	17.48	15.93	14.54	13.30	12.18	11.17	10.27	9.45	8.71	67
68	20.79	18.98	17.36	15.90	14.59	13.41	12.35	11.39	10.51	9.72	9.01	68
69	20.44	18.76	17.25	15.88	14.65	13.54	12.53	11.61	10.78	10.02	9.33	69
70	20.11	18.55	17.15	15.87	14.72	13.67	12.72	11.85	11.05	10.33	9.66	70
71	19.78	18.35	17.05	15.87	14.79	13.81	12.91	12.09	11.34	10.65	10.01	71
72	19.46	18.14	16.95	15.86	14.86	13.95	13.11	12.34	11.63	10.98	10.38	72
73	19.13	17.93	16.84	15.84	14.93	14.08	13.31	12.59	11.93	11.32	10.75	73
74	18.80	17.72	16.74	15.83	15.00	14.23	13.51	12.86	12.24	11.68	11.15	74
75	18.48	17.53	16.64	15.83	15.08	14.38	13.74	13.14	12.58	12.06	11.58	75

Table 27: Discounting factors for term certain

Term	-2.0%	-1.5%	-1.0%	-0.5%	0.0%	0.5%	1.0%	1.5%	2.0%	2.5%	3.0%	Term
	Factor to discount value of multiplier for a period of deferment											
1	1.0204	1.0152	1.0101	1.0050	1.0000	0.9950	0.9901	0.9852	0.9804	0.9756	0.9709	1
2	1.0412	1.0307	1.0203	1.0101	1.0000	0.9901	0.9803	0.9707	0.9612	0.9518	0.9426	2
3	1.0625	1.0464	1.0306	1.0152	1.0000	0.9851	0.9706	0.9563	0.9423	0.9286	0.9151	3
4	1.0842	1.0623	1.0410	1.0203	1.0000	0.9802	0.9610	0.9422	0.9238	0.9060	0.8885	4
5	1.1063	1.0785	1.0515	1.0254	1.0000	0.9754	0.9515	0.9283	0.9057	0.8839	0.8626	5
6	1.1289	1.0949	1.0622	1.0305	1.0000	0.9705	0.9420	0.9145	0.8880	0.8623	0.8375	6
7	1.1519	1.1116	1.0729	1.0357	1.0000	0.9657	0.9327	0.9010	0.8706	0.8413	0.8131	7
8	1.1754	1.1285	1.0837	1.0409	1.0000	0.9609	0.9235	0.8877	0.8535	0.8207	0.7894	8
9	1.1994	1.1457	1.0947	1.0461	1.0000	0.9561	0.9143	0.8746	0.8368	0.8007	0.7664	9
10	1.2239	1.1632	1.1057	1.0514	1.0000	0.9513	0.9053	0.8617	0.8203	0.7812	0.7441	10
11	1.2489	1.1809	1.1169	1.0567	1.0000	0.9466	0.8963	0.8489	0.8043	0.7621	0.7224	11
12	1.2743	1.1989	1.1282	1.0620	1.0000	0.9419	0.8874	0.8364	0.7885	0.7436	0.7014	12
13	1.3004	1.2171	1.1396	1.0673	1.0000	0.9372	0.8787	0.8240	0.7730	0.7254	0.6810	13
14	1.3269	1.2356	1.1511	1.0727	1.0000	0.9326	0.8700	0.8118	0.7579	0.7077	0.6611	14
15	1.3540	1.2545	1.1627	1.0781	1.0000	0.9279	0.8613	0.7999	0.7430	0.6905	0.6419	15
16	1.3816	1.2736	1.1745	1.0835	1.0000	0.9233	0.8528	0.7880	0.7284	0.6736	0.6232	16
17	1.4098	1.2930	1.1863	1.0889	1.0000	0.9187	0.8444	0.7764	0.7142	0.6572	0.6050	17
18	1.4386	1.3126	1.1983	1.0944	1.0000	0.9141	0.8360	0.7649	0.7002	0.6412	0.5874	18
19	1.4679	1.3326	1.2104	1.0999	1.0000	0.9096	0.8277	0.7536	0.6864	0.6255	0.5703	19
20	1.4979	1.3529	1.2226	1.1054	1.0000	0.9051	0.8195	0.7425	0.6730	0.6103	0.5537	20
21	1.5285	1.3735	1.2350	1.1110	1.0000	0.9006	0.8114	0.7315	0.6598	0.5954	0.5375	21
22	1.5596	1.3944	1.2475	1.1166	1.0000	0.8961	0.8034	0.7207	0.6468	0.5809	0.5219	22
23	1.5915	1.4157	1.2601	1.1222	1.0000	0.8916	0.7954	0.7100	0.6342	0.5667	0.5067	23
24	1.6240	1.4372	1.2728	1.1278	1.0000	0.8872	0.7876	0.6995	0.6217	0.5529	0.4919	24
25	1.6571	1.4591	1.2856	1.1335	1.0000	0.8828	0.7798	0.6892	0.6095	0.5394	0.4776	25
26	1.6909	1.4814	1.2986	1.1392	1.0000	0.8784	0.7720	0.6790	0.5976	0.5262	0.4637	26
27	1.7254	1.5039	1.3117	1.1449	1.0000	0.8740	0.7644	0.6690	0.5859	0.5134	0.4502	27
28	1.7606	1.5268	1.3250	1.1507	1.0000	0.8697	0.7568	0.6591	0.5744	0.5009	0.4371	28
29	1.7966	1.5501	1.3384	1.1565	1.0000	0.8653	0.7493	0.6494	0.5631	0.4887	0.4243	29
30	1.8332	1.5737	1.3519	1.1623	1.0000	0.8610	0.7419	0.6398	0.5521	0.4767	0.4120	30
31	1.8706	1.5976	1.3656	1.1681	1.0000	0.8567	0.7346	0.6303	0.5412	0.4651	0.4000	31
32	1.9088	1.6220	1.3793	1.1740	1.0000	0.8525	0.7273	0.6210	0.5306	0.4538	0.3883	32
33	1.9478	1.6467	1.3933	1.1799	1.0000	0.8482	0.7201	0.6118	0.5202	0.4427	0.3770	33
34	1.9875	1.6717	1.4074	1.1858	1.0000	0.8440	0.7130	0.6028	0.5100	0.4319	0.3660	34
35	2.0281	1.6972	1.4216	1.1918	1.0000	0.8398	0.7059	0.5939	0.5000	0.4214	0.3554	35
36	2.0695	1.7230	1.4359	1.1978	1.0000	0.8356	0.6989	0.5851	0.4902	0.4111	0.3450	36
37	2.1117	1.7493	1.4504	1.2038	1.0000	0.8315	0.6920	0.5764	0.4806	0.4011	0.3350	37
38	2.1548	1.7759	1.4651	1.2098	1.0000	0.8274	0.6852	0.5679	0.4712	0.3913	0.3252	38
39	2.1988	1.8030	1.4799	1.2159	1.0000	0.8232	0.6784	0.5595	0.4619	0.3817	0.3158	39
40	2.2437	1.8304	1.4948	1.2220	1.0000	0.8191	0.6717	0.5513	0.4529	0.3724	0.3066	40
41	2.2894	1.8583	1.5099	1.2282	1.0000	0.8151	0.6650	0.5431	0.4440	0.3633	0.2976	41
42	2.3362	1.8866	1.5252	1.2343	1.0000	0.8110	0.6584	0.5351	0.4353	0.3545	0.2890	42
43	2.3838	1.9153	1.5406	1.2405	1.0000	0.8070	0.6519	0.5272	0.4268	0.3458	0.2805	43
44	2.4325	1.9445	1.5561	1.2468	1.0000	0.8030	0.6454	0.5194	0.4184	0.3374	0.2724	44
45	2.4821	1.9741	1.5719	1.2530	1.0000	0.7990	0.6391	0.5117	0.4102	0.3292	0.2644	45
46	2.5328	2.0042	1.5877	1.2593	1.0000	0.7950	0.6327	0.5042	0.4022	0.3211	0.2567	46
47	2.5845	2.0347	1.6038	1.2657	1.0000	0.7910	0.6265	0.4967	0.3943	0.3133	0.2493	47
48	2.6372	2.0657	1.6200	1.2720	1.0000	0.7871	0.6203	0.4894	0.3865	0.3057	0.2420	48
49	2.6911	2.0971	1.6363	1.2784	1.0000	0.7832	0.6141	0.4821	0.3790	0.2982	0.2350	49
50	2.7460	2.1291	1.6529	1.2848	1.0000	0.7793	0.6080	0.4750	0.3715	0.2909	0.2281	50
51	2.8020	2.1615	1.6696	1.2913	1.0000	0.7754	0.6020	0.4680	0.3642	0.2838	0.2215	51
52	2.8592	2.1944	1.6864	1.2978	1.0000	0.7716	0.5961	0.4611	0.3571	0.2769	0.2150	52
53	2.9175	2.2278	1.7035	1.3043	1.0000	0.7677	0.5902	0.4543	0.3501	0.2702	0.2088	53
54	2.9771	2.2617	1.7207	1.3109	1.0000	0.7639	0.5843	0.4475	0.3432	0.2636	0.2027	54
55	3.0378	2.2962	1.7381	1.3174	1.0000	0.7601	0.5785	0.4409	0.3365	0.2572	0.1968	55

Table 27: Discounting factors for term certain *continued*

Term	Factor to discount value of multiplier for a period of deferment											Term
	−2.0%	−1.5%	−1.0%	−0.5%	0.0%	0.5%	1.0%	1.5%	2.0%	2.5%	3.0%	
56	3.0998	2.3312	1.7556	1.3241	1.0000	0.7563	0.5728	0.4344	0.3299	0.2509	0.1910	56
57	3.1631	2.3667	1.7733	1.3307	1.0000	0.7525	0.5671	0.4280	0.3234	0.2448	0.1855	57
58	3.2277	2.4027	1.7913	1.3374	1.0000	0.7488	0.5615	0.4217	0.3171	0.2388	0.1801	58
59	3.2935	2.4393	1.8094	1.3441	1.0000	0.7451	0.5560	0.4154	0.3109	0.2330	0.1748	59
60	3.3607	2.4764	1.8276	1.3509	1.0000	0.7414	0.5504	0.4093	0.3048	0.2273	0.1697	60
61	3.4293	2.5141	1.8461	1.3577	1.0000	0.7377	0.5450	0.4032	0.2988	0.2217	0.1648	61
62	3.4993	2.5524	1.8647	1.3645	1.0000	0.7340	0.5396	0.3973	0.2929	0.2163	0.1600	62
63	3.5707	2.5913	1.8836	1.3713	1.0000	0.7304	0.5343	0.3914	0.2872	0.2111	0.1553	63
64	3.6436	2.6308	1.9026	1.3782	1.0000	0.7267	0.5290	0.3856	0.2816	0.2059	0.1508	64
65	3.7180	2.6708	1.9218	1.3852	1.0000	0.7231	0.5237	0.3799	0.2761	0.2009	0.1464	65
66	3.7938	2.7115	1.9412	1.3921	1.0000	0.7195	0.5185	0.3743	0.2706	0.1960	0.1421	66
67	3.8713	2.7528	1.9608	1.3991	1.0000	0.7159	0.5134	0.3688	0.2653	0.1912	0.1380	67
68	3.9503	2.7947	1.9806	1.4061	1.0000	0.7124	0.5083	0.3633	0.2601	0.1865	0.1340	68
69	4.0309	2.8373	2.0007	1.4132	1.0000	0.7088	0.5033	0.3580	0.2550	0.1820	0.1301	69
70	4.1132	2.8805	2.0209	1.4203	1.0000	0.7053	0.4983	0.3527	0.2500	0.1776	0.1263	70
71	4.1971	2.9243	2.0413	1.4275	1.0000	0.7018	0.4934	0.3475	0.2451	0.1732	0.1226	71
72	4.2827	2.9689	2.0619	1.4346	1.0000	0.6983	0.4885	0.3423	0.2403	0.1690	0.1190	72
73	4.3702	3.0141	2.0827	1.4418	1.0000	0.6948	0.4837	0.3373	0.2356	0.1649	0.1156	73
74	4.4593	3.0600	2.1038	1.4491	1.0000	0.6914	0.4789	0.3323	0.2310	0.1609	0.1122	74
75	4.5503	3.1066	2.1250	1.4564	1.0000	0.6879	0.4741	0.3274	0.2265	0.1569	0.1089	75
76	4.6432	3.1539	2.1465	1.4637	1.0000	0.6845	0.4694	0.3225	0.2220	0.1531	0.1058	76
77	4.7380	3.2019	2.1682	1.4710	1.0000	0.6811	0.4648	0.3178	0.2177	0.1494	0.1027	77
78	4.8347	3.2507	2.1901	1.4784	1.0000	0.6777	0.4602	0.3131	0.2134	0.1457	0.0997	78
79	4.9333	3.3002	2.2122	1.4859	1.0000	0.6743	0.4556	0.3084	0.2092	0.1422	0.0968	79
80	5.0340	3.3504	2.2345	1.4933	1.0000	0.6710	0.4511	0.3039	0.2051	0.1387	0.0940	80

Table 28: Multipliers for pecuniary loss for term certain

Term	Multiplier for regular frequent payments for a term certain at rate of return of											Term
	-2.0%	*-1.5%*	*-1.0%*	*-0.5%*	*0.0%*	*0.5%*	*1.0%*	*1.5%*	*2.0%*	*2.5%*	*3.0%*	
1	1.01	1.01	1.01	1.00	1.00	1.00	1.00	0.99	0.99	0.99	0.99	1
2	2.04	2.03	2.02	2.01	2.00	1.99	1.98	1.97	1.96	1.95	1.94	2
3	3.09	3.07	3.05	3.02	3.00	2.98	2.96	2.93	2.91	2.89	2.87	3
4	4.17	4.12	4.08	4.04	4.00	3.96	3.92	3.88	3.85	3.81	3.77	4
5	5.26	5.19	5.13	5.06	5.00	4.94	4.88	4.82	4.76	4.70	4.65	5
6	6.38	6.28	6.18	6.09	6.00	5.91	5.82	5.74	5.66	5.58	5.50	6
7	7.52	7.38	7.25	7.12	7.00	6.88	6.76	6.65	6.54	6.43	6.32	7
8	8.68	8.50	8.33	8.16	8.00	7.84	7.69	7.54	7.40	7.26	7.12	8
9	9.87	9.64	9.42	9.21	9.00	8.80	8.61	8.42	8.24	8.07	7.90	9
10	11.08	10.80	10.52	10.25	10.00	9.75	9.52	9.29	9.07	8.86	8.66	10
11	12.32	11.97	11.63	11.31	11.00	10.70	10.42	10.15	9.88	9.63	9.39	11
12	13.58	13.16	12.75	12.37	12.00	11.65	11.31	10.99	10.68	10.39	10.10	12
13	14.87	14.37	13.89	13.43	13.00	12.59	12.19	11.82	11.46	11.12	10.79	13
14	16.18	15.59	15.03	14.50	14.00	13.52	13.07	12.64	12.23	11.84	11.46	14
15	17.52	16.84	16.19	15.58	15.00	14.45	13.93	13.44	12.98	12.54	12.12	15
16	18.89	18.10	17.36	16.66	16.00	15.38	14.79	14.24	13.71	13.22	12.75	16
17	20.28	19.38	18.54	17.75	17.00	16.30	15.64	15.02	14.43	13.88	13.36	17
18	21.71	20.69	19.73	18.84	18.00	17.22	16.48	15.79	15.14	14.53	13.96	18
19	23.16	22.01	20.94	19.93	19.00	18.13	17.31	16.55	15.83	15.17	14.54	19
20	24.64	23.35	22.15	21.04	20.00	19.03	18.14	17.30	16.51	15.78	15.10	20
21	26.16	24.71	23.38	22.15	21.00	19.94	18.95	18.03	17.18	16.39	15.65	21
22	27.70	26.10	24.62	23.26	22.00	20.84	19.76	18.76	17.83	16.97	16.17	22
23	29.28	27.50	25.88	24.38	23.00	21.73	20.56	19.48	18.47	17.55	16.69	23
24	30.88	28.93	27.14	25.50	24.00	22.62	21.35	20.18	19.10	18.11	17.19	24
25	32.53	30.38	28.42	26.63	25.00	23.50	22.13	20.87	19.72	18.65	17.67	25
26	34.20	31.85	29.71	27.77	26.00	24.38	22.91	21.56	20.32	19.19	18.14	26
27	35.91	33.34	31.02	28.91	27.00	25.26	23.68	22.23	20.91	19.71	18.60	27
28	37.65	34.86	32.34	30.06	28.00	26.13	24.44	22.90	21.49	20.21	19.04	28
29	39.43	36.40	33.67	31.21	29.00	27.00	25.19	23.55	22.06	20.71	19.47	29
30	41.24	37.96	35.01	32.37	30.00	27.86	25.94	24.20	22.62	21.19	19.89	30
31	43.10	39.54	36.37	33.54	31.00	28.72	26.67	24.83	23.17	21.66	20.30	31
32	44.99	41.15	37.74	34.71	32.00	29.58	27.41	25.46	23.70	22.12	20.69	32
33	46.91	42.79	39.13	35.89	33.00	30.43	28.13	26.07	24.23	22.57	21.08	33
34	48.88	44.45	40.53	37.07	34.00	31.27	28.85	26.68	24.74	23.01	21.45	34
35	50.89	46.13	41.95	38.26	35.00	32.12	29.56	27.28	25.25	23.43	21.81	35
36	52.94	47.84	43.37	39.45	36.00	32.95	30.26	27.87	25.74	23.85	22.16	36
37	55.03	49.58	44.82	40.65	37.00	33.79	30.95	28.45	26.23	24.26	22.50	37
38	57.16	51.34	46.28	41.86	38.00	34.62	31.64	29.02	26.70	24.65	22.83	38
39	59.34	53.13	47.75	43.07	39.00	35.44	32.32	29.58	27.17	25.04	23.15	39
40	61.56	54.95	49.24	44.29	40.00	36.26	33.00	30.14	27.63	25.42	23.46	40
41	63.83	56.79	50.74	45.52	41.00	37.08	33.67	30.69	28.08	25.78	23.76	41
42	66.14	58.66	52.26	46.75	42.00	37.89	34.33	31.23	28.52	26.14	24.06	42
43	68.50	60.56	53.79	47.99	43.00	38.70	34.98	31.76	28.95	26.49	24.34	43
44	70.91	62.49	55.34	49.23	44.00	39.51	35.63	32.28	29.37	26.83	24.62	44
45	73.36	64.45	56.90	50.48	45.00	40.31	36.27	32.80	29.78	27.17	24.88	45
46	75.87	66.44	58.48	51.74	46.00	41.10	36.91	33.30	30.19	27.49	25.15	46
47	78.43	68.46	60.08	53.00	47.00	41.90	37.54	33.80	30.59	27.81	25.40	47
48	81.04	70.51	61.69	54.27	48.00	42.69	38.16	34.30	30.98	28.12	25.64	48
49	83.70	72.59	63.32	55.54	49.00	43.47	38.78	34.78	31.36	28.42	25.88	49
50	86.42	74.70	64.96	56.82	50.00	44.25	39.39	35.26	31.74	28.72	26.11	50
51	89.20	76.85	66.62	58.11	51.00	45.03	40.00	35.73	32.10	29.00	26.34	51
52	92.03	79.03	68.30	59.41	52.00	45.80	40.60	36.20	32.47	29.28	26.56	52
53	94.92	81.24	69.99	60.71	53.00	46.57	41.19	36.66	32.82	29.56	26.77	53
54	97.86	83.48	71.71	62.01	54.00	47.34	41.78	37.11	33.17	29.82	26.97	54
55	100.87	85.76	73.44	63.33	55.00	48.10	42.36	37.55	33.51	30.08	27.17	55

Table 28: Multipliers for pecuniary loss for term certain *continued*

Term	Multiplier for regular frequent payments for a term certain at rate of return of											Term
	−2.0%	**−1.5%**	**−1.0%**	**−0.5%**	**0.0%**	**0.5%**	**1.0%**	**1.5%**	**2.0%**	**2.5%**	**3.0%**	
56	103.94	88.08	75.18	64.65	56.00	48.86	42.93	37.99	33.84	30.34	27.37	56
57	107.07	90.43	76.95	65.98	57.00	49.61	43.50	38.42	34.17	30.59	27.56	57
58	110.27	92.81	78.73	67.31	58.00	50.36	44.07	38.84	34.49	30.83	27.74	58
59	113.53	95.23	80.53	68.65	59.00	51.11	44.63	39.26	34.80	31.06	27.92	59
60	116.85	97.69	82.35	70.00	60.00	51.85	45.18	39.67	35.11	31.29	28.09	60
61	120.25	100.18	84.19	71.35	61.00	52.59	45.73	40.08	35.41	31.52	28.26	61
62	123.71	102.72	86.04	72.71	62.00	53.33	46.27	40.48	35.70	31.74	28.42	62
63	127.25	105.29	87.91	74.08	63.00	54.06	46.81	40.88	36.00	31.95	28.58	63
64	130.85	107.90	89.81	75.46	64.00	54.79	47.34	41.26	36.28	32.16	28.73	64
65	134.53	110.55	91.72	76.84	65.00	55.52	47.86	41.65	36.56	32.36	28.88	65
66	138.29	113.24	93.65	78.23	66.00	56.24	48.39	42.02	36.83	32.56	29.02	66
67	142.12	115.97	95.60	79.62	67.00	56.95	48.90	42.40	37.10	32.75	29.16	67
68	146.03	118.75	97.57	81.03	68.00	57.67	49.41	42.76	37.36	32.94	29.30	68
69	150.02	121.56	99.56	82.44	69.00	58.38	49.92	43.12	37.62	33.13	29.43	69
70	154.10	124.42	101.57	83.85	70.00	59.09	50.42	43.48	37.87	33.31	29.56	70
71	158.25	127.32	103.61	85.28	71.00	59.79	50.91	43.83	38.12	33.48	29.68	71
72	162.49	130.27	105.66	86.71	72.00	60.49	51.41	44.17	38.36	33.65	29.80	72
73	166.82	133.26	107.73	88.15	73.00	61.19	51.89	44.51	38.60	33.82	29.92	73
74	171.23	136.30	109.82	89.59	74.00	61.88	52.37	44.85	38.83	33.98	30.03	74
75	175.74	139.38	111.94	91.04	75.00	62.57	52.85	45.18	39.06	34.14	30.15	75
76	180.33	142.51	114.07	92.50	76.00	63.26	53.32	45.50	39.29	34.30	30.25	76
77	185.02	145.69	116.23	93.97	77.00	63.94	53.79	45.82	39.51	34.45	30.36	77
78	189.81	148.92	118.41	95.45	78.00	64.62	54.25	46.14	39.72	34.60	30.46	78
79	194.69	152.19	120.61	96.93	79.00	65.29	54.71	46.45	39.93	34.74	30.56	79
80	199.68	155.52	122.83	98.42	80.00	65.97	55.16	46.75	40.14	34.88	30.65	80

ACTUARIAL FORMULAE AND BASIS

The functions tabulated are:

Tables 1 and 2 $\bar{a}_x$

Tables 3 and 4 $\bar{a}_{x:\overline{50-x}|}$

Tables 5 and 6 $\bar{a}_{x:\overline{55-x}|}$

Tables 7 and 8 $\bar{a}_{x:\overline{60-x}|}$

Tables 9 and 10 $\bar{a}_{x:\overline{65-x}|}$

Tables 11 and 12 $\bar{a}_{x:\overline{70-x}|}$

Tables 13 and 14 $\bar{a}_{x:\overline{75-x}|}$

Tables 15 and 16 $(50-x)|\bar{a}_x$

Tables 17 and 18 $(55-x)|\bar{a}_x$

Tables 19 and 20 $(60-x)|\bar{a}_x$

Tables 21 and 22 $(65-x)|\bar{a}_x$

Tables 23 and 24 $(70-x)|\bar{a}_x$

Tables 25 and 26 $(75-x)|\bar{a}_x$

Table 27 $1/(1+i)^n$

Table 28 $a_{\overline{n}|}$

- Mortality assumptions for 2008-based official population projections for the United Kingdom.
- Loadings: None.
- Rate of return: As stated in the tables.

A9: The Lord Chancellor's statement, July 27, 2001

THE LORD CHANCELLOR'S DEPARTMENT
Discount Rate
Setting the Discount Rate
Lord Chancellor's Reasons
July 27, 2001

Introduction

On June 25, 2001 I made the Damages (Personal Injury) Order 2001 ("the 2001 Order") pursuant to s.1 of the Damages Act 1996. In setting a rate of 2.5% in the 2001 Order I had regard to what I believed to be the accurate figure for the average gross redemption yield on Index-Linked Government Stock for the three years leading up to June 8, 2001. Following my announcement of the discount rate, questions were raised as to the correctness of the three-year average yield figure upon which I had relied.

These questions led me to have the information about the three-year average yield figure checked thoroughly. Those checks revealed certain limited inaccuracies in the information underlying the average yield figure on which I had based my reasoning in making the 2001 Order. In the light of the correction of that average yield figure, I think it right that I should consider completely afresh, on the basis of the accurate average yield figure, what rate I should have set when I made the 2001 Order on June 25, 2001, in order to determine whether the 2001 Order should be withdrawn.

Decision

Having considered all the material available to me, including the accurate, corrected average yield figure, I have come to the conclusion that a discount rate of 2.5% was the appropriate rate to set. Therefore, I do not consider that the 2001 Order should be withdrawn. This statement sets out my reasons for coming to that conclusion.

Reasons

In determining the discount rate, I have applied the appropriate legal principle laid down authoritatively by the courts, and in particular by the House of Lords in *Wells v Wells*.[1]

I also consider that it is highly desirable to exercise my powers under the Act so as to produce a situation in which claimants and defendants may have a reasonably clear idea about the impact of the discount rate upon their cases, so as to facilitate negotiation of settlements and the presentation of cases in court. In order to promote this objective, I have concluded that I should:

a set a single rate to cover all cases. This accords with the solution adopted by the House of Lords in *Wells v Wells*. It will eliminate scope for uncertainty and argument about the applicable rate. Similarly, I consider it is preferable to have a fixed rate, which promotes certainty and which avoids the complexity and extra costs that a formula would entail;

b set a rate which is easy for all parties and their lawyers to apply in practice and which reflects the fact that the rate is bound to be applied in a range of different circumstances over a period of time.

---

[1] [1999] 1 A.C. 345.

For this reason, I consider it appropriate to set the discount rate to the nearest half per cent, so as to ensure that the figure will be suitable for use in conjunction with the Ogden Tables, which are a ready means for parties to take into account actuarial factors in computing the quantum of damages;

c set a rate which should obtain for the foreseeable future. I consider it would be very detrimental to the reasonable certainty which is necessary to promote the just and efficient resolution of disputes (by settlement as well as by hearing in court) to make frequent changes to the discount rate. Therefore, whilst I will remain ready to review the discount rate whenever I find there is a significant and established change in the relevant real rates of return to be expected, I do not propose to tinker with the rate frequently to take account of every transient shift in market conditions.

(I consider that the reasoning and conclusions in the above paragraph, which appeared in my original reasons for setting the discount rate in the 2001 Order, continue to apply.)

The principle which I must strive to apply is clear: " . . . the object of the award of damages for future expenditure is to place the injured party as nearly as possible in the same financial position he or she would have been in but for the accident. The aim is to award such a sum of money as will amount to no more, and at the same time no less, than the net loss." (*Wells v Wells* at 390A–B per Lord Hope of Craighead). I acknowledge that claimants who have suffered severe injuries are not in the position of ordinary investors. Such claimants have a pressing need for a dependable source of income to meet the costs of their future care. It is accordingly unrealistic to require severely injured claimants to take even moderate risks when they invest their damages awards.

Setting a single rate to cover all cases, whilst highly desirable for the reasons given above, has the effect that the discount rate has to cover a wide variety of different cases, and claimants with widely differing personal and financial characteristics. Moreover, as has become clear from the consultation exercise (including responses by expert financial analysts to questions which I posed them), the real rate of return on investments of any character (including investments in Index-Linked Government Securities) involves making assumptions for the future about a wide variety of factors affecting the economy as a whole, including for example the likely rate of inflation. In these circumstances, it is inevitable that any approach to setting the discount rate must be fairly broad-brush. Put shortly, there can be no single "right" answer as to what rate should be set. Since it is in the context of larger awards, intended to cover longer periods, that there is the greatest risk of serious discrepancies between the level of compensation and the actual losses incurred if the discount rate set is not appropriate, I have had this type of award particularly in mind when considering the level at which the discount rate should be set. (The above paragraphs also formed a part of my original reasons for setting the discount rate, and I consider that they continue to apply.)

The House of Lords in *Wells v Wells* determined the real rate of return obtainable by claimants through low-risk investment by reference to the gross redemption yields on Index-Linked Government Stock. Their Lordships assumed that a claimant would use his damages award to purchase the right portfolio of Index-Linked Government Stock to ensure that in future years the sums which he received from his portfolio by way of coupon payments and payments on redemption would be sufficient to meet his financial needs. The risk that an early sale of Index-Linked Government Stock might cause capital losses was removed by assuming that such a claimant would hold all his Index-Linked Government Stock until redemption.

The House of Lords thought it appropriate to set the discount rate by reference to the average yields on Index-Linked Government Stock. There is no single correct method by which this average yield may be calculated. Among other factors, the calculation will depend upon the length of the period under consideration, the stocks which are to be included within the average, the inflation assumption made and the form of average taken.

The majority of their Lordships considered it appropriate to set a discount rate by taking a three-year average of Index-Linked Government Stock yields. I agree that, having regard to the benefits to be obtained in setting the discount rate for the foreseeable future, three years is an appropriate period over which to take an average. I note that Lord Lloyd of Berwick preferred a one-year period; this confirms the need for judgements to be made in determining the appropriate average yield.

It appears from the speech of Lord Hope at 393E–F that his Lordship had regard to an average of gross redemption yields on Index-Linked Government Stock with lives of over five years. He did not give reasons for adopting that particular approach. I am aware that this approach has also been favoured by the Ogden Working Party. However, having regard to the basic reasoning of the House of Lords in *Wells v Wells*, I do not consider that I am obliged to follow it. As noted above, the House of Lords in *Wells v Wells* assumed that a claimant would generally hold all his Index-Linked Government Stock until redemption. Further, as was stated by Lord Clyde at 395H–396A, it was to be assumed that in each year of loss a proportion of the capital would have to be used. If these two assumptions are to be rendered consistent then it will be necessary for the claimant to purchase Index-Linked Government Stock which will mature in the short term, for otherwise the claimant would have to sell a proportion of his Index-Linked Government Stock prior to redemption in order to realise, in the short term, some of the capital value of his investments. Some claimants, whose losses extend over periods of about five years or so or less, would have to purchase all or most of their Index-Linked Government Stock (if that is what they chose to do with the damages paid to them) in this category of stock. I have therefore decided that it is proper to take an average over all Index-Linked Government Stock rather than to exclude Index-Linked Government Stock with less than five years to maturity.

Nevertheless, I consider that it would be inappropriate to include the gross redemption yields of such stock which is very near maturity ("near maturity ILGS"—which is stock for which the nominal value of the final coupon and redemption payments have become known with certainty). The gross redemption yield on such near maturity ILGS is a nominal yield rather than a real yield. Accordingly, I asked for a calculation of the size of the real yield element in the gross redemption yields of the near maturity ILGS and have included those real yields within my calculation of the average yield.

The average yield figure upon which Lord Hope relied at 393E–F in *Wells v Wells* was based on an inflation assumption of 5%. I consider that, given both the current rate of inflation and the Government's policy aim of maintaining that rate within an upper limit of 2.5%, an assumption of 3% is to be preferred for present purposes.

The House of Lords in *Wells v Wells* did not discuss what form of average should be taken of Index-Linked Government Stock yields. One method is to take an average which is weighted in accordance with the market value of each stock. To my mind, such a weighted average is not relevant to the present circumstances, as the choice of Index-Linked Government Stock portfolio which is necessary to ensure that the future financial needs of a claimant are adequately and promptly met does not depend upon the prevailing market values of Index-Linked Government Stock. I have therefore decided that it is appropriate to take a simple average of Index-Linked Government Stock yields.

A calculation of the simple average of the gross redemption yields of an Index-Linked Government Stock (with an appropriate adjustment for the yields of near maturity ILGS) at an assumed rate of inflation of 3% produces an average yield figure of 2.46%. Accordingly, I conclude that the net average yield on Index-Linked Government Stock, as adjusted to take account of tax, lies in the range between 2% and 2.5%. In my opinion, following *Wells v Wells*, the discount rate should be set within this range. Further, given that the rate is to be set to the nearest 0.5%, it is clear that the discount rate should either be 2% or 2.5%. I do not consider that the choice whether a rate of 2% or one of 2.5% is appropriate is a simple arithmetical matter, nor that *Wells v Wells* requires me to set one rate or the other. I must have regard to the basic principle to which I have referred above, and I have taken account of matters which I consider are relevant to the setting of a discount rate which is just as between claimants as a group and defendants as a group.

In the light of all the information now available to me, and considering the matter completely afresh, I have decided that on June 25, 2001 I should have set the discount rate at 2.5%.

In doing so, I have noted that the real rate of return to be expected from Index-Linked Government Securities tends to be higher the lower the rate of inflation is assumed to be (figures at assumed rates of inflation of 3% and 5% are readily available for comparison). The average gross redemption yield figure of 2.46% assumes an inflation figure of 3% extending into the future. But over recent years inflation has been kept close to or below the 2.5% target set by the Government, and Government policy and the function of the Bank of England remains firmly to maintain inflation according to that target. Although economists differ as to what inflation rates may be expected for the future, I note that the market's general expectation as to the rate of inflation for the future (as implied by market valuations of gilts) is well below 3%. I consider that it is reasonable to assume an inflation rate for the foreseeable future somewhere below 3%, and this in turn provides comfort that a discount rate set at 2.5% is reasonable. (The above paragraph and the larger part of the following four paragraphs were contained in my original reasons for setting the discount rate. They set out considerations which I consider continue to apply).

I am further supported in my conclusion that a discount rate of 2.5% is reasonable by indications that the rate of return in respect of Index-Linked Government Securities does not represent a pure and undistorted measure of the real rate of return which markets would afford in relation to investments with minimal risk which have emerged from the information which was provided in the responses to the consultation paper and the responses from expert financial analysts which I obtained, and by consideration of rates of return on other investments which are available at low risk to claimants. I have treated the following points as significant.

First, some responses to the consultation maintained that the market in Index-Linked Government Securities is at present distorted so that the prevailing yields are artificially low, and do not necessarily give a reliable indication of the real rate of return which markets would afford in relation to investments with minimal risk. The expert financial analysts whom I consulted concurred that the market is distorted at present. This appears to be a result of the minimum funding requirement introduced by the Pensions Act 1995 (which has, in effect, created additional demand for such securities on the part of pension funds) combined with a reduced supply of government securities generally, as the Government has reduced the national debt. The market in Index-Linked Government Securities has changed significantly since *Wells v Wells* was argued and decided. It is widely held that the continuing high demand for Index-Linked Government Stock and the scarcity of supply has led to yields being artificially low as compared with both past record and the yields presently available on similar investment instruments issued by other, comparable, national governments. I consider that the fact that yields in Index-Linked Government Stock appear to be artificially low at present militates against the suggestion that these yields over recent years should be taken as the sole indication of the rates of return that can be achieved through low risk investment in the market. Also, I consider that there is some reasonable prospect of a return to higher rates of return in respect of Index-Linked Government Stock when the Government's already announced plans to abolish the minimum funding requirement are carried into effect. Any distorting effect of the minimum funding requirement would be expected to be particularly pronounced in relation to the longer maturity stocks, whose yields have recently been lower than shorter maturity stocks.

Second, I have noted that the Court of Protection, even in the wake of *Wells v Wells*, has continued to invest, on the behalf of claimants, in multi-asset portfolios, including an equity element. Investment in this manner could be expected to produce real rates of return well in excess of 2.5%. The Court of Protection has specific responsibility to ensure that the financial needs of those for whose benefit it acts will be met, ie its investment objectives are closely similar to those of the prudent claimant which the House of Lords identified in *Wells v Wells*. The Court of Protection takes competent financial advice as to the investment strategy which will best secure those objectives. Despite the decision of the House of Lords in *Wells v Wells* to set the discount rate by reference to yields on Index-Linked Government Securities, the Court of Protection has continued its former policy, with the agreement of the families concerned, of investing in portfolios comprising of a mixture of equities, gilts and cash. Master Lush of the Court of Protection has stated that none of the families of the Court's patients have chosen to invest in Index-Linked Government Stock since *Wells v Wells*, despite having been offered that option. Thus it appears that there are sensible, low risk investment strategies available to claimants which would enable them comfortably to achieve a real rate of return at 2.5% or above, without their being unduly exposed to risk in the equity markets. Although the House of Lords in *Wells v Wells* chose not to be guided by the practice of the Court of Protection, this was principally on the grounds that what the Court of Protection might do in the future was uncertain, and not on the grounds that its practice was irrelevant. I consider it is appropriate to take account of what has happened in the period since that decision.

Third, I consider that it is likely that real claimants with a large award of compensation, who sought investment advice and instructed their advisers as to the particular investment objectives which they needed to fulfil (as they could reasonably be expected to do) would not be advised to invest solely or even primarily in Index-Linked Government Securities, but rather in a mixed portfolio, in which any investment risk would be managed so as to be very low. This view is supported by the experience of the Court of Protection as to the independent financial advice they receive. It is also supported by the responses of the expert financial analysts whom I have consulted. No one responding to the consultation identified a single case in which the claimant had invested solely in Index-Linked Government Securities and doubts were expressed as to whether there was any such case. This suggests that setting the discount rate at 2.5% would not place an intolerable burden on claimants to take on excessive, i.e. moderate or above, risk in the equity markets, and would be a rate more likely to accord with real expectations of returns, particularly at the higher end of awards.

Finally, in deciding that a single rate of 2.5% should have been set by me on June 25, 2001, I have borne in mind that it will, of course, remain open for the Courts under s.1(2) of the Damages Act 1996 to adopt a different rate in any particular case if there are exceptional circumstances which justify it in doing so.

Irvine of Lairg
Lord Chancellor
July 27, 2001

Group B
Damages

B

B1: General damages table following Heil v Rankin and Jackson

B2: Bereavement damages

B3: Auty analysis (pension claims)

B4: Roberts v Johnstone analysis (accommodation claims)

B5: "Model Order" for periodical payments

B6: Step-by-step guide to finding the annual estimates for hourly pay in ASHE SOC2000 6115

B1: General damages table following Heil v Rankin and Jackson

General introduction

On the following pages are two tables for use in updating awards of general damages in the light of the Court of Appeal's judgments in *Heil v Rankin*[1] and in *Simmons v Castle*.[2] At Table E2 will be found an inflation table.

Notes to tables

Annexed to the Court of Appeal's judgment in *Heil* was a rather smudged graph provided to show "very approximately" the scale of the increase.

1. The difficulty comes in applying the tapered increase in the graph. Putting a straight-edge along the top line of the court's graph (the "uplifted" line) shows the line to be a shallow curve. In discussion after judgment was given, their Lordships said that they had not intended to lay down a mathematical formula. We must therefore assume that the top line was intended to fit around what had actually been done in *Heil* (i.e. nothing) and the other seven cases.

2. Despite this, and with a little diffidence (though some confidence) we suggest the following formula. It is calculated on the following assumptions—

    a. the highest award of general damages at March 23, 2000 was around £150,000: awards of this amount or higher were increased by $33\frac{1}{3}$ per cent;

    b. there is no increase in awards that were worth up to £10,000 before that date; and

    c. the uplift is 0% at £10,000 and rises *in a straight line* to $33\frac{1}{3}$ per cent.

3. To find the value of an *old* award in *new* terms, that award must first be updated to March 23, 2000 using the Retail Price Index (reproduced below), in the usual way. Let us call this updated figure A. The formula is:

$$£A + [£A{-}10{,}000/420{,}000 \times £A]$$

The part in square brackets is the *Heil* uplift.

4. In *Simmons v Castle* the Court of Appeal decided that general damages for personal injury (and certain other losses) will increase by 10 per cent (as proposed in the Final Report on Civil Litigation Costs by Sir Rupert Jackson), unless the claimant falls within s.44(6) of the Legal Aid, Sentencing and Punishment of Offenders Act 2012. The effect of this is that in a case where the claimant entered into a Conditional Fee Agreement before April 1, 2013, he recovers the success fee as part of his costs (as before) but does not get the 10 per cent increase in general damages: in any other case the claimant gets the 10 per cent increase in damages but does not get the success fee.

5. For example:

    a. On January 26, 1988, McNeill J. awarded the claimant in *Chan v Chan* general damages of £75,000.

    b. Updating £75,000 to March 23, 2000 in line with the Retail Price Index gives £120,800.

    c. Subtract £10,000 from £120,800, and divide it by 420,000. This gives $110{,}800/420{,}000 = 0.26$. This is the percentage uplift.

---

[1] [2000] 2 W.L.R. 1173.
[2] [2012] EWCA Civ 1039 and [2012] EWCA Civ 1288.

  d. Applying this uplift to the original award gives [0.26 × £120,800] = £31,400.

  e. The award in *Chan v Chan* was therefore worth [£120,800 + £31,400] = **£152,200** on March 23, 2000.

  f. The £152,200 should then be updated from March 23, 2000 to the present and, unless s.44(6) applies, it should also be increased by 10 per cent. Multiply by [present RPI] × 1.10 / [RPI March 2000].

6. Because the degree of uplift varies with the size of the old award, it is inaccurate to apply the *Heil v Rankin* uplift to a figure already adjusted for inflation to a date later than March 23, 2000. The *Simmons v Castle* uplift of 10 per cent does not depend on the size of the award. In April 2013 the RPI was 249.5.

TABLES FOR UPDATING GENERAL DAMAGES

The table on this page shows the factor to allow for inflation from an earlier judgment date to March 23, 2000. The table overleaf shows the appropriate new figure, following *Heil v Rankin* in relation to the conventional level of damages at £1,000 intervals up to £150,000.

Note that the uplift should be applied to the damages adjusted for inflation to March 23, 2000, thus:

(1) Damages awarded, say, January 1990 × Inflation increase January 1, 1990–March 23, 2000 (from first table) = old award as at March 23, 2000.

(2) Award uplifted under *Heil v Rankin* (from second table).

(3) Then multiply by an inflation uplift from March 23, 2000 onwards to the date of trial; plus the additional 10 per cent (unless s.44(6) applies).

TABLE TO UPDATE FOR INFLATION TO MARCH 2000

	J	F	M	A	M	J	J	A	S	O	N	D	
1980	2.708	2.670	2.634	2.547	2.424	2.500	2.480	2.474	2.459	2.443	2.424	2.411	1980
1981	2.396	2.374	2.339	2.274	2.259	2.246	2.236	2.220	2.207	2.188	2.165	2.151	1981
1982	2.139	2.138	2.120	2.078	2.063	2.057	2.057	2.056	2.057	2.047	2.037	2.041	1982
1983	2.038	2.030	2.026	1.998	1.990	1.985	1.974	1.965	1.957	1.950	1.943	1.938	1983
1984	1.939	1.931	1.925	1.900	1.893	1.888	1.890	1.872	1.869	1.857	1.852	1.853	1984
1985	1.846	1.832	1.815	1.777	1.769	1.765	1.768	1.764	1.764	1.762	1.756	1.753	1985
1986	1.750	1.743	1.741	1.724	1.721	1.722	1.727	1.722	1.713	1.711	1.696	1.690	1986
1987	1.684	1.677	1.674	1.654	1.653	1.653	1.650	1.649	1.645	1.637	1.629	1.630	1987
1988	1.630	1.624	1.618	1.592	1.586	1.580	1.578	1.561	1.554	1.538	1.531	1.527	1988
1989	1.517	1.506	1.500	1.473	1.464	1.459	1.458	1.454	1.444	1.433	1.421	1.418	1989
1990	1.409	1.401	1.387	1.346	1.334	1.329	1.328	1.315	1.302	1.292	1.295	1.296	1990
1991	1.293	1.286	1.282	1.265	1.261	1.256	1.259	1.256	1.251	1.246	1.242	1.241	1991
1992	1.242	1.236	1.232	1.213	1.209	1.209	1.213	1.212	1.208	1.204	1.205	1.210	1992
1993	1.221	1.213	1.209	1.198	1.193	1.194	1.197	1.192	1.187	1.188	1.189	1.187	1993
1994	1.192	1.185	1.182	1.168	1.164	1.164	1.169	1.164	1.161	1.160	1.159	1.153	1994
1995	1.153	1.146	1.142	1.130	1.126	1.124	1.129	1.123	1.118	1.124	1.124	1.117	1995
1996	1.121	1.116	1.112	1.104	1.101	1.101	1.105	1.100	1.095	1.095	1.094	1.091	1996
1997	1.091	1.086	1.084	1.077	1.073	1.069	1.069	1.062	1.057	1.056	1.055	1.053	1997
1998	1.056	1.051	1.047	1.036	1.030	1.031	1.033	1.029	1.024	1.024	1.024	1.024	1998
1999	1.031	1.029	1.029	1.019	1.017	1.017	1.020	1.018	1.013	1.011	1.010	1.007	1999
2000	1.010	1.005											2000
	J	F	M	A	M	J	J	A	S	O	N	D	

UPLIFT FOR INFLATION, AND JACKSON, FROM MARCH 2000 TO THE DATE OF TRIAL

The Retail Prices Index on March 23, 2000 was 168.4. 168.4 ÷ 110% = 153.1.   In April 2013 the RPI was 249.5.

The uplift for inflation from March 2000 is calculated as follows:

£award × (RPI at date of trial) / 153.1.

For an award that was worth £5,000 in March 2000, this would give at April 2013:

£5,000 × 249.5 / 153.1 = £8,148.

From April 1, 2013; uplift as in the previous example, from March 2000 until March 31, 2013, then multiply by 1.100.

	2013						2014						
Month	Jul	Aug	Sep	Oct	Nov	Dec	Jan	Feb	Mar	Apr	May	Jun	Jul
Current RPI													
Uplift (current RPI ÷ 153.1)													

TABLE OF UPLIFTS FOLLOWING *HEIL v RANKIN*

Old	New	Old	New	Old	New
0–10,000	No change	57,000	63,378	104,000	127,276
11,000	11,026	58,000	64,628	105,000	128,745
12,000	12,057	59,000	65,883	106,000	130,229
13,000	13,092	60,000	67,142	107,000	131,712
14,000	14,133	61,000	68,407	108,000	133,200
15,000	15,178	62,000	69,676	109,000	134,693
16,000	16,228	63,000	70,949	110,000	136,190
17,000	17,283	64,000	72,228	111,000	137,693
18,000	18,342	65,000	73,511	112,000	139,200
19,000	19,407	66,000	74,799	113,000	140,712
20,000	20,476	67,000	76,092	114,000	142,229
21,000	21,549	68,000	77,390	115,000	143,750
22,000	22,628	69,000	78,692	116,000	142,276
23,000	23,711	70,000	79,999	117,000	146,807
24,000	24,799	71,000	81,311	118,000	148,343
25,000	25,892	72,000	82,628	119,000	149,883
26,000	26,990	73,000	83,950	120,000	151,428
27,000	28,092	74,000	85,276	121,000	152,979
28,000	29,199	75,000	86,607	122,000	154,533
29,000	30,311	76,000	87,942	123,000	156,093
30,000	31,428	77,000	89,283	124,000	157,657
31,000	32,550	78,000	90,629	125,000	159,226
32,000	33,676	79,000	91,979	126,000	160,800
33,000	34,807	80,000	93,333	127,000	162,379
34,000	35,942	81,000	94,693	128,000	163,962
35,000	37,083	82,000	96,057	129,000	165,549
36,000	38,228	83,000	97,426	130,000	167,143
37,000	39,378	84,000	98,800	131,000	168,740
38,000	40,533	85,000	100,179	132,000	170,343
39,000	41,692	86,000	101,562	133,000	171,950
40,000	42,857	87,000	102,945	134,000	173,562
41,000	44,026	88,000	104,343	135,000	175,179

TABLE OF UPLIFTS FOLLOWING *HEIL v RANKIN continued*

Old	New	Old	New	Old	New
42,000	45,199	89,000	105,740	136,000	176,800
43,000	46,378	90,000	107,142	137,000	178,426
44,000	47,561	91,000	108,549	138,000	180,057
45,000	48,750	92,000	109,961	139,000	181,692
46,000	49,942	93,000	111,378	140,000	183,333
47,000	51,140	94,000	112,800	141,000	184,978
48,000	52,342	95,000	114,226	142,000	186,628
49,000	53,549	96,000	115,657	143,000	188,283
50,000	54,761	97,000	117,092	144,000	189,942
51,000	55,978	98,000	118,533	145,000	191,607
52,000	57,200	99,000	119,978	146,000	193,276
53,000	58,426	100,000	121,428	147,000	194,949
54,000	59,657	101,000	122,883	148,000	196,628
55,000	60,892	102,000	124,342	149,000	198,311
56,000	62,133	103,000	125,807	150,000	200,000

B2: Bereavement damages

1. Damages for bereavement are awarded under s.1A of the Fatal Accidents Act 1976. This is a fixed sum, set by statute as amended (see below).

2. The claim for bereavement damages can only be brought by:

    (i) a bereaved spouse, or

    (ii) where the deceased was a minor who never married, by:
    (a) either of his parents if the deceased was legitimate; or
    (b) the mother if the deceased was illegitimate.

3. Where there is a claim for damages for bereavement for the benefit of the parents of the deceased, s.1A(4) of the Fatal Accidents Act 1976 provides that:

    "The sum awarded shall be divided equally between them (subject to any deduction falling to be made in respect of costs not recovered from the defendant)."

    Where the parents are divorced or separated and only one parent makes the claim, that parent will hold half of the bereavement damages on trust for the other parent.

4. The Administration of Justice Act 1982 contains a provision (at s.1A(5)) for the Lord Chancellor to vary the statutory sum. The original statute fixed the sum at £3,500, and that was raised by three subsequent statutory instruments (SI 1990/2575, SI 2002/644 and SI 2013/510). Hence the relevant dates and statutory sums are as follows:

    – if the death was before January 1, 1983, the award is **nil**,

    – if the death was between January 1, 1983 and March 31, 1991, the award is **£3,500**,

    – if the death was between April 1, 1991 and March 31, 2002, the award is **£7,500**,

    – if the death was between April 1, 2002 and December 31, 2007, the award is **£10,000**,

    – if the death was on or after January 1, 2008, the award is **£11,800**, and

    – if the death was on or after April 1, 2013, the award is **£12,980**.

5. The claimant is entitled to interest on bereavement damages from the date of death to the date of trial or settlement of the action—see *Prior v Hastie*.[1]

---

[1] [1987] C.L.Y. 1219.

B3: Auty analysis (pension claims)

In *Wells v Wells*, the House of Lords made only passing reference to the calculation of future pension losses. The implication is that the multipliers for such losses are to be taken from the Ogden Tables, as are those for pecuniary losses for life and for loss of earnings. There is no justification for adopting a different approach. Since the mid-1980s, however, such claims have often been based on the principles set out in *Auty v National Coal Board*.[1] This Analysis is a guide to those principles, but is included with the caution that it has almost certainly been superseded by *Wells v Wells*.

It is important to remember that the trial judge in *Auty* was not working from the Ogden Tables, but from a table of life expectation.

1.   The net annual pension loss after tax: £433.

2.   The claimant and his wife were both aged 34 at the date of trial.

3.   The life tables showed that the claimant's life expectation beyond the age of 65 was 6.68 years, and his wife's life expectation beyond the age of 65 was 10.4 years. She was therefore expected to survive him by 3.75 years.

4.   ***First discount***: the judge rounded 10.4 years down to seven. This is the equivalent of the discounting calculation (now 2.5 per cent) that has already been performed for one when one uses the Ogden Tables.

5.   The basic pension loss at 65 was therefore [7 × £443] = £3,101.

6.   Loss of lump sum gratuity: £1,899.

7.   Total capital value of loss at retirement age [£3,101 + £1,899] = £5,000.

8.   ***Second discount***: Mr Auty was 34 years old. He was therefore being compensated for his pension loss 31 years prematurely. The judge discounted the sum of £5,000 at 5 per cent over 31 years, leaving £1,100. This discount would now be performed by Ogden Table 27 at 2.5 per cent.

9.   ***Third discount***: The Ogden Tables are based on mortality figures, discounted by −2% – +3%. The Tables do not take the other contingencies of life—e.g. sickness, injury at work, redundancy —into account. Paragraphs 33–44 of the Explanatory Notes to the Tables shows how to adjust for "Contingencies other than Mortality". *These contingencies apply only to claims for loss of earnings, not to pension losses.* However, in *Auty* the judge discounted the pension claim by a further 27 per cent for contingencies. This brought the sum of £1,100 down to £800. Of this stage the Court of Appeal said[2]:

     "The discount for imponderables which the judge made in Auty's case was 27 per cent. The judge said that the imponderables included voluntary wastage, redundancy, dismissal, supervening ill-health, disablement or death before 65, and said that death was the major discount."

10. Add value of loss of death in service benefit (£200).

11. Total value of award: **£1,000**.

Note: The three discounts bring the pension element alone (ignoring the lump sum and the death in service benefit) down to £500. If one simply applied Ogden Table 22 and a 2.5 per cent discount to the above pension loss the claimant would receive [7.75 × £433] = £3,356.

Employment tribunals have developed a different approach to the calculation of pension loss. Those interested are referred to the guidelines in Sneath, Sara, Daykin and Gallop, *Industrial Tribunals: Compensation for loss of pension rights* (2003, 3rd edn) HMSO, approved by the Employment Appeal Tribunal in *Benson v Dairy Crest*.[3]

[1] [1985] 1 All E.R. 930.
[2] Waller L.J. in *Auty*, at 937.
[3] (EAT/192/89).

B4: Roberts v Johnstone analysis (accommodation claims)

1. Seriously injured claimants will often require special accommodation which may have to be adapted for their particular needs. This will often mean that they have to move to a more expensive house. The applicable principles of law were set out by the Court of Appeal in *Roberts v Johnstone*.[1]

2. **Example**: A paraplegic claimant lives in an unsuitable house with a market value of £150,000. She wishes to buy a more suitable house for £230,000 and alter it (because of her disabilities) at a cost of £20,000. The alterations will not (in themselves) make any difference to the value of the adapted house. The claimant will continue to live in the adapted house for the rest of her life and the agreed life multiplier is 10. Following *Roberts v Johnstone*, the claim for accommodation costs is calculated as follows:

    (i) Costs of adaption: **£20,000**
        Recovered in full because wholly attributable to injuries and will not add value to the house.

    (ii) Costs of moving house: **£10,000**
        Recovered in full if the claimant would not have moved house but for the accident.

    (iii) Loss of Use of Capital:
        As a result of the move, the claimant is obliged to invest in the house, thereby foregoing the use of a part of her capital. The discount rate of 2.5% is taken as the annual loss caused by this. Hence the claim is:

        £80,000 (extra cost of the house) × 2.5% (discount rate) × 10 (agreed life multiplier) = **£20,000**

        Note that the claimant does not recover the full additional capital cost of the house; if she did, the estate would derive a windfall benefit.

    (iv) Extra Annual Costs of Accommodation:
        If the costs of living in the more expensive house are higher, the claimant can claim them. Items might include council tax, decorating costs and water charges. If these costs were £500 p.a., the claim would be:

        £500 (extra annual costs) × 10 (agreed life multiplier) =   **£5,000**

3. The total claim for accommodation in the example is therefore **£55,000**.

4. If the discount rate is varied from the present figure of 2.5 per cent, *Roberts v Johnstone* claims will also change. For instance, if the rate were to be reduced to 1 per cent, the calculation of loss of capital in para.2 (iii), above, would be £80,000 × 1% × 10 = £8,000.

[1] [1989] Q.B. 878.

B5: "Model Order" for periodical payments

In a judgment given on December 2, 2008, Sir Christopher Holland approved a "model" schedule for use in those NHSLA cases in which the claimant is to receive periodical payments which are to be uprated by reference to ASHE 6115.[1] In such cases, the payments will be made annually in advance on December 15, in each year; and the annual uprating will take effect on that date also.

If the defendant is not the NHSLA, the model order will be a useful starting point, but variations may be appropriate. In particular:

(1)   Administrative provisions are needed as to the method of payment, the provision of notices and similar. These provisions do not appear in the NHSLA model schedule; for such cases, they are left to be incorporated in the body of the order.

(2)   Variations may be appropriate to the date and frequency of payments.[2] The provision of one annual payment in advance is favourable to the claimant and costly to the defendant.

   If, for example, the parties agree that the annual sum due shall be paid by quarterly instalments in advance, four quarterly dates must be fixed. When doing this, particular regard should be paid to two matters:

   (i)   The first date must be set so as to allow sufficient time after the date of approval/judgment for the administrative arrangements to be set up. For the intervening period, a pro rata lump sum can be added to the lump sum part of the award.

   (ii) If stepped rates are to become payable in later years (rising or falling as the claimant ages), one of the quarterly dates should coincide with the claimant's birthday. Transition from one level of payment to the next will then be straightforward.

(3)   Variation may also be appropriate to the date when the annual uprating is to take effect. A date needs to be fixed, which should obviously be one of the quarterly dates. But an automatic selection of the date closest to December 15[3] might again be unduly favourable to the claimant if (for example) the order is being made in October. The appropriate date will depend on the individual facts of the case; it may or may not be the anniversary date of the first quarterly payment.

A useful draft order which incorporates the suggestions above may be seen at: *http://www.guildhall chambers.co.uk/practice_areas/pi.cfm?s=369*.

In that Order, Pt 1 of the Schedule contains the administrative provisions.

Part 2 sets out the provisions for any RPI-linked payments. These may now be rare, but may still arise in certain cases. If not applicable, Pt 2 can be deleted.

Part 3 sets out the provisions for ASHE 6115-linked payments, to include attempted provision for any re-classification of the ASHE groups in future years. The various provisions will be self-explanatory to those familiar with the indexation procedures.

In *Long v Norwich Union*,[4] Mackay J. held that a claimant was not entitled to recover the cost of proving that he was still alive at the date of periodical payment. The court held that this cost would be covered by the award for the costs of deputyship; alternatively, it might be said that modest costs of this type borne by the claimant will be covered by the interest generated on the advance payments to be made under the order.

The editors gratefully acknowledge the assistance of Mr Adrian Palmer QC of Guildhall Chambers, Bristol, for permission to précis his article "Periodical Payments: The Form of the Order", which appeared in Kemp News, July 10, 2009.

---

[1] [2009] P.I.Q.R. P153.

[2] Damages Act 1996 s.2(1), as amended, does not stipulate the frequency of payments. But Pt 41.8(1)(a) of the CPR requires that where periodical payments are to be made, the order must specify the amount, the method and the intervals between payments.

[3] Being the date used in the NHSLA model schedule.

[4] [2009] EWHC 715 QB.

B6: Step-by-step guide to finding the annual estimates for hourly pay in ASHE SOC2000 6115

The data collection point for the Annual Survey of Hours and Earnings (ASHE) is April each year. The data are collected over the summer and the first release of estimates takes place in November of that year. These are provisional estimates which are revised and published as final estimates the following November. The following estimates were published for ASHE SOC2000 6115 on November 7, 2007, December 4, 2008, November 4, 2009, December 8, 2010, and November 23, 2011 and November 22, 2012. Estimates for 2012 are provisional and will be replaced by final estimates in November 2013.

ASHE SOC2000 6115 Centile estimates for hourly earnings £ for UK employees

Centile	10	20	25	30	40	50	60	70	75	80	90
ASHE 6115 2006 Final release	5.37	5.84	6.05	6.24	6.65	7.15	7.70	8.33	8.71	9.25	10.67
ASHE 6115 2007 Final release	5.65	6.15	6.36	6.55	7.01	7.53	8.12	8.80	9.21	9.79	11.38
ASHE 6115 2008 Final release	5.85	6.30	6.49	6.70	7.20	7.71	8.33	9.12	9.56	10.11	11.68
ASHE 6115 2009 Final release	6.00	6.47	6.68	6.90	7.42	7.93	8.51	9.33	9.82	10.36	12.10
ASHE 6115 2010 Final release	6.06	6.55	6.80	7.04	7.50	8.07	8.70	9.45	9.91	10.44	12.16
ASHE 6115 2011 First release	6.09	6.51	6.75	6.98	7.40	7.93	8.52	9.32	9.80	10.33	12.03
ASHE 6115 2011* Final release	6.05	6.44	6.65	6.87	7.28	7.83	8.45	9.17	9.67	10.22	11.92
ASHE 6115 2012* First release	6.21	6.55	6.78	7.00	7.42	7.90	8.50	9.19	9.69	10.24	11.98

Source: ONS ASHE published November 7, 2007, December 4, 2008, November 4, 2009, December 8, 2010; November 23, 2011; November 22, 2012.
Notes: * based on 2010 occupational weights.

ASHE estimates are only available online. They can be found on the website of the UK Statistics Authority. This requires some navigation from the home page. Step-by-step instructions appear below. You need not follow all these instructions each time you consult the tables as you can either download the tables as an Excel file or you can save the web link to the tables in bookmarks.

Reclassification of occupational categories occurs every ten years and occurred in ASHE (SOC 2010) 2011 released in March 2012. The reclassification of occupations introduces a time discontinuity into the statistical series which creates two problems for calculating an annual escalation in a PPO. First, the occupational weights upon which all the ASHE estimates are based change between 2011 and 2012 from SOC 2000 to SOC 2010. Estimates are available for 2011 using both sets of weights. When calculating a growth rate care must be taken that estimates in different years are made on the basis of the same occupational weights. When comparing earnings in any year from 2011 onwards with 2011, use the final 2011 release. When comparing earnings in any year before 2011, use the first 2011 release. Secondly, the classification for carers changed in SOC 2010 to include two separate categories, ASHE 6145 care workers and home carers and ASHE 6146 senior care workers. Aside from the potential escalation difficulty, this new classification introduces problems associated the definition of the "senior" care workers who would populate the additional group and the small sample size of the group. Fortunately, for the purposes of the indexation of future care, the new classification for care can be ignored. From 2011 until at least 2022, the ASHE team at ONS has agreed to continue to publish statistics relating to the SOC 2000 classification of carers, that is occupational group 6115. The occupational earnings tables for 6115 can be found at Table 26.5a.

1. Find the home page of the UK Statistics Authority at *www.statistics.gov.uk*

2. Select the Office for National Statistics (ONS) link at the top right-hand side of the page and click.

3. Type in ASHE 2012 in the search box at the top of this page and click Search.

4. All the ASHE spreadsheets (1–26) are listed in the search results together with other documents. To restrict your search to the statistical tables, check the box marked Reference tables under Filter Results on the right hand side of the screen.

5. Scroll down the list to find the Reference table that you require. For hourly rates for care, you need Table 26.5a which provides earnings estimates disaggregated to the four-digit SOC 2000 classification for 6115.

6   Click on the table title and click on the Open option. This will take you to the contents list of a ZIP file. Each excel file contains an occupational breakdown of a different set of earnings estimates.

7. Double click on Table 26.5a Hourly Pay-Gross. Click on the Open option. This will take you to a worksheet in an excel file. If you are sure that you have located the file that you want, save it using file save in excel.

8. Once in the Excel file, check the bottom tab. 'All' refers to all employees (male and female, part and full-time).

9. Read across the centile estimates. The shading indicates the reliability of the estimate. Where the estimate of the error is less than 5 per cent, there is no shading. The key to the shading can be found at the bottom and at the right hand side of the table.

10. If you have not already saved this file at step 7 above, this table can be saved now either in part or in full. If the file is saved make a note that the 2012 estimates are provisional. They will be replaced in the final release in November 2013 under the same title.

10. If you have not already saved this file at step 7 above, this table can be saved now either in part or in full. If the file is saved make a note that the 2012 estimates are provisional. They will be replaced in the final release in November 2013 under the same title.

11. Details of any changes to the estimates and/or to the step-by-step guide which occur after publication of Fact & Figures 2013 and links to sources of further information on reclassification can be found on *www.victoriawass-laboureconomics.co.uk* under Indexation.

This guide has been prepared by Dr Victoria Wass, Cardiff Business School, June 2013.

Group C
Interest Rates

C

C1:   Interest base rates

C2:   Real and nominal interest rates and
        price inflation

C3:   Special investment account rates

C4:   Special and general damages interest

C5:   Base rate + 10%

C6:   Number of days between two dates

C7:   Decimal years

C8:   Judgment debt interest rates (England
        and Wales)

C9:   Judicial rates of interest (Scotland)

C1: Interest base rates

Introductory notes

1. The data for this table are obtained from retail banks Barclays, Lloyds TSB, HSBC and National Westminster.

2. Where these banks' base rates did not change on the same day, an average rate is shown (and asterisked in the table).

3. Since August 3, 2006, these retail banks' base rates have been identical to the Bank of England's Official Bank Rate.

Date	New rate (%)	Date	New rate (%)	Date	New rate (%)
1982		**1986**		March 25	12.50
August 2	11.50	January 9	12.50	April 12	12.00
August 18	11.00	March 19	11.50	May 24	11.50
August 31	10.50	April 8	11.25*	July 12	11.00
October 7	10.00	April 9	11.00	September 4	10.50
October 14	9.50	April 24	10.50		
November 4	9.00	May 27	10.00	**1992**	
November 26	10.125*	October 14	11.00	May 5	10.00
				September 16	12.00
1983		**1987**		September 17	10.00
January 12	11.00	March 10	10.50	September 22	9.00
March 15	10.50	March 19	10.00	October 16	8.00
April 15	10.00	April 29	9.50	November 13	7.00
June 15	9.50	May 11	9.00		
October 4	9.00	August 7	10.00	**1993**	
		October 26	9.50	January 26	6.00
1984		November 5	9.00	November 23	5.50
March 7	8.875*	December	8.50		
March 15	8.625*			**1994**	
May 10	9.125*	**1988**		February 8	5.25
June 27	9.25	February 2	9.00	September 12	5.75
July 9	10.00	March 17	8.50	December 7	6.25
July 11	11.00*	April 11	8.00		
July 12	12.00	May 18	7.50	**1995**	
August 9	11.50	June 3	8.00	February 2	6.75
August 10	11.00	June 6	8.25*	December 13	6.50
August 20	10.50	June 7	8.50		
November 7	10.00	June 22	9.00	**1996**	
November 20	9.875*	June 29	9.50	January 18	6.25
November 23	9.625*	July 5	10.00	March 8	6.00
		July 19	10.50	June 6	5.75
1985		August 8	10.75*	October 30	6.00
January 11	10.50	August 9	11.00		
January 14	12.00	August 25	11.50	**1997**	
January 28	14.00	August 26	12.00	May 7	6.25
March 20	13.75*	November 25	13.00	June 9	6.50
March 21	13.50			July 11	6.75
March 29	13.25*	**1989**		August 8	7.00
April 2	13.125*	May 24	14.00	November 7	7.25
April 12	12.875*	October 5	15.00		
April 19	12.675*			**1998**	
June 12	12.50	**1990**		June 5	7.50
July 7	12.25*	October 8	14.00	October 9	7.25
July 16	12.00			November 6	6.75
July 29	11.75*	**1991**		December 1	6.25
July 30	11.50	February 13	13.50		
		February 27	13.00		

Date	New rate (%)	Date	New rate (%)	Date	New rate (%)
1999		November 8	4.00	**2007**	
January 8	6.00			January 11	5.25
February 5	5.50	**2003**		May 10	5.50
April 8	5.25	February 7	3.75	July 5	5.75
June 10	5.00	July 10	3.50	December 6	5.50
September 8	5.25	November 6	3.75		
November 4	5.50			**2008**	
		2004		February 7	5.25
2000		February 5	4.00	April 10	5.00
January 13	5.75	May 6	4.25	October 8	4.50
February 10	6.00	June 10	4.50	November 6	3.00
		August 5	4.75	December 4	2.00
2001					
February 8	5.75	**2005**		**2009**	
April 5	5.50	August 4	4.50	January 8	1.50
May 10	5.25			February 5	1.00
August 2	5.00	**2006**		March 5	0.50
September 18	4.75	August 10	4.75		
October 4	4.50	November 9	5.00		

C2: Real and nominal interest rates and price inflation

Introductory notes

1. Price inflation is calculated as the rate of change of the Retail Price Index.
2. The nominal interest rate is based on the rate on 20-year British Government Securities.
3. No account has been taken of tax in these figures.

	Price Inflation %	Nominal Interest Rate %	Real Interest Rate %
1970	6.52	9.21	2.69
1971	9.18	8.85	(0.33)
1972	7.48	8.90	1.42
1973	9.13	10.71	1.58
1974	15.94	14.77	(1.17)
1975	24.05	14.39	(9.66)
1976	16.62	14.43	(2.19)
1977	15.91	12.73	(3.18)
1978	8.20	12.47	4.27
1979	13.45	12.99	(0.46)
1980	18.03	13.78	(4.25)
1981	11.88	14.74	2.86
1982	8.70	12.88	4.18
1983	4.44	10.80	6.36
1984	5.01	10.69	5.68
1985	6.04	10.62	4.58
1986	3.40	9.87	6.47
1987	4.16	9.47	5.31
1988	4.92	9.36	4.44
1989	7.79	9.58	1.79
1990	9.44	11.08	1.64
1991	5.91	9.92	4.01
1992	3.73	9.12	5.39
1993	1.57	7.87	6.30
1994	2.48	8.05	5.57
1995	3.41	8.26	4.85
1996	2.44	8.10	5.66
1997	3.12	7.09	3.97
1998	3.42	5.45	2.03
1999	1.56	4.70	3.14
2000	2.93	4.68	1.75
2001	1.84	4.78	2.94
2002	1.62	4.83	3.21
2003	2.91	4.64	1.73
2004	2.96	4.77	1.81
2005	2.84	4.39	1.55
2006	3.20	4.27	1.07
2007	4.26	4.73	0.47
2008	4.00	4.68	0.68
2009	(0.53)	4.26	4.79
2010	4.61	4.25	(0.36)
2011	5.21	3.83	(1.38)
2012	3.22	2.87	(0.35)
Averages:			
1970–79	12.65	11.95	(0.70)
1980–89	7.44	11.18	3.74
1990–99	3.71	7.96	4.25
2000–09	2.60	4.60	2.00
2010–12	4.34	3.65	(0.69)

Real Interest Rates 1970–2010

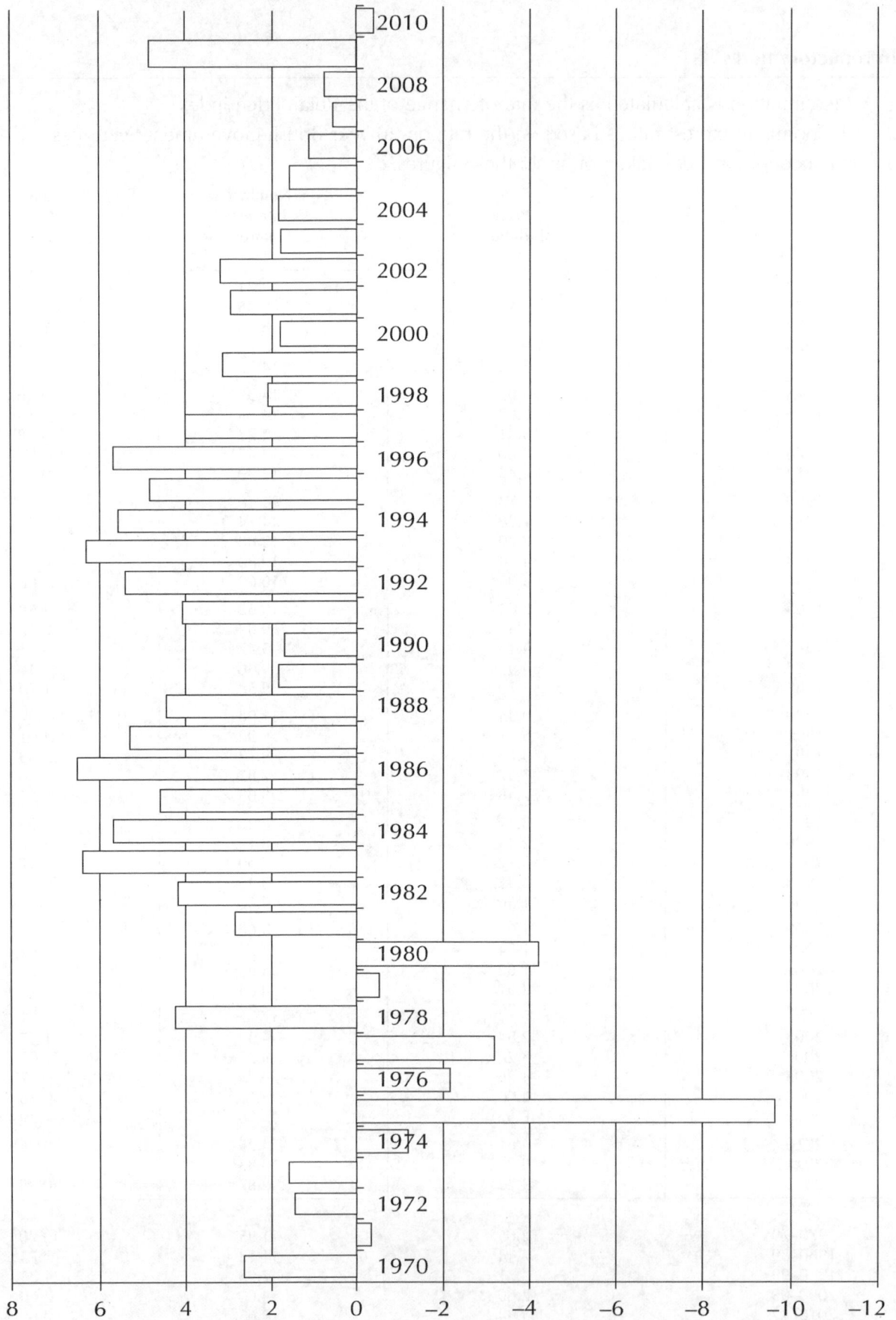

Real Interest Rates 1970–2010

C3: Special investment account rates

Introductory notes

This is a composite table including both the Short-term Investment Account rate and the succeeding High Court Special Investment Account rate.

The manner of crediting interest is set out in Court Fund Rules 1987 r.27. Interest accruing to a special investment account is credited without the deduction of income tax.

From:		%
October 1	1965	5.0
September 1	1966	5.5
March 1	1968	6.0
March 1	1969	6.5
March 1	1970	7.0
April 1	1971	7.5
March 1	1973	8.0
March 1	1974	9.0
February 1	1977	10.0
March 1	1979	12.5
January 1	1980	15.0
January 1	1981	12.5
December 1	1981	15.0
March 1	1982	14.0
July 1	1982	13.0
April 1	1983	12.5
April 1	1984	12.0
August 1	1986	11.5
January 1	1987	12.25
April 1	1987	11.75
November 1	1987	11.25
December 1	1987	11.0
May 1	1988	9.5
August 1	1988	11.0
November 1	1988	12.25
January 1	1989	13.0
November 1	1989	14.25
April 1	1991	12.0
October 1	1991	10.25
February 1	1993	8.0
August 1	1999	7.0
February 1	2002	6.0
February 1	2009	3.0
June 1	2009	1.5
July 1	2009	0.5

C4: Special and general damages interest

Introductory notes

Special damages

The appropriate rate of interest for special damages is the rate, over the period for which the interest is awarded, which is payable on the court special account. This rate was reduced to 0.5 per cent on July 1, 2009. Interest since June 1987 has been paid daily on a 1/365th basis, even in a leap year such as 2004.

In cases of continuing special damages, half the appropriate rate from the date of injury to the date of trial is awarded. In cases where the special damages have ceased and are thus limited to a finite period, there are conflicting Court of Appeal decisions as to whether the award should be half the appropriate rate from injury to trial (*Dexter v Courtaulds*[1]) or the full special account rate from the date within the period to which the special damages are limited (*Prokop v DHSS*[2]).

The relevant rates since 1965 are set out in Table C3.

The table on the next page records the total of these rates from January 1981. In the left-hand column is shown the month from the first day of which interest is assumed to run. The right-hand column shows the percentage interest accumulated from the first day of each month to July 1, 2013.

Continued use may be made of this table by adding to the figures in it 1/365th of the special account rate for each day from July 1, 2013 onwards, using Table C6 which records the number of days between two dates in a two-year period.

Suppose that interest runs from January 1, 2001 to October 13, 2013. The total to July 1, 2013 is 52.66 per cent. From Table C6, July 1 to October 13 is 286–182 days. If the rate remains at 0.5 per cent p.a., the appropriate addition will be 0.5 per cent × 104/365 = 0.14 per cent. Thus the grand total from January 1, 2001 to October 13, 2013 will be 52.66 + 0.14 = 52.80 per cent.

General damages

In personal injury cases, the normal rate of interest on general damages for pain, suffering and loss of amenity was by convention 2 per cent per annum. In *Lawrence v Chief Constable of Staffordshire*[3] the Court of Appeal held that in spite of *Wells v Wells*,[4] the rate should remain at 2 per cent. Interest runs from the date of service of proceedings.

---

[1] [1984] 1 All E.R. 70.
[2] [1985] C.L.Y. 1037.
[3] CA, transcript June 29, 2000.
[4] [1999] A.C. 345.

Table of cumulative interest at the special account rate from the first day of each month to July 1, 2013.

	1981	1982	1983	1984	1985	1986	1987	1988	1989	1990
January	262.85	250.13	236.48	223.85	211.73	199.73	187.94	176.17	165.31	152.10
February	261.79	248.86	235.37	222.79	210.71	198.71	186.90	175.24	164.21	150.89
March	260.83	247.71	234.38	221.93	209.79	197.79	185.96	174.36	163.21	149.79
April	259.76	246.52	233.27	220.77	208.77	196.77	184.92	173.43	162.11	148.59
May	258.74	245.37	232.24	219.79	207.79	195.79	183.95	172.53	161.04	147.42
June	257.68	244.18	231.18	218.77	206.77	194.77	182.96	171.72	159.93	146.22
July	256.65	243.03	230.14	217.78	205.78	193.78	181.99	170.94	158.86	145.04
August	255.59	241.93	229.09	216.76	204.76	192.76	180.99	170.13	157.76	143.82
September	254.53	240.82	228.03	215.74	203.74	191.78	179.99	169.20	156.66	142.61
October	253.50	239.75	227.00	214.76	202.76	190.84	179.03	168.29	155.59	141.44
November	252.44	238.65	225.94	213.74	201.74	189.86	178.03	167.36	154.48	140.23
December	251.41	237.58	224.92	212.75	200.75	188.92	177.11	166.35	153.31	139.06

	1991	1992	1993	1994	1995	1996	1997	1998	1999	2000
January	137.85	125.74	115.46	107.27	99.27	91.27	83.25	75.25	67.25	59.67
February	136.64	124.87	114.59	106.59	98.59	90.59	82.57	74.57	66.57	59.08
March	135.54	124.05	113.97	105.97	97.97	89.95	81.95	73.95	65.95	58.52
April	134.34	123.18	113.29	105.29	97.29	89.27	81.27	73.27	65.27	57.93
May	133.35	122.34	112.64	104.64	96.64	88.62	80.62	72.62	64.62	57.35
June	132.33	121.47	111.96	103.96	95.96	87.94	79.94	71.94	63.94	56.76
July	131.35	120.63	111.30	103.30	95.30	87.28	79.28	71.28	63.28	56.18
August	130.33	119.75	110.62	102.62	94.62	86.60	78.60	70.60	62.60	55.59
September	129.31	118.88	109.94	101.94	93.94	85.92	77.92	69.92	62.01	54.99
October	128.32	118.04	109.28	101.28	93.28	85.26	77.26	69.26	61.43	54.42
November	127.45	117.17	108.60	100.60	92.60	84.58	76.58	68.58	60.84	53.82
December	126.61	116.33	107.95	99.95	91.95	83.93	75.93	67.93	60.26	53.25

	2001	2002	2003	2004	2005	2006	2007	2008	2009	2010
January	52.66	45.66	39.57	33.57	27.55	21.56	15.56	9.56	3.62	1.75
February	52.06	45.06	39.06	33.06	27.05	21.05	15.05	9.05	3.11	1.71
March	51.60	44.60	38.60	32.58	26.58	20.59	14.59	8.57	2.88	1.67
April	51.09	44.09	38.09	32.08	26.08	20.08	14.08	8.06	2.63	1.62
May	50.60	43.60	37.60	31.58	25.58	19.58	13.58	7.56	2.38	1.58
June	50.09	43.09	37.09	31.07	25.07	19.07	13.07	7.05	2.12	1.54
July	49.60	42.60	36.60	30.58	24.58	18.58	12.58	6.65	2.00	1.50
August	49.09	42.09	36.09	30.07	24.07	18.07	12.07	6.14	1.96	1.46
September	48.58	41.58	35.58	29.56	23.56	17.56	11.56	5.63	1.92	1.42
October	48.08	41.08	35.08	29.07	23.07	17.07	11.07	5.13	1.87	1.37
November	47.57	40.57	34.57	28.56	22.56	16.56	10.56	4.62	1.83	1.33
December	47.08	40.08	34.08	28.06	22.06	16.06	10.06	4.13	1.79	1.29

	2011	2012	2013
January	1.25	0.75	0.25
February	1.21	0.71	0.21
March	1.17	0.67	0.17
April	1.12	0.62	0.12
May	1.08	0.58	0.08
June	1.04	0.54	0.04
July	1.00	0.50	0.50
August	0.96	0.46	0.04
September	0.92	0.42	0.08
October	0.88	0.37	0.13
November	0.83	0.33	0.17
December	0.79	0.29	0.21

If the rate remains at 0.5 per cent, interest **up to** the first day of successive later months can be found by adding the following figures.

	2014 (%)
January	0.25
February	0.29
March	0.33
April	0.38
May	0.42
June	0.46
July	0.50

C5: Base rate + 10%

Introductory notes

1. Under the Civil Procedure Rules 1998 r.36.21, where the judgment against a defendant is more advantageous to the claimant than the proposals in a claimant's Pt 36 offer, the court may order interest on the sum awarded and on the costs, for some or all of the period starting with the latest date on which the defendant could have accepted the Pt 36 offer without needing the permission of the court, at a rate not exceeding 10% above base rate. In *All-in-One Design & Build Ltd v Motcomb Estates Ltd*,[1] it was held that r.36.21 is not ultra vires.

2. Rule 36.21(4) provides that where the rule applies, the court will make those orders unless it considers it unjust to do so; sub-rule (5) sets out the factors to be considered in deciding whether it would be unjust.

3. Since 1998 base rates have been as follows:

		Rate + 10%			Rate + 10%			Rate + 10%
1997	November 7	17.25%	**2001**	April 5	15.50%	**2006**	August 3	14.75%
1998	June 4	17.50%		May 10	15.25%		November 9	15.00%
	October 8	17.25%		August 2	15.00%	**2007**	January 11	15.25%
	November 5	16.75%		September 18	14.75%		May 10	15.50%
	December 10	16.25%		October 4	14.50%		July 5	15.75%
1999	January 7	16.00%		November 8	14.00%		December 6	15.50%
	February 4	15.50%	**2002**	February 6	13.75%	**2008**	February 7	15.25%
	April 8	15.25%	**2003**	July 10	13.50%		April 10	15.00%
	June 10	15.00%		November 6	13.75%		October 8	14.50%
	September 8	15.25%	**2004**	February 5	14.00%		November 6	13.00%
	November 4	15.50%		May 6	14.25%		December 4	12.00%
2000	January 13	15.75%		June 10	14.50%	**2009**	January 8	11.50%
	February 10	16.00%		August 5	14.75%		February 5	11.00%
2001	February 8	15.75%	**2005**	August 4	14.50%		March 5	10.50%

The following table shows cumulative interest at 10 per cent above base rate from the first day of each month until July 1, 2013. Interest for parts of a month can be found by following the method in the notes to Table C4.

	2002	2003	2004	2005	2006	2007	2008	2009	2010	2011	2012	2013
January	149.00	135.00	121.31	106.89	92.24	77.60	62.09	47.38	36.74	26.24	15.74	5.21
February	147.81	133.81	120.14	105.64	91.01	76.31	60.77	46.39	35.84	25.34	14.84	4.32
March	146.74	132.76	119.03	104.50	89.90	75.14	59.56	45.54	35.04	24.54	14.01	3.51
April	145.55	131.59	117.84	103.25	88.67	73.85	58.26	44.65	34.15	23.65	13.12	2.62
May	144.40	130.46	116.69	102.04	87.47	72.59	57.02	43.78	33.28	22.78	12.25	1.75
June	143.21	129.29	115.49	100.79	86.24	71.28	55.75	42.89	32.39	21.89	11.36	0.86
July	142.06	128.16	114.30	99.57	85.05	70.01	54.52	42.03	31.53	21.03	10.50	0.88
August	140.87	127.01	113.07	98.32	83.82	68.68	53.24	41.14	30.64	20.14	9.61	0.89
September	139.68	125.86	111.82	97.09	82.57	67.34	51.97	40.25	29.75	19.25	8.72	1.78
October	138.53	124.75	110.61	95.90	81.36	66.04	50.74	39.38	28.88	18.38	7.85	2.65
November	137.34	123.60	109.35	94.66	80.10	64.71	49.50	38.49	27.99	17.49	6.96	3.54
December	136.19	122.48	108.14	93.47	78.88	63.41	48.41	37.63	27.13	16.63	6.10	4.40

If there are no further changes of rate after that on March 5, 2009, interest **up to** the first day of successive later months can be found by adding the figure from the following table:

Januay 2014	5.29
February 2014	6.18
March 2014	6.99
April 2014	7.88
May 2014	8.75
June 2014	9.64
July 2014	10.50

[1] *The Times*, April 4, 2000.

C6: Number of days between two dates

Introductory notes

Deduct the number of the opening date from the number of the closing date (where necessary adding a day for February 29).
Example: October 14th–March 19th is 443 – 287 = 156 days.

Day numbers

Day of month	Jan	Feb	Mar	Apr	May	Jun	Jul	Aug	Sep	Oct	Nov	Dec	Jan	Feb	Mar	Apr	May	Jun	Jul	Aug	Sep	Oct	Nov	Dec	Day of month
1	1	32	60	91	121	152	182	213	244	274	305	335	366	397	425	456	486	517	547	578	609	639	670	700	1
2	2	33	61	92	122	153	183	214	245	275	306	336	367	398	426	457	487	518	548	579	610	640	671	701	2
3	3	34	62	93	123	154	184	215	246	276	307	337	368	399	427	458	488	519	549	580	611	641	672	702	3
4	4	35	63	94	124	155	185	216	247	277	308	338	369	400	428	459	489	520	550	581	612	642	673	703	4
5	5	36	64	95	125	156	186	217	248	278	309	339	370	401	429	460	490	521	551	582	613	643	674	704	5
6	6	37	65	96	126	157	187	218	249	279	310	340	371	402	430	461	491	522	552	583	614	644	675	705	6
7	7	38	66	97	127	158	188	219	250	280	311	341	372	403	431	462	492	523	553	584	615	645	676	706	7
8	8	39	67	98	128	159	189	220	251	281	312	342	373	404	432	463	493	524	554	585	616	646	677	707	8
9	9	40	68	99	129	160	190	221	252	282	313	343	374	405	433	464	494	525	555	586	617	647	678	708	9
10	10	41	69	100	130	161	191	222	253	283	314	344	375	406	434	465	495	526	556	587	618	648	679	709	10
11	11	42	70	101	131	162	192	223	254	284	315	345	376	407	435	466	496	527	557	588	619	649	680	710	11
12	12	43	71	102	132	163	193	224	255	285	316	346	377	408	436	467	497	528	558	589	620	650	681	711	12
13	13	44	72	103	133	164	194	225	256	286	317	347	378	409	437	468	498	529	559	590	621	651	682	712	13
14	14	45	73	104	134	165	195	226	257	287	318	348	379	410	438	469	499	530	560	591	622	652	683	713	14
15	15	46	74	105	135	166	196	227	258	288	319	349	380	411	439	470	500	531	561	592	623	653	684	714	15
16	16	47	75	106	136	167	197	228	259	289	320	350	381	412	440	471	501	532	562	593	624	654	685	715	16
17	17	48	76	107	137	168	198	229	260	290	321	351	382	413	441	472	502	533	563	594	625	655	686	716	17
18	18	49	77	108	138	169	199	230	261	291	322	352	383	414	442	473	503	534	564	595	626	656	687	717	18
19	19	50	78	109	139	170	200	231	262	292	323	353	384	415	443	474	504	535	565	596	627	657	688	718	19
20	20	51	79	110	140	171	201	232	263	293	324	354	385	416	444	475	505	536	566	597	628	658	689	719	20
21	21	52	80	111	141	172	202	233	264	294	325	355	386	417	445	476	506	537	567	598	629	659	690	720	21
22	22	53	81	112	142	173	203	234	265	295	326	356	387	418	446	477	507	538	568	599	630	660	691	721	22
23	23	54	82	113	143	174	204	235	266	296	327	357	388	419	447	478	508	539	569	600	631	661	692	722	23
24	24	55	83	114	144	175	205	236	267	297	328	358	389	420	448	479	509	540	570	601	632	662	693	723	24
25	25	56	84	115	145	176	206	237	268	298	329	359	390	421	449	480	510	541	571	602	633	663	694	724	25
26	26	57	85	116	146	177	207	238	269	299	330	360	391	422	450	481	511	542	572	603	634	664	695	725	26
27	27	58	86	117	147	178	208	239	270	300	331	361	392	423	451	482	512	543	573	604	635	665	696	726	27
28	28	59	87	118	148	179	209	240	271	301	332	362	393	424	452	483	513	544	574	605	636	666	697	727	28
29	29		88	119	149	180	210	241	272	302	333	363	394		453	484	514	545	575	606	637	667	698	728	29
30	30		89	120	150	181	211	242	273	303	334	364	395		454	485	515	546	576	607	638	668	699	729	30
31	31		90		151		212	243		304		365	396		455		516		577	608		669		730	31

C7: Decimal years

An alternative way of calculating interest is with a table expressing intervals as decimals of a year. It is in some respects a simpler method than the Number of Days Table (Table C6) as it avoids the need to divide by 365.

The first table below gives days, weeks and months as decimals of a year.

The second table gives the period between corresponding days of two months, with the earlier month down the left-hand side and the later month across the top. Thus from the two figures in bold one sees that from April 1–June 1 is 0.167 years; from June 1 to the next April 1 is 0.833 years.

Days, weeks and months expressed as decimals of a year

Days

1	0.003	2	0.005	3	0.008	4	0.011	5	0.014	6	0.016	7	0.019	8	0.022	9	0.025	10	0.027
11	0.030	12	0.033	13	0.036	14	0.038	15	0.041	16	0.044	17	0.047	18	0.049	19	0.052	20	0.055
21	0.058	22	0.060	23	0.063	24	0.066	25	0.068	26	0.071	27	0.074	28	0.077	29	0.079	30	0.082

Weeks

1	0.019	2	0.038	3	0.058	4	0.077	5	0.096	6	0.115	7	0.134	8	0.153	9	0.173	10	0.192

Months

28 days	0.077	29 days	0.079	30 days	0.082	31 days	0.085

Intervals between corresponding days of months as decimals of a year

Earlier month	Later month					
	Jan	Feb	Mar	Apr	May	Jun
Jan	1.000	0.085	0.162	0.247	0.329	0.414
Feb	0.915	1.000	0.077	0.162	0.244	0.329
Mar	0.838	0.923	1.000	0.085	0.167	0.252
Apr	0.753	0.838	0.915	1.000	0.082	**0.167**
May	0.671	0.756	0.833	0.918	1.000	0.085
Jun	0.586	0.671	0.748	**0.833**	0.915	1.000
Jul	0.504	0.589	0.666	0.751	0.833	0.918
Aug	0.419	0.504	0.581	0.666	0.748	0.833
Sept	0.334	0.419	0.496	0.581	0.663	0.748
Oct	0.252	0.337	0.414	0.499	0.581	0.666
Nov	0.167	0.252	0.329	0.414	0.496	0.581
Dec	0.085	0.170	0.247	0.332	0.414	0.499

Earlier month	Jul	Aug	Sept	Oct	Nov	Dec
Jan	0.496	0.581	0.666	0.748	0.833	0.915
Feb	0.411	0.496	0.581	0.663	0.748	0.830
Mar	0.334	0.419	0.504	0.586	0.671	0.753
Apr	0.249	0.334	0.419	0.501	0.586	0.668
May	0.167	0.252	0.337	0.419	0.504	0.586
Jun	0.082	0.167	0.252	0.334	0.419	0.501
Jul	1.000	0.085	0.170	0.252	0.337	0.419
Aug	0.915	1.000	0.085	0.167	0.252	0.334
Sept	0.830	0.915	1.000	0.082	0.167	0.249
Oct	0.748	0.833	0.918	1.000	0.085	0.167
Nov	0.663	0.748	0.833	0.915	1.000	0.082
Dec	0.581	0.666	0.751	0.833	0.918	1.000

Example: to calculate interest at 8 per cent from June 3, 2012 to April 15, 2013

3.6.10 –15.6.10	=	12 days	=	0.033 years		
15.6.10–15.4.11	=			0.833		
Total	3.6.10–15.4.11		=	0.866 years		
Interest at 8% from 3.6.10–15.4.11			=	0.866 × 8	=	6.928%

C8: Judgment debt interest rates (England and Wales)

Introductory notes

Interest rates under the Judgments Act 1838 s.17.

This table sets out the interest rates as determined by the Judgment Debts (Rate of Interest) Orders. Such orders are made under the Administration of Justice Act 1970 s.44.

By virtue of The County Courts (Interest on Judgment Debts) Order 1991, the general rule is that every judgment debt of not less than £5,000 carries interest from the date on which it was given, at the same rate as that payable on High Court judgments.

From	At %	Order
April 20, 1971	7.5	SI 1971/491
March 1, 1977	10	SI 1977/141
December 3, 1979	12.5	SI 1979/1382
June 9, 1980	15	SI 1980/672
June 8, 1982	14	SI 1982/696
November 10, 1982	12	SI 1982/1427
April 16, 1985	15	SI 1985/437
April 1, 1993 to date	8	SI 1993/564

C9: Judicial rates of interest (Scotland)

From	At %	Act of Sederunt
May 4, 1965 – January 5, 1970	5	SI 1965/321
January 6, 1970 – January 6, 1975	7	SI 1969/1819
January 7, 1975 – April 4, 1983	11	SI 1974/2090
April 5, 1983 – August 15, 1985	12	SI 1983/398
August 16, 1985 – March 31, 1993	15	SI 1985/1178
April 1, 1993 to date	8	SI 1993/770 and SI 1994/1443

Group D

Investment

D

D1:   **Share price index (FTSE 100)**

D2:   **Barclays Equity Index**

D3:   **Index-linked stock**

D1: Share price index (FTSE 100)

FTSE® 100 (on last day of month)

	1987	1988	1989	1990	1991	1992	1993	1994
January	1808.20	1790.80	2052.10	2337.30	2170.30	2571.20	2807.20	3491.80
February	1979.20	1768.80	2002.40	2255.40	2380.90	2562.10	2868.00	3328.10
March	1997.50	1742.50	2075.00	2247.90	2456.50	2440.10	2878.70	3086.40
April	2050.50	1802.20	2118.00	2103.40	2486.20	2654.10	2813.10	3125.30
May	2203.00	1784.40	2114.40	2345.10	2499.50	2707.60	2840.70	2970.50
June	2284.10	1857.60	2151.00	2374.60	2414.80	2521.20	2900.00	2919.20
July	2360.90	1853.60	2297.00	2326.20	2588.80	2399.60	2926.50	3082.60
August	2249.70	1753.60	2387.90	2162.80	2645.70	2312.60	3100.00	3251.30
September	2366.00	1826.50	2299.40	1990.20	2621.70	2553.00	3037.50	3026.30
October	1749.80	1852.40	2142.60	2050.30	2566.00	2658.30	3171.00	3097.40
November	1579.90	1792.40	2276.80	2149.40	2420.20	2778.80	3166.90	3081.40
December	1712.70	1793.10	2422.70	2143.50	2493.10	2846.50	3418.40	3065.50

	1995	1996	1997	1998	1999	2000	2001	2002
January	2991.60	3759.30	4275.80	5458.50	5896.00	6268.50	6297.50	5164.80
February	3009.30	3727.60	4308.30	5767.30	6175.10	6232.60	5917.90	5101.00
March	3137.90	3699.70	4312.90	5932.20	6295.30	6540.20	5633.70	5271.80
April	3216.70	3817.90	4436.00	5928.30	6552.20	6327.40	5966.90	5165.60
May	3319.40	3747.80	4621.30	5870.70	6226.20	6359.30	5796.10	5085.10
June	3314.60	3711.00	4604.60	5832.50	6318.50	6312.70	5642.50	4656.40
July	3463.30	3703.20	4907.50	5837.00	6231.90	6365.30	5529.10	4246.20
August	3477.80	3867.60	4817.50	5249.40	6246.40	6672.70	5345.00	4227.30
September	3508.20	3953.70	5244.20	5064.40	6029.80	6294.20	4903.40	3721.80
October	3529.10	3979.10	4842.30	5438.40	6255.70	6438.40	5039.70	4039.70
November	3664.30	4058.00	4831.80	5743.90	6597.20	6142.20	5203.60	4169.40
December	3689.30	4118.50	5135.50	5882.60	6930.20	6222.50	5217.40	3940.40

	2003	2004	2005	2006	2007	2008	2009	2010
January	3567.40	4390.70	4852.30	5760.30	6203.10	5879.78	4149.64	5188.52
February	3655.60	4492.20	4968.50	5791.50	6171.50	5818.62	3830.09	5354.52
March	3613.30	4385.70	4894.40	5964.60	6308.00	5852.58	3926.14	5679.64
April	3926.00	4489.70	4801.70	6023.10	6449.20	6087.25	4243.71	5553.29
May	4048.10	4430.70	4964.00	5723.80	6621.40	6053.50	4417.94	5188.43
June	4031.20	4464.10	5113.20	5833.40	6607.90	5625.90	4249.21	4916.87
July	4157.00	4413.10	5282.30	5928.30	6360.10	5411.90	4608.36	5258.02
August	4161.10	4459.30	5296.90	5906.10	6303.30	5636.61	4908.90	5225.22
September	4091.30	4570.80	5477.70	5960.80	6466.80	4902.45	5133.90	5548.62
October	4287.60	4624.20	5317.30	6129.20	6721.60	4377.34	5044.55	5675.16
November	4342.60	4703.20	5423.20	6048.80	6432.50	4288.01	5190.68	5528.27
December	4476.90	4814.30	5618.80	6220.80	6456.90	4434.17	5412.88	5899.94

	2011	2012	2013
January	5862.94	5681.60	5897.80
February	5994.01	5871.50	6347.20
March	5908.76	5768.50	6378.60
April	6069.90	5737.80	6490.70
May	5990.00	5320.90	
June	5945.70	5571.10	
July	5815.20	5662.60	
August	5394.50	5712.80	
September	5128.50	5758.40	
October	5544.20	5820.50	
November	5505.40	5861.90	
December	5527.30	5866.80	

D2: Barclays Equity Index

Year	Equity Price Index December %		Equity Income Index December %		Income Yield %	Equity Price Index Adjusted for Cost of Living %		Equity Income Index Adjusted for Cost of Living %	
1956	220	−13.9	183	+2.2	5.7	62	−16.5	53	−0.8
1957	205	−7.0	188	+2.8	6.3	55	−11.1	52	−1.7
1958	289	+41.1	202	+7.5	4.8	76	+38.5	55	+5.5
1959	432	+49.5	227	+12.1	3.6	113	+49.5	61	+12.1
1960	421	−2.6	276	+21.7	4.5	108	−4.4	73	+19.5
1961	409	−3.0	286	+3.5	4.8	101	−7.0	73	−0.8
1962	391	−4.4	285	−0.4	5.0	94	−6.9	71	−3.0
1963	450	+15.2	266	−6.5	4.1	106	+13.1	65	−8.2
1964	405	−10.0	303	+13.7	5.1	91	−14.2	70	+8.5
1965	428	+5.9	326	+7.7	5.2	92	+1.3	73	+3.1
1966	389	−9.3	328	+0.5	5.8	81	−12.5	70	−3.1
1967	500	+28.7	319	−2.5	4.4	101	+25.6	67	−4.8
1968	718	+43.5	339	+6.1	3.2	137	+35.4	67	+0.2
1969	609	−15.2	342	+0.8	3.9	111	−19.0	65	−3.7
1970	563	−7.5	360	+5.5	4.4	95	−14.3	63	−2.3
1971	799	+41.9	379	+5.1	3.3	124	+30.2	61	−3.6
1972	901	+12.8	414	+9.3	3.2	130	+4.8	62	+1.6
1973	619	−31.4	430	+3.9	4.8	81	−37.9	58	−6.0
1974	276	−55.3	472	+9.6	11.7	30	−62.5	53	−8.0
1975	653	+136.3	521	+10.4	5.5	57	+89.2	47	−11.6
1976	628	−3.9	588	+12.8	6.4	48	−16.5	46	−2.0
1977	886	+41.2	682	+16.1	5.3	60	+25.9	48	+3.5
1978	910	+2.7	768	+12.6	5.8	57	−5.3	50	+3.9
1979	949	+4.3	951	+23.8	6.9	51	−11.0	53	+5.6
1980	1206	+27.1	1073	+12.8	6.1	56	+10.4	52	−2.0
1981	1294	+7.2	1111	+3.5	5.9	54	−4.3	48	−7.6
1982	1579	+22.1	1211	+9.0	5.3	62	+15.8	49	+3.4
1983	1944	+23.1	1309	+8.1	4.6	73	+16.9	51	+2.7
1984	2450	+26.0	1578	+20.6	4.4	88	+20.5	58	+15.3
1985	2822	+15.2	1781	+12.8	4.3	95	+9.0	62	+6.8
1986	3452	+22.3	2033	+14.1	4.0	112	+17.9	68	+10.0
1987	3596	+4.2	2264	+11.4	4.3	113	+0.4	74	+7.4
1988	3829	+6.5	2628	+16.1	4.7	113	−0.3	80	+8.7
1989	4978	+30.0	3076	+17.0	4.2	136	+20.7	87	+8.7
1990	4265	−14.3	3401	+10.5	5.5	107	−21.6	88	+1.1
1991	4907	+15.1	3591	+5.6	5.0	117	+10.1	89	+1.1
1992	5635	+14.8	3573	−0.5	4.4	131	+11.9	86	−3.0
1993	6951	+23.3	3414	−4.4	3.4	159	+21.0	81	−6.2
1994	6286	−9.6	3684	+7.9	4.0	140	−12.1	85	+4.9
1995	7450	+18.5	4127	+12.0	3.8	161	+14.8	92	+8.5
1996	8320	+11.7	4536	+9.9	3.7	175	+9.0	99	+7.3
1997	9962	+19.7	4690	+3.4	3.2	202	+15.5	98	−0.2
1998	11048	+10.9	4026	−14.2	2.5	218	+7.9	82	−16.5
1999	13396	+21.2	4140	+2.8	2.1	260	+19.1	83	+1.0
2000	12329	−8.0	4007	−3.2	2.2	233	−10.6	78	−5.9
2001	10428	−15.4	3998	−0.2	2.6	195	−16.0	77	−0.9
2002	7825	−25.0	4049	+1.3	3.6	142	−27.1	76	−1.6
2003	9121	+16.6	4121	+1.8	3.1	161	+13.4	75	−1.0
2004	9961	+9.2	4428	+7.5	3.1	170	+5.5	78	+3.8
2005	11764	+18.1	5058	+14.2	3.0	197	+15.5	87	+11.8
2006	11311	+13.2	5549	+9.7	2.9	213	+8.3	92	+5.0
2007	13580	+2.0	5978	+7.7	3.0	209	−1.9	95	+3.5
2008	9129	−32.8	5974	−0.1	4.5	139	−33.5	94	−1.1
2009	11407	+25.0	5321	−10.9	3.3	170	+22.0	82	−13.0
2010	12655	+10.9	5331	+0.2	2.9	180	+5.9	78	+4.4
2011	11808	−6.7	6059	+13.6	3.5	160	−11.0	85	+8.4

Note: original investment of £100 December 1945, gross income reinvested.
Reproduced here with the kind permission of Barclays Capital.

D3: Index-linked stock

Return on index-linked government securities

	1999		2000		2001		2002		2003	
	Gross %	Net %	Gross %	Net %	Gross %	Net %	Gross %	Net %	Gross %	Net %
January	1.96%	1.67%	2.13%	1.81%	1.99%	1.69%	2.36%	2.01%	1.99%	1.69%
February	1.96%	1.67%	1.99%	1.69%	2.02%	1.72%	2.35%	2.00%	1.87%	1.59%
March	1.84%	1.56%	1.95%	1.66%	2.33%	1.98%	2.36%	2.01%	1.94%	1.65%
April	1.93%	1.64%	1.96%	1.67%	2.60%	2.21%	2.38%	2.03%	2.00%	1.70%
May	1.94%	1.65%	2.02%	1.72%	2.56%	2.18%	2.34%	1.99%	1.82%	1.55%
June	1.98%	1.68%	1.91%	1.63%	2.50%	2.13%	2.23%	1.89%	1.85%	1.57%
July	2.03%	1.73%	2.06%	1.75%	2.40%	2.04%	2.41%	2.05%	2.06%	1.75%
August	2.23%	1.90%	2.09%	1.78%	2.20%	1.87%	2.12%	1.80%	2.02%	1.72%
September	2.21%	1.88%	2.10%	1.79%	2.46%	2.09%	2.10%	1.78%	1.93%	1.64%
October	2.09%	1.78%	2.11%	1.80%	2.20%	1.87%	2.22%	1.89%	2.19%	1.86%
November	1.92%	1.64%	1.95%	1.66%	2.26%	1.92%	2.35%	2.00%	2.19%	1.86%
December	1.88%	1.60%	2.01%	1.71%	2.38%	2.03%	2.11%	1.79%	1.92%	1.63%

	2004		2005		2006		2007		2008	
	Gross %	Net %	Gross %	Net %	Gross %	Net %	Gross %	Net %	Gross %	Net %
January	1.97%	1.68%	1.69%	1.44%	1.04%	0.79%	1.50%	1.25%	0.98%	0.73%
February	1.84%	1.56%	1.68%	1.43%	1.05%	0.80%	1.27%	1.02%	0.95%	0.70%
March	1.75%	1.49%	1.69%	1.44%	1.25%	1.00%	1.45%	1.20%	0.87%	0.62%
April	1.91%	1.62%	1.64%	1.39%	1.44%	1.19%	1.70%	1.45%	0.99%	0.74%
May	1.99%	1.69%	1.62%	1.37%	1.42%	1.17%	1.75%	1.50%	1.06%	0.81%
June	1.96%	1.67%	1.46%	1.21%	1.50%	1.25%	1.74%	1.49%	0.92%	0.67%
July	2.00%	1.70%	1.57%	1.32%	1.31%	1.06%	1.54%	1.29%	1.01%	0.76%
August	1.84%	1.56%	1.38%	1.13%	1.18%	0.93%	1.37%	1.12%	0.64%	0.39%
September	1.79%	1.53%	1.40%	1.15%	1.22%	0.97%	1.39%	1.14%	1.01%	0.76%
October	1.77%	1.51%	1.37%	1.12%	1.10%	0.85%	1.36%	1.11%	1.61%	1.36%
November	1.70%	1.44%	1.30%	1.05%	1.11%	0.86%	1.17%	0.92%	1.73%	1.48%
December	1.62%	1.37%	1.14%	0.89%	1.29%	1.04%	1.06%	0.81%	1.02%	0.77%

	2009		2010		2011		2012		2013	
	Gross %	Net %	Gross %	Net %	Gross %	Net %	Gross %	Net %	Gross %	Net %
January	1.03%	0.78%	0.76%	0.51%	0.72%	0.47%	−0.23%	−0.48%	−0.24%	−0.49%
February	1.26%	1.01%	0.81%	0.56%	0.64%	0.39%	−0.15%	−0.40%	−0.23%	−0.48%
March	1.05%	0.80%	0.68%	0.43%	0.66%	0.41%	−0.09%	−0.34%	−0.41%	−0.66%
April	1.09%	0.84%	0.72%	0.47%	0.57%	0.32%	−0.06%	−0.31%	−0.45%	−0.70%
May	0.99%	0.74%	0.76%	0.51%	0.53%	0.28%	−0.18%	−0.43%	−0.27%	−0.52%
June	0.88%	0.63%	0.71%	0.46%	0.51%	0.26%	−0.08%	−0.33%	−0.01%	−0.26%
July	0.96%	0.71%	0.84%	0.59%	0.35%	0.10%	−0.09%	−0.34%		
August	0.74%	0.49%	0.51%	0.26%	0.38%	0.13%	0.10%	−0.35%		
September	0.73%	0.48%	0.51%	0.26%	0.18%	−0.07%	0.11%	−0.14%		
October	0.60%	0.35%	0.63%	0.38%	0.24%	−0.01%	0.11%	−0.14%		
November	0.52%	0.27%	0.65%	0.40%	−0.11%	−0.36%	0.01%	−0.26%		
December	0.72%	0.47%	0.52%	0.27%	−0.23%	−0.48%	0.05%	−0.30%		

Notes:

1. The above table shows the month end gross redemption yields of British Government index-linked stocks with over five years to maturity assuming 3 per cent inflation (the standard assumption in recent years). (Source: Financial Times or FT website). This is not the same basis that the Lord Chancellor used when he set the discount rate in July 2001 under s.1(1) of the Damages Act 1996.

2. The net percentage yield shown above up to 2004 is stated after deducting tax at 15 per cent (this was the assumption used in *Wells v Wells* and by the Lord Chancellor when he set the discount rate in 2001). This is an oversimplification because the yield comprises interest which is taxable and capital gains or losses which are not.

3. From 2005 a fixed deduction of 0.25 per cent has been allowed for tax instead of a percentage. This is because in spite of reducing yields in recent years, taxable interest remains high so that applying a percentage to the combined gross yield would understate the deduction for tax. The actual average tax rate will vary depending on the size of the award.

Index-linked stock (April 1999 – April 2012)

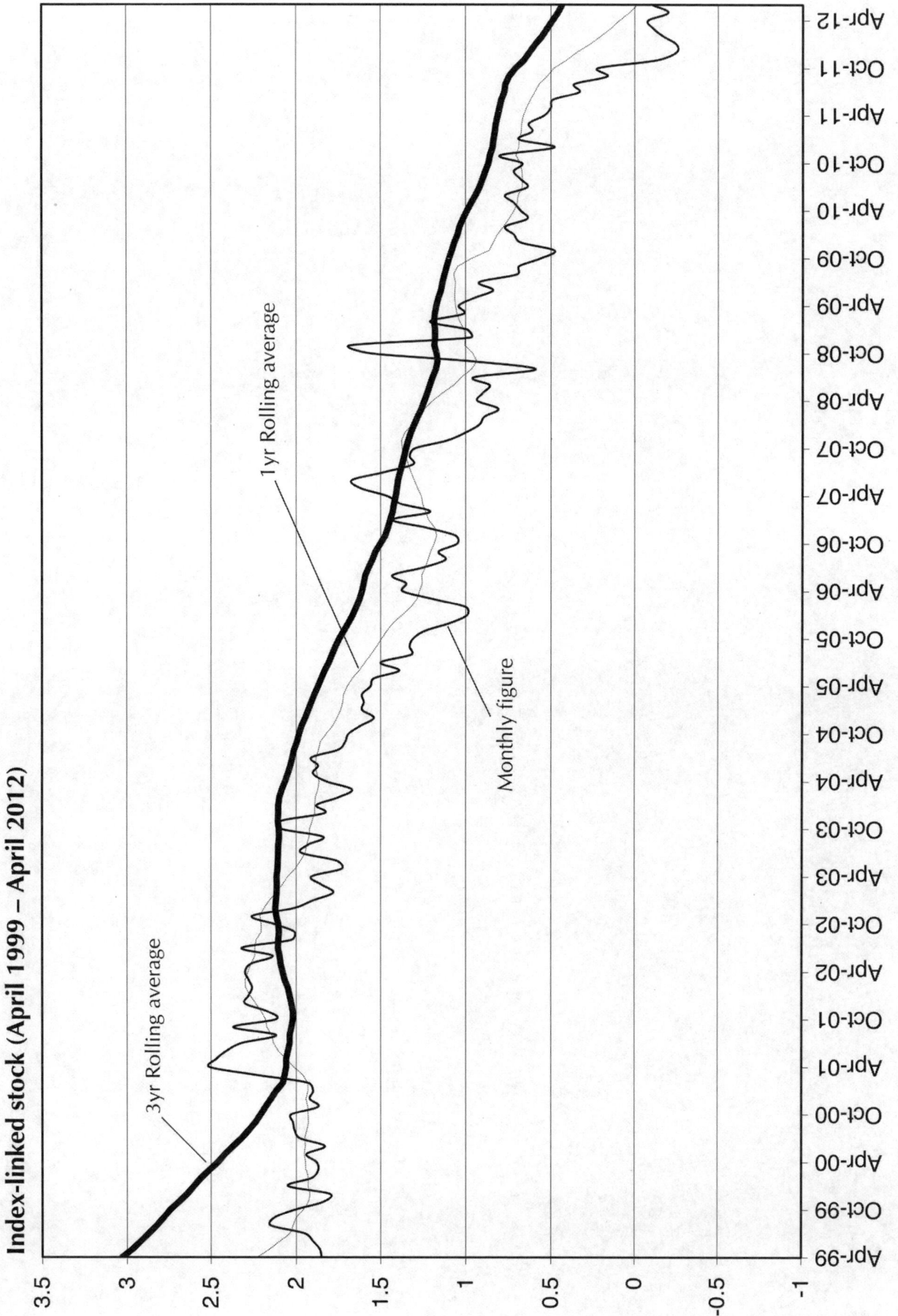

3yr Rolling average

1yr Rolling average

Monthly figure

Group E
Prices

E

E1:   **Retail prices index**

E2:   **Inflation table**

E3:   **House price indices**

E4:   **Average semi-detached house prices by region**

E5:   **How prices have changed over 12 years**

E1: Retail prices index

Year	Jan	Feb	Mar	Apr	May	June	July	Aug	Sept	Oct	Nov	Dec
2013	245.80	247.60	248.70	249.50	250.00	249.70						
2012	238.00	239.90	240.80	242.50	242.40	241.80	242.10	243.00	244.20	245.60	245.60	246.80
2011	229.00	231.30	232.50	234.40	235.20	235.20	234.70	236.10	237.90	238.00	238.50	239.40
2010	217.90	219.20	220.70	222.80	223.60	224.10	223.60	224.50	225.30	225.80	226.80	228.40
2009	210.10	211.40	211.30	211.50	212.80	213.40	213.40	214.40	215.30	216.00	216.60	218.00
2008	209.80	211.40	212.10	214.00	215.10	216.80	216.50	217.20	218.40	217.70	216.00	212.90
2007	201.60	203.10	204.40	205.40	206.20	207.30	206.10	207.30	208.00	208.90	209.70	210.90
2006	193.40	194.20	195.00	196.50	197.70	198.50	198.50	199.20	200.10	200.40	201.10	202.70
2005	188.90	189.60	190.50	191.60	192.00	192.20	192.20	192.60	193.10	193.30	193.60	194.10
2004	183.10	183.80	184.60	185.70	186.50	186.80	186.80	187.40	188.10	188.60	189.00	189.90
2003	178.40	179.30	179.90	181.20	181.50	181.30	181.30	181.60	182.50	182.60	182.70	183.50
2002	173.30	173.80	174.50	175.70	176.20	176.20	175.90	176.40	177.60	177.90	178.20	178.50
2001	171.10	172.00	172.20	173.10	174.20	174.40	173.30	174.00	174.60	174.30	173.60	173.40
2000	166.60	167.50	168.40	170.10	170.70	171.10	170.50	170.50	171.70	171.60	172.10	172.20
1999	163.40	163.70	164.10	165.20	165.60	165.60	165.10	165.50	166.20	166.50	166.70	167.30
1998	159.50	160.30	160.80	162.60	163.50	163.40	163.00	163.70	164.40	164.50	164.40	164.40
1997	154.40	155.00	155.40	156.30	156.90	157.50	157.50	158.50	159.30	159.50	159.60	160.00
1996	150.20	150.90	151.50	152.60	152.90	153.00	152.40	153.10	153.80	153.80	153.90	154.40
1995	146.00	146.90	147.50	149.00	149.60	149.80	149.10	149.90	150.60	149.80	149.80	150.70
1994	141.30	142.10	142.50	144.20	144.70	144.70	144.00	144.70	145.00	145.20	145.30	146.00
1993	137.90	138.80	139.30	140.60	141.10	141.00	140.70	141.30	141.90	141.80	141.60	141.90
1992	135.60	136.30	136.70	138.80	139.30	139.30	138.80	138.90	139.40	139.90	139.70	139.20
1991	130.20	130.90	131.40	133.10	133.50	134.10	133.80	134.10	134.60	135.10	135.60	135.70
1990	119.50	120.20	121.40	125.10	126.20	126.70	126.80	128.10	129.30	130.30	130.00	129.90
1989	111.00	111.80	112.30	114.30	115.00	115.40	115.50	115.80	116.60	117.50	118.50	118.80
1988	103.30	103.70	104.10	105.80	106.20	106.60	106.70	107.90	108.40	109.50	110.00	110.30
1987	100.00	100.40	100.60	101.80	101.90	101.90	101.80	102.10	102.40	102.90	103.40	103.30
1986	96.25	96.60	96.73	97.67	97.85	97.79	97.52	97.82	98.30	98.45	99.29	99.62
1985	91.20	91.94	92.80	94.78	95.21	95.41	95.23	95.49	95.44	95.59	95.92	96.05
1984	86.84	87.20	87.48	88.64	88.97	89.20	89.10	89.94	90.11	90.67	90.95	90.87
1983	82.61	82.97	83.12	84.28	84.64	84.84	85.30	85.68	86.06	86.36	86.67	86.89
1982	78.73	78.76	79.44	81.04	81.62	81.85	81.88	81.90	81.85	82.26	82.66	82.51
1981	70.29	70.93	71.99	74.07	74.55	74.98	75.31	75.87	76.30	76.98	77.79	78.28
1980	62.18	63.07	63.93	66.11	66.72	67.35	67.91	68.06	68.49	68.92	69.48	69.86
1979	52.52	52.95	53.38	54.30	54.73	55.67	58.07	58.53	59.11	59.72	60.25	60.68
1978	48.04	48.31	48.62	49.33	49.61	49.99	50.22	50.54	50.75	50.98	51.33	51.76
1977	43.70	44.13	44.56	45.70	46.06	46.54	46.59	46.82	47.07	47.28	47.50	47.76
1976	37.49	37.97	38.17	38.91	39.34	39.54	39.62	40.18	40.71	41.44	42.03	42.59
1975	30.39	30.90	31.51	32.72	34.09	34.75	35.11	35.31	35.61	36.12	36.55	37.01
1974	25.35	25.78	26.01	26.89	27.28	27.55	27.81	27.83	28.14	28.69	29.20	29.63
1973	22.64	22.78	22.92	23.35	23.52	23.64	23.75	23.82	24.03	24.50	24.69	24.87
1972	21.01	21.12	21.19	21.38	21.49	21.63	21.70	21.87	21.99	22.30	22.37	22.49
1971	19.43	19.53	19.69	20.11	20.25	20.39	20.51	20.52	20.55	20.67	20.79	20.89
1970	17.91	18.00	18.11	18.38	18.44	18.49	18.62	18.61	18.70	18.90	19.03	19.16

	Jan	Feb	Mar	Apr	May	June	July	Aug	Sept	Oct	Nov	Dec	
1969	17.06	17.15	17.22	17.41	17.38	17.46	17.46	17.42	17.47	17.60	17.64	17.76	1969
1968	16.07	16.15	16.20	16.49	16.51	16.57	16.59	16.61	16.63	16.71	16.74	16.97	1968
1967	15.66	15.67	15.67	15.79	15.78	15.85	15.75	15.71	15.70	15.82	15.91	16.02	1967
1966	15.11	15.12	15.15	15.33	15.44	15.48	15.41	15.50	15.48	15.52	15.61	15.63	1966
1965	14.47	14.47	14.52	14.80	14.85	14.89	14.89	14.92	14.93	14.95	15.01	15.08	1965
1964	13.84	13.85	13.90	14.02	14.14	14.19	14.19	14.25	14.25	14.26	14.38	14.43	1964
1963	13.57	13.69	13.71	13.74	13.73	13.73	13.65	13.61	13.65	13.71	13.74	13.77	1963
1962	13.22	13.23	13.28	13.47	13.51	13.60	13.55	13.43	13.41	13.40	13.45	13.52	1962
1961	12.63	12.63	12.68	12.74	12.78	12.89	12.89	13.01	12.99	13.01	13.15	13.17	1961
1960	12.36	12.36	12.34	12.41	12.41	12.47	12.50	12.42	12.43	12.53	12.59	12.62	1960
1959	12.42	12.41	12.41	12.32	12.27	12.29	12.26	12.29	12.23	12.28	12.37	12.40	1959
1958	12.16	12.10	12.19	12.33	12.28	12.40	12.20	12.18	12.19	12.31	12.35	12.40	1958
1957	11.74	11.73	11.71	11.75	11.77	11.89	11.99	11.97	11.93	12.05	12.11	12.17	1957
1956	11.25	11.25	11.39	11.55	11.53	11.52	11.47	11.51	11.48	11.55	11.60	11.63	1956
1955	10.70	10.70	10.70	10.76	10.74	10.97	11.00	10.93	11.00	11.11	11.29	11.29	1955
1954	10.28	10.26	10.35	10.39	10.36	10.42	10.60	10.53	10.51	10.56	10.61	10.66	1954
1953	10.14	10.17	10.24	10.33	10.30	10.35	10.35	10.29	10.27	10.27	10.30	10.26	1953
1952	9.71	9.72	9.77	9.93	9.93	10.09	10.08	10.02	10.00	10.09	10.08	10.15	1952
1951	8.60	8.68	8.74	8.88	9.10	9.13	9.27	9.31	9.38	9.44	9.48	9.54	1951
1950	8.28	8.30	8.32	8.35	8.37	8.33	8.33	8.30	8.35	8.44	8.47	8.52	1950
1949	7.99	8.01	7.98	7.96	8.11	8.14	8.15	8.16	8.19	8.23	8.23	8.25	1949
1948	7.64	7.78	7.80	7.91	7.90	8.04	7.92	7.92	7.93	7.95	7.97	7.98	1948
1947	–	–	–	–	–	7.33	7.38	7.34	7.37	7.43	7.58	7.60	1947
	Jan	Feb	Mar	Apr	May	June	July	Aug	Sept	Oct	Nov	Dec	

Source: Office for National Statistics licensed under the Open Government Licence V.I.O.

Note:

To calculate the equivalent value of a lump sum, divide by the RPI at the time and multiply the result by the current RPI. Thus £460 in June 1981 would be calculated as:

$$\left(\frac{460}{74.98} \right) \times \text{current RPI}$$

to show the relative value of that amount in "today's money".

E2: Inflation table

Introductory notes

The table shows the value each January in earlier years equivalent to £1 in January 2013, after taking account of inflation over time.

Price inflation is measured by reference to the Retail Price Index.

Year	Multiplier	Year	Multiplier
1948	32.18	1981	3.50
1949	30.76	1982	3.12
1950	29.70	1983	2.98
		1984	2.83
1951	28.59	1985	2.70
1952	25.31		
1953	24.24	1986	2.55
1954	23.92	1987	2.46
1955	22.96	1988	2.38
		1989	2.21
1956	21.85	1990	2.06
1957	20.93		
1958	20.22	1991	1.89
1959	19.79	1992	1.81
1960	19.88	1993	1.78
		1994	1.74
1961	19.46	1995	1.68
1962	18.60		
1963	18.11	1996	1.64
1964	17.76	1997	1.59
1965	16.98	1998	1.54
		1999	1.50
1966	16.27	2000	1.48
1967	15.69		
1968	15.29	2001	1.44
1969	14.41	2002	1.42
1970	13.73	2003	1.38
		2004	1.34
1971	12.65	2005	1.30
1972	11.70		
1973	10.86	2006	1.27
1974	9.70	2007	1.22
1975	8.09	2008	1.17
		2009	1.17
1976	6.56	2010	1.13
1977	5.62		
1978	5.12	2011	1.07
1979	4.68	2012	1.03
1980	3.95	2013	1.00

E3: House price indices

1. There are several price indices available in April 2013. These include the Halifax, Nationwide, the Financial Times, the Royal Institute of Chartered Surveyors, Hometrack, Rightmove, the Government Index and the Land Registry index.

2. The editors of "Facts & Figures" have used the Halifax table in previous editions and continue to do so. The Index Year for the Halifax table is 1983. In certain circumstances, the data offered by other indices may be useful. For example the Land Registry figures are broken down regionally and contain information about the numbers of first-time buyers. However, they exclude cash purchases which account for about a quarter of all transactions. Each table has strengths and weaknesses of this sort.

3. None of the indices should be treated as definitive. They can only be used as guides to the movement of prices over longer periods of time. Readers should be cautious about over-interpreting the analysis of short-term price changes.

All Houses

| Year | U.K. | | |
	Index	%	Average Price £
92	208.1	−5.6	64,309
93	202.1	−2.9	62,455
94	203.1	0.5	62,750
95	199.6	−1.7	61,666
96	208.6	4.5	64,441
97	221.7	6.3	68,504
98	233.7	5.4	72,196
99	250.5	7.2	77,405
00	275.1	9.8	85,005
01	298.6	8.5	92,256
02	350.6	17.4	108,342
03	429.1	22.4	132,589
04	507.6	18.3	156,831
05	536.6	5.7	165,807
06	581.3	8.3	179,601
07	635.9	9.4	196,478
08	585.9	−7.9	181,032
09	524.6	−10.5	162,085
10	539.6	2.9	166,739
11	524.5	−0.1	162,064
12	522.1	−0.6	161,308

Year	North Index	%	Yorks/Humb Index	%	N. West Index	%	E. Midlands Index	%
92	210.1	−1.6	231.9	−3.6	226.1	−4.3	214.4	−5.9
93	206.3	−1.8	228.3	−1.6	219.3	−3.0	208.3	−2.8
94	203.6	−1.3	226.3	−0.9	215.8	−1.6	209.1	0.4
95	195.9	−3.8	219.2	−3.1	207.8	−3.7	203.9	−2.5
96	201.9	3.1	224.5	2.4	210.7	1.4	209.4	2.7
97	206.5	2.3	228.5	1.8	216.7	2.9	221.5	5.8
98	211.2	2.3	229.8	0.5	220.4	1.7	229.9	3.8
99	220.1	4.2	236.5	2.9	231.0	4.8	244.8	6.5
00	221.9	0.8	243.9	3.2	242.6	5.0	265.0	8.2
01	234.0	5.5	257.5	5.6	255.7	5.4	287.3	8.4
02	271.4	16.0	297.7	15.6	292.8	14.5	361.7	25.9
03	370.6	36.5	395.6	32.9	366.3	25.1	457.5	26.5
04	490.3	32.3	495.0	25.1	472.8	29.1	541.4	18.3
05	533.3	8.8	549.3	11.0	523.7	10.8	564.9	4.3
06	567.3	6.4	602.4	9.7	565.1	7.9	599.4	6.1
07	601.8	6.1	640.5	6.3	596.8	5.6	632.4	5.5
08	547.2	−9.1	580.0	−9.5	558.3	−6.5	582.0	−8.0
09	500.2	−8.6	526.3	−9.3	492.8	−11.7	518.2	−11.0
10	511.5	2.3	538.2	2.3	486.7	−1.3	541.7	4.5
11	505.4	3.9	493.6	−4.9	478.3	−1.4	524.6	−1.2
12	478.1	−1.0	509.1	−0.8	468.6	−3.4	523.1	1.0

Year	W. Midlands Index	%	E. Anglia Index	%	S. West Index	%	S. East Index	%
92	229.4	−4.6	198.5	−7.4	193.9	−7.8	192.8	−8.5
93	219.1	−4.5	193.2	−2.7	185.9	−4.1	186.4	−3.3
94	218.3	−0.4	195.8	1.3	186.6	1.5	189.8	1.8
95	215.6	−1.2	193.5	−1.1	186.1	−1.3	190.3	0.3
96	224.6	4.2	197.7	2.1	195.1	4.8	199.9	5.0
97	237.3	5.6	211.0	6.7	209.7	7.5	221.2	10.7
98	250.0	5.4	224.4	6.4	226.4	8.0	244.2	10.4
99	254.7	1.9	241.1	7.5	248.8	9.9	271.2	11.0
00	282.2	10.8	279.7	16.0	291.0	17.0	318.3	17.4
01	301.5	6.8	322.6	15.4	327.8	12.6	354.7	11.4
02	363.7	20.7	386.0	19.6	403.4	23.0	413.7	16.6
03	460.7	26.7	465.0	20.5	477.7	18.4	483.8	17.0
04	540.5	17.3	522.3	12.3	545.4	14.2	528.8	9.3
05	565.4	4.6	536.0	2.6	552.6	1.3	537.0	1.5
06	602.8	6.6	581.1	8.4	587.5	6.3	571.2	6.4
07	640.4	6.2	637.3	9.7	641.9	9.3	636.9	11.5
08	591.9	−7.6	600.8	−5.7	583.2	−9.1	588.6	−7.6
09	534.1	−9.8	520.2	−13.4	540.0	−7.4	532.1	−9.6
10	549.5	2.9	540.9	−4.0	568.5	5.3	561.4	5.5
11	533.8	0.9	548.1	−1.4	538.3	0.4	561.1	2.3
12	528.8	−0.4	540.7	−0.6	553.1	1.1	558.8	1.0

Year	Gr. London Index	%	Wales Index	%	Scotland Index	%	N. Ireland Index	%
92	202.0	−9.4	207.7	−4.3	193.2	0.2	145.5	−1.0
93	192.0	−4.9	204.5	−1.6	196.4	1.6	151.7	4.3
94	195.5	1.8	201.9	−1.2	199.4	1.6	162.1	6.9
95	194.9	−0.4	194.2	−3.8	199.4	0.0	172.8	6.6
96	212.4	9.0	205.5	5.9	204.9	2.8	204.5	18.3
97	246.3	16.0	212.0	3.1	204.7	0.1	210.6	3.0
98	272.3	10.5	220.2	3.8	209.8	2.5	235.6	11.9
99	317.9	16.8	232.3	5.5	212.8	1.4	248.8	5.6
00	373.6	17.5	245.0	5.5	214.2	0.7	264.4	6.3
01	428.3	14.7	263.8	7.7	220.0	2.7	296.8	12.2
02	499.4	16.6	299.8	13.6	238.5	8.4	307.4	3.6
03	563.3	12.8	397.2	32.5	274.5	15.1	340.3	10.7
04	608.5	8.0	516.3	30.0	330.6	20.4	397.9	16.9
05	621.4	2.1	553.7	7.3	375.7	13.6	486.0	22.1
06	680.9	9.6	589.7	6.5	421.7	12.2	581.3	32.6
07	777.6	14.2	640.7	8.7	488.2	15.8	844.5	31.1
08	705.3	−9.3	579.4	−9.6	478.2	−2.1	679.2	−19.6
09	622.0	−11.8	512.0	−11.6	426.6	−10.8	563.7	−17.0
10	659.9	6.1	530.3	3.6	421.4	−1.2	506.2	−10.2
11	681.3	2.4	530.8	−1.7	384.5	−5.8	412.5	−2.8
12	674.4	2.2	505.6	−3.0	384.3	−5.5	405.4	−8.7

E4: Average semi-detached house prices by region

Prices are as of fourth quarter of 2012.

Region	£
North	118,525
North West	136,152
West Midlands	141,625
South East	240,299
Greater London	333,601
Yorkshire & Humberside	124,579
East Midlands	126,541

E5: How prices have changed over 12 years

PRICE COMPARISON 2001–2013

Item	Price in 2001	Price in 2013	% change	Source
Milk (pint)	36p	49p	36%	ONS
Loaf of white sliced bread (800g)	71p	£1.35	90%	ONS
Sugar (kg)	57p	99p	63%	ONS
Draught lager (pint)	£2.20	£4.25	63%	ONS
Cigarettes (20 king sized)	£4.22	£7.98	89%	ONS
Unleaded petrol per litre	83.5p	135.8p	63%	Petrol Prices
House prices	£96,337	£163,356	69.5%	Halifax House Price Index & Historical House Price Data
Average mortgage size (new loans)	£59,200	£144,141	143.4%	Council of Mortgage Lenders
Weekly state pension	£72.50	£110.15	51.9%	The Pensions Advisory Service
Level of UK consumer debt	£900.5 billion	£1,347.4 billion	49.6%	Bank of England Statistics
Price of oil (per barrel)	$19.40	$102.88	430.3%	Price of Oil & WTRG
Price of gold (per ounce)	$276.80	$1,454.75	425%	Digital Look
Ford Focus (latest model)	£15,700	£19,545	24.4%	Ford
McDonald's Big Mac	£1.99	£2.29	15%	McDonald's

Read more: *http://www.thisismoney.co.uk/historic-inflation-calculator#ixzz1Bm4ygOL6*

Group F
Earnings

F1:   **Earnings losses in personal injury and fatal accident cases**

F2:   **Payroll documents**

F3:   **National minimum wage**

F4:   **Regional unemployment statistics**

F5:   **Average weekly earnings index**

F6:   **Average weekly earnings**

F7:   **Average earnings statistics**

F8:   **Public sector comparable earnings**

F9:   **Public sector earnings websites**

F

F1: Earnings losses in personal injury and fatal accident cases

1. Purpose of note

The purpose of this note is to provide some basic guidance on what information to request from a claimant in order to make an initial assessment as to whether an earnings loss is likely to arise.

2. Nature of occupation

Identify at an early stage into which category of occupation the claimant falls:

Employment
— Employee without ownership rights.
— Director/shareholder (of private company).

Self-employment
— Sole trader.
— Partner.

3. Relevant dates

For the purposes of proposing the periods for which information should be requested, relevant dates will be identified as follows:

For an individual in employment
(References here are to tax years ending on April 5, although the tax for many salaried employees will often effectively run from April 1 to March 31.)

D1 April 6 three years before D2
D2 April 5 immediately preceding D3
D3 Incident date
D4 April 5 immediately preceding D5
D5 Present time

For business accounts
D6 Date of beginning of accounting period three years before D7
D7 Date of end of accounting period immediately preceding D3
D8 Date of end of accounting period immediately preceding D5

A full three years' pre-accident financial information should often be sufficient (having regard to the need for proportionality), although documentation for a longer period may be appropriate if it emerges that business results have been volatile.

For an individual in employment

D1		D2	[D3] Incident		D4	D5
April 6 April 5	April 6 April 5	April 6 April 5	April 6 April 5	April 6 April 5	April 6 April 5	April 6 Present time
Tax year −3	Tax year −2	Tax year −1	Tax year 0	Tax year +1	Current tax year −1	Current tax year

For business accounts

D6	D7	D3 [Incident]		D8	D5
Beginning End	Beginning End	Beginning End	Beginning End	Beginning End	Beginning End	Beginning End	Beginning Present time
Accounts year −3	Accounts year −2	Accounts year −1	Accounts year 0	Accounts year +1	Current accounts year −1	Current accounts year

4. **Employment: Employee without ownership rights**

This is the likely category for most employees—but excluding in particular those who are directors and/or shareholders with a degree of control over private companies.

In the absence of detailed representations from the employer, or from an employment expert, the earnings history may be the only useful guide to potential earnings but for the incident giving rise to the claim.

The most useful documentation will usually be a comprehensive set of pay advices (monthly, sometimes four-weekly, or weekly) because these may be expected to show:

- basic pay level (and dates/amounts of periodic increases),
- overtime (if paid) and any other regular or periodic enhancements,
- bonuses (and dates/amounts paid),
- sick pay (and dates), and
- employee pension contributions.

Request:

- **Pay advices (whether from employment or subsequent pension) from D1 to D5.**
- **Details of benefits other than pay for each tax year between D1 and D2 and for each tax year since D2.**

5. **Employment: Director/shareholders**

This category relates mainly to those individuals who have a degree of ownership or control, probably in a private company, and whose remuneration as such may not be a fair reflection of the personal reward available from the business.

For instance:

- profits may have been drawn by way of dividend for reasons of tax efficiency; or
- profits (which the claimant could have drawn) have been re-invested in the business.

It may well be appropriate to assess loss along the lines that would be adopted in relation to a sole trader or partner, that is:

- first to identify whether a business loss has occurred that is attributable to the claim incident, and
- if so, go on to identify the share of the business loss suffered personally by the claimant.

In such a case, it will often be appropriate to review not only the remuneration history of the individual but also the dividend history. Benefits history may also be important.

Thank you for purchasing Facts and Figures: Tables for the Calculation of Damages 2013/14

☑ Don't miss important updates

So that you have all the latest information, **Facts and Figures: Tables for the Calculation of Damages** is published annually. Sign up today for a Standing Order to ensure you receive the updating copies as soon as they publish. Setting up a Standing Order with Sweet & Maxwell is hassle-free, simply tick, complete and return this FREEPOST card and we'll do the rest.

You may cancel your Standing Order at any time by writing to us at Thomson Reuters, PO Box 1000, Andover, SP10 9AH stating the Standing Order you wish to cancel.

Alternatively, if you have purchased your copy of **Facts and Figures: Tables for the Calculation of Damages 2013/14** from a bookshop or other trade supplier, please ask your supplier to ensure that you are registered to receive the new editions.

All goods are subject to our 30 day Satisfaction Guarantee (applicable to EU customers only)

Yes, please send me new editions of **Facts and Figures: Tables for the Calculation of Damages** to be invoiced on publication, until I cancel the standing order in writing.

☐ All new editions

Title   Name ....

Organisation ....

Job title ....

Address ....

Postcode ....

Telephone ....

Email ....

S&M account number (if known) ....

PO number ....

All orders are accepted subject to the terms of this order form and our Terms of Trading. (see www.sweetandmaxwell.co.uk). By submitting this order form I confirm that I accept these terms and I am authorised to sign on behalf of the customer.

Signed ....   Job Title ....

Print Name ....   Date ....

UK VAT Number: GB 900 5487 43. Irish VAT Number: IE 9513874E. For customers in an EU member state (except UK & Ireland) please supply your VAT Number. VAT No [   ]

(BC007) V9 (07.2013) JL / JK

Facts and Figures: Tables for the Calculation of Damages 2013/14. charges are not made for titles supplied to mainland UK. Non-mainland UK please add £4/€5 per delivery. Europe - please add £10/€13 for first item, £2.50/€3 for each additional item. Rest of World - please add £30/€38 for first item, £15/€19 for each additional item. For deliveries outside Europe please add £30/€42 for first item, £15/€21 for each additional item.

SWEET & MAXWELL   THOMSON REUTERS

THOMSON REUTERS

FREEPOST

PO BOX 1000

ANDOVER

SP10 9AH

UNITED KINGDOM

Request:

Regarding the Business

- **full accounts (including detailed profit and loss accounts) from D6 to D8,**

  and consider requesting

- **figures for monthly (preferably) or quarterly sales from D6 to D5.**
  (Important if the claimant's role is likely to have influenced sales levels; the figures should show up trends and seasonality, etc.)

Regarding the claimant

- **pay advices (whether from employment or pension) from D1 to D5, and**
- **tax returns from D1 to D4.**
  (Mainly to check remuneration and dividends received in each tax year, but also benefits and any personal pension contributions, etc.)

6. **Self-employment: Sole trader**

Request:

- **full accounts from D6 to D8,**
- **figures for monthly or quarterly sales from D6 to D5, and**
- **tax returns from D1 to D4.**
  (Mainly to check private usage deductions from business expenses, capital allowances, personal pension contributions, etc.)

7. **Self-employment: Partner**

Approach will be:

- first to identify whether a business loss has occurred that is attributable to the claim incident, and
- if so, go on to identify the share of the business loss suffered personally by the claimant.

Request:

Regarding the Business

- **full partnership accounts from D6 to D8, and**
- **figures for monthly (preferably) or quarterly sales from D6 to D5.**

Regarding the claimant

- **personal tax returns from D1 to D4.**
  (Mainly to check personal pension contributions, etc.)

8. **Benefits other than pay (employees)**

In the first instance, it is probably sufficient simply to ask, in relation to any employee (including a company director), for:

- **details of any non-pecuniary benefits in employment, and any pension benefits.**

9. Other points

• Company searches

Searches of small UK limited companies seldom yield helpful results as regards accounts because the contents of the accounts to be filed are invariably in shortened form, sometimes only a balance sheet.

In cases where there are doubts about full disclosure, a search may be useful in identifying whether a claimant has more directorships than advised, or possibly a history of connections with insolvent companies.

• Permanent Health Insurance income

Where a claimant receives insurance money through his employer, this will usually be evident from review of the pay advices.

As to whether credit needs to be given by the claimant for such insurance money for claim purposes will probably depend on the nature of the underlying policy.

• Ill-health pension

Where a claimant receives an ill-health pension following an incident, this should again be evident from review of the pay advices.

Generally, no credit is to be given for actual pension in a loss of earnings claim: *Parry v Cleaver*.[1]

• Partnerships

There may be cases where the profit-sharing arrangements do not reflect the realistic commercial input of the respective partners. This issue may arise particularly where spouses are business partners. The court may be prepared to put aside the historic arrangements in assessing loss: *Ward v Newall Insulation Co Ltd*.[2]

[1] [1970] A.C. 1.
[2] [1998] 1 W.L.R. 1722.

F2: Payroll documents

Employee name		Employer name	
MR D CAMERON		FirstLord Limited	

Pay date	Tax period	Tax code
31 MARCH 2013	12	810L

Pay and allowances (* non-taxable)	£	Deductions/(Refunds)	£	Totals to date	£
Salary	2,500.00			Taxable gross	33,800.00
Car allowance *	275.00			Car allowance *	1,650.00
		Income tax	344.90	Income tax	5,139.00
		National insurance	197.80	National insurance	2,435.00
		Pension	100.00	Pension	1,200.00
Total	2,775.00	Total	642.70	Net pay	2,132.30

Points to note

1   As good a starting point as any is usually a pay advice for the **last full tax year**, but try also to obtain all subsequent pay advices whether to date of trial in a personal injury case or to date of death if a fatal accident.

2   It is worth bearing in mind that some employers pay every four weeks, and on rare occasions every two weeks, rather than necessarily monthly or weekly. The **tax period** should help to identify payment frequency.

3   The tax code, 810L, represents the basic tax allowance of £8,105. This indicates that the tax inspector has no reason to make any adjustment to the standard code to collect additional tax due in the year.

This in turn implies that the employee has no taxable benefits from the employer.

The most common taxable benefits are probably health insurance cover and those related to private use of motor vehicles.

By way of example, were the employee enjoying benefits to a value of £1,000 pa, the code could be expected to be 710L. Application of this code would result in the tax due on the benefit being collected under PAYE over the course of the tax year.

4   In the illustration shown above, the **gross taxable income** figure requires some reconciliation to other figures.

The year-end figures suggest that salary has probably been running consistently at £2,500 per month, with a £100 per month pension contribution; that would produce a taxable total of £28,800 in the year, suggesting that there has been additional pay of £5,000 in arriving at the taxable gross figure of £33,800.

The figure for the year's total **National Insurance** for the year is consistent with a salary of £2,500 per month, with a single addition of £5,000.

So the gross taxable appears likely to comprise £30,000 salary, a one-off addition of £5,000 less £1,200 pension.

5   The combination of a **pension deduction** which appears to represent exactly 4 per cent of salary, together with the fact that it can readily be established that the national insurance contributions are at contracted out rates, suggests that the employee is a member of a final salary pension scheme which may give rise to a pension loss claim.

(In the case of a money purchase pension scheme, the deductions are made less basic rate tax, 20 per cent in 2013/14, so it is unlikely that the amount of £100.00 is a monthly contribution to such a scheme.)

6   A **car allowance** is shown, but it is marked as non-taxable.

Note also that the totals to date suggest that the allowance has been in payment for only six months in the year.

Generally, if an allowance is non-taxable, it is unlikely to represent a valuable benefit. Perhaps the car allowance in this case is a fixed level reimbursement of business costs on a prescribed formula which will be adjusted after the year-end in accordance with actual business mileage or the like.

Nevertheless it would be worth establishing why the car allowance was not in payment through-out the year.

F3: National minimum wage

Introductory notes

1. The National Minimum Wage became law on April 1, 1999.

2. The National Minimum Wage is the minimum amount of pay to which workers over a specified age are entitled. Up to September 30, 2004, the minimum age was 18. Since October 1, 2004 a new rate has been available to workers under 18 who are no longer of compulsory school age.

3. Most adult workers who are resident in the UK, who have a written, oral or implied contract and who are not genuinely self-employed, are entitled to the National Minimum Wage.

4. The National Minimum Wage is enforced by HM Revenue and Customs.

5. There are currently four levels of National Minimum Wage: a development rate for those aged between 18 and 20; a main rate for workers aged 21 or over; from October 1, 2004, a rate for workers under 18 who are no longer of compulsory school age; and, from October 1, 2010, an apprentice minimum wage (see note 8, below).

6. The main rate was extended to workers aged 21 or over from October 2010. Prior to that the qualifying age for the main rate was 22. Correspondingly the development rate has been available to those aged between 18 and 20 from October 2010. Prior to that it was available to those aged between 18 and 21.

7. A development rate available, subject to various conditions, to workers aged 22 or over who started a new job with a new employer and did accredited training, being a course approved by the UK government to obtain a vocational qualification, was abolished for pay reference periods starting on or after October 1, 2006. When applicable, the accredited training rate could only be paid for the first six months of the new job, after which the National Minimum Wage main rate applied.

8. A new apprentice minimum wage was introduced with effect from October 1, 2010, available to apprentices aged under 19, or apprentices aged 19 or over but in the first year of their apprenticeship.

	Pay reference periods starting on or after October 1					
	2007 £/hr	2008 £/hr	2009 £/hr	2010 £/hr	2011 £/hr	2012 £/hr
Workers under 18 who are no longer of compulsory school age (notes 2 and 5)	3.53	3.57	3.64	3.68	3.68	3.72
Development rate for workers aged 18–21 years/18–20 years (from October 2010) (notes 5 and 6)	4.77	4.83	4.92	4.98	4.98	5.03
Rate for apprentices aged under 19, or 19 or over but in the first year of their apprenticeship (note 8)	N/A	N/A	2.50	2.60	2.65	2.68
Main rate for workers aged 22 or over (21 or over from October 2010) (notes 5 and 6)	5.73	5.80	5.93	6.08	6.19	6.31

F4: Regional unemployment statistics

In previous years, tables showing the average duration of claims for Jobseeker's Allowance have been drawn from the Office of National Statistics Economic and Labour Market Review. This is no longer being produced.

The tables below have been based on data available on the Nomis website for June 2013.

North East
Median duration (weeks)

Age	Female	Male	All
Under 17	5.0	13.0	6.0
17	7.4	5.7	6.5
18	13.1	13.1	13.1
19	24.7	23.5	23.9
20–24	25.5	26.3	26.0
25–29	25.5	29.5	28.2
30–34	28.5	33.4	31.4
35–39	31.3	36.1	34.1
40–44	35.0	38.1	36.8
45–49	34.7	41.0	38.0
50–54	31.1	38.0	35.5
55–59	28.3	41.1	36.2
60 and over	35.6	29.2	31.1
All ages	27.8	30.9	29.7

North West
Median duration (weeks)

Age	Female	Male	All
Under 17	7.0	4.0	5.8
17	7.2	6.9	7.1
18	10.4	10.8	10.6
19	17.6	17.9	17.8
20–24	19.3	19.7	19.6
25–29	20.9	21.7	21.5
30–34	23.6	24.2	24.0
35–39	26.8	26.8	26.8
40–44	29.3	29.6	29.5
45–49	28.7	32.8	31.2
50–54	24.9	33.3	30.0
55–59	23.4	34.8	30.4
60 and over	27.2	26.9	27.0
All ages	22.7	24.0	23.5

Yorkshire and the Humber
Median duration (weeks)

Age	Female	Male	All
Under 17	3.7	8.0	5.2
17	5.6	6.2	6.0
18	12.0	11.2	11.6
19	21.6	19.6	20.4
20–24	23.5	22.4	22.7
25–29	23.3	24.7	24.2
30–34	26.5	27.0	26.8
35–39	29.6	31.4	30.7
40–44	32.1	33.6	32.9
45–49	31.6	34.0	33.1
50–54	29.4	34.7	32.6
55–59	26.5	38.0	33.8
60 and over	28.9	27.6	28.0
All ages	25.4	26.0	25.8

East Midlands
Median duration (weeks)

Age	Female	Male	All
Under 17	3.3	5.3	4.8
17	6.0	5.1	5.5
18	11.7	10.6	11.1
19	19.3	17.8	18.3
20–24	19.7	19.8	19.8
25–29	20.6	21.6	21.2
30–34	22.9	23.8	23.5
35–39	26.0	25.0	25.3
40–44	26.2	27.2	26.8
45–49	25.4	29.5	27.6
50–54	24.4	31.2	28.1
55–59	23.1	31.5	27.4
60 and over	24.6	24.0	24.2
All ages	22.1	23.0	22.7

West Midlands
Median duration
(weeks)

Age	Female	Male	All
Under 17	5.0	3.6	5.0
17	5.3	6.3	5.7
18	11.6	11.0	11.3
19	20.3	18.7	19.3
20–24	22.6	21.6	21.9
25–29	22.5	23.9	23.4
30–34	24.9	26.2	25.7
35–39	28.0	28.0	28.0
40–44	30.5	33.8	32.4
45–49	30.1	34.0	32.5
50–54	29.8	36.8	34.3
55–59	26.6	38.2	34.1
60 and over	30.3	29.5	29.7
All ages	24.6	25.6	25.3

East
Median duration
(weeks)

Age	Female	Male	All
Under 17	7.3	7.0	7.6
17	6.0	7.1	6.7
18	11.4	11.1	11.2
19	17.9	17.0	17.3
20–24	18.5	19.0	18.9
25–29	19.5	20.4	20.1
30–34	22.1	22.3	22.2
35–39	25.4	24.3	24.8
40–44	27.5	25.8	26.5
45–49	27.0	26.3	26.6
50–54	23.4	28.2	25.9
55–59	23.5	29.5	26.4
60 and over	23.3	23.3	23.3
All ages	21.8	22.2	22.1

London
Median duration
(weeks)

Age	Female	Male	All
Under 17	3.2	7.0	4.9
17	6.3	5.6	5.8
18	9.8	10.3	10.1
19	15.4	15.2	15.3
20–24	17.8	17.8	17.8
25–29	19.2	20.4	19.9
30–34	22.1	22.5	22.4
35–39	27.2	25.7	26.4
40–44	31.8	30.0	30.9
45–49	34.6	34.6	34.6
50–54	36.3	37.8	37.2
55–59	34.7	43.4	38.8
60 and over	42.7	39.3	40.5
All ages	25.0	24.8	24.9

South East
Median duration
(weeks)

Age	Female	Male	All
Under 17	8.5	6.0	8.0
17	8.2	5.9	7.1
18	10.5	9.9	10.2
19	15.7	16.1	15.9
20–24	16.2	17.4	17.0
25–29	17.8	19.8	19.1
30–34	20.4	20.5	20.5
35–39	22.4	22.1	22.2
40–44	25.1	24.8	24.9
45–49	24.6	25.8	25.3
50–54	23.0	26.4	25.1
55–59	22.0	28.6	25.3
60 and over	25.3	24.1	24.4
All ages	20.2	21.3	20.9

South West
Median duration
(weeks)

Age	Female	Male	All
Under 17	5.0	10.5	9.7
17	10.9	9.2	9.9
18	11.0	10.6	10.8
19	16.2	16.4	16.3
20–24	17.1	18.2	17.9
25–29	15.9	18.5	17.7
30–34	20.0	20.0	20.0
35–39	20.6	21.0	20.8
40–44	22.3	23.3	23.0
45–49	21.8	24.3	23.3
50–54	19.8	24.7	22.9
55–59	19.1	24.8	22.6
60 and over	21.7	20.6	20.9
All ages	18.6	20.3	19.7

England
Median duration
(weeks)

Age	Female	Male	All
Under 17	5.6	6.8	6.1
17	7.1	6.4	6.8
18	11.2	10.9	11.0
19	18.7	18.0	18.3
20–24	20.0	20.2	20.1
25–29	20.6	22.1	21.6
30–34	23.3	24.1	23.8
35–39	26.4	26.0	26.2
40–44	29.3	29.5	29.4
45–49	29.5	31.6	30.8
50–54	27.3	32.9	30.8
55–59	25.2	34.9	31.2
60 and over	28.8	26.8	27.4
All ages	23.3	24.1	23.8

Wales
Median duration (weeks)

Age	Female	Male	All
Under 17	7.0	6.0	6.7
17	6.4	3.8	5.2
18	11.2	11.5	11.4
19	19.2	19.7	19.5
20–24	20.0	21.1	20.7
25–29	20.5	23.2	22.4
30–34	24.4	23.7	23.9
35–39	25.6	27.9	27.0
40–44	27.7	29.6	28.8
45–49	27.3	30.3	29.2
50–54	23.8	31.2	27.8
55–59	23.3	32.7	28.5
60 and over	23.9	25.1	24.8
All ages	22.4	24.0	23.5

Scotland
Median duration (weeks)

Age	Female	Male	All
Under 17	5.3	5.6	5.5
17	8.4	8.3	8.3
18	10.8	12.0	11.5
19	18.3	19.9	19.4
20–24	19.0	20.7	20.2
25–29	20.0	21.5	21.0
30–34	23.1	24.0	23.7
35–39	25.5	26.8	26.2
40–44	27.6	30.2	29.2
45–49	27.2	32.4	30.6
50–54	24.0	32.3	28.8
55–59	24.1	34.5	30.5
60 and over	28.9	24.7	25.4
All ages	22.0	24.0	23.4

Northern Ireland
Median duration (weeks)

Age	Female	Male	All
Under 17	19.5	6.0	17.3
17	9.7	8.8	9.0
18	16.3	17.2	16.9
19	24.4	25.2	25.0
20–24	20.7	23.1	22.5
25–29	22.3	28.7	27.1
30–34	28.8	31.6	31.0
35–39	31.5	33.9	33.2
40–44	36.9	37.4	37.3
45–49	37.4	37.5	37.5
50–54	35.3	36.9	36.4
55–59	36.3	40.5	38.8
60 and over	38.1	44.6	43.0
All ages	28.2	30.0	29.5

United Kingdom
Median duration (weeks)

Age	Female	Male	All
Under 17	5.7	6.5	6.0
17	7.5	7.0	7.2
18	11.3	11.2	11.2
19	19.0	18.6	18.7
20–24	19.9	20.5	20.3
25–29	20.6	22.4	21.8
30–34	23.4	24.3	24.0
35–39	26.4	26.6	26.5
40–44	29.4	30.0	29.5
45–49	29.6	32.0	31.0
50–54	27.0	33.0	30.8
55–59	25.4	35.1	31.4
60 and over	29.0	27.3	27.8
All ages	23.4	24.4	24.0

F4: Regional unemployment statistics

Thousands, seasonally adjusted

Labour Force Survey (April–June 2012)

	Total aged 16–64	Economically active						Employment						Unemployment					
	Total	Total		Men		Women		Total		Men		Women		Total		Men		Women	
	Level	Level	Rate (%)*	Level	Rate(%)*	Level	Rate (%)*	Level	Rate (%)*	Level	Rate (%)*	Level	Rate (%)**	Level	Rate (%)**	Level	Rate (%)**	Level	Rate (%)**
	1	2	3	4	5	6	7	8	9	10	11	12	13	14	15	16	17	18	19
North East	1,694	1,262	74.5	686	81.5	576	67.6	1,129	66.6	601	71.3	528	62.0	133	10.6	85	12.4	48	8.3
North West	4,440	3,408	76.8	1,820	82.1	1,589	71.4	3,089	69.6	1,625	73.3	1,465	65.8	319	9.4	195	10.7	124	7.8
Yorkshire & the Humber	3,455	2,658	76.9	1,438	83.3	1,221	70.6	2,393	69.3	1,279	74.1	1,114	64.4	265	10.0	159	11.0	107	8.7
East Midlands	2,877	2,251	78.2	1,209	84.3	1,042	72.2	2,060	71.6	1,103	76.9	957	66.4	191	8.5	106	8.8	84	8.1
West Midlands	3,433	2,589	75.4	1,401	81.9	1,189	69.0	2,358	68.7	1,273	74.5	1,085	62.9	231	8.9	128	9.1	104	8.7
East	3,715	2,986	80.4	1,602	86.2	1,384	74.5	2,783	74.9	1,490	80.2	1,294	69.6	203	6.8	112	7.0	91	6.5
London	5,422	4,096	75.5	2,277	83.3	1,819	67.7	3,733	68.8	2,077	75.9	1,656	61.6	363	8.9	201	8.8	162	8.9
South East	5,421	4,335	80.0	2,301	85.6	2,304	74.4	4,054	74.8	2,162	85.6	1,892	74.4	281	6.5	138	6.0	142	7.0
South West	3,280	2,592	79.0	1,385	84.9	1,207	73.3	2,438	74.3	1,294	79.3	1,144	69.4	154	6.0	91	6.6	63	5.2
England	**33,737**	**26,178**	**77.6**	**14,119**	**85.8**	**12,060**	**71.4**	**24,037**	**71.2**	**12,903**	**76.6**	**11,134**	**65.9**	**2,141**	**8.2**	**1,215**	**8.6**	**926**	**7.7**
Wales	1,894	1,423	75.1	758	80.9	665	69.5	1,299	68.6	689	73.5	610	63.8	124	8.7	69	9.1	55	8.2
Scotland	3,397	2,644	77.9	1,387	83.3	1,257	72.6	2,431	71.6	1,263	75.8	1,168	67.5	213	8.1	124	8.9	89	7.1
N Ireland	1,158	843	72.7	454	79.0	389	66.6	777	67.1	409	71.2	368	63.0	66	7.8	45	9.8	21	5.5
United Kingdom[1]	**40,186**	**31,088**	**77.4**	**16,718**	**83.5**	**14,370**	**71.3**	**28,544**	**71.0**	**15,265**	**76.3**	**13,279**	**65.8**	**2,544**	**8.2**	**1,453**	**8.7**	**1,091**	**7.6**

Data source: Labour Force Survey

Labour market statistics enquiries: labour.market@ons.gov.uk

Relationship between columns: 2 = 4+6 = 8+14; 8 = 10+12; 14 = 16+18

[1] Due to slight methodological differences between the way the national and regional LFS estimates have been interim adjusted for the 2001 Census, there may be small differences between the UK totals and the sum of the regional components.

* Denominator = all persons of working age

** Denominator = Total economically active

Labour Force Survey

The table reports headline labour market indicators for the UK and its constituent regions and nations. These are reported for the working age population (16–64 years) and include the number economically active in the working age population, the number in employment or self-employment (or Government employment scheme) and the number unemployed. The statistics are derived from the Labour Force Survey (LFS) for April to June 2012 which were released on August 12, 2012. Updated statistics are available on NOMIS (*www.nomisweb.co.uk*). The UK statistics are reported in Table A02 and the regional statistics are reported in Tables HI01 to HI11.

Unemployment is defined using the ILO definition and includes those who were without work during the reference week but who are currently available for work and who were either actively seeking work in the past four weeks or who had already found a job to start within the next three months. This definition of unemployment is independent of whether or not the individual is eligible to claim benefit.

Those who are either employed or unemployed (and looking for work) are defined as economically active. The economically inactive are calculated by the difference between the estimate in column 1, the working age population and the estimate in column 2, the economically active working age population. Many people who are disabled will be inactive rather than unemployed.

Non-employment includes unemployment and inactivity. It is the difference between column 1 and column 8.

Claimant Count v ILO Unemployment

Along with a large number of other countries, the United Kingdom publishes two defined measures of unemployment that complement each other.

One comes from a monthly count of those claiming unemployment-related benefits. This administrative measure is known as the "Claimant Count".

The other comes from a quarterly survey of households, the Labour Force Survey (LFS). This survey measure is accepted as an international standard because it is based on methods recommended by the International Labour Organisation (ILO). It is known as the p and is used by the European Union (EU) and the Organisation for Economic Co-operation and Development (OECD).

Both measures have their advantages and disadvantages.

The advantage of the Claimant Count is that it is available quickly and monthly and because it is a 100% count, it also provides precise information on very small areas.

The ILO measure on the other hand as well as being internationally standard, springs from a data source (the Labour Force Survey) which allows unemployment to be analysed in the context of other labour market information and a variety of demographic characteristics.

A disadvantage of the Claimant Count is that it can be affected if there are changes to the benefit system from which it is derived.

Although changes in the benefit system may also affect the labour market behaviour of respondents to the LFS, the ILO definition itself is entirely independent of the benefit system. Comparatively the LFS results, based on the ILO measure, are not reliable for areas smaller than counties or the larger local authority districts, because of sample size restrictions. Estimates of less than 10,000 persons unemployed (after grossing up) are not shown in published tables because they are subject to unacceptably high sampling error and are, therefore, unreliable.

This said, government statistics apply recognised statistical procedures in order to minimise these disadvantages and maintain the relevance of both measures as accurate labour market indicators.

Claimant Count Rates

Area	2003	2004	2005	2006	2007	2008	2009	2010	2011	2012
North East	4.9	4.0	3.9	4.1	4.1	4.5	6.9	6.7	4.7	5.4
North West	3.4	2.9	2.9	3.4	3.2	3.4	5.4	5.2	4.0	4.4
Yorkshire and the Humber	3.5	2.9	3.0	3.4	3.1	3.4	5.7	5.6	4.2	4.7
East Midlands	2.9	2.5	2.5	2.9	2.6	2.8	4.9	4.6	3.4	3.7
West Midlands	3.6	3.3	3.4	3.9	3.8	3.9	6.3	5.9	4.6	4.7
East	2.2	2.0	2.1	2.3	2.1	2.2	4.0	3.8	2.9	3.0
London	3.7	3.5	3.5	3.5	3.0	2.8	4.3	4.5	4.0	4.1
South East	1.8	1.6	1.6	1.9	1.6	1.7	3.3	3.1	2.5	2.5
South West	1.9	1.6	1.6	1.8	1.6	1.7	3.4	3.1	2.5	2.6
England	3.0	2.6	2.7	2.9	2.7	2.8	4.7	4.5	3.7	3.9
Wales	3.5	3.0	3.0	3.1	2.9	3.3	5.5	5.2	3.8	4.0
Scotland	3.8	3.5	3.2	3.2	2.8	2.9	4.6	4.9	4.0	4.2
Northern Ireland	4.3	3.6	3.4	3.2	2.8	3.1	5.5	6.4	6.1	5.3
United Kingdom	**3.1**	**2.7**	**2.7**	**3.0**	**2.7**	**2.8**	**4.7**	**4.6**	**3.7**	**3.9**

Percentages, seasonally adjusted annual averages

ILO Unemployment Rates

Area	2003	2004	2005	2006	2007	2008	2009	2010	2011	2012
North East	6.5	6.3	5.5	6.6	5.8	8.6	9.5	10.2	9.8	10.8
North West	4.5	4.9	4.8	5.2	5.9	7.7	8.5	7.7	8.5	9.5
Yorkshire and the Humber	4.6	5.0	4.2	5.7	5.5	7.1	9.6	9.3	8.7	9.7
East Midlands	4.3	4.5	4.3	5.2	5.7	6.4	7.8	8.0	7.9	8.3
West Midlands	5.6	5.5	4.6	5.8	6.3	7.9	9.5	9.9	8.7	8.5
East	4.1	3.3	3.9	4.8	5.0	5.5	6.6	6.2	6.7	6.6
London	6.6	6.9	6.7	7.8	6.4	7.5	8.9	9.4	9.4	8.9
South East	3.8	3.8	3.7	4.5	4.6	4.8	6.4	6.3	5.7	6.3
South West	3.7	2.8	3.5	3.7	3.9	5.1	6.4	6.3	5.7	5.9
England	5.0	4.7	4.6	5.5	5.4	6.6	8.0	7.9	7.8	8.1
Wales	4.8	4.9	4.5	3.7	5.1	7.6	6.4	8.7	7.9	9.0
Scotland	5.7	5.7	5.5	5.2	4.6	5.1	7.8	8.1	7.7	7.9
Northern Ireland	5.5	5.6	4.7	4.4	4.0	5.7	6.4	8.0	7.1	6.9
United Kingdom	**5.1**	**4.8**	**4.7**	**5.6**	**5.3**	**6.5**	**8.0**	**8.0**	**7.8**	**8.1**

Percentages, Spring each year, seasonally adjusted

F5: Average weekly earnings index

Average weekly earnings index

Whole economy, excluding bonuses and arrears, and seasonally adjusted.

	2000	2001	2002	2003	2004	2005
January	99.0	102.5	107.1	110.8	114.6	119.3
February	98.9	102.5	107.9	111.1	114.7	119.5
March	98.7	103.2	108.1	111.3	115.1	120.2
April	98.7	104.0	108.4	111.7	115.6	120.6
May	99.3	104.1	108.4	112.0	116.0	120.8
June	99.4	104.3	109.1	112.2	116.3	121.2
July	99.7	105.0	109.3	112.5	116.7	121.9
August	100.1	105.7	109.0	112.9	117.2	122.4
September	100.9	105.8	109.3	113.3	117.4	122.8
October	101.3	106.2	109.5	113.6	118.0	123.0
November	101.7	106.6	109.8	114.0	118.3	123.3
December	102.2	106.7	109.8	114.5	119.1	123.6
Yearly Average	100.0	104.7	108.8	112.5	116.6	121.6

	2006	2007	2008	2009	2010	2011
January	124.2	128.9	134.2	138.0	140.4	143.7
February	124.6	129.4	134.8	138.3	140.4	143.4
March	124.8	130.0	135.3	138.2	141.0	143.7
April	125.0	130.0	136.2	138.6	140.7	143.4
May	125.7	131.0	135.9	139.0	140.7	144.1
June	126.3	131.6	136.2	139.0	141.0	144.0
July	126.3	132.1	136.6	138.5	141.7	144.1
August	126.5	132.7	137.0	138.7	142.0	144.3
September	127.2	132.9	137.3	139.2	142.4	144.8
October	128.0	133.0	137.8	139.4	142.4	145.2
November	128.2	133.6	137.9	139.4	142.7	145.4
December	128.7	133.8	138.0	140.0	142.7	145.6
Yearly Average	126.3	131.6	136.4	138.9	141.5	144.3

	2012	2013
January	145.2	146.8
February	145.9	147.0
March	146.3	147.2
April	146.2	
May	146.6	
June	146.9	
July	146.9	
August	147.4	
September	147.1	
October	147.1	
November	147.4	
December	147.4	

Index base: 2000 = 100.0

ONS index reference: K54L

F5: Average weekly earnings index

Notes

This table has previously shown the Average Weekly Earnings Index for the whole economy, including bonuses and not seasonally adjusted.

The Average Earnings Index has been withdrawn and replaced as the lead measure of short-term changes in average earnings in Great Britain by the Average Weekly Earnings ["AWE"] statistic.

The index figures which now feature in this table are for the whole economy, excluding bonuses and seasonal adjustments.

F6: Average weekly earnings

These figures are the average (mean) gross weekly earnings of full-time employees on adult rates whose pay was not affected by absence.

	Men	Women
	£	£
1985	192.40	126.40
1986	207.50	137.20
1987	224.00	148.10
1988	245.80	164.20
1989	269.50	182.30
1990	295.60	201.50
1991	318.90	222.40
1992	340.10	241.10
1993	353.50	252.60
1994	362.10	261.50
1995	374.60	269.80
1996	391.60	283.00
1997	408.70	297.20
1998	427.10	309.60
1999	442.40	326.50
2000	453.30	337.60
2001	490.50	366.80
2002	513.80	383.20
2003	525.00	396.00
2004	556.80	420.20
2005	568.00	435.60
2006	589.80	450.00
2007	606.10	462.80
2008	631.10	485.50
2009	643.00	501.20
2010	653.30	513.10
2011	658.10	515.40
2012	660.10	524.40

Until 2004 these figures were taken from the New Earnings Survey.
In 2004 the Annual Survey of Hours and Earnings (ASHE) was developed to replace the New Earnings Survey.
Both the New Earnings Survey and ASHE are published by HMSO.

F7: Average earnings statistics

Introductory notes

1. It will usually be possible to obtain agreement, or a direction, that the earnings shown in the Annual Survey of Hours and Earnings (ASHE) may be adduced in evidence without formal proof but occasionally it is necessary to adduce formal proof. This is done by calling a witness from the Office for National Statistics (ONS).

2. ASHE provides information about the levels, distribution and make-up of earnings and hours for paid employees. The data are collected and published by the ONS. ASHE replaced the New Earnings Survey (NES) in 2004.

3. ASHE is based upon a one per cent sample of employee taken from HM Revenue and Customs PAYE records. ASHE does not cover the self-employed nor employees not covered in the reference period.

4. ASHE is collected in April of each year and is published as a first release the following November. A second release is published a year later which includes any revisions to the estimates which may be required. The revisions are usually small.

5. The Tables reproduced here relate to a sample restricted to full-time employees on adult rates of pay whose pay was not affected by absence. The estimates are disaggregated by sex and by a four digit occupational classification. They are first release estimates.

6. The earnings information relates to weekly and annual gross pay before tax, national insurance or other deductions and excludes payments in kind. Earnings are reported for full-time employees who are defined as those who work more than 30 paid hours per week.

7. Two measures of typical earnings are reported, the mean and median. The median is ONS's preferred measure of average earnings as it is less affected by the relatively small number of very high earners which skews the distribution of earnings. The median provides a better indication of typical earnings than does the mean.

8. It is helpful to understand the Standard Occupational Classification (SOC) as an ordered taxonomy of jobs in which narrowly defined jobs at the four digit level (unit groups) are included within a wider definition at the three digit level which in turn are included within a wider category at the two digit level and a still wider category at the one digit level. The hierarchy is based upon the concepts of the type of job and on the level of skill. There are 369 four digit occupational unit groups in SOC 2010 which cluster to form 90 minor groups, 25 sub major groups and 9 major groups. As an example, Rail Travel Assistants, 6215, are included within the three digit group Leisure and Travel Services (621) and at the two digit level, within Leisure, Travel and Related Personal Service Occupations (62), and, at the one digit level, within Caring, Leisure and other Personal Service Occupations (6). n.e.c. stands for 'not elsewhere classified'.

9. Reclassification of occupational categories occurs every ten years and occurred in ASHE 2011 released in March 2012. For 2011 there is a dual set of tables, one using the SOC 2000 and the second using SOC 2010.

10. Statistics derived from samples are called 'estimates' because they estimate the population parameters that we are interested in. All sample estimates are subject to a degree of unreliability due to sampling variation. This is measured by ONS in the form of the coefficient of variation (CV) and is

published in the series of Tables b which accompany the sample estimates in the series of Tables a. The CV is the ratio of the standard error of the estimate to the estimate itself. The smaller is the CV, the higher the precision (or quality) of the estimate. The ONS define four standards of reliability in relation to the size of the CV: less than 5 per cent, 5–10 per cent, 10 to 20 per cent and greater than 20 per cent. An estimate with a CV of less than 5 per cent is the most reliable. Estimates with CVs of greater than 20 per cent are considered insufficiently reliable and are not published. Those in-between are shaded in the ONS publication, though not in the reproduction here.

11. Tables of ASHE estimates are published online where alternative breakdowns can be found, for example by region, age group, industrial sector etc. After November 2013, the estimates published online for 2012 will be the revised final release ones. A further advantage of the online source is the shading according to the levels of reliability referred to in 10. above. The tables can be found on the website of the UK Statistics Authority. This requires some navigation from the Home page. Step-by-step instructions to find the estimates produced here are provided below. You need not follow all these step-by-step instructions each time you consult the tables as you can either download the tables as an Excel file or you can save the web link to bookmarks/favourites.

11. Find the home page of the UK Statistics Authority at: *http://www.statistics.gov.uk*

12. Select the Office for National Statistics (ONS) link at the top right hand side of the page and click.

13. Type in ASHE 2011 in the search box at the top right hand side of this page and click Search.

14. All the ASHE spreadsheets (1–26) are listed in the search results together with other documents. To restrict your search to the statistical tables, check the box marked Reference tables under Filter Results on the right hand side of the screen.

15. Scroll down the list to find the Reference table that you require. Table 14 provides earnings estimates disaggregated by Occupation at the level of the four digit Standard Occupation Classification (SOC). There are two sets of occupational tables in 2011, one under SOC 2000 and the second under SOC 2010. If you are interested in carers' earnings you should consult the advice at B6. Estimates after 2011 will use SOC 2010.

16. Click on the table title and click on the Open option. This will take you to the contents list of a ZIP file. Each excel file contains an occupational breakdown of a different set of earnings estimates.

17. For example, click on Table 14.1a for Weekly Pay–Gross or Table 14.7a Annual Pay–Gross. Click on the Open option. This will take you to a worksheet in an excel file. If you are sure that you have located the file that you want, save it using file save in excel.

18. Note that all files marked with a file extension 'b' report the coefficient of variation on the estimate (see 10. above)

19. Once in the Excel file, check the bottom tabs. Choose 'Male Full-time' or 'Female Full-time' to view the tables reproduced here. The median is reported in column three and the mean in column 5.

20. The shading indicates the reliability of the estimate. Where the estimate of the error is less than 5 per cent, there is no shading. The key to the shading can be found at the bottom and at the right hand side of the table. The shading is not reproduced here.

21. If you have not already saved this file at step 17 above, this table can be saved now either in part or in full. If the file is saved make a note that the 2012 estimates are provisional. They will be replaced in the final release in November 2013 under the same title.

This guide has been prepared by Dr Victoria Wass, Cardiff Business School, July 2013.

Full-time males on adult rates (where pay was not affected by absence)

	Gross weekly pay (in April) 2012		Gross annual earnings (in April) 2012	
n.e.c. = not elsewhere classified X = unreliable				
	Median £	Mean £	Median £	Mean £
Occupation SOC 2010				
All Employees	538.1	658.1	28,374	36,415
Managers, directors and senior officials	787.9	1,006.5	41,500	60,664
Corporate managers and directors	831.3	1,053.9	43,748	63,851
Chief executives and senior officials	1,518.5	1,897.1	85,019	142,706
Chief executives and senior officials	1,549.6	1,944.5	86,725	146,446
Elected officers and representatives	X	675.5	X	X
Production managers and directors	801.3	959.2	41,844	54,726
Production managers and directors in manufacturing	824.5	992.7	43,116	57,078
Production managers and directors in construction	737.8	830.1	37,993	45,964
Production managers and directors in mining and energy	750.5	1,051.0	X	56,829
Functional managers and directors	1,135.9	1,335.0	60,642	86,340
Financial managers and directors	1,200.1	1,459.7	63,699	100,940
Marketing and sales directors	1,245.7	1,413.5	69,489	91,515
Purchasing managers and directors	832.4	927.5	43,767	53,645
Advertising and public relations directors	X	1,479.9	X	X
Human resource managers and directors	958.8	1,150.5	50,332	66,473
Information technology and telecommunications directors	1,167.5	1,228.4	60,063	67,790
Functional managers and directors n.e.c.	997.6	1,148.4	50,538	67,042
Financial institution managers and directors	1,026.5	1,306.3	55,057	83,589
Managers and directors in transport and logistics	594.1	682.9	31,950	36,743
Managers and directors in transport and distribution	656.9	736.1	34,994	38,903
Managers and directors in storage and warehousing	553.2	636.3	29,250	34,803
Senior officers in protective services	1,040.3	1,118.2	54,231	58,175
Officers in armed forces	X	1,279.0	X	81,634
Senior police officers	1,094.4	1,226.8	57,875	60,526
Senior officers in fire, ambulance, prison and related services	871.3	880.5	43,040	43,909
Health and social services managers and directors	869.2	1,026.1	45,934	53,682
Health services and public health managers and directors	892.3	1,047.3	46,592	55,101
Social services managers and directors	818.8	950.6	41,885	49,048
Managers and directors in retail and wholesale	515.1	620.0	26,873	32,967
Other managers and proprietors	584.5	726.3	31,086	41,364
Managers and proprietors in agriculture related services	574.9	639.3	29,328	35,107
Managers and proprietors in agriculture and horticulture	572.3	631.4	28,927	33,793
Managers and proprietors in forestry, fishing and related services	X	X	X	X
Managers and proprietors in hospitality and leisure services	462.1	590.9	24,872	32,604
Hotel and accommodation managers and proprietors	527.4	740.4	29,177	41,022
Restaurant and catering establishment managers and proprietors	412.0	469.0	21,741	24,529
Publicans and managers of licensed premises	403.8	484.6	21,144	26,584
Leisure and sports managers	521.3	626.8	26,884	33,415
Travel agency managers and proprietors	673.7	873.4	X	X
Managers and proprietors in health and care services	599.2	642.9	30,588	33,625
Health care practice managers	622.5	673.7	30,368	35,582
Residential, day and domiciliary care managers and proprietors	596.4	633.7	30,800	33,153
Managers and proprietors in other services	673.7	829.8	36,162	48,042
Property, housing and estate managers	719.7	845.3	38,673	47,471
Garage managers and proprietors	554.0	596.7	30,466	32,176

Full-time males on adult rates (where pay was not affected by absence)

n.e.c. = not elsewhere classified
X = unreliable

Occupation SOC 2010	Gross weekly pay (in April) 2012		Gross annual earnings (in April) 2012	
	Median £	Mean £	Median £	Mean £
Hairdressing and beauty salon managers and proprietors	X	X	X	X
Shopkeepers and proprietors – wholesale and retail	X	709.4	X	39,242
Waste disposal and environmental services managers	642.1	766.5	34,192	40,147
Managers and proprietors in other services n.e.c.	678.6	877.8	36,117	53,658
Professional occupations	729.1	842.0	38,292	45,687
Science, research, engineering and technology professionals	723.3	794.0	38,256	42,310
Natural and social science professionals	685.9	767.4	37,217	40,210
Chemical scientists	610.4	687	32,005	35,363
Biological scientists and biochemists	769.6	810.4	40,072	41,385
Physical scientists	777.1	933.1	41,346	48,505
Social and humanities scientists	513.0	555.1	29,779	30,410
Natural and social science professionals n.e.c.	685.9	739.7	36,498	39,755
Engineering professionals	697.3	756.9	37,506	40,816
Civil engineers	693.4	778.0	36,208	40,136
Mechanical engineers	766.9	807.4	40,612	44,456
Electrical engineers	759.7	817.6	41,932	43,024
Electronics engineers	707.1	729.8	33,738	39,410
Design and development engineers	680.3	744.9	35,590	39,373
Production and process engineers	645.7	693.2	35,821	36,949
Engineering professionals n.e.c.	686.7	755.9	38,153	41,806
Information technology and telecommunications professionals	750.6	824.3	39,338	43,774
IT specialist managers	827.5	932.6	44,922	50,134
IT project and programme managers	991.4	1,023.2	49,658	53,153
IT business analysts, architects and systems designers	765.6	828.1	39,189	43,340
Programmers and software development professionals	705.2	750.6	36,784	39,381
Web design and development professionals	599.1	631.4	32,103	33,882
Information technology and telecommunications professionals n.e.c.	710.5	786.0	37,729	41,073
Conservation and environment professionals	590.7	647.4	30,368	33,805
Conservation professionals	585.8	600.2	30,102	30,797
Environment professionals	590.9	657.9	30,389	34,454
Research and development managers	880.9	942.1	45,840	50,490
Health professionals	795.9	1,071.1	40,312	57,737
Health professionals	1,109.1	1,345.3	65,557	76,738
Medical practitioners	1,352.5	1,523.0	88,422	90,912
Psychologists	X	864.4	X	45,315
Pharmacists	833.6	825.8	45,127	43,728
Ophthalmic opticians	X	784.5	X	33,364
Dental practitioners	1,227.0	1,179.6	70,924	69,874
Veterinarians	X	986.5	X	X
Medical radiographers	680.9	720.5	37,652	40,127
Podiatrists	677.1	648.7	34,326	34,253
Health professionals n.e.c.	622.8	725.7	30,752	36,420
Therapy professionals	601.7	654.8	30,720	34,124
Physiotherapists	570.4	603.8	28,310	31,533
Occupational therapists	550.5	600.8	27,263	30,371
Speech and language therapists				
Therapy professionals n.e.c.	X	934.0	X	49,184
Nursing and midwifery professionals	626.1	650.4	32,974	32,688
Nurses	625.4	649.5	32,850	32,636
Midwives	689.4	712.8	36,106	37,422
Teaching and educational professionals	752.3	801.1	38,996	41,538
Higher education teaching professionals	901.3	995.1	46,229	50,329

F7: Average earnings statistics

Full-time males on adult rates (where pay was not affected by absence)

Occupation SOC 2010	Gross weekly pay (in April) 2012		Gross annual earnings (in April) 2012	
n.e.c. = not elsewhere classified X = unreliable	Median £	Mean £	Median £	Mean £
Further education teaching professionals	672.7	705.1	34,481	35,774
Secondary education teaching professionals	738.3	755.3	38,287	38,881
Primary and nursery education teaching professionals	714.5	742.8	38,327	38,810
Special needs education teaching professionals	746.2	717.8	38,664	38,657
Senior professionals of educational establishments	966.2	1,024.80	49,642	54,465
Education advisers and school inspectors	725.3	864.2	39,102	47,671
Teaching and other educational professionals n.e.c.	596.3	617.8	31,066	31,782
Business, media and public service professionals	708.3	841.6	37,022	48,356
Legal professionals	957.9	1,168.8	51,108	65,284
Barristers and judges	X	1,042.5	X	54,664
Solicitors	876.3	1,084.2	45,689	59,899
Legal professionals n.e.c.	1,220.8	1,363.5	72,326	78,298
Business, research and administrative professionals	766.6	887.5	40,000	54,736
Chartered and certified accountants	766.6	850.3	39,533	45,750
Management consultants and business analysts	786.3	897.3	42,758	53,334
Business and financial project management professionals	877.9	981.6	46,317	54,817
Actuaries, economists and statisticians	958.1	X	X	X
Business and related research professionals	603.7	635.9	30,845	33,369
Business, research and administrative professionals n.e.c.	625.2	740.9	32,865	38,032
Architects, town planners and surveyors	679.0	752.2	35,405	39,866
Architects	709.9	824.1	39,442	46,253
Town planning officers	600.2	626.9	31,977	33,361
Quantity surveyors	739.7	754.7	37,553	38,646
Chartered surveyors	656.2	707.8	33,779	37,056
Chartered architectural technologists	471.2	537.2	25,620	29,327
Construction project managers and related professionals	753.9	848.9	39,183	44,241
Welfare professionals	528.2	552.1	25,455	27,809
Social workers	608.6	605.4	30,122	30,343
Probation officers	642.6	657.9	33,137	33,358
Clergy	440.8	468.8	22,412	24,049
Welfare professionals n.e.c.	595.0	650.4	28,610	32,887
Librarians and related professionals	556.1	608.9	28,483	31,289
Librarians	569.2	556.4	27,841	29,193
Archivists and curators	X	668.5	28,770	33,762
Quality and regulatory professionals	676.7	770.5	35,296	41,066
Quality control and planning engineers	619.3	670.7	31,874	34,820
Quality assurance and regulatory professionals	751.8	856.0	39,468	46,418
Environmental health professionals	629.1	681.7	30,811	36,109
Media professionals	629.1	766.6	33,122	39,916
Journalists, newspaper and periodical editors	615.3	753.8	32,240	38,082
Public relations professionals	579.8	675.7	31,122	37,859
Advertising accounts managers and creative directors	801.4	952.0	46,859	50,972
Associate professional and technical occupations	614.8	715.4	32,936	40,446
Science, engineering and technology associate professionals	547.3	592.4	28,423	30,923
Science, engineering and production technicians	545.9	580.0	28,260	30,200
Laboratory technicians	468.2	534.4	25,154	27,763
Electrical and electronics technicians	575.0	614.5	29,487	32,336
Engineering technicians	609.0	642.1	31,682	33,023
Building and civil engineering technicians	542.3	661.8	29,024	37,864
Quality assurance technicians	492.4	526.8	26,911	28,112
Planning, process and production technicians	555.2	598.2	29,157	31,678

Full-time males on adult rates (where pay was not affected by absence)

n.e.c. = not elsewhere classified X = unreliable Occupation SOC 2010	Gross weekly pay (in April) 2012		Gross annual earnings (in April) 2012	
	Median £	Mean £	Median £	Mean £
Science, engineering and production technicians n.e.c.	499.4	545.1	26,342	28,244
Draughtspersons and related architectural technicians	532.4	569.4	28,072	29,702
Architectural and town planning technicians	520.6	551.5	26,135	29,133
Draughtspersons	536.6	576.3	28,392	29,895
Information technology technicians	556.2	621.8	28,763	32,655
IT operations technicians	559.7	629.7	29,578	33,430
IT user support technicians	549.0	614.3	28,299	31,943
Health and social care associate professionals	519.8	560.3	26,749	29,226
Health associate professionals	636.1	645.6	34,044	34,296
Paramedics	715.1	754.9	38,401	39,364
Dispensing opticians	X	X	X	X
Pharmaceutical technicians	506.6	514.5	26,550	27,800
Medical and dental technicians	509.3	578.9	28,808	30,202
Health associate professionals n.e.c.	545.6	556.8	28,000	30,499
Welfare and housing associate professionals	496.8	521.8	24,817	26,866
Youth and community workers	489.2	518.0	25,437	26,763
Child and early years officers	454.4	476.5	24,442	25,412
Housing officers	532.4	520.5	26,179	26,084
Counsellors	468.2	534.0	X	29,034
Welfare and housing associate professionals n.e.c.	501.2	542.7	24,311	27,667
Protective service occupations	699.9	721.8	36,519	37,221
NCOs and other ranks	822.1	766.9	36,716	38,449
Police officers (sergeant and below)	771.3	793.3	40,633	40,622
Fire service officers (watch manager and below)	577.8	618.5	30,456	31,330
Prison service officers (below principal officer)	553.1	529.6	28,990	27,679
Police community support officers	498.2	497.3	25,902	26,019
Protective service associate professionals n.e.c.	633.5	688.4	34,097	38,023
Culture, media and sports occupations	500.5	663.1	27,277	36,158
Artistic, literary and media occupations	583.6	722.5	31,057	39,470
Artists	494.2	563.1	X	30,980
Authors, writers and translators	536.2	675.2	X	35,629
Actors, entertainers and presenters	X	X	X	X
Dancers and choreographers	X	710.1	42,746	43,818
Musicians	737.1	803.0	37,391	40,098
Arts officers, producers and directors	661.4	858.8	36,407	48,967
Photographers, audio-visual and broadcasting equipment operators	498.3	548.2	26,663	28,161
Design occupations	488.2	534.7	26,558	29,062
Graphic designers	479.3	529.6	25,001	28,123
Product, clothing and related designers	498.1	543.7	29,954	30,613
Sports and fitness occupations	383.2	X	19,598	X
Sports players	X	X	X	X
Sports coaches, instructors and officials	398.7	455.1	20,219	20,899
Fitness instructors	315.5	355.5	16,576	17,882
Business and public service associate professionals	654.4	788.5	35,679	47,733
Transport associate professionals	1,159.5	1,327.5	61,874	65,553
Air traffic controllers	1,329.4	1,315.8	X	66,793
Aircraft pilots and flight engineers	1,459.9	1,602.9	74,437	75,746
Ship and hovercraft officers	687.9	718.6	37,600	38,519
Legal associate professionals	592.9	758.1	31,688	43,336
Business, finance and related associate professionals	709.1	890.1	38,000	59,695
Estimators, valuers and assessors	574.9	655.9	31,124	35,699
Brokers	1,084.9	1,411.4	X	138,377
Insurance underwriters	576.5	813.9	31,027	48,468
Finance and investment analysts and advisers	728.3	896.8	38,535	X

Full-time males on adult rates (where pay was not affected by absence)

n.e.c. = not elsewhere classified
X = unreliable

Occupation SOC 2010	Gross weekly pay (in April) 2012		Gross annual earnings (in April) 2012	
	Median £	Mean £	Median £	Mean £
Taxation experts	952.6	1,236.4	49,180	70,715
Importers and exporters	489.9	569.7	25,968	28,903
Financial and accounting technicians	859.6	965.0	45,562	55,126
Financial accounts managers	795.1	972.1	44,844	64,653
Business and related associate professionals n.e.c.	583.3	682.3	30,708	39,119
Sales, marketing and related associate professionals	670.8	786.6	36,772	45,587
Buyers and procurement officers	578.6	632.8	30,017	33,294
Business sales executives	558.4	670.4	31,340	36,354
Marketing associate professionals	561.1	664.1	28,577	35,378
Estate agents and auctioneers	490.0	549.7	27,294	32,382
Sales accounts and business development managers	783.9	897.7	42,632	53,869
Conference and exhibition managers and organisers	505.2	581.7	28,682	33,283
Conservation and environmental associate professionals	412.4	443.6	23,013	24,314
Public services and other associate professionals	548.8	610.0	30,005	33,968
Public services associate professionals	546.8	598.3	32,402	36,297
Human resources and industrial relations officers	499.8	617.9	28,285	38,176
Vocational and industrial trainers and instructors	536.8	597.1	27,842	30,657
Careers advisers and vocational guidance specialists	501.4	627.1	X	32,254
Inspectors of standards and regulations	557.3	580.3	28,528	29,317
Health and safety officers	673.0	693.6	35,156	35,899
Administrative and secretarial occupations	432.2	519.1	23,468	28,017
Administrative occupations	434.6	519.2	23,531	28,097
Administrative occupations: Government and related organisations	441.7	478.8	24,526	25,952
National government administrative occupations	398.2	454.8	23,163	25,117
Local government administrative occupations	498.4	513.1	25,534	26,779
Officers of non-governmental organisations	533.2	581.2	29,220	30,222
Administrative occupations: Finance	444.6	542.3	24,259	30,434
Credit controllers	385.0	451.3	20,000	24,650
Book-keepers, payroll managers and wages clerks	525.1	575.5	27,500	31,112
Bank and post office clerks	389.5	471.6	22,277	27,280
Finance officers	537.3	793.4	27,493	X
Financial administrative occupations n.e.c.	430.2	552.4	22,944	30,979
Administrative occupations: Records	421.6	488.2	22,387	25,784
Records clerks and assistants	424.7	483.5	22,766	25,690
Pensions and insurance clerks and assistants	425.5	552.9	23,473	30,787
Stock control clerks and assistants	401.9	451.4	21,240	23,352
Transport and distribution clerks and assistants	455.3	517.1	23,575	27,311
Library clerks and assistants	349.3	443.3	17,809	20,871
Human resources administrative occupations	395.9	419.4	21,916	23,755
Other administrative occupations	383.3	457.9	20,262	23,914
Sales administrators	426.8	484.5	22,424	25,443
Other administrative occupations n.e.c.	378.6	454.6	19,950	23,726
Administrative occupations: Office managers and supervisors	636.3	749.1	34,217	40,091
Office managers	675.0	799.9	36,523	43,234
Office supervisors	512.8	535.9	25,835	27,353
Secretarial and related occupations	404.4	517.9	21,879	27,643
Medical secretaries	391.8	506.8	X	27,259
Legal secretaries				
School secretaries	496.7	494.0	23,597	22,982
Company secretaries	829.0	926.1	X	X
Personal assistants and other secretaries	509.1	612.9	28,144	33,071
Receptionists	318.9	351.2	17,575	18,631
Typists and related keyboard occupations	392.2	517.2	21,589	24,618

Full-time males on adult rates (where pay was not affected by absence)

n.e.c. = not elsewhere classified
X = unreliable

Occupation SOC 2010	Gross weekly pay (in April) 2012		Gross annual earnings (in April) 2012	
	Median £	Mean £	Median £	Mean £
Skilled trades occupations	472.3	516.9	24,716	26,523
Skilled agricultural and related trades	345.4	378.3	18,281	19,753
Agricultural and related trades	345.4	378.3	18,281	19,753
Farmers	484.3	565.5	24,460	30,008
Horticultural trades	338.1	367.7	15,818	18,068
Gardeners and landscape gardeners	353.7	379.6	18,518	19,540
Groundsmen and greenkeepers	334.4	356.3	17,612	18,903
Agricultural and fishing trades n.e.c.	349.7	388.5	18,221	20,644
Skilled metal, electrical and electronic trades	522.2	560.8	27,263	28,747
Metal forming, welding and related trades	494.8	560.4	25,598	27,364
Smiths and forge workers	459.9	456.0	22,494	22,502
Moulders, core makers and die casters	349.1	390.8	X	19,963
Sheet metal workers	470.0	490.5	25,149	25,251
Metal plate workers, and riveters	527.0	624.0	25,985	29,439
Welding trades	478.6	550.7	25,078	27,198
Pipe fitters	649.6	772.0	X	X
Metal machining, fitting and instrument making trades	514.5	556.2	26,847	28,296
Metal machining setters and setter-operators	489.9	525.2	24,556	26,070
Tool makers, tool fitters and markers-out	516.5	538.0	26,453	27,478
Metal working production and maintenance fitters	519.7	560.4	27,259	28,646
Precision instrument makers and repairers	549.5	616.1	29,402	31,205
Air-conditioning and refrigeration engineers	616.1	574.7	29,306	29,868
Vehicle trades	462.8	504.2	24,410	26,081
Vehicle technicians, mechanics and electricians	452.2	491.6	24,108	25,539
Vehicle body builders and repairers	423.9	452.7	22,808	23,552
Vehicle paint technicians	467.3	477.3	24,416	24,890
Aircraft maintenance and related trades	614.1	622.3	32,534	32,826
Boat and ship builders and repairers	533.6	580.8	26,612	29,394
Rail and rolling stock builders and repairers	613.3	657.8	28,882	31,725
Electrical and electronic trades	544.3	576.9	28,938	29,928
Electricians and electrical fitters	559.9	582.9	29,390	30,003
Telecommunications engineers	544.5	570.8	28,072	29,629
TV, video and audio engineers	455.3	484.8	X	24,804
IT engineers	526.7	594.2	27,122	29,894
Electrical and electronic trades n.e.c.	536.8	574.6	28,945	30,159
Skilled metal, electrical and electronic trades supervisors	607.5	661.2	31,424	34,378
Skilled construction and building trades	468.8	517.7	23,953	25,830
Construction and building trades	465.3	509.2	23,633	25,233
Steel erectors	462.4	494.9	24,777	26,225
Bricklayers and masons	443.8	498.7	22,452	23,419
Roofers, roof tilers and slaters	436.4	453.8	22,038	22,269
Plumbers and heating and ventilating engineers	540.9	565.9	27,905	28,712
Carpenters and joiners	442.5	468.3	22,654	23,343
Glaziers, window fabricators and fitters	377.4	411.8	19,642	20,698
Construction and building trades n.e.c.	498.1	587.6	25,141	28,646
Building finishing trades	418.9	455.7	21,485	23,193
Plasterers	410.7	409.4	21,365	20,640
Floorers and wall tilers	409.3	452.1	21,697	23,133
Painters and decorators	425.3	470.4	21,622	23,976
Construction and building trades supervisors	600.0	637.9	30,702	32,346
Textiles, printing and other skilled trades	372.3	411.9	19,678	21,539
Textiles and garments trades	428.1	454.0	21,361	21,661
Weavers and knitters	367.0	392.9	20,749	20,450
Upholsterers	427.7	436.9	20,714	20,720
Footwear and leather working trades	451.3	495.5	21,303	23,011

Full-time males on adult rates (where pay was not affected by absence)

	Gross weekly pay (in April) 2012		Gross annual earnings (in April) 2012	
n.e.c. = not elsewhere classified X = unreliable **Occupation SOC 2010**	Median £	Mean £	Median £	Mean £
Tailors and dressmakers	X	425.6	X	22,088
Textiles, garments and related trades n.e.c.	X	533.9	X	23,318
Printing trades	460.2	502.3	22,990	25,665
Pre-press technicians	429.2	462.3	21,603	22,786
Printers	499.2	524.8	25,811	27,545
Print finishing and binding workers	406.5	472.4	20,813	22,904
Food preparation and hospitality trades	348.6	382.6	18,023	20,003
Butchers	337.0	365.2	17,766	18,442
Bakers and flour confectioners	350.4	373.8	17,426	18,548
Fishmongers and poultry dressers	279.4	325.8	14,491	16,998
Chefs	346.2	374.5	18,015	19,831
Cooks	329.6	378.6	X	21,102
Catering and bar managers	392.9	435.6	20,058	22,948
Other skilled trades	393.2	439.7	20,736	22,985
Glass and ceramics makers, decorators and finishers	350.4	381.4	16,966	19,205
Furniture makers and other craft woodworkers	381.2	403.1	19,785	20,608
Florists				
Other skilled trades n.e.c.	424.2	485.6	23,398	26,087
Caring, leisure and other service occupations	370.1	405.2	19,515	20,981
Caring personal service occupations	362.3	389.0	19,066	19,899
Childcare and related personal services	326.9	364.3	17,665	19,164
Nursery nurses and assistants	324.6	324.6	17,058	17,328
Childminders and related occupations				
Playworkers	320.8	350.3	X	18,403
Teaching assistants	298.3	358.0	15,484	18,482
Educational support assistants	364.7	397.2	18,817	X
Animal care and control services	353.6	371.3	17,800	18,968
Veterinary nurses				
Pest control officers	418.1	414.2	20,000	20,815
Animal care services occupations n.e.c.	312.6	352.8	15,565	18,123
Caring personal services	369.1	393.7	19,271	20,055
Nursing auxiliaries and assistants	378.3	401.4	19,902	20,584
Ambulance staff (excluding paramedics)	473.7	495.6	22,572	24,727
Dental nurses	X	X	X	X
Houseparents and residential wardens	401.4	436.9	21,143	22,906
Care workers and home carers	343.6	362.9	17,409	18,123
Senior care workers	404.9	424.3	21,188	22,068
Care escorts	X	370.8	X	18,487
Undertakers, mortuary and crematorium assistants	425.4	419.7	21,270	21,671
Leisure, travel and related personal service occupations	381.2	433.0	20,492	22,717
Leisure and travel services	431.9	481.0	23,726	25,683
Sports and leisure assistants	322.1	345.3	16,935	17,851
Travel agents	371.8	398.6	20,018	20,514
Air travel assistants	524.7	569.3	30,028	29,922
Rail travel assistants	586.2	616.2	30,858	32,248
Leisure and travel service occupations n.e.c.	X	634.3	X	34,430
Hairdressers and related services	310.8	342.3	15,669	17,366
Hairdressers and barbers	307.4	342.1	15,669	17,366
Beauticians and related occupations				
Housekeeping and related services	356.1	374.2	18,612	19,545
Housekeepers and related occupations	281.4	332.9	14,261	17,839
Caretakers	366.5	379.1	19,140	19,748
Cleaning and housekeeping managers and supervisors	406.8	454.6	20,678	22,999

Full-time males on adult rates (where pay was not affected by absence)

n.e.c. = not elsewhere classified
X = unreliable

Occupation SOC 2010	Gross weekly pay (in April) 2012		Gross annual earnings (in April) 2012	
	Median £	Mean £	Median £	Mean £
Sales and customer service occupations	334.6	400.4	17,607	21,453
Sales occupations	318.9	379.1	16,759	20,284
Sales assistants and retail cashiers	301.8	347.6	15,824	18,199
Sales and retail assistants	297.1	344.5	15,567	18,087
Retail cashiers and check-out operators	274.8	304.2	14,143	15,210
Telephone salespersons	347.7	391.9	19,670	20,713
Pharmacy and other dispensing assistants	288.1	345.5	14,509	17,643
Vehicle and parts salespersons and advisers	361.6	393.8	19,096	20,952
Sales related occupations	381.2	491.6	20,892	31,117
Collector salespersons and credit agents	X	X	X	X
Debt, rent and other cash collectors	328.0	362.0	18,469	19,918
Roundspersons and van salespersons	402.0	426.3	20,783	22,081
Market and street traders and assistants	X	X	X	X
Merchandisers and window dressers	473.4	519.0	21,438	26,603
Sales related occupations n.e.c.	421.6	595.7	25,396	X
Sales supervisors	379.1	453.0	20,071	22,823
Customer service occupations	375.9	444.6	20,078	23,942
Customer service occupations	348.0	387.4	18,854	20,604
Call and contact centre occupations	314.3	386.2	X	X
Telephonists	339.3	363.9	18,731	20,218
Communication operators	518.1	560.3	27,312	28,827
Market research interviewers	X	399.6	X	19,758
Customer service occupations n.e.c.	345.1	375.5	18,804	19,957
Customer service managers and supervisors	616.1	693.3	31,834	37,262
Process, plant and machine operatives	440.4	472.7	22,800	24,116
Process, plant and machine operatives	426.4	464.7	25,553	24,035
Process operatives	384.1	424.5	20,331	22,131
Food, drink and tobacco process operatives	350.9	391.4	18,715	20,317
Glass and ceramics process operatives	355.4	411.3	17,704	20,963
Textile process operatives	384.7	422.4	18,460	21,220
Chemical and related process operatives	405.4	477.0	24,197	25,824
Rubber process operatives	472.6	461.6	23,510	23,837
Plastics process operatives	409.8	444.4	21,685	22,608
Metal making and treating process operatives	504.5	502.7	25,583	26,143
Electroplaters	411.2	443.1	20,257	22,163
Process operatives n.e.c.	458.5	483.4	25,191	25,143
Plant and machine operatives	455.6	492.9	23,421	25,000
Paper and wood machine operatives	414.0	432.8	19,885	21,849
Coal mine operatives	721.6	711.9	X	37,922
Quarry workers and related operatives	622.1	720.0	27,290	34,109
Energy plant operatives	534.4	537.0	26,865	28,215
Metal working machine operatives	439.7	468.3	22,524	23,803
Water and sewerage plant operatives	543.6	566.9	28,146	29,184
Printing machine assistants	446.0	484.3	22,236	23,370
Plant and machine operatives n.e.c.	432.4	485.0	24,043	25,446
Assemblers and routine operatives	425.4	461.1	22,715	23,857
Assemblers (electrical and electronic products)	385.3	433.2	20,753	21,773
Assemblers (vehicles and metal goods)	533.8	562.5	27,411	28,130
Routine inspectors and testers	465.1	498.2	24,502	26,114
Weighers, graders and sorters	371.0	393.0	21,380	22,009
Tyre, exhaust and windscreen fitters	343.2	382.6	19,482	20,280
Sewing machinists	402.9	398.3	21,327	19,844
Assemblers and routine operatives n.e.c.	375.5	412.2	19,919	21,370
Construction operatives	468.6	512.4	24,791	26,462
Scaffolders, stagers and riggers	587.1	615.1	30,190	31,373
Road construction operatives	499.4	536.3	25,307	27,203

Full-time males on adult rates (where pay was not affected by absence)

n.e.c. = not elsewhere classified
X = unreliable

Occupation SOC 2010	Gross weekly pay (in April) 2012		Gross annual earnings (in April) 2012	
	Median £	Mean £	Median £	Mean £
Rail construction and maintenance operatives	562.3	606.8	31,808	33,582
Construction operatives n.e.c.	435.5	469.6	22,626	23,900
Transport and mobile machine drivers and operatives	453.9	480.0	23,043	24,191
Road transport drivers	441.0	458.7	22,243	22,903
Large goods vehicle drivers	497.3	507.6	25,281	25,222
Van drivers	393.7	423.0	19,715	21,011
Bus and coach drivers	431.5	462.5	22,029	23,487
Taxi and cab drivers and chauffeurs	341.9	443.4	17,570	22,644
Driving instructors	466.5	503.7	25,341	27,459
Mobile machine drivers and operatives	463.1	498.5	23,736	24,855
Crane drivers	622.3	634.5	29,518	31,556
Fork-lift truck drivers	364.0	401.8	19,530	20,765
Agricultural machinery drivers	465.1	490.0	25,030	24,235
Mobile machine drivers and operatives n.e.c.	492.2	529.4	24,904	26,094
Other drivers and transport operatives	654.5	659.4	35,532	34,589
Train and tram drivers	813.2	819.9	42,521	41,633
Marine and waterways transport operatives	547.1	524.3	32,013	31,025
Air transport operatives	455.3	489.6	24,423	26,056
Rail transport operatives	655.5	672.3	34,957	35,447
Other drivers and transport operatives n.e.c.	507.1	515.3	26,544	27,145
Elementary occupations	351.7	376.7	18,692	19,574
Elementary trades and related occupations	365.0	397.1	19,029	20,235
Elementary agricultural occupations	365.0	389.8	18,963	19,665
Farm workers	369.7	400.5	19,820	20,346
Forestry workers	399.7	422.9	20,585	21,760
Fishing and other elementary agriculture occupations n.e.c.	336.6	355.4	16,874	17,436
Elementary construction occupations	389.9	425.5	19,856	21,161
Elementary process plant occupations	353.3	385.7	18,521	19,938
Industrial cleaning process occupations	352.6	372.0	17,562	18,688
Packers, bottlers, canners and fillers	331.2	364.3	17,504	19,331
Elementary process plant occupations n.e.c.	366.4	398.1	19,202	20,388
Elementary administration and service occupations	346.5	370.4	18,570	19,377
Elementary administration occupations	406.2	430.0	22,698	23,003
Postal workers, mail sorters, messengers and couriers	427.5	449.4	23,646	24,030
Elementary administration occupations n.e.c.	302.9	344.5	15,849	17,640
Elementary cleaning occupations	315.1	338.3	16,561	17,548
Window cleaners	320.5	348.6	X	17,863
Street cleaners	338.7	364.8	17,707	19,001
Cleaners and domestics	303.5	324.5	15,467	16,470
Launderers, dry cleaners and pressers	272.5	304.5	14,252	15,589
Refuse and salvage occupations	365.9	384.8	19,171	20,304
Vehicle valeters and cleaners	279.1	291.5	14,554	15,163
Elementary cleaning occupations n.e.c.	354.9	404.0	X	X
Elementary security occupations	409.8	427.7	21,147	22,197
Security guards and related occupations	412.7	430.9	21,447	22,379
Parking and civil enforcement occupations	350.4	379.6	17,748	19,404
School midday and crossing patrol occupations	X	501.5	X	26,221
Elementary security occupations n.e.c.	412.5	434.9	21,599	22,563
Elementary sales occupations	326.5	340.7	16,919	17,160
Shelf fillers	330.7	345.2	17,030	17,405
Elementary sales occupations n.e.c.	239.5	290.5	X	14,800
Elementary storage occupations	349.7	375.1	18,608	19,334
Other elementary services occupations	261.4	280.3	12,997	13,654
Hospital porters	348.6	360.9	18,063	18,213

Full-time males on adult rates (where pay was not affected by absence)

	Gross weekly pay (in April) 2012		Gross annual earnings (in April) 2012	
	Median	Mean	Median	Mean
Occupation SOC 2010	£	£	£	£
Kitchen and catering assistants	252.0	272.9	12,265	12,956
Waiters and waitresses	250.5	275.4	12,684	14,182
Bar staff	261.2	274.8	12,575	12,943
Leisure and theme park attendants	266.3	294.2	13,682	15,285
Other elementary services occupations n.e.c.	299.0	312.9	14,896	15,862
Not classified				

n.e.c. = not elsewhere classified
X = unreliable

Full-time females on adult rates (where pay was not affected by absence)

	Gross weekly pay (in April) 2012		Gross Annual earnings in (April) 2012	
	Median £	**Mean** £	**Median** £	**Mean** £
Occupation SOC 2010				
All Employees	440.0	515.4	22,604	26,648
Managers, directors and senior officials	599.9	729.5	30,646	39,347
Corporate managers and directors	639.8	775.3	32,718	42,131
Chief executives and senior officials	1,040.5	1,256.8	54,464	69,664
Chief executives and senior officials	1,083.6	1,316.4	55,020	73,807
Elected officers and representatives	X	X	X	X
Production managers and directors	659.0	786.0	32,967	40,919
Production managers and directors in manufacturing	662.5	791.2	33,105	41,078
Production managers and directors in construction	593.3	739.4	29,364	39,455
Production managers and directors in mining and energy				
Functional managers and directors	824.4	964.6	42,045	54,562
Financial managers and directors	800.6	942.5	40,895	52,404
Marketing and sales directors	1,005.8	1,115.7	52,129	69,842
Purchasing managers and directors	763.8	905.0	36,895	50,648
Advertising and public relations directors	1,322.0	1,452.7	X	X
Human resource managers and directors	781.2	902.5	40,163	49,372
Information technology and telecommunications directors	X	1,182.9	X	60,157
Functional managers and directors n.e.c.	724.9	827.3	X	47,411
Financial institution managers and directors	638.1	819.2	33,493	44,585
Managers and directors in transport and logistics	479.4	568.4	25,584	29,377
Managers and directors in transport and distribution	593.7	694.0	28,703	34,690
Managers and directors in storage and warehousing	442.0	515.6	23,916	26,930
Senior officers in protective services	987.7	929.9	52,789	50,141
Officers in armed forces	X	X	X	X
Senior police officers	1,048.9	1,023.9	54,949	52,680
Senior officers in fire, ambulance, prison and related services	880.3	943.1	45,143	50,172
Health and social services managers and directors	779.8	852.7	40,155	43,493
Health services and public health managers and directors	842.3	898.0	42,518	46,187
Social services managers and directors	698.5	715.4	34,878	35,755
Managers and directors in retail and wholesale	377.2	450.3	19,722	23,753
Other managers and proprietors	517.5	578.1	26,338	30,291
Managers and proprietors in agriculture related services	494.6	539.0	X	27,927
Managers and proprietors in agriculture and horticulture	494.3	520.2	24,719	24,322
Managers and proprietors in forestry, fishing and related services	X	X	X	X
Managers and proprietors in hospitality and leisure services	409.1	476.1	22,000	25,077
Hotel and accommodation managers and proprietors	450.9	542.1	25,010	28,149
Restaurant and catering establishment managers and proprietors	392.7	426.4	20,455	22,412
Publicans and managers of licensed premises	349.8	401.2	X	22,365
Leisure and sports managers	442.9	512.0	22,240	26,558
Travel agency managers and proprietors	X	474.4	X	26,498
Managers and proprietors in health and care services	562.5	582.0	28,758	29,794
Health care practice managers	570.7	599.4	32,293	31,915
Residential, day and domiciliary care managers and proprietors	560.5	577.7	28,636	29,234
Managers and proprietors in other services	559.2	649.8	27,519	34,485
Property, housing and estate managers	573.0	623.3	29,908	33,070
Garage managers and proprietors	X	519.2	X	24,988

Full-time females on adult rates (where pay was not affected by absence)

n.e.c. = not elsewhere classified
X = unreliable

Occupation SOC 2010	Gross weekly pay (in April) 2012		Gross Annual earnings in (April) 2012	
	Median £	Mean £	Median £	Mean £
Hairdressing and beauty salon managers and proprietors	X	482.1	19,613	22,990
Shopkeepers and proprietors – wholesale and retail	X	575.9	X	X
Waste disposal and environmental services managers	695.9	757.4	X	42,207
Managers and proprietors in other services n.e.c.	563.8	707.6	27,577	38,093
Professional occupations	644.6	688.8	32,828	34,968
Science, research, engineering and technology professionals	630.7	697.6	32,306	36,080
Natural and social science professionals	634.8	694.4	32,490	35,672
Chemical scientists	587.8	600.6	27,383	30,192
Biological scientists and biochemists	657.7	702.9	32,863	36,244
Physical scientists	X	780.9	X	41,609
Social and humanities scientists	543.3	522.1	25,899	27,278
Natural and social science professionals n.e.c.	613.7	699.9	32,357	35,441
Engineering professionals	584.1	656.3	29,824	33,866
Civil engineers	504.4	618.5	X	34,469
Mechanical engineers	X	632.8	X	33,323
Electrical engineers	585.0	640.7	29,330	32,099
Electronics engineers				
Design and development engineers	632.6	636.6	28,868	29,937
Production and process engineers	557.9	696.5	28,568	X
Engineering professionals n.e.c.	584.3	670.5	30,470	34,360
Information technology and telecommunications professionals	678.2	732.9	34,386	37,797
IT specialist managers	745.0	810.2	38,401	42,065
IT project and programme managers	710.5	771.5	36,954	40,106
IT business analysts, architects and systems designers	649.9	730.1	33,587	39,121
Programmers and software development professionals	676.8	702.6	33,341	35,133
Web design and development professionals	531.1	558.1	28,768	30,135
Information technology and telecommunications professionals n.e.c.	615.6	706.1	X	34,230
Conservation and environment professionals	534.6	563.4	27,673	29,765
Conservation professionals	547.6	551.3	26,622	28,171
Environment professionals	530.5	567.1	27,813	30,144
Research and development managers	677.2	735.0	35,516	39,384
Health professionals	617.4	683.1	31,415	34,096
Health professionals	769.6	903.8	38,098	47,156
Medical practitioners	946.5	1,123.5	X	64,188
Psychologists	637.6	705.7	32,398	36,045
Pharmacists	717.5	712.9	36,618	36,321
Ophthalmic opticians	X	605.7	X	29,475
Dental practitioners	X	867.6	X	X
Veterinarians	639.6	681.9	32,815	34,782
Medical radiographers	737.3	721.1	37,003	36,368
Podiatrists	539.5	600.6	28,000	31,207
Health professionals n.e.c.	558.2	578.2	27,456	28,450
Therapy professionals	585.3	599.1	30,380	31,029
Physiotherapists	590.5	597.4	30,903	31,067
Occupational therapists	563.6	588.2	29,061	30,225
Speech and language therapists	594.7	592.5	X	31,123
Therapy professionals n.e.c.	607.3	680.9	X	35,179
Nursing and midwifery professionals	600.4	618.5	30,742	30,901
Nurses	596.4	615.7	30,372	30,688
Midwives	661.4	664.5	34,477	34,300
Teaching and educational professionals	679.3	688.7	34,840	34,755
Higher education teaching professionals	784.9	817.7	40,568	41,559
Further education teaching professionals	636.2	647.7	31,647	32,204
Secondary education teaching professionals	702.3	696.6	35,777	35,048

Full-time females on adult rates (where pay was not affected by absence)

n.e.c. = not elsewhere classified
X = unreliable

Occupation SOC 2010	Gross weekly pay (in April) 2012		Gross Annual earnings in (April) 2012	
	Median £	Mean £	Median £	Mean £
Primary and nursery education teaching professionals	660.9	675.7	34,557	34,189
Special needs education teaching professionals	654.3	641.5	34,740	32,449
Senior professionals of educational establishments	776.3	791.6	38,072	39,162
Education advisers and school inspectors	679.3	756.8	33,450	39,032
Teaching and other educational professionals n.e.c.	459.8	493.6	24,439	24,883
Business, media and public service professionals	625.2	693.7	31,929	36,192
Legal professionals	766.6	900.1	40,737	49,101
Barristers and judges	613.0	677.9	31,066	33,568
Solicitors	747.4	862.8	40,706	46,408
Legal professionals n.e.c.	848.6	1,078.8	44,310	61,481
Business, research and administrative professionals	636.3	702.1	32,547	36,697
Chartered and certified accountants	629.5	666.2	32,078	33,793
Management consultants and business analysts	686.1	784.7	35,234	40,995
Business and financial project management professionals	683.2	744.2	33,793	39,116
Actuaries, economists and statisticians	661.8	856.7	36,052	X
Business and related research professionals	557.3	569.9	28,728	29,008
Business, research and administrative professionals n.e.c.	625.2	645.1	32,376	33,225
Architects, town planners and surveyors	580.0	622.7	28,169	30,694
Architects	633.4	720.2	X	X
Town planning officers	564.3	598.6	28,998	29,992
Quantity surveyors	609.6	655.2	29,180	32,204
Chartered surveyors	553.3	615.8	28,148	30,092
Chartered architectural technologists				
Construction project managers and related professionals	450.0	486.2	22,034	23,065
Welfare professionals	593.4	592.6	30,537	30,265
Social workers	604.6	598.5	30,851	30,592
Probation officers	578.8	598.2	30,201	30,777
Clergy	447.5	506.5	23,203	26,724
Welfare professionals n.e.c.	509.3	579.2	26,239	29,025
Librarians and related professionals	493.3	530.6	X	27,440
Librarians	470.8	509.1	23,998	25,994
Archivists and curators	581.0	583.9	29,963	31,192
Quality and regulatory professionals	656.0	692.6	34,458	35,932
Quality control and planning engineers	628.9	637.2	30,228	32,322
Quality assurance and regulatory professionals	669.4	727.0	36,477	38,556
Environmental health professionals	639.8	660.7	29,963	32,762
Media professionals	574.9	640.3	30,195	33,964
Journalists, newspaper and periodical editors	570.8	614.2	30,568	33,429
Public relations professionals	539.4	597.9	X	32,712
Advertising accounts managers and creative directors	678.0	752.1	30,142	36,654
Associate professional and technical occupations	499.8	563.7	26,276	29,803
Science, engineering and technology associate professionals	445.2	482.9	22,664	24,698
Science, engineering and production technicians	401.0	447.4	20,369	22,815
Laboratory technicians	355.0	388.4	18,344	20,113
Electrical and electronics technicians	473.5	517.6	23,829	26,285
Engineering technicians	482.8	514.8	25,043	25,478
Building and civil engineering technicians	X	515.3	X	X
Quality assurance technicians	461.0	503.2	23,273	26,296
Planning, process and production technicians	467.7	484.5	22,322	23,035
Science, engineering and production technicians n.e.c.	377.8	436.8	19,274	22,381
Draughtspersons and related architectural technicians	477.0	557.8	25,014	27,928
Architectural and town planning technicians	478.4	X	25,048	29,758

Full-time females on adult rates (where pay was not affected by absence)

n.e.c. = not elsewhere classified
X = unreliable

Occupation SOC 2010	Gross weekly pay (in April) 2012		Gross Annual earnings in (April) 2012	
	Median £	Mean £	Median £	Mean £
Draughtspersons	449.9	487.7	25,000	26,158
Information technology technicians	495.9	517.4	25,174	26,653
IT operations technicians	505.4	533.9	26,003	27,557
IT user support technicians	484.4	500.1	24,399	25,705
Health and social care associate professionals	456.4	481.5	23,336	24,558
Health associate professionals	500.0	531.3	25,360	27,214
Paramedics	661.8	691.1	32,692	34,323
Dispensing opticians	398.2	457.3	18,876	19,929
Pharmaceutical technicians	378.4	420.3	20,872	21,837
Medical and dental technicians	434.7	519.9	24,869	27,097
Health associate professionals n.e.c.	545.4	558.4	27,430	30,027
Welfare and housing associate professionals	454.4	470.4	23,032	23,984
Youth and community workers	474.6	493.3	23,970	24,983
Child and early years officers	412.4	437.5	21,308	22,331
Housing officers	459.8	471.7	23,708	24,102
Counsellors	506.2	524.0	24,647	26,609
Welfare and housing associate professionals n.e.c.	447.2	462.2	22,958	23,611
Protective service occupations	634.8	646.7	32,679	32,941
NCOs and other ranks				
Police officers (sergeant and below)	687.4	695.4	35,107	35,224
Fire service officers (watch manager and below)	575.2	589.2	28,658	29,987
Prison service officers (below principal officer)	436.8	468.4	22,517	23,737
Police community support officers	467.3	472.5	24,781	24,602
Protective service associate professionals n.e.c.	628.4	685.6	32,830	36,471
Culture, media and sports occupations	455.5	529.1	24,643	28,817
Artistic, literary and media occupations	468.7	582.2	27,049	32,698
Artists	466.2	544.3	X	28,448
Authors, writers and translators	435.4	558.3	X	31,026
Actors, entertainers and presenters	X	X		
Dancers and choreographers	482.4	552.8	X	X
Musicians	502.0	529.1	X	27,016
Arts officers, producers and directors	567.0	660.7	33,194	38,855
Photographers, audio-visual and broadcasting equip- ment operators	367.8	426.4	19,618	23,231
Design occupations	442.0	501.1	23,548	26,767
Graphic designers	420.7	453.8	21,868	24,033
Product, clothing and related designers	487.2	544.3	X	29,276
Sports and fitness occupations	379.6	422.8	19,193	22,167
Sports players				
Sports coaches, instructors and officials	428.7	504.5	X	26,445
Fitness instructors	320.5	337.6	16,591	18,190
Business and public service associate professionals	511.3	589.5	27,043	31,751
Transport associate professionals	1,016.1	1,019.6	49,675	49,358
Air traffic controllers	X	1,017.5	X	48,867
Aircraft pilots and flight engineers				
Ship and hovercraft officers				
Legal associate professionals	460.0	550.9	24,674	29,677
Business, finance and related associate professionals	535.2	620.2	27,779	33,181
Estimators, valuers and assessors	449.7	480.3	22,698	25,721
Brokers	X	X	X	X
Insurance underwriters	489.4	519.7	25,444	27,929
Finance and investment analysts and advisers	552.6	659.5	29,998	35,790
Taxation experts	728.5	854.2	X	45,939
Importers and exporters	383.4	433.1	X	22,620
Financial and accounting technicians	607.7	689.2	30,010	35,964
Financial accounts managers	579.7	674.3	31,351	37,141
Business and related associate professionals n.e.c.	477.6	523.1	24,657	26,718
Sales, marketing and related associate professionals	535.7	616.8	27,993	33,441
Buyers and procurement officers	488.3	558.2	25,208	30,299

Full-time females on adult rates (where pay was not affected by absence)

	Gross weekly pay (in April) 2012		Gross Annual earnings in (April) 2012	
n.e.c. = not elsewhere classified X = unreliable				
Occupation SOC 2010	Median £	Mean £	Median £	Mean £
Business sales executives	424.0	493.4	23,082	27,217
Marketing associate professionals	477.0	537.9	24,359	27,879
Estate agents and auctioneers	382.8	467.7	19,517	23,892
Sales accounts and business development managers	653.8	737.6	34,113	40,002
Conference and exhibition managers and organisers	491.9	560.4	26,028	30,427
Conservation and environmental associate professionals	415.9	429.3	19,224	21,870
Public services and other associate professionals	479.4	527.2	25,809	27,842
Public services associate professionals	467.9	513.3	27,844	29,018
Human resources and industrial relations officers	494.9	552.3	24,884	28,554
Vocational and industrial trainers and instructors	475.5	509.5	24,338	26,021
Careers advisers and vocational guidance specialists	512.8	510.9	26,687	26,578
Inspectors of standards and regulations	467.2	502.8	24,147	27,330
Health and safety officers	508.5	587.5	26,807	29,227
Administrative and secretarial occupations	376.0	418.4	19,700	21,658
Administrative occupations	376.1	420.1	19,720	21,696
Administrative occupations: Government and related organisations	387.1	419.5	20,882	22,259
National government administrative occupations	373.2	404.2	20,261	21,985
Local government administrative occupations	417.8	434.9	21,744	22,408
Officers of non-governmental organisations	425.0	473.6	22,509	24,100
Administrative occupations: Finance	383.7	427.5	20,204	22,161
Credit controllers	383.0	408.5	19,580	21,204
Book-keepers, payroll managers and wages clerks	397.7	444.7	20,521	22,684
Bank and post office clerks	366.8	406.4	19,887	21,672
Finance officers	418.6	460.8	22,089	23,708
Financial administrative occupations n.e.c.	366.5	412.6	19,132	21,511
Administrative occupations: Records	373.5	410.2	19,319	20,939
Records clerks and assistants	370.3	405.3	19,042	20,452
Pensions and insurance clerks and assistants	370.8	440.8	19,647	23,163
Stock control clerks and assistants	360.8	401.4	18,419	20,362
Transport and distribution clerks and assistants	406.3	428.4	20,809	22,078
Library clerks and assistants	348.7	371.0	18,496	19,170
Human resources administrative occupations	395.3	410.8	20,216	20,986
Other administrative occupations	353.4	388.3	18,281	19,683
Sales administrators	364.9	404.9	18,764	20,787
Other administrative occupations n.e.c.	352.0	386.8	18,201	19,587
Administrative occupations: Office managers and supervisors	487.7	541.4	25,117	28,399
Office managers	491.0	552.9	25,302	28,994
Office supervisors	420.1	470.1	23,067	24,671
Secretarial and related occupations	375.0	412.2	19,602	21,522
Medical secretaries	398.7	390.8	20,005	19,668
Legal secretaries	360.7	391.5	18,816	20,403
School secretaries	359.3	386.6	18,413	19,818
Company secretaries	479.6	592.7	25,198	32,984
Personal assistants and other secretaries	446.1	474.2	23,171	24,722
Receptionists	303.6	320.0	15,792	16,441
Typists and related keyboard occupations	326.5	361.1	17,690	18,951
Skilled trades occupations	332.7	375.3	17,102	19,246
Skilled agricultural and related trades	310.1	358.1	X	17,653
Agricultural and related trades	310.1	358.1	X	17,653
Farmers	X	437.0		
Horticultural trades	303.2	352.8	X	X
Gardeners and landscape gardeners	307.0	344.1	15,332	17,832
Groundsmen and greenkeepers	314.0	350.2		
Agricultural and fishing trades n.e.c.				
Skilled metal, electrical and electronic trades	412.9	469.5	20,993	24,745
Metal forming, welding and related trades	258.3	279.7	13,797	14,439

Full-time females on adult rates (where pay was not affected by absence)

n.e.c. = not elsewhere classified
X = unreliable

Occupation SOC 2010	Gross weekly pay (in April) 2012		Gross Annual earnings in (April) 2012	
	Median £	Mean £	Median £	Mean £
Smiths and forge workers				
Moulders, core makers and die casters				
Sheet metal workers	253.6	277.7		
Metal plate workers, and riveters				
Welding trades				
Pipe fitters				
Metal machining, fitting and instrument making trades	369.7	415.4	18,567	20,993
Metal machining setters and setter-operators	X	359.4	X	17,914
Tool makers, tool fitters and markers-out				
Metal working production and maintenance fitters	369.8	426.7	18,505	21,659
Precision instrument makers and repairers	412.6	478.9	X	24,389
Air-conditioning and refrigeration engineers				
Vehicle trades	337.7	351.4	16,638	18,303
Vehicle technicians, mechanics and electricians	303.9	311.5	15,157	16,146
Vehicle body builders and repairers				
Vehicle paint technicians				
Aircraft maintenance and related trades				
Boat and ship builders and repairers				
Rail and rolling stock builders and repairers				
Electrical and electronic trades	508.9	542.8	26,343	28,874
Electricians and electrical fitters	502.3	491.6	23,281	25,915
Telecommunications engineers	454.5	541.5	X	X
TV, video and audio engineers				
IT engineers	X	606.5	X	X
Electrical and electronic trades n.e.c.	516.5	555.4	28,633	28,341
Skilled metal, electrical and electronic trades supervisors	X	539.6	X	29,653
Skilled construction and building trades	437.5	457.2	20,872	21,484
Construction and building trades	450.3	457.6	21,706	21,410
Steel erectors				
Bricklayers and masons				
Roofers, roof tilers and slaters				
Plumbers and heating and ventilating engineers	493.4	511.7	X	X
Carpenters and joiners	385.3	415.4	16,221	17,364
Glaziers, window fabricators and fitters				
Construction and building trades n.e.c.	442.4	472.9	22,328	23,636
Building finishing trades	X	X	X	X
Plasterers				
Floorers and wall tilers				
Painters and decorators				
Construction and building trades supervisors	X	405.3	X	19,657
Textiles, printing and other skilled trades	312.9	344.0	16,253	17,588
Textiles and garments trades	280.0	340.8	14,187	15,422
Weavers and knitters	257.8	290.0		
Upholsterers	X	341.6	X	X
Footwear and leather working trades	269.1	283.7	13,929	13,932
Tailors and dressmakers	272.1	302.2	14,144	14,372
Textiles, garments and related trades n.e.c.	X	434.8	X	17,305
Printing trades	312.4	368.8	16,647	19,722
Pre-press technicians	X	373.8	X	X
Printers	X	366.2	X	X
Print finishing and binding workers	312.9	368.2	X	20,097
Food preparation and hospitality trades	316.3	341.2	16,561	17,591
Butchers	271.9	288.5		
Bakers and flour confectioners	280.0	303.7	14,165	15,631
Fishmongers and poultry dressers				
Chefs	314.9	339.8	16,793	17,650
Cooks	280.8	293.0	14,685	15,008
Catering and bar managers	353.0	379.9	18,304	19,560

Full-time females on adult rates (where pay was not affected by absence)

n.e.c. = not elsewhere classified X = unreliable	Gross weekly pay (in April) 2012		Gross Annual earnings in (April) 2012	
Occupation SOC 2010	Median £	Mean £	Median £	Mean £
Other skilled trades	291.7	351.9	14,637	17,195
Glass and ceramics makers, decorators and finishers	274.9	299.5	14,338	14,921
Furniture makers and other craft woodworkers	378.5	438.1	X	X
Florists	266.9	286.5	12,960	14,224
Other skilled trades n.e.c.	X	492.6	X	23,755
Caring, leisure and other service occupations	322.5	348.0	16,504	17,352
Caring personal service occupations	324.8	347.0	16,612	17,290
Childcare and related personal services	298.4	322.0	15,256	16,143
Nursery nurses and assistants	279.4	308.5	14,294	15,464
Childminders and related occupations	335.7	365.0	16,045	18,604
Playworkers	318.9	333.2	15,436	16,434
Teaching assistants	301.4	321.2	15,408	16,005
Educational support assistants	320.7	339.4	16,684	17,417
Animal care and control services	309.2	344.6	16,070	17,388
Veterinary nurses	325.2	341.4	16,694	17,080
Pest control officers				
Animal care services occupations n.e.c.	299.8	347.3	15,040	17,652
Caring personal services	335.2	358.0	17,131	17,814
Nursing auxiliaries and assistants	356.0	379.1	18,181	18,917
Ambulance staff (excluding paramedics)	427.6	463.8	21,657	24,034
Dental nurses	330.9	346.7	16,840	17,492
Houseparents and residential wardens	386.5	423.3	19,508	21,275
Care workers and home carers	313.7	337.3	15,961	16,604
Senior care workers	387.6	411.7	19,729	20,294
Care escorts	252.7	289.0	12,893	13,758
Undertakers, mortuary and crematorium assistants	402.9	434.7	21,296	23,402
Leisure, travel and related personal service occupations	310.5	353.6	15,799	17,698
Leisure and travel services	358.2	400.1	19,321	20,840
Sports and leisure assistants	309.9	334.7	16,524	17,692
Travel agents	340.8	371.8	18,021	19,560
Air travel assistants	402.7	450.7	X	X
Rail travel assistants	507.4	537.1	25,694	27,504
Leisure and travel service occupations n.e.c.	342.3	424.6	X	19,301
Hairdressers and related services	250.7	291.5	12,280	13,822
Hairdressers and barbers	236.1	271.7	11,765	13,163
Beauticians and related occupations	287.7	331.9	14,457	15,443
Housekeeping and related services	310.3	337.9	15,312	16,946
Housekeepers and related occupations	283.4	315.3	14,330	15,952
Caretakers	329.7	386.2	17,202	19,008
Cleaning and housekeeping managers and supervisors	312.7	336.1	X	16,724
Sales and customer service occupations	304.1	341.1	15,622	17,369
Sales occupations	277.9	309.3	14,103	15,541
Sales assistants and retail cashiers	269.5	297.7	13,660	14,883
Sales and retail assistants	264.3	295.2	13,509	14,658
Retail cashiers and check-out operators	253.6	261.8	12,702	13,101
Telephone salespersons	335.1	357.5	18,779	20,551
Pharmacy and other dispensing assistants	292.2	309.6	14,884	15,494
Vehicle and parts salespersons and advisers	X	360.0	X	X
Sales related occupations	345.5	385.6	18,216	20,390
Collector salespersons and credit agents	X	415.8	17,693	17,661
Debt, rent and other cash collectors	306.4	340.0	16,257	18,163
Roundspersons and van salespersons	250.5	302.2		
Market and street traders and assistants				
Merchandisers and window dressers	409.4	463.6	21,281	23,829
Sales related occupations n.e.c.	331.6	359.8	17,845	19,700
Sales supervisors	298.0	336.5	15,434	16,950
Customer service occupations	353.0	392.3	18,682	20,501

Full-time females on adult rates (where pay was not affected by absence)

Occupation SOC 2010	Gross weekly pay (in April) 2012		Gross Annual earnings in (April) 2012	
n.e.c. = not elsewhere classified X = unreliable	Median £	Mean £	Median £	Mean £
Customer service occupations	339.1	362.7	17,946	18,745
Call and contact centre occupations	321.5	341.0	16,937	17,918
Telephonists	326.4	360.1	16,489	17,774
Communication operators	494.4	500.9	25,222	25,698
Market research interviewers	X	X	X	X
Customer service occupations n.e.c.	336.8	358.2	17,914	18,484
Customer service managers and supervisors	488.2	549.0	25,737	29,131
Process, plant and machine operatives	318.6	351.4	16,132	17,651
Process, plant and machine operatives	312.9	339.5	15,889	17,025
Process operatives	303.9	327.1	15,534	16,510
Food, drink and tobacco process operatives	298.7	320.3	15,531	16,199
Glass and ceramics process operatives	325.9	336.7	X	18,253
Textile process operatives	328.2	343.9	15,648	16,735
Chemical and related process operatives	327.1	360.3	15,885	19,103
Rubber process operatives			13,536	14,866
Plastics process operatives	295.9	351.5	15,227	16,393
Metal making and treating process operatives				
Electroplaters				
Process operatives n.e.c.	313.1	337.8	15,900	16,382
Plant and machine operatives	300.5	353.9	15,027	17,833
Paper and wood machine operatives	X	358.9	X	16,112
Coal mine operatives				
Quarry workers and related operatives				
Energy plant operatives	318.2	319.9	16,326	16,396
Metal working machine operatives	274.6	297.5	14,268	15,869
Water and sewerage plant operatives	553.0	575.3	27,108	29,438
Printing machine assistants	298.2	395.5	X	20,286
Plant and machine operatives n.e.c.	280.9	330.5	X	16,804
Assemblers and routine operatives	316.0	342.5	16,031	17,006
Assemblers (electrical and electronic products)	314.5	315.1	16,346	16,280
Assemblers (vehicles and metal goods)	383.1	409.7	17,877	19,302
Routine inspectors and testers	357.2	397.4	17,652	19,034
Weighers, graders and sorters	254.1	278.2	X	X
Tyre, exhaust and windscreen fitters				
Sewing machinists	293.3	322.5	14,110	15,139
Assemblers and routine operatives n.e.c.	295.5	329.9	15,639	16,829
Construction operatives	349.3	417.6	19,376	21,138
Scaffolders, stagers and riggers				
Road construction operatives				
Rail construction and maintenance operatives				
Construction operatives n.e.c.	338.8	394.9	17,412	19,322
Transport and mobile machine drivers and operatives	366.1	420.7	18,633	21,222
Road transport drivers	353.9	378.6	17,405	18,959
Large goods vehicle drivers	493.4	507.9	X	25,091
Van drivers	286.5	328.8	14,595	15,892
Bus and coach drivers	385.5	426.3	20,034	22,264
Taxi and cab drivers and chauffeurs	X	352.8	X	X
Driving instructors				
Mobile machine drivers and operatives	269.1	297.7	15,284	16,082
Crane drivers				
Fork-lift truck drivers				
Agricultural machinery drivers				
Mobile machine drivers and operatives n.e.c.	262.2	297.9	13,321	15,851
Other drivers and transport operatives	759.3	669.1	33,312	33,059
Train and tram drivers	813.2	809.9	42,165	40,894
Marine and waterways transport operatives				
Air transport operatives				
Rail transport operatives	X	658.9	X	31,886
Other drivers and transport operatives n.e.c.	X	X	X	24,799

Full-time females on adult rates (where pay was not affected by absence)

	Gross weekly pay (in April) 2012		Gross Annual earnings in (April) 2012	
n.e.c. = not elsewhere classified X = unreliable				
	Median £	Mean £	Median £	Mean £
Occupation SOC 2010				
Elementary occupations	275.6	302.7	14,225	15,171
Elementary trades and related occupations	290.8	312.4	15,145	16,058
Elementary agricultural occupations	294.5	308.3	14,718	14,922
Farm workers	303.2	300.5	14,767	14,976
Forestry workers				
Fishing and other elementary agriculture occupations				
n.e.c.	280.4	311.9	13,728	14,342
Elementary construction occupations	328.0	303.2	17,379	17,768
Elementary process plant occupations	290.3	313.0	15,263	16,168
Industrial cleaning process occupations	302.3	310.0	14,627	14,364
Packers, bottlers, canners and fillers	291.9	313.6	15,207	16,075
Elementary process plant occupations n.e.c.	276.6	312.0	15,503	16,704
Elementary administration and service occupations	273.0	301.1	14,070	15,014
Elementary administration occupations	323.2	347.8	16,973	18,428
Postal workers, mail sorters, messengers and couriers	387.1	409.2	21,446	21,764
Elementary administration occupations n.e.c.	269.4	282.6	14,103	14,360
Elementary cleaning occupations	261.6	281.6	13,254	13,634
Window cleaners				
Street cleaners				
Cleaners and domestics	257.5	280.0	13,155	13,497
Launderers, dry cleaners and pressers	267.9	286.4	13,580	13,946
Refuse and salvage occupations	321.8	321.6	17,225	17,238
Vehicle valeters and cleaners	290.2	307.7	14,839	15,830
Elementary cleaning occupations n.e.c.	267.9	295.2	14,218	16,132
Elementary security occupations	444.2	451.3	22,359	22,335
Security guards and related occupations	471.5	487.4	23,906	24,570
Parking and civil enforcement occupations	383.3	422.8	20,060	20,985
School midday and crossing patrol occupations	281.3	303.2	X	13,707
Elementary security occupations n.e.c.	402.7	429.6	20,215	19,510
Elementary sales occupations	315.1	314.1	15,522	15,707
Shelf fillers	317.4	315.4	15,531	15,760
Elementary sales occupations n.e.c.	287.2	307.2	14,066	15,402
Elementary storage occupations	301.1	323.3	15,867	16,464
Other elementary services occupations	247.0	261.8	12,334	12,485
Hospital porters	X	355.5	15,460	17,751
Kitchen and catering assistants	249.0	264.9	12,459	12,568
Waiters and waitresses	241.7	255.1	11,503	11,934
Bar staff	242.2	255.2	12,117	12,347
Leisure and theme park attendants	265.2	271.6	14,455	14,263
Other elementary services occupations n.e.c.	266.1	277.4	12,565	13,024
Not classified				

F8: Public sector comparable earnings

The gross-income equivalent of net sums and some comparable salaries: 2013–14 tax rates

Net (£)	Gross[1] (£)	Comparable gross salaries[2]
10,000	11,303	
10,900	12,646	*National Minimum Wage (adults) £12,646*, Army (new entrant) £14,145
12,000	14,288	*Healthcare Assistant £16,918*
14,000	17,273	*Army Private (B) £17,515*
16,000	20,258	*Nurse (newly qualified) £21,336*, Junior Hospital Doctor (B) £22,412
18,000	23,243	Teacher (newly qualified, B) £24,724
20,000	26,228	Nurse Grade F £26,603, Army Private (T) £28,940, NHS Registrar (B) £29,411
22,500	29,960	Sergeant (B) £30,013, Nurse (A) £31,135, *Bishop (B) £31,430*, Sister Grade G (T) £32,557
25,000	33,691	*Dean (T) £33,170*, Teacher (Upper scale, B) £34,179, Sergeant (T) £36,929
27,500	37,422	Captain (B) £37,916, Head Teacher (B) £38,399, *Bishop (T) £40,410*
30,000	41,154	
32,500	44,895	Captain (T) £45,090, NHS Registrar (T) £46,246, Major (B) £47,760
35,000	49,343	
37,500	53,791	Teacher (Advanced Skills, T) £56,949, Major (T) £57,199, *Bishop of London £57,590*
40,000	58,240	Civil Service Band 1 (B) £58,200
42,500	62,688	*Archbishop of York £62,830*, MP £65,737, Lieutenant Colonel (B) £67,032
45,000	67,137	
47,500	71,585	*Archbishop of Canterbury £74,450*, NHS Consultant (B) £74,504
50,000	76,033	Lieutenant Colonel (T) £77,617
52,500	80,482	Colonel (B) £81,310, Civil Service Band 2 (B) £81,600
55,000	84,930	
57,500	89,379	Colonel (T) £89,408
60,000	93,827	Junior Government Minister £94,228, Brigadier (B) £97,030
62,500	98,275	Civil Service Band 3 (B) £99,960, Brigadier (T) £100,964
65,000	102,724	Minister of State £104,050, District Judge (PRFD) £106,921, Major General (B) £108,201
67,500	109,323	GP (A) £112,459
70,000	116,116	Civil Service Band 2 (T) £117,740, NHS Consultant (A) £119,200, Major General (T) £119,214
72,500	121,838	Lieutenant General (B) £125,908
75,000	126,286	Circuit Judge £128,296
77,500	130,734	
80,000	135,183	Senior Circuit Judge £138,548
82,500	139,631	Permanent Secretary (B) £139,740, Cabinet Minister £141,866
85,000	144,080	
87,500	148,528	Lieutenant General (T) £152,642
90,000	152,976	Head Teacher (T) £153,450
92,500	158,006	
95,000	163,382	General (B) £165,284
97,500	168,759	High Court Judge £172,753
100,000	174,135	
105,000	184,888	General (T) £185,184, Prime Minister £194,250
110,000	195,640	Lord Justice of Appeal £196,707, Civil Service Band 3 (T) £205,000
115,000	206,393	Supreme Court Justice & Family Division President £206,857, Master of the Rolls £214,165
120,000	217,146	Chief of Defence Staff (B) £238,123
130,000	238,651	Lord Chief Justice £239,845, Chief of Defence Staff (T) £252,698
140,000	260,156	Permanent Secretary (T) £273,250
150,000	281,662	
175,000	335,425	

[1] Assumptions for the grossed-up equivalent: 3% contributory pension; contracted out of S2P for Class 1 NIC.
Salaries effective April 2012. Public service pay rates over £21,000 are frozen for the second year at 2010 rates. *Changed pay rates and recipients are italicised.*

[2] All categories are subject to varying terms and conditions, and some benefit from expenses. (A), (B) and (T) indicate average, bottom and top of range or seniority for post or rank.

F9: Public sector earnings websites

Websites and other sources that provide helpful information about pay and retirement benefits in the public sector include:

Sector/ annual review date	Sources of information
Armed forces (April 1)	*http://www.army.mod.uk* *http://www.royalnavy.mod.uk* *http://www.raf.mod.uk*
Health service (April 1)	*http://www.nhscareers.nhs.co.uk* *http://www.nhsemployers.org*
Police (September 1)	*http://www.police-information.co.uk*
Teachers (September 1)	*http://www.teachers.org.uk* *http://www.atl.org.uk*
Local government (April 1)	*http://www.navca.org.uk* [National Association for Voluntary and Community Action] *http://www.lgps.org.uk* [Local Government Pension Scheme]
Civil service (April 1)	*http://www.civilservice.gov.uk*

Group G

Tax and National Insurance

G1:   Net equivalents to a range of gross annual income figures

G2:   Illustrative net earnings calculations

G3:   Income tax reliefs and rates

G4:   National Insurance contributions

G5:   VAT registration thresholds and rates

G

G1: Net equivalents to a range of gross annual income figures

Gross income £pa	2004/05 Net equivalent income		2005/06 Net equivalent income		2006/07 Net equivalent income	
	Employed £pa	Self-employed £pa	Employed £pa	Self-employed £pa	Employed £pa	Self-employed £pa
1,000	1,000	1,000	1,000	1,000	1,000	1,000
2,000	2,000	2,000	2,000	2,000	2,000	2,000
3,000	3,000	3,000	3,000	3,000	3,000	3,000
4,000	4,000	4,000	4,000	4,000	4,000	4,000
5,000	4,946	4,847	4,977	4,872	5,000	4,891
6,000	5,736	5,667	5,767	5,692	5,797	5,717
7,000	6,498	6,459	6,556	6,511	6,587	6,537
8,000	7,168	7,159	7,226	7,211	7,280	7,260
9,000	7,838	7,859	7,896	7,911	7,950	7,960
10,000	8,508	8,559	8,566	8,611	8,620	8,660
11,000	9,178	9,259	9,236	9,311	9,290	9,360
12,000	9,848	9,959	9,906	10,011	9,960	10,060
13,000	10,518	10,659	10,576	10,711	10,630	10,760
14,000	11,188	11,359	11,246	11,411	11,300	11,460
15,000	11,858	12,059	11,916	12,111	11,970	12,160
16,000	12,528	12,759	12,586	12,811	12,640	12,860
17,000	13,198	13,459	13,256	13,511	13,310	13,560
18,000	13,868	14,159	13,926	14,211	13,980	14,260
19,000	14,538	14,859	14,596	14,911	14,650	14,960
20,000	15,208	15,559	15,266	15,611	15,320	15,660
21,000	15,878	16,259	15,936	16,311	15,990	16,360
22,000	16,548	16,959	16,606	17,011	16,660	17,060
23,000	17,218	17,659	17,276	17,711	17,330	17,760
24,000	17,888	18,359	17,946	18,411	18,000	18,460
25,000	18,558	19,059	18,616	19,111	18,670	19,160
26,000	19,228	19,759	19,286	19,811	19,340	19,860
27,000	19,898	20,459	19,956	20,511	20,010	20,560
28,000	20,568	21,159	20,626	21,211	20,680	21,260
29,000	21,238	21,859	21,296	21,911	21,350	21,960
30,000	21,908	22,559	21,966	22,611	22,020	22,660
31,000	22,578	23,259	22,636	23,311	22,690	23,360
32,000	23,276	23,979	23,306	24,011	23,360	24,060
33,000	24,046	24,749	23,976	24,728	24,030	24,760
34,000	24,816	25,519	24,646	25,498	24,746	25,492
35,000	25,586	26,288	25,541	26,268	25,516	26,262
40,000	28,742	29,444	28,904	29,631	29,066	29,812
45,000	31,692	32,394	31,854	32,581	32,016	32,762
50,000	34,642	35,344	34,804	35,531	34,966	35,712
55,000	37,592	38,294	37,754	38,481	37,916	38,662
60,000	40,542	41,244	40,704	41,431	40,866	41,612
65,000	43,492	44,194	43,654	44,381	43,816	44,562
70,000	46,442	47,144	46,604	47,331	46,766	47,512
75,000	49,392	50,094	49,554	50,281	49,716	50,462
80,000	52,342	53,044	52,504	53,231	52,666	53,412
85,000	55,292	55,994	55,454	56,181	55,616	56,362
90,000	58,242	58,944	58,404	59,131	58,566	59,312
95,000	61,192	61,894	61,354	62,081	61,516	62,262
100,000	64,142	64,844	64,304	65,031	64,466	65,212
150,000	93,642	94,344	93,804	94,531	93,966	94,712
200,000	123,142	123,844	123,304	124,031	123,466	124,212
250,000	152,642	153,344	152,804	153,531	152,966	153,712
300,000	182,142	182,844	182,304	183,031	182,466	183,212

G1: Net equivalents to a range of gross annual income figures

	2007/08 Employed				2007/08 Self–employed		
Gross income £pa	Net equivalent income £pa	Net per £100 extra £pa	Reason	Gross income £pa	Net equivalent income £pa	Net per £100 extra £pa	Reason
1,000	1,000	100		1,000	1,000	100	
2,000	2,000	100		2,000	2,000	100	
3,000	3,000	100		4,000	4,000	100	
4,000	4,000	100		4,635	4,635	*	← £114 NIC Class 2
5,000	5,000	100		5,000	4,886	–	payable
5,225	5,225	79	← 10% tax payable and	5,225	5,111	82	← 10% tax payable and
6,000	5,837	79	11% NIC	6,000	5,747	82	8% NIC Class 4 payable
7,000	6,627	79	Class 1 payable	7,000	6,567	82	
7,455	6,986	67	← 22% tax payable	7,455	6,940	70	← 22% tax payable
8,000	7,352	67		8,000	7,321	70	
9,000	8,022	67		9,000	8,021	70	
10,000	8,692	67		10,000	8,721	70	
11,000	9,362	67		11,000	9,421	70	
12,000	10,032	67		12,000	10,121	70	
13,000	10,702	67		13,000	10,821	70	
14,000	11,372	67		14,000	11,521	70	
15,000	12,042	67		15,000	12,221	70	
16,000	12,712	67		16,000	12,921	70	
17,000	13,382	67		17,000	13,621	70	
18,000	14,052	67		18,000	14,321	70	
19,000	14,722	67		19,000	15,021	70	
20,000	15,392	67		20,000	15,721	70	
21,000	16,062	67		21,000	16,421	70	
22,000	16,732	67		22,000	17,121	70	
23,000	17,402	67		23,000	17,821	70	
24,000	18,072	67		24,000	18,521	70	
25,000	18,742	67		25,000	19,221	70	
26,000	19,412	67		26,000	19,921	70	
27,000	20,082	67		27,000	20,621	70	
28,000	20,752	67		28,000	21,321	70	
29,000	21,422	67		29,000	22,021	70	
30,000	22,092	67		30,000	22,721	70	
31,000	22,762	67		31,000	23,421	70	
32,000	23,432	67		32,000	24,121	70	
33,000	24,102	67		33,000	24,821	70	
34,000	24,772	67		34,000	25,521	70	
34,840	25,335	77	← NIC Class 1 reduced to 1%	34,840	26,109	77	← NIC Class 4 reduced
35,000	25,458	77		35,000	26,233	77	to 1%
37,500	27,382	77		37,500	28,157	77	
39,825	29,172	59	← 40% tax payable	39,825	29,947	59	← 40% tax payable
40,000	29,276	59		40,000	30,051	59	
45,000	32,226	59		45,000	33,001	59	
50,000	35,176	59		50,000	35,951	59	
55,000	38,126	59		55,000	38,901	59	
60,000	41,076	59		60,000	41,851	59	
65,000	44,026	59		65,000	44,801	59	
70,000	46,976	59		70,000	47,751	59	
75,000	49,926	59		75,000	50,701	59	
80,000	52,876	59		80,000	53,651	59	
85,000	55,826	59		85,000	56,601	59	
90,000	58,776	59		90,000	59,551	59	
95,000	61,726	59		95,000	62,501	59	
100,000	64,676	59		100,000	65,451	59	
150,000	94,176	59		150,000	94,951	59	*£2.20 x 52 weeks =£114 pa
200,000	123,676	59		200,000	124,451	59	fixed for any level of income
250,000	153,176	59		250,000	153,951	59	in excess of £4,635 pa. So
300,000	182,676	59		300,000	183,451	59	net equivalent of £4,650
							gross is £4,536.

	2008/09				2008/09		
	Employed				Self–employed		
	Net equivalent income	Net per £100 extra	Reason		Net equivalent income	Net per £100 extra	Reason
Gross income £pa	£pa	£pa		Gross income £pa	£pa	£pa	
1,000	1,000	100		1,000	1,000	100	
2,000	2,000	100		2,000	2,000	100	
3,000	3,000	100		4,000	4,000	100	
4,000	4,000	100		4,825	4,825	*	← £120 NIC Class 2
5,000	5,000	100		5,000	4,880	100	payable
5,435	5,435	89	← 11% NIC	5,435	5,315	92	←8% NIC Class 4 payable
6,000	5,938	89	Class 1 payable	6,000	5,835	92	
6,035	5,969	69	← 20% tax payable	6,035	5,867	72	← 20% tax payable
7,000	6,635	69		7,000	6,562	72	
8,000	7,325	69		8,000	7,282	72	
9,000	8,015	69		9,000	8,002	72	
10,000	8,705	69		10,000	8,722	72	
11,000	9,395	69		11,000	9,442	72	
12,000	10,085	69		12,000	10,162	72	
13,000	10,775	69		13,000	10,882	72	
14,000	11,465	69		14,000	11,602	72	
15,000	12,155	69		15,000	12,322	72	
16,000	12,845	69		16,000	13,042	72	
17,000	13,535	69		17,000	13,762	72	
18,000	14,225	69		18,000	14,482	72	
19,000	14,915	69		19,000	15,202	72	
20,000	15,605	69		20,000	15,922	72	
21,000	16,295	69		21,000	16,642	72	
22,000	16,985	69		22,000	17,362	72	
23,000	17,675	69		23,000	18,082	72	
24,000	18,365	69		24,000	18,802	72	
25,000	19,055	69		25,000	19,522	72	
26,000	19,745	69		26,000	20,242	72	
27,000	20,435	69		27,000	20,962	72	
28,000	21,125	69		28,000	21,682	72	
29,000	21,815	69		29,000	22,402	72	
30,000	22,505	69		30,000	23,122	72	
31,000	23,195	69		31,000	23,842	72	
32,000	23,885	69		32,000	24,562	72	
33,000	24,575	69		33,000	25,282	72	
34,000	25,265	69		34,000	26,002	72	
35,000	25,955	69		35,000	26,722	72	
37,500	27,680	69		37,500	28,522	72	
40,000	29,405	69		40,000	30,322	72	
40,040	29,432	79	← NIC Class 1 reduced to 1%	40,040	30,351	79	← NIC Class 4 reduced to 1%
40,835	30,060	59	← 40% tax payable	40,835	30,979	59	← 40% tax payable
45,000	32,518	59		45,000	33,436	59	
50,000	35,468	59		50,000	36,386	59	
55,000	38,418	59		55,000	39,336	59	
60,000	41,368	59		60,000	42,286	59	
65,000	44,138	59		65,000	45,236	59	
70,000	47,268	59		70,000	48,186	59	
75,000	50,218	59		75,000	51,136	59	
80,000	53,168	59		80,000	54,086	59	
85,000	56,118	59		85,000	57,036	59	
90,000	59,068	59		90,000	59,986	59	
95,000	62,018	59		95,000	62,936	59	*£2.30 x 52 weeks
100,000	64,968	59		100,000	65,886	59	=£120 pa fixed for any
150,000	94,468	59		150,000	95,386	59	level of income in
200,000	123,968	59		200,000	124,886	59	excess of £4,635 pa.
250,000	153,468	59		250,000	154,386	59	So net equivalent of
300,000	182,968	59		300,000	183,886	59	£4,650 gross is £4,730.

G1: Net equivalents to a range of gross annual income figures

	2009/10				2009/10		
	Employed				Self–employed		
Gross income £pa	Net equivalent income	Net per £100 extra	Reason	Gross income £pa	Net equivalent income	Net per £100 extra	Reason
£pa	£pa	£pa		£pa	£pa	£pa	
1,000	1,000	100		1,000	1,000	100	
2,000	2,000	100		2,000	2,000	100	
3,000	3,000	100		3,000	3,000	100	
4,000	4,000	100		4,000	4,000	100	
5,000	5,000	100		5,075	5,075	*	← £125 NIC Class 2 payable
5,715	5,715	89	← 11% NIC Class 1	5,715	5,590	92	← 8% NIC Class 4 payable
6,000	5,969	89	payable	6,000	5,852	92	
6,475	6,391	69	← 20% tax payable	6,475	6,289	72	← 20% tax payable
7,000	6,754	69		7,000	6,667	72	
8,000	7,444	69		8,000	7,387	72	
9,000	8,134	69		9,000	8,107	72	
10,000	8,824	69		10,000	8,827	72	
11,000	9,514	69		11,000	9,547	72	
12,000	10,204	69		12,000	10,267	72	
13,000	10,894	69		13,000	10,987	72	
14,000	11,584	69		14,000	11,707	72	
15,000	12,274	69		15,000	12,427	72	
16,000	12,964	69		16,000	13,147	72	
17,000	13,654	69		17,000	13,867	72	
18,000	14,344	69		18,000	14,587	72	
19,000	15,034	69		19,000	15,307	72	
20,000	15,724	69		20,000	16,027	72	
21,000	16,414	69		21,000	16,747	72	
22,000	17,104	69		22,000	17,467	72	
23,000	17,794	69		23,000	18,187	72	
24,000	18,484	69		24,000	18,907	72	
25,000	19,174	69		25,000	19,627	72	
26,000	19,864	69		26,000	20,347	72	
27,000	20,554	69		27,000	21,067	72	
28,000	21,244	69		28,000	21,787	72	
29,000	21,934	69		29,000	22,507	72	
30,000	22,624	69		30,000	23,227	72	
31,000	23,314	69		31,000	23,947	72	
32,000	24,004	69		32,000	24,667	72	
33,000	24,694	69		33,000	25,387	72	
34,000	25,384	69		34,000	26,107	72	
35,000	26,074	69		35,000	26,827	72	
37,500	27,799	69		37,500	28,627	72	
40,000	29,524	69		40,000	30,427	72	
43,875	32,197	59	← NIC Class 1 reduced	43,875	33,217	59	← NIC Class 4 reduced
45,000	32,861	59	to 1% and 40% tax	45,000	33,881	59	to 1% and 40% tax
50,000	35,811	59	payable	50,000	36,831	59	payable
55,000	38,761	59		55,000	39,781	59	
60,000	41,711	59		60,000	42,731	59	
65,000	44,661	59		65,000	45,681	59	
70,000	47,611	59		70,000	48,631	59	
75,000	50,561	59		75,000	51,581	59	
80,000	53,511	59		80,000	54,531	59	
85,000	56,461	59		85,000	57,481	59	
90,000	59,411	59		90,000	60,431	59	
95,000	62,361	59		95,000	63,381	59	
100,000	65,311	59		100,000	66,331	59	*£2.40 x 52 weeks
150,000	94,811	59		150,000	95,831	59	=£125 pa fixed for
200,000	124,311	59		200,000	125,331	59	any level of income in
250,000	153,811	59		250,000	154,831	59	excess of £5,075 pa.
300,000	183,311	59		300,000	184,331	59	So net equivalent of £5,100 gross is £4,975.

	2010/11				2010/11		
	Employed				**Self–employed**		
	Net equivalent income	Net per £100 extra	Reason		Net equivalent income	Net per £100 extra	Reason
Gross income £pa	**£pa**	**£pa**		**Gross income £pa**	**£pa**	**£pa**	
1,000	1,000	100		1,000	1,000	100	
2,000	2,000	100		2,000	2,000	100	
3,000	3,000	100		3,000	3,000	100	
4,000	4,000	100		4,000	4,000	100	
5,000	5,000	100		5,075	5,075	Note 2	← £125 NIC Class 2 payable
5,715	5,715	89	← 11% NIC Class 1 payable	5,715	5,590	92	← 8% NIC Class 4 payable
6,000	5,969	89		6,000	5,852	92	
6,475	6,391	69	← 20% tax payable	6,475	6,289	72	← 20% tax payable
7,000	6,754	69		7,000	6,667	72	
8,000	7,444	69		8,000	7,387	72	
9,000	8,134	69		9,000	8,107	72	Note 2 £2.40 x 52 weeks
10,000	8,824	69		10,000	8,827	72	= £125 pa fixed for any
11,000	9,514	69		11,000	9,547	72	level of income in excess of
12,000	10,204	69		12,000	10,267	72	£5,075 pa. So net
13,000	10,894	69		13,000	10,987	72	equivalent of £5,100
14,000	11,584	69		14,000	11,707	72	gross is £4,975.
15,000	12,274	69		15,000	12,427	72	
16,000	12,964	69		16,000	13,147	72	
17,000	13,654	69		17,000	13,867	72	
18,000	14,344	69		18,000	14,587	72	
19,000	15,034	69		19,000	15,307	72	
20,000	15,724	69		20,000	16,027	72	
21,000	16,414	69		21,000	16,747	72	
22,000	17,104	69		22,000	17,467	72	
23,000	17,794	69		23,000	18,187	72	
24,000	18,484	69		24,000	18,907	72	
25,000	19,174	69		25,000	19,627	72	
26,000	19,864	69		26,000	20,347	72	
27,000	20,554	69		27,000	21,067	72	
28,000	21,244	69		28,000	21,787	72	
29,000	21,934	69		29,000	22,507	72	
30,000	22,624	69		30,000	23,227	72	
31,000	23,314	69		31,000	23,947	72	
32,000	24,004	69		32,000	24,667	72	
33,000	24,694	69		33,000	25,387	72	
34,000	25,384	69		34,000	26,107	72	
35,000	26,074	69		35,000	26,827	72	
37,500	27,799	69		37,500	28,627	72	
40,000	29,524	69		40,000	30,427	72	
43,875	32,197	59	← NIC Class 1 reduced	43,875	33,217	59	← NIC Class 4 reduced to
45,000	32,861	59	to 1% and 40% tax	45,000	33,881	59	1% and 40% tax payable
50,000	35,811	59	payable	50,000	36,831	59	
55,000	38,761	59		55,000	39,781	59	
60,000	41,711	59		60,000	42,731	59	
65,000	44,661	59		65,000	45,681	59	
70,000	47,611	59		70,000	48,631	59	
75,000	50,561	59		75,000	51,581	59	
80,000	53,511	59		80,000	54,531	59	
85,000	56,461	59		85,000	57,481	59	
90,000	59,411	59		90,000	60,431	59	
95,000	62,361	59		95,000	63,381	59	
100,000	65,311	Note 1		100,000	66,331	Note 1	
150,000	92,221	49	← 50% tax payable	150,000	93,241	49	← 50% tax payable
200,000	116,721	49	Note 1 Personal allowance	200,000	117,741	49	
250,000	141,221	49	reduced to nil between	250,000	142,241	49	
300,000	165,721	49	£100,000 and £112,950	300,000	166,741	49	

G1: Net equivalents to a range of gross annual income figures

	2011/12 Employed				2011/12 Self–employed		
Gross income £pa	Net equivalent income £pa	Net per £100 extra £pa	Reason	Gross income £pa	Net equivalent income £pa	Net per £100 extra £pa	Reason
1,000	1,000	100		1,000	1,000	100	
2,000	2,000	100		2,000	2,000	100	
3,000	3,000	100		3,000	3,000	100	
4,000	4,000	100		4,000	4,000	100	
5,000	5,000	100		5,315	5,315	Note 2	← £130 NIC Class 2 payable
6,000	6,000	100		6,000	5,870	Note 2	
7,000	7,000	100		7,000	6,870	Note 2	
7,225	7,225	88	← 12% NIC Class 1 payable	7,225	7,095	91	← 9% NIC Class 4 payable
7,475	7,445	68	← 20% tax payable	7,475	7,322	71	← 20% tax payable
8,000	7,802	68		8,000	7,695	71	
9,000	8,482	68		9,000	8,405	71	Note 2 £2.50 x 52 weeks
10,000	9,162	68		10,000	9,115	71	= £130 pa fixed for any
11,000	9,842	68		11,000	9,825	71	level of income in excess of
12,000	10,522	68		12,000	10,535	71	£5,315 pa. So net
13,000	11,202	68		13,000	11,245	71	equivalent of £5,400
14,000	11,882	68		14,000	11,955	71	gross is £5,270.
15,000	12,562	68		15,000	12,665	71	
16,000	13,242	68		16,000	13,375	71	
17,000	13,922	68		17,000	14,085	71	
18,000	14,602	68		18,000	14,795	71	
19,000	15,282	68		19,000	15,505	71	
20,000	15,962	68		20,000	16,215	71	
21,000	16,642	68		21,000	16,925	71	
22,000	17,322	68		22,000	17,635	71	
23,000	18,002	68		23,000	18,345	71	
24,000	18,682	68		24,000	19,055	71	
25,000	19,362	68		25,000	19,765	71	
26,000	20,042	68		26,000	20,475	71	
27,000	20,722	68		27,000	21,185	71	
28,000	21,402	68		28,000	21,895	71	
29,000	22,082	68		29,000	22,605	71	
30,000	22,762	68		30,000	23,315	71	
31,000	23,442	68		31,000	24,025	71	
32,000	24,122	68		32,000	24,735	71	
33,000	24,802	68		33,000	25,445	71	
34,000	25,482	68		34,000	26,155	71	
35,000	26,162	68		35,000	26,865	71	
37,500	27,862	68		37,500	28,640	71	
40,000	29,562	68		40,000	30,415	71	
42,475	31,245	58	← NIC Class 1 reduced	42,475	32,172	58	← NIC Class 4 reduced to
45,000	32,709	58	to 2% and 40% tax	45,000	33,636	58	2% and 40% tax payable
50,000	35,609	58	payable	50,000	36,536	58	
55,000	38,509	58		55,000	39,436	58	
60,000	41,409	58		60,000	42,336	58	
65,000	44,309	58		65,000	45,236	58	
70,000	47,209	58		70,000	48,136	58	
75,000	50,109	58		75,000	51,036	58	
80,000	53,009	58		80,000	53,936	58	
85,000	55,909	58		85,000	56,836	58	
90,000	58,809	58		90,000	59,736	58	
95,000	61,709	58		95,000	62,636	58	
100,000	64,609	Note 1		100,000	65,536	Note 1	
150,000	90,619	48	← 50% tax payable	150,000	91,546	48	← 50% tax payable
200,000	114,619	48	Note 1 Personal allowance	200,000	115,546	48	
250,000	138,619	48	reduced to nil between	250,000	139,546	48	
300,000	162,619	48	£100,000 and £114,950	300,000	163,546	48	

Gross income £pa	2012/13 Employed Net equivalent income £pa	Net per £100 extra £pa	Reason	Gross income £pa	2012/13 Self-employed Net equivalent income £pa	Net per £100 extra £pa	Reason
1,000	1,000	100		1,000	1,000		
2,000	2,000	100		2,000	2,000		
3,000	3,000	100		3,000	3,000		
4,000	4,000	100		4,000	4,000		
5,000	5,000	100		5,595	5,595	Note 2	← £130 NIC Class 2 payable
6,000	6,000	100		6,000	5,862	Note 2	
7,000	7,000	100		7,000	6,862	Note 2	
7,605	7,605	88	← 12% NIC Class 1 payable	7,605	7,467	91	← 9% NIC Class 4 payable
8,000	7,953	88		8,000	7,826	91	
8,105	8,045	68	← 20% tax payable	8,105	7,922	71	← 20% tax payable
9,000	8,654	68		9,000	8,557	71	Note 2 £2.65 x 52 weeks
10,000	9,334	68		10,000	9,267	71	= £138 pa fixed for any
11,000	10,014	68		11,000	9,977	71	level of income in excess of
12,000	10,694	68		12,000	10,687	71	£5,595 pa. So net
13,000	11,374	68		13,000	11,397	71	equivalent of £5,600
14,000	12,054	68		14,000	12,107	71	gross is £5,462.
15,000	12,734	68		15,000	12,817	71	
16,000	13,414	68		16,000	13,527	71	
17,000	14,094	68		17,000	14,237	71	
18,000	14,774	68		18,000	14,947	71	
19,000	15,454	68		19,000	15,657	71	
20,000	16,134	68		20,000	16,367	71	
21,000	16,814	68		21,000	17,077	71	
22,000	17,494	68		22,000	17,787	71	
23,000	18,174	68		23,000	18,497	71	
24,000	18,854	68		24,000	19,207	71	
25,000	19,534	68		25,000	19,917	71	
26,000	20,214	68		26,000	20,627	71	
27,000	20,894	68		27,000	21,337	71	
28,000	21,574	68		28,000	22,047	71	
29,000	22,254	68		29,000	22,757	71	
30,000	22,934	68		30,000	23,467	71	
31,000	23,614	68		31,000	24,177	71	
32,000	24,294	68		32,000	24,887	71	
33,000	24,974	68		33,000	25,597	71	
34,000	25,654	68		34,000	26,307	71	
35,000	26,334	68		35,000	27,017	71	
37,500	28,034	68		37,500	28,792	71	
40,000	29,734	68		40,000	30,567	71	
42,475	31,417	58	← NIC Class 1 reduced	42,475	32,325	58	← NIC Class 4 reduced to
45,000	32,881	58	to 2% and 40% tax	45,000	33,789	58	2% and 40% tax payable
50,000	35,781	58	payable	50,000	36,689	58	
55,000	38,681	58		55,000	39,589	58	
60,000	41,581	58		60,000	42,489	58	
65,000	44,481	58		65,000	45,389	58	
70,000	47,381	58		70,000	48,289	58	
75,000	50,281	58		75,000	51,189	58	
80,000	53,181	58		80,000	54,089	58	
85,000	56,081	58		85,000	56,989	58	
90,000	58,981	58		90,000	59,889	58	
95,000	61,881	58		95,000	62,789	58	
100,000	64,781	Note 1		100,000	65,689	Note 1	
150,000	90,539	48	← 50% tax payable	150,000	91,447	48	← 50% tax payable
200,000	114,539	48	Note 1 Personal allowance	200,000	115,447	48	
250,000	138,539	48	reduced to nil between	250,000	139,447	48	
300,000	162,539	48	£100,000 and £116,210	300,000	163,447	48	

G1: Net equivalents to a range of gross annual income figures

	2013/14 Employed				2013/14 Self-employed		
Gross income £pa	Net equivalent income £pa	Net per £100 extra £pa	Reason	Gross income £pa	Net equivalent income £pa	Net per £100 extra £pa	Reason
1,000	1,000	100		1,000	1,000		
2,000	2,000	100		2,000	2,000		
3,000	3,000	100		3,000	3,000		
4,000	4,000	100		4,000	4,000		
5,000	5,000	100		5,725	5,725	Note 2	← £140 NIC Class 2 payable
6,000	6,000	100		6,000	5,860	Note 2	
7,000	7,000	100		7,000	6,860	Note 2	
7,755	7,755	88	← 12% NIC Class 1 payable	7,755	7,615	91	← 9% NIC Class 4 payable
8,000	7,971	88		8,000	7,838	91	
9,000	8,851	88		9,000	8,748	91	
9,440	9,238	68	← 20% tax payable	9,440	9,148	71	← 20% tax payable
10,000	9,619	68		10,000	9,546	71	Note 2 £2.70 x 52 weeks
11,000	10,299	68		11,000	10,256	71	= £140 pa fixed for any
12,000	10,979	68		12,000	10,966	71	level of income in excess of
13,000	11,659	68		13,000	11,676	71	£5,725 pa. So net
14,000	12,339	68		14,000	12,386	71	equivalent of £6,100
15,000	13,019	68		15,000	13,096	71	gross is £5,960.
16,000	13,699	68		16,000	13,806	71	
17,000	14,379	68		17,000	14,516	71	
18,000	15,059	68		18,000	15,226	71	
19,000	15,739	68		19,000	15,936	71	
20,000	16,419	68		20,000	16,646	71	
21,000	17,099	68		21,000	17,356	71	
22,000	17,779	68		22,000	18,066	71	
23,000	18,459	68		23,000	18,776	71	
24,000	19,139	68		24,000	19,486	71	
25,000	19,819	68		25,000	20,196	71	
26,000	20,499	68		26,000	20,906	71	
27,000	21,179	68		27,000	21,616	71	
28,000	21,859	68		28,000	22,326	71	
29,000	22,539	68		29,000	23,036	71	
30,000	23,219	68		30,000	23,746	71	
31,000	23,899	68		31,000	24,456	71	
32,000	24,579	68		32,000	25,166	71	
33,000	25,259	68		33,000	25,876	71	
34,000	25,939	68		34,000	26,586	71	
35,000	26,619	68		35,000	27,296	71	
37,500	28,319	68		37,500	29,071	71	
40,000	30,019	68		40,000	30,846	71	
41,450	31,005	58	← NIC Class 1 reduced	41,450	31,875	58	← NIC Class 4 reduced to
45,000	33,064	58	to 2% and 40% tax	45,000	33,934	58	2% and 40% tax payable
50,000	35,964	58	payable	50,000	36,834	58	
55,000	38,864	58		55,000	39,734	58	
60,000	41,764	58		60,000	42,634	58	
65,000	44,664	58		65,000	45,534	58	
70,000	47,564	58		70,000	48,434	58	
75,000	50,464	58		75,000	51,334	58	
80,000	53,364	58		80,000	54,234	58	
85,000	56,264	58		85,000	57,134	58	
90,000	59,164	58		90,000	60,034	58	
95,000	62,064	58		95,000	62,934	58	
100,000	64,964	Note 1		100,000	65,834	Note 1	
150,000	90,188	53	← 45% tax payable	150,000	91,058	53	← 45% tax payable
200,000	116,688	53	Note 1 Personal allowance	200,000	117,558	53	
250,000	143,188	53	reduced to nil between	250,000	144,058	53	
300,000	169,688	53	£100,000 and £118,880	300,000	170,558	53	

G2: Illustrative net earnings calculations

Man under 65 at 2013/14 tax rates

		Employed person					Self-employed person				
		£pa	£pa	£pa	£pa	£pa	£pa	£pa	£pa	£pa	£pa
Gross income	[a]	15,000	35,000	50,000	110,000	160,000	15,000	35,000	50,000	110,000	160,000
Income tax											
Gross		15,000	35,000	50,000	110,000	160,000	15,000	35,000	50,000	110,000	160,000
Personal allowance		(9,440)	(9,440)	(9,440)	(4,440)	–	(9,440)	(9,440)	(9,440)	(4,440)	–
Taxable		5,560	25,560	40,560	105,560	160,000	5,560	25,560	40,560	105,560	160,000
Tax payable											
– At 20%		1,112	5,112	6,402	6,402	6,402	1,112	5,112	6,402	6,402	6,402
– At 40%				3,420	29,420	47,196			3,420	29,420	47,196
– At 45%						4,500					4,500
	[b]	1,112	5,112	9,822	35,822	58,098	1,112	5,112	9,822	35,822	58,098
National insurance											
Class 1											
– At 12%		869	3,269	4,043	4,043	4,043					
– At 2%				171	1,371	2,371					
Class 2							140	140	140	140	140
Class 4											
– At 9%							652	2,452	3,033	3,033	3,033
– At 2%									171	1,371	2,371
	[c]	869	3,269	4,214	5,414	6,414	792	2,592	3,344	4,544	5,544
Net income	[a–b–c]	13,019	26,619	35,964	68,764	95,488	13,096	27,296	36,834	69,634	96,358
Net % of gross		86.8%	76.1%	71.9%	62.5%	59.7%	87.3%	78.0%	73.7%	63.3%	60.2%
Note 1: personal allowance											
Personal allowance		9,440	9,440	9,440	9,440	9,440	9,440	9,440	9,440	9,440	9,440
Restriction for excess of income over limit*		–	–	–	(5,000)	(9,440)	–	–	–	(5,000)	(9,440)
Net allowance		9,440	9,440	9,440	4,440	–	9,440	9,440	9,440	4,440	–

*If gross pay does not exceed £100,000, no restriction.
If gross pay does exceed £100,000, restriction is the lower of:
(a) (gross pay–£100,000)/2; and
(b) £9,440

G3: Income tax reliefs and rates

Introductory notes

Personal allowance

Every taxpayer resident in the UK (as well as certain non-UK residents) is entitled to a personal allowance.

From 2010/11, the personal allowance has been subject to an income limit of £100,000. Where total income exceeds this limit, the personal allowance is reduced by 50 per cent of the excess. Accordingly, no personal allowance is available on incomes in excess of £118,880 in 2013/14.

Age-related personal allowance

Higher personal allowances are available to taxpayers who are 65 or more in the tax year, subject to an income limit—£26,100 for 2013/14.

Where total income exceeds the prescribed income limit, the higher personal allowance is reduced by 50 per cent of the excess, although for years up to and including 2009/10 the allowance cannot be reduced below the ordinary personal allowance. However, from 2010/11, the personal allowance for people aged 65–74—and that for people aged 75 and over—can be reduced below the ordinary personal allowance where the income exceeds £100,000.

For 2013/14, the higher personal allowances available are:

Age 65–74 (at any time during the year)	£10,500
Age 75 and above	£10,660

The age-related personal allowance has been frozen from 2012/13 onwards.

Age-related married couple's allowance

Where a couple married before December 5, 2005, live together and at least one spouse was born before April 6, 1935, the husband can claim married couple's allowance.

Where a couple married or entered into a civil partnership on or after December 5, 2005, live together and at least one spouse or partner was born before April 6, 1935, the person with the higher income can claim married couple's allowance.

For 2013/14, the allowance is £7,915 and the rate of tax relief is 10 per cent.

The same income limit applies as in the case of the age-related personal allowance (£26,100 for 2013/14).

Where the claimant's income exceeds the income limit, the married couple's allowance is reduced by 50 per cent of the excess less any reduction of the personal allowance (as above), until the allowance is equal to the following amounts:

Tax year 2006/07	Minimum allowance £2,350	Tax relief £235
Tax year 2007/08	Minimum allowance £2,440	Tax relief £244
Tax year 2008/09	Minimum allowance £2,540	Tax relief £254
Tax year 2009/10	Minimum allowance £2,670	Tax relief £267
Tax year 2010/11	Minimum allowance £2,670	Tax relief £267
Tax year 2011/12	Minimum allowance £2,800	Tax relief £280
Tax year 2012/13	Minimum allowance £2,960	Tax relief £296
Tax year 2013/14	Minimum allowance £3,040	Tax relief £304

Child Tax Credit

Child Tax Credit is a means-tested benefit paid directly into the bank account of the main carer of the child(ren), on a weekly or four-weekly basis.

Child Tax Credit neither is affected by, nor affects, Child Benefit (see below).

Child Tax Credit is based initially on the income of the previous tax year.

The claim is corrected to actual income basis in due course.

Before April 2012 Child Tax Credit was usually available if income did not exceed a limit of £41,300. From April 6, 2012 this limit is lower for most people and depends on the claimant's individual circumstances. As a rough guide, no Child Tax Credit will be available from April 6, 2012 where the claimant has:

—one child and annual income of more than about £26,000; or

—two children and annual income of more than about £32,200.

Taxation of savings income

Savings income is subdivided into dividends and other savings income, with dividends treated as the top slice of savings income.

Tax is payable on dividend income at the dividend ordinary rate of 10 per cent up to the basic rate limit, and at the dividend upper rate of 32.5 per cent thereafter up to the higher rate limit.

From 2010/11, in addition to these rates tax is payable on dividend income falling into the additional rate band at the dividend additional rate, as follows:

Tax year 2010/11	42.5 per cent
Tax year 2011/12	42.5 per cent
Tax year 2012/13	42.5 per cent
Tax year 2013/14	37.5 per cent

Tax is payable on other savings income at 10 per cent on income in the starting rate band, at 20 per cent on income in the basic rate band, and at 40 per cent thereafter up to the higher rate limit.

From 2010/11, in addition to these rates tax is payable on other savings income falling into the additional rate band at the following rates:

Tax year 2010/11	50 per cent
Tax year 2011/12	50 per cent
Tax year 2012/13	50 per cent
Tax year 2013/14	45 per cent

From 2008/09, there has been a new 10 per cent starting rate for savings income only, with the following limits:

Tax year 2008/09	£2,320
Tax year 2009/10	£2,440
Tax year 2010/11	£2,440
Tax year 2011/12	£2,560
Tax year 2012/13	£2,710
Tax year 2013/14	£2,790

If the taxpayer's non-savings income exceeds these limits, the 10 per cent savings rate does not apply. This does not affect the dividend ordinary, upper and additional rates applicable for the year.

2006/07 to 2013/14

Fiscal year:	2006/07 £	2007/08 £	2008/09 £	2009/10 £	2010/11 £	2011/12 £	2012/13 £	2013/14 £
Income tax reliefs								
Personal allowance	5,035	5,225	6,035	6,475	6,475*	7,475*	8,105*	9,440*
Income tax rates								
Starting rate band – Payable at 10%	2,150	2,230	–	–	–	–	–	–
Basic rate band – Payable at 20%	–	–	34,800	37,400	37,400	35,000	34,370	32,010
Basic rate band – Payable at 22%	31,150	32,370	–	–	–	–	–	–
Higher rate band – Payable at 40%	Balance	Balance	Balance	Balance	112,600	115,000	115,630	117,990
Additional rate band – Payable at 45%	–	–	–	–	–	–	–	Balance
– Payable at 50%	–	–	–	–	Balance	Balance	Balance	–

* Please refer to the preceding note on personal allowance.

G4: National Insurance contributions

Introductory notes

1. Married women and widows have been able to elect to pay a reduced contribution as follows:

   - 4.85 per cent on earnings between primary threshold and upper earnings limit, and 1 per cent on earnings above upper earnings limit from 2003/04 to 2010/11.

   - 5.85 per cent on earnings between primary threshold and upper earnings limit, and 2 per cent on earnings above upper earnings limit in 2011/12 and 2013/14.

2. Class 1 employee contributions and Class 2 contributions cease to be payable when a man has reached 65 and a woman 60.

3. Class 4 contributions are not payable in respect of any fiscal year that starts after pensionable age has been reached.

4. Class 3 contributions are voluntary at a flat weekly rate (£13.55pw in 2013/14).

5. From April 6, 2009 an Upper Accrual Point (UAP) was introduced at a frozen rate of £770.00 per week for the calculation of the State Second Pension (S2P) and Class 1 National Insurance rebates under contracted-out schemes. From the same date the Upper Earnings Limit (UEL) previously used for these purposes was aligned with the higher rate threshold for income tax.

2006/07 to 2009/10

Fiscal year:	2006/07 £	2007/08 £	2008/09 £	2009/10 £
Class 1 contributions (Employees)				
Lower earnings limit (LEL) (pa)	4,368	4,524	4,680	4,940
Primary threshold (PT) (pa)	5,035	5,225	5,435	5,715
Upper Accrual Point				40,040
Upper earnings limit (UEL) (pa)	33,540	34,840	40,040	43,875
Standard rate				
If earnings below LEL:	Nil	Nil	Nil	Nil
If earnings at or above LEL: – Contribution rate on earnings up to PT	Nil	Nil	Nil	Nil
– Contribution rate on earnings between PT and UEL	11%	11%	11%	11%
– Contribution rate on earnings above UEL	1%	1%	1%	1%
Maximum contribution (pa)	3,135 +1% of excess over UEL	3,258 +1% of excess over UEL	3,807 +1% of excess over UEL	4,198 +1% of excess over UEL
Contracted out rate				
As standard rate except – Contribution rate on earnings between PT and UEL	9.4%	9.4%	9.4%	
– Contribution rate on earnings between PT and UAP				9.4%
– Contribution rate on earnings between UAP and UEL				11.0%
Maximum contribution (pa)	2,679 +1% of excess over UEL	2,784 +1% of excess over UEL	3,253 +1% of excess over UEL	3,648 +1% of excess over UEL
Class 2 contributions (Self-employed)				
Small earnings exception limit	4,465	4,635	4,825	5,075
Fixed weekly contributions (pw)	2.10	2.20	2.30	2.40
Class 4 contributions (Self-employed)				
Lower profits limit (LPL) (pa)	5,035	5,225	5,435	5,715
Upper profits limit (UPL) (pa)	33,540	34,840	40,040	43,875
Contribution rate on profits between LPL and UPL	8.0%	8.0%	8.0%	8.0%
Contribution rate on profits above UPL	1.0%	1.0%	1.0%	1.0%
Maximum contribution (pa)	2,280 +1% of excess over UPL	2,369 +1% of excess over UPL	2,768 +1% of excess over UPL	3,053 +1% of excess over UPL

2010/11 to 2013/14

Fiscal year:	2010/11 £	2011/12 £	2012/13 £	2013/14 £
Class 1 contributions (Employees)				
Lower earnings limit (LEL) (pa)	5,044	5,304	5,564	5,668
Primary threshold (PT) (pa)	5,715	7,225	7,605	7,755
Upper Accrual Point	40,040	40,040	40,040	40,040
Upper earnings limit (UEL) (pa)	43,875	42,475	42,475	41,450
Standard rate				
If earnings below LEL:	Nil	Nil	Nil	Nil
If earnings at or above LEL: – Contribution rate on earnings up to PT	Nil	Nil	Nil	Nil
– Contribution rate on earnings between PT and UEL	11%	12%	12%	12%
– Contribution rate on earnings above UEL	1%	2%	2%	2%
Maximum contribution (pa)	4,198 +1% of excess over UEL	4,230 +2% of excess over UEL	4,184 +2% of excess over UEL	4,043 +2% of excess over UEL
Contracted out rate				
As standard rate except – Contribution rate on earnings between PT and UEL				
– Contribution rate on earnings between PT and UAP	9.4%	10.4%	10.6%	10.6%
– Contribution rate on earnings between UAP and UEL	11.0%	12.0%	12.0%	12.0%
Maximum contribution (pa)	3,648 +1% of excess over UEL	3,705 +2% of excess over UEL	3,730 +2% of excess over UEL	3,591 +2% of excess over UEL
Class 2 contributions (Self-employed)				
Small earnings exception limit	5,075	5,315	5,595	5,725
Fixed weekly contributions (pw)	2.40	2.50	2.65	2.70
Class 4 contributions (Self-employed)				
Lower profits limit (LPL) (pa)	5,715	7,225	7,605	7,755
Upper profits limit (UPL) (pa)	43,875	42,475	42,475	41,450
Contribution rate on profits between LPL and UPL	8.0%	9.0%	9.0%	9.0%
Contribution rate on profits above UPL	1.0%	2.0%	2.0%	2.0%
Maximum contribution (pa)	3,053 +1% of excess over UPL	3,173 +2% of excess over UPL	3,138 +2% of excess over UPL	3,033 +2% of excess over UPL

G5: VAT registration thresholds and rates

Registration is required when a person's turnover (taxable supplies from all the person's businesses) exceeds prescribed limits.

Past and future turnover limits apply (looking one year back and one year forward).

Registration is also required if a turnover limit is to be exceeded in a period of 30 days.

De-registration depends on satisfying HM Revenue & Customs that the future annual limit (e.g. £79,000 from April 1, 2013) will not be exceeded.

The registration levels are:

	Past turnover		Future turnover
	one year	Unless turnover for next year will not exceed	30 days
	£	£	£
From April 1, 2013	79,000	77,000	79,000
April 1, 2012 to March 31, 2013	77,000	75,000	77,000
April 1, 2011 to March 31, 2012	73,000	71,000	73,000
April 1, 2010 to March 31, 2011	70,000	68,000	70,000
May 1, 2009 to March 31, 2010	68,000	66,000	68,000
April 1, 2008 to April 30, 2009	67,000	65,000	67,000
April 1, 2007 to March 31, 2008	64,000	62,000	64,000
April 1, 2006 to March 31, 2007	61,000	59,000	61,000
April 1, 2005 to March 31, 2006	60,000	58,000	60,000
April 1, 2004 to March 31, 2005	58,000	56,000	58,000

Note:

These limits can be of particular relevance in considering likely turnover levels for businesses such as taxis and driving schools, where VAT registration may render charges uncompetitive (because most such businesses operate below the registration limits).

VAT Rates

Date	VAT Rate
From January 4, 2011	20.0%
January 1, 2010 to January 3, 2011	17.5%
December 1, 2008 to December 31, 2009	15.0%
April 1, 1991 to November 30, 2008	15.0%

Group H
Pension

H1:   **Net equivalents to a range of gross annual pension figures**

H2:   **Illustrative net pension calculations**

H3:   **Note on pension losses**

H

H1: Net equivalents to a range of gross annual pension figures

Introductory notes

1. The following table sets out the net equivalents to a range of annual pension figures in 2013/14, distinguishing between:

   - a single person aged under 65;

   - a single person aged 65–74 at any time during the tax year;

   - a single person aged 75 or over at any time during the tax year;

   - a married person aged under 65;

   - a married person aged 65–74 at any time during the tax year; and

   - a married person aged 75 or over at any time during the tax year.

2. The table is followed by illustrative net pension calculations for each marital status and age category, at income levels of £15,000, £20,000, £30,000, £50,000, £110,000 and £160,000 per annum.

3. The age ranges selected reflect the availability of age-related personal and married couple's allowances, as detailed in G3.

4. Since pensions are not subject to National Insurance contributions, the net equivalent figures represent the gross pension less income tax. Given that liability to primary Class 1 National Insurance contributions falls away when the earner has reached pensionable age [note 2 of G4], it follows that the net equivalent figures for those aged 65 and over apply equally to earnings from employment and pensions.

   Similarly, given that Class 4 contributions are not payable in respect of any fiscal year that starts after pensionable age has been reached [note 3 of G4], it follows that the net equivalent figures for those aged 65 and over apply also to earnings from self-employment where pensionable age has been reached in a prior fiscal year.

H1: Net equivalents to a range of gross annual pension figures

	2013/14 Net equivalent pension					
	Single, or married where neither spouse was born before 6.4.35			Married, where either spouse was born before 6.4.35		
Gross pension £pa	Aged under 65 £pa	Aged 65–74 £pa	Aged 75 or over £pa	Aged under 65 £pa	Aged 65–74 £pa	Aged 75 or over £pa
1,000	1,000	1,000	1,000	1,000	1,000	1,000
2,000	2,000	2,000	2,000	2,000	2,000	2,000
3,000	3,000	3,000	3,000	3,000	3,000	3,000
4,000	4,000	4,000	4,000	4,000	4,000	4,000
5,000	5,000	5,000	5,000	5,000	5,000	5,000
6,000	6,000	6,000	6,000	6,000	6,000	6,000
7,000	7,000	7,000	7,000	7,000	7,000	7,000
8,000	8,000	8,000	8,000	8,000	8,000	8,000
9,000	9,000	9,000	9,000	9,000	9,000	9,000
10,000	9,888	10,000	10,000	9,888	10,000	10,000
11,000	10,688	10,900	10,932	10,688	10,900	11,000
12,000	11,488	11,700	11,732	11,488	11,700	12,000
13,000	12,288	12,500	12,532	12,288	12,500	13,000
14,000	13,088	13,300	13,332	13,088	13,300	14,000
15,000	13,888	14,100	14,132	13,888	14,100	14,924
16,000	14,688	14,900	14,932	14,688	14,900	15,724
17,000	15,488	15,700	15,732	15,488	15,700	16,524
18,000	16,288	16,500	16,532	16,288	16,500	17,324
19,000	17,088	17,300	17,332	17,088	17,300	18,124
20,000	17,888	18,100	18,132	17,888	18,100	18,924
21,000	18,688	18,900	18,932	18,688	18,900	19,724
22,000	19,488	19,700	19,732	19,488	19,700	20,524
23,000	20,288	20,500	20,532	20,288	20,500	21,324
24,000	21,088	21,300	21,332	21,088	21,300	22,124
25,000	21,888	22,100	22,132	21,888	22,100	22,924
26,000	22,688	22,900	22,932	22,688	22,900	23,724
27,000	23,488	23,610	23,642	23,488	23,610	24,434
28,000	24,288	24,310	24,342	24,288	24,310	25,134
29,000	25,088	25,088	25,088	25,088	25,088	25,857
30,000	25,888	25,888	25,888	25,888	25,888	26,607
31,000	26,688	26,688	26,688	26,688	26,688	27,357
32,000	27,488	27,488	27,488	27,488	27,488	28,107
33,000	28,288	28,288	28,288	28,288	28,288	28,857
34,000	29,088	29,088	29,088	29,088	29,088	29,607
35,000	29,888	29,888	29,888	29,888	29,888	30,357
40,000	33,888	33,888	33,888	33,888	33,888	34,192
45,000	37,178	37,178	37,178	37,178	37,178	37,482
50,000	40,178	40,178	40,178	40,178	40,178	40,482
55,000	43,178	43,178	43,178	43,178	43,178	43,482
60,000	46,178	46,178	46,178	46,178	46,178	46,482
65,000	49,178	49,178	49,178	49,178	49,178	49,482
70,000	52,178	52,178	52,178	52,178	52,178	52,482
75,000	55,178	55,178	55,178	55,178	55,178	55,482
80,000	58,178	58,178	58,178	58,178	58,178	58,482
85,000	61,178	61,178	61,178	61,178	61,178	61,482
90,000	64,178	64,178	64,178	64,178	64,178	64,482
95,000	67,178	67,178	67,178	67,178	67,178	67,482
100,000	70,178	70,178	70,178	70,178	70,178	70,482
120,000	78,402	78,402	78,402	78,402	78,402	78,706
140,000	90,402	90,402	90,402	90,402	90,402	90,706
160,000	101,902	101,902	101,902	101,902	101,902	102,206

H2: Illustrative net pension calculations

Single person aged under 65 at 2013/14 rates

		£pa	£pa	£pa	£pa	£pa	£pa
Gross pension	[a]	15,000	20,000	30,000	50,000	110,000	160,000
Income tax							
Gross		15,000	20,000	30,000	50,000	110,000	160,000
Personal allowance		(9,440)	(9,440)	(9,440)	(9,440)	(4,440)	–
Taxable		5,560	10,560	20,560	40,560	105,560	160,000
Tax payable							
– At 20%		1,112	2,112	4,112	6,402	6,402	6,402
– At 40%					3,420	29,420	47,196
– At 45%							4,500
	[b]	1,112	2,112	4,112	9,822	35,822	58,098
Net income	[a–b]	13,888	17,888	25,888	40,178	74,178	101,902
Net % of gross		92.6%	89.4%	86.3%	80.4%	67.4%	63.7%
Note 1: personal allowance							
Personal allowance		9,440	9,440	9,440	9,440	9,440	4,440
Restriction for excess of income over limit*		–	–	–	–	(5,000)	(9,440)
Net allowance		9,440	9,440	9,440	9,440	4,440	–

*If gross pay does not exceed £100,000, no restriction.
If gross pay does exceed £100,000, restriction is the lower of:
(a) (gross pay–£100,000)/2; and
(b) £9,440.

Single person aged between 65 and 74 at 2013/14 rates

		£pa	£pa	£pa	£pa	£pa	£pa
Gross pension	[a]	15,000	20,000	30,000	50,000	110,000	160,000
Income tax							
Gross		15,000	20,000	30,000	50,000	110,000	160,000
Personal allowance (note 1)		(10,500)	(10,500)	(9,440)	(9,440)	(5,500)	–
Taxable		4,500	9,500	20,560	40,560	104,500	160,000
Tax payable							
– At 20%		900	1,900	4,112	6,402	6,402	6,402
– At 40%					3,420	28,996	47,196
– At 45%							4,500
	[b]	900	1,900	4,112	9,822	35,398	58,098
Net income	[a–b]	14,100	18,100	25,888	40,178	74,602	101,902
Net % of gross		94.0%	90.5%	86.3%	80.4%	67.8%	63.7%
Note 1: personal allowance							
Allowance for age 65–74		10,500	10,500	10,500	10,500	10,500	10,500
Restriction for excess of income over limits*		–	–	(1,060)	(1,060)	(5,000)	(10,500)
Net allowance		10,500	10,500	9,440	9,440	5,500	–

*If gross pension does not exceed £26,100, no restriction.
If gross pension does exceed £26,100, but does not exceed £100,000,
restriction is the lower of:
(a) (gross pension–£26,100)/2; and
(b) £10,500 – £9,440 = £1,060
If gross pension exceeds £100,000, restriction is the lower of:
(a) (gross pension–£100,000)/2; and
(b) £10,500

Single person aged 75 or over at 2013/14 rates

		£pa	£pa	£pa	£pa	£pa	£pa
Gross pension	[a]	15,000	20,000	30,000	50,000	110,000	160,000
Income tax							
Gross		15,000	20,000	30,000	50,000	110,000	160,000
Personal allowance (note 1)		(10,660)	(10,660)	(9,440)	(9,440)	(5,660)	–
Taxable		4,340	9,340	20,560	40,560	104,340	160,000
Tax payable							
– At 20%		868	1,868	4,112	6,402	6,402	6,402
– At 40%					3,420	28,932	47,196
– At 45%							4,500
	[b]	868	1,868	4,112	9,822	35,334	58,098
Net income	[a–b]	14,132	18,132	25,888	40,178	74,666	101,902
Net % of gross		94.2%	90.7%	86.3%	80.4%	67.9%	63.7%
Note 1: personal allowance							
Allowance for age 75 and over		10,660	10,660	10,660	10,660	10,660	10,660
Restriction for excess of income over limits*		–	–	(1,220)	(1,220)	(5,000)	(10,660)
Net allowance		10,660	10,660	9,440	9,440	5,660	–

*If gross pension does not exceed £26,100, no restriction.
If gross pension does exceed £26,100, but does not exceed £100,000, restriction is the lower of:
(a) (gross pension–£26,100)/2; and
(b) £10,660 – £9,440 = £1,220
If gross pension exceeds £100,000, restriction is the lower of:
(a) (gross pension–£100,000)/2; and
(b) £10,660

Married person aged under 65 at 2013/14 rates

		£pa	£pa	£pa	£pa	£pa	£pa
Gross pension	[a]	15,000	20,000	30,000	50,000	110,000	160,000
Income tax							
Gross		15,000	20,000	30,000	50,000	110,000	160,000
Personal allowance		(9,440)	(9,440)	(9,440)	(9,440)	(4,440)	–
Taxable		5,560	10,560	20,560	40,560	105,560	160,000
Tax payable							
– At 20%		1,112	2,112	4,112	6,402	6,402	6,402
– At 40%					3,420	29,420	47,196
– At 45%							4,500
	[b]	1,112	2,112	4,112	9,822	35,822	58,098
Net income	[a–b]	13,888	17,888	25,888	40,178	74,178	101,902
Net % of gross		92.6%	89.4%	86.3%	80.4%	67.4%	63.7%
Note 1: personal allowance							
Personal allowance		9,440	9,440	9,440	9,440	9,440	9,440
Restriction for excess of income over limit*		–	–	–	–	(5,000)	(9,440)
Net allowance		9,440	9,440	9,440	9,440	4,440	–

*If gross pension does not exceed £100,000, no restriction.
If gross pension does exceed £100,000, restriction is the lower of:
(a) (gross pay–£100,000)/2; and
(b) £9,440

Married person aged between 65 and 74 at 2013/14 rates

		£pa	£pa	£pa	£pa	£pa	£pa
Gross pension	[a]	15,000	20,000	30,000	50,000	110,000	160,000
Income tax							
Gross		15,000	20,000	30,000	50,000	110,000	160,000
Personal allowance (note 1)		(10,500)	(10,500)	(9,440)	(9,440)	(5,500)	–
Taxable		4,500	9,500	20,560	40,560	104,500	160,000
Tax payable							
– At 20%		900	1,900	4,112	6,402	6,402	6,402
– At 40%					3,420	28,996	47,196
– At 45%							4,500
	[b]	900	1,900	4,112	9,822	35,398	58,098
Net income	[a–b]	14,100	18,100	25,888	40,178	74,602	101,902
Net % of gross		94.0%	90.5%	86.3%	80.4%	67.8%	63.7%

Note 1: personal allowance

	£pa	£pa	£pa	£pa	£pa	£pa
Personal allowance for age 65 to 74	10,500	10,500	10,500	10,500	10,500	10,500
Restriction for excess of income over limits*	–	–	(1,060)	(1,060)	(5,000)	(10,500)
Net allowance	10,500	10,500	9,440	9,440	5,500	–

*If gross pension does not exceed £26,100, no restriction.
If gross pension does exceed £26,100, but does not exceed £100,000,
restriction is the lower of:
(a) (gross pension–£26,100)/2; and
(b) £10,500 – £9,440 = £1,060
If gross pension exceeds £100,000, restriction is the lower of:
(a) (gross pension–£100,000)/2; and
(b) £10,500

Married person aged 75 or over at 2013/14 rates

		£pa	£pa	£pa	£pa	£pa	£pa
Gross pension	[a]	15,000	20,000	30,000	50,000	110,000	160,000
Income tax							
Gross		15,000	20,000	30,000	50,000	110,000	160,000
Personal allowance (note 1)		(10,660)	(10,660)	(9,440)	(9,440)	(5,660)	–
Taxable		4,340	9,340	20,560	40,560	104,340	160,000
Tax payable							
– At 20%		868	1,868	4,112	6,402	6,402	6,402
– At 40%					3,420	28,932	47,196
– At 45%							4,500
		868	1,868	4,112	9,822	35,334	58,098
Relief for married couple's allowance (note 2)		(792)	(792)	(719)	(304)	(304)	(304)
	[b]	77	1,077	3,394	9,518	35,030	57,794
Net income	[a–b]	14,924	18,924	26,607	40,482	74,970	102,206
Net % of gross		99.5%	94.6%	88.7%	81.0%	68.2%	63.9%

Note 1: personal allowance

	£pa	£pa	£pa	£pa	£pa	£pa
Personal allowance for age 75 and over	10,660	10,660	10,660	10,660	10,660	10,660
Restriction for excess of income over limits*	–	–	(1,220)	(1,220)	(5,000)	(10,660)
Net allowance	10,660	10,660	9,440	9,440	5,660	–

*If gross pension does not exceed £26,100, no restriction.
If gross pension does exceed £26,100, but does not exceed £100,000, restriction is the lower of:
(a) (gross pension–£26,100)/2; and
(b) £10,660 – £9,440 = £1,220
If gross pension exceeds £100,000, restriction is the lower of:
(a) (gross pension–£100,000)/2; and
(b) £10,660

Note 2: married couple's allowance

Assumptions:
1 at least one spouse born before April 6, 1935; and
2 full married couple's allowance allocated to pensioner.

	£pa	£pa	£pa	£pa	£pa	£pa
Married couple's allowance for age 75 and over	7,915	7,915	7,915	7,915	7,915	7,915
Retriction for excess of income over limit*	–	–	(730)	(4,875)	(4,875)	(4,875))
Net allowance	7,915	7,915	7,185	3,040	3,040	3,040
Relief at 10%	792	792	719	304	304	304

*If gross pension does not exceed £26,100, no restriction.
If gross pension does exceed £26,100, restriction is the lower of:
(a) (gross pension–£26,100)/2] **less** restriction of personal allowance; and
(b) £7,915 – £3,040 = £4,875

H3: Note on pension losses

1. Purpose of note

The purpose of this note is to provide some basic guidance to practitioners who need to consider whether a pension loss is likely to arise in any specific case.

2. "Final Salary" or "Money Purchase" scheme?

Ascertain which type of scheme was being contributed to.

Final Salary schemes (also known as Deferred Benefit schemes)

- benefits are defined in advance, usually in terms of:

  - final salary,
  - number of years of service,
  - a factor (often 1/60th or 1/80th for each year of service), and

- the financial risk of ensuring that benefits are paid lies with the employer.

Money Purchase schemes (also known as Personal Pensions and/or Defined Contribution schemes)

- benefits depend on a combination of:

  - the amounts paid in by the member,
  - any amounts paid in by the employer (if there is one),
  - the investment returns achieved up to retirement,
  - the annuity rates available on retirement, and

- the financial risk lies with the member.

By definition, a self-employed person will have no employer contributions.

3. Is there likely to be a loss?

Start by assuming that there will be a loss to be evaluated, if:

  - the claimant was contributing to a pension scheme;
  - there is a claim for loss of earnings; and
  - there was an employer contribution.

4. Final salary scheme member

Potential pension:

- Obtain a copy of the members' guide (which will often be in simple terms).

- Obtain a copy of the most recent statement of the individual members' scheme benefits (an estimate of pension at normal retirement age based on current salary).

- With these documents, and the projection of final salary being used for evaluating loss of earnings, it should be possible to calculate the expected pension at retirement date (at its present day value).

Actual pension:

- Establish the actual (reduced) pension that will be payable at normal retirement date (at its present day value).

Proceed by:

- Applying *Wells v Wells* principles.[1] Table A8 refers.

- Calculating loss of annual pension (after tax). Table H1 will assist.

- Applying an appropriate multiplier drawn from the Ogden tables. Tables A1 and A8 refer.

Calculations incorporating a loss of lump sum benefit can be complex and will only be possible if the effect that taking the lump sum has on the annual pension can be ascertained with reasonable certainty. (Public pension schemes usually provide separately for lump sum and annual pension benefits, so the figures are generally straightforward to ascertain.)

5. **Money purchase scheme member**

A forensic accountant will often approach evaluation of loss along the following lines:

Potential pension:

- Ascertain current value of pension fund.

- Calculate contributions foregone (payable by member and by employer if applicable).

- Calculate value of potential pension fund at retirement, based on contributions foregone and an assumed rate of investment return within the fund.

- Calculate in turn:

    ■ the lump sum benefit available on retirement (discounted to present day value), and
    ■ the gross annual pension (based on annuity tables).

Actual pension:

- Calculate value of actual pension fund at retirement, based on any future contributions to the scheme and the assumed rate of investment return within the fund.

- Calculate in turn:

    ■ the lump sum benefit available (discounted to present day value), and
    ■ the gross annual pension.

Proceed by:

- Calculating the loss of lump sum (at present day value).

- Calculating the loss of annual pension (after tax). Table H1 will assist.

[1] [1999] 1 A.C. 345.

- Applying an appropriate multiplier drawn from the Ogden tables.

- Consider whether any further adjustments should be applied, of the sort discussed at Table A8.

6. Important cases

Have regard to:

- *Parry v Cleaver*[1]:

Briefly: pension loss only runs from anticipated retirement age.

So that: no credit need be given against earnings losses for an early/ill health pension

- *Longden v British Coal Corporation*[2]:

Briefly: explains how to apportion an actual tax-free lump sum received ahead of expected retirement age between pre- and post-retirement periods.

So that: treatment of the actual lump sum is brought into line with *Parry v Cleaver* principles.

- *Aboul-Hosn v Trustees of the Italian Hospital*[3]:

Briefly: allows for a simple calculation in which pension loss is based on the tax relief foregone on the claimant's potential personal pension contributions.

(This would only be appropriate in a case where there are no employer contributions foregone.)

7. Further points

- Do not rely on quotations from pension providers; they invariably incorporate inflation and are not therefore compatible with conventional multipliers.

- Keep in mind the reality of life expectancy. If life expectancy is impaired, pension loss will be reduced.

- That said, do not overlook the possibility of a "lost years" claim in respect of pension losses between the end of the post-accident life expectancy and the end of the pre-accident life expectancy.

- Do not assume that males necessarily retire at 65 and females at 60.

- Bear in mind that, between April 2010 and April 2020, the state pension age for women will gradually increase from 60–65. The state pension age is then set to increase from 65 to 68 between 2024 and 2046. There is a state pension age calculator at *http://www.the pensionservice.gov.uk*.

- Claims for loss of state pension may arise, particularly in relation to the State Second Pension (S2P).

- Smaller pension losses may sometimes not be worth pursuing, given the safety net of the State Pension Credit. See Table I2.

[1] [1970] A.C. 1.
[2] [1998] A.C. 653.
[3] (1987) (unreported).

Group I
Benefits, Allowances, Charges

I1:   **Social security benefits (non-means-tested)**

I2:   **Social security benefits and tax credits (means-tested)**

I3:   **Personal injury trusts**

I4:   **Claims for loss of earnings and maintenance at public expense**

I5:   **Foster care allowances**

I

I1: Social Security benefits (non-means-tested)

How they work

Generally, all of these benefits may be claimed independently of each other. However, there are overlapping benefit rules which prevent more than one income replacement benefit being payable. If the claimant is entitled to more than one income replacement benefit, then the amount of the highest will be payable.

Many benefits are contributory, entitlement being dependent on satisfying conditions as to amount of national insurance contributions paid.

Until April 2003, increases were payable for many benefits for dependent children, subject to an earnings limit. The increases have now been replaced by child tax credit (see section I2) but people in receipt of the increases on April 5, 2003 have transitional protection.

Entitlement to non-means-tested benefits is frequently affected if claimants are in hospital or in full-time care.

Claims for all benefits must be made in writing. Claims can be backdated only to a limited extent (varying according to the type of benefit).

A. Income replacement

1. Retirement

Retirement Pension	2013–2014
Claimant (Category A)	£110.15
(Category B)	£66.00
Adult dependant	£66.00

Either spouse/civil partner may qualify in their own right (Category A) or as a spouse or civil partner (Category B). Special rules apply for parents, carers, divorced people, widows and widowers. Women's State Pension age is gradually increasing to 65 by November 2018.

Highly variable rates according to contribution history.

Contributory and taxable.

For information for Form E submit Form BR20 (for valuation of additional state pension); or Form BR19 (for benefit forecast): downloadable at *http://www.direct.gov.uk*

2. Ill Health

i. Statutory Sick Pay	2013–2014
Standard rate	£86.70

Paid by the employer for up to 168 days (28 six-day weeks), to employees earning not less than £107 gross p.w. Taxable.

ii. Incapacity Benefit (IB)   2013–2014

Employment and Support Allowance (ESA, below) has replaced IB for new claimants. Surviving IB claimants to have moved to ESA by March 2014.

Short-term (under pension age)	
Lower rate	£76.45
Higher rate	£9.50
Adult dependant—extra	£44.85
Short-term (over pension age)	
Lower rate	£97.25
Higher rate	£101.35
Adult dependant—extra	£56.65
Long-term (under pension age)	£99.15
Increase for age Higher rate	£11.70
Lower rate	£6.00
Adult dependant—extra	£57.60

Higher rate applies from week 29. Long-term IB payable after first 52 weeks.

Increase for age arises at higher rate when incapacity began under 35; lower rate if under 45. Higher rate being reduced to come into line with ESA allowances.

Restrictions apply to dependants' allowances.

Contributory (save for those incapacitated in youth). Taxable, except short-term lower rate and transitional benefits.

iii. Employment and Support Allowance (ESA)   2013–2014

(Replaces IB and IS (Table 29) paid on disability grounds for claims made since October 2008)

Maximum Basic Rate	
Single claimant	£71.70
Couple	£112.55
Work-related component	£28.45
(for those meeting new limited capability for work test)	
Support component	£34.80
(for those assessed as more severely disabled)	
Premiums (means-tested)	
Enhanced disability—single	£15.15
Enhanced disability—couple	£21.75
Severe disability—single/couple (lower rate)	£59.50
Severe disability—couple (higher rate)	£119.00
Carer premium	£33.30

Includes both contributory and "income-related" (means-tested) benefit, based on either limited capability for work (placed in "work-related activity

Entitlement to contributory benefits depends on payment of National Insurance Contributions. Amounts are per week.

group", helped to prepare for suitable work) or limited capability for work-related activity (not expected to work, placed in support group).

Benefit paid at basic rate during 13-week assessment phase. Lower rates for under 25s during assessment period; youth ESA abolished for new claimants from April 2012; existing claimants able to go on claiming, but only for one year from entitlement, disregarding time in support group. Contributory ESA: time-limited to one year for those in work-related activity group; also no age or spouse's additions, and no housing costs allowances. Income related ESA (IRESA): assessment, housing costs and capital rules modelled on IS (Table 29). Child maintenance and up to £20 earnings p.w. disregarded (or 16 hours p.w. earning up to £97.50 p.w. for 52 weeks). Passport to other benefits including full HB and CTB (HB & CTB: Table 29). Contributory ESA taxable: IRESA not.

iv. Carer's Allowance

	2013–2014
Claimant	£59.75
Adult dependant—extra	£35.15

Paid to people over 16 who spend at least 35 hours p.w. caring for recipient of higher or middle rates of Care Component of Disability Living Allowance, Attendance Allowance, or Constant Attendance Allowance at or above the normal rate with a related pension. Claimant can earn no more than £100 p.w. net and must not be in full-time education; however, entitled to offset against earnings up to half any sums paid to someone else (not close relative) to care for either recipient of allowances or carer's children under 16. Adult dependency increase abolished for new claims from April 2010. Non-contributory; not means-tested.

Claimant's benefit and adult dependency increases are taxable; child dependency increases are not.

3. Unemployment—Jobseeker's Allowance (JSA)

i. Contribution-based JSA

		2013–2014
Claimant	18–24	£56.25
	25 and over	£71.00

ii. Income-based JSA (IBJSA)

		2013–2014
Claimant	16–24	£56.80
	25 and over	£71.70
Couple Both over 18		£112.55
Dependent children		
—(existing claimants only—		
others see Child Tax Credit)		
till day before 20th birthday		£65.62

Premiums: as for IS (Table 29)

Contributory JSA is age-related flat-rate payment; without dependant allowances: paid for up to 26 weeks. IBJSA is paid with, or from expiry of, contributory JSA, with IS-style rules for income, capital, premiums and mortgage interest.

Personal allowance payments and premiums for children being phased out (replaced by child tax credit). Child maintenance is disregarded. Claimants must be under State Pension age, available for and actively seeking work, and have a current Jobseeker's Agreement: IBJSA is a passport to other benefits including full HB & CTB. Men are eligible for Pension Credit (PC) although those who are not yet 65 may claim PC instead.

Main rates only given. Not usually available for those under 18 or those working 16+ hours p.w. Only main rates shown.

Personal allowance taxable.

4. Maternity/paternity/adoption

i. Statutory Maternity Pay (SMP)

	2013–2014
Average earnings threshold	£109.00
Higher rate (first 6 weeks)	90 per cent of average weekly wage
Lower rate (for up to next 33 weeks)	£136.78[2]

Paid by employer for a maximum of 39 weeks. Taxable.

ii. Statutory Paternity Pay (SPP)

	2013–2014
Average earnings threshold	£109.00
Rate	£136.78[2]

Payable for up to two weeks. Additional SPP at same rate if upon mother's return to work, baby 20 weeks old and she would otherwise still be entitled to SMP, SAP or MA. Not payable beyond mother's 39-week maternity period. Taxable.

iii. Maternity Allowance

	2013–2014
Average earnings threshold	£30.00
Standard rate	£136.78[2]

Paid to claimants not entitled to SMP but employed or self-employed for at least 26 weeks in 66 weeks before due date, and average pay over earnings threshold. Maximum 39 weeks (during which may work up to 10 days). Adult dependency increases no longer paid. Non-taxable.

iv. Statutory Adoption Pay[1]

	2013–2014
Average earnings threshold	£109.00
Standard rate	£136.78

Paid by employer for a maximum of 39 weeks. Taxable.

[1] *Qualifying conditions based on length of service and average earnings*
[2] *Or (if less) 90% of the parent's weekly average earnings*

Entitlement to contributory benefits depends on payment of National Insurance Contributions. Amounts are per week.

v. Surestart Maternity Grant

	2013–2014
Standard one-off payment	£500.00

Subject to complex conditions. Available only for first child.

5. ADDITIONAL CHILD PAYMENTS FOR SPECIFIED BENEFITS

	2013–2014
Oldest child with child benefit	£8.10
Each other child with child benefit	£11.35

Mostly abolished.

6. BEREAVEMENT

i. Bereavement Benefit

	2013–2014
Lump sum	£2,000.00

ii. Bereavement allowance (age-related)

32.49 to £108.30

Available to bereaved spouses/civil partners over 45 but under State Pension age who do not remarry or cohabit and who are not bringing up children. Standard rate £108.30 for those 55 and over.

Payable for up to 52 weeks from date of bereavement.

iii. Widowed Parent's Allowance £108.30

Available to bereaved spouses/civil partners under State Pension age and in receipt of child benefit who do not remarry or cohabit.

Widowed Parent's Allowance and Bereavement Allowance cannot be claimed together.

All benefits are contributory and (save lump sum) taxable.

B. Special needs

1. PERSONAL INDEPENDENCE PAYMENT (PIP)

		2013–2014
Care Component	Highest	£79.15
	Middle	£53.00
	Lowest	£21.00
Mobility Component	Higher	£55.25
	Lower	£21.00

The claimant must qualify before reaching 65. Available to under-16s too.

2. ATTENDANCE ALLOWANCE

	2013–2014
Higher rate	£79.15
Lower rate	£53.00

Paid for care needs of those over 65.

Both allowances are based on need, but there are no restrictions on how they are used. Both allowances are non-contributory, non-means-tested, non-taxable and are ignored as income for means-tested benefits

C. Children

1. CHILD BENEFIT (CB)

	2013
Only/elder/eldest child	£20.30
Each subsequent child	£13.40

A child must be under 16, or under 20 and in full-time secondary education, or under 18 and registered for work or work-based training. Will no longer be available to all high rate tax payers from 2013 onwards. Non-contributory and non-taxable.

Administered by HMRC.

2. GUARDIAN'S ALLOWANCE

	2013–2014
Guardian's allowance	£15.90

Payable with child benefit to those raising the children of deceased (or, sometimes, unavailable) parents. Non-contributory, non-taxable. Administered by HMRC.

Entitlement to contributory benefits depends on payment of National Insurance Contributions.

Amounts are per week except for the Surestart Maternity Grant payment and Bereavement benefit lump sum.

I2: Social security benefits and tax credits (means-tested)

Income Support (IS) 2012–2013

For reduced cohort of those under pension age on low income, working less than 16 hrs p.w. (e.g. lone parents of young children, carers, some sick workers and some students). Not for the unemployed (see JSA: Table 28) or new claimants who are sick/disabled (see ESA: ibid.) or most childless people under 18. Children remain dependent while CB (ibid.) is payable, but replacement of allowances by CTC continues.

With some exceptions for existing claimants, new conditions restrict entitlement for lone parents as youngest child reaches threshold age: 5+.

Main rates only are shown.

IS brings automatic entitlement on income grounds to other benefits including maximum HB and CTC.

A need level is established from the allowances and Premiums right, plus mortgage interest at Bank of England's published monthly average mortgage rate (currently 3.63 per cent) on loans of up to £200,000 (with restrictions on increases during a claim and a reduction for resident non-dependants; current maximum interest payment is £139 p.w.). IS is then paid to supplement other income to the need level. There are detailed rules on the application of premiums and disregarded income. Payments from a former partner may disqualify, including a lump sum payment of any amount (treated as income) but all child maintenance disregarded. No disregard for childcare costs.

Capital up to £6,000 is disregarded (£10,000 for those in residential/nursing homes; £3,000 for child). Capital between £6,000 and £16,000 is deemed to produce tariff income of £1 for each £250 (or part) over £6,000. There is no entitlement to IS if capital exceeds £16,000, disregarding value of home. Notional capital rules penalise deliberate deprivation of capital to obtain IS.

Non-contributory. Rarely taxable.

Personal allowances

		p.w.	p.a.
Single person	16–24	56.80	2,953.00
	25 or over	71.70	3,728.40
Lone parent	Under 18	56.80	2,953.00
	Over 18	71.70	3,728.40
Couple	Both over 18	112.55	5,852.60
Dependent children			
(existing untransferred claimants only—others see CTC)			
till day before 20th birthday/end of secondary education (if earlier)		65.62	3,412.24

Main Premiums

		p.w.	p.a.
Carer		34.40	1,788.80
Enhanced disability			
	Single	15.15	787.80
	Disabled child	23.45	1,190.28
	Couple	21.75	1,131.00

Severe disability

	Single (or one of couple)	59.50	3,094.00
	Couple (both qualifiying)	119.00	6,188.00

Existing claimants only (others see CTC):

Family/lone parent family	17.40	904.80
Disabled child	57.89	3,010.28
Enhanced disability (child)	23.45	1,219.40

Pension Credit (PC) 2013–2014

PC comprises two elements: Guarantee Credit (GC) for those of qualifying age whose income is below the "standard minimum guarantee"; and Savings Credit for those 65 and over with modest savings or income. Either or both are claimable.

Age at which GC available is rising gradually in line with increases in State Pension age; this is key date for other benefits and retirement age-related provisions: for current law see Pensions Act 1995 Sch.4.

Means-tested, some income disregarded. No upper capital limit. £10,000 disregarded; thereafter tariff income is £1 for every £500 (or part).

Not a tax credit. State pension is not affected. Administered by the Pension Service. Child maintenance disregarded; other maintenance disregarded only for savings credit. No provision for childcare costs. Housing costs as for IS. Guarantee Credit is a passport to maximum HB and CTB.

Non-contributory. Not taxable.

Standard Minimum Guarantee		**p.w.**
	Single	145.40
	Couple	222.05
	Additional amount for severe disability	
	Single	59.50
	Couple (both qualify)	119.00
	Additional amount for carers	33.30

Savings Credit			
	Threshold	Single	115.30
		Couple	183.90
	Maximum	Single	18.06
		Couple	22.89

Working Tax Credit (WTC) 2013–2014

		p.a.
First Income threshold		6,420.00
Withdrawal rate	41%	
Basic element		1,920.00
Additional couple's/lone parent element		1,970.00
30 hours element		790.00
Disabled worker element		2,855.00
Severe disability element		1,220.00

I2: Social security benefits and tax credits (means-tested)

Childcare element   **p.w.**

Percentage of eligible costs covered   70%
Maximum eligible cost   300.00
  (maximum payable £210 p.w.)
Maximum eligible cost for one child   175.00
  (maximum payable £122.50 p.w.)

Based on gross annual income: in-work support for families with child/children where lone parent over 16 works at least 16 hours p.w., or couple's combined work hours total 24 hours p.w., with one parent working at least 16 hours p.w. Extra payment for working at least 30 hours p.w. Also in-work support for some households without child, including those 25+ working at least 30 hours p.w., and those 60+ or with disability working at least 16 hours p.w. Up to first threshold, claimants receive the maximum. Credit then tapers by 41p per £1 of income as income rises. Above first threshold, claimant loses main element of WTC first, then childcare element, then child element of any CTC.

Elements are cumulative. Complex assessment rules. Maintenance ignored. Assessment on annual income, joint incomes for couples (disregarding £300 of certain types of unearned income).

Awards provisional until end of year notice identifies under/overpayments. Disregard of £2,500 before in-year falls in income affect entitlement; disregard of £10,000 before in-year rises in income affect entitlement. Administered by HMRC.

Child Tax Credit (CTC) 2013–2014

                                                                                   p.a.
First Income threshold for those entitled to CTC only   15,910.00
Withdrawal rate   41%

Family elements

          Family element   545.00

Child elements

          Child element (per child)   2,720.00
          Disabled child additional element   3,015.00
          Severely disabled child additional element   1,220.00

Based on gross annual income, support for families with child/children. First the per child element then the family element taper by 41p per £1 of income once income above £15,860 (WTC abated first).

One family element per family. The child elements are cumulative, including any disabled child or severely disabled child additional elements. Paid to nominated main carer.

Replaces most benefit additions for children.

Administered by HMRC.

Housing (HB) and Council Tax (CTB) Benefits 2013–2014

HB for "eligible" housing costs (not mortgages). Since April 7, 2008, eligible housing costs in respect of private rentals based on local housing allowance (LHA): LHA for new claims is flat rate using "30th percentile" (cheapest 30 per cent of properties in an area), rather than median, for relevant local rents, based on household size/composition (bedrooms). Maximum housing allowance four bedroom rate (£400), with individual caps dependent on number of bedrooms. Most under 35s restricted to bed-sit/ shared accommodation rate. Eligible housing costs for council/social housing tenants based on contractual rent not LHA. Benefit reduced if any non-dependants reside with claimant.

250   PNBA

CTB is paid to those on low income to assist with payment of council tax (so not under 18s or most full-time students). Award for HB and CTB depends on: money coming in; amount of savings; personal circumstances (children, disability, others in household); eligible charge.

Those on IS, IBJSA, Pension Credit Guarantee (PCG) or IRESA usually eligible automatically. For others, some income disregarded, e.g. £5 p.w. single claimant/£10 p.w. couple/£20 p.w. claimant eligible for disability or carer premium/£25 p.w. single parent. Child benefit and maintenance fully disregarded. Childcare costs paid by single parents and working/disabled couples may be disregarded, up to £175 p.w. for one child and £300 p.w. for more than one child.

If income is greater than the claimant's applicable amount, a tapered reduction applies. HB is reduced by 65 per cent of excess income; CTB by 20 per cent.

Usual upper savings limit £16,000; if on Pension Credit GC no upper limit (but tariff income). Capital up to £6,000 is disregarded. (£10,000 if above qualifying age for PC). For claimants under women's pension age: each £250 (or part) over £6,000 is deemed to produce tariff income of £1 p.w. For claimants over women's pension age rate is £1 per £500 (or part). Different capital limits for those in residential homes and for children. Where other adult residents preclude the single person discount for CTB, an alternative maximum CTB (Second Adult Rebate) may apply, based on their income and status. Non-contributory and non-taxable. Administered by Local Authorities.

Non-contributory and non-taxable. Administered by Local Authorities.

		p.w.
Claimant	18–24	56.80
	25 or over	71.70
Lone parent	Under 18	56.80
	18 or over	71.70
Couple	Both under 18	85.80
	One or both over 18	112.55
Dependent children to day before 20th birthday		65.62
Pensioner	Single women's pension age to 64	145.40
	Couple one or both women's pension age to 64	222.05
	Single 65 and over	163.50
	Couple one or both 65 and over	244.95

Premiums
As for IS *opposite* **except**

	Family/lone parent family premium	17.40
Protected lone parent family premiumum		22.20
ESA components		
	Work-related activity	28.45
	Support	34.80

13: Personal injury trusts

Introduction

Following a serious personal injury a client may receive substantial sums of money, be they from a claim for damages, personal accident insurance payouts, charitable gifts, or other sources.

Such clients often have to live for many years, if not the rest of their lives, with the personal, social and financial repercussions that arise because of their injury. They may be left unable to work, their family members may give up jobs to provide care, and they may have expensive ongoing costs to pay for; such as the costs of private care, case management, specialist aids and equipment. They will also continue have their regular living costs to meet, including the maintenance of any children or dependant relatives.

Therefore, it is important to ensure that each client is provided with proper and complete advice, and practical support where required, to ensure that:

- they get the best possible award from their personal injury claim;
- they are able to claim all of the state benefits and public care funding that they may be entitled to, both now and in years to come; and
- they have a suitable structure in place to properly manage and invest their award in the future.

It is, of course, important for any legal advisor to ensure that they have given each and every client the proper advice with regard to each of these matters. To fail to do so has in the past led to a number of personal injury lawyers being found to have been negligent because they have not provided their clients with proper advice about the possible use of personal injury trusts.

What is a personal injury trust?

A person injury trust is a formal structure in which to hold and manage any funds which the client has received as a consequence of their personal injury.

A formal trust deed should be put in place, which sets out the rules for the management of the funds. It is important that it is the right kind of trust, that best suits the client's requirements in their particular circumstances.

The trust deed should specify the trustees; two or more people, or a trust corporation, who are then in charge of the trust. The trustees should together make decisions about the management of the trust funds, including any payments made out of those funds, and are under an obligation to exercise their powers for the benefit of those named as beneficiaries. In most cases there will only be one beneficiary, the injured person.

The benefits of a personal injury trust

There are several benefits of having a personal injury trust in place, which include the following (albeit not an exhaustive list):

- If held in a personal injury trust, assets arising as a consequence of a personal injury are disregarded for the purpose of many means-tested state benefits and services.

  Therefore, a client (and their partner if they claim benefits together) can continue to receive these benefits, despite having funds within the trust which, if held by them personally, would have left them with too much capital to remain entitled.

  These means-tested state benefits include Income Support, Income Related Employment Support Allowance, Income Based Job Seekers Allowance, Housing Benefit and Council Tax Benefit. A trust can also protect entitlement to Local Authority funding for residential care and should protect funding for domiciliary care where the Local Authority operates a capital means test (the position with regard to the treatment of income depends upon the policy of the relevant local authority).

- The trust structure can help to protect the interests of young, older, disabled or otherwise vulnerable clients.

  Because of the requirement to have trustees in place who must each authorise all transactions within the trust, a client can be protected if their trustees are vigilant to any inappropriate proposals for the use of the funds.

  A steadfast trustee, be they a solicitor, interested family friend or parent, can exercise their effective veto against the use of trust funds to ensure that the funds are only applied in the client's best interests. The balance of power will depend on the type of trust chosen, and clients who fear that they may need extra safeguards should be advised carefully about this.

- A client can benefit from the knowledge, experience and wisdom of their trustees.

  Having appropriate trustees appointed can provide a client with important advice and support when making big decisions. Particularly when dealing with a large lump sum, this can be invaluable to ensure that decisions are appropriate to protect and ensure the long-term interests of the client.

  Some clients prefer to have an appropriately experienced solicitor appointed as one of their trustees, so that they can give advice on matters such as investment decisions, budgeting, and large items of capital expenditure.

- The personal injury trust helps to define and "ring fence" the funds that arise as a consequence of the client's personal injury, keeping them separate from other assets that may belong to the client.

  This can be of help if the client's circumstances change in the future and they suddenly find that they may be eligible for means-tested benefits or care funding; for example, if they have to go in to a care home, or if they separate from a working partner.

  The personal injury trust "wrapper" can also help to define what funds were awarded for their future needs. This can help to differentiate the funds if the client goes through a divorce or any other process where their personal finances are taken into consideration.

The basic rules for entitlement to means-tested benefits

As you may imagine, the rules for assessing a client's entitlement to means-tested benefits are detailed and complex.

However, when considering how personal injury funds may affect a client's entitlement to means-tested benefits, the key principles for Income Support, Income Related Employment Support Allowance, Income Based Job Seeker's Allowance, Housing Benefit and Council Tax Benefit are, broadly speaking, as follows:

- When considering a client's capital, it is important to consider both the personal injury funds that they are due to receive, as well as any savings or investments that they already hold.
- The first payment of any money derived from a personal injury will be ignored for 52 weeks from the date of receipt. An interim payment, or indeed any other payment received as a consequence

of the injury, will qualify as the first payment. The intention of this disregard is that the claimant will have an appropriate period to seek advice and set up the trust.

- If a client has capital below £6,000, then their capital will not affect their entitlement. This lower threshold is £10,000 for those living in a care home or independent hospital.
- If a client has capital between £6,000 and £16,000, then their entitlement will be reduced. For capital between those two thresholds they will be treated as having income of £1 for every £250 or part thereof above £6,000.
- If a client has capital over £16,000 they will be excluded from entitlement altogether.
- A client and their partner (with whom they live) will share a capital allowance, so it is important to look at their capital together. They should ideally have less than £6,000 between them both, if they are to maintain full entitlement.
- Certain assets, such as the value of the home a client lives in and their personal possessions, are disregarded when calculating capital.
- Any income received by the client, including that received by their partner, is deducted from the amount of benefits payable, albeit subject to some personal disregards and allowances.

The basic rules for entitlement to means-tested benefits for elderly clients

For Pension Credit, (currently available for new claimants after age 61, which age will increase gradually to 65 by 2018) the lower capital threshold is £10,000, and above that amount tariff income from a client's capital is assumed at a rate of £1 for every £500, or part thereof. There is no upper capital threshold. Income derived from a personal injury settlement is ignored, whether paid from a trust or otherwise. Actual capital is ignored, except to the extent that it creates assumed tariff income.

For Housing Benefit and Council Tax Benefit, if a client is in receipt of Pension Guarantee Credit, all capital, including partner's capital, is ignored. The effect is that personal injury funds are also ignored. If a client is over 60 and not receiving a qualifying benefit (such as Income Support, Income Related Employment Support Allowance, Income Based Job Seekers Allowance), the lower capital threshold is £6,000 and the capital threshold is £16,000. However, personal injury monies are ignored completely, whether in a trust or not, both in respect of capital and income.

Welfare reform

Since the implementation of the Welfare Reform Act 2012 in March 2013, Council Tax Benefit has been replaced by a discretionary scheme designed by local authorities. For people of working age the scheme is less generous in many areas than under the old Council Tax Benefit system and many people who have previously received full Council Tax Benefit will now have to make a contribution towards their Council Tax.

The primary income related benefits will be replaced by Universal Credit for new claims after October 2013. There will be no new claims for Income Support, Income Related Employment Support Allowance and Income Based Job Seeker's Allowance, after October 2013 and no new claims for Housing Benefit after April 2014. Current claimants for these benefits will be migrated to Universal Credit by 2017.

This will result in substantial regulatory change and it remains to be seen how far this will have a knock on effect on social care funding, the calculation of which is closely tied to the existing income related benefits regulations.

The rules for residential care home funding

When a client moves into a residential or nursing care home, they are assessed to see if they should contribute towards some or all of the care home costs. The means-testing regulations are the National Assistance (Assessment of Resources) Regulations 1992 (the "assessment regulations") and there is statutory guidance entitled the "Charging for Residential Accommodation guidance". The assessment regulations also apply in Wales but Wales has its own version of CRAG. The principal difference between the English and Welsh versions of CRAG is that there is no lower capital limit in Wales and therefore no tariff income scheme.

The key principles are as follows:

- The means-test applies to the resident only. Any capital or income belonging to their partner beneficially is ignored.
- The value of any assets of the client will be included in the capital calculation, unless they are disregarded under the regulations.
- Changes to the personal injury claimant's residence are common so it is useful to set out the disregards applying to domestic real property.
  The resident's main residence before moving into residential care is subject to a number of potential disregards which include the following:
  - occupation by the client's partner, former partner or civil partner (except where they are estranged).
  - A lone parent who is the client's estranged or divorced partner.
  - A member of the client's family who is either:
  - aged 60 or over;
  - a child under 16 whom the client is responsible to maintain; or
  - incapacitated.
- Where the stay in the accommodation is temporary, i.e. less than 52 weeks and the resident either intends to return to their home or sell it and buy other accommodation to move into within 52 weeks.
- During the first 12 weeks of a permanent stay.
- A house purchased for the resident within the last 26 weeks or such longer period as is reasonable to allow and which they are taking steps to occupy.
- The proceeds of sale of the former residence if sold within the last 26 weeks or such longer period as is reasonable to allow, where the resident intends to use the proceeds to buy another property for their occupation.

- When considering a resident's capital, the following thresholds are applicable in England:

  - lower threshold   £14,250
  - upper threshold   £23,250

If a resident's capital is above the upper threshold then they pay the costs in full, until or unless their capital is reduced to that amount.

If a resident's capital falls between those two thresholds then they are treated as having income of £1 for every £250 of capital over the lower threshold.

For residents living in Wales, there is only one capital threshold of £23,250, above which clients pay the costs of their care in full, until or unless their capital is reduced to that amount. There is no tariff income on capital in Wales.

a) Income received by the client is taken into account subject to the definitions of income contained in the assessment regulations and the disregards contained in Sch.3 to the regulations. A personal allowance of £23.50 per week (£24 per week in Wales) is also disregarded. Income on capital invested under the personal injury trust is disregarded.

b) The first capital payment made to the resident which is derived from a personal injury to them is disregarded for 52 weeks whether or not it is within a personal injury trust but any sum which a court has specifically identified as being for care is excluded from the disregard (see below for further information).

c) Income paid to the resident from their personal injury trust is disregarded unless it was intended for use and actually used for the payment of those elements of the fees that were taken into account when the local authority standard rate was fixed for the accommodation. The standard rate is the cost of accommodation provided by the local authority. This provision is likely to be intended to apply also to the "usual rate" the local authority charges when placing a resident in independent residential accommodation but the regulation does not make this clear.

The rules for domiciliary care funding

In England local authorities have discretionary powers under the Health and Social Services and Social Security Adjudications Act 1983 s.17 to make reasonable charges for adult service users where care is provided at home. The Department of Health has issued mandatory guidance on the operation of such charging schemes entitled "Fairer Charging".

In the case of *Crofton v NHSLA*,[1] the Court of Appeal held that the Fairer Charging guidance incorporates CRAG, but only in so far as CRAG deals with capital. This means that the income provisions of CRAG do not apply to assessments of income and so are at the discretion of the relevant local authority.

Periodical payments would normally be treated as income and therefore fall to be treated at the local authority's discretion. Where the local authority takes account of income, they will rarely if ever be disregarded. It may be possible to avoid this result and specialist advice should be taken if this is likely to impact on the client's ability to afford their care, for example in a reduced liability case.

The capital within personal injury trusts should, following *Crofton*, be disregarded as this is a capital asset which is disregarded as per CRAG. In England, the assessment of investment income to the trust appears to be a matter for the local authority's discretion. Specialist advice should be sought in relation to setting up a personal trust for those who may need to claim local authority funding for domiciliary care in cases where there is only partial recovery of loss.

In Wales charges for domiciliary care are subject to the Social Care Charges (Wales) Measure 2010 and associated regulations. Section 1 of the measure provides a power to charge for chargeable care services which are defined in s.13, broadly speaking, as domiciliary care services. At present the maximum weekly charge for domiciliary care is £50.

The provisions of Pt 3 of the assessment regulations relating to capital are incorporated in the means-test by regulation save that the main residence is disregarded in any event and the requirements of the assessment regulations are without prejudice to any policy of the local authority to adopt more generous provision. Regulations also provide for the manner in which income is to be assessed. Earnings are disregarded. Investment income to a trust is probably potentially assessable. The Fairer Charging guidance no longer applies in Wales, having been replaced in April 2011 by new statutory

---

[1] [2007] EWCA Civ 71.

guidance. The case of *Crofton* is thus not authority on the question of the applicability of CRAG to a person living in Wales.

What funds can go into a personal injury trust?

The benefits regulations take a wide definition, allowing any sums of capital to be disregarded if they arise "as a consequence of a personal injury".

This means that the use of personal injury trusts are not just limited to awards of damages, and can include:

- A personal injury award, including interim payments received during the course of a claim.
- A Criminal Injuries Compensation Authority award.
- A Motor Insurers' Bureau award.
- Payments from the Armed Forces Compensation Scheme, and similar schemes.
- Payments from various "no fault" schemes, sometimes set up by government bodies both here and abroad, such as payments from the Irish Residential Institutions Redress Board.
- Funds received from a Periodical Payment or Structured Settlement.
- Charitable or public donations following an accident.
- Funds received from accident or travel insurance.
- Funds received from a professional negligence claim paid to compensate for an undervalued personal injury claim.

It is vitally important to remember that, although the capital disregard is quite wide, the income disregard is rather more restricted. Where a person receives income from, for example, a personal accident policy or an occupational ill health pension, it is unlikely that those funds would be able to be disregarded or enter a personal injury trust. The author is aware of at least one case working its way through the court process at the moment on this very point.

When to set up a personal injury trust

It is important that, if at all possible, a personal injury trust is set up before a client receives their funds.

Lawyers should be aware that any client funds held on their Client Account may be treated as the client's money by the benefits agency and local authority. Therefore, any funds held on Client Account can jeopardise a client's benefit entitlement and consideration should be given to the suitability of a personal injury trust straight away.

Lawyers also run the risk that if funds remain on their client account, and they are aware that the client has not notified the benefits agency, they could find their firm obliged to report the client's non-disclosure as defrauding the benefits agency. Furthermore, they run the risk that they may be construed as aiding and abetting the client in a possible benefits fraud.

While it is usually best advice that a personal injury trust should be set up sooner rather than later, it is possible to set up a trust after the funds have been received and held personally by the client for some time. There is no restriction upon when personal injury funds must be placed into a trust; so funds can be held for months, or years, before a client arranges to place them in a trust. This does not allow the client to claim retrospectively for any benefits that they have missed out on prior to the trust being set up.

However, a client will have to demonstrate to the satisfaction of the benefits agency, or local authority, that the funds placed into the trust are purely those arising from their personal injury. There is a risk that the funds may over time have been mixed up with, or diluted by, other income or capital belonging to the client. Therefore, clients may find that they have some difficulty persuading the authorities that all of the funds should be disregarded.

Setting up a personal injury trust

It will be necessary to appoint appropriate trustees. There should be at least two trustees, and no more than four. They must be over 18 years of age and mentally capable of acting as a trustee. It is usually best to avoid trustees whose health and age might make them incapable of fulfilling their obligations in the foreseeable future.

The choice of trustees is an important one, as they will for all intents and purposes have full control over the personal injury trust and the assets held within it. It is important to consider whether they will be able to work well together and continue to act in the best interests of the beneficiaries. For this reason, some caution should be exercised before appointing partners, spouses, or other family members as trustees, if there is a risk of the relationship breaking down in the future.

Some clients may prefer to have an appropriately experienced solicitor appointed as one of their trustees. This allows an impartial and professional person to assist in the trustees' deliberations and decision making. It can help to ensure that the trustees are making decisions together which are appropriate to the needs of the beneficiaries, as well as providing the professional expertise and experience that can be invaluable when making difficult decisions.

It is also important that a client receives the correct advice about the right kind of trust to put in place. Consideration needs to be given to the client's particular circumstances, their potential liability to tax and the provision that they may wish to make for their family in the future. This will in turn affect whether the client is named as the sole beneficiary of the trust, or whether other beneficiaries are named and, if so, whether the trustees have any discretion in how they apply funds for their benefit.

The client being advised about Personal Injury Trusts should be advised about wills at the same time.

Once the advice is given, and the necessary decisions are made, the trust deed will need to be prepared by the instructed lawyer, before being signed in the presence of witnesses, and dated. The personal injury trust will usually have a suitable title, such as the "Josephine Anne Bloggs Personal Injury Trust."

Once a personal injury trust is set up

Once a personal injury trust is set up, the trustees' first act will usually be to open a bank or building society account to hold the trust funds. The account should be suitably named, such as the "Josephine Anne Bloggs Personal Injury Trust". The account should usually require that each and every one of the trustees is required to sign to authorise all transactions on account, including all cheques.

Once the trustees have set up the trust bank account, the personal injury lawyer can confidently arrange for a cheque to be issued for the personal injury funds, ensuring that the cheque is made payable to the trust, i.e. payable to the "Josephine Anne Bloggs Personal Injury Trust", and not to the client personally.

The trustees will need to keep to certain rules in order to be able to use funds from the trust without affecting the client's benefit entitlement, namely:

- Any income arising from the funds in the trust, such as interest or dividends, should be paid into a trust account, and not paid to the client personally.
- The trustees can transfer funds into the client's own personal account, but should take care to ensure that the client's capital (including the capital held by their partner if they are claiming benefits as a couple) stays below £6,000 at all times, which is the lower capital threshold for most means-tested benefits.
- Possibly the simplest way to use funds from the trust is to make direct payments from the trust to third parties. This way the funds go directly from the trust account, to the third party and do not go through the client's hands in any way.
- Any further assets set up to be held by the trustees, be they bank accounts, investments or property, should be set up with the same restrictions as the original trust bank account, namely:
  - in the name of the trust, or trustees; and
  - with the restriction that each and every one of the trustees is required to sign all transactions with regard to that asset.

Is a client likely to benefit from a personal injury trust in the future?

For many clients it is easy to determine that they are entitled to means-tested benefits, or care funding, at the time that they receive their funds, and so it makes sense to protect their entitlement straight away by setting up a personal injury trust.

However, some clients may at the time have no entitlement to means-tested benefits, and so a personal injury trust may not seem immediately relevant. In such cases careful consideration should be given to the client's potential to claim means-tested benefits in the future.

A client may become entitled to means-tested benefits in the future if their relevant circumstance change, which may include:

- If they need to move to live in a care home.
- If they move out of the family home to live on their own.
- If they leave full- or part-time education.
- If they are discharged from hospital or residential care.
- If they and their spouse divorce or separate.
- When they reach a significant age for benefits purposes, such as 16, 18 or 60 years of age.
- If they or their partner lose their job, retire or are medically unable to continue to work.
- If they, or their partner, lose their entitlement to another benefit or source of income.
- If they, or their partner, find their health deteriorates and they become entitled to higher rates of disability benefits, which in turn have a knock-on effect for some means-tested benefits.
- If they, or their partner, find that they have used up their pre-existing savings (those which have not arisen from the personal injury claim and which have previously prevented them claiming means-tested benefits) and so find that they would become entitled to means-tested benefits if their personal injury funds were disregarded as capital.

In such cases clients should be advised to use up their pre-existing savings with some caution. The benefits agency or local authority can ask to look at a person's history of expenditure, and any gifts made, to see if the client has in the opinion of the authority, deliberately depleted their estate in order to gain entitlement to means-tested benefits or services. If the authority feels that a client has deliberately depleted their estate in such a manner, they can decide to treat the spent funds as "notional capital", essentially treating the client as if they still have the funds and leaving them with no entitlement to the means-tested benefit or service which they have applied for. Therefore, it is important that clients keep a careful record of their expenditure to demonstrate that their use of funds has been reasonable and not a deliberate attempt to deplete their estate.

The 52-week rule

Payments received as a consequence of a personal injury are disregarded for the purpose of assessing entitlement to means tested benefits for the first 52 weeks after they are received.

However, that disregard applies only to the first payment received as a consequence of that personal injury, which may often be the client's first interim payment. It is also important to check to see a client has received other earlier payments, which may count as their "first payment", such as payments from an accident insurance policy or even a capital payment from a charity.

Any later payments, including further interim payments, are not protected by this disregard after the expiry of the original 52-week period.

Therefore, when receiving a first payment as a consequence of a personal injury, a client may choose not to set up a trust if they anticipate spending enough of that sum to bring their capital below the relevant threshold by the end of the 52-week period. However, they should be advised to hold that payment in a bank account separate from any other funds. That way, if towards the end of period they find that they unexpectedly have funds remaining, they can still arrange to place them into a personal injury trust safe in the knowledge that the funds have not become mixed up with other capital in any way.

However, in many cases it will be appropriate to set up a personal injury trust as soon as any funds are received, regardless of the 52-week rule. Where the amount of funds due to the client overall are almost certainly going to last longer than that period, there is little if no benefit in delaying the setting up of a personal injury trust which is likely to remain in place to manage the client's funds for many years to come.

Personal injury trusts for children and protected parties

In most cases the decision as to whether or not to set up a personal injury trust is one for the client to make for themselves, albeit with the benefit of good advice from a lawyer. The matter does not require court approval in any way.

However, if a client is unable to make their own decision it will be necessary to obtain approval from the appropriate court with authority to make a decision on behalf of the client (CPR r.21.11 and supplementary Practice Direction), namely:

- The High Court will need to approve the establishment of a personal injury trust to manage an infant's funds until the infant reaches 18 years of age.

- In cases involving mentally incapable people, the Court of Protection will need to approve the establishment of a personal injury trust, in preference to the appointment of a Deputy for Property and Affairs. Following the case of *Re HM*,[2] the court is likely to approve the establishment of trusts in limited circumstances only. However, it is important to note that the disregards which apply for benefits and care purposes for funds derived from a personal injury are also available for injury derived funds held under the auspices of the Court of Protection.

[2] (2011) C.O.P. 11875043 April 11, 2011.

14: Claims for loss of earnings and maintenance at public expense

The Administration of Justice Act 1982 s.5 provides that where an injured claimant seeks to recover damages for loss of earnings, the defendant can set off against that claim any saving attributable to maintenance (either wholly or partly) at public expense in a hospital, nursing home or other institution.

This deduction is comparable to (but not the same as) the common law principle that where a claimant is in a private hospital or home (in respect of which damages are claimed from the defendant), credit must be giving for the domestic expenses thereby saved. This is the "domestic element" which was discussed in *Fairhurst v St Helens and Knowsley Health Authority*.[1]

15: Foster care allowances

Introductory notes:

Every April the Fostering Network publishes the cost of bringing up a child in its own home for the next 12 months. Contact Fostering Network Publications, 87 Blackfriars Road, London SE1 8HA (tel: 020 7620 6400; *http://www.fostering.net*).

The Fostering Network publishes Foster Care Finance, with recommended minimum weekly allowances for fostering in the UK and a full survey of allowances paid by each local authority. The Fostering Network's recommended minimum allowance depends on the age of the child and whether or not the placement is in London. The allowances do not include any form of reward for carers themselves. The Fostering Network recommends four extra weeks' payment, to cover the cost of birthdays, holidays and a religious festival. It encourages local authorities to pay allowances to all carers at least in line with its recommended rates. Despite such encouragement the majority of local authorities give foster carers less than the Fostering Network's recommended minimum allowances for spending on the care of fostered children. From a survey published by the Fostering Network in September 2003, 53 per cent of local authorities in England and 87 per cent of local authorities in Wales paid below the Fostering Network's recommended minimum allowance.

Fostering Network recommended costs of bringing up a child in its own home for the year beginning April 6, 2013

Age of child (years)	National (£ per week)	London (£ per week)
0–4	122.00	140.00
5–10	134.00	157.00
11–15	154.00	178.00
16+	179.00	209.00

In *Spittle v Bunney*[2] it was said that the cost of fostering services is not an appropriate measure for the value of the loss of a (deceased) mother's services, but the case is not uncontroversial.

---

[1] [1995] P.I.Q.R. Q1, at Q8 and Q9.
[2] [1988] 1 W.L.R. 847.

Group J
Court of Protection

J1:   Note on the Court of Protection

J2:   The incidence of Deputyship costs over a claimant's life

J3:   Deputyship costs

J

J1: Note on the Court of Protection

The Mental Capacity Act 2005 and the Court of Protection

It is important to understand some of the background to, and the purpose of, the legislation. The original bill was known as the Mental Incapacity Bill. This became the Mental Capacity Act (the Act). That change is critical in that the removal of those two letters make all the difference to the tone of the Act. The Act is very much intended to empower incapacitated adults. All of us practitioners in this field need to acknowledge that fact and continually keep the principles as set out in s.1 of the Act in the forefront of our minds at all times:

1. A person must be assumed to have capacity unless it is established that he lacks capacity.
2. A person is not to be treated as unable to make a decision unless all practicable steps to help him to do so have been taken without success.
3. A person is not to be treated as unable to make a decision merely because he makes an unwise decision.
4. An act done, or decision made, under this Act for or on behalf of a person who lacks capacity must be done, or made, in his best interests.
5. Before the act is done, or the decision is made, regard must be had to whether the purpose for which it is needed can be as effectively achieved in a way that is less restrictive of the person's rights and freedom of action.

It is easy to assume that, because the Court of Protection has not changed its name and the Public Guardianship Office has only changed slightly to the Office of the Public Guardian, nothing much occurred on October 1, 2007 when the Act came fully into force. In fact fundamental changes took place.

It is also important to note that there is a complete separation now between the Office of the Public Guardian (OPG) and the Court of Protection.

The old Court of Protection was merely an Office of the Supreme Court, whereas the new court is a superior Court of Record with equal authority to that of the High Court. Indeed certain functions of the High Court concerning termination of life cases have been transferred to the new Court of Protection. However, it is important to remember that an application to the court is the last remedy to consider. The Code of Practice established under the Act sets out clearly that matters should, wherever possible, be reached by negotiation rather than an application to the court.

The PGO was the administrative office of the old court, whereas the new Office of the Public Guardian has no connection with the court. Its role is purely to act on behalf of the Public Guardian and its role so far as this note is concerned is to supervise the conduct of Deputies. It has no part in the administration of cases.

The new court has no administrative arm and has no continuing record of clients, or case workers dealing with their affairs. Its role is purely to make decisions by the issuing of declarations or orders which might or might not involve the appointment of a Deputy.

The new court has wider powers than the old court and can make orders about welfare issues as well as financial matters.

The aim of the court is always to resolve matters in the manner least intrusive into a person's affairs. As a result the process of appointing a Financial Deputy is only to be pursued when it is quite clear, based on medical evidence, that a client lacks capacity to manage his financial affairs. The Mental Capacity Act is an evolving piece of legislation. Since coming fully into force on October 1, 2007 the Act has had significant amendments to it. The Mental Health Act 2008 amended the Act in respect of

Deprivation of Liberty issues and brought in a second Code of Practice on Deprivation of Liberty safeguards. Furthermore, from the outset the OPG announced an intention to review the implementation of the Act 12 months after coming into force in order to review its aims and ambitions, of both empowering and protecting those who lacked capacity, were being met.

This has resulted in a series of consultation papers which have amended from time to time the numerous statutory instruments supporting the principle legislation. The first related to "Forms, supervision and fees". This resulted in two new statutory instruments coming into force on May 1, 2010. One related to Enduring Powers of Attorney. The other made minor amendments to the fees exemption region and the bonding process.

This was followed by a consultation on rule changes. Recommendations were made as a result of that consultation but as yet no changes have been implemented.

A third consultation ended in May 2011 in relation to OPG fees and a new structure of fees came in to effect from October 1, 2011.

1. The scope and authority of the Court of Protection

As mentioned above it is important to remember that the court is a solution of last resort in most respects. However, as far as the Personal Injury/Clinical Negligence lawyer is concerned it is the first resort to obtain the appointment of a Deputy to deal with an incapacitated client's financial affairs.

To make an application it has to be established that a person lacks capacity in accordance with the definition as set out in s.2 of the Act:

"A person lacks capacity in relation to a matter if at the material time he is unable to make a decision for himself in relation to the matter because of an impairment of, or a disturbance, in the functioning of the mind or brain".

It is important to remember that there is no general level below which a client lacks capacity and above which he does not. The statement that a person "lacks capacity" in itself is meaningless. When and in connection with what issues does a person lack capacity? Clearly some clients will lack capacity concerning all their financial affairs but most clients retain some capacity and it is for the Deputy to establish the areas and the extent to which the client has capacity and ensure that he does not trespass there. All Deputyship Orders make it absolutely clear that the Deputy has no authority to decide any matters on which the client retains capacity.

The second part of the test is equally important. One must establish that the lack of capacity is as a result of "an impairment of, or a disturbance in the functioning of the mind or brain". A COP3 Assessment of Capacity form establishing both heads is required in support of the application.

Section 3 of the Act sets out that for the purposes of establishing the lack of capacity it is necessary to show that the client is unable:

"(a) to understand the information relevant to the decision;
 (b) to retain that information;
 (c) to use or weigh that information as part of the process of making the decision;
     or;
 (d) to communicate his decision (whether by talking, using sign language or any other means)."

In essence failing to meet any one of the first three tests will establish the lack of capacity on a specific decision. However, someone who passes all three tests yet is unable to communicate his decision also is deemed to lack capacity in this context, even though medically he may have full capacity.

Putting all this in the context of Personal Injury or Clinical Negligence litigation one of the first occasions where capacity may be an issue, apart from the actual commencement of proceedings, is when the first interim payment is to be made. Can the client manage this? It is quite possible that a head-injured client may have capacity to manage modest funds of say a few thousand pounds. However, when a significant interim payment is made, he may not. A Deputy is not needed until you reach the point where the client cannot manage the funds available. However, if a Deputy is appointed knowing a significant settlement is due eventually, then the role of the Deputy in respect of minor interims may be just to stand aside and let the client deal with them.

2. The appointment of a property and affairs Deputy

Practitioners need to understand that the role of a Deputy is different to that of the pre-MCA Receiver. The appointment of a receiver was based on the concept of a one-off assessment of capacity. If it was found that the client "lacked capacity" then the power of the Receiver meant that the Receiver could take over all financial decision-making from the client and there was no need to re-consider the matter again. All Deputyship orders make it quite clear that whilst the Deputy may have wide powers to manage all of a client's financial affairs, under no circumstances can a Deputy make a decision on a matter where the client has the capacity to make his own decision. Furthermore, if the Deputy did do so then that decision would be invalid. A Deputy's authority only extends to matters where it is "established" that the client lacks capacity himself. As a result a lot more time and effort needs to be taken on a decision-by-decision basis for many clients to establish a lack of capacity.

Often there can be conflicting medical evidence as to the question of capacity. If that is the case then all such evidence must be put before the court when making an application. This can be a problem for litigators because there may be contrary evidence in existence which they do not wish to disclose in the litigation. It has to be disclosed in the Court of Protection application.

3. The timing of an application

It is important not to apply sooner than necessary. For instance, a client may have capacity to manage small interim payments but not to manage a larger sum.

Applications will usually be dealt with within the terms of the court's service levels of 21 weeks. However, Orders can be issued more quickly in some cases. As from September 1, 2010 Orders are only issued once the surety bond is in place. Previously the Order was issued but did not come into force until one calendar month after issue to allow for the bond to be put in place. This change in procedure means a slight delay in the issuing of Orders but it means the Order is fully effective from the date of its issue.

4. Professional or lay Deputy

In cases involving recovery of large amounts of say £500,000 or more (excluding Deputyship costs) it is reasonable to apply for the appointment of a professional Deputy and recover the costs of the Professional Deputyship as a specific head of future loss. There is no prescribed figure for the application for the appointment of a professional Deputy. A lot will depend on the circumstances of the individual claimant. However, in larger damages cases it is suggested that a professional is preferred as it can often remove family tensions that get in the way when a family member is appointed. Also if no professional costs are claimed at the outset then, if in later life a professional is needed, his costs are a real drain on the funds of the claimant.

5. Decision making by Deputies

When a Deputy makes a decision on behalf of a person he needs to make that decision in the person's best interests. There is no definition of "best interests" under the Act; merely guidelines of what to consider in deciding what is in a person's best interests. These guidelines are set out in s.4 of the Act. The overriding rule is that the decision maker must consider all relevant circumstances. In that respect the client has a role to play in the decision making process. The Deputy *must* consider whether it is likely that the client will have capacity at some time in relation to the decision and if so, when. Also the Deputy "so far as reasonably practicable" *must* permit and encourage the client to be involved as far as possible in the decision making process. He must also "if it is practicable" *and appropriate* consult certain others such as family, and carers, etc. The need to consult these others is often referred to whereas the need to consult and involve the client, which is a stronger obligation, is often forgotten. It may be uncomfortable but it is required.

6. The role of the financial Deputy

It is often assumed that the role of the financial Deputy is akin to that of a bank manager or book keeper. This is not so. Whilst there is a high element of routine involved, in high value cases there is a lot of highly technical and complex work to be carried out in connection with such things as house adaptations, carer employment, and investments. It is important to allocate the lowest appropriate grade or fee earner to each piece of work. As a result the Deputy will probably only be able to charge at grade A or B for small amounts of work.

In summary, the routine work of a professional Deputyship includes the following, amongst other things:

(a) liaison with an application to the Court of Protection and the Office of the Public Guardian where necessary;
(b) preparation of annual accounts/reports to the Office of the Public Guardian;
(c) completion of tax returns and payment to the Inland Revenue as necessary;
(d) dealing with requests for capital expenditure;
(e) setting appropriate budgets and regular payments as appropriate;
(f) considering and approving investment proposals;
(g) overseeing and arranging the employment and retention of care workers and other employed staff, and liaison as appropriate with the case manager;
(h) overseeing and arranging payment of national insurance contributions and PAYE tax in respect of any employees' wages;
(i) liaising with the person whose affairs are being dealt with and, wherever possible, taking all practical steps to enable them to make their own decisions;
(j) liaising with the person's family, associates, care managers and other parties as appropriate (in accordance with the "best interests" criteria);
(k) ensuring that the person receives the correct state benefits, council tax benefits and exemptions, housing benefit and local authority/public funding for care; and
(l) payment of bills, fees and regular expenses.

Most of these items should be carried out at grade C or D where possible. If there is not such a grade fee earner available then higher grade fee earners will only recover the lower grade hourly rates. The Supreme Court Costs Office are becoming very focused on the proportionality of charges.

7. Welfare Deputies

When the Act came into being there was much talk about appointing welfare Deputies in some numbers. However, in reality very few welfare Deputies have been appointed. This is because if you follow through the principles of the Act and in particular the concept of dealing with decisions in a way which is least restrictive of the person's rights and freedoms then the idea of having a welfare Deputy is, in fact, the most restrictive way of dealing with welfare matters. Accordingly, welfare Deputyships are only really for the most severely disabled who require constant welfare decisions made for them. The concept of a professional welfare Deputy is also extremely rare and the payment structure under the court's rules extremely limited as a consequence.

8. Approval of damages awards by the Court of Protection
Prior to October 2007 the Master of the Court of Protection would often provide email approval of a personal injury settlement, but this procedure has now ceased as from October 1, 2007. The Civil Procedure (Amendment) Rules 2007 set out amendments to CPR Pt 21 which provides that only a Master, designated Civil Judge or his nominee should normally hear applications for the approval of a settlement or compromise involving a "protected beneficiary" (a person who lacks capacity to manage or control any money recovered by him or on his behalf in the proceedings). Therefore, the approval of the Court of Protection is no longer required.

9. Charges for the appointment of Deputies and management by professional Deputies.
The costs of a professional Deputy is a significant item of any large personal injury or clinical negligence claim (including CICA and MIB) involving a head-injured client.

It is important to put together the claim for Deputyship costs extremely carefully as they will be a significant item of any claim. Even if you have the in-house experience to prepare your own costs statement there is a line of argument that an independent expert's statement is to be preferred merely to establish objectivity.

Whilst many elements of a claim will be standard, e.g. court fees and OPG fees, the annual costs of acting as a professional Deputy will vary from case to case. It may well be that a "difficult" client's costs will be significantly higher than those of a very passive head-injured client. Costs will vary between the early and late years of a case. It is impossible to be prescriptive about the costs of a professional Deputy. The role is not like that of a carer or even a case manager where exact numbers of hours are claimed each month. It is therefore prudent in the case of a Deputy to include some contingency for unexpected events. It is very difficult to weigh up accurately how many head-injured clients will behave on a long-term basis. A lot comes down to experience.

The requirements of the MCA and the Code of Practice means in ensuring that a Deputy does not make decisions which the client can make for himself mean a lot more time can be spent on assessing capacity now. When it is established that there is a lack of capacity in respect of a specific decision, it is necessary for the Deputy to assess what will be in the client's best interests. All this takes time.

It is a requirement for the Deputy, or at least someone on his behalf, to visit the client at least once a year at home, but it may be that such visits are necessary more frequently for some clients. It would be usual for more visits to be required in the early stages, particularly after settlement, owing to the number of decisions which will be required at that time.

Regarding the terms of the Deputyship Order, it should also be borne in mind that a Deputy may need to make further applications from time to time to the court. Orders can be limited as to time and the amount of funds that can be spent in a year. Time-limited Orders are typically given at the outset before a compensation claim has been settled. Financially limited Orders may be given to reduce the surety bond costs or for many other reasons. All Orders are not the same.

10. Fixed costs in the Court of Protection
A new Practice Direction lays down categories of fixed costs effective from February 1, 2011. They provide an alternative in low cost cases to having your bills assessed. Court Orders will state whether fixed costs are to apply. Normally Deputyship Orders will give the option to take fixed costs or have detailed assessment.

The Practice Direction deals with the following:

(a) Payments on account—where detailed assessment applies, a professional Deputy may take payments on account for the first three quarters of the year which are proportionate to the work undertaken but which must not exceed 20 per cent of the estimated annual charges. The balance is then recovered following the detailed assessment. The only bill submitted for assessment is at the end of the Deputyship year.

(b) Solicitors costs in court proceedings:

(i) Work up to and including the making of the Order appointing a Deputy for Property and Affairs—an amount not exceeding £850 plus VAT.
(ii) Annual management fees for the first year of Deputyship—an amount not exceeding £1,500 plus VAT: for the second and subsequent years £1,185 plus VAT.
(iii) Preparation and lodgement of accounts—an amount up to £235 plus VAT.
(iv) Preparation of HMRC Income Tax return—an amount up to £235 plus VAT.

(c) Conveyancing costs—for the first time for many years there are fixed fees for conveyancing. On sales or purchases a value element of 0.15 per cent of the consideration may be charged subject to a minimum of £350 and a maximum of £1,500 plus VAT and disbursements. This is a reduction from previous fixed rates. There are other fixed fees in the Practice Direction—see the details on the HMCS website.

11. Court fees in relation to Deputyship

As mentioned previously the OPG's fees are undergoing review in a consultation that ends on May 21, 2011. The new fees are intended to apply from July 1, 2011. The editors do not know what they will be but the proposals are outlined below.

The current fees are:

OPG fees

1. Deputy Assessment fee   £100

A one-off fee for carrying out a risk assessment to decide the level of supervision to apply.

2. Supervision fees:

- Type I supervision (highest)   £320 per annum
- Type IIA (intermediate)   £320 per annum
- Type II supervision (lower)   £320 per annum
- Type III supervision (minimal)   £35 per annum

Supervision will vary. Typically on larger cases with a professional Deputy there will be Type 1 Supervision until the case settles and then it will move to II or IIA. Type III applies to small value cases for which the capital threshold is currently £18,000 increasing to £19,500 in April 2013 and then £21,000 in April 2014.

Court of Protection fees

- Application fee for the appointment of a Deputy   £400
- Application fee for any other application, e.g. statutory will   £400
- Appeal fee for filing a notice appealing a court decision   £400
- Hearing fee—in addition to the application fee   £500

Fee remissions and exemptions

There are fee exemptions and remissions available for both the OPG and Court of Protection fees.

For both OPG and Court of Protection fees a full exemption is available if a person is in receipt of any of the following means-tested benefits:

- Income Support /ESA.
- Income-based Jobseeker's Allowance.
- State Pension Guarantee Credit.
- A combination of Working Tax Credit and either Child Tax Credit, Disability Element or Severe Disability Element.
- Housing Benefit.
- Council Tax Benefit.

AND the person has not been awarded damages of more than £16,000 which were disregarded in calculating chargeability for any of the above benefits.

For Court of Protection fees a person is eligible for the relevant fee remission if their gross annual income falls within the following bands

Up to £12,000	Full remission
£12,001–£13,500	75% remission
£13,501–£15,000	50% remission
£15,501–£16,500	25% remission
£16,501 and above	No remission

For OPG fees a person is eligible for a 50 per cent reduction if their gross annual income is less than £12,000.

12. Surety Bonds for Deputies

Initially, there was a great deal of uncertainty about Surety Bonds. Judicial independence meant that there was no set scale and there was clear evidence that different judges had different attitudes to bonding and the amount of surety required. As a result of the case of *Re H*[1] (COP) this has now been resolved. Judge Hazel Marshall laid down clear guidelines to be followed in calculating a suitable level of surety.

Typically, bond premiums for solicitors acting as professional Deputies in high value Personal Injury/Clinical Negligence claims are no more than £250–£350 per annum, even where settlement levels are several million pounds. (This takes account of the existence of the solicitors' professional indemnity policy.) Where a large portion of a settlement is met by periodic payments then that will serve to reduce the level of bonding.

13. Wills and statutory wills

No one under the age of 18 may make a will. This principle cannot be avoided even by the use of trusts for minors who, it may be thought, will not survive beyond 18.

If a person of 18 or over has testamentary capacity he can make a will for himself and give his own instructions. If not, then it is possible for a statutory will to be made.

In order to give instructions for a will a person must be able to understand the following:

(a) The nature of the document to be executed.
(b) The extent of his property and estate.
(c) The nature of the claims of those he proposes to benefit or exclude from participation in the will.

These are the criteria set down in the case of *Banks v Goodfellow*.[2]

---

[1] [2009] EWHC B31.
[2] (1870) L.R. 5 Q.B.

Many clients whose financial affairs are dealt with by a Deputy have such testamentary capacity. If the Deputy obtains a certificate of testamentary capacity the client can give instructions and execute his will in the usual way. However, if it is established that the client lacks testamentary capacity then an application to the Court of Protection for a statutory will to be executed on his behalf should be made.

Practice Direction F supplemental to Pt 9 of the Court of Protection Rules 2007 sets out the detailed procedure.

The cost of such an application can be significant as the procedure requires the involvement of the Official Solicitor on behalf of the client and the notification of anyone adversely affected by the applications, e.g. those who might lose their entitlement under an intestacy by the terms of the proposed will.

A Medical Certificate will be required. The court fee of £400 will apply to the application and if it goes to a hearing a further £500 court fee will apply. Many applications are dealt with on the papers and no attendance is required. Hearings will normally only be required if there are serious disputes over the proposed will. Costs can amount in the simplest of cases to a few thousand pounds and in the most difficult of cases tens of thousands of pounds. The usual rule about costs is that all parties' costs are paid out of the testator's estate. However, the court has discretion to order costs against any party if it believes he has acted unreasonably. It is important to claim this item properly in the compensation claim.

14. Keeping up to date
As from April 2011 the OPG website has closed. Information about the OPG is now found in the DIRECTGOV site and that for the Court of Protection on the HMCS website. Neither is as easy to navigate as the OPG site but hopefully that will change.

SOME IMPORTANT INFORMATION ABOUT BENEFITS RELEVANT TO DEPUTIES

Income Support (Amended) Regulations 1987 as amended.

52-week disregard

Under para.12A of Sch.10 to the Regulations (which since April 7, 2008 extend to means testing for Local Authority funded care or Direct Payments) practitioners have to be careful when receiving interim payments.

In essence there is a period of 52 weeks running from the day of receipt of the first payment (no matter how small) in consequence of a personal injury claim, during which the capital received will be disregarded. However, you do not receive a separate 52-week period on future payments.

e.g.   £10,000 interim received six months ago.
£100,000 final compensation received today.

The 52-week period starts on the date of the first payment, so that the disregard for the £100,000 will actually expire in 26 weeks' time.

In most cases interims are received over a much longer period such that the disregard will run out well before the interim is exhausted. As a result the funds received do have to be disclosed. However, if the funds are held by the Deputy under the Deputyship order then they are disregarded regardless of the 52-week period. There is no need to put funds in a personal injury trust if they are held by a Deputy under a Court of Protection Order.

Payments other than the interim may also trigger the 52-week disregard period if they are paid "in consequence of" a personal injury, e.g. personal accident insurance or a statutory "no fault" scheme.

Funds held in or out of court

Under the Regulations funds received as a consequence of a personal injury are disregarded entirely if they are either held in trust or are under the control of the Court of Protection.

Most practitioners are aware of the trust exception but may not fully understand the Court of Protection exemption. Originally, in order to qualify for the exemption the funds of a Deputy had to be held in court, i.e. actually be invested through Court Funds Office. However, since April 7, 2008 as a result of SI 593/2008 that restriction no longer applies. Now funds held "to the Order of the Court" are disregarded. As a result funds invested more freely, including in property, remain disregarded as long as they are in the Deputy's name. Accordingly there is no need to contemplate personal injury trusts where there is a Deputyship.

J2: The incidence of Deputyship costs over a claimant's life

1. The appointment of a Deputy is likely to arise for a personal injury/clinical negligence claimant when he lacks capacity to manage his financial and property affairs, i.e. he is a protected person for the purpose of the Mental Capacity Act 2005 prior to the index injury or insult or as a consequence thereof. In either case Deputyship costs are a recoverable head of loss:

   - where the incapacity preceeded the index injury or insult, but it is only in consequence of that injury or insult that the claimant has financial affairs and property of sufficient size and complexity to warrant the appointment of a Deputy, and
   - where the incapacity is a direct consequence of the injury/insult.

2. Minority is not of itself an incapacity for these purposes but it is the Court of Protection's practice to appoint a Deputy for infants where the damages are significant and the probability is that the infant will not acquire legal capacity on attaining his majority.

3. At the latest admission of liability and/or judgement an application should be made without delay. This is in order that a decision maker, i.e. the Deputy, can be put in place as soon as possible to enable interim funds to be applied for the claimant's benefit. An application may be made earlier if the circumstances in which an eventual award is a probability.

4. The process of application for a Deputy will involve the solicitor concerned in undertaking a fact-find with the claimant and his family for preparation and completion of the application; service in person upon the claimant and close members of family of notice of intention to apply; and of the application itself once issued. Fees will arise for the Court of Protection on application; and on appointment with the office of the public guardian. Work may typically be undertaken by the Deputy and/or solicitors acting on his behalf on an interim basis in relation to the management of the claimant's property and affairs either in anticipation of, or with the benefit of, interim authorities provided on application by the court.

5. The order appointing a Deputy is also authority for assessment of costs involved in the application. Cost Draftsman and SCCO assessment fees will arise accordingly to the claimant's account.

6. The court will in addition require the Deputy to enter into a security bond. The extent of the bond appropriate is in the discretion of the judge. Considerations are detailed in the case of *Re H*. They include whether the Deputy is a professional and has the benefit of PII and in a Solicitor's case of the compensation fund; the extent of the annual income; and the size of assets generally which are readily accessible by the Deputy without further reference to the court. The figure provided in the accompanying cost breakdown is an estimate in a typical cerebral palsy and/or catastrophic brain injury case.

7. It is important to check the terms in which the first general order is made to ensure that it provides the Deputy with the authorities sought on the application and/or likely to be required, for example to purchase a property and/or to invest. Failing this, short of the court's accepting an error which requires correction, a separate application for amendment will be required and will attract a fee and costs associated with its preparation and conduct. Applications will generally be dealt with on paper without a hearing but nonetheless can take three months to be processed even on that basis. The initial application can be anticipated to take at least six months as will an application for appointment of a new Deputy.

8. The management of the claimant's property and affairs then proceeds in annual stages—Deputyship years. The anniversary of the initial order appointing the Deputy is authority for the Deputy's assessment of his/her costs of the preceding year. The Deputy can take payments on account during the year at quarterly intervals: currently the amount is 20 per cent of the total anticipated

annual costs per quarter, for the first three quarters of the Deputyship year, which will be set-off against the eventual bill once approved by the SCCO.

9. The security bond will be renewed on an annual basis and in addition an OPG annual supervision fee will be payable. This is charged according to a scale and depends upon the level of supervision deemed appropriate by the OPG. It will generally be higher in the case of a lay, as opposed to a professional, Deputy. Initially a claim is ongoing and in the immediate post-settlement years the level of supervision may also be set at a higher level (probably type 2A intermediate), being reduced once a routine is in place (down to type 2 light touch). The figures given in the accompanying breakdown are for a type 2A (intermediate) level of supervision.

10. In the initial years of a Deputyship, costs can be anticipated to be higher than they will be in subsequent years. Costs are given in the accompanying breakdown for the "first two Deputyship years" within which it is contemplated that significant structural issues will be addressed including;

    *   acquisition and adaptation of accommodation,
    *   the major/initial investment decisions, and
    *   the establishment, through Case Managers or otherwise, of care and other support regimes.

11. The impact of the litigation should be factored in while this is being undertaken. Litigation will inevitably increase costs because:

    *   long-term budgeting even on an annual basis will not generally be possible while the Deputyship is in its infancy and the claimant is dependent upon interim payments,
    *   liaison with the litigation team will be required including as to the claimant's requirements for interim funding; the adequacy of offers made in these connections; the provision of evidence in support of applications; the provision of copy financial and other records and their appropriate collation; and the consideration of the eventual form of order and of financial advice in relation thereto, and
    *   Stresses will occur to the claimant and his family. These can be anticipated to extend beyond settlement of the action/final judgment. It is a commonplace that the first year or two post-litigation are likely to be unsettled.

12. Thus "the first two Deputyship years" may extend over a greater period of time. When the conclusion of the assessment of damages approaches, there are likely to be a number of years that are already "history". When concluding assessment of damages approaches, these are likely to be a number of years for which the bills for Deputyship costs have been assessed and paid. Heightened costs associated with the litigation itself and the major structural adjustments in prospect will extend beyond the end of the litigation. At least one year should be allowed for the major investment decisions and for the claimant and family to settle down (even if relocation to suitable alternative accommodation has already taken place).

13. The general management costs identified for "the first two Deputyship years" are for a case of medium level complexity. Depending on all the circumstances and needs of the claimant including importantly the interplay and relationship with his/her family, the costs could be greater or less. All is contingent upon the level of activity required of the Deputy and their team. The range might be between £12/13,000 and £30,000 or more for general management costs.

14. Matters usually settle down to a general routine after that period. A range of £8,000–12,000 for general management costs might be anticipated in a typical cerebral palsy/acquired brain injury claim. Decisions may have to be taken about the claimant and his best interest and those of the family. Previous decisions should be revised.

15. It must be borne in mind that the MCA requires the deputy to consult on decisions to be made. A claimant will often require face-to-face meetings so that the Deputy is able to provide him with

appropriate explanations for decisions. The time and cost of dealing with this appropriately should not be underestimated.

16. Such issues may arise periodically. Some claimants will have behavioural problems, these include excessive contact, abusive behaviour and the claimant working against the Deputy. The claimant may feel that the Deputy is intruding into his life and taking his money. In addition it would not be unexpected if there were periodic disruption to the care team. A contingency sum has been allowed in the accompanying schedule.

17. On attaining majority the claimant requires a will. If he has testamentary capacity (as opposed to capacity to manage financial and property affairs), the will can be prepared on his instructions and subject to the court's approval, signed on his behalf by the Deputy. If not, a statutory will must be made by the court on application. The Official Solicitor will be appointed to act on behalf of the claimant. In either case the application will need to be supported by evidence as to those who might be required as having a claim upon the claimant's natural love and affection, and as to the claimant's best interest (*Re P*). In either case a medical report will be required concerning capacity. The costs given in the accompanying breakdown are estimated on the assumption that an attended hearing will be required. Depending upon the degree of contention, the costs may be greater or smaller. All parties that may be affected by any new will must be notified. If the claimant would have been intested this will include a natural parent even if the parent has re-married and estranged children from former relationships, etc. If the proposed will is contested the cost will increase significantly.

18. The will will require periodic review in the light of changed circumstances and provision is accordingly made for the preparation of a further will every 10 years.

19. The application for a new Deputy amounts to a fresh application, but as much of the information will already be available, the costs incurred are likely to be lower. A medical certificate will be required concerning capacity and the application might be expected to take up to six months, again. The appointment of a new Deputy will give rise to an authority for assessment of the existing/retiring Deputy's costs.

20. The Deputyship will come to an end either on: (a) application by the claimant for discharge on the footing that he or she now has sufficient capacity to manage his or her own finances and affairs; or (b) death. In either case there will be winding-up costs associated with accounting to the protected person or to the representatives of their estate. An application for discharge on the ground of regained capacity of the protected person will generally require to be supported by a Medical Certificate.

21. No provision has been made in the accompanying breakdown for incidental applications for additional or special authority but each will cost £400 in application fee.

22. A professional Deputy will be required to submit an annual bill of costs to the Senior Court Costs Office (SCCO) on the anniversary of each deputyship year. The bill will need to be prepared by a Costs Draftsman and the costs of the bill being prepared will be around 5.5 per cent of the profit costs claimed. Additionally there is an assessment fee of £220 which is payable to the SCCO on application for the assessment.

J3: Deputyship costs

One-off cost of application for a Deputy to be appointed

1	Solicitors' costs	£4,000	
2	*Plus VAT*	£800	
3	Disbursements (medical cert/travel)	£400	
4	*Plus VAT*	£80	Total setup costs: £6,845
5	Court of Protection Application fee	£400	
6	Office of the Public Deputy Assessment Fee	£100	
7	Marsh Ltd. Security Bond	£625	
8	Cost Draftsman's fees	£220	
9	SCCO Assessment Fee	£220	

Estimated annual costs for each of the first two Deputyship years

10	General management costs	£18,000	
11	*Plus VAT*	£3,600	
12	Plus Disbursements	£150	Total annual cost for each of the first two years: £23,935 pa
13	*Plus VAT*	£30	
14	Costs Draftsman's fee	£990	
15	SCCO Annual Assessment fee	£220	
16	Marsh Ltd. Security Bond	£625	
17	OPG Annual Supervision fee	£320	

Estimated annual costs for following years

18	General management costs	£10,000	
19	*Plus VAT*	£2,000	
20	Plus Disbursements	£150	
21	*Plus VAT*	£30	Total annual cost: £13,895
22	Costs Draftsman's fee	£550	
23	SCCO Annual Assessment fee	£220	
24	Marsh Ltd. Security Bond	£625	
25	OPG Annual Supervision fee	£320	

Other future costs

26	Solicitors' costs in dealing with a statutory will application (assuming a hearing is required)	£5,500	
27	*Plus VAT*	£1,100	
28	Official Solicitor's costs in dealing with statutory will (assuming a hearing is required)	£2,500	
29	*Plus VAT*	£500	Each of these items to be incurred every 10 years = total of £12,600 every 10 years
30	Court of Protection fee for statutory will	£400	
31	Disbursements involved in statutory will	£400	
32	*Plus VAT*	£80	
33	Solicitors' Costs for appointment of new Deputy/Obtaining new order	£1,200	
34	*Plus VAT*	£240	
35	Disbursements (Medical Cert)	£150	
36	*Plus VAT*	£30	
37	CP Application Fee for appointment of a new Deputy	£400	
38	OPG Deputy Assessment Fee	£100	
39	Winding-up costs	£1,500	One off
40	*Plus VAT*	£300	One off
41	Contingency sum	£30,000	One off
42	*Plus VAT*	£6,000	One off

Group K
Carer Rates and Rehabilitation

K1:   **Care and attendance**

K2:   **Nannies, cleaners and school fees**

K3:   **DIY, gardening and housekeeping**

K4:   **Hospital self-pay (uninsured) charges**

K5:   **NHS charges**

K6:   **The 2007 Rehabilitation Code**

K7:   **Rehabilitation: a practitioner's guide**

K

K1: Care and attendance

Introduction

1. Although a series of cases since 2005 involving injuries of the utmost severity has led to highly developed claims for care and attendance including case management,[1] the underlying principles are relatively straightforward. This section aims to be a source of practical assistance to practitioners and courts setting about the task of assessing damages for care and attendance.

Past non-commercial care

2. Damages awarded in respect of non-commercial care, usually by family members, are governed by the following rules/practical advice.
3. The aim is to award the reasonable value of / proper recompense for gratuitous services rendered—*Hunt v Severs*.[2]
4. Accordingly, a claimant holds the damages on trust for those who provided the care.[3]
5. If a tortfeasor has himself provided the care, there can be no recovery of damages on that score.[4]
6. If a claimant has fallen out with the care provider so that the recovery on trust will not be honoured, again there will be no recovery.[5]
7. There is no threshold requirement, in terms of either severity of injury/case or type/level of care, to be satisfied before an award can be made.[6] Extra domestic services are sufficient.[7]
8. While there is no threshold to satisfy, there must be actual care. So, when a claimant is still in hospital, damages are not to be awarded for mere visiting—only for any periods of care given during the course of the visit.[8]

---

[1] Readers interested in the finer detail of big cases can find it set out in the paper by James Rowley QC, "Serious PI litigation—a Quantum Update" with the accompanying tables at: *http://www.byromstreet.com/seminars-and-papers.php#archive*.

[2] [1994] 2 A.C. 350, 363A et seq. These are special damages. While not referred to expressly in the speeches, the rationale in *Daly v General Steam Navigation Co Ltd* 1981] 1 W.L.R. 120 CA—awarding general damages in respect of past non-commercial domestic services—was overruled by the House of Lords through the result in *Hunt v Severs*.

[3] *Hunt v Severs*, above, also expressly over-ruled the line of authority derived from *Donnelly v Joyce* [1974] QB 454 in favour of that derived from Lord Denning's judgment in *Cunningham v Harrison* [1973] QB 942. No longer is an award for services considered as a claimant's damages (based on his need for the care) for him then to make a present to the carer. Rather it is recompense to the carer and only held by a claimant on trust.

[4] Ibid., 363D. This is a common occurrence when passengers are suing a member of the family who was the negligent driver. Where liability is split, there is no known authority but also there is no reason in principle why a tortfeasor carer cannot recover to the extent of another tortfeasor's share of the blame.

[5] See *ATH v MS* [2003] PIQR Q1, [30] as to the principle; but in this case of fatal accident, the court was already ordering damages to be paid into court for investment on behalf of dependent children and felt able to enforce the trust through the investment control of the court. It would be otherwise if the monies were simply to be paid over to a claimant and the court really felt that the trust would not be honoured.

[6] The Court of Appeal in *Giambrone v Sunworld Holidays Ltd* [2004] PIQR Q4, Q36 decided that dicta in *Mills v British Rail Engineering Ltd* [1992] PIQR Q130 to the effect that there was a threshold of devoted care or care well beyond the ordinary call of duty (and similar phrases) were obiter and not to be followed.

[7] The Court of Appeal in *Mills* had overlooked a passage from Lord Denning in *Cunningham v Harrison*—quoted with apparent approval by Lord Bridge in *Hunt v Severs*, above at 360E—"Even though she had not been doing paid work but only domestic duties in the house, nevertheless all extra attendance on him certainly calls for compensation." [1973] QB 942, 952B–C.

[8] *Havenhand v Jeffrey* (unreported, February 24, 1997 CA); *Tagg v Countess of Chester Hospital Foundation NHS Trust* [2007] EWHC 509 (QB), [85]; *Huntley v Simmons* [2009] EWHC 405 (QB), [65].

---

9. Compensable care must relate to the person—the claimant himself or, under the rule in *Lowe v Guise*,[9] another disabled member of the same household, usually cared for by the claimant but who, because of the claimant's injury, is cared for by another. So, where the provision spreads out into non-commercial cover for the claimant in his business, different considerations apply; there is no compensable claim here for the hours provided by analogy with real care.[10]

10. Claims are rarely put on the following footing but where a carer has lost earnings in the provision of services, the value of the services can be assessed as the lost net earnings up to a ceiling of the commercial value of the care provided.[11]

11. In the majority of cases the exercise is to examine the care and make a fair assessment of the number of hours in fact provided. (In doing this, one will in passing register if care has in fact been given at anti-social hours or has been particularly demanding.) The assessment is easy in respect of discrete blocks of care; but calls for more subtle evidence/judgment when care is given in multiple short bursts over the course of day and night or constitutes more general supervision/ support in the home while daily life continues.

12. Hourly rates are then applied to the determined number of hours.

13. Many different scales have been used in the past; but now there is uniformity in taking rates derived from Local Authority Spinal Point 8.

14. The suggested starting points are the basic (daytime weekday) rate or the enhanced aggregate rate (which takes into account care in the evenings, at night and at weekends). Both are set out in the table.

15. The aggregate rate balances all the hours of the week by their relative number and appropriate rate. It is logically entirely apt only when care is spread out evenly through the whole week and the hours of the day and night. The odd hour here and there in the evening will not justify an aggregate rate; but intensive care given only at night and not by day, seven days a week (for example, when commercial daytime care has been purchased but a relative left to care at night), would logically justify more than the aggregate rate. Where a spouse has gotten up early to provide care before going to work and then carried on in the evenings on returning home, no care has been given when the daytime weekday rate is applicable.

16. There is no reason in principle why different rates cannot be used in different periods—the aggregate rate during more intensive care in early convalescence and the basic rate afterwards; or a rate over the whole period averaged somewhere between the two. No doubt the exercise would have to be relatively broad brush but it may be none the worse for that. The overarching aim is to attach a reasonable value to the actual care and award proper recompense.

17. Notwithstanding the logical attraction, however, of choosing a rate close to the circumstances of the actual provision, following *Fairhurst v St Helens & Knowsley HA*[12] the basic rate was used for

---

[9] [2002] QB 1369, [38]. What the ratio of this case is (and how widely or narrowly the rule established should be construed) is a fertile area for argument. Is it really confined to care of a disabled member or will care of a baby or child suffice? Is the element of provision being within the same household essential to the legal rule? Is it an important difference if a disabled mother has come to rely on her daughter's care while living in the next street; or in a self-contained granny-flat within the curtilage of the daughter's house; or in the spare room of her house?

[10] *Hardwick v Hudson* [1999] 1 W.L.R. 1770.

[11] *Housecroft v Burnett* [1986] 1 All E.R. 332 O'Connor L.J. at 343e albeit his view of the *Cunningham v Harrison* and *Donnelly v Joyce* debate was over-ruled in *Hunt v Severs*. The ceiling of the commercial rate has sometimes been criticised on the basis that it would have been enough simply to apply a wider test of reasonableness to the evaluation of the mother's claim for care of her daughter. However, that evaluation was at the very heart of the appeal and it would be difficult to contend that the invocation of the commercial ceiling was not part of the ratio.

[12] Averaging things with a broad brush appealed to Stuart-Smith J in *Ali v Caton & MIB* [2013] EWHC 1730 (Q.B.) at [323b–d] and he effectively reached a rate between the aggregate and basic ones. He took the starting point of the claimant's expert's figures and discounted them by 25% on account of arguments over both rates and the number of hours. " . . . *Adoption of a basic rate throughout would lead to under-compensation while adoption of the enhanced rate would have the opposite effect.*" See below at para.44 for more about the nature of this case.

over a decade in reported cases, even those of maximum severity when the care was of an onerous nature and much of it provided at nights and at weekends.[13]

18. Notwithstanding *Wells v Wells*[14] and modernisation of the assessment of damages for personal injuries, it took until *Massey v Tameside*[15] for there to be a reported case at the aggregate rate. Since then there has been a move away from using the basic rate as the universal starting point in very serious cases at least.[16]

19. It is unclear whether, in more routine cases where a significant proportion of the care has been carried out at anti-social times, a rate other than the basic rate is being awarded in unreported decisions; or if the basic rate still rules.

20. It is increasingly common for experts in very valuable cases to break the past down into a large number of periods with minor fluctuations in hours and annual increases in rates. It may be fine in that type of case, albeit use of properly considered averages would surely simplify things considerably at no significant cost in overall accuracy. In cases without experts, practical experience suggests focussing on fewer distinct periods of care and taking into account minor fluctuations through the reasoned choice of an average number of hours or average rate rather than embarking on over-elaborate calculation. Where cases involve gradually diminishing care from a point on hospital discharge to recovery or a plateau of continuing need, looking to the level of care midway through that period has much to commend it as a starting point in picking an overall average.

21. Since personal injury damages are awarded net of tax and NI, there is now invariably an appropriate reduction in respect of past non-commercial care.[17] It is usually 25 per cent[18] but the bracket appears to be between 20 per cent and 33 per cent.[19]

22. A sum equivalent to any Carer's Allowance received is to be deducted from an award for non-commercial care.[20] The value of direct payments also stands to be deducted.[21] There is no loss to the extent that there is NHS continuing care.

Example schedule[22]

Care while an in-patient—two weeks
Average of two hours actual care at the bedside

---

[13] Many settlements were negotiated with an enhancement for a higher rate, but there was no reported case until *Massey v Tameside* [2007] EWHC 317 (QB).

[14] [1999] 1 A.C. 345.

[15] [2007] EWHC 317 (QB).

[16] See also *Ali v Caton & MIB*, above fn 12.

[17] At a time when the basic rate was being used as the universal starting point, a few very serious cases emerged where it was felt that a deduction from such a low rate would leave a carer with inadequate recompense; and some courts refused to make a deduction. Now that the quality and difficulty of care is beginning to be reflected through higher rates, this method of achieving a fair result is no longer required. Choose the appropriate rate for the quality/intensity of care; but then make the principled deduction for tax and NI. As with any rule, however, there is the odd reasoned departure to be found: in *AC v Farooq & MIB* [2012] EWHC 1484 QB) King J. did not make deduction from the £7.11 rate used by one of the nursing experts since it already represented a compromise over what was the appropriate commercial rate—see [131].

[18] This was the considered reduction in *Whiten v St George's Healthcare NHS Trust* [2011] EWHC 2066 (QB) from the already chosen aggregate rate—see [144].

[19] *Evans v Pontypridd Roofing Limited* [2002] PIQR Q5 is the leading general authority on the non-commercial reduction.

[20] Teare J. in *Massey*, above, at [52]:
"To the extent that the carer has received benefits in respect of his or her voluntary care the claimant does not need a sum of money to give proper recompense for that care. It therefore seems to me that the Defendant's contention is right in principle."

[21] *Crofton v NHS Litigation Authority* [2007] 1 W.L.R. 923.

[22] The example will pick up the threads of the "logical" approach as outlined in the text. No doubt a counter schedule, as well as attempting to reduce the number of hours, would take a point that the basic rate only should be allowed in a case beneath that of maximum severity. Readers should report decided cases on the issue of hourly rate applied and kindly inform the writer when a case reference is available via james.rowley@byromstreet.com.

---

each evening (including Saturday and Sunday):
2 hours x 14 days @ the aggregate rate (£8.98)   251

Care during four weeks intensive convalescence at
home: six hours provided daily, including weekends and evenings: 6 hours x 28 days @ the aggre-
gate rate (£8.98)   1,509

Further six months of care gradually diminishing
from six hours a day to nil, more during the evenings and weekends at the beginning than at the
end:
Average of 3 hours a day care x 365/2 x the average
of the basic and aggregate rates (£7.91)   4,331

                                                               6,091
Non-commercial discount   x0.75
                                                                              4,568

No continuing personal care but assistance still
required in respect of heavier DIY, gardening, etc.
chores
Making allowance from £1,500 pa[23] for the chores
still possible:
£750 pa x 10 (discounted lifetime multiplier to say
70):   7,500

Total   £12,068

---

[23] Mackay J. in *Fleet v Fleet* [2009] EWHC 3166 (QB):
"25. This is claimed based on a multiplicand of £1500 p.a. I do not understand the multiplier to be controversial. The defendant contends for between £750 and £1000 per annum as a "more conventional sum" than the £1500 sought by the Claimant. The evidence on this issue is that Mr Fleet did all the DIY in the house and had in the past installed a new bathroom according to his wife. He was a skilled man albeit he was busy and worked long days and sometimes long weeks. He also said that he had plans to redecorate the house, and Mrs Fleet said that the living room now needs redecoration; though she could do some of the preparatory work, and did do so when her husband did the work, she could not in my judgement be reasonably expected to fill the gap left by him.
26. Equally, there is considerable garden at the house which Mrs Fleet tends but she cannot manage the trimming of the trees a screen of which separates the house from its neighbours and which has to be kept in order, or cut the grass.
27. I believe I am justified in saying that I can take into account the general level of awards under this head of damage from past experience. It would be dismal if experts had to be called to say how much it costs to mow a lawn or paint a room; after all judges do have some experience of that kind of activity and what it cost to buy it in the market place.
28. I see nothing wrong with the figure of £1,500 per annum claimed by the plaintiff and I think that is the right sum."

Past commercial care

23. Where there has been actual expenditure in the past on commercial care, it should be capable of easy proof (or reasonably accurate estimation if records have not been kept).
24. It will usually be awarded in full unless the defendant raises issues of unreasonable provision (or elements of separate causation leading to unrelated provision).[24]
25. The primary measure of damage against which to judge the claimed level of provision is one of reasonable care to meet a claimant's needs.[25]
26. If, at first blush, the claim in the past appears to exceed the primary measure of damage, principles of mitigation of loss may yet come to a claimant's aid if some evidence is adduced to explain the apparent over-spend. Once a claimant raises such arguments, the burden of proof lies on a

---

[24] In *O'Brien v Harris* (transcript of February 22, 2001) the BIRT rehabilitation costs (£21,860) significantly exceeded those originally estimated (£13,700) (see [191]). There was no evidence from BIRT explaining the difference or resiling from the estimate (see [192]). The case manager was not called to justify the additional case management costs (£10,834 v £6,461) (see [193]). Some increased costs were allowed based on inferences from the invoices to the effect that a higher quality of support worker had been provided than in the estimate (see [195]). There had, however, been inadequate management of cost (see [194]) (but by whom?—see below) and Pitchford J. made an overall award of £18,500 (see [196]).

In the very recent case of *Loughlin v Singh* [2013] EWHC 1641 (QB), Parker J. was invited (see [62]) to disallow the costs of past care and case management on the basis that *the standard of such care and management fell significantly below that which could reasonably be expected to meet the exigencies of the claimant's condition and circumstances.* The full submission was rejected as *wholly disproportionate and unjust*; but the claim was reduced by 20% with a broad brush on account of the case manager's failure to address the claimant's need for a specific and effective sleep hygiene regime in timely fashion. Parker J. made a finding that *the efforts made on this fundamental aspect of the rehabilitation were simply not adequate* (see [61]). . . . *Principle requires that I should take due account of the fact, that I have found, that the standard of the care and case management services did, in an important respect, fall significantly below the standard that could reasonably have been expected. In other words, the objective value of what the claimant received was less than the amount of the charges made for the relevant services* (see [62]).

There was no finding in *Loughlin* that the claimant through his Financial Deputy had knowingly appointed an incompetent case manager. Parker J. made no finding of failure to mitigate against the claimant/Financial Deputy in the handling/funding of the case manager (although this may have been an under-current in the case). As long as Parker J.'s findings amounted to *gross* negligence on the part of the case manager, his observations can be squared with wider principles of novus actus under *Rahman v Arearose Ltd* [2001] QB 351: insofar as the increased costs of failing to implement a sleep hygiene regime were caused by the gross negligence of a third party, they were separately caused. It is difficult to see, however, why a finding of mere negligence as against gross negligence in the past on the part of a case manager should break the chain of causation and lead to the dis-allowance of part of the claim.

In the even more recent case of *Ali v Caton & MIB*, above fn. 12, Stuart-Smith J. awarded the full claim for past support workers, the regime having been set up in accordance with apparently competent third party advice. *The position of a significantly brain-damaged claimant who acts on the basis of apparently reasonable advice is strong, though not always impregnable, when seeking to recover the costs of doing so from a tortfeasor. On this item, the balance of the argument strongly favours the claimant* [323f–h]. This approach is in keeping with the writer's understanding of the real legal issue set out in the previous paragraph.

[25] The principle was put succinctly by Lord Lloyd in *Wells v Wells* [1999] 1 A.C. 345, 377F in just 17 words:
"Plaintiffs are entitled to a reasonable standard of care to meet their requirements, but that is all."

Stephenson L.J. traced in *Rialis v Mitchell* (Court of Appeal transcript July 6, 1984) how the 100% principle was finessed through a series of Victorian cases involving accidents on the railways to reflect the recovery of reasonable rather than perfect compensation. Reasonable compensation is now 100% compensation since it is the primary measure of damage.

Swift J. reminded herself in *Whiten* (see [4]) of the judgment of Lord Woolf M.R. in *Heil v Rankin et al* [2001] 2 QB 272, [22–3] and [27]:

" . . . the aim of an award of damages for personal injuries is to provide compensation. The principle is that 'full compensation' should be provided. . . . This principle of 'full compensation' applies to pecuniary and non-pecuniary damages alike. . . . The compensation must remain fair, reasonable and just. Fair compensation for the injured person. The level must also not result in injustice to the defendant, and it must not be out of accord with what society as a whole would perceive as being reasonable."

She continued at [5]:

"The claimant is entitled to damages to meet his reasonable needs arising from his injuries. In considering what is 'reasonable', I have had regard to all the relevant circumstances, including the requirement for proportionality as between the cost to the defendant of any individual item and the extent of the benefit which would be derived by the claimant from that item."

defendant to prove a failure in mitigation; and the standard against which to judge a claimant's actions is not a harsh one.[26]

Future non-commercial care

27. If non-commercial care is to be carried on long into the future, the potential break down of the package is a contingency to be assessed. Where there is detailed expert evidence, there will often be an alternative package laid out drawing on greater commercial care. It will then be a matter for the judge to reach a fair balanced assumption in monetary terms between two or more packages, weighting the award according to the available evidence.[27]

28. Where the evidence is not so detailed and there is no provision elsewhere in the calculations for a break down in the non-commercial care package, it may well be appropriate to reflect adverse contingencies by refusing to apply the usual non-commercial discount. In this way some allowance is made with a broad brush for the possibility of more expensive commercial care on separation/ill health/death in the family member who is to supply the care.[28]

Future commercial care

Care—hourly rates

29. There is no "conventional" hourly rate for future commercial care, whether recruited through direct employment or an agency. All depends on the nature/difficulty of the required care; the level of need for continuity in carers; and the prevailing rates local to a claimant's home. Evidence on all three scores is highly desirable.[29] Examples of recent hourly rates in the biggest cases (direct employment not agency rates) are as follows:

Case[30]	Weekday - £	Weekend - £	Location
Whiten (agreed – mid-2011)	13	15	"Good" London rates
Sklair (agreed – late 2009)	11	13	Beckenham, Kent
C v Dixon (determined – evidence as at mid '08)	10	11	Barnsley
Huntley (determined – aggregate rate for late 2008)	9.50	9.50	Portsmouth Cosham/Hillsea

[26] The topic is beyond the scope of this chapter; an obvious source of assistance lies in *McGregor on Damages*, 18th edn (London: Sweet & Maxwell, 2012), para.7–070 and in the surrounding paragraphs.

[27] In *C v Dixon* [2009] EWHC 708 (QB) King J. assessed damages where the relationship between the claimant and his partner was far from assured in the long run. He took an assumed period of 10 years before break up as a fair reflection of the chances and proceeded to do the arithmetic from that starting point.

[28] See *Willbye v Gibbons* [2004] PIQR P1, [12] and [16] in which, on a quality of evidence which was insufficient to warrant fine alternative contingency calculations in the event of breakdown in the non-commercial package, Kennedy L.J. varied the sum awarded by removing the non-commercial discount allowed by the Recorder.

[29] Jack J. bewailed the lack of evidence of decent quality in *XXX* [2008] EWHC 2727 (QB), [16].

[30] Full case references can be found in wider text of this chapter.

Case[30]	Weekday - £	Weekend - £	Location
XXX (agreed – late 2008)	12	14	Guildford
Smith (determined – mid 2008)	10	12	Herts.
Crofts (agreed composite rate – summer 2008)	12	12	Herts.

Case management—hourly rate

30. As with support worker rates there is no "conventional" hourly rate for case management; but the rate for this (as against the number of hours required) is usually uncontroversial. The rate has crept up gradually and £90 an hour+ travel time (£45 an hour plus mileage) was agreed in *Whiten*. £95 an hour was awarded in *Ali v Canton*.[31] The required number of hours varies greatly and will be lower where there is agency care as against direct employment.

Provision for holidays, sick pay, etc.

31. Where future care is to be provided through direct employment rather than agency provision, it is now customary to take into account: (i) paid holidays, (ii) higher hourly rates paid on Bank holidays, (iii) sick leave, and (iv) down time in the package for training days by adopting calculations based on a notional 60 weeks in the year.[32] While a few experts continue to use it, the alternative method of taking 52 weeks in the year and a percentage uplift to cover the required extras (which started at around 27 per cent and rose steadily) has fallen out of favour in reported cases.

ERNIC

32. Calculation of ERNIC on carer's wages is often misunderstood. It is currently (tax year 2013/14) payable at 13.8 per cent on wages above the secondary threshold[33] (£148 a week × 52 weeks = £7,696 pa). So, to reach the annual sum of ERNIC, calculate the annual wage's bill and deduct from it (£7,696 × the likely number of carers in the package) to give the sum on which 13.8 per cent is likely to be paid.

---

[31] See fn. 12.

[32] See: *XXX* [2008] EWHC 2727 (QB), [24] and *Whiten v St George's Healthcare NHS Trust* [2011] EWHC 2066 (QB) at [167]–[168]. For the evolution of the 60-week calculation, see the paper at n.1. It is clear that down time for training days, additional pay for bank holidays, etc. are included in the 60-week calculation. Those care experts who take 60 weeks and routinely bill for training time and so on in addition might be said to be trying too hard. The taking of 60 weeks, however, might be distinguished up or down for the specific training, etc. requirements of any case since it has evolved out of the bigger cases—it might be easier to distinguish down rather than up (or the attempt not worth the effort).

[33] There is an upper ceiling; but no carer is ever paid enough to bring it into play.

NEST pension contributions

33. The following table[34] shows the workers who are or may be (at their instigation) to be enrolled. The qualifying compulsory threshold for earnings keeps going up and has now reached £9,440 pa. Enrolment is compulsory between the ages of 22 and State Retirement Age; optional at the behest of the employee either side of those ages from age 16 upwards of a lower threshold of £5,668 pa. The percentage contribution of the employer is payable on earnings above the relevant threshold, so it is to be calculated in a similar way to ERNIC—see above.

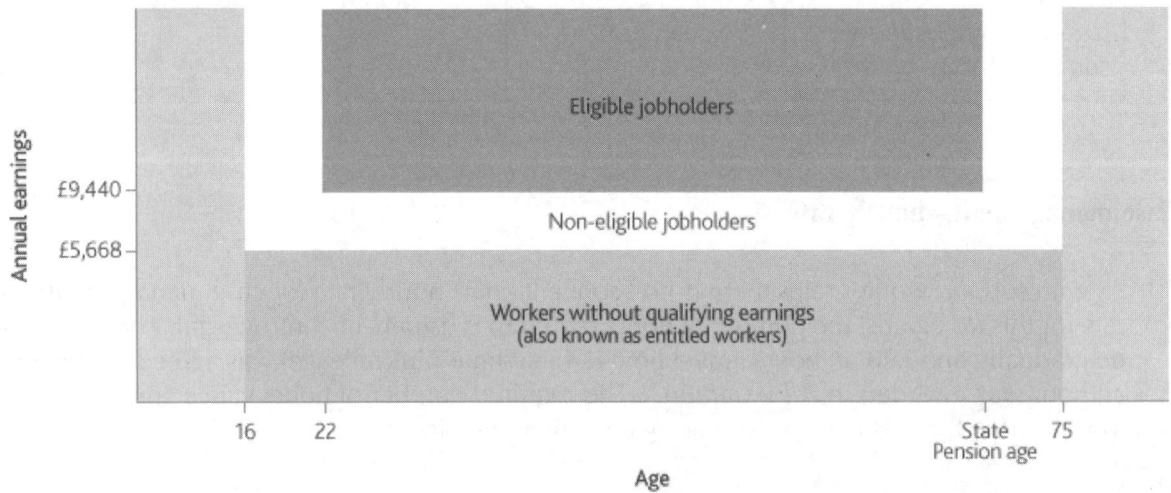

34. There will be a staged introduction of the duties depending on the size of the employer; but all care packages have fewer than 30 employees so will stand to be introduced into the scheme late on. The detail of this now appears in a downloadable guide.[35] The earliest date for an existing package to be brought under the NEST provisions is June 2015 and timing depends on the last two characters of the PAYE reference number of the employer. The date for a care package being started up now is July 1, 2017.

35. Once the duties have bitten on an employer, the full impact of the contributions is also to be phased in: the plan at time of writing is:

	Minimum percentage of qualifying earnings that must be paid in total	Minimum percentage of qualifying earnings that *employers* must pay
To end September 2017	2%	**1%**
October 2017 to end September 2018	5%	**2%**
October 2018 onwards	8%	**3%**

Parental contribution to the future care package

36. The court's attitude to any fair offset from future commercial care of very severely damaged children on account of parental involvement has evolved since 2006. The seeds sown by Sir Rodger Bell in *Iqbal*[36]—to the effect that parents are not to be presumed to take part in the care of grievously injured children requiring onerous care—have grown on strongly via Teare J. in

---

[34] Taken from the NEST website—see: *http://www.nestpensions.org.uk/schemeweb/NestWeb/public/NESTforEmployers/contents/assessing-your-workers.html.*
[35] At: *http://www.thepensionsregulator.gov.uk/employers/staging-date-timeline.aspx.*
[36] [2006] EWHC 3111 (QB), [20].

Massey [64], Lloyd Jones J. in *A v Powys* [57] and HHJ Collender QC (sitting as a Deputy High Court judge) in *Crofts* [120]. By the time of *Whiten* (2011) the NHSLA was no longer apparently arguing for any real offset: the only point at which the parents' potential contribution was considered relevant was in allowing for a single night sleeper in the commercial package on the basis that they would be available in an emergency (see [205]).

Offset for care required anyway?

37. In *Sklair v Haycock*,[37] the claimant (aged 49 and looked after informally by his "Bohemian" father) had suffered with Asperger's Syndrome and Obsessive Compulsive Disorder before the accident. The defence focussed on and valued what were described as merely the few extra hours of care required as a result of the accident.

38. The narrow approach of the defence was rejected. Edwards-Stuart J. found that the claimant's elderly father would have continued to look after him for 5–10 years longer, when his wider family would have looked after him at a financial cost to them of £150–£200 per week for 5–10 years, after which a residential placement in local authority care would have been likely.

39. The accident had turned (as a matter of fact) the claimant's need for this lower level of care into a reasonable need for 24–hour commercial care (see [80]). There was no question in the judge's mind (see [78]) after *Peters v East Midlands SHA*[38] of the claimant now having to mitigate into local authority care: he could pursue the tortfeasor as of right. The only real issue, therefore, was how, if at all, to credit the mixture of family non-commercial care and family-funded commercial care he would have received anyway against the full cost of 24-hour commercial care.

40. As to family non-commercial care, Edwards-Stuart J. rejected any offset at all (see [89]).

41. As to family expenditure on commercial care, Edwards-Stuart J. gave credit for its net value, reasoning at [91] that if the family had lent the claimant money to pay for care (and he had paid for it himself) he would have had to give credit for the value of that care. It should make no difference whether the family channel the money through the claimant or pay for the care directly.

Resident carers

42. The old arguments for residential agency care have completely fallen away in the most serious cases. There may still be a place for such a provision, however, in cases requiring a lighter touch, as with care of the partial tetraplegic claimant in *Davies*[39] (between the ages of 70 and 75, after which extensive top up for double up hours was added). The last gasp of the argument for residential care in the most serious cases came when the NHSLA in *Whiten* tried to run a *Davies*-post-75-style argument in the case of a grievously injured child with mixed spastic-dystonic, severe, quadriplegic cerebral palsy. It suggested the bedrock of a care package through a residential agency carer with extensive hourly top up.   Swift J. rejected that potential solution without hesitation (see [204]).

Risk/benefit applied to care regimes

43. *Davies*[40] and *C v Dixon*[41] have also been interesting in the detailed way in which Wilkie J. and King J. balanced risk and benefit to the claimant in reaching the appropriate care package. In each

---

[37] [2009] EWHC 3328 (QB).
[38] [2009] 3 W.L.R. 737.
[39] [2008] EWHC 740 (QB), Wilkie J.
[40] [2008] EWHC 740 (QB), Wilkie J.
[41] [2008] EWHC 740 (QB), Wilkie J., at 24.

case the defendant argued that the package suggested by the claimant's experts amounted to substantial over-provision and would be stifling of the claimant. In *Davies* some risk of falling was found to be acceptable without a resident carer always on hand before the age of 70: a resident carer package before that age did not take into account the contribution which a degree of self-reliance has to a person's sense of worth and well-being. In *C v Dixon* the claimant was not to be wrapped in cotton wool with unnecessary commercial and double up provision—he could have the required 24-hour care in a looser sense, including some down time in the package as long he had someone to contact in an emergency. Since his partner was assumed to be with him for the next 10 years, there was no need for commercial overnight care during that period.

44. In the moderate (general damages £147,500 – July 2013) brain injury case of *Ali v Caton & MIB*[42] Stuart-Smith J described scope of the care package there allowing 15 hours a week of support as follows [331ii)]:

"The purpose of the future care regime should be to provide sufficient support to enable [the Claimant] to pursue a structured and constructive existence so far as possible, reinforcing constructive routines and being available to assist when he is confronted by the new, the unfamiliar or the complex."

Two carers throughout the day

45. Whether two carers are required throughout the day has not been litigated to a formal decision recently. In *A v B*[43] two carers were required throughout waking hours (essentially in respect of transfers for toileting which could not be forecast as to timing) in a case of severe compromise in dystonic athetoid tetraplegic cerebral palsy. A similar result ensued in *XXX*. In both cases the claimants had little or no appreciation of their predicament but swift availability of changing was necessary for their health and comfort. The result was the same in *Massey* for a different reason: here the claimant had substantially retained intellect in a grossly mal-functioning body: for him the availability of two carers was essential for transfers and transport so that he could exercise autonomy and make decisions to act on impulse rather than live in the straight-jacket of double-up provision which was less than continuous and at fixed hours of the day.

46. The case for two carers in respect of a sentient adult who can give basic co-operation with hoisted transfers (in the sense of not lashing out or being subject to spasm) has not yet been clearly made out for transfers within the home. While the NHS commonly uses two nurses for such transfers even with a hoist on hospital wards, that appears to be at least partly because two nurses are available in such a setting and the use of two speeds things up.

Day centre provision

47. The argument for offset from a commercial care package for down time while a claimant attends a local authority day centre was never strong. With its lack of forensic success and further funding cuts and closure of day centres, the argument is not currently being aired.

Team leaders

48. Although the payment of a higher rate to a member of the support worker team did not find favour over five years ago in *Crofton* or *Iqbal*, the allowance of a team leader (reducing the amount and cost of case management intervention) has become pretty standard more recently in really serious cases. £2 an hour extra was conceded in *XXX*. In *Whiten* the principle was disputed; and as a fall

---

[42] See fn. 12.
[43] [2006] EWHC 1178 (QB).

back it was suggested by the defendant that any provision could be by reference to a small proportion of the hours worked by the team leader, i.e. only those hours when in fact engaged on team leader duties. Swift J. at [164] rejected that line and allowed 30 hours a week at a weekday rate enhanced by £3 an hour (London). The whole point was to attract someone to the post with experience and ability: the defendant's suggestion would not achieve the aim.

Handover meetings

49. Claiming handover periods of up to half an hour at the conclusion of each shift has never appeared an attractive argument and is not generally being run at the moment.

Liaison/team meetings

50. Recently, these were not contended for in *Whiten*; allowed as to merely one hour a month in *C v Dixon*, and substantially conceded in *XXX*. There may have been oversight when these allowances have been made or conceded: as the "60 weeks in the year" evolved, it was probably supposed to take into account a routine allowance for training and team meetings—see the discussion of the evidence in the judgment of Penry-Davy J. in *Smith*.[44]

Chance contingencies and PPOs for care

51. Huntley[45] illustrates that the essential chance assessment of damages for future loss has survived the new PPO regime, which purports to trace everything back to a claimant's needs. There the claimant, who had suffered a frontal lobe injury and whose rehabilitation had not gone well up to trial, contended for 24 hours of care per day as the long-term solution: the defendant submitted for 21 hours per week. Underhill J. approached matters by evaluating first of all the hard-core minimum level that he thought was reasonable, which he assessed at six hours a day (see [109]). This hardcore cost he would have put within a PPO (see [114]) but not the full chance reasonable amount that he went on to evaluate as follows. He uplifted the package by 50 per cent from six hours to nine hours a day with a broad brush for all the possibilities of needing greater care. He then discounted that back by one hour to eight hours a day for the chance that the claimant would not in fact engage all the care that he might reasonably require. There was a real chance that he would reject care (as he would if he entered a stable relationship) and small chances of imprisonment and detention under the Mental Health Act. The resulting additional two hours a day beyond the core six hours Underhill J. would have provided within an additional lump sum award; but the whole PPO submission was withdrawn when the claimant did not recover for 24-hour care.

Burden of proof/correct measure of damage—most basic legal principles

52. It was fashionable four or five years ago for claimants to run an argument along the following lines in order to give themselves an edge in the expert dispute over future care: while the legal test in relation to allowing claims is reasonableness,[46] there may be a range of reasonable options to meet a claimant's care needs and that, provided the care package for which the claimant contends falls within this range, it should be accepted by the court. It was said that in order to mount an acceptable attack on a claimant's case a defendant had to do a good deal more than show that the

[44] [2008] EWHC 2234 (QC)—the transcript lacks numbered paragraphs.
[45] [2009] EWHC 405 (QB).
[46] See above at n.22 for some more recent dicta.

odd element is a little higher than might be paid in some circumstances. The effect of the argument was to turn issues of evaluation of future care into those equivalent to mitigation of past loss—would be it be an unreasonable decision to implement eight hours a day rather than six (with the burden on a defendant to disprove the decision with a generous ambit in favour of a claimant)?

53. If the argument is traced back[47] it might be thought to amount to a conjuring trick, mixing principles of mitigation with what is really an issue covered by the court's evaluation of the primary/normal measure of damage for future loss—an exercise in which the court rather than a claimant holds the ring.

---

[47] See the paper at n.1.

Year	Time of day	Hourly rate £	Hours pw	Cost pw £	Divided by hours pw	Aggregate rate
Nov 1976 to Oct 1977	Basic Time $+\frac{1}{4}$ Time $+\frac{1}{2}$	£1.02 £1.28 £1.53	—	—	—	£1.24
Nov 1977 to Oct 1978	Basic Time $+\frac{1}{4}$ Time $+\frac{1}{2}$	£1.12 £1.40 £1.68	—	—	—	£1.36
Nov 1978 to Jul 1979	Basic Time $+\frac{1}{4}$ Time $+\frac{1}{2}$	£1.21 £1.51 £1.82	—	—	—	£1.47
Aug to Oct 1979	Basic Time $+\frac{1}{4}$ Time $+\frac{1}{2}$	£1.29 £1.61 £1.94	—	—	—	£1.57
Nov 1979 to Mar 1980	Basic Time $+\frac{1}{4}$ Time $+\frac{1}{2}$	£1.46 £1.83 £2.19	—	—	—	£1.78
Apr 1980 to Oct 1980	Basic Time $+\frac{1}{4}$ Time $+\frac{1}{2}$	£1.54 £1.93 £2.31	—	—	—	£1.87
Nov to Dec 1980	Basic Time $+\frac{1}{4}$ Time $+\frac{1}{2}$	£1.66 £2.08 £2.49	—	—	—	£2.02
Jan to Oct 1981	Basic Time $+\frac{1}{4}$ Time $+\frac{1}{2}$	£1.88 £2.35 £2.82	—	—	—	£2.29
Nov 1981 to Oct 1982	Basic Time $+\frac{1}{4}$ Time $+\frac{1}{2}$	£2.00 £2.50 £3.00	—	—	—	£2.43
Nov 1982 to Oct 1983	Basic Time $+\frac{1}{4}$ Time $+\frac{1}{2}$	£2.10 £2.63 £3.15	—	—	—	£2.56
Nov 1983 to Oct 1984	Basic Time $+\frac{1}{4}$ Time $+\frac{1}{2}$	£2.19 £2.74 £3.29	—	—	—	£2.67
Nov 1984 to Aug 1985	Basic Time $+\frac{1}{4}$ Time $+\frac{1}{2}$	£2.29 £2.86 £3.44	—	—	—	£2.79
Sep 1985 to Aug 1986	Basic Time $+\frac{1}{4}$ Time $+\frac{1}{2}$	£2.44 £3.05 £3.66	—	—	—	£2.97
Sep 1986 to Jun 1987	Basic Time $+\frac{1}{4}$ Time $+\frac{1}{2}$	£2.60 £3.25 £3.90	—	—	—	£3.16
Jul 1987 to Aug 1988	Basic Time $+\frac{1}{4}$ Time $+\frac{1}{2}$	£2.90 £3.63 £4.35	—	—	—	£3.53
Sep 1988 to Aug 1989	Basic Time $+\frac{1}{4}$ Time $+\frac{1}{2}$	£3.07 £3.84 £4.61	—	—	—	£3.74
Sep 1989 to Aug 1990	Basic Time $+\frac{1}{4}$ Time $+\frac{1}{2}$	£3.34 £4.18 £5.01	—	—	—	£4.07
Sep 1990 to Jun 1991	Basic Evening Weekend	£3.66 £4.58 £5.50	55 65 48	£201.30 + £297.70 + £264.00 = £763.00	168	£4.54
Jul 1991 to Jun 1992	Basic Evening Weekend	£3.89 £4.87 £5.84	55 65 48	£213.95 + £316.55 + £280.32 = £810.82	168	£4.83

Year	Time of day	Hourly rate £	Hours pw	Cost pw £	Divided by hours pw	Aggregate rate
Jul 1992 to Jun 1993	Basic Evening Weekend	£4.04 £5.05 £6.06	55 65 48	£222.20 + £328.25 + £290.88 = £841.33	168	£5.01
Jul 1993 to Aug 1994	Basic Evening Weekend	£4.21 £5.26 £6.32	55 65 48	£231.55 + £341.90 + £303.36 = £876.81	168	£5.22
Sep 1994 to May 1995	Basic Evening Saturday Sunday	£4.44 £5.55 £6.66 £8.88	55 65 24 24	£244.20 + £360.75 + £159.84 + £213.12 = £977.91	168	£5.82
Jun 1995 to Mar 1996	Basic Evening Saturday Sunday	£4.56 £5.70 £6.84 £9.12	55 65 24 24	£250.80 + £370.50 + £164.16 + £218.88 = £1,004.34	168	£5.98
Apr 1996 to Mar 1997	Basic Evening Saturday Sunday	£4.69 £5.86 £7.03 £9.38	55 65 24 24	£257.95 + £380.90 + £168.72 + £225.12 = £1,032.69	168	£6.15
Apr 1997 to Mar 1998	Basic Evening Saturday Sunday	£4.84 £6.05 £7.26 £9.68	55 65 24 24	£266.20 + £393.25 + £174.24 + £232.32 = £1,066.01	168	£6.35
Apr 1998 to Mar 1999	Basic Evening Saturday Sunday	£4.98 £6.22 £7.47 £9.96	55 65 24 24	£273.90 + £404.30 + £179.28 + £239.04 = £1,096.52	168	£6.53
Apr 1999 to Mar 2000	Basic Evening Saturday Sunday	£5.13 £6.41 £7.69 £10.26	55 65 24 24	£282.15 + £416.65 + £184.56 + £246.24 = £1,129.60	168	£6.72
Apr 2000 to Mar 2001	Basic Evening Saturday Sunday	£5.29 £6.61 £7.93 £10.58	55 65 24 24	£290.95 + £429.65 + £190.32 + £253.92 = £1,164.84	168	£6.93
Apr 2001 to Mar 2002	Basic Evening Saturday Sunday	£5.49 £6.86 £8.23 £10.97	55 65 24 24	£301.95 + £455.90 + £197.52 + £263.28 = £1,208.61	168	£7.19
Apr 2002 to Sep 2002	Basic Evening Saturday Sunday	£5.65 £7.06 £8.47 £11.30	55 65 24 24	£310.75 + £458.90 + £203.28 + £271.20 = £1,244.13	168	£7.41
Oct 2002 to Mar 2003	Basic Evening Saturday Sunday	£5.71 £7.14 £8.56 £11.42	55 65 24 24	£314.05 + £464.10 + £205.44 + £274.08 = £1,257.67	168	£7.49
Apr 2003 to Mar 2004	Basic Evening Saturday Sunday	£5.90 £7.37 £8.85 £11.80	55 65 24 24	£324.50 + £479.05 + £212.40 + £283.20 = £1,299.15	168	£7.73

Year	Time of day	Hourly rate £	Hours pw	Cost pw £	Divided by hours pw	Aggregate rate
Apr 2004 to Mar 2005	Basic Evening Saturday Sunday	£6.06 £7.57 £9.09 £12.12	55 65 24 24	£333.30 + £492.05 + £218.16 + £290.88 = £1,334.39	168	£7.94
Apr 2005 to Mar 2006	Basic Evening Saturday Sunday	£6.24 £7.80 £9.36 £12.48	55 65 24 24	£343.20 + £507.00 + £224.64 + £299.52 = £1,374.36	168	£8.18
Apr 2006 to Mar 2007	Basic Evening Saturday Sunday	£6.43 £8.04 £9.65 £12.86	55 65 24 24	£353.65 + £522.60 + £231.60 + £308.64 = £1,416.49	168	£8.43
Apr 2007 to Mar 2008	Basic Evening Saturday Sunday	£6.59 £8.24 £9.88 £13.18	55 65 24 24	£362.45 + £535.60 + £237.12 + £316.32 = £1,451.49	168	£8.64
Apr 2008 to Mar 2009	Basic Evening Saturday Sunday	£6.75 £8.44 £10.13 £13.50	55 65 24 24	£371.25 + £548.60 + £243.12 + £324.00 = £1,486.97	168	£8.85
Apr 2009 to Mar 2013	Basic Evening Saturday Sunday	£6.85 £8.56 £10.28 £13.70	55 65 24 24	£376.75 £556.40 £246.72 £328.80 = £1,508.67	168	£8.98
Apr 2013	Basic Evening Saturday Sunday	£6.92 £9.23 £10.38 £13.84	70 50 24 24	£484.40 £461.50 £249.12 £332.16 = £1,527.18	168	£9.09

K2: Nannies, cleaners and school fees

The death or incapacity of a spouse frequently involves incurring the costs of a nanny or a housekeeper or of sending a child to boarding school so that the surviving parent can continue working. Also, with some employments, typically when they involve overseas postings or frequent moves, school fees are part of the remuneration and will be lost if the employee dies or is disabled from that particular employment.

Nannies

| | Daily | | Live-in | |
	Weekly net	Annual gross	Weekly net	Annual gross
Central London	£495	£34,124	£389	£26,017
Outer London/Home Counties	£428	£28,995	£336	£21,963
Other areas	£389	£26,017	£317	£20,509

The figures are derived from the 2012 survey by *Nannytax*. The total cost to the client will be more than the gross wage as it is necessary to pay for holidays, sickness, employer's national insurance contribution, agency fees and so on. (See the discussion of *A v B Hospitals Trust*[1] at note 7 to Table K1: Carer rates.)

Cleaners

The services of cleaners in London are currently advertised at the following rates (as at June 2013). These are commonly for three or more hours a week: one-off visits usually cost more.

Homeclean	£8.45 per hour	(three hours a week)
	£9.18 per hour	(two hours a week: the cleaner is paid separately avoiding VAT; and there is an annual agency fee)
MK Londyn	£12.00 per hour	(£10.00 plus VAT)
Amy Cleaning	£9.99 per hour	(Varies. The cleaner is paid separately, avoiding VAT; there is also an agency fee).

School fees

Annual school fees for a three-term year are as follows.

Public school (average)		Independent Schools Council	
Boarders (Upper school)	£31,350	Boarder	£27,612
Day pupils (Upper school)	£21,708	Day pupil (boarding school)	£15,636
Day pupils (Under school or preparatory school)	£15,114	Day pupil (day school)	£11,505

Notes:

1. Fees for pupils entering in the sixth form may be higher.

2. Fees for weekly as opposed to full-time boarders may be lower.

The information has been obtained from the websites of Nannytax, Homeclean, MK Londyn, Amy Cleaning, Westminster School, and the Independent Schools Council.

[1] [2006] EWHC 1178.

K3: DIY, gardening and housekeeping

1. Claimants are entitled to damages for the loss of the ability to do these tasks. Anyone who is responsible for the running of a house knows that there is a real cost in bringing in an electrician, tiler, carpenter, joiner, plumber or other skilled tradesmen to carry out tasks that they themselves cannot do. "The loss of ability to do work in the home is a recoverable head of damages and includes 'services' such as general housekeeping, gardening and maintenance".[1]

2. The same principle applies to loss of housekeeping skills. Claimants can be compensated for their inability to carry out the tasks which occur in most households—e.g. cleaning, shopping, laundry, ironing, cooking, and washing up. Even sewing on buttons, cleaning the windows, and performing the mundane routines of daily existence, such as putting out the bins and dealing with the milkman, all have to be carried out by someone, though it is too easy to forget them.

3. The loss can be valued commercially. In *Phipps v Brooks Dry Cleaning Services*[2] Stuart-Smith L.J. says that such skills have "a real money value", and Brandon J. in *Daly v General Steam Navigation Co Ltd*[3] says:

    "The loss occurred and the cost of employing someone else is no more than a way of measuring it".

4. The difficulty is always in finding an appropriate rate and working out a number of hours every week which such housekeeping tasks take to perform. Whether as a "jury award" or by using a multiplier/multiplicand approach, a judge is perfectly able to assess the evidence and make an award which reflects the reality of the loss to the claimant or the dependants. The courts have made a wide range of awards, which are analysed in *Kemp & Kemp*, Vol.1, Ch.17. In *Lawrence v Osborn*,[4] the defendant insurers accepted an annual rate of £750 per annum as the standard figure for inability to perform DIY functions. In *Wells v Wells*,[5] the Court of Appeal accepted an award under this head of £1,000 per annum. In *Dixon v Wene*,[6] Gross J. awarded £15,000 (a global sum), for loss of services: gardening and DIY.

5. Evidence is needed to support such a claim, photographs being an excellent addition to witness statement evidence. A report from a local surveyor and/or an independent agency can also strengthen this claim.

6. It should be borne in mind that often, as people get older, their appetite and energy for such tasks diminishes. This is not true for all, however; some 70- and 80-year-olds seem to have an undiminished enthusiasm for these activities.

7. A claimant need not prove an actual intention to employ replacement services (paid or unpaid). It is worth remembering the words of Bridge L.J. in *Daly v General Steam Navigation Co*[7]:

    "It has been energetically argued by Mr Bennett, for the defendants, that before future loss of capacity to undertake housekeeping duties can properly be assessed at the estimated cost of

[1] Damages for Personal Injury: Medical, Nursing and Other Expenses; Law Commission, Law Com. No.262 (1999), para.2.34.
[2] [1996] P.I.Q.R. Q 100.
[3] [1979] 1 Lloyd's Rep. 257.
[4] Unreported November 7, 1997, Anthony May J., QBD.
[5] [1997] 1 W.L.R. 652.
[6] [2004] EWHC 2273 (QB).
[7] [1981] W.L.R. 120, 127.

employing some third person to come in and do that which the plaintiff is unable to do for herself, the plaintiff has to satisfy the court that she has a firm intention in any event that such a person shall be employed. For my part, I am quite unable to see why that should be so. Once the judge had concluded, as this judge did, that, to put the plaintiff, so far as money could do so, in the position in which she would have been if she had never been injured, she was going to need, in the future, domestic assistance for eight hours a week, it seems to me that it was entirely reasonable and entirely in accordance with principle in assessing damages, to say that the estimated cost of employing labour for that time, for an appropriate number of years having regard to the plaintiff's expectation of life, was the proper measure of her damages under this heading. It is really quite immaterial, in my judgment, whether having received those damages, the plaintiff chooses to alleviate her own housekeeping burden, which is an excessively heavy one, having regard to her considerable disability to undertake housekeeping tasks, by employing the labour which has been taken as the basis of the estimate on which damages have been awarded, or whether she chooses to continue to struggle with the housekeeping on her own and to spend the damages which have been awarded to her on other luxuries which she would otherwise be unable to afford".

		Hourly range	Daily range
Handymen	London	£25–£50	£180–£240
	Outside London	£15–£35	£100–£180
Gardeners	London	£25–£30	n/a
	Outside London	£15–£20	n/a

Charges will vary depending on the complexity of the work undertaken.

Charges often increase for the first hour of work undertaken and/or at weekends.

Companies that cater exclusively to seniors or those on low income and consequently charge a much reduced rate have not been included in these ranges.

Handyman charges are exclusive of plumbing or electrical charges which are invariably set at a higher rate.

K4: Hospital self-pay (uninsured) charges

The following figures are inclusive of hospital charges and surgeons' and anaesthetists' fees. The charges are approximate, as certain factors affecting cost, such as length of stay or prosthesis used, vary from patient to patient.

Private Healthcare Charges

Investigation—CT—single system	from £500
Investigation—MRI—single investigation	from £500
Scar revision	£510–£5,750
Therapy—physiotherapy (hourly rate)	from £60
Outpatient consultation (consultant charge)	£60–£200

Treatment	Cost
breast lump removal	£2,040–£5,295
cardiac catheterisation	£1,827–£2,472
carpal tunnel release	£1,751–£2,370
cataract removal (one eye)	£3,006–£4,067
circumcision	£1,627–£2,202
colonoscopy (bowel examination)	£1,976–£2,673
colposcopy (cervix examination)	£765–£1,035
coronary angioplasty	£3,191–£4,318
coronary artery bypass graft	£14,195–£19,205
cruciate ligament repair (ACL)	£4,420–£5,979
cystoscopy (bladder examination)	£1,171–£2,375
epidural injection	£855–£1,156
gall bladder removal (cholecystectomy—laparoscopic)	£4,973–£6,728
facet joint injection under x-ray and anaesthetic	£858–£1,161
ganglion removal	£1,032–£1,465
gastric banding (weight loss surgery)	£6,073–£8,216
gastric balloon insertion	£3,400–£7,273
gastric bypass (weight loss surgery)	£9,273–£12,546
gastroscopy	£1,759–£2,380
grommets insertion	£2,208–£2,987
haemorrhoids removal	£2,106–£4,057
hernia repair (laparoscopic inguinal)	£2,140–£2,895
hip replacement	£10,798–£14,609
hip resurfacing	£8,797–£18,746
hysterectomy	£5,174–£7,001
hysteroscopy	£1,915–£2,592
knee arthroscopy	£3,178–£4,299
knee replacement	£11,047–£14,946
laparoscopy	£1,906–£4,125
prostate removal (TURP)	£4,595–£6,218
sigmoidoscopy	£1,640–£2,219
sterilisation (female)	£4,866–£6,583
termination of pregnancy	£1,479–£3,091
tonsillectomy	£1,836–£3,849
vaginal repair	£3,944–£5,336

varicose vein surgery (both legs)	£2,530–£3,423
varicose vein surgery (one leg)	£1,729–£2,340
varicose vein laser treatment—EVLT (both legs)	£3,632–£4,913
varicose vein laser treatment—EVLT (one leg)	£3,030–£4,099
vasectomy	£467–£1,420
vasectomy reversal	£2,609–£3,530
wisdom teeth extraction replacement	£1,917–£2,587

These figures are drawn from around the country. Charges vary from hospital to hospital and between different areas of the country. They are generally higher in London than elsewhere.

K5: NHS charges

NHS prescriptions (from April 1, 2013)

Charge per prescribed item		£7.85
Prescription prepayment certificate:	three months	£29.10
	12 months	£104.00

For items dispensed in combination (duo) packs, there is a charge for each different drug in the pack.

NHS dental treatment (from April 1, 2013)

If a patient is not exempt from charges, he should pay one of the following rates for each course of treatment he receives:

Course of treatment	Cost	Scope
Band 1	£18.00	This covers an examination, diagnosis (e.g. x-rays), advice on how to prevent future problems, and a scale and polish if needed.
Band 2	£49.00	This covers everything listed in Band 1, plus any further treatment such as fillings, root canal work or extractions.
Band 3	£214.00	This covers everything listed in Bands 1 and 2 above, plus crowns, dentures or bridges.

Notes

1. These are the only charges for NHS dental treatment.
2. A patient only has to pay one charge for each course of treatment, even if it takes more than one visit to the dentist to finish it.
3. If the patient needs more treatment within the same or lower charge band (e.g. an additional filling), within two months of completing a course of treatment, there is no extra charge.
4. There is no charge for repairing dentures or for having stitches removed.
5. Children under 18, and many adults, do not have to pay NHS charges. (See form HC11, "Help with Health Costs", which can be found on the Department of Health website: *http:/ /www.dh.gov.uk*.)

NHS wigs and fabric supports (from April 1, 2013)

Stock modacrylic wig	£64.95
Partial wig—human hair	£172.00
Full bespoke wig—human hair	£251.55
Abdominal support	£39.75
Spinal support	£39.75
Surgical brassière	£26.35

K6: The 2007 Rehabilitation Code

(Code of Best Practice on Rehabilitation, Early Intervention and Medical Treatment in Personal Injury Claims)

The aim of this code is to promote the use of rehabilitation and early intervention in the compensation process so that the injured person makes the best and quickest possible medical, social and psychological recovery. This objective applies whatever the severity of the injuries sustained by the claimant. The Code is designed to ensure that the claimant's need for rehabilitation is assessed and addressed as a priority, and that the process of so doing is pursued on a collaborative basis by the claimant's lawyer and the compensator.

Therefore, in every case, where rehabilitation is likely to be of benefit, the earliest possible notification to the compensator of the claim and of the need for rehabilitation will be expected.

1. INTRODUCTION

1.1 The purpose of the personal injury claims process is to put the individual back into the same position as he or she would have been in had the accident not occurred, insofar as money can achieve that objective. The purpose of the rehabilitation code is to provide a framework within which the claimant's health, quality of life and ability to work are restored as far as possible before, or simultaneously with, the process of assessing compensation.

1.2 Although the Code is recognised by the Personal Injury Pre-Action Protocol, its provisions are not mandatory. It is recognised that the aims of the Code can be achieved without strict adherence to the terms of the Code, and therefore it is open to the parties to agree an alternative framework to achieve the early rehabilitation of the claimant.

1.3 However, the Code provides a useful framework within which claimant's lawyers and the compensator can work together to ensure that the needs of injured claimants are assessed at an early stage.

1.4 In any case where agreement on liability is not reached it is open to the parties to agree that the Code will in any event operate, and the question of delay pending resolution of liability should be balanced with the interests of the injured party. However, unless so agreed, the Code does not apply in the absence of liability or prior to agreement on liability being reached.

1.5 In this code the expression "the compensator" shall include any loss adjuster, solicitor or other person acting on behalf of the compensator.

2. THE CLAIMANT'S SOLICITOR

2.1 It should be the duty of every claimant's solicitor to consider, from the earliest practicable stage, and in consultation with the claimant, the claimant's family, and where appropriate the claimant's treating physician(s), whether it is likely or possible that early intervention, rehabilitation or medical treatment would improve their present and/or long-term physical and mental well being. This duty is ongoing throughout the life of the case but is of most importance in the early stages.

2.2 The claimant's solicitors will in any event be aware of their responsibilities under section 4 of the Pre-Action Protocol for Personal Injury Claims.

2.3 It shall be the duty of a claimant's solicitor to consider, with the claimant and/or the claimant's family, whether there is an immediate need for aids, adaptations, adjustments to employment to enable the claimant to keep his/her existing job, obtain suitable alternative employment with the same employer or retrain for new employment, or other matters that would seek to alleviate problems caused by disability, and then to communicate with the compensators as soon as practicable about any such rehabilitation needs, with a view to putting this Code into effect.

2.4 It shall not be the responsibility of the solicitor to decide on the need for treatment or rehabilitation or to arrange such matters without appropriate medical or professional advice.

2.5 It is the intention of this Code that the claimant's solicitor will work with the compensator to address these rehabilitation needs and that the assessment and delivery of rehabilitation needs shall be a collaborative process.

2.6 It must be recognised that the compensator will need to receive from the claimant's solicitors sufficient information for the compensator to make a proper decision about the need for intervention, rehabilitation or treatment. To this extent the claimant's solicitor must comply with the requirements of the Pre-Action Protocol to provide the compensator with full and adequate details of the injuries sustained by the claimant, the nature and extent of any or any likely continuing disability and any suggestions that may have already have been made concerning the rehabilitation and/or early intervention.

2.7 There is no requirement under the Pre-Action Protocol, or under this code, for the claimant's solicitor to have obtained a full medical report. It is recognised that many cases will be identified for consideration under this code before medical evidence has actually been commissioned or obtained.

3. THE COMPENSATOR

3.1 It shall be the duty of the compensator, from the earliest practicable stage in any appropriate case, to consider whether it is likely that the claimant will benefit in the immediate, medium or longer-term from further medical treatment, rehabilitation or early intervention. This duty is ongoing throughout the life of the case but is most important in the early stages.

3.2 If the compensator considers that a particular claim might be suitable for intervention, rehabilitation or treatment, the compensator will communicate this to the claimant's solicitor as soon as practicable.

3.3 On receipt of such communication, the claimant's solicitor will immediately discuss these issues with the claimant and/or the claimant's family pursuant to his duty set out above.

3.4 Where a request to consider rehabilitation has been communicated by the claimant's solicitor to the compensator, it will usually be expected that the compensator will respond to such request within 21 days.

3.5 Nothing in this or any other code of practice shall in any way modify the obligations of the compensator under the Protocol to investigate claims rapidly and in any event within three months (except where time is extended by the claimant's solicitor) from the date of the formal claim letter. It is recognised that, although the rehabilitation assessment can be done even where liability investigations are outstanding, it is essential that such investigations proceed with the appropriate speed.

4. ASSESSMENT

4.1 Unless the need for intervention, rehabilitation or treatment has already been identified by medical reports obtained and disclosed by either side, the need for and extent of such intervention, rehabilitation or treatment will be considered by means of an assessment by an appropriately qualified person.

4.2 An assessment of rehabilitation needs may be carried out by any person or organisation suitably qualified, experienced and skilled to carry out the task. The claimant's solicitor and the compensator should endeavour to agree on the person or organisation to be chosen.

4.3 No solicitor or compensator may insist on the assessment being carried out by a particular person or organisation if (on reasonable grounds) the other party objects, such objection to be raised within 21 days from the date of notification of the suggested assessor.

4.4 The assessment may be carried out by a person or organisation which has a direct business connection with the solicitor or compensator, only if the other party agrees. The solicitor or compensator will be expected to reveal to the other party the existence of and nature of such a business connection.

5. THE ASSESSMENT PROCESS

5.1 Where possible, the agency to be instructed to provide the assessment should be agreed between the claimant's solicitor and the compensator. The method of providing instructions to that agency will be agreed between the solicitor and the compensator.

5.2 The assessment agency will be asked to carry out the assessment in a way that is appropriate to the needs of the case and, in a simple case, may include, by prior appointment, a telephone interview but in more serious cases will probably involve a face-to-face discussion with the claimant. The report will normally cover the following headings:

1. The injuries sustained by the claimant.
2. The current disability/incapacity arising from those injuries. Where relevant to the overall picture of the claimant's needs, any other medical conditions not arising from the accident should also be separately annotated.
3. The claimant's domestic circumstances (including mobility accommodation and employment) where relevant.
4. The injuries/disability in respect of which early intervention or early rehabilitation is suggested.
5. The type of intervention or treatment envisaged.
6. The likely cost.
7. The likely outcome of such intervention or treatment.

5.3 The report should not deal with issues relating to legal liability and should therefore not contain a detailed account of the accident's circumstances.

5.4 In most cases it will be expected that the assessment will take place within 14 days from the date of the letter of referral to the assessment agency.

5.5 It must be remembered that the compensator will usually only consider such rehabilitation to deal with the effects of the injuries that have been caused in the relevant accident and will normally not be expected to fund treatment for conditions which do not directly relate to the accident unless the effect of such conditions has been exacerbated by the injuries sustained in the accident.

6. THE ASSESSMENT REPORT

6.1 The report agency will, on completion of the report, send copies on to both the claimant's solicitor and compensator simultaneously. Both parties will have the right to raise questions on the report, disclosing such correspondence to the other party.

6.2 It is recognised that for this assessment report to be of benefit to the parties, it should be prepared and used wholly outside the litigation process. Neither side can therefore, unless they agree in writing, rely on its contents in any subsequent litigation.

6.3 The report, any correspondence related to it and any notes created by the assessing agency to prepare it, will be covered by legal privilege and will not be disclosed in any legal proceedings unless the parties agree. Any notes or documents created in connection with the assessment process will not be disclosed in any litigation, and any person involved in the preparation of the report or involved in the assessment process, shall not be a compellable witness at court. This principle is also set out in para.4.4, above, of the Pre-Action Protocol.

6.4 The provision in para.6.3, above as to treating the report, etc. as outside the litigation process is limited to the assessment report and any notes relating to it. Any notes and reports created during the subsequent case management process will be covered by the usual principle in relation to disclosure of documents and medical records relating to the claimant.

6.5 The compensator will pay for the report within 28 days of receipt.

6.6 This code intends that the parties will continue to work together to ensure that the rehabilitation which has been recommended proceeds smoothly and that any further rehabilitation needs are also assessed.

7. RECOMMENDATIONS

7.1 When the assessment report is disclosed to the compensator, the compensator will be under a duty to consider the recommendations made and the extent to which funds will be made available to implement all or some of the recommendations. The compensator will not be required to pay for intervention treatment that is unreasonable in nature, content or cost or where adequate and timely provision is otherwise available. The claimant will be under no obligation to undergo intervention, medical or investigation treatment that is unreasonable in all the circumstances of the case.

7.2 The compensator will normally be expected to respond to the claimant's solicitor within 21 days from the date upon which the assessment report is disclosed as to the extent to which the recommendations have been accepted and rehabilitation treatment would be funded and will be expected to justify, within that same timescale, any refusal to meet the cost of recommended rehabilitation.

7.3 If funds are provided by the compensator to the claimant to enable specific intervention, rehabilitation or treatment to occur, the compensator warrants that they will not, in any legal proceedings connected with the claim, dispute the reasonableness of that treatment, nor the agreed costs, provided of course that the claimant has had the recommended treatment. The compensator will not, should the claim fail or be later discontinued, or any element of contributory negligence be assessed or agreed, seek to recover from the claimant any funds that they have made available pursuant to this Code.

K7: Rehabilitation: a practitioner's guide

Compiled by the Bodily Injury Claims Management Association

Norman W. Cottington, The Injury Care Clinics (President)
David Blofeld, past Claims Manager, Hart Re
Christopher Crook, Solicitor, Edwards Duthie
Tony Goff, Solicitor, George Ide Phillips
Graham Plumb, Claims Manager, AXA Insurance
Keith O. Popperwell, Solicitor Silverbeck Rymer
Bernard Rowe, Solicitor, Lyons Davidson (Treasurer)
Martin Saunders, Allianz Cornhill Insurance
Martin Staples, Solicitor, Vizards
Janet Tilley, Solicitor, Colemans CTTS (Secretary)
Ian Walker, Solicitor, Russell Jones and Walker (Vice President)

CONTENTS

1. Case Management
2. Immediate Needs Assessment
3. Emotional and Psychological Care
4. Physiotherapy, Osteopathy and Chiropractic
5. Accommodation
6. Nursing, Care and Equipment
7. Social Services
8. Social Security Benefits
9. Mobility
10. Vocational

1. CASE MANAGEMENT

One of the first decisions to make is who will manage the rehabilitative process. The various specialist disciplines are outlined below. The task of organising so many disciplines may seem daunting, but help can be found.

One way is to use a case manager to act as case co-ordinator.

The appointment of a case manager at an early stage in the claim will need to be discussed and preferably agreed with the claimant and the insurer. A case manager must have close contact with the claimant and his/her family.

A case manager must have the time available to deal with the claimant and preferably be based close to the claimant.

Case managers can come from a variety of disciplines, but look for someone trained and committed to the standards laid down by the Case Management Society of the UK (CMSUK).

There are a number of specialist case management organisations in the UK, although the number of claimants is likely to outweigh the availability of specialists for some time to come.

A case manager will co-ordinate all of the available services and should be required as appropriate to:

- assess the personal circumstances and needs of the claimant and his/her family;
- monitor medical rehabilitation and, if necessary, provide for multi-disciplinary assessment;
- liaise with the DSS and claim appropriate benefits;
- liaise with the local authority for interim support prior to a statutory assessment (currently Community Care Act 1990); review such assessment and negotiate the provision of services and financial assistance from the local authority;
- arrange for therapies;
- monitor the needs of the claimant's family and arrange for respite care, if necessary;
- assist the claimant in obtaining training and monitoring carers;
- facilitate employment rehabilitation;
- arrange appropriate accommodation;
- review personal transport arrangements;
- consider mobility issues; and
- consider funding arrangements for rehabilitation.

Cost
Following an initial assessment, case management will normally be charged on an hourly basis (expect to pay between £65 and £85 per hour). Input by a case manager should reduce once rehabilitation needs have been addressed.

2. IMMEDIATE NEEDS ASSESSMENT

Why?
Rehabilitation in the long-term will be difficult, if not impossible, if short-term needs are overlooked. "First Aid" support is essential to overcome the immediate aftermath of an injury and to provide a platform on which to build long-term rehabilitation.

At what level?
As a rule of thumb, an immediate needs assessment is applicable to claimants who have sustained injuries likely to cause incapacity for several months or longer.

When?
The assessment should be done as soon as possible, even before discharge from hospital, with a view to ensuring the home environment to which the claimant will be discharged is suitable at least for the basic needs of the claimant and his/her family. However, an assessment undertaken years after the event of the injury can still help.

What to expect
The report should provide preliminary background information about the claimant's circumstances, including the following:

a. the nature and extent of the injury;
b. any relevant medical background;
c. family circumstances;
d. immediate home adaptation needs;

e. steps to improve the claimant's quality of life and support for family carers; and
f. how, and at what cost, recommendations can be implemented.

Relatively simple and inexpensive measures can make a big difference, for example, stair handrails, ramps for wheelchair access, raised toilet seats, widened doorways, and lowered light switches or doorknobs.

Recommendations should be capable of being put into immediate effect and at proportionate, reasonable cost.

Do not confuse an immediate needs assessment with long-term care needs and costs, which will be addressed by appropriate experts in the claim.

By whom?
A case manager trained and committed to the standards laid down by the Case Management Society of the UK (CMSUK) is the most obvious choice.

An occupational therapist or anyone with a social care background, for example, a community care nurse, a social worker or a general practitioner, may similarly be able to conduct the assessment.

Cost
The Code requires that the insurer be responsible for the cost.

The charge will depend upon the complexity of the report and travel expenses, but expect to pay between £750 and £1,750.

The defendant's insurer should usually fund reasonable recommendations by way of an interim payment (see section 7 of the Code).

Liability
Only a complete denial of liability should prevent a defendant's insurer from considering an immediate needs assessment (but also consider an assessment via Social Services).

If the dispute is confined to contributory negligence, the comparatively low cost of an assessment will be justified.

3. EMOTIONAL AND PSYCHOLOGICAL CARE

Why?
Anyone who has suffered a serious injury has experienced a major life event. The injured person, his/her family and close friends will be totally unprepared for either the injury or what follows.

Those who have suffered a serious injury will need to come to terms with what has happened to them. There may also be psychological disorders triggered by the accident, which must be recognised and dealt with. Failure to do so may prevent other treatments from being effective and may hinder a return to work.

Emotional, and in many cases psychological support needs to be given to help the claimant and those upon whom he/she depends.

When?

Support should be offered as soon as possible. Often this will be determined by the willingness of the injured claimant and/or his/her family to accept outside help. Many people are frightened by their feelings or by the idea of sharing them with someone. Proper counselling can also be of great assistance to relatives acting as carers.

An early assessment can in itself help identify problems or potential problems in time to prevent prolonged post-traumatic stress disorder.

An assessment and, where needed, counselling or psychological treatment are best considered soon after the injury and/or return home from hospital (i.e. within the first three months of injury). The need for emotional and psychological support may last much longer than the medical treatment.

By whom?

Clinical psychologists should normally carry out an initial assessment. If there is any suggestion of brain injury, then a neuropsychologist should be used.

It is useful to check first whether the claimant's hospital team has already involved a psychologist to help with rehabilitation or whether there is a facility within the GP's practice.

Arrangements should be made with a clinical psychologist close to the claimant's home. Where necessary, appointments can be arranged at the claimant's home, which is important if the claimant is distressed by travel.

There are a number of agencies that have panels of psychologists available or you can contact the British Psychological Society at St. Andrew's House, 48 Princess Road East, Leicester LE1 7DR or by telephone on 0116 254 9568.

What to expect

Most assessments involve some psychological testing. This is necessary to determine what help is needed. Better insight and understanding by the claimant and/or his/her family of what to expect of themselves and their feelings will help to achieve maximum recovery.

Cost

A clinical psychologist's assessment and recommendations will cost between £200 and £500.

A neuropsychologist's assessment will cost between £750 and £1,750.

Psychological therapy costs between £75 and £150 per session.

4. PHYSIOTHERAPY, OSTEOPATHY AND CHIROPRACTIC

Why?

Early mobilisation following injury is now widely recognised as an important part of treatment and needs to be encouraged, provided that it is consistent with medical advice. Damaged tissue needs careful handling. Injury victims need to be shown how to regain movement and function as soon as possible. Whilst treatment methods vary amongst the different professions, these all work towards maximising useful function and can help prevent an injury from becoming a permanent disability.

When?

In the case of serious injuries, this type of treatment is normally determined by the hospital medical team. After discharge from hospital, it is all too easy to overlook the benefit to be gained from continuing physiotherapy and other treatments. Treatment is not just about relieving pain, but equally about achieving the best possible recovery of movement, strength and function. In the case of soft tissue injuries, treatment should be assessed as soon as possible, i.e. within a few weeks, not months, of the injury. In more serious cases, initial treatment should be considered as part of the overall medical management of the patient. After discharge, treatment should be considered as part of the overall nursing plan or by direct referral to a practitioner.

By whom?

This type of treatment is provided by chartered physiotherapists, osteopaths or chiropractors. Increasingly, it is possible to find that two or more of these disciplines are offered at the same clinic. There are a number of specialist agencies that will provide and co-ordinate treatment. Details of local practitioners can also be found in the Yellow Pages. Alternatively, information is available from:

- Chartered Society of Physiotherapists: 0207 306 6666
- General Council of Osteopaths: 0207 357 6655
- British Chiropractic Association: 0118 950 5950

What to expect

Make sure the practitioner is a member of a relevant professional body and that there are well-equipped treatment rooms. All practitioners will want to assess the patient before offering treatment. The assessment may involve x-rays as well as a physical examination.

If treatment is offered, a treatment plan should be prepared that identifies the number of treatments and when they are to be given. Often a patient will be taught exercises to help speed up the recovery process.

Cost

The cost will vary from clinic to clinic. Average costs for an assessment will be in the order of £40–£60. Treatment is likely to cost in the order of £30–£45 per session depending upon locality.

5. ACCOMMODATION

Why?

A secure, comfortable and accessible home is likely to be a pre-requisite for any home-based rehabilitation plan. Accommodation that was suitable for a claimant before an injury may be unsuitable after injury.

When?

Assessment of accommodation needs should be undertaken as soon as possible. For many patients, the only obstacle to being discharged from hospital is their inability to access their own home.

The need for substantial adaptations to accommodation or even a purpose-built property is normally a long-term consideration. Permanent arrangements are best dealt with when it is reasonably clear what the long-term requirements will be.

Physical needs will be identified in medical, occupational therapist and nursing reports.

Short-term needs are as important a consideration as long-term needs. Short-term may, in fact, mean several months or even longer. Immediate needs may have been dealt with under an immediate needs report, but this will need to be updated.

By whom?
A case manager or occupational therapist may be able to advise upon minor alterations that are needed until permanent needs become clear. Once these needs have been identified, a good local builder will be able to carry out minor works such as installing rails, ramps and widening doorways.

If major alterations are needed, a report will be required from an accommodation expert, usually a surveyor or architect, and preferably one with experience of designing accommodation for use by people with disabilities. Whoever carries out the assessment should be familiar with and liaise with the local authority, from which grants may be available. This is particularly relevant in cases where damages may be reduced as a result of an apportionment of liability.

What to expect
A visit to the claimant's home or proposed home, after consideration of the medical and other reports. This will lead to a report detailing the physical requirements of the property that are necessary in order for the claimant to maximise his/her potential for independent living. In addition, it will take into account the possibility that a carer might need accommodation.

The report should detail the work needed, together with costs, including likely maintenance and/or replacement costs.

Cost
The cost of this report will vary from case to case. Hourly charge-out rates will be in the order of £100–£150 per hour. A detailed report is likely to cost £1,000 or more.

6. NURSING, CARE AND EQUIPMENT

Why?
The objective will be to establish the most beneficial regime, aimed at ensuring the health and welfare of the injured person, and optimising independence and self-esteem by the most cost-effective means.

When?
It is important to establish in advance what arrangements will be beneficial at each stage of the recovery process, and not address each stage as it occurs. At each stage, it is vital that the case manager, or those reporting, are fully aware of the current medical prognosis, including any anticipated changes.

By whom?
The appointed case manager is likely to be the best choice, as they often possess all of the relevant experience. The person chosen must have an understanding of the medical and physical needs of the claimant, and how to provide for them. Not all nursing/care experts may deal with aids and equipment. Separate advice may be needed from an occupational therapist.

What to expect

The expert will need to see all existing reports and it may be beneficial for the different disciplines to confer.

The expert will need to speak to the claimant and his/her family and carers as well as those responsible for medical treatment. The report should address:

- the injured person's capacity for coping with the challenges of his/her injury and impairment;
- existing care, by whom and in what environment;
- external features impacting on the situation, e.g. accommodation, social contact, locality and family dynamics;
- the level of nursing care required;
- vulnerabilities—health and safety issues for the claimant and his/her carers at present and in the future;
- the need for an enabler;
- the need for domestic assistance;
- details of equipment needed;
- detailed cost of recommendations and suggested providers; and
- objectives and their timescales.

Cost

This will depend upon the circumstances and the complexity of each case. Reports will cost from £1,000. Hourly charging rates are likely to range from £65–£90 per hour, but could possibly be higher.

7. SOCIAL SERVICES

Social services are provided pursuant to the National Health Service Community Care Act 1990 by local authorities' Social Services departments, which are entitled to call upon:

- Health Authorities.
- Housing Departments.

The trigger for support is an assessment by the local authority pursuant to s.47 of the NHS and Community Care Act 1990. The right to an assessment is absolute.

Once an assessment has been carried out, a written copy must be provided to the Social Services department. A complaints and review procedure is available if the assessment is considered unsatisfactory.

Following assessment, the local authority will make a decision about whether to provide services and the type of services to be provided.

Social services available include:

- home helps or carers;
- respite breaks for carers;
- laundry service;
- therapies;
- odd job scheme;
- rehabilitation;

- carer support;
- residential care;
- transport;
- housing adaptation; and
- provision of accommodation suitable to the claimant's needs.

The provision of services may be dependent upon the resources of the local authority. Each local authority publishes eligibility criteria. Certain services must be provided under a legal duty. Other services may be provided on a discretionary basis, but there is no duty to do so.

Section 2 of the Chronically Sick and Disabled Persons Act sets out services that must be supplied as a legal duty:

- home help;
- provision of radio, television, library or residential services;
- home adaptations for greater safety, comfort or convenience;
- holidays;
- meals; and
- telephone.

The local authority will formulate a case plan, which will be administered by a case manager. This will specify all needs, including those that cannot be met due to budget restraints.

Local authorities are empowered to make direct cash payments to disabled persons so that they can purchase care services for themselves (Community Care (Direct Payments) Act 1996). In addition, cash payments are available from Independent Living Funds and from the DWP.

If the claimant needs suitable accommodation, the local authority has a duty to provide this pursuant to s.21 of the National Assistance Act.

Residential care can be arranged by both local authorities and health authorities. Provision of residential care by a health authority is free, but DWP benefits are treated as if the claimant were in hospital. Local authority residential care is subject to means testing. Residential care includes the provision of basic accommodation.

A claimant can choose his/her preferred accommodation and can ask a third party (e.g. an insurer or tortfeasor) to meet any shortfall if the cost is more than the local authority would normally pay.

If a local authority provides services free of charge, a claimant cannot make a claim against the insurer in respect of such services.

A local authority has discretion to charge for services other than residential care.

The right to charge for services is subject to a two-stage test:

1. whether it is reasonable in all the circumstances; and
2. whether the claimant has sufficient means to pay for the services.

Where residential accommodation is provided by a local authority, there is a duty to charge, subject to means testing.

However, such charges can be avoided by the creation of a trust or if the damages are administered by the court (see Preservation of Benefits, below).

8. SOCIAL SECURITY BENEFITS

Aim
To maximise benefits and to preserve the right to means-tested benefits.

Non-means-tested benefits
There are four main groups of non-means-tested benefits that are payable as a consequence of disability:

1. Incapacity for Work
   Incapacity Benefit
   Severe Disablement Allowance

2. Care and Supervision
   Disability Living Allowance
   Care Component
   Constant Attendance Allowance

3. Mobility
   DLA Mobility Component

4. Degree of Disablement
   Severe Disablement Allowance
   Industrial Disablement Benefit

Income Support
This is paid to the claimant if he/she is incapable of working, and to a carer if regularly and substantially engaged in caring for another person.

If the claimant has capital in excess of £8,000 (or £16,000 if in residential care), he/she does not qualify for income support.

Disability Working Allowance
This is intended to encourage people with disabilities to return to work. It is paid to people who work 16 hours or more per week. If a claimant (or his/her partner) has capital of more than £16,000, the claimant does not qualify for this allowance.

Disability Living Allowance
The DLA is not means-tested.

This allowance comprises a care component and a mobility component. The care component is for personal care needs and is paid at three different rates. The mobility component is paid at two different rates.

Tests are administered by an Adjudication Officer.

Receipt of the DLA acts as a gateway to the following benefits:

- Disability Premium.

- Severe Disability Premium.
- Independent Living Funds.
- Motability Scheme.

Industrial Injuries Benefit
This benefit is paid to those who are disabled by a loss of physical and mental capacity caused by an industrial accident or disease.

It is paid in addition to any other non means-tested benefit.

Incapacity Benefit
This is paid to those who are unable to work due to disability. It is non-means-tested, but it is only payable if sufficient national insurance contributions (NIC) have been made.

Severe Disablement Allowance
This allowance is paid for 28 weeks to those who are incapable of working but have made insufficient NIC to qualify for the incapacity benefit.

How to claim
Benefit is generally paid from the date that a claim is received by a DWP Office.

There is discretion to accept anything in writing "as sufficient" in the circumstances of a particular case.

The DLA is paid from the date a claim form is requested, so long as the claim form is returned within six weeks.

Income support is paid from the date of notifying the DWP, so long as the claim form is returned within one month. There is discretion to extend time limits in some cases.

Claims should be made to a local DWP Office or by telephoning the Benefit Enquiry Line on 0800 882200.

Appeals are made to the local DWP Office. An appeal can be made within three months of any decision. There is some discretion to extend the time limit up to six years, but it is difficult to make a late appeal.

The effect of receipt of damages on income-related benefits
Lump sum payments of compensation are treated as capital and are added to any other capital that the claimant may have. The effect is that:

- a claimant or partner may have up to £8,000 (£16,000 if in residential care) in capital and benefit will not be affected;
- deductions are made on a sliding scale in Income Support, DLA, Housing Benefit and Council Tax Benefit, depending on the amount of capital;
- income support is not payable where there is capital in excess of £8,000 (or £16,000 if in residential care); and
- no Housing Benefit, Council Tax Benefit or DLA is payable if capital exceeds £16,000.

Preservation of benefits

Benefits paid to a claimant can be managed by creating a trust or ensuring the damages fund is administered by the court.

Trusts

The trust may be set up by the claimant or someone acting on behalf of the claimant. If a trust is created:

- the capital value of the trust fund is wholly disregarded;
- payments from the trust fund to the claimant or on his/her behalf will be treated as income or capital, depending on frequency of payment and the terms of the trust; and
- regular discretionary payments will be disregarded, provided they are used for needs other than those intended to be covered by benefits.[1]

Funds administered by the court

A decision of the Social Security Commissioner[2] makes it clear that money in the Court of Protection should not be taken into account for entitlement to Income Support under the terms of para.12 to Sch.120 to the Income Support (General) Regulations (as amended).

9. MOBILITY

Why?

Restricted mobility emphasises impairment and threatens independence. Mobility contributes toward independence.

When?

Immediate thought should be given to mobility within the home, which is often effectively achieved by simple steps such as providing ramps and widening doorways for wheelchair users.

Longer-term projects, such as specialised wheelchairs or appropriate motor vehicles, may have to await medical recovery.

What to expect?

A driving assessment can identify and address any barriers to independent driving ability, and can identify aids, adaptations or controls required to overcome those barriers.

The Disability Living centres identify and cost aids and equipment for mobility and dexterity.

By whom?

Personal mobility can be assessed by an occupational therapist.

Disability Living centres exhibit and assist in identifying appropriate aids, including wheelchairs, vehicles and prosthetic appliances.

---

[1] This is no longer so. It was changed by the 2006 Regulations. See H4.
[2] (1996) 3 J.S.S.L.D. 136.

Driving Assessment centres can assist in determining the right choice of vehicle and wheelchair.

The claimant or his/her family can apply to the DWP for a Mobility Allowance and/or payment under the Motability Scheme to defray the cost of a vehicle.

Disabled living experts, usually architects, can advise on property alterations to ensure ease of access.

Cost

A driving assessment is unlikely to cost £50–£100 or more, at a mobility centre.

The Disability Living centres provide their services at no cost, although the equipment they recommend can cost anything from a few pounds for a wide-handled toothbrush to more than £1,000 for a suitable wheelchair.

10. VOCATIONAL

Why?

A return to work is more likely to raise a claimant's self-esteem than anything else. It provides independence and self-respect.

When?

A claimant should be helped to return to work, if appropriate, as soon as possible.

It is vital to:

- take early steps to consider, with the involvement of the employer, the preservation of the claimant's pre-accident job, by adapting the workplace or duties in accordance with the Equality Act 2010; and
- if remaining with the pre-accident employer is not possible, then consider all alternative avenues.

Insurers may be willing to fund the necessary steps to achieve these goals.

By whom?

A vocational or employment rehabilitation expert should assess the claimant's suitability to return to work and his/her requirements.

A vocational report should not be confused with the reports commonly commissioned from employment consultants. The latter are generally designed to assist in the quantification of loss, whereas the former is intended to identify the injured person's potential and motivation for employment, and to recommend how to achieve a return to suitable work. The expert should know the local area and sympathetic employers, whilst having a good working relationship with the Disability Employment Advisor.

What to expect

A detailed interview should be undertaken to identify the claimant's former work experience abilities and qualifications, his/her aspirations, and a general assessment of his/her current physical and mental ability.

The next stage should, ideally, be a meeting between the vocational assessor and the previous employer with a view to identifying whether re-employment is possible, either in full or reduced capacity; whether other placements may be available; and/or whether adaptations to the work place may be necessary to facilitate such employment.

If employment with the pre-accident employer is not possible for whatever reason, then consideration will be given to other suitable local job opportunities.

If no such opportunities exist, a more detailed vocational assessment, carried out over a period of one week, may be recommended.

There are numerous facilities nationwide where such assessments can take place either on a day or residential basis. Assessments take place in a working environment and measure dexterity, co-ordination, ability, communication skills, confidence, and motivation. Speed, ability and quality of work is recorded, assessed and reported upon.

Following assessment, recommendations may include finding a work placement properly suited to the claimant's skills and abilities or sending the claimant on a training scheme to learn new skills. Another possibility is for the claimant to be supported by a trainer or friend, who would work alongside him/her in a work placement until confidence is gained in employment skills.

A return to some form of remunerative employment is the most effective way an injured person can regain his/her self-esteem and achieve an improved quality of life.

Cost
This will vary depending upon the type of assessment and the time it takes. Expect charges of £750–£1,500 for a vocational interview and report. More detailed assessments will cost more. A residential five-day assessment is likely to cost £2,000 or more.

Case management—the early days
As health care options, delivery methods and financing mechanisms became more complex, with inconsistent incentives and accountability, the need for assistance in obtaining timely and appropriate care to achieve recovery and optimal functioning has become increasingly evident.

The first Case Management Society was established in America in 1990 (CMSA) after recognition of the need for a supportive body for this rapidly expanding profession. In 1996, the Case Management Society International was established to provide an umbrella for global affiliation. Canada, Australia, South Africa and a number of European countries already have their own case management societies.

In response to this growth in case management, an informal group of care professionals involved in case management practice started meeting during 2000 to explore the possibility of a national, non-profit, professional membership association for case managers.

About CMSUK
The overall goals and ambitions are to:

* advise on the development of a professional case management qualification;
* develop and encourage consistent professional standards of best practice, competence, service and conduct of case managers;

- provide comprehensive continuing education programmes;
- provide support for its members;
- instil confidence for purchasers when employing the services of a CMSUK member;
- development of case managers within existing public/private health and social environment; and
- one of our main aims is to be affiliated with and accredited by the main professional bodies that currently register practising case managers.

With evolving care structures, CMSUK will play an integral part in setting and upholding standards to ensure that cost-effective and timely outcomes are achieved.

If you would like to know more about CMSUK, please write to: CMSUK, 100 Fetter Lane, London, EC4A 1BN. Email: cmsukltd@yahoo.co.uk

Group L
Motoring and Allied Material

L

L1:   **AA motoring costs**

L2:   **Taxation of car and fuel benefits**

L3:   **The Motability Scheme**

L4:   **Calculations involving motor cars**

L5:   **Time, speed and distance**

L1: AA motoring costs

Petrol cars

	Cost New (£)				
	Up to £13,000	£13,000 to £18,000	£18,000 to £25,000	£25,000 to £32,000	Over £32,000
Standing charges per annum (£s)					
Vehicle Excise Duty (Road tax)	125.00	175.00	200.00	260.00	455.00
Insurance	667.00	806.00	1078.00	1617.00	3395.00
Cost of capital	227.00	313.00	389.00	548.00	966.00
Depreciation	1223.00	2006.00	2597.00	3857.00	8159.00
Breakdown cover	50.00	50.00	50.00	50.00	50.00
Total, standing charges only (£s)	2292.00	3350.00	4314.00	6332.00	13025.00
Standing charges per mile (pence)					
5,000	45.35	66.20	85.24	125.10	257.24
10,000	22.92	33.50	43.14	63.32	130.25
15,000	15.61	22.87	29.45	43.24	89.01
20,000	12.07	17.75	22.87	33.59	69.20
25,000	9.76	14.36	18.50	27.18	56.02
30,000	8.17	12.04	15.51	22.78	46.95
Running costs per mile (pence)					
Petrol*	12.67	14.19	15.77	17.32	21.80
Tyres	1.28	1.83	2.16	2.90	3.75
Service labour costs	4.85	4.98	4.55	4.32	7.32
Replacement parts	2.50	2.75	2.88	3.50	3.63
Parking and tolls	2.00	2.00	2.00	2.00	2.00
Total, running costs only (pence)	23.30	25.75	27.36	30.04	38.50
* Unleaded Petrol @ 133.7 p/litre. For every penny more or less, add or subtract	0.10	0.11	0.13	0.14	0.17

Total of standing charges and running costs (in pence) based on annual mileage of:

5,000 miles	68.65	91.95	112.60	155.14	295.74
10,000 miles	46.22	59.25	70.50	93.36	168.75
15,000 miles	38.90	48.62	56.81	73.28	127.51
20,000 miles	35.37	43.50	50.23	63.63	107.70
25,000 miles	33.05	40.11	45.86	57.22	94.52
30,000 miles	31.47	37.79	42.87	52.82	85.45

Please see the associated notes for more detail. These figures are typical but do not represent all types of vehicle and conditions of use. The figures change from time to time.

Diesel cars

	Cost New (£)				
	Up to £16,000	£16,000 to £22,000	£22,000 to £26,000	£26,000 to £36,000	Over £36,000
Standing charges per annum (£s)					
Vehicle Excise Duty (Road tax)	30.00	140.00	175.00	220.00	475.00
Insurance	700.00	840.00	1100.00	1495.00	1930.00
Cost of capital	253.00	374.00	453.00	582.00	959.00
Depreciation					
(at 10,000 miles/annum)	1487.00	2301.00	2824.00	3713.00	7438.00
Breakdown cover	50.00	50.00	50.00	50.00	50.00
Total, standing charges only (£s)	2520.00	3705.00	4602.00	6060.00	10852.00
Standing charges per mile (pence)					
5,000	49.81	73.18	90.91	119.71	214.06
10,000	25.20	37.05	46.02	60.60	108.52
15,000	17.20	25.31	31.43	41.39	74.33
20,000	13.34	19.68	24.42	32.16	57.98
25,000	10.79	15.92	19.76	26.02	46.98
30,000	9.04	13.35	16.56	21.81	39.40
Running costs per mile (pence)					
Diesel*	10.03	12.19	13.59	15.44	19.97
Tyres	1.20	1.80	1.95	3.30	3.90
Service labour costs	4.35	4.45	4.77	4.81	7.46
Replacement parts	2.91	2.81	2.88	3.43	3.72
Parking and tolls	2.00	2.00	2.00	2.00	2.00
Total, running costs only (pence)	20.49	23.25	25.19	28.98	37.05
* Diesel @ 142.6 p/litre.					
For every penny more or less,					
add or subtract	0.07	0.08	0.10	0.11	0.14

Total of standing charges and running costs (in pence) based on annual mileage of:

5,000 miles	70.29	96.43	116.10	148.69	241.12
10,000 miles	45.69	60.30	71.21	89.58	145.57
15,000 miles	37.68	48.57	56.62	70.37	111.38
20,000 miles	33.83	42.93	49.61	61.13	95.03
25,000 miles	31.28	39.18	44.95	55.00	84.03
30,000 miles	29.53	36.60	41.76	50.78	76.45

Notes to the AA tables:

The AA tables are published annually as a guide to the likely cost to the average private user to run a car. (In previous years tables were also produced for motorcycles and scooters.) The figures given can only be a guide, as individual vehicles will vary: for instance fuel consumption will depend on traffic conditions and the type of journey, and repairs can be very unpredictable. The aim is to show a representative cost that reflects all the important items, so that the motorist can see how it all adds up. This should help make the most suitable choice of economical and environmentally less damaging transport.

Standing Charges   The basic costs which you have to pay whether you use the car or not. They include the Road Tax (annual VED), insurance, the cost of the capital used for the vehicle, the loss of value of the vehicle or depreciation, and AA breakdown cover. Depreciation is affected by mileage.

Running Costs   The actual costs of using the car include petrol, oil, tyres, routine servicing, repairs and parking.

Vehicle Groups   Cars are put into groups depending on the new car price, as this is a better guide to what they cost to run than for instance the engine size. Take the new car list price when it was first registered (including the main options such as automatic gearbox, air conditioning etc supplied with the car), not the current list price. If in doubt, used-car price guides will give the original list prices.

Claiming Mileage   How much an employer pays for mileage is a matter for negotiation between them and the employees, as circumstances will vary. The Inland Revenue operates the Approved Mileage Allowance Payment (AMAP) system (in our Table L2)—further details from your local tax office or:

http://www.hmrc.gov.uk/mileage/index.htm, and
http://www.inlandrevenue.gov.uk/cars/fuel_company_cars.htm.

The figures given in our tables are VAT inclusive.

The AA Website   The Motoring Costs tables are also on the AA website at *http://www.theaa.com* Here some of the data will be updated throughout the year, and there is an interactive version that can tailor the costs to an individual car model and, for instance, the actual insurance premium paid.

Road Tax   For cars registered after 1st March 2001 the rate of Vehicle Excise Duty depends on their fuel type and their emissions of carbon dioxide in the legislated Type Approval tests. In the tables, averages for the price groups are used for the VED rate. For older (pre-March 2001) cars, if the engine capacity is 1,549 cc or less the duty is £140, and if it is over 1,549 cc the duty is £225.

Insurance   The UK average cost for a comprehensive policy with a 60% no-claims discount.

Cost of capital   This represents the loss of income from the owners having money tied up in a vehicle, which could otherwise be earning interest in a deposit account, calculated at 2.4% (the AA's online saving rate) of the average value for the car cost group. If the money is borrowed, the cost of capital will instead consist of the charges for loans or hire-purchase finance.

Depreciation   Cars lose value at different rates, depending on make, age, mileage, condition and even colour. Older cars will in general depreciate at a slower rate. The tables assume that depreciation costs are averaged over four years from purchase, and include typical adjustments for the different annual mileage in that period. Different rates are used for mileages differing from 10,000 miles per annum.

AA breakdown cover   For AA "Roadside" annual vehicle based cover.

Fuel cost   Based on the average UK price, but can be adjusted for price changes using the factors given. The fuel consumption figures taken are typical for each of the car bands listed.

Tyres   Based on using six tyres in a four-year period. Actual tyre life will vary with individual driving style. The prices in each car category are based on online prices for a well-known brand: they include valve, balance, and the disposal charge for the old tyre. The prices at main dealers will be higher.

Service and labour costs   Average cost for each car cost group for normal servicing and parts replacement at a dealer, taking average UK labour rates. Actual labour rates vary between different parts of the country and different brands.

Replacement parts   The replacement parts included cover those likely to be needed under normal driving conditions, such as brake materials, oils, filters, bulbs, wipers, and hoses.

Parking and tolls   The allowance for parking and road tolls is based on a national average for an urban driver. You may pay more or less depending on patterns of use.

Editors' note:

1.   The AA notes have been re-arranged by us, with the AA's permission, in the interests of space.
2.   Figures for the taxation of car and fuel benefits are at Table L2.
3.   The current Vehicle Excise Duty bands are as follows:

| Bands | CO_2 Emission | Petrol or Diesel Car | |
| | | Standard rate | First year rate |
	(g/km)	£	£
Band A	Up to 100	0	0
Band B	101–110	20.00	0
Band C	111–120	30.00	0
Band D	121–130	105.00	0
Band E	131–140	125.00	125.00
Band F	141–150	140.00	140.00
Band G	151–165	175.00	175.00
Band H	166–175	200.00	285.00
Band I	176–185	220.00	335.00
Band J	186–200	260.00	475.00
Band K	201–225	280.00	620.00
Band L	226–255	475.00	840.00
Band M	Over 255	490.00	1065.00

An alternative fuel car has a discount of £10 for all Bands.

The first year rate applies to new car purchases only. The duty reverts to the standard rate in subsequent years.

The CO_2 emission of a particular vehicle can be found at a website provided by the Vehicle Certification Agency (VCA): *www.vcacarfueldata.org.uk//ved_calculator.asp*. It is also on the V5 registration document.

L2: Taxation of car and fuel benefits

Car benefit 2006/07 to 2013/14

			CO$_2$ emissions (g/km)						Percentage of car's price taxed if car does not run solely on diesel (%)	Percentage of car's price taxed if car does run solely on diesel (%)
2006/07	2007/08	2008/09	2009/10	2010/11	2011/12	2012/13	2013/14			
N/A	N/A	N/A	N/A	1-75	1-75	1-75	1-75	5	8
N/A	N/A	0-120	0-120	76-120	76-120	76-99	76-94	10	13
N/A	N/A	N/A	N/A	N/A	N/A	100	95	11	14
N/A	N/A	N/A	N/A	N/A	N/A	105	100	12	15
N/A	N/A	N/A	N/A	N/A	N/A	110	105	13	16
N/A	N/A	N/A	N/A	N/A	N/A	115	110	14	17
0-144	0-144	121-139	121-139	121-134	121-129	120	115	15	18
145	145	140	140	135	130	125	120	16	19
150	150	145	145	140	135	130	125	17	20
155	155	150	150	145	140	135	130	18	21
160	160	155	155	150	145	140	135	19	22
165	165	160	160	155	150	145	140	20	23
170	170	165	165	160	155	150	145	21	24
175	175	170	170	165	160	155	150	22	25
180	180	175	175	170	165	160	155	23	26
185	185	180	180	175	170	165	160	24	27
190	190	185	185	180	175	170	165	25	28
195	195	190	190	185	180	175	170	26	29
200	200	195	195	190	185	180	175	27	30
205	205	200	200	195	190	185	180	28	31
210	210	205	205	200	195	190	185	29	32
215	215	210	210	205	200	195	190	30	33
220	220	215	215	210	205	200	195	31	34
225	225	220	220	215	210	205	200	32	35
230	230	225	225	220	215	210	205	33	35
235	235	230	230	225	220	215	210	34	35
240	240	235	235	230	225	220	215	35	35

Notes

1. From April 6, 2002, although the benefit of a company car is still to be calculated as a percentage of the price of the car (normally list price), the percentage is graduated according to carbon dioxide (CO_2) emissions and adjustments for business mileage and older cars no longer apply.
2. There are discounts for certain cleaner alternatively-propelled cars, which may reduce the minimum charge to that shown in the table.
3. The diesel supplement and the discounts for cleaner alternatives apply only to cars first registered on January 1, 1998 or later.
4. Cars without an approved CO_2 emissions figure are taxed according to engine size. This includes all cars registered before 1998 but only a tiny proportion of those registered 1998 and later.
5. Except where otherwise indicated, the exact CO_2 figure is rounded down to the nearest 5 grams per kilometre when using the above table.
6. From April 6, 2008 there was a new lower rate of 10 per cent (13 per cent for diesel) for cars with CO_2 emissions of 120 grams per kilometre or less.
7. From April 6, 2010 cars and vans with zero CO_2 emissions were exempt from company car tax for five tax years.
8. From April 6, 2010 an ultra low carbon cars band was introduced for five years.

Car fuel benefit—petrol and diesel—cash equivalent 2003/04 to 2013/14

Notes

1. From April 6, 2003, the car fuel benefit is, like the car benefit, linked directly to the CO_2 emissions of the company car.
2. There are the same diesel supplement and discounts for cleaner alternatively-propelled cars as there are in calculating the car benefit.
3. To calculate the car fuel benefit the percentage in the table used for calculating car benefit is multiplied against a set figure for the year:

   2003/04 to 2007/08   £14,400.
   2008/09 to 2009/10   £16,900.
   2010/11   £18,000.
   2011/12   £18,800.
   2012/13   £20,200.
   2013/14   £21,100.

   Thus, if the car benefit percentage for 2013/14 is 23%, the fuel benefit would be £21,100 × 23% = £4,853.
4. For cars registered before January 1, 1998 and cars with no approved CO_2 emissions figure, the percentage to be applied is the same as that used to calculate the car benefit.

Authorised mileage allowance payments—tax-free rates in pence per mile
2002/03 to 2010/11

Annual mileage	Pence per mile
Up to 10,000	40p
10,001 +	25p

2011/12 to 2013/14

Annual mileage	Pence per mile
Up to 10,000	45p
10,001 +	25p

L3: The Motability Scheme

Disabled people who need a motor vehicle may obtain one by utilising most if not all of the Higher Rate component of the Disability Living Allowance or the War Pensioner's Mobility Supplement. Motability is only available to those in receipt of either of these benefits who assign all or some of them to the scheme for the duration of the contract. Because of the very wide range of physical and mental disabilities of those in receipt of them the scheme does not require the person seeking to use it to be a driver: anyone in receipt of either allowance who is over three is entitled to use it. Under the Scheme there are four available options:

1. A new car can be obtained on a three-year hire lease contract, or three or five years for a wheelchair accessible vehicle (WAV).
2. A new, or used, car can be taken on hire purchase over two to five years.
3. A quadricycle can be obtained on a five-year lease (a quadricycle is a light steering three-door vehicle that can be driven on a motorcycle licence).
4. A powered wheelchair or scooter may be taken on a three-year contract hire.

A national network of some 4,500 dealers provides a wide range of suitably adapted new and used cars. In the case of option (1) (three- or five-year contract hire), the scheme requires a capital sum and a monthly payment which is provided for by the assignment of the relevant state benefit to the scheme. As well as the adapted vehicle, all maintenance is provided to include the cost of tyres, as is insurance for two named drivers who are over 25, annual road fund disc and roadside recovery. Fuel, oil and other incidentals are the responsibility of the driver. There is a 60,000-mile limit on use over the three years of the contract or 100,000 miles for a WAV, and an annual limit of 20,000 miles. Any mileage over that limit attracts a penalty of 5p per mile. At the end of the contract period the car reverts to the scheme. In the case of option (2) (hire purchase) the scheme provides only for the hire purchase of the vehicle, with any necessary adaptation, in return for a capital payment and the assignment of the relevant state benefit. It does not provide for maintenance, roadside recovery or insurance. There is no mileage restriction. At the end of the period the car belongs to the disabled person. Hire purchase is not actively encouraged by the scheme but is available if persistence is shown. In the case of option (4) (wheelchair or scooter) only contract hire is now available.

When costing, care must be taken to distinguish between the three elements of any claim:

(i) the capital cost of both purchase and adaptation which recur every three years;
(ii) the monthly running costs covered by the Motability Scheme; and
(iii) the running costs not covered by the scheme such as oil, petrol and car washes.

Not all cars are available and advice must be obtained as to whether what is available adequately meets the needs of the disabled person. When experts have recommended that a car be obtained under the scheme practitioners should ensure that they are clear which option is being recommended and ensure that they compare like for like.

The condition precedent for using the Motability Scheme is that the beneficiary is in receipt of a state benefit which falls within the Second Schedule of the Social Security (Recovery of Benefits) Act 1997. It is now clear, following *Eagle v Chambers (No.2)*[1], that s.17 of the Act precludes a court from insisting that the mobility component of the Disabled Living Allowance should be used by any recipient to mitigate her loss. Henceforth no defendant can insist that a claimant use the mobility allowance to participate in the Motability Scheme.

Further reading and assistance in specific cases can be obtained at:
http://www.motabilitycarscheme.co.uk and Customer Services (0845) 456 4566.

---

[1] [2004] EWCA Civ 1033.

L4: Calculations involving motor cars

There are a number of commonly encountered calculations involving the cost of motor cars. This section contains tables and examples of calculations dealing with the following and should be read along with the table of AA motoring costs in section L1:

1. New car prices.

2. Cost of future replacements.

3. Cost of more frequent replacement.

4. Cost of automatic cars.

5. Cost of additional mileage.

We have classified cars as follows:

Mini: Most cars of 1.1 litre or under, such as Toyota Aygo 1.0, Vauxhall Corsa 1.0
Super mini: Similar cars between 1.1 and 1.4, Ford Fiesta 1.25, Suzuki Swift 1.2
Small: Cars of the smaller Ford Focus, VW Golf type, mostly 1.3–1.6 litre
Medium: The Ford Mondeo, VW Passat type, mostly cars from 1.6–1.9 litre
Executive: The larger Passat, Volvo S60 type, mostly 2.0–2.8 litre
Prestige: The BMW 330d, Jaguar 3.0, mostly up to 3.5 litre
Luxury: The Jaguar XJ, Audi A8 4.2, mostly over 3.5 litre and expensive
Estate etc: Self-explanatory

Notes:

1. The first table is intended to convey in broad terms the purchase costs of motor cars across a range of models. The material is taken from *Parker's Car Price Guide* and *What Car?* with the kind permission of the publishers.

    The *New Price* is the recommended retail price (including VAT) according to the latest manu-facturer's price list: all prices stated are "on the road" and include delivery charges, 12 months' road fund licence, number plates and £25 registration tax. *VED band* is the vehicle excise duty band.

2. Depreciation: Different cars, even produced by the same manufacturer, depreciate at different rates. As a model of car may change after a few years even if the same name is retained, losses over a long period cannot be calculated for individual models but only by reference to the general position.

3. Automatics: The comparison of manual and automatic cars is similarly a generalisation. The calculation for depreciation assumes that the new price of the automatic is *higher* than for the manual model. There is considerable variation, even among cars of similar type with similar new prices, in the rate at which the premium for the automatic version is eroded. With some cars the gap disappears very quickly: with some the premium for the automatic version is actually greater for used cars than for new ones.

4. Where the current new price of the manual and automatic versions is the same, which is often the case with expensive cars, the used automatic tends to retain its value *better* than the manual model. It may nevertheless have higher fuel consumption but whether it will be more expensive overall may depend on the mileage.

1. New Car Prices

	New Price (£)	VED band
Mini		
Citroën C1 1.0i VT 3d	7,995	A
Toyota Aygo 1.0 3d	8,535	A
Vauxhall Corsa 1.0 ecoFLEX S 3d	11,625	C
Super Mini		
Citroën DS3 1.2 VT 82 Dsign 3d	12,700	B
Ford Fiesta 1.25 82 Style 3d	11,995	C
Suzuki Swift 1.2 SZ2 3d	10,799	C
Vauxhall Corsa 1.2 S 3d	11,970	D
Volkswagen Polo 1.2 70 S 3d	11,290	D
Small		
Citroën C4 1.6v 90 VTR 5d	16,095	B
Ford Focus 1.6 Zetec 5d	17,305	E
Honda Civic 1.4 i VTEC SE 5d	16,955	D
Renault Megane 1.6 110 Expr 5d	16,280	G
Toyota Auris 1.6 Icon 5d	17,495	E
Vauxhall Astra 1.6i SE 16v 5d	20,105	F
Volkswagen Golf 1.6 105 S 5d	19,565	A
Medium		
BMW 316i ES 4d	25,180	E
Ford Mondeo 2.0 Edge 5d	20,195	C
Toyota Avensis 1.8 T2 4d	18,895	G
Vauxhall Insignia 1.8 ES 5d	18,040	H
Volkswagen Passat 1.8 TSI S 4d	20,795	G
Volvo V40 2.0 D3 SE 5d	23,845	H
Executive		
BMW 320i SE 4d	26,195	F
Honda Accord 2.0i VTEC EX 4d	26,130	G
Toyota Avensis 2.2 D-4D TR 4d	23,045	F
Volkswagen Passat 2.0 TDi 140 Highline 4d	23,010	C
Volvo S60 2.0 D3 SE 4d	26,745	C

1. New Car Prices

	New Price (£)	VED band
Prestige Audi Quattro A4 3.0 245 SE 4d	34,755	F
BMW 330d SE 5d	35,030	E
Jaguar XF 3.0 V6 Luxury 4d	35,855	G
Mercedes-Benz E250 SE 4d	35,115	G
Volvo S80 2.4 DS SE Lux 4d	34,320	C
Luxury Audi Quattro A8 4.2 SE 4d	65,865	J
BMW 550i SE 5d	56,710	K
Jaguar XJ 3.0 V6 Prem Lux 4d	60,060	G
Mercedes-Benz S 350 Blue Eff 4d	50,505	I
Estate Citroën C5 1.6 HDi 110 115 VTR 5d	21,295	D
Ford Mondeo Estate 2.0 Zetec 5d	22,445	C
Honda Accord 2.0i VTEC ES 5d	24,265	G
Mercedes-Benz E250 CDI SE 5d	38,400	F
Vauxhall Insignia 2.0 130 ES 5d	20,950	D
Volkswagen Passat 2.0 TDi 140 S 5d	23,155	C
4 x 4 Honda CR-V 2.0 i-VTEC 5d	22,605	H
Nissan X-Trail 2.0 dCi 150 Tekna 5d	31,700	J
Toyota Landcruiser 3.0 D-4D LC3 5d	36,995	K
Volkswagen Touareg 3.0 SE TDi 5d	40,690	I
Volvo XC90 2.4 DS SE Lux 5d	43,095	K
People carriers Chrysler Grand Voyager 2.8 LE Auto 5d	36,265	K
Citroën C4 Grand Picasso HDi 150 VTR 5d	23,405	E
Ford Galaxy 2.0 Zetec 5d	26,155	F
Renault Grand Scenic 1.6 dCi 130 Dyn 5d	22,725	C
Toyota Verso 2.0 D-4D Icon 5d	21,445	D
Vauxhall Zafira 1.8 VVT Design 5d	23,115	H

2. Cost of future replacements

Table 1 below has representative trade-in values of used *manual* cars expressed as a proportion of the *current* new price (calculated from material in *Parker's Car Price Guide*). Automatic cars may depreciate faster. Where the new price of an automatic car is *higher* than that of the corresponding manual car, there is a tendency for the automatic to depreciate by about 1 per cent more (altogether, not per year).

Table 1 Trade-in values of used manual cars

Age of car	Residual value	Loss of value	Equivalent annual depreciation
1	0.64	0.36	0.360
2	0.50	0.50	0.256
3	0.41	0.59	0.204
4	0.36	0.64	0.168
5	0.33	0.67	0.143
Adjustment for automatics	−0.01	+0.01	

The table can be used to calculate the future net costs of replacements where the replacements will be second hand as well as where they will be new.

Example 1: The claimant is 54 and needs a people carrier such as a Chrysler Grand Voyager 3.3 LE Auto 5d, automatic version. He will need to replace it every four years, the final replacement being when he is 70. He would not otherwise have had a car (or the car is additional to whatever vehicle would have been bought in any event).

Initial price of people carrier, say		£32,995.00
Proportion of price lost at each replacement (Table 1 above, + 0.01)	0.65	
Cost of each replacement	0.65 × 32,995 = 21,446.75	
Multiplier for 16 years (Table A5, 2.5%, four-yearly)	3.14	
Cost of future replacements	3.14 × 21,446.75 =	£67,342.80
Total		£100,337.80

Example 2: The same claimant currently runs a manual Volvo S80 2.4 SE and will replace it with the Chrysler people carrier. The additional cost is the future cost of the Chryslers *minus* the corresponding figure saved on Volvos. (If either both cars are manual or both automatic the calculation is simpler.)

Initial price of Volvo saved, say		£28,245.00
Proportion of price saved at each replacement (Table 1 above, manual)	0.64	
Cost of each replacement	0.64 × 28,245.00 =	18,076.80
Multiplier for 16 years (Table A5, 2.5%, four-yearly)	3.14	
Cost of future replacements saved	3.14 × 18,076.80	= £56,761.15
Total saved		£85,006.15
Net future cost of Chryslers instead of Volvos (100,337.80 − 85,006.15)		= £15,331.64

3. Cost of more frequent replacement

Claimants are sometimes advised that because of their condition they need a more reliable car and should therefore replace it more often than they needed to do before the injury. Table 2, which is derived from Table 1, shows the additional annual cost, expressed as a proportion of the new price. Find the row corresponding to the new interval in years and the column corresponding to the old interval.

Note that the table expresses the multiplier as an *annual* cost, not the cost *on each exchange*. Thus in row 2, column 4, the figure 0.088 means that the additional expense of replacing a car every two years, instead of every four years, is 8.8 per cent of the price of the car per year for however long the claimant continues to drive.

Table 2 Multipliers for additional annual cost of replacing car more frequently

		Old interval in years				
		1	2	3	4	5
	1	0	0.104	0.156	0.192	0.217
New	2		0	0.052	0.088	0.113
interval	3			0	0.036	0.061
in	4				0	0.025
years	5					0

Example: The claimant is 40 and drives a car currently costing £11,995 new. She has just bought one. She can continue to drive a similar car, with modifications. She has been advised that because of her disability she should now change it every three years rather than every five as she has until now. She should stop driving at about 73, so the last change will be at about age 70.

Multiplier for additional annual cost from table above		
– new frequency three years, old frequency five years	0.061	
Multiplier for woman of 40 until age 70 (Ogden Table 28, at 2.5%)	20.50	
Multiplier for additional cost of more frequent replacement	0.061 × 20.50	= 1.25
Current cost of car		£11,995.00
Additional cost of replacing car more frequently until age 70		£14,993.75

4. Cost of automatic cars

Claimants' injuries sometimes make it necessary for them to have an automatic car which they would not otherwise have needed. Generally this involves additional costs in three respects: the automatic car is more expensive to buy, is more expensive to run and tends to depreciate faster than the corresponding manual model (but see the notes in the introduction).

Table 3 Added cost of automatic cars

		Mini and Super Mini	Small	Medium and Executive	Prestige and Luxury	Estate, 4×4 and MPV
Added cost of new car in £		850	1,075	1,145	1,275	1,245
Petrol @ 137.7p per litre	In pence per mile	3.65	1.85	1.52	0.44	–
	For every penny more/less, add/subtract	0.030	0.015	0.012	0.004	–

Greater depreciation

Where the new price of an automatic model of a car is *higher* than that of the corresponding manual car, there is a tendency for the automatic to depreciate by about 1 per cent more (altogether, not per year)—see Table 1 above. Thus:

New manual model	£11,000	three-year-old manual	$11,000 \times 0.41 = £4,510$
New automatic	£12,000	three-year-old automatic	$12,000 \times 0.40 = £4,800$

Example: The claimant is 48. He drives a manual car of medium type whose price new is about £16,000. He drives about 10,000 miles a year and changes his car every three years. Because of his injury he now needs an automatic. He is likely to stop driving in about 30 years.

Extra cost of automatic car:
On first purchase (from Table 3, column 3 above): £1,145.00

Cost at each replacement of automatic (Table 1, row 3): $17,145 \times 0.60 =$ 10,293.00
less cost at each replacement of manual $16,000 \times 0.59 =$ 9,440.00
Additional cost at each replacement £ 853.00
Crude multiplier for replacements (Table A5, 27 years, three-yearly) 6.33
Multiplier for 27 years certain (Table A5, cont's loss) 19.71
Multiplier for man of 48 until age 75 (Table A1) 18.24
Multiplier discounted for mortality $(6.33 \times 18.24/19.71) =$ 5.86 £4,996.79

Extra cost per mile, petrol at 136.4 p/litre = $1.52 + (-1.3 \times 0.012) = 1.50$ pence
Extra running cost 10,000 miles pa £150.00
Crude multiplier (table A5, 30 years, cont's loss) 21.19
Multiplier discounted for mortality $(21.19 \times 18.24/19.71) =$ 19.61 £2,941.50

Total extra cost: £9,083.29

5. Cost of additional mileage

The AA figures for *running* costs at Table L1 do not include depreciation. Mileage reduces the value of a car by a factor which varies with the type of car and its age on resale. Age on resale is not necessarily the length of time the claimant had the car. The categories A, B, C, etc. are derived from *Parker's Price Guide*.

The table may not be appropriate for mileages below 1,000 miles a year or above 30,000 miles a year.

Table 4   Adjustment for depreciation for extra mileage

Age on resale	Depreciation in pence per mile							
	A	B	C	D	E	F	G	H
1	3.00	4.00	5.00	6.00	7.00	8.50	10.50	13.50
2	2.50	3.50	4.50	5.50	6.50	7.50	9.00	11.00
3	2.00	3.00	3.50	4.50	5.00	6.00	7.50	10.00
4	1.20	2.00	2.50	3.50	4.00	5.00	6.00	8.00
5	1.00	1.50	2.00	2.50	3.00	4.00	5.00	7.00
6	0.70	1.20	1.50	2.00	2.50	3.00	4.00	6.00
7	0.50	0.90	1.00	1.50	2.00	2.50	3.50	5.00
8	0.40	0.60	0.90	1.00	1.50	2.00	2.50	4.00

Example: The claimant would have had a car anyway. His mileage is increased by 4,000 miles a year because of his injury. He buys a one-year-old car and changes it after four years costing about £14,500 in category C in the mileage adjustment table. Petrol costs 136.6 pence per litre.

Running cost per mile from AA figures (Table L1)	25.75 pence
Adjustment for petrol price (from Table L1) ($-1.1p \times 0.11$)	(0.12)
Adjustment for mileage (category C, Four years old)	2.50
Total per mile	28.13 pence
Total annual cost ($4,000 \times 28.13$)	£1,125.20

6. Cost of professional servicing

Some claimants will have carried out the routine servicing of their cars themselves, but their injury may make that impracticable and they will in future need to have the car serviced professionally.

The resulting increased cost consists essentially in the labour element in the cost of servicing. Costs such as the cost of the Ministry of Transport test itself will remain the same and will not form an element of the loss. There will be *some* increase in the cost of materials such as replacement parts and oil, as these may be less expensive online or at a supermarket rather than at a garage. On the other hand, particularly with newer models, the more complex servicing tasks may not be feasible without specialised equipment, and so even mechanically minded car owners may be unable to do these jobs themselves. This section therefore takes the loss as equivalent to the cost of labour and treats these other factors as neutral overall.

Labour costs vary between main dealers and independent garages, and between different parts of the country. They are generally cheaper in the north and away from London, but do not conform to any clear pattern. In a 2011 survey Gwynedd was one of the most expensive areas, but Clwyd, not far away, was one of the cheapest. Also, as will be seen from the figures in Table L1: AA Motoring Costs, the most expensive cars involve higher labour costs but the cheapest cars to buy are not the cheapest to service. For those reasons it is not straightforward to try to produce figures independently on the basis of time estimates and hourly labour charges, and the editors recommend using the following figures derived from Table L1.

Table 5 Additional cost of professional servicing

Cost of car new	Additional cost in pence per mile				
	Up to £13,000	£13–18,000	£18–25,000	£25–32,000	over £32,000
Petrol cars	4.85	4.98	4.55	4.32	7.32
Cost of car new	Up to £16,000	£16–22,000	£22–26,000	£26–36,000	over £36,000
Diesel cars	4.35	4.45	4.77	4.81	7.46

Example: The same claimant as in section 5 used to do his own servicing and because of his injury is now unable to do so. His car cost £14,500 new. Before the accident he drove 12,000 miles a year, but because of the accident he must now drive a further 4,000 miles, making 16,000 miles in all. He incurs the additional cost of professional servicing, as well as the additional cost of extra mileage.

Extra cost of professional servicing per mile	4.98 pence
Annual cost (for *12,000* miles)[1] 12,000 × 4.98 pence	£ 597.60
Cost of additional 4,000 mileage (from section 5 example)	£1,125.20
Total annual cost	£1,722.80

Sections 2–5 are based on figures in *Parker's Car Price Guide* and from the websites of the *Vehicle Certification Agency* and the *United States Department of Transportation*.

---

[1] Note that the figure for running costs used to calculate the cost of additional mileage already includes service labour costs. The extra cost of servicing must therefore be based on the pre-accident 12,000 miles: there will be double counting if it is calculated on the basis of the post-accident 16,000 miles.

L5: Time, speed and distance

Table of speeds and distances

Speeds				Distances in yards																			
mph	km/h	yd/sec	m/sec	5	10	15	20	25	30	40	50	60	75	100	125	150	175	200	225	250	300	400	500
5	8.0	2.44	2.24	2.0	4.1	6.1	8.2	10.2	12.3	16.4	20.5	24.5	30.7	40.9	51.1	61.4	71.6	81.8	92.0	102.3	122.7	163.6	204.5
10	16.1	4.89	4.47	1.0	2.0	3.1	4.1	5.1	6.1	8.2	10.2	12.3	15.3	20.5	25.6	30.7	35.8	40.9	46.0	51.1	61.4	81.8	102.3
15	24.1	7.33	6.71	0.7	1.4	2.0	2.7	3.4	4.1	5.5	6.8	8.2	10.2	13.6	17.0	20.5	23.9	27.3	30.7	34.1	40.9	54.5	68.2
20	32.2	9.78	8.94	0.5	1.0	1.5	2.0	2.6	3.1	4.1	5.1	6.1	7.7	10.2	12.8	15.3	17.9	20.5	23.0	25.6	30.7	40.9	51.1
25	40.2	12.22	11.18	0.4	0.8	1.2	1.6	2.0	2.5	3.3	4.1	4.9	6.1	8.2	10.2	12.3	14.3	16.4	18.4	20.5	24.5	32.7	40.9
30	48.3	14.67	13.41	0.3	0.7	1.0	1.4	1.7	2.0	2.7	3.4	4.1	5.1	6.8	8.5	10.2	11.9	13.6	15.3	17.0	20.5	27.3	34.1
35	56.3	17.11	15.65	0.3	0.6	0.9	1.2	1.5	1.8	2.3	2.9	3.5	4.4	5.8	7.3	8.8	10.2	11.7	13.1	14.6	17.5	23.4	29.2
40	64.4	19.56	17.88	0.3	0.5	0.8	1.0	1.3	1.5	2.0	2.6	3.1	3.8	5.1	6.4	7.7	8.9	10.2	11.5	12.8	15.3	20.5	25.6
45	72.4	22.00	20.12	0.2	0.5	0.7	0.9	1.1	1.4	1.8	2.3	2.7	3.4	4.5	5.7	6.8	8.0	9.1	10.2	11.4	13.6	18.2	22.7
50	80.5	24.44	22.35	0.2	0.4	0.6	0.8	1.0	1.2	1.6	2.0	2.5	3.1	4.1	5.1	6.1	7.2	8.2	9.2	10.2	12.3	16.4	20.5
60	96.6	29.33	26.82	0.2	0.3	0.5	0.7	0.9	1.0	1.4	1.7	2.0	2.6	3.4	4.3	5.1	6.0	6.8	7.7	8.5	10.2	13.6	17.0
70	112.7	34.22	31.29	0.1	0.3	0.4	0.6	0.7	0.9	1.2	1.5	1.8	2.2	2.9	3.7	4.4	5.1	5.8	6.6	7.3	8.8	11.7	14.6
80	128.7	39.11	35.76	0.1	0.3	0.4	0.5	0.6	0.8	1.0	1.3	1.5	1.9	2.6	3.2	3.8	4.5	5.1	5.8	6.4	7.7	10.2	12.8
90	144.8	44.00	40.23	0.1	0.2	0.3	0.5	0.6	0.7	0.9	1.1	1.4	1.7	2.3	2.8	3.4	4.0	4.5	5.1	5.7	6.8	9.1	11.4
100	160.9	48.89	44.70	0.1	0.2	0.3	0.4	0.5	0.6	0.8	1.0	1.2	1.5	2.0	2.6	3.1	3.6	4.1	4.6	5.1	6.1	8.2	10.2

Seconds

Notes:

1. The table shows the time taken to cover a given distance at a given speed, to the nearest $\frac{1}{10}$ second.

2. The table can also be used to ascertain the approximate speed of a vehicle, if the time and distance are known.

3. As an example, to find how long it would take to cover 125 yards at 35 mph, follow the vertical column down from the figure 125 and follow the horizontal row across from the figure 35: they meet at the figure 7.3, which is the number of seconds taken to cover the distance.

4. A speed of z miles per hour approximately equals [0.5z] yards per second.

5. The general formula for the number of seconds to cover a given distance at a given speed is approximately:

$$\frac{\text{distance in yards} \times 2.04545}{\text{speed in miles per hour}}$$

Typical Stopping Distances (average car length = 4 metres)

Speed (mph)	Thinking Distance (metres)	Braking Distance (metres)	Total Stopping Distance (metres)	(car lengths)
20	6	6	12	3
30	9	14	23	6
40	12	24	36	9
50	15	38	53	13
60	18	55	73	18
70	21	75	96	24

Extracted from The Highway Code, published by the Stationery Office.

Group M

Other Information

M

M1:   **Senior Court Costs Office Guideline Rates for Summary Assessment**

M2:   **Conversion formulae**

M3:   **Perpetual calendar**

M4:   **Religious festivals**

M5:   **Medical reference intervals and scales**

M6:   **Websites**

M7:   **Addresses of useful organisations**

M1: Senior Court Costs Office Guideline Rates for Summary Assessment

Band One	A	B	C	D
2011	217	192	161	118
2010	217	192	161	118
2009	213	189	158	116
2008	203	180	151	110
2007	195	173	145	106
2005	184	163	137	100

Aldershot, Farnham, Bournemouth (including Poole), Birmingham Inner, Bristol, Cambridge City, Harlow, Canterbury, Maidstone, Medway and Tunbridge Wells, Cardiff (Inner), Chelmsford South, Essex and East Suffolk, Chester, Fareham, Winchester, Hampshire, Dorset, Wiltshire, Isle of Wight, Kingston, Guildford, Reigate, Epsom, Leeds Inner (within two-kilometers radius of the City Art Gallery), Lewes, Liverpool, Birkenhead, Manchester Central, Newcastle—City Centre (within a two-mile radius of St Nicholas Cathedral), Norwich City, Nottingham City, Oxford, Thames Valley, Southampton, Portsmouth, Swindon, Basingstoke, Watford.

Band Two	A	B	C	D
2011	201	177	146	111
2010	201	177	146	111
2009	198	174	144	109
2008	191	168	139	105
2007	183	161	133	101
2005	173	152	126	95

Bath, Cheltenham and Gloucester, Taunton, Yeovil, Bury, Chelmsford North, Cambridge County, Peterborough, Bury St E, Norfolk, Lowestoft, Cheshire and North Wales, Coventry, Rugby, Nuneaton, Stratford and Warwick, Exeter, Plymouth, Hull (City), Leeds Outer, Wakefield and Pontefract, Leigh, Lincoln, Luton, Bedford, St Albans, Hitchin, Hertford, Manchester Outer, Oldham, Bolton, Tameside, Newcastle (other than City Centre), Nottingham and Derbyshire, Sheffield, Doncaster and South Yorkshire, Southport, St Helens, Stockport, Altrincham, Salford, Swansea, Newport, Cardiff (Outer), Wigan, Wolverhampton, Walsall, Dudley and Stourbridge, York, Harrogate.

Band Three	A	B	C	D
2011	201	177	146	111
2010	201	177	146	111
2009	198	174	144	109
2008	174	156	133	99
2007	167	150	128	95
2005	158	142	121	90

Birmingham Outer, Bradford (Dewsbury, Halifax, Huddersfield, Keighley and Skipton), Cumbria, Devon, Cornwall, Grimsby, Skegness, Hull Outer, Kidderminster, Northampton and Leicester, Preston, Lancaster, Blackpool, Chorley, Accrington, Burnley, Blackburn, Rawenstall and Nelson, Scarborough and Ripon, Stafford, Stoke, Tamworth, Teesside, Worcester, Hereford, Evesham and Redditch, Shrewsbury, Telford, Ludlow, Oswestry, South and West Wales.

London City [EC1–4]	A	B	C	D
2011	409	296	226	138
2010	409	296	226	138
2009	402	291	222	136
2008	396	285	219	134
2007	380	274	210	129
2005	359	259	198	122

London Central [W1, WC1, WC2, SW1]	A	B	C	D
2011	317	242	196	126
2010	317	242	196	126
2009	312	238	193	124
2008	304	231	189	121
2007	292	222	181	116
2005	276	210	171	110
London Outer [N, E, SE, W, SW, NW, Bromley, Croydon, Dartford, Gravesend and Uxbridge]	A	B	C	D
2011	229–267	172–229	165	121
2010	229–267	172–229	165	121
2009	263–225	225–169	162	119
2008	256–219	219–165	158	116
2007	246–210	210–158	152	111
2005	232–198	198–149	144	105

A – Solicitors with over eight years' post-qualification experience including at least eight years' litigation experience.
B – Solicitors and legal executives with over four years' post-qualification experience including at least four years' litigation experience.
C – Other solicitors and legal executives and fee earners of equivalent experience.
D – Trainee Solicitors, para legals and fee earners of equivalent experience.
Note: "Legal Executive" means a Fellow of the Institute of Legal Executives.

Entitlement to VAT on Costs

DATE	VAT RATE
April 1, 1991–November 30, 2008	17.5%
December 1, 2008–December 31, 2009	15%
January 1, 2010–January 3, 2011	17.5%
January 4, 2011 to date	20%

Costs PD 44 para.2.3 deals with entitlement to VAT on Costs. It provides:

"VAT should not be included in a claim for costs if the receiving party is able to recover the VAT as input tax. Where the receiving party is able to obtain credit from HM Revenue and Customs for a proportion of the VAT as input tax, only that proportion which is not eligible for credit should be included in the claim for costs."

Costs PD 44 para.2.7 deals with the form of a Bill of Costs where the VAT Rate changes. It provides:

"Where there is a change in the rate of VAT, suppliers of goods and services are entitled by ss.88 (1) and 88(2) of the VAT Act 1994 in most circumstances to elect whether the new or the old rate of VAT

should apply to a supply where the basic and actual tax points span a period during which there has been a change in VAT rates."

Costs PD 44 para.2.8 provides:

"It will be assumed, unless a contrary indication is given in writing, that an election to take advantage of the provisions mentioned in paragraph 2.7 and to charge VAT at the lower rate has been made. In any case in which an election to charge at the lower rate is not made, such a decision must be justified to the court assessing the costs."

Costs PD 44 para.2.9 deals with apportionment. It provides:

"Subject to 2.7 & 2.8 all bills of costs, fees and disbursements on which VAT is included must be divided into separate parts so as to show work done before, on and after the date or dates from which any change in the rate of VAT takes effect. Where, however, a lump sum charge is made for work which spans a period during which there has been a change in VAT rates, and paragraphs 2.7 and 2.8 above do not apply, reference should be made to paragraphs 30.7 or 30.8 of the VAT Guide (Notice 700) (or any revised edition of that notice) published by HMRC. If necessary, the lump sum should be apportioned. The totals of profit costs and disbursements in each part must be carried separately to the summary."

M2: Conversion formulae

	To convert	Multiply by
Area	square inches to square centimetres	6.452
	square centimetres to square inches	0.1555
	square metres to square feet	10.7638
	square feet to square metres	0.0929
	square yards to square metres	0.8361
	square metres to square yards	1.196
	square miles to square kilometres	2.590
	square kilometres to square miles	0.3861
	acres to hectares	0.4047
	hectares to acres	2.471
Length	inches to centimetres	2.540
	centimetres to inches	0.3937
	feet to metres	0.3048
	metres to feet	3.281
	yards to metres	0.9144
	metres to yards	1.094
	miles to kilometres	1.609
	kilometres to miles	0.6214
Temperature	Centigrade to Fahrenheit	$\times\, 9 \div 5 + 32$
	Fahrenheit to Centigrade	$-32 \times 5 \div 9$
Volume	cubic inches to cubic centimetres	16.39
	cubic centimetres to cubic inches	0.06102
	cubic feet to cubic metres	0.02832
	cubic metres to cubic feet	35.31
	cubic yards to cubic metres	0.7646
	cubic metres to cubic yards	1.308
	cubic inches to litres	0.01639
	litres to cubic inches	61.024

	To convert	Multiply by
Weight	gallon to litres	4.545
	litres to gallons	0.22
	grains to grams	0.0647
	grams to grains	15.43
	ounces to grams	28.35
	grams to ounces	0.03527
	pounds to grams	453.592
	grams to pounds	0.0022
	pounds to kilograms	0.4536
	kilograms to pounds	2.2046
	tons to kilograms	1016.05
	kilograms to tons	0.0009842
Speed	miles per hour to kilometres per hour	1.6093
	kilometres per hour to miles per hour	0.6214
Fuel cost	pence per litre to pounds per gallon	0.045
	pounds per gallon to pence per litre	22.00
USA measures	Dry USA pint to UK pint	0.9689
	UK pint to USA pint	1.1032
	USA pint to litres	0.5506
	litres to USA pint	1.816
	USA bushel to UK bushel	0.9689
	UK bushel to USA bushel	1.032
	USA bushel to litres	35.238
	litres to USA bushel	0.0283
	Liquid USA pint (16 fl oz) to UK pint	0.8327
	UK pint to USA pint	1.2
	USA pint to litres	0.4732
	litres to USA pint	2.113
	USA gallon to UK gallon	0.8327
	UK gallon to USA gallon	1.2
	USA gallon to litres	3.7853
	litres to USA gallons	0.2641

Clothing

Shirts

UK/USA	14	$14\frac{1}{2}$	15	$15\frac{1}{2}$	16	$16\frac{1}{2}$	17	$17\frac{1}{2}$
Europe	36	37	38	39	40	41	42	43

Ladies clothes

UK

Size code	10	12	14	16	18	20	22
Bust/hip inches	32/34	34/36	36/38	38/40	40/42	42/44	44/46
Bust/hip cm	84/89	88/93	92/97	97/102	102/107	107/112	112/117

USA

Size code	6	8	10	12	14	16	18
Bust/hip inches	$34\frac{1}{2}/36\frac{1}{2}$	$35\frac{1}{2}/37\frac{1}{2}$	$36\frac{1}{2}/38\frac{1}{2}$	$37\frac{1}{2}/39\frac{1}{2}$	38/40	$39\frac{1}{2}/41\frac{1}{2}$	41/43

European sizes vary from country to country

Footwear—Men

British	6	7	8	9	10	11	12
American	$6\frac{1}{2}$	$7\frac{1}{2}$	$8\frac{1}{2}$	$9\frac{1}{2}$	$10\frac{1}{2}$	$11\frac{1}{2}$	$12\frac{1}{2}$
Continental	40	41	42	43	44	45	46

Footwear—Women

British	3	4	5	6	7	8	9
American	$4\frac{1}{2}$	$5\frac{1}{2}$	$6\frac{1}{2}$	$7\frac{1}{2}$	$8\frac{1}{2}$	$9\frac{1}{2}$	$10\frac{1}{2}$
Continental	36	37	38	39	40	42	43

Children's clothes

UK

Age	1	2	3	4	5	6	7	8	9	10	11	12
Height/inches	32	36	38	40	43	45	48	50	53	55	58	60
Height/cm	80	92	98	104	110	116	122	128	134	140	146	152

USA

Boys' size code	1	2	3	4	5	6	8		10		12	
Girls' size code	2	3	4	5	6	6x	7	8	10		12	

Europe

Height/cm	80	92	98	104	110	116	122	128	134	140	146	152

M3: Perpetual calendar

The number opposite each of the years in the list below indicates which of the calendars on the following pages is the one for that year. Thus the number opposite 2000 is 14, so calendar 14 can be used as a 2000 calendar.

Leap years

Years divisible by four without remainder are leap years with 366 days instead of 365 (29 days in February instead of 28). However, the first year of the century is not a leap year except when divisible by 400.

Year	Calendar	Year	Calendar	Year	Calendar	Year	Calendar	Year	Calendar	Year	Calendar
1980	10	1992	11	2004	12	2016	13	2028	14	2040	8
1981	5	1993	6	2005	7	2017	1	2029	2	2041	3
1982	6	1994	7	2006	1	2018	2	2030	3	2042	4
1983	7	1995	1	2007	2	2019	3	2031	4	2043	5
1984	8	1996	9	2008	10	2020	11	2032	12	2044	13
1985	3	1997	4	2009	5	2021	6	2033	7	2045	1
1986	4	1998	5	2010	6	2022	7	2034	1	2046	2
1987	5	1999	6	2011	7	2023	1	2035	2	2047	3
1988	13	2000	14	2012	8	2024	9	2036	10	2048	11
1989	1	2001	2	2013	3	2025	4	2037	5	2049	6
1990	2	2002	3	2014	4	2026	5	2038	6	2050	7
1991	3	2003	4	2015	5	2027	6	2039	7	2051	1

1

January
M	2	9	16	23 30
T	3	10	17	24 31
W	4	11	18	25
T	5	12	19	26
F	6	13	20	27
S	7	14	21	28
S	1 8	15	22	29

February
M	6	13	20	27
T	7	14	21	28
W	1 8	15	22	
T	2 9	16	23	
F	3 10	17	24	31
S	4 11	18	25	
S	5 12	19	26	

March
M	6	13	20	27
T	7	14	21	28
W	1 8	15	22	29
T	2 9	16	23	30
F	3 10	17	24	31
S	4 11	18	25	
S	5 12	19	26	

April
M	3	10	17	24
T	4	11	18	25
W	5	12	19	26
T	6	13	20	27
F	7	14	21	28
S	1 8	15	22	29
S	2 9	16	23	30

May
M	1 8	15	22	29
T	2 9	16	23	30
W	3 10	17	24	31
T	4 11	18	25	
F	5 12	19	26	
S	6 13	20	27	
S	7 14	21	28	

June
M	5	12	19	26
T	6	13	20	27
W	7	14	21	28
T	1 8	15	22	29
F	2 9	16	23	30
S	3 10	17	24	
S	4 11	18	25	

July
M	3	10	17	24 31
T	4	11	18	25
W	5	12	19	26
T	6	13	20	27
F	7	14	21	28
S	1 8	15	22	29
S	2 9	16	23	30

August
M	7	14	21	28
T	1 8	15	22	29
W	2 9	16	23	30
T	3 10	17	24	31
F	4 11	18	25	
S	5 12	19	26	
S	6 13	20	27	

September
M	4	11	18	25
T	5	12	19	26
W	6	13	20	27
T	7	14	21	28
F	1 8	15	22	29
S	2 9	16	23	30
S	3 10	17	24	

October
M	2	9	16	23 30
T	3	10	17	24 31
W	4	11	18	25
T	5	12	19	26
F	6	13	20	27
S	7	14	21	28
S	1 8	15	22	29

November
M	6	13	20	27
T	7	14	21	28
W	1 8	15	22	29
T	2 9	16	23	30
F	3 10	17	24	
S	4 11	18	25	
S	5 12	19	26	

December
M	4	11	18	25
T	5	12	19	26
W	6	13	20	27
T	7	14	21	28
F	1 8	15	22	29
S	2 9	16	23	30
S	3 10	17	24	31

2

January
M	1 8	15	22	29
T	2 9	16	23	30
W	3 10	17	24	31
T	4 11	18	25	
F	5 12	19	26	
S	6 13	20	27	
S	7 14	21	28	

February
M	5	12	19	26
T	6	13	20	27
W	7	14	21	28
T	1 8	15	22	
F	2 9	16	23	
S	3 10	17	24	
S	4 11	18	25	

March
M	5	12	19	26
T	6	13	20	27
W	7	14	21	28
T	1 8	15	22	29
F	2 9	16	23	30
S	3 10	17	24	31
S	4 11	18	25	

April
M	2	9	16	23 30
T	3	10	17	24
W	4	11	18	25
T	5	12	19	26
F	6	13	20	27
S	7	14	21	28
S	1 8	15	22	29

May
M	7	14	21	28
T	1 8	15	22	29
W	2 9	16	23	30
T	3 10	17	24	31
F	4 11	18	25	
S	5 12	19	26	
S	6 13	20	27	

June
M	4	11	18	25
T	5	12	19	26
W	6	13	20	27
T	7	14	21	28
F	1 8	15	22	29
S	2 9	16	23	30
S	3 10	17	24	

July
M	2	9	16	23 30
T	3	10	17	24 31
W	4	11	18	25
T	5	12	19	26
F	6	13	20	27
S	7	14	21	28
S	1 8	15	22	29

August
M	6	13	20	27
T	7	14	21	28
W	1 8	15	22	29
T	2 9	16	23	30
F	3 10	17	24	31
S	4 11	18	25	
S	5 12	19	26	

September
M	3 10	17	24	
T	4 11	18	25	
W	5 12	19	26	
T	6 13	20	27	
F	7 14	21	28	
S	1 8	15	22	29
S	2 9	16	23	30

October
M	1 8	15	22	29
T	2 9	16	23	30
W	3 10	17	24	31
T	4 11	18	25	
F	5 12	19	26	
S	6 13	20	27	
S	7 14	21	28	

November
M	5	12	19	26
T	6	13	20	27
W	7	14	21	28
T	1 8	15	22	29
F	2 9	16	23	30
S	3 10	17	24	
S	4 11	18	25	

December
M	3	10	17	24 31
T	4	11	18	25
W	5	12	19	26
T	6	13	20	27
F	7	14	21	28
S	1 8	15	22	29
S	2 9	16	23	30

3

	January	February	March	April
M	7 14 21 28	4 11 18 25	4 11 18 25	1 8 15 22 29
T	1 8 15 22 29	5 12 19 26	5 12 19 26	2 9 16 23 30
W	2 9 16 23 30	6 13 20 27	6 13 20 27	3 10 17 24
T	3 10 17 24 31	7 14 21 28	7 14 21 28	4 11 18 25
F	4 11 18 25	1 8 15 22	1 8 15 22	5 12 19 26
S	5 12 19 26	2 9 16 23	2 9 16 23 30	6 13 20 27
S	6 13 20 27	3 10 17 24	3 10 17 24 31	7 14 21 28

	May	June	July	August
M	6 13 20 27	3 10 17 24	1 8 15 22 29	5 12 19 26
T	7 14 21 28	4 11 18 25	2 9 16 23 30	6 13 20 27
W	1 8 15 22 29	5 12 19 26	3 10 17 24 31	7 14 21 28
T	2 9 16 23 30	6 13 20 27	4 11 18 25	1 8 15 22 29
F	3 10 17 24 31	7 14 21 28	5 12 19 26	2 9 16 23 30
S	4 11 18 25	1 8 15 22 29	6 13 20 27	3 10 17 24 31
S	5 12 19 26	2 9 16 23 30	7 14 21 28	4 11 18 25

	September	October	November	December
M	2 9 16 23 30	7 14 21 28	4 11 18 25	2 9 16 23 30
T	3 10 17 24	1 8 15 22 29	5 12 19 26	3 10 17 24 31
W	4 11 18 25	2 9 16 23 30	6 13 20 27	4 11 18 25
T	5 12 19 26	3 10 17 24 31	7 14 21 28	5 12 19 26
F	6 13 20 27	4 11 18 25	1 8 15 22 29	6 13 20 27
S	7 14 21 28	5 12 19 26	2 9 16 23 30	7 14 21 28
S	1 8 15 22 29	6 13 20 27	3 10 17 24	1 8 15 22 29

4

	January	February	March	April
M	6 13 20 27	3 10 17 24	3 10 17 24 31	7 14 21 28
T	7 14 21 28	4 11 18 25	4 11 18 25	1 8 15 22 29
W	1 8 15 22 29	5 12 19 26	5 12 19 26	2 9 16 23 30
T	2 9 16 23 30	6 13 20 27	6 13 20 27	3 10 17 24
F	3 10 17 24 31	7 14 21 28	7 14 21 28	4 11 18 25
S	4 11 18 25	1 8 15 22	1 8 15 22 29	5 12 19 26
S	5 12 19 26	2 9 16 23	2 9 16 23 30	6 13 20 27

	May	June	July	August
M	5 12 19 26	2 9 16 23 30	7 14 21 28	4 11 18 25
T	6 13 20 27	3 10 17 24	1 8 15 22 29	5 12 19 26
W	7 14 21 28	4 11 18 25	2 9 16 23 30	6 13 20 27
T	1 8 15 22 29	5 12 19 26	3 10 17 24 31	7 14 21 28
F	2 9 16 23 30	6 13 20 27	4 11 18 25	1 8 15 22 25
S	3 10 17 24 31	7 14 21 28	5 12 19 26	2 9 16 23 30
S	4 11 18 25	1 8 15 22 29	6 13 20 27	3 10 17 24 31

	September	October	November	December
M	1 8 15 22 29	6 13 20 27	3 10 17 24	1 8 15 22 29
T	2 9 16 23 30	7 14 21 28	4 11 18 25	2 9 16 23 30
W	3 10 17 24	1 8 15 22 29	5 12 19 26	3 10 17 24 31
T	4 11 18 25	2 9 16 23 30	6 13 20 27	4 11 18 25
F	5 12 19 26	3 10 17 24 31	7 14 21 28	5 12 19 26
S	6 13 20 27	4 11 18 25	1 8 15 22 29	6 13 20 27
S	7 14 21 28	5 12 19 26	2 9 16 23 30	7 14 21 28

5

	January	February	March	April
M	5 12 19 26	2 9 16 23	2 9 16 23 30	6 13 20 27
T	6 13 20 27	3 10 17 24	3 10 17 24 31	7 14 21 28
W	7 14 21 28	4 11 18 25	4 11 18 25	1 8 15 22 29
T	1 8 15 22 29	5 12 19 26	5 12 19 26	2 9 16 23 30
F	2 9 16 23 30	6 13 20 27	6 13 20 27	3 10 17 24
S	3 10 17 24 31	7 14 21 28	7 14 21 28	4 11 18 25
S	4 11 18 25	1 8 15 22	1 8 15 22 29	5 12 19 26

	May	June	July	August
M	4 11 18 25	1 8 15 22 29	6 13 20 27	3 10 17 24 31
T	5 12 19 26	2 9 16 23 30	7 14 21 28	4 11 18 25
W	6 13 20 27	3 10 17 24	1 8 15 22 29	5 12 19 26
T	7 14 21 28	4 11 18 25	2 9 16 23 30	6 13 20 27
F	1 8 15 22 29	5 12 19 26	3 10 17 24 31	7 14 21 28
S	2 9 16 23 30	6 13 20 27	4 11 18 25	1 8 15 22 29
S	3 10 17 24 31	7 14 21 28	5 12 19 26	2 9 16 23 30

	September	October	November	December
M	7 14 21 28	5 12 19 26	2 9 16 23 30	7 14 21 28
T	1 8 15 22 29	6 13 20 27	3 10 17 24	1 8 15 22 29
W	2 9 16 23 30	7 14 21 28	4 11 18 25	2 9 16 23 30
T	3 10 17 24	1 8 15 22 29	5 12 19 26	3 10 17 24 31
F	4 11 18 25	2 9 16 23 30	6 13 20 27	4 11 18 25
S	5 12 19 26	3 10 17 24 31	7 14 21 28	5 12 19 26
S	6 13 20 27	4 11 18 25	1 8 15 22 29	6 13 20 27

6

	January	February	March	April
M	4 11 18 25	1 8 15 22	1 8 15 22 29	5 12 19 26
T	5 12 19 26	2 9 16 23	2 9 16 23 30	6 13 20 27
W	6 13 20 27	3 10 17 24	3 10 17 24 31	7 14 21 28
T	7 14 21 28	4 11 18 25	4 11 18 25	1 8 15 22 29
F	1 8 15 22 29	5 12 19 26	5 12 19 26	2 9 16 23 30
S	2 9 16 23 30	6 13 20 27	6 13 20 27	3 10 17 24
S	3 10 17 24 31	7 14 21 28	7 14 21 28	4 11 18 25

	May	June	July	August
M	3 10 17 24 31	7 14 21 28	5 12 19 26	2 9 16 23 30
T	4 11 18 25	1 8 15 22 29	6 13 20 27	3 10 17 24 31
W	5 12 19 26	2 9 16 23 30	7 14 21 28	4 11 18 25
T	6 13 20 27	3 10 17 24	1 8 15 22 29	5 12 19 26
F	7 14 21 28	4 11 18 25	2 9 16 23 30	6 13 20 27
S	1 8 15 22 29	5 12 19 26	3 10 17 24 31	7 14 21 28
S	2 9 16 23 30	6 13 20 27	4 11 18 25	1 8 15 22 29

	September	October	November	December
M	6 13 20 27	4 11 18 25	1 8 15 22 29	6 13 20 27
T	7 14 21 28	5 12 19 26	2 9 16 23 30	7 14 21 28
W	1 8 15 22 29	6 13 20 27	3 10 17 24	1 8 15 22 29
T	2 9 16 23 30	7 14 21 28	4 11 18 25	2 9 16 23 30
F	3 10 17 24	1 8 15 22 29	5 12 19 26	3 10 17 24 31
S	4 11 18 25	2 9 16 23 30	6 13 20 27	4 11 18 25
S	5 12 19 26	3 10 17 24 31	7 14 21 28	5 12 19 26

7

	January	February	March	April
M	3 10 17 24 31	7 14 21 28	7 14 21 28	4 11 18 25
T	4 11 18 25	1 8 15 22	1 8 15 22 29	5 12 19 26
W	5 12 19 26	2 9 16 23	2 9 16 23 30	6 13 20 27
T	6 13 20 27	3 10 17 24	3 10 17 24 31	7 14 21 28
F	7 14 21 28	4 11 18 25	4 11 18 25	1 8 15 22 29
S	1 8 15 22 29	5 12 19 26	5 12 19 26	2 9 16 23 30
S	2 9 16 23 30	6 13 20 27	6 13 20 27	3 10 17 24

	May	June	July	August
M	2 9 16 23 30	6 13 20 27	4 11 18 25	1 8 15 22 29
T	3 10 17 24 31	7 14 21 28	5 12 19 26	2 9 16 23 30
W	4 11 18 25	1 8 15 22 29	6 13 20 27	3 10 17 24 31
T	5 12 19 26	2 9 16 23 30	7 14 21 28	4 11 18 25
F	6 13 20 27	3 10 17 24	1 8 15 22 29	5 12 19 26
S	7 14 21 28	4 11 18 25	2 9 16 23 30	6 13 20 27
S	1 8 15 22 29	5 12 19 26	3 10 17 24 31	7 14 21 28

	September	October	November	December
M	5 12 19 26	3 10 17 24 31	7 14 21 28	5 12 19 26
T	6 13 20 27	4 11 18 25	1 8 15 22 29	6 13 20 27
W	7 14 21 28	5 12 19 26	2 9 16 23 30	7 14 21 28
T	1 8 15 22 29	6 13 20 27	3 10 17 24	1 8 15 22 29
F	2 9 16 23 30	7 14 21 28	4 11 18 25	2 9 16 23 30
S	3 10 17 24	1 8 15 22 29	5 12 19 26	3 10 17 24 31
S	4 11 18 25	2 9 16 23 30	6 13 20 27	4 11 18 25

8

	January	February	March	April
M	2 9 16 23 30	6 13 20 27	5 12 19 26	2 9 16 23 30
T	3 10 17 24 31	7 14 21 28	6 13 20 27	3 10 17 24
W	4 11 18 25	1 8 15 22 29	7 14 21 28	4 11 18 25
T	5 12 19 26	2 9 16 23	1 8 15 22 29	5 12 19 26
F	6 13 20 27	3 10 17 24	2 9 16 23 30	6 13 20 27
S	7 14 21 28	4 11 18 25	3 10 17 24 31	7 14 21 28
S	1 8 15 22 29	5 12 19 26	4 11 18 25	1 8 15 22 29

	May	June	July	August
M	7 14 21 28	4 11 18 25	2 9 16 23 30	6 13 20 27
T	1 8 15 22 29	5 12 19 26	3 10 17 24 31	7 14 21 28
W	2 9 16 23 30	6 13 20 27	4 11 18 25	1 8 15 22 29
T	3 10 17 24 31	7 14 21 28	5 12 19 26	2 9 16 23 30
F	4 11 18 25	1 8 15 22 29	6 13 20 27	3 10 17 24 31
S	5 12 19 26	2 9 16 23 30	7 14 21 28	4 11 18 25
S	6 13 20 27	3 10 17 24	1 8 15 22 29	5 12 19 26

	September	October	November	December
M	3 10 17 24	1 8 15 22 29	5 12 19 26	3 10 17 24 31
T	4 11 18 25	2 9 16 23 30	6 13 20 27	4 11 18 25
W	5 12 19 26	3 10 17 24 31	7 14 21 28	5 12 19 26
T	6 13 20 27	4 11 18 25	1 8 15 22 29	6 13 20 27
F	7 14 21 28	5 12 19 26	2 9 16 23 30	7 14 21 28
S	1 8 15 22 29	6 13 20 27	3 10 17 24	1 8 15 22 29
S	2 9 16 23 30	7 14 21 28	4 11 18 25	2 9 16 23 30

9

	January	February	March	April
M	1 8 15 22 29	5 12 19 26	4 11 18 25	1 8 15 22 29
T	2 9 16 23 30	6 13 20 27	5 12 19 26	2 9 16 23 30
W	3 10 17 24 31	7 14 21 28	6 13 20 27	3 10 17 24
T	4 11 18 25	1 8 15 22 29	7 14 21 28	4 11 18 25
F	5 12 19 26	2 9 16 23	1 8 15 22 29	5 12 19 26
S	6 13 20 27	3 10 17 24	2 9 16 23 30	6 13 20 27
S	7 14 21 28	4 11 18 25	3 10 17 24 31	7 14 21 28

	May	June	July	August
M	6 13 20 27	3 10 17 24	1 8 15 22 29	5 12 19 26
T	7 14 21 28	4 11 18 25	2 9 16 23 30	6 13 20 27
W	1 8 15 22 29	5 12 19 26	3 10 17 24 31	7 14 21 28
T	2 9 16 23 30	6 13 20 27	4 11 18 25	1 8 15 22 29
F	3 10 17 24 31	7 14 21 28	5 12 19 26	2 9 16 23 30
S	4 11 18 25	1 8 15 22 29	6 13 20 27	3 10 17 24 31
S	5 12 19 26	2 9 16 23 30	7 14 21 28	4 11 18 25

	September	October	November	December
M	2 9 16 23 30	7 14 21 28	4 11 18 25	2 9 16 23 30
T	3 10 17 24	1 8 15 22 29	5 12 19 26	3 10 17 24 31
W	4 11 18 25	2 9 16 23 30	6 13 20 27	4 11 18 25
T	5 12 19 26	3 10 17 24 31	7 14 21 28	5 12 19 26
F	6 13 20 27	4 11 18 25	1 8 15 22 29	6 13 20 27
S	7 14 21 28	5 12 19 26	2 9 16 23 30	7 14 21 28
S	1 8 15 22 29	6 13 20 27	3 10 17 24	1 8 15 22 29

10

	January	February	March	April
M	7 14 21 28	4 11 18 25	3 10 17 24 31	7 14 21 28
T	1 8 15 22 29	5 12 19 26	4 11 18 25	1 8 15 22 29
W	2 9 16 23 30	6 13 20 27	5 12 19 26	2 9 16 23 30
T	3 10 17 24 31	7 14 21 28	6 13 20 27	3 10 17 24
F	4 11 18 25	1 8 15 22 29	7 14 21 28	4 11 18 25
S	5 12 19 26	2 9 16 23	1 8 15 22 29	5 12 19 26
S	6 13 20 27	3 10 17 24	2 9 16 23 30	6 13 20 27

	May	June	July	August
M	5 12 19 26	2 9 16 23 30	7 14 21 28	4 11 18 25
T	6 13 20 27	3 10 17 24	1 8 15 22 29	5 12 19 26
W	7 14 21 28	4 11 18 25	2 9 16 23 30	6 13 20 27
T	1 8 15 22 29	5 12 19 26	3 10 17 24 31	7 14 21 28
F	2 9 16 23 30	6 13 20 27	4 11 18 25	1 8 15 22 29
S	3 10 17 24 31	7 14 21 28	5 12 19 26	2 9 16 23 30
S	4 11 18 25	1 8 15 22 29	6 13 20 27	3 10 17 24 31

	September	October	November	December
M	1 8 15 22 29	6 13 20 27	3 10 17 24	1 8 15 22 29
T	2 9 16 23 30	7 14 21 28	4 11 18 25	2 9 16 23 30
W	3 10 17 24	1 8 15 22 29	5 12 19 26	3 10 17 24 31
T	4 11 18 25	2 9 16 23 30	6 13 20 27	4 11 18 25
F	5 12 19 26	3 10 17 24 31	7 14 21 28	5 12 19 26
S	6 13 20 27	4 11 18 25	1 8 15 22 29	6 13 20 27
S	7 14 21 28	5 12 19 26	2 9 16 23 30	7 14 21 28

11

	January	February	March	April
M	6 13 20 27	3 10 17 24	2 9 16 23 30	6 13 20 27
T	7 14 21 28	4 11 18 25	3 10 17 24 31	7 14 21 28
W	1 8 15 22 29	5 12 19 26	4 11 18 25	1 8 15 22 29
T	2 9 16 23 30	6 13 20 27	5 12 19 26	2 9 16 23 30
F	3 10 17 24 31	7 14 21 28	6 13 20 27	3 10 17 24
S	4 11 18 25	1 8 15 22 29	7 14 21 28	4 11 18 25
S	5 12 19 26	2 9 16 23	1 8 15 22 29	5 12 19 26

	May	June	July	August
M	4 11 18 25	1 8 15 22 29	6 13 20 27	3 10 17 24 31
T	5 12 19 26	2 9 16 23 30	7 14 21 28	4 11 18 25
W	6 13 20 27	3 10 17 24	1 8 15 22 29	5 12 19 26
T	7 14 21 28	4 11 18 25	2 9 16 23 30	6 13 20 27
F	1 8 15 22 29	5 12 19 26	3 10 17 24 31	7 14 21 28
S	2 9 16 23 30	6 13 20 27	4 11 18 25	1 8 15 22 29
S	3 10 17 24 31	7 14 21 28	5 12 19 26	2 9 16 23 30

	September	October	November	December
M	7 14 21 28	5 12 19 26	2 9 16 23 30	7 14 21 28
T	1 8 15 22 29	6 13 20 27	3 10 17 24	1 8 15 22 29
W	2 9 16 23 30	7 14 21 28	4 11 18 25	2 9 16 23 30
T	3 10 17 24	1 8 15 22 29	5 12 19 26	3 10 17 24 31
F	4 11 18 25	2 9 16 23 30	6 13 20 27	4 11 18 25
S	5 12 19 26	3 10 17 24 31	7 14 21 28	5 12 19 26
S	6 13 20 27	4 11 18 25	1 8 15 22 29	6 13 20 27

12

	January	February	March	April
M	5 12 19 26	2 9 16 23	1 8 15 22 29	5 12 19 26
T	6 13 20 27	3 10 17 24	2 9 16 23 30	6 13 20 27
W	7 14 21 28	4 11 18 25	3 10 17 24 31	7 14 21 28
T	1 8 15 22 29	5 12 19 26	4 11 18 25	1 8 15 22 29
F	2 9 16 23 30	6 13 20 27	5 12 19 26	2 9 16 23 30
S	3 10 17 24 31	7 14 21 28	6 13 20 27	3 10 17 24
S	4 11 18 25	1 8 15 22 29	7 14 21 28	4 11 18 25

	May	June	July	August
M	3 10 17 24 31	7 14 21 28	5 12 19 26	2 9 16 23 30
T	4 11 18 25	1 8 15 22 29	6 13 20 27	3 10 17 24 31
W	5 12 19 26	2 9 16 23 30	7 14 21 28	4 11 18 25
T	6 13 20 27	3 10 17 24	1 8 15 22 29	5 12 19 26
F	7 14 21 28	4 11 18 25	2 9 16 23 30	6 13 20 27
S	1 8 15 22 29	5 12 19 26	3 10 17 24 31	7 14 21 28
S	2 9 16 23 30	6 13 20 27	4 11 18 25	1 8 15 22 29

	September	October	November	December
M	6 13 20 27	4 11 18 25	1 8 15 22 29	6 13 20 27
T	7 14 21 28	5 12 19 26	2 9 16 23 30	7 14 21 28
W	1 8 15 22 29	6 13 20 27	3 10 17 24	1 8 15 22 29
T	2 9 16 23 30	7 14 21 28	4 11 18 25	2 9 16 23 30
F	3 10 17 24	1 8 15 22 29	5 12 19 26	3 10 17 24 31
S	4 11 18 25	2 9 16 23 30	6 13 20 27	4 11 18 25
S	5 12 19 26	3 10 17 24 31	7 14 21 28	5 12 19 26

13

	January	February	March	April
M	4 11 18 25	1 8 15 22 29	7 14 21 28	4 11 18 25
T	5 12 19 26	2 9 16 23	1 8 15 22 29	5 12 19 26
W	6 13 20 27	3 10 17 24	2 9 16 23 30	6 13 20 27
T	7 14 21 28	4 11 18 25	3 10 17 24 31	7 14 21 28
F	1 8 15 22 29	5 12 19 26	4 11 18 25	1 8 15 22 29
S	2 9 16 23 30	6 13 20 27	5 12 19 26	2 9 16 23 30
S	3 10 17 24 31	7 14 21 28	6 13 20 27	3 10 17 24

	May	June	July	August
M	2 9 16 23 30	6 13 20 27	4 11 18 25	1 8 15 22 29
T	3 10 17 24 31	7 14 21 28	5 12 19 26	2 9 16 23 30
W	4 11 18 25	1 8 15 22 29	6 13 20 27	3 10 17 24 31
T	5 12 19 26	2 9 16 23 30	7 14 21 28	4 11 18 25
F	6 13 20 27	3 10 17 24	1 8 15 22 29	5 12 19 26
S	7 14 21 28	4 11 18 25	2 9 16 23 30	6 13 20 27
S	1 8 15 22 29	5 12 19 26	3 10 17 24 31	7 14 21 28

	September	October	November	December
M	5 12 19 26	3 10 17 24 31	7 14 21 28	5 12 19 26
T	6 13 20 27	4 11 18 25	1 8 15 22 29	6 13 20 27
W	7 14 21 28	5 12 19 26	2 9 16 23 30	7 14 21 28
T	1 8 15 22 29	6 13 20 27	3 10 17 24	1 8 15 22 29
F	2 9 16 23 30	7 14 21 28	4 11 18 25	2 9 16 23 30
S	3 10 17 24	1 8 15 22 29	5 12 19 26	3 10 17 24 31
S	4 11 18 25	2 9 16 23 30	6 13 20 27	4 11 18 25

14

	January	February	March	April
M	3 10 17 24 31	7 14 21 28	6 13 20 27	3 10 17 24
T	4 11 18 25	1 8 15 22 29	7 14 21 28	4 11 18 25
W	5 12 19 26	2 9 16 23	1 8 15 22 29	5 12 19 26
T	6 13 20 27	3 10 17 24	2 9 16 23 30	6 13 20 27
F	7 14 21 28	4 11 18 25	3 10 17 24 31	7 14 21 28
S	1 8 15 22 29	5 12 19 26	4 11 18 25	1 8 15 22 29
S	2 9 16 23 30	6 13 20 27	5 12 19 26	2 9 16 23 30

	May	June	July	August
M	1 8 15 22 29	5 12 19 26	3 10 17 24 31	7 14 21 28
T	2 9 16 23 30	6 13 20 27	4 11 18 25	1 8 15 22 29
W	3 10 17 24 31	7 14 21 28	5 12 19 26	2 9 16 23 30
T	4 11 18 25	1 8 15 22 29	6 13 20 27	3 10 17 24 31
F	5 12 19 26	2 9 16 23 30	7 14 21 28	4 11 18 25
S	6 13 20 27	3 10 17 24	1 8 15 22 29	5 12 19 26
S	7 14 21 28	4 11 18 25	2 9 16 23 30	6 13 20 27

	September	October	November	December
M	4 11 18 25	2 9 16 23 30	6 13 20 27	4 11 18 25
T	5 12 19 26	3 10 17 24 31	7 14 21 28	5 12 19 26
W	6 13 20 27	4 11 18 25	1 8 15 22 29	6 13 20 27
T	7 14 21 28	5 12 19 26	2 9 16 23 30	7 14 21 28
F	1 8 15 22 29	6 13 20 27	3 10 17 24	1 8 15 22 29
S	2 9 16 23 30	7 14 21 28	4 11 18 25	2 9 16 23 30
S	3 10 17 24	1 8 15 22 29	5 12 19 26	3 10 17 24 31

M4: Religious festivals

2013

☬	Birthday of Guru Gobind Singh	January 5
☽	Mawlid-al-Nabi	January 24
✝	Ash Wednesday	February 13
✡	Purim	February 24
✡	Passover	March 26
ॐ	Holi	March 27
☬	Hola Mohalla	March 28
✝	Good Friday	March 29
✝	Easter Sunday	March 31
✝	Easter Monday	April 1
☬	Baisakhi Day	April 14
✝	Ascension Day	May 9
✡	Shavuot	May 15
✝	Pentecost	May 19
☽	Ramadan begins	July 9
☽	Eid al-Fitr	August 8
✡	Rosh Hashanah	September 5
✡	Yom Kippur	September 14
✡	Succot	September 19
ॐ	Dasarah	October 14
☽	Eid al-Adha	October 15
ॐ	Diwali	November 3
☽	Hijra – New year	November 4
☽	Ashurah	November 13
☬	Birthday of Guru Nanak	November 17
✡	Chanukah	November 28
✝	Christmas Day	December 25

2014

☬	Birthday of Guru Gobind Singh	January 5
☽	Mawlid-al-Nabi	January 13
✝	Ash Wednesday	March 5
✡	Purim	March 16
ॐ	Holi	March 17
☬	Hola Mohalla	March 17
☬	Birthday of Guru Nanak	April 14
☬	Baisakhi Day	April 14
✡	Passover	April 15
✝	Good Friday	April 18
✝	Easter Sunday	April 20
✝	Easter Monday	April 21
✝	Ascension Day	May 29
✡	Shavuot	June 4
✝	Pentecost	June 8
☽	Ramadan begins	June 28
☽	Eid al-Fitr	July 28
✡	Rosh Hashanah	September 25
✡	Yom Kippur	October 4
ॐ	Dasarah	October 4
☽	Eid al-Adha	October 4
✡	Succot	October 9
ॐ	Diwali	October 23
☽	Ashurah	November 3
☽	Hijra – New year	November 15
✡	Chanukah	December 17
✝	Christmas Day	December 25

2015

☬	Birthday of Guru Gobind Singh	January 5
✝	Ash Wednesday	February 25
✡	Purim	March 6
ॐ	Holi	March 6
☬	Hola Mohalla	March 6
✝	Good Friday	April 3
✡	Passover	April 4
✝	Easter Sunday	April 5
✝	Easter Monday	April 6
☬	Baisakhi Day	April 14
✝	Ascension Day	May 2
✝	Pentecost	May 24
✡	Shavuot	May 24
☽	Ramadan begins	June 18
☽	Eid al-Fitr	July 18
✡	Rosh Hashanah	September 14
✡	Yom Kippur	September 23
☽	Eid al-Adha	September 23
✡	Succot	September 28
☽	Hijra – New year	October 14
ॐ	Dasarah	October 22
☽	Ashurah	October 23
ॐ	Diwali	November 11
☬	Birthday of Guru Nanak	November 25
✡	Chanukah	December 7
☽	Mawlid-al-Nabi	December 23
✝	Christmas Day	December 25

✝ Christian
ॐ Hindu
✡ Jewish
☽ Muslim
☬ Sikh

Note: all Islamic and Jewish holidays begin at sundown on the preceding day.

M5: Medical reference intervals and scales

Haematology—reference intervals

Measurement	Reference interval
White cell count	$4.0–11.0 \times 10^9/l$
Red cell count – Male: Female:	$4.5–6.5 \times 10^{12}/l$ $3.9–5.6 \times 10^{12}/l$
Haemoglobin – Male: Female:	13.5–18.0g/dl 11.5–16.0g/dl
Platelet count	$150.0–400.0 \times 10^9/l$
Erthrocyte sedimentation rate (ESR) – Male: Female:	Up to age in years divided by two. Up to (age in years plus 10) divided by two.
Prothrombin time (factors II, VII, X)	10–14 seconds
Activated partial thromboplastic time (VIII, IX, XI, XII)	35–45 seconds

Proposed therapeutic ranges for prothrombin time (British Society for Haematology guidelines on oral anticoagulants, 1984)

British ratio (NR)	Clinical state
2.0–2.5	Prophylaxis of deep vein thrombosis including high risk surgery (e.g. for fractured femur).
2.5–3.0	Treatment of deep vein thrombosis, pulmonary embolism, transient ischaemic attacks.
3.0–4.5	Recurrent deep vein thrombosis an pulmonary embolism, arterial disease including myocardial infarction, arterial grafts, cardiac prosthetic valves and grafts.

Cerebrospinal fluid—reference intervals

| Opening pressure (mmCSF) | Infants: < 80; children: < 90; adults: < 210 |

Substance	Reference interval
Glucose	3.3–4.4 mmol/l or ≥ 2/3 of plasma glucose
Chloride	122–128 mmol/l
Lactate	< 2.8 mmol/l

Biochemistry—reference intervals

Substance	Specimen	Reference Interval
Albumin	P	*35–50 g/l
a-amylase	P	0–180 Somogyi U/dl
Bicarbonate	P	*24–30 mmol/l
C reactive protein (CRP)	P	< 6 mg/l
Calcium (ionised)	P	1.0–1.25 mmol/l
Calcium (total)	P	*2.12–2.65 mmol/l
Chloride	P	98–107 mmol/l
Cholesterol	P	3.3–6.2 mmol/l
Creatinine	P	*58–110 mmol/l
Glucose (fasting)	P	3.5–5.5 mmol/l
Glycosylated haemoglobin	B	5–8%
Phosphate	P	0.8–1.45 mmol/l
Potassium	P	3.6–5.0 mmol/l
Protein (total)	P	60–80 g/l
Sodium	P	*137–145 mmol/l
Urea	P	*2.5–7.5 mmol/l

Key: P = plasma; B = whole blood

* Reference intervals for these substances differ in pregnancy. Reference intervals in pregnancy are not reproduced here.

Arterial blood gases—reference intervals

pH:	7.35–7.45
PaO$_2$:	>10.6 kPa
PaCO$_2$:	4.7–6.0 kPa
Base excess	±2 mmol/l
NB: 7.6 mmHg = 1 kPa (atmospheric pressure = 100 kPa)	

Apgar scoring chart

A baby's condition is assesed at one and five minutes after birth by means of the Apgar score. This system observes five signs. A score of nought, one or two is awarded for each sign.

Sign	0	1	2
Heart rate	absent	slow (below 100)	over 100
Respiratory effect	absent	weak cry, hypoventilation	good cry
Muscle tone	limp	some flexion of extremities	well flexed
Reflex irritability	no response	some motion	cry
Colour	blue, pale	body pink, extremities blue	completely pink

NB: An Apgar score of 10 represents optimal condition. A score of three or less indicates a markedly asphyxiated infant.

Glasgow coma scale

Three types of response are assessed:

	Score	
Best motor	6	Obeys commands
response	5	Localises to pain
	4	Flexion/withdrawal to pain
	3	Abnormal flexion
	2	Abnormal extension
	1	None
Best verbal	5	Oriented
response	4	Confused
	3	Inappropriate words
	2	Incomprehensible sounds
	1	None
Eye opening	4	Spontaneously
	3	To speech
	2	To pain
	1	None

The overall score is the sum of the scores in each area, e.g. no response to pain + no verbal response + no eye opening = three.

In severe injury the score is eight or under.
In moderate injury the score is nine–12.
In minor injury the score is 13–15.

PULHHEEMS rating

This is a system of physical and mental grading used by all three branches of the British Armed Forces. It is taken from the joint Services publication JSP 346 which is issued to all Service and Civilian medical practitioners required to examine applicants for entry to the Armed Forces. It is carried out on new recruits, and repeated at five-yearly intervals after the age of 30. After the age of 50, it is performed at two-yearly intervals.

PULHHEEMS is an abbreviation for the factors to be tested. These include:

P	Physique
U	Upper limbs
L	Locomotion—i.e. lower limbs and back
H	Hearing in the left ear
H	Hearing in the right ear
E	Visual acuity—left eye
E	Visual acuity—right eye
M	Mental function
S	Stability (emotional)

The maximum score is eight (excellent) and the minimum one (unfit for service). In the form this appears in a table as follows (Lord Nelson taken as an example):

P	U	L	H	H	E	E	M	S
8	4	8	8	8	8	1	8	5

FDI World Dental Federation notation

FDI Two-Digit Notation

Permanent Teeth

upper right								upper left							
18	17	16	15	14	13	12	11	21	22	23	24	25	26	27	28
48	47	46	45	44	43	43	41	31	32	33	34	35	36	37	38
lower right								lower left							

Deciduous teeth (baby teeth)

upper right					upper left				
55	54	53	52	51	61	62	63	64	65
85	84	83	82	81	71	72	73	74	75
lower right					lower left				

Codes, names and usual number of roots

	Codes	Names	Usual number of roots
11	21	maxillary central incisor	1
41	31	mandibular central incisor	1
12	22	maxillary lateral incisor	1
42	32	mandibular lateral incisor	1
13	23	maxillary canine	1
43	33	mandibular canine	1
14	24	maxillary first premolar	2
44	34	mandibular first premolar	1
15	25	maxillary second premolar	1
45	35	mandibular second premolar	1
16	26	maxillary first molar	3
46	36	mandibular first molar	2
17	27	maxillary second molar	3
47	37	mandibular second molar	2
18	28	maxillary third premolar	3
48	38	mandibular third premolar	2

How the codes are constructed

Syntax: <quadrant code><tooth code>

Quadrant codes		**Tooth codes**	
1	upper right	1	central incisors
2	upper left	2	lateral incisors
3	lower left	3	canines
4	lower right	4	1st premolars
		5	2nd premolars
		6	1st molars
		7	2nd molars
		8	3rd molars

M6: Websites

Useful web sites

Site	Address
Acts of Parliament	*http://www.legislation.gov.uk*
Australasian Legal Information Institute	*http://www.austlii.edu.au*
Bank of England	*http://www.bankofengland.co.uk*
Bar Council	*http://www.barcouncil.org.uk*
British and Irish Legal Information Institute	*http://www.bailii.org*
CGT Indexation Allowance	*http://www.number7.demon.co.uk/cgt/allow.htm*
Child Support Agency	*http://www.csa.gov.uk*
Social Security and Child Support Commissioners' Decisions	*http://www.justice.gov.uk/guidance/courts-and-tribunals/ aa/decisions*
Companies House	*http://www.companies-house.gov.uk*
Court of Justice of the European Union	*http://www.curia.europa.eu/jcms/jems/j-61*
Her Majesty's Court and Tribunals Service	*https://www.hmcourts-service.gov.uk/*
Carers Trust	*https://www.carers.org/merger*
Delia Venables Legal Resources	*http://www.venables.co.uk*
DCA Human Rights site	*http://www.dca.gov.uk/peoples-rights/human-rights/ index.htm*
Department of Health	*http://www.dh.gov.uk*
Electronic Share Information (iii)	*http://www.iii.co.uk*
European Court of Human Rights	*http://www.echr.coe.int*
Financial Times	*http://www.ft.com*
Government Actuary's Department	*http://www.gad.gov.uk*
Government Information Service	*http://www.direct.gov.uk*
Hague Conference on Private International Law	*http://www.hcch.net/index_en.php*
Hague Convention on Child Abduction	*http://www.hcch.net/index_ en.php?act=text.display&tid=21*
Hansard: House of Commons Debates	*http://www.parliament.uk/business/publications/ hansard/commons*
House of Lords Debates	*http://www.parliament.uk/business/publications/ hansard/lords*
Land Registry	*http://www.landregistry.gov.uk*
Legislation.gov.uk	*http://www.legislation.gov.uk*
House of Commons	*http://www.parliament.uk/commons*
House of Lords	*http://www.parliament.uk/business/lords*
House Price Indices (Halifax)	*http://www.lloydsbankinggroup.com/media1/economic- insight/halifax-house-price-index-page.asp allundersonhalifax_hpi.asp*
Information for Lawyers	*http://www.infolaw.co.uk*
HM Revenue & Customs	*http://www.hmrc.gov.uk/home.htm*
Judicial Committee of the Privy Council	*http://www.jcpc.gov.uk*
Laurie West-Knights' homepage	*http://www.lawonline.cc*
Law Society	*http://www.lawsociety.org.uk/home.law*
Legal Services Commission	*http://www.legalservices.gov.uk/*
Ministry of Justice	*http://www.justice.gov.uk*
National Savings & Investments	*http://www.nsandi.com/*
Official Solicitor and Public Trustee Office	*http://www.justice.gov.uk/about/ospt*
ONS–Consumer Price Index and Retail Price Index	*http://www.ONS.gov.uk/ons/guide-method/user- guidance/prices/cpi-and-rpi/index.html*
Pension annuity quotes	*http://www.annuity-bureau.co.uk*
RPI (full table)	*http://www.statistics.gov.uk/cci/nugget.asp?id=21*
Smith Bernal (transcripts of judgments)	*http://www.merrillcorp.com*
Statutory Instruments	*http://www.legislation.gov.uk/uksi*
Sweet & Maxwell	*http://www.sweetandmaxwell.co.uk*
The Stationery Office	*http://www.tso.co.uk*
The Supreme Court	*http://www.supremecourt.gov.uk/*
The Times	*http://www.thetimes.co.uk*
UK Parliament	*http://www.parliament.uk*
Upmystreet (regional data)	*http://www.zoopla.co.uk*

M7: Addresses of useful organisations

Part 1—Medical

British Medical Association

BMA House
Tavistock Square
London WC1H 9JP
Tel: 020 7387 4499
Fax: 020 7383 6400
Website: *http://www.bma.org.uk*

General Dental Council

37 Wimpole Street
London W1G 8DQ
Tel: 020 7887 3800
Fax: 020 7224 3294
Email: information@gdc-uk.org
Website: *http://www.gdc-uk.org*

British Association for Accident and Emergency Medicine—merged with the College of Emergency Medicine

The Royal College of Surgeons of England
35–43 Lincoln's Inn Fields
London WC2A 3PN
Tel: 020 7831 9405
Fax: 020 7405 0318
Email: communications@rceng.ac.uk

The College of Emergency Medicine

7–9 Breams Buildings
London, EC4A 1DT
Tel: 020 7404 1999
Fax: 020 7067 1267
Website: *http://www.collemergencymed.ac.uk*

General Medical Council

Regent's Place
350 Euston Road
London NW1 3JN
Tel: 0161 923 6602
Fax: 020 7189 5401
Email: gmc@gmc-uk.org
Website: *http://www.gmc-uk.org*

General Optical Council

41 Harley Street
London W1G 8DJ
Tel: 020 7580 3898
Fax: 020 7307 3939
Email: goc@optical.org
Website: *http://www.optical.org*

Nursing and Midwifery Council

23 Portland Place
London W1B 1PZ
Tel: 020 7637 7181
Fax: 020 7436 2924
Email: advice@nmc-uk.org
Website: *http://www.nmc-uk.org*

Accidents

Royal Society for the Prevention of Accidents
(RoSPA)
RoSPA House
28 Calthorpe Road
Edgbaston
Birmingham B15 1RP
Tel: 0121 248 2000
Fax: 0121 248 2001
Email: help@rospa.co.uk
Website: *http://www.rospa.com*

Alcoholism

Medical Council on Alcohol
5 St. Andrew's Place
Regent's Park
London NW1 4LB
Tel: 020 7487 4445
Fax: 020 7935 4479
Email: mca@medicouncilalcol.demon.co.uk
Website: *http://www.m-c-a.org.uk*

Alzheimer's disease

Alzheimer's Society
Devon House
58 St Katherine's Way
London E1W 1LB
Tel: 020 7423 3500
Fax: 020 7423 3501
Email: enquiries@alzheimers.org.uk

Anaesthetics

Obstetric Anaesthetists' Association
21 Portland Place
London W1B 1PY
Tel: 020 7631 8883
Fax: 020 7631 4352
Email: secretariat@oaa-anaes.ac.uk

Asthma

Asthma UK
Summit House
70 Wilson Street
London EC2A 2DB
Tel: 0800 121 62 55
Fax: 020 7256 6075
Email: info@asthma.org.uk

Bereavement

Child Bereavement Charity
The Saunderton Estate
Wycombe Road
Saunderton
Buckinghamshire HP14 4BF
Tel: 01494 568 900
Fax: 01494 568 920
Email: enquiries@childbereavement.org.uk

The Compassionate Friends
(counselling for bereaved parents)
National Office
53 North Street
Bristol BS3 1EN
Tel: 0845 120 3785
Fax: 0845 120 3786
Email: info@tcf.org.uk

Biochemistry

Biochemical Society
Charles Darwin House
12 Roger Street
London WC1N 2JU
Tel: 020 7685 2400
Fax: 020 7685 2467
Email: genadmin@biochemistry.org

Blindness

Royal National Institute of the Blind
105 Judd Street
London WC1H 9NE
Tel: 020 7388 1266
Fax: 020 7388 2034
Email: helpline@rnib.org.uk

Brain

Brain Research Trust
Dutch House, 307–308 High Holborn
London WC1V 7LL
Tel: 020 7404 9982
Fax: 020 7404 9983
Email: info@brt.org.uk

British Association of Brain Injury Case
Managers (BABICM)
PO Box 199
Bury
BL8 9EJ
Tel: 0700 2222 426
Email: secretary@babicm.org

Centre for Brain Injury, Rehabilitation and
Development (BIRD)
The Old Coach House
Church Road
Eccleston, Chester
Tel: 01244 678 629

Brittle bone disease

Brittle Bone Society
30 Guthrie Street
Dundee DD1 5BS
Tel: 01382 204 446
Fax: 01382 206 771
Email: bbs@brittlebone.org

Cancer

British Association of Cancer United
Patients (BACUP)
3 Bath Place
Rivington Street
London EC2A 3RJ
Tel: 020 7696 9003
Fax: 020 7696 9002
Email: info@cancerbacup.org.uk

The Association for Cancer Surgery
Royal College of Surgeons
35–43 Lincoln's Inn Fields
London WC2A 3PE
Tel: 020 7869 6817
Fax: 020 7869 6851
Email: admin@baso.org.uk

Macmillan Cancer Relief
89 Albert Embankment
London SE1 7UQ
Tel: 020 7840 7840
Fax: 020 7840 7841
Email: cancerline@macmillan.org.uk

Cancer Research UK
Angel Building
407 St John Street
London EC1V 4AD
Tel: 020 7242 0200
Fax: 020 3469 6400

Marie Curie Cancer Care
89 Albert Embankment
London SE1 7TP
Tel: 0800 716 146
Fax: 020 7599 7708
Email: supporter.services@mariecurie.org.uk

Cardiology

British Cardiovascular Society
9 Fitzroy Square
London W1T 5HW
Tel: 020 7383 3887
Fax: 020 7388 0903
Email: enquiries@bcs.com

British Heart Foundation
Greater London House
180 Hampstead Road
London, NW1 7AW
Tel: 020 7554 0000
Website: http://www.bhf.org.uk

Society of Cardiothoracic Surgeons in Great
Britain & Ireland
The Royal College of Surgeons
35–43 Lincoln's Inn Fields
London WC2A 3PE
Tel: 020 7869 6893
Fax: 020 7869 6890

Childbirth

The Association for Post-Natal Illness
145 Dawes Road, Fulham
London SW6 7EB
Tel: 020 7386 0868
Fax: 020 7386 8885
Email: info@apni.org

The National Childbirth Trust
Alexandra House
Oldham Terrace
London W3 6NH
Tel: 0800 330 0700
Email: enquiries@nct.org.uk

Royal College of Midwives
15 Mansfield Street
London W1G 9NH
Tel: 020 7312 3535
Fax: 020 7312 3536
Email: info@rcm.org.uk

Stillbirth and Neonatal Death Society (SANDS)
28 Portland Place
London W1B 1LY
Tel: 020 7436 7940
Fax: 020 7436 3715
Email: support@UK-sands.org

Children

The National Association for Children with
Lower Limb Abnormalities (STEPS)
Warrington Lane
Lymm
Cheshire WA13 OSA
Tel: 01925 750 271
Email: info@steps-charity.org.uk

Barnardo's
Tanners Lane
Barkingside
Ilford
Essex IG6 1QG
Tel: 020 8550 8822
Website: http://www.barnardos.org.uk

Baby Life Support Systems (Bliss)
9 Holyrood Street
London SE1 2EL
Tel: 020 7378 1122
Fax: 020 7403 0673
Email: information@bliss.org.uk

Child Accident Prevention Trust
Canterbury Court (1.09)
1–3 Brixton Road
London SW9 6DE
Tel: 020 7608 3828
Fax: 020 7608 3674
Email: safe@capt.org.uk

Child Poverty Action Group (CPAG)
94 White Lion Street
London N1 9PF
Tel: 020 7837 7979
Fax: 020 7837 6414
Email: info@cpag.org.uk

(see also **Paediatric**)

Chiropody

Institute of Chiropodists & Podiatrists
150 Lord Street
Southport
Merseyside PR9 0TL
Tel: 01704 546 141
Fax: 01704 500 477
Email: secretary@iocp.org.uk

Society of Chiropodists & Podiatrists
1 Fellmonger's Pass
Tower Bridge Road
London SE1 3LY
Tel: 020 7234 8620
Fax: 0845 450 3721
Website: *http://www.feetforlife.org*

Colostomy

Colostomy Association
Enterprise House
95 London Street
Reading RG1 4QA
Tel: 0118 939 1537
Email: cass@colostomyassociation.org.uk
Website: *http://www.colostomyassociation.org.uk*

Counselling

British Association for Counselling and
Psychotherapy
BACP House
15 St John's Business Park
Lutterworth LE17 4HB
Tel: 01455 883 300
Fax: 01455 550 243
Email: bacp@bacp.co.uk

Cystic fibrosis

Cystic Fibrosis Trust
11 London Road
Bromley
Kent BR1 1BY
Tel: 020 8464 7211
Fax: 020 8313 0472
Email: enquiries@cftrust.org.uk

Day surgery

British Association of Day Surgery
The Royal College of Surgeons
35–43 Lincoln's Inn Fields
London WC2A 3PE
Tel: 020 7973 0308
Fax: 020 7973 0314
Email: bads@bads.co.uk

Deafness

Royal Association for Deaf People
Century House South, Riverside Office Centre
North Station Road, Colchester, Essex CO1 1RE
Tel: 0845 688 2525
Fax: 0845 688 2526
Email: info@royaldeaf.org.uk

Royal National Institute for Deaf People
19–23 Featherstone Street
London EC1Y 8SL
Tel: 020 7296 8000
Minicom: 020 7296 8001
Fax: 020 7296 8199
Email: informationline@hearingloss.org.uk

Dentists

British Dental Association
64 Wimpole Street
London W1G 8YS
Tel: 020 7935 0875
Fax: 020 7487 5232
Email: enquiries@bda.org

Dermatology

British Association of Dermatologists
Willan House
4 Fitzroy Square
London W1T 5HQ
Tel: 020 7383 0266
Fax: 020 7388 5263
Email: admin@bad.org.uk

Development

British Association for Developmental
Disabilities
5 Handsworth Drive
Great Barr
Birmingham B43 6ED
Tel/Fax: 0121 360 2027

Diabetes

Diabetes UK Central Office
Macleod House
10 Parkway
London NW1 7AA
Tel: 020 7424 1000
Fax: 020 7424 1001
Email: info@diabetes.org.uk

Diagnostics

Cellmark Diagnostics
PO Box 265
Abingdon OX14 1YX
Tel: 0800 362 522
Fax: 01235 528 141
Email: info@cellmark.co.uk

University Diagnostics Ltd
Queens Road
Teddington
Middx TW11 0NJ
Tel: 020 8943 8400

Dietetics

British Dietetic Association
5th Floor Charles House
148–9 Great Charles Street
Queensway
Birmingham B3 3HT
Tel: 0121 200 8080
Fax: 0121 200 8081
Email: info@bda.uk.com

British Nutrition Foundation
High Holborn House
52–54 High Holborn
London WC1V 6RQ
Tel: 020 7404 6504
Fax: 020 7404 6747
Email: postbox@nutrition.org.uk

Digestion

Digestive Disorders CORE Foundation
3 Saint Andrew's Place
London NW1 4LB
Tel: 020 7486 0341
Fax: 020 7224 2012
Email: info@corecharity.org.uk

Disability

Disabled Living Foundation
380–384 Harrow Road
London W9 2HU
Tel: 020 7289 6111
Fax: 020 7226 2922 [111]
Email: info@dlf.org.uk

Royal Association for Disability and
Rehabilitation (RADAR)
12 City Forum
250 City Road
London EC1V 8AF
Tel: 020 7250 3222
Fax: 020 7250 0212
Email: enquiries@disabilityrightsuk.org

Disfigurement

Changing Faces
(Charity for Facially Disfigured People)
The Squire Centre
33–37 University Street
London WC1E 6JN
Tel: 0845 4500 275
Fax: 0845 4500 276
Email: info@changingfaces.org.uk

Down's Syndrome

Down's Syndrome Association (DSA)
Langdon Down Centre
2a Langdon Park
Teddington TW11 9PS
Tel: 0845 230 0372
Fax: 0845 230 0373
Email: info@downs-syndrome.org.uk

Drugs

Committee on Safety of Medicines (for
adverse reaction reports)
151 Buckingham Palace Road
Victoria, London SW1W 9SZ
Tel: 020 3080 6000
Fax: 020 3118 9803
Email: info@mhra.gsi.gov.uk

Dyslexia

Dyslexia Action
Egham Centre, Park House
Wick Road, Egham
Surrey TW20 0HH
Tel: 01784 222 300
Fax: 01784 222 333
Email: info@dyslexiaaction.org.uk

Ear, nose and throat

British Association of Otorhinolaryngologists
ENT UK at The Royal College of Surgeons
35–43 Lincoln's Inn Fields
London WC2A 3PE
Tel: 020 7404 8373
Fax: 020 7404 4200
Email: entuk@entuk.org

(see also **Deafnes**s)

Elderly

British Geriatrics Society
Marjory Warren House
31 St John's Square
London EC1M 4DN
Tel: 020 7608 1369
Fax: 020 7608 1041
Email: general.information@bgs.org.uk

British Association for Service to the Elderly (BASE)
119 Hassell Street
Newcastle-under-Lyme
Staffordshire ST5 1AX
Tel: 01782 661 033
Fax: 01782 661 033
Email: basenul@intonet.co.uk

Endocrinology

Society for Endocrinology
22 Apex Court
Woodlands
Bradley Stoke
Bristol BS32 4JT
Tel: 01454 642 200
Fax: 01454 642 222
Email: info@endocrinology.org

Epilepsy

Epilepsy Action
New Anstey House
Gate Way Drive
Yeadon
Leeds LS19 7XY
Tel: 0113 210 8800
Fax: 0113 391 0300
Email: epilepsy@epilepsy.org.uk

Forensic science

British Academy of Forensic Sciences
Anaesthetic Unit
Royal London Hospital
London E1 1BB
Tel: 020 7377 9201

Gastroenterology

British Society of Gastroenterology
3 Saint Andrew's Place
Regent's Park
London NW1 4LB
Tel: 020 7935 3150
Fax: 020 7487 3734
Email: j.rother@bsg.org.uk

Glaucoma

International Glaucoma Association
Woodcote House
15 Highpoint Business Village
Henwood
Ashford
Kent TN24 8DH
Tel: 01233 648 170
Fax: 01233 648 179
Email: info@iga.org.uk

General information

Health Information (will provide a wide
range of health information for both
doctors and their patients)
The Mapels
Level 2
The Lister Hospital
Coreys Mill Lane
Stevenage
Hertfordshire SG1 4AB
Tel: 0800 665 544

Haematology

British Society for Haematology
100 White Lion Street
London N1 9PF
Tel: 020 7713 0990
Fax: 020 7837 1931
Email: info@b-s-h.org.uk

Haemophilia

The Haemophilia Society
First Floor
Petersham House
57a Hatton Garden
London EC1N 8JG
Tel: 020 7713 0990
Fax: 020 7405 4824
Email: info@haemophilia.org.uk

Hand surgery

British Society of Surgery of the Hand
Royal College of Surgeons of England
35–43 Lincoln's Inn Fields
London WC2A 3PE
Tel: 020 7831 5162
Fax: 020 7831 4041
Email: secretariat@bssh.ac.uk

Head injuries

Headway (The Brain Injuries Association)
Bradbury House
190 Bagnall Road, Old Basford
Nottingham
NG6 8SF
Tel: 0115 924 0800
Fax: 0115 958 4446
Email: enquiries@headway.org.uk

Health visitors

Community Practitioners' and Health Visitors
Association (Amicus/CPHVA)—Unite
Unite
128 Theobold's Road
Holborn
London WC1X 8TN
Tel: 020 7611 2500
Fax: 020 7611 2555
Website: *http://www.unitetheunion.org*

Hysterectomy

Hysterectomy Association
West View, West Street
Broadwindsor
Dorset DT1 3QQ
Email: info@hysterectomy-association.org.uk

Injury

(See **Rehabilitation**)

Kidneys

National Kidney Federation
The Point, Coach Road,
Shireoaks, Worksop
Nottinghamshire S81 8BW
Tel: 01909 544 999
Helpline: 0845 601 0209
Email: nfk@kidney.org.uk

The National Kidney Research Fund
Kings Chambers
Priestgate
Peterborough PE1 1FG
Tel: 0845 070 7601
Email: info@kidneyresearch.uk.org

Kidney Research UK
Nene Hall
Lynch Wood Park
Peterborough PE2 6FZ
Tel: 0845 300 1499
Email: kidneyhealth@kidneyresearchuk.org

Lungs

(See **Thoracic**)

Lupus

Lupus UK
St James House
Eastern Road
Romford
Essex RM1 3NH
Tel: 01708 731 251
Fax: 01708 731 252
Email: headoffice@lupusuk.org.uk

Maxillofacial surgery

(See **Oral**)

M.E.

Myalgic Encephalomyelitis Association
4 Top Angel
Buckingham Industrial Park
Buckingham MK18 1TH
Tel: 0870 444 8233
Fax: 01280 821 602
Email: enquiries@meassociation.org.uk

Medicine

Committee on Safety of Medicines
151 Buckingham Palace Road
Victoria
London SW1W 9SZ
Tel: 020 3080 6000
Fax: 020 3118 9803
Email: info@mhra.gsi.gov.uk

Medical Society of London
Lettsom House
11 Chandos Street
London W1G 9EB
Tel: 020 7580 1043
Fax: 020 7631 4817

Medicines Commission
151 Buckingham Palace Road
Victoria London SW1W 9SZ
Tel: 020 3080 6000
Fax: 020 3118 9803
Email: info@mhra.gsi.gov.uk

The Royal Society of Medicine
1 Wimpole Street
London W1G 0AE
Tel: 020 7290 2991
Website: *http://www.rsm.ac.uk*

Meningitis

The National Meningitis Trust
Fern House
Bath Road
Stroud
Gloucestershire GL5 3TJ
Tel: 01453 768 000
Fax: 01453 768 001
Email: info@meningitis-trust.org.uk

Menopause (premature)

The Menopause Amarant Trust
80 Lambeth Road
London SE1 7PW
Tel: 01293 413 000 (Advice Line)
Website: *http://www.amarantmenopausetrust.org.uk*

Mental health

National Association for Mental Health (MIND)
Granta House
15/19 Broadway
London E15 4BQ
Tel: 020 8519 2122
Fax: 020 8522 1725
Email: contact@mind.org.uk

Royal Society for Mentally Handicapped
Children and Adults (MENCAP)
Mencap National Centre
123 Golden Lane
London EC1Y 0RT
Tel: 020 7454 0454
Fax: 020 7696 5540
Email: information@mencap.org.uk

Midwives

(See **Childbirth**)

Migraine

Migraine Trust
52–53 Russell Square
London WC1B 4HP
Tel: 020 7631 6970
Fax: 020 7436 2886
Email: info@migrainenetrust.org

Mobility

Banstead Mobility Centre
Damson Way
Fountain Drive
Carshalton
Surrey SM5 4NR
Tel: 020 8770 1151
Fax: 020 8770 1211
Website: *http://www.bansteadmobility.co.uk*

Motor Neurone Disease

Motor Neurone Disease Association
PO Box 246
Northampton NN1 2PR
Tel: 01604 250 505
Tel: 0845 7626 262 (helpline)
Fax: 01604 638 289/624 726
Email: enquiries@mndassociation.org

Multiple Sclerosis

MS Society
MS National Centre
372 Edgware Road
London NW2 6ND
Tel: 020 8438 0700
Fax: 020 8430 0701
Email: info@mssociety.org.uk

Muscular Dystrophy

Muscular Dystrophy Campaign
61 Southwark Street
London SE1 0HL
Tel: 020 7803 4800
Email: info@muscular-dystrophy.org

Narcolepsy

Narcolepsy UK
PO Box 13842
Penicuik
EH26 8WX
Tel: 0845 450 0394
Fax: 0870 777 3039
Email: info@narcolepsy.org.uk

Neurology

Association of British Neurologists
Ormond House
27 Boswell Street
London WC1W 3JZ
Tel: 020 7405 4060
Fax: 020 7405 4070
Email: info@theabn.org

Neurosurgery

Society of British Neurological Surgeons
35–43 Lincoln's Inn Fields
London WC2A 3PE
Tel: 020 7869 6892
Fax: 020 7869 6890
Email: admin@sbns.org.uk

Nursing

Royal College of Nursing of the United
Kingdom
20 Cavendish Square
London W1G 0RN
Tel: 020 7409 3333
Fax: 020 7647 3435
Website: *http://www.rcn.org.uk*

BNA Care Assessment Services
The Colonnades
Beaconsfield Road
Hatfield
Hertfordshire AL10 8YD
Tel: 01707 255 658
Fax: 01707 255 660
Email: bna@dial.pipex.com

Carers Trust
Unit 14, Bourne Court
Southend Road, Woodford Green
Essex 1G8 8HD
Tel: 0844 800 4361
Fax: 0844 800 4362
Email: info@carers.org
Website: *http://carersorg*

Occupational medicine

Society of Occupational Medicine
Hamilton House
Mabledon Place
London WC1H 9BB
Tel: 020 7554 8628 (or 8627)
Fax: 020 7554 8526
Email: admin@som.org.uk

Occupational therapy

British Association of Occupational Therapists/
College of Occupational Therapists
106–114 Borough High Street
Southwark
London SE1 1LB
Tel: 020 7357 6480
Email: reception@cot.co.uk
Website: *http://www.cot.co.uk*

Oncology

(See **Cancer**)

Oral

British Association of Oral & Maxillofacial
Surgeons
Royal College of Surgeons
35–43 Lincoln's Inn Fields
London WC2A 3PE
Tel: 020 7405 8074
Fax: 020 7430 9997
Email: office@baoms.org.uk

Orthopaedic

British Orthopaedic Association
Royal College of Surgeons
35–43 Lincoln's Inn Fields
London WC2A 3PE
Tel: 020 7405 6507
Fax: 020 7831 2676
Email: secretary@boa.ac.uk

Osteoporosis

National Osteoporosis Society
Camerton
Bath BA2 OPJ
Tel: 01761 471 771
Fax: 01761 471 104
Website: *http://www.nos.org.uk*
Email: info@nos.org.uk

Pain

The British Pain Society
Third Floor
Churchill House
35 Red Lion Square
London WC1R 4SG
Tel: 020 7269 7840
Fax: 020 7831 0859
Email: info@britishpainsociety.org

National Back Pain Association
Backcare
16 Elmtree Road
Teddington
Middlesex TW11 8ST
Tel: 020 8977 5474
Fax: 020 8943 5318
Email: info@backcare.org.uk

Parkinson's disease

Parkinson's UK
215 Vauxhall Bridge Road
London SW1V 1EJ
Tel: 020 7931 8080
Fax: 020 7233 9908
Email: hello@parkinsons.org.uk

Pathology

Pathological Society of Great Britain &
Ireland
2 Carlton House Terrace
London SW1Y 5AF
Tel: 020 7976 1260
Fax: 020 7930 2981
Email: admin@pathsoc.org.uk

Royal College of Pathologists
2 Carlton House Terrace
London SW1Y 5AF
Tel: 020 7451 6700
Fax: 020 7451 6701
Email: info@rcpath.org

Patients

Patients Association
PO Box 935
Harrow HA1 3YJ
Tel: 020 8423 9111
Fax: 020 8423 9119
Email: helpline@patients-association.com

Physiotherapy

Chartered Society of Physiotherapy
14 Bedford Row
London WC1R 4ED
Tel: 020 7306 6666
Fax: 020 7306 6611
Email: csp@csphysio.org.uk

Plastic surgery

British Association of Plastic Surgeons
The Royal College of Surgeons
35–43 Lincoln's Inn Fields
London WC2A 3PE
Tel: 020 7831 5161
Fax: 020 7831 4041
Email: secretariat@baps.co.uk

Polio

British Polio Fellowship
Ground Floor
Unit A
Eagle Office Centre
The Runway
South Ruislip
Middlesex HA4 6SE
Tel: 0800 018 0586
Fax: 020 8842 0555
Email: info@britishpolio.org

Post-natal illness

(See **Childbirth**)

Psoriasis

Psoriasis Association
Dick Coles House
2 Queensbridge
Northampton NN4 7BZ
Tel: 0845 676 0076
Fax: 01604 251 621
Email: mail@psoriasis-association.org.uk

Psychiatry

Royal College of Psychiatrists
17 Belgrave Square
London SW1X 8PG
Tel: 020 7235 2351
Fax: 020 7245 1231
Email: reception@rcpsych.ac.uk

Psychology

British Psychological Society
Saint Andrew's House
48 Princess Road East
Leicester LE1 7DR
Tel: 0116 254 9568
Fax: 0116 227 1314
Email: enquiries@bps.org.uk

David McGlown
Clinical Psychologist Public Trust Office
Stewart House
24 Kingsway
London WC2B 6JX
Tel: 020 7269 7085

Psychotherapy

British Association of Psychotherapists
37 Mapesbury Road
London NW2 4HJ
Tel: 020 8452 9823
Fax: 020 8452 0310
Email: mail@bap-psychotherapy.org

Radiography and Radiology

Society and College of Radiographers
207 Providence Square
Mill Street
London SE1 2EW
Tel: 020 7740 7200
Fax: 020 7740 7204
Email: info@sor.org

Royal College of Radiologists
38 Portland Place
London W1B 4JQ
Tel: 020 7636 4432
Fax: 020 7323 3100
Email: enquiries@rcr.ac.uk

Rehabilitation

British Society of Rehabilitation Medicine
c/o Royal College of Physicians
11 Saint Andrew's Place
London NW1 4LE
Tel: 01992 638 865
Fax: 01992 638 674
Email: admin@bsrm.co.uk

REMEDI (Rehabilitation and Medical
Research Trust for Relief of Disability)
c/o Winterflood Securities Ltd
The Atrium Building
Cannon Bridge
25 Dowgate Hill
London EC4R 2GA
Tel: 0207 384 2929
Email: info@remedies.org.uk

The Injury Care Clinics Ltd
Carnac House, Carnac Court
Carns Estate, Fareham
Hampshire PO16 8UZ
Tel: 0870 050 1710
Fax: 0844 493 5035
Email: info@ticcs.co.uk

Research

Medical Research Society
Dr Afzal Chaudhry
Academic Secretary
Box 118, Dialysis Centre
Addenbrooke's Hospital
Hills Road

Cambridge CB2 2QQ
Tel: 07092 388 555
Email: anc35@cam.ac.uk

Rheumatology

British Society for Rheumatology
Bride House
18–20 Bride Lane
London EC4Y 8EE
Tel: 020 7842 0900
Fax: 020 7842 0901
Email: bsr@rheumatology.org.uk

Schizophrenia

Rethink
Head Office
89 Albert Embankment
London SE1 7TP
Tel: 0300 500 0927
Email: info@rethink.org

SCOPE

Scope
6 Market Road
London N7 9PW
Tel: 020 7619 7100
(Helpline: 11am–9pm Mon-Fri,
2–6pm weekend)
Fax: 020 7619 7399
Email: cphelpline@scope.org.uk

Speech

Royal College of Speech & Language Therapists
2 White Hart Yard
London SE1 1NX
Tel: 020 7378 3012
Email: info@rcslt.org

Association for all Speech-Impaired
Children (AFASIC)
1st Floor
20 Bowling Green Lane
London EC1R 0BD
Tel: 020 7490 9410
Fax: 020 7251 2834
Email: info@afasic.org.uk
Website: *http://www.afasicengland.org.uk*

Spinal injuries

Spinal Injuries Association
SIA House
2 Trueman Place
Oldbrook
Milton Keynes MK6 3HH
Tel: 0845 678 6633

Fax: 0845 070 6911
Freephone Helpline: 0800 980 0501
Email: sia@spinal.co.uk

(See also **Back pain under Pain**)

Stroke

The Stroke Association
Stroke House
240 City Road
London EC1V 2PR
Tel: 020 7566 0300
Fax: 020 7490 2686
Email: info@stroke.org.uk

Torture

Freedom from Torture
111 Isledon Road
London N7 7JW
Tel: 020 7697 7777
Fax: 020 7697 7739
Website: *http://www.freedomfromtorture.org*

Thoracic

British Thoracic Society
17 Doughty Street
London WC1N 2PL
Tel: 020 7831 8778
Fax: 020 7831 8766
Email: bts@brit-thoracic.org.uk

British Lung Foundation
Lung Foundation House
73–75 Goswell Road
London EC1V 7ER
Tel: 0207 688 5555
Website: *http://www.blf.org.uk/home*

Society of Cardiothoracic Surgeons of Great
Britain & Ireland
35–43 Lincoln's Inn Fields
London WC2A 3PE
Tel: 020 7869 6893
Fax: 020 7869 6890
Email: sctsadmin@scts.org

(See also **Asthma**)

Transplants

NHS Blood and Transplant Organ Donation and
Transplantation Directorate
Fox Den Road
Stoke Gifford BS34 8RR
Tel: 0117 975 7575
Fax: 0117 975 7577
Email: enquiries@nhsbt.nhs.uk

Tropical Medicine

Liverpool School of Tropical Medicine
Pembroke Place
Liverpool L3 5QA
Tel: 0151 705 3100
Fax: 0151 705 3370
Website: *http://www.liv.ac.uk/lstm*

London School of Hygiene and Tropical Medicine
Keppel Street
London WC1E 7HT
Tel: 020 7636 8636
Fax: 020 7436 5389
Email: registry@lshtm.ac.uk
Website: *http://www.lshtm.ac.uk*

HPA Malaria Reference Laboratory (for advice on prophylaxis)
London School of Hygience and Tropical Medicine
Keppel Street
London WC1E 7HT
Tel: 020 7636 7921
Email: red.team@hPa.org.uk
Website: *http://www.malaria-reference.co.uk*

Urology

British Association of Urological Surgeons
Royal College of Surgeons
35–43 Lincoln's Inn Fields
London WC2A 3PE
Tel: 020 7869 6950
Fax: 020 7404 5048
Email: admin@baus.org.uk

Part 2—Litigation

Action Against Medical Accidents (AvMA)

44 High St
Croydon
Surrey CR0 17B
Tel: 020 8688 9555
Fax: 020 8667 9065
Email: advice@avma.org.uk
Website: *http://www.avma.org.uk*

Association of Personal Injury Lawyers (APIL)

3 Alder Court
Rennie Hogg Road
Nottingham N62 1RX
Tel: 0115 958 0585
Fax: 0115 958 0885
Email: mail@apil.org.uk

Association of Trial Lawyers of America

777 6th Street
NW Suite 200
Washington DC 20001
USA
Tel: 001 800 424 2725
Email: help@justice.org

Clinical Disputes Forum

Chairman: Dr Alastair Scotland
Medical Director and Chief Officer
National Clinical Assessment Authority
9th Floor, Market Towers
London SW8 5NQ
Tel: 0115 947 4700
Fax: 0115 958 0885
Email: margaret.dangoor@blueyonder.co.uk

Compensation Recovery Unit (CRU)

Compensation Recovery Unit
Durham House
Washington
Tyne & Wear NE38 7SF
Tel: 0191 225 2005
Fax: 0191 225 2048
Email: cru-info-management@dwp.gsi.gov.uk

Disability Law Service

(free advice for the disabled on legal matters, benefits and grants)
39–45 Cavell Street
London E1 2BP
Tel: 020 7791 9800
Fax: 020 7791 9802
Email: advice@dls.org.uk

General Council of the Bar (Bar Council)

289–293 High Holborn
London WC1V 7HZ
Tel: 020 7242 0082
Fax: 020 7831 9217
Website: *http://www.generaloffice @barcouncil.org.uk*
Email: Contactus@barcouncil.org.uk

Incorporated Council of Law Reporting for England and Wales

Megarry House
119 Chancery Lane
London WC2A 1PP
Tel: 020 7242 6471
Fax: 020 7831 5247
Email: enquiries@iclr.co.uk

Inquest

89–93 Fonthill Road
London N4 3JH
Tel: 020 7263 1111
Fax: 020 7561 0799
Email: inquest@inquest.org.uk

Law Society

113 Chancery Lane
London WC2A 1PL
Tel: 020 7242 1222
Fax: 020 7831 0344
Website: *http://www.lawsociety.org.uk*

Legal Services Commisson

Legal Services Commission Head Office
102 Petty France
London SW1H 9AJ
Tel: 020 7718 8000
Email: london@legalservices.gsi.gov.uk
Website: *http://www.legalservices.gov.uk*

Legal Services Commission London/South
Exchange Tower (Area No. 1)
2 Harbour Exchange Square
London E14 9GE
Tel: 020 7718 8466
Email: london@legalservices.gov.uk

Legal Services Commission (Area No. 2)
3rd and 4th Floors Invicta House
Trafalgar Place
Cheapside
Brighton BN1 4FR
Tel: 01273 878 800

Legal Services Commission (Area No. 3)
Old Shire Hall
The Forbury
Reading
Berkshire RG1 3EH
Tel: 020 7715 3991

Legal Services Commission Wales and the
West Group Area Offices (Area No. 4)
33–35 Queen Square
Bristol BS1 4LU
Tel: 0117 302 3000

Legal Services Commission (Area No. 5)
2nd Floor, Churchill House
17 Churchill Way
Cardiff
South Glamorgan CF10 2HH
Tel: 0300 200 2020
Email: Cardiff@legalservices.gsi.co.uk

Legal Services Commission Midlands Group
Area Offices (Area No. 6)
1st Floor, Cannon House
18 The Priory Queensway
Birmingham B4 6BS
Tel: 0121 232 5500
Email: Birmingham@legalservices.gsi.co.uk

Legal Services Commission (Area No. 7)
2nd Floor Lee House
90 Great Bridgewater Street
Manchester M1 5JW
Tel: 0300 200 2020
Email: manchester@legalservices.gsi.co.uk

Legal Services Commission (Area No. 9)
Harcourt House
Chanceller House
21 The Calls
Leeds LS2 7EH
Tel: 0113 390 7300
Email: leeds@legalservices.gsi.co.uk

Legal Services Commission (Area No. 10)
2nd Floor, Fothergill House
16 King Street
Nottingham NG1 2AS
Tel: 0115 908 4200

Legal Services Commission (Area No. 11)
62–68 Hills Road
Cambridge CB2 1LA
Tel: 0300 200 2020
Email: legal-enquiries@legalservices.gsi.co.uk

Legal Services Commission North Western
Group Area Offices (Area No. 12)
2nd Floor, Pepper House
Pepper Row
Chester CH1 1DW
Tel: 01244 404 500
Email: Chester@legalservices.gsi.gov.uk

Legal Services Commission (Area No. 15)
Cavern Walks
8 Matthew Street
Liverpool L2 6RE
Tel: 0151 242 5200
Email: liverpool@legalservices.gsi.gov.uk

Medical Defence Union

230 Blackfriars Road
London SE1 8PG
Tel: 0800 716 376
Fax: 0844 209 0308
Email: advisory@the-mdu.com
Website: *http://www.the-mdu.com*

The Medical Protection Society Ltd

33 Cavendish Square
London W1G OPS
Tel: 020 7399 1300
Fax: 020 7399 1300
Email: info@mps.org.uk

Medico-Legal Society

Dr Jill Crombie
20 Embankment Place
London WC2N 6NN
Tel: 020 7289 0188
Email: E.pygott@zen.co.uk

Motor Insurers Bureau

Linford Wood House
6–12 Capital Drive
Linford Wood
Milton Keynes MK14 6XT
Tel: 01908 830 001
Fax: 01908 671 681
Email: enquiries@mib.org.uk
Website: *http://www.mib.org.uk*

National Association of Guardians ad Litem and Reporting Officers (NAGALRO)

PO Box 264
Esher
Surrey KT10 0WA
Tel: 01372 818 504
Fax: 01372 818 505
Email: nagalro@globalnet.co.uk

Official Solicitor to the Supreme Court

81 Chancery Lane
London WC2A 1DD
Tel: 020 7911 7127
Fax: 020 7911 7105
Email: enquiries@offsol.gsi.gov.uk

The Patients' Association

PO Box 935
Harrow
Middlesex HA1 3YJ
Tel: 020 8423 9111
Fax: 020 8423 9119
Email: mailbox@patients-association.com

Personal Injury Bar Association (PIBA)

Faircroft Avenue
Walmley
Sutton Coldfield
West Midlands B76 1HQ
Tel: 0121 240 8448
Email: admin@piba.org.uk

Professional Negligence Bar Association (PNBA)

Victoria Woodbridge
Crown Office Chambers
London EC4Y 7EP
Tel: 020 7797 8100
Email: woodbridge@crownofficechambers.com

Witnesses Against Abuse by Health and Care Workers

Verulam House
110 Luton Road
Harpenden
Hertfordshire AL5 3BL

Smith Bernal Reporting Ltd

(Court of Appeal Transcribers)
2nd Floor, 101 Finsbury Pavement
London EC2A 1ER
Tel: 020 7422 6100
Fax: 020 7588 7605
Email: London@merrillcorp.com

Part 3—Government

Commission for Local Administration in England

(Local Government Ombudsman)
PO Box 4771
Coventry CV4 0EH
Tel: 0300 061 0614
Fax: 024 7682 0001
Email: training@lgo.org.uk

Department of Health

Richmond House
79 Whitehall
London SW1A 2NS
Tel: 020 7210 4850

Department of Work and Pensions

DWP Litigation Division
2nd Floor
Caxton House
Tothill Street
London SW1H 9NA
Tel: 020 7712 2171
Fax: 020 7712 2386
Email: ministers@dwp.gsi.gov.uk
Website: *http://www.dwp.gov.uk*

Department of Health Social Care Group

Richmond House
79 Whitehall
London SW1A 2NL
Tel: 020 7210 4850

Health & Safety Executive

2 Southwark Bridge
London SE1 9HS
Tel: 020 7556 2100
Fax: 020 7557 2102
Website: *http://www.hse.gov.uk*

Health and Safety Executive—Health Policy Division

Rose Court
2 Southwark Bridge
London SE1 9HS
Tel: 020 7717 6000 (Head Office)
Fax: 020 7717 6717

Home Office

Home Office Direct Communications Unit
Millbank
London SW1P 3JU
Tel: 020 7222 9510
Email: public.enquiries@homeoffice.gsi.gov.uk

HM Inspector of Anatomy

Dept. of Health
Richmond House
79 Whitehall
London SW1A 2HS
Tel: 020 7210 4850
Fax: 020 7210 5952

Lord Chancellor's Department

Selbourne House
54–60 Victoria Street
London SW1E 6QW
Tel: 020 7210 8614

Care Quality Commission

Finsbury Tower
103–105 Bunhill Row
London EC1Y 8TG
Tel: 0300 616161
Email: enquiries@cqc.org.uk

Mental Welfare Commission for Scotland

Thistle House
91 Haymarket Terrace
Edinburgh EH12 5HE
Tel: 0131 313 8777
Email: enquiries@mwcscot.org.uk

National Blood Authority

NHS Blood and Transplant
Head Office
Oak House
Reeds Crescent
Watford
Hertfordshire WD24 4QN
Tel: 01923 486 800
Website: *http://www.nhsbt.nhs.uk*

Scottish Office Home and Health Department

St Andrew's House
Regent Road
Edinburgh EH1 3DG
Tel: 08457 741 741
Fax: 01397 795 001
Email: ceu@scotlan.gsi.gov.uk

London Office: Dover House
Whitehall
London SW1A 2AU
Tel: 020 7270 6754
Fax: 020 7270 6812
Email: scottish.secretary@scotland.gsi.gov.uk

Scottish National Blood Transfusion Service

21 Ellen's Glen Road, Liberton
Edinburgh EH17 7QT
Tel: 0131 536 5700
Fax: 0131 536 5781

Part 4—Courts and Tribunals

The Supreme Court

Parliament Square
London SW1P 3BD
Switchboard: 0207 960 1500/1900
Fax: 020 7960 1901
Email: Enquiries@supremecourt.gsi.gov.uk
Website: *http://www.supremecourt.gov.uk*

Court of Appeal

Civil Division
Room E330
Royal Courts of Justice
Strand
London WC2A 2LL
Tel: 020 7947 6000 (Listings Office)

High Court of Justice

Royal Courts of Justice
Strand
London WC2A 2LL
Tel: 020 7947 6000 (General Office)

Court of Protection

The Royal Courts of Justice
Thomas More Building
Strand
London WC2A 2LL
Tel: 0300 456 4600
Website: *http://www.justice.gov.uk/courts/rcj-rolls-building/court-of-protection*

Criminal Injuries Compensation Authority (CICA)

Winston Solicitors LLP
112 Street Lane
Leeds LS8 2AL
Tel: 0113 320 5000
Website: *http://www.criminal-injuries.co.uk*

Part 5—Other

Child Poverty Action Group

94 White Lion Street
London N1 9PF
Tel: 020 7837 7979
Fax: 020 7837 6414
Email: info@cpag.org.uk

Fostering Network

87 Blackfriars Road
London SE1 8HA
Tel: 020 7620 6400
Fax: 020 7620 6401
Email: info@fostering.net

Leonard Cheshire Disability

66 South Lambeth Road
London SW8 1RL
Tel: 020 3242 0200
Fax: 020 3242 0250
Email: info@LCDisability.org

The Bank of England

Threadneedle Street
London EC2R 8AH
Tel: 020 7601 4444
Fax: 020 7601 5460
Email: enquiries@bankofengland.co.uk